MEASUREMENT AND ASSESSMENT IN TEACHING

Tenth Edition

M. David Miller
University of Florida

Robert L. Linn
Professor Emeritus
University of Colorado at Boulder

Norman E. Gronlund
Professor Emeritus
University of Illinois at Urbana–Champaign

Merrill
is an imprint of

Upper Saddle River, New Jersey
Columbus, Ohio

Library of Congress Cataloging-in-Publication Data

Miller, M. David

    Measurement and assessment in teaching / M. David Miller, Robert L. Linn, Norman E.
       Gronlund.—10th ed.
       p. cm.
    Prev. ed. entered under: Linn, Robert L.
    Includes index.
    ISBN-13: 978-0-13-240893-6
    ISBN-10: 0-13-240893-7
    1. Educational tests and measurements. I. Linn, Robert L. II. Gronlund, Norman Edward
       III. Linn, Robert L. Measurement and assessment in teaching. IV. Title.

    LB3051.L545 2009

    371.26—dc22

                                         2007042418

Vice President and Executive Publisher: Jeffery W. Johnston
Publisher: Kevin M. Davis
Development Editor: Christina Robb
Editorial Assistant: Lauren Reinkober
Production Editor: Mary Harlan
Production Coordinator: Christian Holdener, S4Carlisle Publishing Services
Design Coordinator: Diane C. Lorenzo
Text Design and Illustrations: S4Carlisle Publishing Services
Cover Design: Jason Moore
Cover Image: Super Stock
Production Manager: Laura Messerly
Director of Marketing: Quinn Perkson
Marketing Manager: Erica M. DeLuca
Marketing Coordinator: Brian Mounts

This book was set in Garamond by S4Carlisle Publishing Services. It was printed and bound by R. R. Donnelley & Sons
Company. The cover was printed by The Lehigh Press, Inc.

Pearson Education Ltd.   Pearson Education Australia Pty. Limited
Pearson Education Singapore Pte. Ltd.   Pearson Education North Asia Ltd.
Pearson Education Canada, Inc.   Pearson Educación de Mexico, S.A. de C.V.
Pearson Education–Japan   Pearson Education Malaysia Pte. Ltd.
                                    Pearson Education Upper Saddle River, New Jersey

Merrill
is an imprint of

                                        10 9 8 7 6 5 4 3 2 1
                                   ISBN-13: 978-0-13-240893-6
                                   ISBN-10:   0-13-240893-7

Dedicated to
Anne E. Seraphine,
Joyce E. Linn and
Jim and Dick Gronlund

Preface

Measurement and Assessment in Teaching, Tenth Edition, introduces the classroom teacher to those elements of measurement and assessment that are essential to good teaching. The main theme throughout the book is that the assessment of learning plays an important role in the instructional process and that its effectiveness depends heavily on the ability of teachers to construct and select tests and assessments that provide valid measures of learning outcomes.

The tenth edition is substantially revised to reflect the major changes that have occurred in educational testing and assessment since the last edition. Some of the more significant changes include:

1. Major revisions in Chapter 1 reflect the changing context of testing and assessment now required to meet the state and federal uses of tests for purposes of school accountability, emphasizing in particular the requirements of the No Child Left Behind Act that was signed into law by President Bush in January 2002.
2. Many new examples of classroom assessments have been added.
3. Revisions in Chapter 6 have a stronger emphasis on the development of tests with higher order skills.
4. The discussion of motivation on standardized tests (Chapter 18) is updated.
5. References to many Web sites have been added or updated.
6. Materials on published tests reflect new editions and new approaches to assessment.

This book is designed for the introductory course in educational measurement and assessment at either the undergraduate or graduate level, and assumes no previous knowledge of measurement or statistics. The writing is direct, and numerous examples are used to illustrate concepts and approaches to testing and assessment. Statistical concepts are introduced only where necessary for understanding and discussion, and then the emphasis is on interpretation rather than computation. A section of elementary statistics is provided in Appendix A for those who want to understand how to obtain the statistical results discussed.

As with earlier editions, the focus of the book is best described by a list of general learning outcomes that should result from its use.

- An understanding of the role of measurement and assessment in the instructional process
- The ability to define instructional goals and objectives in ways that facilitate the construction of appropriate tests and assessments
- An understanding of the concepts of validity and reliability and their role in the construction, selection, interpretation, and use of tests and assessments
- The ability to construct classroom tests and assessments that measure a variety of learning outcomes, from simple to complex
- The ability to obtain assessment information from classroom observations, peer appraisals, and self-reports
- The ability to administer tests and assessments properly and to use their results effectively, with due regard to the necessary precautions
- The ability to interpret test and assessment results properly, with full awareness of their meaning and the ever-present error of measurement
- An understanding of both the potentialities and the limitations of the various test and assessment procedures used in the school
- An understanding of how tests and assessments contribute to effective marking and reporting systems and to improved instructional decisions
- The ability to interpret and use results of published tests and state assessments properly and to select ones that are most appropriate for a given purpose
- An understanding of trends and issues in the use of externally mandated tests and assessments

These understandings and abilities are most likely to be attained when reading the book is supplemented by other experiences. The Companion Website, at *http://www.prenhall.com/miller,* offers additional opportunities to review and apply chapter content and helps students explore measurement and assessment topics using the Internet. Practical application of textbook material will enhance learning and contribute to competence in using measurement skills.

An electronic Instructor's Manual with Test Bank is available at *www.pearsonhighered.com.*

Our thanks to the individuals who reviewed the tenth edition of the book: Bruce Frey, University of Kansas; Glenn Snelbecker, Temple University; Sherri Strawser, University of Nevada, Las Vegas, and Mary Carolyn Thies, University of Maryland. We also thank the publishers who generously permitted the use of copyrighted materials. We also are grateful for the patience and support of our wives and for the valuable help of the staff at Merrill/Prentice Hall.

Brief Contents

Contents

PART II   CLASSROOM TESTS AND ASSESSMENTS

PART III   SELECTING AND USING PUBLISHED TESTS

APPENDIXES

NOTE: Every effort has been made to provide accurate and current Internet information in this book.
However, the Internet and information posted on it are constantly changing, so it is inevitable that
some of the Internet addresses listed in this textbook will change.

CHAPTER

1

EDUCATIONAL TESTING AND ASSESSMENT: CONTEXT, ISSUES, AND TRENDS

Federal and state legislation mandate extensive use of student assessments to hold schools, districts, and educators accountable for student achievement. National and international assessment programs, national and state content and performance standards, and global competition have also contributed to increased demands for testing and assessment. These factors have both stimulated and reflected new trends in educational measurement. On-line, computer-based testing is already in use in some places, and has expanded a good deal in the last few years. The increased reliance on testing and assessment as an educational reform tool has also raised issues concerning the fairness of uses and interpretations of tests and assessments. At the same time that externally mandated testing has been expanding, there also has been an increased emphasis on the use of formative assessments by teachers as an integral part of their day-to-day instruction.

Educational testing is pervasive in schools. Standardized paper-and-pencil tests are part of federal, state, and district requirements throughout the United States. These mandated tests and assessments come in a variety of forms and are intended to serve quite a range of purposes. They include machine-scored, multiple-choice tests as well as assessments requiring short or extended answers or possibly even some types of hands-on performance assessment tasks (e.g., a science experiment or the creation of a piece of art).

Statewide testing requirements in selected subjects and grades have been in place in most states for a number of years. Until recently the nature of the tests and patterns of tested grades and subject areas varied substantially from state to state. Federal legislation signed into law on January 8, 2002, however, requires greater uniformity in state testing requirements. The No Child Left Behind (NCLB) Act (Public Law [P.L.] 107-110) required states as of the 2005–2006 school year to test all students in grades 3 through 8 and in at least one grade in high school in reading or language arts and mathematics every year. Starting with the 2007–2008 school year, states also are required to test students annually in science in at least one grade in each of three grade spans (3–5, 6–9, and 10–12).

The testing required by the NCLB Act is used to hold schools, districts, and states accountable for student achievement. The law requires states to set performance standards that are used to establish annual "adequate yearly progress" targets that ensure that all students will perform at the "proficient" level or above by the 2013–2014 school year. Schools that fail to meet adequate yearly progress targets 2 years in a row are placed into a "needs improvement" category. When initially identified as "needs improvement," schools must develop improvement plans, and districts must provide public school choice. When a school is identified 2 years in a row, districts are required to make available tutoring services for low-income students. Schools that continue to be identified for 3, 4, or 5 years in a row are subject to more severe sanctions, leading finally to restructuring and the replacement of teachers and school administrators.

Many states have testing and assessment requirements in addition to those mandated by the accountability provisions of the NCLB Act. The added requirements may be used for school accountability or accreditation. A substantial number of states also require students to pass tests for grade-to-grade promotion and an increasing number of states require students to pass tests for graduation from high school.

Tests and assessments are also administered as part of national surveys (e.g., the National Assessment of Educational Progress [NAEP]), and for international assessments such as the International Mathematics and Science Studies or the Progress in International Reading Literacy Studies. Indeed, the NCLB Act requires states to participate in state-by-state NAEP every other year in both reading and mathematics at grades 4 and 8. For many readers of this textbook, of course, another type of standardized test may come to mind as a result of the not-too-distant experience of taking the SAT or the ACT for admissions to college or taking the Graduate Record Examination for admission to graduate school.

Most students, particularly those educated in the United States, have had considerable experience with a variety of standardized tests before entering college. Standardized tests and assessments have played a prominent role in discussions of the state of education in the United States and in the educational reform initiatives. Standardized tests have also been the focus of intense controversy. Reasons for the controversies vary, including charges that standardized tests are biased against minorities and females and beliefs that they drive instruction in undesirable ways by an overemphasis on factual knowledge and low-level skills. Given the importance of standardized testing for educational policy-makers and the associated issues and controversies, it is essential that teachers understand the technology as well as the uses and abuses of standardized testing and assessment.

Although most of this book focuses on the construction and use of tests and assessments in the classroom, there are several reasons for starting with a discussion of trends and issues related to externally mandated tests and assessments. Externally mandated tests and assessments provide a context for some aspects of classroom assessment. In many cases, such tests and assessments are intended to be a lever of educational reform by making curriculum priorities more explicit and focusing on instructional effort. Furthermore, many of the controversial issues related to standardized tests and assessments are either directly relevant to classroom assessments (e.g., questions of instructional relevance, validity, and fairness) or set the stage for considering the relative strengths and weaknesses of classroom assessments.

Although externally mandated tests receive the lion's share of attention in press coverage and dominate a great deal of political discussions about the quality of education in the United States, they represent only a relatively small fraction of all testing and assessment that goes on in the schools. Formative assessments under the control of classroom teachers comprise a larger fraction of the overall testing and assessment activity in the schools. Formative assessments are frequently referred to as assessments *for* learning to distinguish them from externally mandated standardized tests that are referred to as assessments *of* learning. Teachers need to have a good understanding of both types of assessments.

EDUCATIONAL ASSESSMENT: BAROMETER AND LEVER OF REFORM

Although students spend considerably more time taking teacher-made tests and assessments than they do taking tests that are externally mandated, the latter attract the greater attention of policymakers, the media, and the general public. Attention to externally mandated tests and assessments is nothing new. The United States has a long history of expecting a great deal of such tests and assessments. A 1992 report prepared for Congress by the Office of Technology Assessment (OTA) states,

> From the earliest days of the public school movement, American educators, parents, policymakers, and taxpayers have turned to these tests as multipurpose tools: yardstick of individual progress in classrooms, agent of school reform, filter of educational opportunity, and barometer of the national educational condition. (p. 3)

Many variations exist both in the nature of the tests and assessments and in the uses that have been made of them; however, the OTA report indicates some consistent themes. Educational reformers have used results of mandated tests and assessments to document shortcomings, but, more important, they have used them as instruments of educational reform.

In the barometer role, tests and assessments are expected to provide information about current status and progress of student achievement and the quality of schooling. In the role as a lever of reform, they are also expected to serve as a mechanism of reforming educational practices by clarifying priorities and motivating greater and more focused efforts on the part of students and teachers by holding educators and students accountable for results.

Factors That Make Tests and Assessments Appealing to Educational Policymakers

1. Tests and assessments are relatively inexpensive. Compared to changes that involve increases in instructional time, reduced class size, attracting more able people to teaching, hiring teacher aides, or programmatic changes involving substantial professional development for teachers, testing is cheap.
2. Testing and assessment can be externally mandated. It is far easier to mandate testing and assessment requirements at the state or district level than it is to take actions that involve change in what happens day to day inside the classroom.
3. Testing and assessment changes can be rapidly implemented. Importantly, new test or assessment requirements can be implemented within the term of office of elected officials.
4. Results are visible. Test results routinely are reported by the press.

FIVE DECADES OF TEST-BASED EDUCATIONAL REFORM

Test-based reforms can readily be traced back to the middle of the 19th century, when the Massachusetts state superintendent of instruction used written examinations as a means of holding public schools accountable for results (Resnick, 1982). In the early part of the 20th century, Joseph Rice (1914) administered spelling and mathematics tests to thousands of school children in a series of studies that raised questions about the efficiency of the use of instructional time. Numerous achievement test batteries published following World War I made use of the multiple-choice technology that came into widespread use during the war. Although there was substantial growth in the use of tests between World Wars I and II, the expansion accelerated after World War II, particularly from the 1960s to the present.

Federal Support of Compensatory Education: Title I

In recognition of the large disparities in educational opportunities and in student performance, considerable attention was focused on compensatory education in the mid-1960s. The Elementary and Secondary Education Act (ESEA) of 1965 put in place the largest and most enduring of these federal efforts in this realm commonly known as Title I. Although it was reshaped in some important ways in both the 1994 and 2001 reauthorizations (the Improving America's School Act of 1994 and the NCLB Act of 2001), Title I continues to be the largest federal program of assistance to elementary and secondary education.

The congressional demands for evaluation and accountability for the funds distributed under Title I of ESEA, as well as several other programs of the 1960s, proved to be a boon to test publishers. The testing requirements of the Title I Evaluation and Reporting System (TIERS) contributed to a substantial expansion in the use of published standardized tests. Rather than administering tests once a year in selected grades, TIERS encouraged the administration of tests in both the fall and the spring for Title I students, to evaluate the progress of students participating in the program. Although little use was made of the aggregate test results, these TIERS requirements relieved for a time the pressure from demands for accountability for this major federal program. However, dissatisfaction with the progress made in student achievement, especially for the students that Title I is intended to serve, contributed to the substantial increases in testing and accountability provisions in the NCLB Act of 2001 that were briefly described earlier.

Minimum-Competency Testing

Perceived shortcomings of the skills of high school graduates led to the rapid introduction of additional testing requirements in the 1970s and early 1980s. Minimum-competency testing (MCT) reforms swiftly spread from state to state. In a single decade (1973–1983), the number of states with some form of MCT requirement went from 2 to 34. As the name suggests, MCT programs focused on basic skills that were considered to be the minimal essentials for the next grade level or a high school diploma. Minimal basic skills, although not easy to define or defend, were widely accepted as a reasonable requirement for high school graduation. However, in a landmark case in Florida (*Debra P. v. Turlington*, 1979), the court ruled that students had to be given adequate notice of the testing (2 years) and that the state had to demonstrate that the students had an opportunity to learn the material tested. Although several of the MCT high school graduation requirements instituted by states in the 1970s and 1980s are still in place, the recognition of the need to consider more than minimum levels of performance soon led to other testing and assessment demands.

A Nation at Risk

Another wave of test-based reforms followed closely on the heels of the MCT movement. This round of reform efforts stressed school-level accountability and attempted to push beyond minimums. The test-based reforms of the middle and late 1980s were encouraged by a number of reports on the status of education that were completed in 1983. *A Nation at Risk: The Imperative for Educational Reform*, issued by the National Commission on Excellence in Education (1983), was probably the best known and most influential of these. That report featured tests in two ways: (1) to document shortcomings in student achievement, and (2) as a recommended mechanism of reform.

All 50 states introduced some type of educational reform in the wake of *A Nation at Risk*. Consistent with the emphasis of the report, testing was central in the majority of state-legislated reform efforts. Indeed, in many cases, externally mandated tests were relied on as the major instrument of reform. Many of the reforms involved an expansion of the use of test results for accountability purposes. Accountability programs took a variety of forms but shared the common characteristic that they increased real or perceived stakes of results for teachers and educational administrators.

Building and district "report cards" showing student test performance were used to make educators more accountable for student achievement. As intended, test-based comparisons of schools and districts placed considerable pressure on school superintendents, principals, and teachers to "get the scores up." Test preparation became a major

---

A Nation at Risk

Conclusion of Inadequate Achievement

The educational foundations of our society are presently being eroded by a rising tide of mediocrity that threatens our very future as a Nation and a people. (National Commission on Excellence in Education, 1983, p. 5)

Reliance on Tests as a Mechanism of Reform

A Nation at Risk recommended the use of tests as instruments to improve education through their use to

(a) certify the student's credentials;
(b) identify the need for remedial intervention; and
(c) identify the opportunity for advanced work. (National Commission on Excellence in Education, 1983, p. 28)

---

component in the instructional programs of many schools. Teachers reported in surveys that, as the result of the pressure, they focused their instruction on the skills tested, taught test-taking skills, and used the format of the externally mandated test in their own tests. The focus sometimes narrowed to the specific topics known to be on the mandated test, and practice was provided on items similar to those in the test. Under high-stakes testing conditions, topics corresponding to important instructional objectives not included on the test often were found to fall by the wayside as the testing date approached (see, for example, Nolan, Haladyna, & Hass, 1992; Shepard, 2000; Smith & Rottenberg, 1991).

Although some states and districts contracted for or developed their own tests, the accountability systems of the 1980s relied heavily on published standardized tests. Upward trends in student achievement were reported by an overwhelming majority of states and districts during the first few years of accountability testing programs. A physician, John Cannell (1987), forcefully brought to public attention what came to be known as the "Lake Wobegon effect," that is, the incredible finding that essentially all states and most districts were reporting that their students were scoring above the national norm. The Lake Wobegon effect received considerable publicity. This finding that almost all states using standardized tests in the elementary grades were reporting that the majority of their students were above the national average has generally been attributed to a combination of placing great pressure on getting scores up and the reuse of the same test with old norms year after year (Linn, Graue, & Sanders, 1990). The Lake Wobegon effect raised serious questions about the credibility of test results and about the possible negative side effects of high-stakes accountability uses of standardized test results.

Standards-Based Reform

The wave of reform in the 1990s continued to emphasize accountability but added some significant new features. Perhaps the four most notable of the new features are the emphasis on (a) adopting ambitious, "world-class" standards that both shape the assessments and define levels of acceptable performance; (b) using forms of assessment that require students to perform more substantial tasks (e.g., construct extended essay responses and conduct experiments) rather than only select answers on multiple-choice items; (c) the attachment of high-stakes accountability mechanisms for schools, teachers, and sometimes students; and (d) the inclusion of all students.

Content and Performance Standards.   Educational improvement must begin with a clear idea of what students are expected to learn. This premise underlies the standards-based efforts to improve American education. Standards are statements that specify what should be taught and what students should learn. Standards specify goals or expectations for students, but they do not mandate a particular curriculum, textbook, or instructional approach. There may be many ways of achieving the ends identified in the standards. The key to effective standards, however, is that they be specific enough to identify what students need to learn and to determine when the standards have been met.

These two purposes—identifying what students need to learn and determining when the standards are achieved by students—correspond to the two types of standards that are commonly distinguished: content standards and performance standards. **Content standards** specify the "what," whereas performance standards specify "how well." That is, content standards are public statements that specify what students should know and be able to do in specific content or subject-matter areas at identified points of their education (e.g., grade 4 reading or grade 8 mathematics). **Performance standards** are dependent on content standards but add the specification of the level of performance that students are expected to achieve in relationship to the content standards. In other words, they answer the question, How good is good enough? Ideally, "they indicate both the nature of the evidence (such as an essay, mathematical proof, scientific experiment, project, exam, or combination of these) required to demonstrate that content standards have been met and the quality of student performance that will be deemed acceptable (what merits a passing or an 'A' grade)" (National Educational Goals Panel, 1991, p. 22).

We will have more to say about standards in Chapter 3. For present purposes, however, it is sufficient to note that with encouragement from content-specific teachers' associations (e.g., the National Council of Teachers of Mathematics and the National Council of Teachers of English) and the federal government through the Goals 2000 legislation, almost every state developed and adopted some form of content standards during the 1990s. In many states, the content standards have served as the basis for developing assessments that are intended to be "aligned" with the standards.

Content Standards On-Line

Content standards developed by states and national professional associations may be found on the World Wide Web. A good place to start is:

http://edstandards.org/Standards.html.

Links to other sites organized by content area and state may be found there.

See also the Mid-continent Research for Education and Learning Web site at:

http://www.mcrel.org/standards-benchmarks.

Performance-Based Assessment.   Coinciding with and reinforced by the movement to develop content and performance standards was the substantial press throughout the 1990s for the development and use of "new" approaches to assessment, variously referred to as alternative assessment, authentic assessment, direct assessment, or performance-based assessment. Each qualifier stresses a different aspect of the assessments: *authentic* stresses an emphasis on "real-world" tasks relevant outside the classroom, *alternative* stresses something other than the familiar multiple-choice test, and *performance* stresses the actual doing of a task (e.g., writing an essay or doing a hands-on experiment) rather than merely recognizing or knowing a right answer. Whatever the qualifier, *assessment* is intended to suggest a shift from fixed-response, machine-scored tests to the use of tasks requiring students to construct responses.

Calls for the increased reliance on performance-based assessment generally rest on three premises that were articulated by Resnick and Resnick (1992). The first premise is characterized by the acronym WYTIWYG (What You Test Is What You Get). The second premise is the converse of this: "You do not get what you do not assess." The third premise is a logical conclusion that follows from acceptance of the first two: "Make assessments worth teaching to" (Resnick & Resnick, 1992, p. 59).

These premises are coupled with an acceptance of the argument that high-stakes testing and assessment shapes instruction and student learning. Rather than trying to change that connection, proponents of performance-based assessment argue that it is assessments that need to be modified not only to eliminate the negative effects of teaching to the assessment but also to make that activity have the desired result of enhanced student learning.

High-Stakes Accountability Mechanisms.   Attaching high stakes to the results of assessments, although not new, has become increasingly popular with policymakers in states and districts throughout the country. The high-stakes accountability provisions of the NCLB Act of 2001 differ from the past in that they come from the federal level and now apply to all states, but are in keeping with the trend toward ratcheting up the stakes attached to test results for schools apparent in many states for most of the 1990s. More often than not, the stakes have applied primarily to educators by using the results of tests to determine rewards and sanctions for schools. For example, some programs identified schools that received not only special recognition but also monetary rewards for improved performance of students on the mandated state or district assessments. In some instances, those monetary rewards could be shared by teachers in the school. For schools where performance on assessments did not improve or even declined, various types of sanctions have been imposed by states. Examples of sanctions imposed through assessment-based accountability systems include bringing in an external team to oversee the school, reassigning teachers to other schools, and removing principals. Under the provisions of the NCLB Act, tutoring, expanded time for instruction either after school or during the summer, and public school choice may be provided to students in low-performing schools. Schools where students score below established target levels may be restructured and teachers and administrators may be replaced.

The stakes for individual students have also been increased in a number of states in recent years. Because of phase-in schedules, the requirements for students that may affect high school graduation, the type of diploma a student receives, or grade-to-grade promotion have not been fully implemented in all cases, but the movement toward increased

requirements is widespread. Tougher grade-to-grade promotion and graduation requirements appear at first blush like a replay of the minimum-competency testing movement
of the late 1970s and early 1980s. They differ, however, in that the new requirements that
are envisioned are intended to set more ambitious "world-class" performance standards.

Inclusion of All Students.   A prominent feature of standards-based educational efforts is
the emphasis on high expectations for ***all*** students. Past practices of excluding a relatively
large percentage of students from state and district standardized test programs because of
limited English proficiency, because they recently moved to a state or district, or because
of student disabilities are incompatible with the push to include all students. The goal of
including all students in the assessment requires the use of multiple strategies. First, many
students who would have been excluded in the past can in fact participate in assessments
without any special considerations or adaptations of procedures. For those students, only
a commitment to include is needed rather than allowing students to be excluded when
convenient. Inclusion is a prominent part of the requirements of the NCLB Act. Schools
that test less than 95% of their eligible students will be placed in the needs-improvement
category regardless of how well the students who are tested perform on the tests.

Many students who would likely have been excluded in the past can be included with
minor accommodations of the assessment. Some accommodations, such as extended time
to complete the assessment, are ones that may lead to changes in assessment conditions
that improve the validity of the assessment for all students. For example, when speed is
not the issue, untimed assessments or ones with generous time limits may increase validity and fairness for all students and at the same time reduce the need to offer extended
time to complete the assessment for some students.

More extensive modifications are clearly needed for some students to meaningfully
participate in the assessment. English-language learners who are proficient in another
language, for example, may have knowledge and skills in a content area other than reading or writing in English that can be assessed in the student's first language but cannot be
reasonably assessed in English.

Accommodations are also needed for some students with disabilities. The nature and
extent of accommodation needed clearly depends on the kind and severity of a student's
disability. Large-print and Braille versions of an assessment are obvious adaptations for
students with visual impairments. Students with some types of physical handicaps may
require someone to record their responses for them. However, by far the largest fraction
of students who were excluded from assessments in the past because of disabilities that
require individual education plans (IEPs) are students with learning disabilities.

Many students with IEPs for learning disabilities are likely to be able to take parts or
all of standards-based assessments without special accommodations. No single type of
accommodation will be appropriate for all those students with learning disabilities that
require some kind of accommodation. Rather, several different approaches are likely to be
needed. Among the more common suggested accommodations for students with learning
disabilities are shorter assessments, more time for completing assessment tasks, oral reading of directions, assessment in small groups or individually, and oral responses to tasks.

Classroom teachers face issues of making appropriate accommodations in both their
instruction and classroom assessment in working with students with IEPs. Although the
IEP is the essential source for guiding the decisions that teachers must make in these

regards, it is clear that considerable professional judgment on the part of teachers is also required. The guiding principle for accommodations on an assessment, whether it is externally mandated or one developed by the teacher for classroom use, is that the accommodations be comparable to the ones required by the student's IEP for instruction.

No Child Left Behind

The fifth consecutive decade of test-based educational reform was ushered in by the NCLB Act of 2001. Although this act is a reauthorization of the ESEA of 1965, its extensive testing requirements apply to all public schools, not just to those receiving Title I funds. The NCLB Act reinforces the role of content and performance standards. Specifically, the law requires each state to "demonstrate that the State has adopted challenging content standards and challenging student performance standards that will be used by the State" (P.L. 107-110, Section 1111[b] [1] [A]).

As noted previously, almost every state had adopted content standards, and most states had some tests in place for selected grades and subjects that were intended to measure their content standards. Most states had set performance standards on their tests. There is great variability among the states, however, in the breadth, depth, and specificity of their content standards. There is also considerable variability in the stringency of the performance standards that have been set by states (for a discussion of variability in state performance standards, see Linn, 2003). To satisfy the requirements of the NCLB Act, however, states were required to submit plans justifying the claim that their content standards are challenging and that they have in place challenging performance standards, referred to in the law as student academic achievement standards. The student academic achievement standards must be "aligned with the State's academic content standards . . . describe two levels of high achievement (proficient and advanced) that determine how well children are mastering the State academic content standards; and describe a third level of achievement (basic) to provide complete information about the progress of lower-achieving children toward mastering the proficient and advanced levels of achievement" (P.L. 107-110, Section 1111[b] [1] [D] [ii]).

The performance standards set by states for use under the provisions of the NCLB Act are of consequence because they are used to set intermediate annual achievement targets for student achievement such that all students will be at the "proficient" level or higher by the 2013–2014 school year. The end goal of 100% proficient in 2014, together with

Sources of Information About NCLB

In addition to the U.S. Department of Education's NCLB Web site (http://www.nclb.gov), most state Web sites include links to information about the NCLB Act as well as specific information about the way in which the state has met the requirements of the law.

See also the following:

http://www.mynclb.com

http://www.neirtec.org/products/techbriefs/default.asp

http://www.nga.org/

http://www.cep-dc.org

state-established starting points in 2002, is used to define "adequate yearly progress" (AYP) targets. The comparison of student achievement for a school in reading or language arts and in mathematics to the AYP targets in those subjects determine whether a school will be identified as "needs improvement" and be subject to the sanctions that apply to schools so designated.

The Question of Impact

The degree to which the increased pressure helped or hurt education is controversial. Proponents of high-stakes testing argue that the tests measure objectives that are important for students to learn and that it is desirable for teachers to focus their attention on those objectives. They point with pride to the increases in test scores that were observed in state and district testing programs since the 1990s.

Critics of the increased emphasis on test results argue that an overreliance on test results distorts education. They argue that important objectives are ignored when they are not included on the tests that count. Moreover, they claim that the increased scores paint a misleading picture because teachers teach the specifics of the tests rather than more general content domains (Koretz, 2005).

The proper role of externally mandated tests and assessments in directing instruction is an issue with which you will struggle, especially if the current emphasis on holding educators accountable for results on these instruments continues. What sort of preparation for taking tests or assessments should students have? How much time should be spent in test preparation activities, such as taking practice tests and learning test-taking strategies? To what degree should tested objectives be given emphasis at the expense of objectives that are not tested? These are important educational questions that have no simple answers. They require thought and reflection on the part of individual teachers and principals.

Consider, for example, the seemingly simple issues of "teaching to the test" and "teaching the test itself." We are almost always interested in making inferences that go beyond the specific test that is used. We would like, for example, to be able to say something about the degree of a student's understanding of mathematical concepts based on the score that is obtained on a math concepts test. Because the items on a test only sample the domain of interest, the test score and the inference about the degree of understanding are not the same. A generalization is required, and it is the generalization, not the test score per se, that is important. When the specific items on the test are taught, the validity of the inference about the student's level of achievement is threatened. Teaching the specific test items is apt to result in an exaggerated view of student achievement in the overall domain of interest.

Teaching to the test—that is, emphasizing the objectives that are on the test without teaching the specific test items—has both advantages and disadvantages. Many schools and districts have made teaching to the test more systematic by the introduction of "benchmark" tests. These are tests that are similar to and keyed to the same content standards as the state mandated test, but are administered several times during the year prior to the administration of the state test. The benchmark test results are used to identify students who are likely to have difficulty on the state test, and teachers are expected to devote special attention to those students to help them perform at the proficient level or above on the state test. Inasmuch as the objectives on the test are important, emphasizing those objectives with or without the use of benchmark tests provides a desirable focus. On the other hand, multiple-choice, standardized tests do not cover all the important learning objectives. Hence, narrowing to only those objectives that are covered would be detrimental for education as a whole.

TECHNOLOGICAL ADVANCES IN TESTING AND ASSESSMENT

With the rapid growth in the availability and power of relatively low-cost microcomputers, it is not surprising that the use of computers to administer tests is becoming increasingly common. Indeed, some readers of this text may have taken or be planning to take the computer-administered Graduate Record Examination, the Academic Skills Assessments of the Praxis Series: Professional Assessments for Beginning Teachers, or one of the other computer-based tests offered by the Educational Testing Service. A special issue of *Education Week* titled "Pencils Down: Technology's Answer to Testing," published in May 2003, was devoted to the use of computer technology to administer and score tests. The editors' introduction to the special issue argues that there has been a convergence of education and technology that has vaulted "computer-based testing into the headlines, raising important questions about whether this new mode of assessment is more useful than traditional paper-and-pencil exams" (The Editors, *Education Week*, May 8, 2003, p. 8). The editors note that the NCLB Act has created a new stimulus for schools to find more efficient ways of testing with faster turnaround than is possible with paper-and-pencil testing technology. According to *Education Week*, 12 states and the District of Columbia had already launched some form of computer-based testing or pilot program when the special issue appeared. The use of computer-based testing has continued to grow since the publication of the 2003 special issue of *Education Week*. During the 3 years from May 2003 to May 2006, the number of states with some form of computer-based assessment of students increased from 12 to 22 (Swanson, 2006, p. 55).

Using a computer to administer items from a paper-and-pencil test can have several advantages. Rather than waiting several weeks to receive test results, scores can be obtained immediately. Computer-based testing also provides the means of tailoring the test to individual students by using performance on previously administered items to select the next item to administer. Although the start-up cost can be substantial, on-line, computer-based testing can also result in substantial reductions in printing, distribution, and scoring expenses. The catch, however, is the need to have more computers available for use in the schools than are currently available in many schools. Judging from a recent special issue of *Education Week* on technology in the schools, which indicated that the national average was 3.8 students per instructional computer (Swanson, 2006. p. 51), it is reasonable to believe that the typical school now has enough computers to make it feasible to administer computer-based tests.

Computers to administer tests that count is one use and, in the short term, may not be the most common use of computer-based testing. There is an almost insatiable demand for the use of practice tests and other forms of test preparation. The flexibility and immediate score reporting offered by on-line testing makes the technology especially appealing for purposes of test preparation. As discussed in later chapters, computer-based testing also has substantial potential for teachers for their own classroom assessments.

Illustrative On-Line and Adaptive Testing Software

http://mgb3.quizlab.com/secured/newteacher.cfm

http://www.fscreations.com/

http://www.onlinetesting.net/

http://www.exambuilder.com/

One change that has already been widely implemented is the use of the computer to administer adaptive tests, that is, tests in which the choice of the next item to administer is based on previous responses of the test taker. Adaptive tests can enhance both the efficiency with which information is handled and the quality of that information. The design of an adaptive test usually starts with the administration of an item that is expected to be of middle difficulty. The second and subsequent items to be administered are determined by the responses of the test taker. In general, if a test taker answers an item correctly, then the computer will select a somewhat more difficult item to administer next. Conversely, a somewhat easier item is administered following an incorrect response. Testing is stopped when the estimates of the individual's performance reach some predetermined level of precision or when some pragmatic maximum number of items has been administered. A variety of computer software is available for administering tests (see the box "Illustrative On-Line and Adaptive Testing Software").

It has been demonstrated that adaptive testing can enhance the efficiency and the precision with which certain types of knowledge, skills, and abilities are measured. In some cases, adaptive tests can obtain the same level of reliability of measurement in just over half the time required for a conventional paper-and-pencil test. If adaptive tests only administer items of the type already in use in a better way, however, the full potential of the use of computers for the administration of tests will not be realized. The attraction of computers as testing devices is not limited to doing better what we already do. Their potential to measure proficiencies that are not measured well by conventional paper-and-pencil tests is even more appealing.

In the long run, the potentially more significant changes in testing as the result of computer-based testing depend on using the computer to do things that cannot be reasonably accomplished with paper-and-pencil tests. The technology opens the door to the use of video simulations or problem settings where students access information from the Web or a CD in ways similar to instructional use of that technology.

Simulations can be used to present test takers with problems that have greater realism and more apparent relevance than problems that are commonly found on paper-and-pencil tests. Computer-based examinations that have been used for some time in medical education and in certification testing for physicians provide an illustration of the type of simulation tests that are apt to be seen in the future as computerized test administration becomes more common. Computer problems simulate aspects of the job of a physician. The test taker is initially presented with a limited set of information about a patient, such as a verbal description of symptoms of the type that a patient might provide at the start of a visit. The test taker then has a variety of options, such as getting a patient history, ordering laboratory tests, or deciding on a course of treatment. Requested information is provided, and new options can be followed by the test taker until a diagnosis is made and a course of treatment prescribed.

Computer-administered problem simulations along these lines have potential advantages over current paper-and-pencil tests in many content areas. They provide a means of going beyond the sort of factual recall that is sometimes overemphasized on paper-and-pencil tests. They focus attention on the use of information to solve realistic problems. They can help assess not only the product of a student's thinking but also the process that the student uses to solve a problem, including the way in which the problem is attacked, the efficiency of the solution, and the number of hints that may be needed to solve the problem.

PUBLIC CONCERN ABOUT TESTING AND ASSESSMENT

Decisions about the selection, administration, and use of educational tests and assessments are no longer left to the educator alone. The public has become an active and vocal partner. As discussed previously, externally mandated testing has been imposed on the schools by states or districts as a result of the public demand for evidence of the school programs' effectiveness. In some states, the public at large has participated, through selected groups, in determining the objectives and standards of the statewide assessment programs. In states where testing and assessment has been made the responsibility of the local school district, parent groups often help shape the programs. It is interesting to note that the concern of state legislators and the general public with the quality of school programs has created a demand for *more* testing and assessment in the schools, not less.

During the expansion of testing programs, the concern has been that there may be too much testing in the schools. In addition to taking the tests in the local school program, high school students, for example, may also have to take one or more state competency tests and several college admissions tests. It is feared that the heavy demand on their time and energy might detract from their schoolwork and that the external testing programs may cause undesirable shifts in the school's curriculum. When teachers and schools are judged by how well students perform on state tests and assessments and by how many students are accepted by leading colleges, direct preparation for the tests and assessments is likely to enter into classroom activities and thereby distort the curriculum.

Probably the greatest public concern has been with the social consequences of testing, especially perceived threats to the rights and opportunities of individuals and groups. This concern has shown up in the form of attacks on standardized tests and the testing industry, new legislation affecting testing, calls for a moratorium on standardized testing, and charges that tests are biased and discriminatory. There are certainly some good reasons for the public's concern with the social consequences of testing. It is important, however, to distinguish between negative consequences for individuals or groups that are due to faults in the tests or assessments and ones that are caused by the misinterpretation and misuse of test scores.

Discussed next are four areas of concern resulting in controversy over testing and assessment: (1) the nature and quality of tests, (2) the effects of testing on students,

(3) fairness to minorities, and (4) gender fairness. Some of these issues, particularly the effects of testing and questions of fairness and bias, are also considered in subsequent chapters, in part because they are fundamental issues for all testing and assessment and in part because they can be dealt with more adequately after developing some fundamental concepts of testing and assessment, such as validity (see Chapter 4).

Nature and Quality of Tests

A long-standing criticism of standardized tests is directed primarily at the use of multiple-choice items. In the early 1960s, critics such as Hoffman (1962) contended that the multiple-choice item penalized the more intelligent original thinkers. He supported his claims by reviewing items from standardized tests and showing how some highly able and creative students were likely to see implications in the items not thought of by the test author(s) and thus question the correctness of the keyed answers. Although Hoffman obviously was able to discover some defective items that appeared in standardized tests, his criticisms seemed to go well beyond the evidence presented. He did, however, encourage test publishers to supplement statistical item analysis with a more careful, logical analysis of test items.

Multiple-choice questions continue to bear the brunt of criticisms made by both specialists in educational measurement who seek ways of improving educational tests and critics who would like to eliminate standardized testing. For example, Frederiksen (1984), a major contributor to the field of measurement, has argued that multiple-choice items place too much emphasis on "well structured problems" when problems of greatest interest both in and out of school are often "ill structured" and where skills such as problem identification and hypothesis generation are often as important as problem solution. Such criticisms have led to increased emphasis on open-ended questions and the design of computer simulation tests.

Another type of criticism—that tests **measure only limited aspects** of an individual—has also received considerable attention. This criticism is well founded. Tests do measure specific and limited samples of behavior. Aptitude tests typically measure samples of verbal and quantitative skills useful in predicting school success, and achievement tests measure samples of student performance on particular learning tasks useful in assessing educational progress. Both fulfill their limited functions well, but the difficulty arises when we expect more of them than was intended. For example, both the advocates and the critics of college admissions testing sometimes assume that the tests measure all that is needed for success in college and beyond. This tendency to read into test scores more than they really tell has been called the "whole person fallacy" by W. W. Trunbull, the former president of the Educational Testing Service.

Tests Measure Only a Narrow Segment of Skills and Abilities

Ability and academic achievement occupy an Olympian perch on the prestige ladder. Yet it is widely agreed that motivation, creativity, personal honesty, intuition, even the degree of social consciousness play significant roles in the struggle for the most cherished of American ideals—"success in life." Admission tests thus measure a relatively narrow segment of the human potential. (Educational Testing Service, 1979, p. 6)

Much of the misinterpretation and misuse of test scores could be avoided if the limited nature of the information tests provide was more widely recognized. In college admission decisions, as well as in all other educational decisions, test scores provide just one type of information and always should be supplemented by past records of achievement and other types of assessment data. No major educational decision should ever be based on test scores alone.

To help avoid an overreliance on test scores, it is important to recognize that all assessments are subject to error and that predictions in all areas are fallible. Recognizing the limitations of tests and assessments is a critical component of the proper use of results. To put the limitations in context, it is also important to compare the tests' reliability, validity, and fairness with the alternatives. Would our judgments of aptitude and achievement be more trustworthy and fair without test results? Would our predictions of future school or occupational success be more valid without the additional information supplied by tests? Would our educational decisions be improved if we stopped using tests? Qualified users of tests take into account the possible error in test scores during interpretation and use, and they combine test scores with other relevant information when making educational decisions. To argue that better educational decisions would be made without test scores is to argue that better decisions are made when less information is available. Test scores are certainly fallible, but probably less so than most of the other types of information that enter into educational decisions. See the box "What Are the Consequences of Not Testing?"

Effects of Testing on Students

Critics of testing argue that testing is likely to have certain undesirable effects on students. Some of the most commonly mentioned charges directed toward the use of aptitude and achievement tests are listed here with brief comments.

Criticism 1: Tests Create Anxiety.   There is no doubt that anxiety increases during testing. For most students, it motivates them to perform better. For a few, test anxiety may be so great that it interferes with test performance. These typically are students who are generally anxious, and the test simply adds to their already high level of anxiety. A number of steps can be taken to reduce test anxiety, such as thoroughly preparing for the test, taking practice exercises, and using liberal time limits. Fortunately, many test publishers in recent years have provided practice tests and shifted from speed tests to power tests. This should help, but it is still necessary to observe students carefully during testing and to discount the scores of overly anxious students.

Criticism 2: Tests Categorize and Label Students.   Categorizing and labeling individuals can be a serious problem, particularly when those labels are used as an excuse for poor student achievement rather than a means of providing the extra services and help to ensure better achievement. It is all too easy to place individuals in pigeonholes and apply labels that determine, at least in part, how they are viewed and treated. Classifying students in terms of levels of mental ability has probably caused the greatest concern in education. When students are classified as mentally retarded, for example, it influences how teachers and peers view them, how they view themselves, and the kind of school

What Are the Consequences of Not Testing?

If the use of educational tests were abandoned, the encouragement and reward of individualized efforts to learn would be more difficult. Excellence in programs of education would become less tangible as a goal and less demonstrable as an attainment. Educational opportunities would be extended less on the basis of aptitude and merit and more on the basis of ancestry and influence; social-class barriers would become less permeable.

Decisions on important issues of curriculum and method would be made less on the basis of solid evidence and more on the basis of prejudice or caprice. These, it seems to us, are likely to be the more harmful consequences, by far. Let us not forgo the wise use of good tests.

Source: Ebel, R. L., *Practical Problems in Educational Measurement.* Copyright © 1980 by Houghton Mifflin Company. Used with permission.

programs they receive. When students are mislabeled as mentally retarded, as has been the case with some racial and ethnic minorities, the problem is compounded. At least some of the support for mainstreaming handicapped students has come from the desire to avoid the categorizing and labeling that accompanies special education classes.

Classifying students into various types of learning groups can more efficiently use the teacher's time and the school's resources. However, when grouping, teachers must take into account that tests measure only a limited sample of a student's abilities and that students are continuously changing and developing. By keeping the groupings tentative and flexible and regrouping for different subjects (e.g., reading and math), teachers can avoid most of the undesirable features of grouping. It is when the categories are viewed as rigid and permanent that labeling becomes a serious problem. In such cases, it is not the test that should be blamed but the user of the test.

Criticism 3: Tests Damage Students' Self-Concepts.   This is a concern that requires the attention of teachers, counselors, and other users of tests. The improper use of tests may indeed contribute to distorted self-concepts. The stereotyping of students is one misuse of tests that is likely to have an undesirable influence on a student's self-concept. Another is the inadequate interpretation of test scores that may cause students to make unwarranted generalizations from the results. It is certainly discouraging to receive low scores on tests, and it is easy to see how students might develop a general sense of failure unless the results are properly interpreted. Low-scoring students need to be made aware that aptitude and achievement tests are limited measures and that the results can change. In addition, the possibility of overgeneralizing from low test scores will be lessened if the student's positive accomplishments and characteristics are mentioned during the interpretation. When properly interpreted and used, tests can help students develop a realistic understanding of their strengths and weaknesses and thereby contribute to improved learning and a positive self-image.

Criticism 4: Tests Create Self-Fulfilling Prophecies.   This criticism has been directed primarily toward intelligence or scholastic aptitude tests. The argument is that test scores create teacher expectations concerning the achievement of individual students; the teacher then teaches in accordance with those expectations, and the students respond by achieving to their expected level—a self-fulfilling prophecy. Thus, those who are expected to achieve more do achieve more, and those who are expected to achieve less **do** achieve less. This so-called Pygmalion effect received strong support from a widely heralded study by Rosenthal and Jacobsen (1968), even though the study was later challenged by other researchers (Elashoff & Snow, 1971; West & Anderson, 1976). The belief that teacher expectations enhance or hinder a student's achievement is widely held, and the role of testing in creating these expectations is certainly worthy of further research.

In summary, there is some merit in the various criticisms concerning the possible undesirable effects of tests on students; but more often than not, these criticisms should be directed at the users of the tests rather than the tests themselves. The same persons who misuse test results are likely to misuse alternative types of information that are even less accurate and objective. Thus, the solution is not to stop using tests but to start using tests and other data sources of information more effectively. When tests are used in a positive manner—that is, to help students improve their learning and development—the consequences are likely to be desirable rather than undesirable.

Fairness of Tests to Minorities

The issue of test fairness to racial and ethnic minorities is a critical issue for any assessment program. Fairness has received increasing attention over the years in the literature on testing and assessment. Concern with the fairness of tests has paralleled the general public concern with providing equal rights and opportunities to all U.S. citizens. An analysis of the discussions of fairness in testing and assessment makes it evident that the concept of fairness is used in many different ways. Testing and assessment professionals have often equated fairness with an **absence of bias**—considering, for example, a test use as fair if predictions of nontest performance are comparable for different racial or ethnic groups.

Fairness may also focus on the equity in treatment of persons from different groups in the assessment process. This second notion of fairness is sometimes referred to as **procedural fairness** and involves questions such as the following: Do test takers have an equal opportunity to show what they know and can do on a test? Are responses to essay questions graded comparably by raters without regard to the test taker's group membership?

A third meaning of fairness would require that students be provided with an adequate or equal **opportunity to learn** the material that is assessed. A fourth meaning of fairness that is common in some popular uses of the term is the **equality of results**. From this perspective, a test would be considered fair only if the average performance of different groups (e.g., African Americans, Latinos, and whites) was the same.

These four conceptions of fairness—absence of bias, procedural fairness, opportunity to learn, and equality of results—are consistent with the discussion of the topic in the latest revision of the *Standards for Educational and Psychological Testing* (AERA, APA, & NCME, 1999). The different perspectives can lead to quite different conclusions about the fairness of any test or assessment. The fourth conception, equality of results, is incompatible with other tenets of testing and assessment, such as the goal of getting a valid and reliable measure of what students know and can do regardless of their background or group membership. Inasmuch as different groups of students differ in the instruction they have received, their experiences both in and out of school, and their interest and effort, one cannot expect a valid measure to show no difference between the groups. In other words, a test or assessment that shows average differences in scores for minority and majority group students may fairly reflect the consequences of unfair treatment of minorities by the society.

An absence of bias and procedural fairness is essential for an assessment to have a high level of validity in measuring the knowledge, skills, and understandings that it is intended to measure. In other words, those characteristics are essential to avoid unfairness due to faulty measurement.

Whether professionals in testing and assessment would consider adequacy or equality of opportunity to learn as essential for fairness generally depends not only on the instrument but also on the uses and interpretations that are made of the results. Thus, it would be considered fair to use results of an achievement test to document inequalities in education where there were substantial differences in opportunity to learn. But it would not be fair to use the test results as the basis for rewards or sanctions for students under those conditions. Nor would it be fair to infer that the group that was not provided with an adequate opportunity to learn was intellectually inferior or incapable of learning the material on the assessment.

It is often useful to distinguish between (a) the possible presence of bias in the test content and (b) the possible unfair use of test results. These factors are undoubtedly related, but we discuss them here separately.

In evaluating the possible presence of bias in test content, it is important to distinguish between the performance the test is intended to measure and factors that may distort the scores unfairly. In testing mathematics skills with story problems, for example, it is important to keep the reading level low so that the test scores are not contaminated by reading ability. If the reading level is too difficult, poor readers will obtain lower scores than warranted, and the test will be biased against them. Because a particular minority group may have a disproportionately large number of poor readers, the test may be biased against that minority group. But if the test of mathematics skills is not contaminated by reading or other factors, low scores will simply indicate lack of mathematics skills. Such a test is fair to everyone even if the test scores indicate group differences in the mastery of mathematics.

In the past, standardized tests typically emphasized content and values that were more familiar to white middle-class students than to racial or ethnic minorities and students of lower socioeconomic status. Thus, the content of some scholastic aptitude tests contained vocabulary, pictures, and objects that minorities had less opportunity to learn. Similarly, some reading tests contained stories and situations that were unrelated to their life experiences. Racial and ethnic minorities were seldom represented in pictures, stories, and other test content, and when they were, it was sometimes in an offensive manner. How much these types of bias might have lowered the scores of individual students is impossible to say, but most persons familiar with testing would acknowledge some adverse effect. Fortunately, test publishers have taken steps to correct the situation. Test publishers now employ staff members representing various racial and cultural minorities, and new tests are routinely reviewed for content that might be biased or offensive to minority groups. Statistical analysis is also being used to detect and remove test items that function differently for different groups of test takers (Cole & Moss, 1989).

The most controversial problems concerning the fair use of tests with minority groups are encountered when aptitude tests are used as a basis for educational and vocational selection. Much of the difficulty here is with the definition of fair test use. One view is that a test is fair or unbiased if it predicts as accurately for minority groups as it does for the majority group. This traditional view, which favors a common cutoff score for selection, has been challenged as being unfair to minority groups because they often earn lower test scores, and thus a smaller proportion of qualified individuals tends to be selected. Alternative definitions of test fairness favor some type of adjustment, such as separate cutoff scores or bonus points, for some minorities.

Ultimately, the decision as to whether minority group membership is to be ignored or given special consideration in selection will not be made by educators or psychologists. The fair use of tests in selection is part of a larger issue that must be settled by society through court rulings. Stated in simplified form, the issue is how equal educational and occupational opportunities can best be provided for members of minority groups without infringing on the rights of other individuals.

Gender Fairness

The issues of fairness regarding testing and assessment have also attracted considerable attention in the use and interpretation of tests and assessments for males and females. For example, the use of scores on tests such as the Preliminary SAT (PSAT) as the basis for identifying National Merit Scholars has focused attention on the issue of gender bias in tests in recent years. On the mathematics section of the PSAT, the average score for males has been higher than the average score for females, and there have been more males than females with very high scores for many years. In recent years, the average score for males is also slightly higher than the average for females on the verbal section of these tests. As a consequence, a substantially larger percentage of male National Merit Scholars have been identified than female scholars. As a partial response to this difference, writing scores, on which females tend to score higher than males, have been added to the mix for identifying National Merit Scholars, thereby reducing the gender difference in recognition of scholars.

As in the case of differences in scores of racial or ethnic groups, the existence of a difference in average scores for males and females does not necessarily imply that the test is biased. There are, for example, differences in the number of mathematics courses taken by females and males in high school, and these differences may lead to differences in the scores on the mathematics tests (Willingham & Cole, 1997). Whatever the cause of the differences, however, it does not change the fact that use of the tests alone results in a larger proportion of scholarships being awarded to males than to females despite the fact that females earn higher grades in school than males on average. Judgments about the proper use of test scores must rest on more than technical evaluations of the tests or the degree to which the scores reflect real differences in knowledge, skills, and developed abilities rather than unintentional biases. Such judgments also involve questions of social values and social policy.

Although not a minority group, women have had some of the same problems as minorities have in attempting to obtain equal educational and occupational opportunities. Thus, in the use of test results in career planning, care needs to be taken so that test scores are not unfairly used to direct females away from certain occupations. For example, females tend to score lower than males on mechanical comprehension tests and to have lower mechanical interest scores. Although these differences probably reflect cultural influences rather than sex bias in the tests, it would be unfortunate if such results were used to limit the occupations females might consider as possible careers.

Information About the Construction and Use of Formative Assessments

The Assessment Training Institute (**http://www.assessmentinst.com**) offers books and videos that are designed to help K–12 educators construct and use formative assessments.

Willingham and Cole (1997) have reported a comprehensive set of analyses examining differences in the performance of males and females on a variety of types of tests and assessments. They also have investigated factors related to the differences found and comparability in the validity of the measures when they are used for various purposes, such as predicting subsequent performance of males and females.

Formative Assessments

Several distinctions can be made between formative assessments and mandated tests. First, classroom teachers control the timing and use of formative assessments, whereas mandated tests are controlled from afar and must be administered on a schedule dictated by the state or district. Second, formative assessments are flexible and may be adapted to the instructional needs of individual students, whereas external tests are standardized and uniform for all students. Moreover, as noted, external tests provide evaluations *of* student learning whereas formative assessments provide measures *for* learning; that is, the main purpose of formative assessments is to provide information that can be used to guide instruction and enhance student learning.

To be effective tools of teaching and learning, formative assessments must be consistent with important student learning goals (see, for example, Shepard, 2001). Teachers must be able to control the time that formative assessments are administered and the choice of tasks that students are asked to perform. The assessments must provide feedback to students and teachers (Black & Wiliam, 1998). Rubrics that teachers use to score constructed responses to assessment tasks must be transparent and made part of the feedback to students. Clear instructional goals and specifications of assessment tasks, together with transparent scoring rubrics, can contribute to improved learning by helping students use self-assessments to monitor their own progress.

SUMMARY

You are likely to encounter a number of externally mandated testing and assessment programs in schools. As a teacher, you may be directly involved in some of the programs. Others you may simply need to know about so that you can serve as an informed professional in dealing with students, parents, and the public. These programs have generally contributed to expanded testing and assessment in the schools, which in turn have created new trends and raised concerns. You will also have opportunities to construct and use formative assessments. When properly used, the latter assessments can be effective tools for enhancing instruction and student learning. Subsequent chapters provide elaborations of these ideas.

Demands for accountability have led to substantial increases in the amount of testing and assessment in the schools and in the importance that is attached to the scores. Minimum-competency testing programs that required students to pass tests to receive high school diplomas or to be promoted to the next grade grew rapidly throughout the country in the late 1970s. Demands for comparisons of schools, school districts, and states in terms of student achievement test scores led to the introduction of still more testing and assessment requirements and increased the stakes for teachers and school administrators.

In recent years, emphasis has been placed on establishing demanding content and performance standards for all students. The demanding performance standards have increased the stakes associated with assessment-based accountability systems in a number of states. At the same time, the pressure to include all students has presented new challenges in developing assessments and administration procedures that provide adequate accommodations for students with special needs or students who are English-language learners.

The NCLB Act of 2001 has requirements for increases in the amount of testing that states had mandated before the act became law. It reinforces the role of content and student performance standards. Most important, the act requires states to use student test results to hold schools and districts accountable for student achievement in reading or language arts and mathematics and, beginning with the 2007–2008 school year, in science.

Several changes in educational measurement have been broad enough and persistent enough to be identified as trends. In addition to the expanded uses of tests that have just been summarized, developments are changing the nature of testing and assessment. Most notable of these developments is the increased emphasis on performance-based assessment. Concerns that tests and assessments strongly influence what gets taught have led to increased emphasis on making assessments that correspond as closely as possible to complex learning objectives that are not readily measured by conventional tests. Demands for new forms of assessment have led to changes in approaches being used to measure teacher performance as well as student performance.

Technological developments also promise to change the nature of testing and assessment. Computers provide a means of making tests adaptive to the individual test taker and constructing realistic simulations to test problem-solving skills. On-line, computer-based testing has certain potential advantages over traditional paper-and-pencil tests. In addition to making adaptive testing, on-line testing provides immediate access to results and may be especially useful as part of an early warning system and in preparing for high-stakes tests. On-line testing may also provide cost savings. The biggest hurdle to wider implementation of computer-based, on-line testing is the demand for access to computers in the schools that exceeds current availability in many places.

Critics of testing have raised issues concerning the possible consequences of testing in the schools. Most of the criticism has been directed toward standardized tests, including such issues as the nature and quality of the tests, the possible harmful effects of testing on students, and the fairness of tests to minorities and women. It is important to recognize the multiple perspectives on what constitutes fairness in testing and assessment, including the absence of bias, procedural fairness, adequacy of opportunity to learn, and equality of outcomes. Although the nature of the test or assessment itself requires close attention in considering issues of fairness, in many instances it is the use or misuse of the results of tests and assessments that is most critical to achieving fairness.

Formative assessments constructed by classroom teachers differ from external tests in a number of ways. They are less formal and may be administered at different times throughout the school year as deemed appropriate by the needs of individual students. They can contribute to improvements in instruction and student learning by providing timely feedback and by clarifying expectations in ways that students can use for purposes of ongoing self-assessment.

LEARNING EXERCISES

1. Discuss the potential effects of the pressure to compare schools, districts, and states in terms of student achievement test scores on instruction and student learning.
2. Discuss the pros and cons of teaching to the specific content of externally mandated tests and assessments.
3. What types of testing and assessment do you think should be increased or decreased in the schools? Why?
4. List possible advantages and disadvantages for each of the apparent trends in educational measurement cited in this chapter.
5. Which criticisms of testing do you consider to be most serious? What steps should be taken to correct them?

6. Discuss the potential uses of computer-based, on-line testing and evaluate the potential advantages and disadvantages of those uses.
7. Consider a testing or assessment program with which you have had experience and discuss how the different perspectives on fairness might be evaluated and explained for that program.
8. Discuss distinctions between mandated tests and formative assessments.
9. Describe some of the unique features of formative assessments and explain how these features might contribute to improved teaching and learning.

REFERENCES

American Educational Research Association, American Psychological Association, and the National Council on Measurement in Education. (1999). *Standards for educational and psychological testing.* Washington, DC: American Educational Research Association.

Black, P., & Wiliam, D. (1998). Assessment and classroom learning. *Assessment in Education: Principles, Policy and Practice, 5*(1), 7–74.

Cannell, J. J. (1987). *Nationally normed elementary achievement testing in America's public schools: How all 50 states are above the national average* (2nd ed.). Daniels, WV: Friends of Education.

Cole, N. S., & Moss, P. A. (1989). Bias in test use. In R. L. Linn (Ed.), *Educational measurement* (3rd ed.). New York: Macmillan.

Debra P. v. Turlington. 474 F. Supp. 244 (M.D. Fla. 1979).

Educational Testing Service. (1979). *ETS developments, 26.* Princeton, NJ: Author.

Education Week. (2003, May). *Technology counts 2003.* Executive summary: Pencils down: Technology's answer to testing.

Elashoff, J. D., & Snow, R. E. (Eds.). (1971). *Pygmalion reconsidered.* Worthington, OH: Charles A. Jones.

Frederiksen, N. (1984). The real test bias. *American Psychologist, 39*, 193–202.

Hoffman, B. C. (1962). *The tyranny of testing.* New York: Crowell-Collier.

Koretz, D. (2005). Alignment, high stakes, and the inflation of test scores. In J. L. Herman & E. H. Haertel (Eds.), *Uses and misuses of data for educational accountability and improvement. Yearbook of the National Society for the Study of Education* (Vol. 104, Part 2, pp. 98–118).

Linn, R. L. (2003). Accountability: Responsibility and reasonable expectations. *Educational Researcher, 31*(7), 3–13.

Linn, R. L., Graue, M. E., & Sanders, N. M. (1990). Comparing state and district test results to national norms: The validity of claims that everyone is above average. *Educational Measurement: Issues and Practice, 9*(3), 5–14.

National Commission on Excellence in Education. (1983). *A nation at risk: The imperative for educational reform.* Washington, DC: U.S. Government Printing Office.

National Educational Goals Panel. (1991). *The national education goals report, 1991: Building a nation of learners. Executive summary.* Washington, DC: Author.

Nolan, S. B., Haladyna, T. M., & Hass, N. S. (1992). Uses and abuses of achievement test scores. *Educational Measurement: Issues and Practice, 11*(2), 9–15.

Resnick, D. (1982). History of educational testing. In A. K. Wigdor & W. R. Garner (Eds.), *Ability testing: Uses, consequences, and controversies* (pp. 173–194). Washington, DC: National Academy Press.

Resnick, L. B., & Resnick, D. P. (1992). Assessing the thinking curriculum: New tools for educational reform. In B. G. Gifford & M. C. O'Conner (Eds.), *Changing assessments: Alternative views of aptitude, achievement and instruction* (pp. 37–75). Boston: Kluwer Academic Publishers.

Rice, J. M. (1914). *Scientific management in education.* New York: Noble and Eldrege.

Rosenthal, R., & Jacobsen, L. (1968). *Pygmalion in the classroom.* New York: Holt, Rinehart & Winston.

Shepard, L. (2000). The role of assessment in a learning culture. *Educational Researcher, 29*(7), 4–14.

Shepard, L. (2001). The role of classroom assessment in teaching and learning. In V. Richardson (Ed.), *Handbook of research on teaching* (4th ed.). Washington, DC: American Educational Research Association.

Smith, M. L., & Rottenberg, C. (1991). Unintended consequences of external testing in elementary schools. *Educational Measurement: Issues and Practice, 10*(4), 7–11.

Swanson, C. (2006). Tracking U.S. Trends, *Education Week, 25*(35), 50–55.

United States Congress, Office of Technology Assessment. (1992). *Testing in American schools: Asking the right questions* (OTA-SET-519). Washington, DC: U.S. Government Printing Office.

West, C. K., & Anderson, T. H. (1976). The question of preponderant causation in teacher expectancy research. *Review of Educational Research, 46*, 613–630.

Willingham, W. W., & Cole, N. S. (1997). *Gender and fair assessment.* Mahwah, NJ: Lawrence Erlbaum Associates.

FURTHER READING

Bunderson, C. V., Inouye, D. K., & Olsen, J. B. (1989). The four generations of computerized educational measurement. In R. L. Linn (Ed.), *Educational measurement* (3rd ed.). New York: Macmillan. Discusses uses of computers to administer tests.

Cole, N. S., & Moss, P. A. (1989). Bias in test use. In R. L. Linn (Ed.), *Educational measurement* (3rd ed.). New York: Macmillan. Discusses a wide range of issues related to bias in test use and interpretation.

Stiggins, R., Arter, J., Chappuis, J., & Chappuis, S. (2004). *Classroom assessment for student learning:* *Doing it right—Using it well.* Portland, OR: Assessment Training Institute.

U.S. Congress, Office of Technology Assessment. (1992). *Testing in American schools: Asking the right questions* (OTA-SET-519). Washington, DC: U.S. Government Printing Office. A comprehensive report on the role of externally mandated educational testing and assessment in American education. Presents a discussion of policy issues and arguments for and against various approaches to assessment.

Widgor, A. K., & Garner, W. R. (Eds.). (1982). *Ability testing: Uses, consequences, and controversies, Part I.* Washington, DC: National Academy Press. A report by the Committee on Ability Testing convened by the National Academy of Sciences to study the role of testing in American life. Covers the controversies surrounding testing, the nature of ability testing, the use of tests in education and industry, and the social and legal issues in testing. The final chapter is a summary and review of the role of ability testing.

Willingham, W. W., & Cole, N. S. (1997). *Gender and fair assessment.* Mahwah, NJ: Lawrence Erlbaum Associates. The report provides a comprehensive analysis of gender differences on tests and assessments and the interpretation of those differences.

2

THE ROLE OF MEASUREMENT AND ASSESSMENT IN TEACHING

Assessment of student learning requires the use of techniques for measuring student achievement. Assessment is more than a collection of techniques, however. It is a systematic process that plays a significant role in effective teaching. It begins with the identification of learning goals, monitors the progress students make toward those goals, and ends with a judgment concerning the extent to which those goals have been attained.

The abundance of external mandates for tests and assessments discussed in Chapter 1 make it evident that students in the United States are subjected to a great deal of testing and assessment just as a consequence of those mandates; but measurement and assessment include much more than standardized tests. Students spend considerably more time taking teacher-constructed tests and tests selected by teachers from materials furnished by publishers than they do taking standardized tests. Even the addition of teacher-constructed and teacher-selected tests leaves us with an incomplete picture of the domain of measurement and assessment. Formal assessments of student worksheets, homework assignments, projects, and term papers further expand the concept of the domain but still leave it incomplete because many of the assessments that are critical to the moment-by-moment classroom activities are informal.

Informal classroom observation guides many instructional decisions. For example, oral questioning of students may indicate the need for a complete review of the material, class discussion may reveal misunderstandings that must be corrected on the spot, and interest in a topic may suggest that more time should be spent on it than originally planned. Similarly, in observing individual students, a teacher decides that Sandra needs help in writing a complete paragraph, that Mike needs more practice in doing mathematics problems, that Juan and Donna should be given remedial work in reading, and that Maria should be encouraged to read more challenging books.

Instructional decisions such as these are made continually during the process of teaching. Some are based on students' oral responses, some on the actual performance of a skill, and others on a student's quizzical look, tone of voice, or physical behavior. All are based on the teacher's moment-by-moment observations. Although these observations are informal, they play an indispensable role in effective teaching.

Tests and other procedures for measuring student learning are not intended as replacements for the teacher's informal observations and judgments. Rather, they are intended to complement and supplement the teacher's informal methods of obtaining information about students. The teacher is still the observer and decision maker. Measurement and assessment procedures merely provide more systematic, objective evidence on which to base instructional decisions.

INSTRUCTIONAL DECISIONS REQUIRING ASSESSMENT DATA

Numerous decisions made by teachers require them to supplement their informal observations of students with more systematic measures of aptitudes, achievement, and personal development. It would not be feasible to make an exhaustive list of all such decisions, but it is possible to identify some of the more common ones. The following list of questions illustrates some of the major instructional decisions teachers are likely to encounter during the course of their teaching. Examples of the types of measurement and assessment procedures that might be most helpful in answering the questions are included in parentheses.

1. How realistic are my teaching plans for this particular group of students? (scholastic aptitude tests, past record of achievement)
2. How should the students be grouped for more effective learning? (teacher-constructed tests, past record of achievement, observation)
3. To what extent are the students ready for the next learning experience? (pretests of needed skills, past record of achievement)
4. To what extent are students attaining the learning goals of the course? (teacher-constructed tests, class projects, oral questioning, observation)
5. To what extent are students progressing beyond the minimum essentials? (teacher-constructed tests, general achievement tests, class projects, portfolios of student work, observation)
6. At what point would a review be most beneficial? (periodic quizzes, oral questioning, observation)
7. What types of learning difficulties are the students encountering? (diagnostic tests, observation, oral questioning, portfolios of work products, student conferences)
8. Which students should be referred to counseling, special classes, or remedial programs? (scholastic aptitude tests, achievement tests, diagnostic tests, observation)
9. Which students have poor self-understanding? (self-ratings, student conferences)
10. Which school grade should be assigned to each student? (review of portfolio of all assessment data)

11. What should parents be told about the progress of their child? (review of portfolio of all assessment data)

12. How effective was my teaching? (achievement tests, students' ratings, self-reflection, supervisors' ratings)

This list of questions highlights the need for various types of information in teaching, but instructional decisions are not so neatly ordered. There are always numerous sub-questions to be answered and an overlap among the various decisions. Many different types of assessment data might be useful in a particular situation. The teaching–learning process involves a continuous and interrelated series of instructional decisions concerning ways to enhance student learning. Our main point here, however, is that the effectiveness of the instruction depends to a large extent on the nature and quality of the information on which the decisions are based.

ASSESSMENT, TEST, AND MEASUREMENT

The terms *assessment, test*, and *measurement* are easily confused because all may be involved in a single process. **Assessment** is a general term that includes the full range of procedures used to gain information about student learning (observations, ratings of performances or projects, paper-and-pencil tests) and the formation of value judgments concerning learning progress. A **test** is a particular type of assessment that typically consists of a set of questions administered during a fixed period of time under reasonably comparable conditions for all students. We sometimes use testing and assessment together even though tests are a specific type of assessment. When used in this way, assessment emphasizes the broader array of performances and projects that might not be called to mind by the word *testing*. **Measurement** is the assigning of numbers to the results of a test or other type of assessment according to a specific rule (e.g., counting correct answers or awarding points for particular aspects of an essay). The specific meaning of each term is summarized in the box "Terminology."

TERMINOLOGY

Assessment: Any of a variety of procedures used to obtain information about student performance. Includes traditional paper-and-pencil tests as well as extended responses (e.g., essays), performances of authentic tasks (e.g., laboratory experiments), teacher observations, and student self-report. Assessment answers the question: "How well does the individual perform?"

Test: An instrument or systematic procedure for measuring a sample of behavior by posing a set of questions in a uniform manner. Because a test is a form of assessment, tests also answer the question: "How well does the individual perform—either in comparison with others or in comparison with a domain of performance tasks?"

Measurement: The process of obtaining a numerical description of the degree to which an individual possesses a particular characteristic. Measurement answers the question: "How much?"

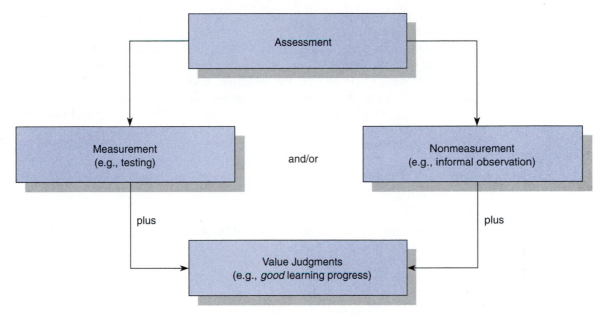

Figure 2.1
The assessment process

Assessment is a much more comprehensive and inclusive term than *measurement* or *testing*. The term *measurement* is limited to quantitative descriptions of students; that is, the results of measurement are always expressed in numbers (e.g., Alex correctly solved 35 of the 40 mathematics problems). It does not include qualitative descriptions (e.g., Laura's work was neat), nor does it imply judgments concerning the worth or value of the obtained results. Assessment, on the other hand, may include both quantitative descriptions (measurement) and qualitative descriptions (nonmeasurement) of students. In addition, assessment always includes value judgments concerning the desirability of the results. Figure 2.1 shows the comprehensive nature of assessment and the role of measurement and nonmeasurement techniques in the assessment process. As noted in the diagram, assessment may or may not be based on measurement; when it is, it goes beyond simple quantitative descriptions.

GENERAL PRINCIPLES OF ASSESSMENT

Assessment is an integrated process for determining the nature and extent of student learning and development. This process will be most effective when the following principles are taken into consideration.

1. Clearly specifying what is to be assessed has priority in the assessment process. The effectiveness of assessment depends as much on a careful description of what to assess as it does on the technical qualities of the assessment procedures used. Thus, specification of the characteristics to be measured should precede the selection or development of assessment procedures. When assessing student learning, this means clearly specifying the intended learning goals before selecting the assessment procedures to use.

General statements from content standards or from course objectives can be a helpful starting point, but in most cases teachers will need to add greater specificity for the assessment process to be effective. For example, a content standard in the area of history might specify that students should "understand ideas and documents within historical contexts." For a content standard stated at that general level, a variety of multiple-choice, short-answer, or essay questions might be considered relevant. To establish assessment priorities for such a standard, teachers need to answer questions such as the following: What ideas? What documents? What historical context? What constitutes adequate evidence of understanding? Such questions are not answered by the general statement in the standard, but they must be answered, either explicitly or implicitly, to develop assessments.

2. **An assessment procedure should be selected because of its relevance to the characteristics or performance to be measured.** Assessment procedures are frequently selected on the basis of their objectivity, accuracy, or convenience. Although these criteria are important, they are secondary to the main criterion: Is this procedure the most effective method for measuring the learning or development to be assessed? Every procedure discussed in subsequent chapters is appropriate for certain uses and inappropriate for others. Any specific test may also be appropriate for certain uses and inappropriate for others. In assessing student achievement, for example, we need a close match between the intended learning goals and the types of assessment tasks used. If the development of the ability to organize ideas and write a well-integrated composition is a learning goal, then a multiple-choice test on the mechanics of writing would be a poor substitute for assessments based on analyses of student writing under a variety of conditions (e.g., in-class essay tests, writing projects, and term papers).

3. **Comprehensive assessment requires a variety of procedures.** No single type of instrument or procedure can assess the vast array of learning and development outcomes emphasized in a school program. Multiple-choice and short-answer tests of achievement are useful for measuring knowledge, understanding, and application outcomes, but essay tests and other written projects are needed to assess the ability to organize and express ideas. Projects that require students to formulate problems, accumulate information through library research, or collect data (e.g., through experimental observations or interviews) are needed to measure certain skills in formulating and solving problems. Observational techniques are needed to assess performance skills and various aspects of student behavior; and self-report techniques are useful for assessing interests and attitudes. A complete picture of student achievement and development requires the use of many different assessment procedures.

4. **Proper use of assessment procedures requires an awareness of their limitations.** Assessment procedures range from highly developed measuring instruments (e.g., standardized aptitude and achievement tests) to rather crude assessment devices (e.g., observational and self-report techniques). Even the best educational and psychological measuring instruments yield results that are subject to various types of measurement error.

No test or assessment asks all the questions or poses all the problems that might appropriately be presented in a comprehensive coverage of the knowledge, skills, and understanding relevant to the content standards or objectives of a course or instructional sequence. Instead, only a sample of the relevant problems or questions is presented. Even in a relatively narrow part of a content domain, such as understanding photosynthesis or the addition and subtraction of fractions, a host of problems might be presented, but any given test or assessment samples but a small fraction of those problems. Consequently, sampling error is one common problem in educational and psychological measurement. An achievement test may not adequately sample a particular domain of instructional content, and even a good sample of items will not completely cover the domain. An observational instrument designed to assess a student's social adjustment may not sample enough behavior for a dependable index of this trait. Fortunately, sampling error can be controlled through careful application of established measurement procedures.

A second source of error is caused by chance factors influencing assessment results, such as guessing on objective tests, subjective scoring on essay tests, errors in judgment on observation devices, and inconsistent responding on self-report instruments (e.g., attitude scales). Because of these problems, students just a few points apart on an educational assessment should not be considered to be different. In fact, no score on an educational or psychological assessment should be treated as a totally accurate measurement of the characteristic in question. Through the careful use of assessment procedures, we are able to keep these errors of measurement to a minimum. (We consider the topic of measurement error in greater detail in Chapter 5.)

The incorrect interpretation of measurement results constitutes another major source of error. Users of educational assessments sometimes interpret results as more precise than they are or as an indication of characteristics beyond those the assessment is designed to measure. For instance, scholastic aptitude scores are sometimes misinterpreted as measures of innate abilities rather than as modifiable abilities or as a measure of general personal worth rather than as a limited measure of verbal and numerical reasoning. Misinterpretation of test results is all too common and is one of the major considerations concerning the validity of an assessment that is considered in Chapter 4. Avoiding misinterpretation requires careful attention to what the test actually measures, how accurately it does so, and its intended uses.

These limitations of assessment procedures do not negate the value of tests and other types of assessments. A keen awareness of the limitations of assessment instruments makes it possible to use them more effectively. Keep in mind that the cruder the instrument, the greater its limitations and, consequently, the more caution required in its use.

5. Assessment is a means to an end, not an end in itself. The use of assessment procedures implies that some useful purpose is being served and that the user is clearly aware of this purpose. To blindly gather data about students and then file the information away is a waste of both time and effort. Wasting time and effort of the students, teachers, and other users of the information will have negative effects on later assessments. Motivation to take assessment seriously will be influenced by the teachers and students understanding the reasons for the assessments and their appropriate use. Assessment is best viewed as a process of obtaining information on which to base important educational decisions.

ASSESSMENT AND THE INSTRUCTIONAL PROCESS

The main purpose of classroom instruction is to help students achieve a set of intended learning goals. These goals should typically include desired changes in the intellectual, emotional, and physical spheres. When classroom instruction is viewed in this light, assessment becomes an integral part of the teaching–learning process. The intended learning outcomes are established by the instructional goals, the desired changes in students are brought about by the planned learning activities, and the students' learning progress is periodically assessed by tests and other assessment devices. Although the interdependent nature of teaching and learning is beyond dispute, the interdependent nature of teaching, learning, and assessment is less often recognized.

The statements in the box "Measurement and Assessment—Essential Components of Effective Teaching" attest to the fact that leaders in the advancement of teaching as a profession recognize the critical role of assessment as an integral part of effective teaching. The interdependence of these three facets of education can be clearly seen in the following steps included in the instructional process.

Identifying Instructional Goals

The first step in both teaching and assessment is determining the learning outcomes to be expected from classroom instruction. How should students think and act when they complete the learning experience? What knowledge and understanding should the students possess? What skills should they be able to display? What interests and attitudes should they have developed? What changes in habits of thinking, feeling, and doing should have taken place? In short, for what specific changes are we striving, and what are students like when we have succeeded in bringing about these changes? Content standards and curriculum guidelines established by a state or district provide a useful starting point for specifying instruction goals, but they almost always require elaboration and additional specificity in order to identify specific goals for students and to guide the details of assessment development. Chapter 3 provides guidance in the process of clarifying instructional goals and objectives.

Preassessing the Learners' Needs

When the instructional goals have been clearly specified, it is usually desirable to make some assessment of the learners' needs in relation to the learning outcomes to be achieved. Do the students possess the abilities and skills needed to proceed with the instruction? Have the students already developed the skills and understanding intended? Assessing students' knowledge and skills at the beginning of instruction enables us to answer such questions. This information is useful in planning work for students who lack the prerequisite skills and in modifying our instructional plans to fit the needs of the learners.

Providing Relevant Instruction

Relevant instruction takes place when course content and teaching methods are integrated into planned instructional activities designed to help students achieve the intended learning outcomes. During this instructional phase, measurement and assessment provide

Measurement and Assessment—Essential Components of Effective Teaching

INTASC: Interstate New Teacher Assessment and Support Consortium, a group created to develop standards for effective teaching for new teachers and to collaborate on assessment procedures for use by states' teacher certification: "The teacher understands and uses formal and informal assessment strategies to evaluate and ensure the continuous intellectual, social, and physical development of the learner."

Source: Principle 8 of the INTASC Model Standards for Teacher Licensing. Available:

http://www.ccsso.org/content/pdfs/ corestrd.pdf

NBPTS: National Board of Professional Teaching Standards, a group created to provide certification of highly accomplished professional teachers, lists five core propositions. Proposition "III. Teachers are responsible for managing and monitoring student learning." Under Proposition III, teachers "use multiple methods for measuring student growth and understanding, and they can clearly explain student performance to parents." Available:

http://www.nbpts.org/the_standards/ the_five_core_propositio

IRA: International Reading Association lists five standards for reading professionals. The standards show the necessary skills for educators (i.e., "candidates") to teach reading. "Standard 3: Assessment, Diagnosis and Evaluation. Candidates use a variety of assessment tools and practices to plan and evaluate effective reading instruction." Available:

http://www.reading.org/resources/issues/ reports/professional_standards.html

NCTM: National Council of Teachers of Mathematics lists six principles for school mathematics and a series of standards associated with the principles including a set of assessment standards. The Assessment Principle is: "Assessment should support the learning of important mathematics and furnish useful information to both teachers and students." Available:

http://www.nctm.org/execsummary.aspx

NAS: National Academy of Sciences has published *The National Science Education Standards*. Teaching Standard A is: "Teachers of science plan an inquiry-based science program for their students. In doing this, teachers . . . select teaching and assessment strategies that support the development of student understanding and nurture a community of science learners." Available:

http://darwin.nap.edu/books/0309053269/ html/30.html

a means of monitoring learning progress and diagnosing learning difficulties. Thus, periodic assessment during instruction provides a type of feedback-corrective procedure that aids in continuously adapting instruction to group and individual needs.

Many of the assessments that take place during instruction that enable teachers to monitor and make adjustments are seamlessly integrated into instructional activities. For example, the instructional activity might be group work on a science problem, but during the group activity a teacher may observe that Noah is doing most of the talking and hands-on work with the apparatus while others in the group are largely passive observers. Such observations allow teachers to make adjustments as the work progresses. On the other hand, a short quiz or question-and-answer period may be used to check on the understanding that each individual student is acquiring through the group activity.

Assessing the Intended Learning Outcomes

The final step in the instructional process is to determine the extent to which the learning objectives were achieved by the students. This is accomplished by using tests and other types of assessments that are specifically designed to measure the intended learning outcomes. Ideally, the content standards and instructional goals will clearly specify the desired changes in students, and the assessment instruments will provide a relevant measure or description of the extent to which those changes have taken place. Matching a range of assessment procedures to the intended learning outcomes, with particular emphasis on those that are judged to be most important, is basic to effective classroom assessment, and the link between the assessment procedures and the intended learning outcomes receives considerable attention in later chapters.

Using the Results

Student assessment is often regarded as being essentially for the benefit of teachers and administrators. This attitude overlooks the direct contribution that assessment can make to students. Properly used assessment procedures can contribute directly to improved student learning by (a) clarifying the nature of the intended learning outcomes, (b) providing short-term goals to work toward, (c) providing feedback concerning learning progress, (d) providing information for overcoming learning difficulties and for selecting future learning experiences, and (e) identifying the next instructional goal. Although these purposes are probably best served by the periodic assessment during instruction, the final assessment of intended outcomes also should contribute to these ends.

Information from carefully developed tests and other types of assessments also can be used to improve instruction. Such information can aid in judging (a) the appropriateness and attainability of the instructional goals, (b) the usefulness of the instructional materials, and (c) the effectiveness of the instructional methods. Thus, assessment procedures can contribute to improvements in the teaching–learning process itself and contribute directly to improved student learning.

Assessment results are, of course, also used for assigning marks and reporting student progress to parents. As discussed in Chapter 12, portfolios of student work can provide an effective mechanism for communicating student progress to parents in ways that not only give greater meaning to traditional marks or grades but also illustrate the areas where

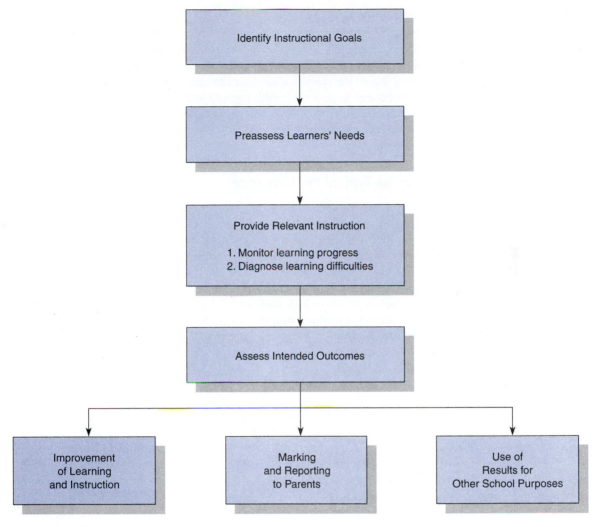

Figure 2.2
Simplified instructional model

parents may help students with their learning. The systematic use of a wide range of assessment procedures provides an objective and comprehensive basis for reporting on each student's learning progress. In addition to marking and reporting, assessment results also are used in the school for various administrative and guidance functions. They are useful in curriculum development, in aiding students with educational and vocational decisions, and in assessing the effectiveness of the school program. The simplified instructional model shown in Figure 2.2 summarizes the basic steps in the instructional process and illustrates the interrelated nature of teaching, learning, and assessment.

TYPES OF ASSESSMENT PROCEDURES

The assessment process may include a wide variety of procedures. These may be classified and described in many different ways, depending on the frame of reference used. Here we present those bases for classification that are most useful for understanding and using assessment procedures in teaching. Although the categories are not discrete, they provide a good general overview of assessment procedures and a useful introduction to some basic terms. The specific procedures used in classroom assessment are described and illustrated in later chapters.

Maximum Performance Versus Typical Performance

Tests and other types of assessments may be placed in two broad categories on the basis of the nature of the measurement. These have been labeled by Cronbach (1990) as **measures of maximum performance** and **measures of typical performance**. In the first category are those procedures used to determine a person's developed abilities or achievements. Procedures of this type are concerned with how well individuals perform when they are motivated to obtain as high a score as possible. In short, the assessment results indicate what individuals can do when they put forth their best effort. Aptitude and achievement tests are included in this category. A distinction between these two types of tests is commonly made in terms of the use of the results rather than of the qualities of the tests themselves. An aptitude test is designed primarily to predict success in some future learning activity, whereas an achievement test is designed to indicate degree of success in some past learning activity.

Because some tests may be used for both purposes, however, it is obvious that the difference is mainly a matter of emphasis. For example, an algebra test designed to measure achievement at the end of the course also may be used to predict success in future mathematics courses. Such overlapping of function prevents distinct classification, but the terms *aptitude* and *achievement* provide useful designations for discussions of measures of ability.

Although the intent of assessments of student achievement is to measure "maximum performance," they can do so only if students attempt to do their best when taking the assessment. If students are not motivated to try their best on a test, then the results obviously may underestimate each student's maximal performance. Thus, the notion of maximal performance refers to the intent of the assessment rather than what may be validly concluded from the score obtained by a student. Student motivation to try their best on the test will be necessary for the results to be interpretable and useful.

The second category in this classification of procedures includes those designed to reflect a person's typical behavior. Procedures of this type are concerned with what individuals *will* do rather than what they *can* do. Methods designed to assess interests, attitudes, adjustment, and various personality traits are included in this category. Here the emphasis is on obtaining representative responses rather than high scores. Although this is an extremely important area in which to appraise students, assessments of typical behavior are fraught with difficulties. The limitations of testing instruments in this field have led to wide use of interviews, questionnaires, anecdotal records, ratings, and various other self-report and observational techniques. None of these techniques alone provides an adequate appraisal of typical behavior, but the combined results of a number of them enable the teacher to make fairly accurate judgments concerning student progress and change in these areas.

Portfolios can be used as a measure of either typical or maximum performance. A portfolio can be prepared to show what a student can do by selecting "best" pieces of work, particularly to show the learning that has occurred. In contrast, a portfolio might include typical work from the year so that parents can understand the progress that a student has made. The purpose of the portfolio (maximum versus typical) will guide the types of work that are selected to be included and the interpretations and uses of the resulting portfolio.

Fixed-Choice Tests and Complex-Performance Assessments

The format of tests and assessments has been the subject of considerable debate and controversy in recent years. The multiple-choice test item has been the most widely used format on standardized tests used in the United States for more than half a century. Multiple-choice and other variations of selected-response test items (e.g., true–false, matching) are highly efficient because students can respond to a relatively large number of questions in a brief period of time and the responses can be machine scored. Objective scoring, high reliability for a given period of time, and cost effectiveness are major advantages of this technique.

Although selected-response tests have always had their critics, several perceived weaknesses of this testing format have attracted widespread attention in recent years. Of particular concern are the beliefs that (a) selected-response tests tend to overemphasize factual knowledge and low-level skills at the expense of higher-order problem-solving and conceptual skills and (b) such tests drive instruction in ways that are inconsistent with current understandings of cognition and learning that emphasize the importance of engaging students in the construction of knowledge and their own understandings rather than the accumulation of discrete facts and procedural skills (Resnick & Resnick, 1992).

During the 1990s, there was a groundswell of support for a quite different approach to measurement and assessment, one that relies on extended tasks and the analysis of complex student performances. Performance-assessment tasks are intended to closely reflect long-term instructional goals and require students to solve problems of importance outside the confines of the classroom or to perform in ways that are valued in their own right. Written essays are one example of a complex-performance task that reflects the instructional goal of effective communication more than a selected-response test could. Other examples include open-ended mathematics problems requiring extended responses, laboratory experiments in science, creation of a piece of art, oral presentations, projects, and exhibitions of student work.

Fixed-choice tests and complex-performance assessments represent two ends of a continuum. Tests requiring the construction of short answers fall between the extremes. Even an essay test may fall short of the intent of a complex-performance assessment if students are allowed only a brief period to respond, have no choice of topic, and have no chance to revise. On the other hand, a fixed-choice item can require more complex performance than recall of facts when carefully constructed.

Performance assessments are frequently referred to as "authentic assessments" to emphasize that they assess performance while students are engaged in problem-solving and learning experiences that are valued in their own right, not just as a means of appraising student achievement. However, not all performance assessments are "authentic" in the sense that they engage students in solving real problems.

Performance assessments are more time consuming to administer and score than fixed-choice tests. Human judgment is a critical part of scoring and requires a high degree of expertise and training. Selected-response tests and complex-performance assessment, as well as a range of intermediate techniques, are useful for assessing student achievement. As is highlighted in subsequent chapters, a full range of assessment procedures is needed, and the particular mix must be carefully tailored to the purposes of the assessment and to its impact on teaching and learning.

Placement, Formative, Diagnostic, and Summative Assessment

Tests and other assessment procedures can also be classified in terms of their functional role in classroom instruction. Identified some time ago by Airasian and Madaus (1972), one such classification system follows the sequence in which assessment procedures are likely to be used in the classroom. Their categories continue to be relevant today. They classified the assessment of student performance in the following manner.

1. **Placement assessment**: To determine student performance at the beginning of instruction
2. **Formative assessment**: To monitor learning progress during instruction
3. **Diagnostic assessment**: To diagnose learning difficulties during instruction
4. **Summative assessment**: To assess achievement at the end of instruction

Although a single instrument may sometimes be useful for more than one purpose (e.g., for both formative and summative assessment purposes), each of these types of classroom assessment typically requires instruments specifically designed for the intended use.

Placement Assessment.   Placement assessment is concerned with the student's entry performance and typically focuses on questions such as the following: (a) Does the student possess the knowledge and skills needed to begin the planned instruction? For example, is a student's reading comprehension at a level that he or she can do the expected independent reading for a unit in history, or does the beginning algebra student have a sufficient command of essential mathematics concepts? (b) To what extent has the student already developed the understanding and skills that are the goals of the planned instruction? Sufficient levels of comprehension and proficiencies might indicate the desirability of skipping certain units or of being placed in a more advanced course. (c) To what extent do the student's interests, work habits, and personality characteristics indicate that one mode of instruction might be better than another (e.g., group instruction versus independent study)? Answers to questions such as these require the use of a variety of techniques: records of past achievement, pretests on course objectives, self-report inventories, observational techniques, and so on. The goal of placement assessment is to determine for each student the position in the instructional sequence and the mode of instruction that is most beneficial.

Formative Assessment.   Formative assessment is used to monitor learning progress during instruction. Its purpose is to provide continuous feedback to both students and teachers concerning learning successes and failures. Feedback to students provides reinforcement of successful learning and identifies the specific learning errors and misconceptions that are in need of correction. Feedback to teachers provides information for modifying instruction and for prescribing group and individual work. Formative assessment depends heavily on specially prepared tests and assessments for each segment of instruction (e.g., unit, chapter). Tests and other types of assessment tasks used for formative assessment are most frequently teacher made, but customized tests made available by publishers of textbooks and other instructional materials also can serve this function. Observational techniques are, of course, also useful in monitoring student progress and identifying learning errors. Because formative assessment is directed toward improving learning and instruction, the results are typically not used for assigning course grades.

Diagnostic Assessment.   Diagnostic assessment is a highly specialized procedure. It is concerned with the persistent or recurring learning difficulties that are left unresolved by the standard corrective prescriptions of formative assessment. If a student continues to experience failure in reading, mathematics, or other subjects despite the use of prescribed alternative methods of instruction, then a more detailed diagnosis is indicated. To use a medical analogy, formative assessment provides first-aid treatment for simple learning problems, and diagnostic assessment searches for the underlying causes of those problems that do not respond to first-aid treatment. Thus, diagnostic assessment is much more comprehensive and detailed. It involves the use of specially prepared diagnostic tests as well as various observational techniques. Serious learning disabilities also are likely to require the services of educational, psychological, and medical specialists and, given the appropriate diagnosis, the development of an individualized education plan for the student. The aim of diagnostic assessment is to determine the causes of persistent learning problems and to formulate a plan for remedial action.

Summative Assessment.   Summative assessment typically comes at the end of a course (or unit) of instruction. It is designed to determine the extent to which the instructional goals have been achieved and is used primarily for assigning course grades or for certifying student mastery of the intended learning outcomes. The techniques used in summative assessment are determined by the instructional goals, but they typically include teacher-made achievement tests, ratings on various types of performance (e.g., laboratory, oral report), and assessments of products (e.g., themes, drawings, research reports). These various sources of information about student achievement may be systematically collected into a portfolio that may be used to summarize or showcase the student's accomplishments and progress. Although the main purpose of summative assessment is grading or the certification of student achievement, it also provides information for judging the appropriateness of the course objectives and the effectiveness of the instruction.

Norm-Referenced and Criterion-Referenced Measurement

How the results of tests and other assessment procedures are interpreted also provides a method of classifying these instruments. There are two basic ways of interpreting student performance. **Norm-referenced** interpretation describes the performance in terms of the relative position held in some known group (e.g., typed better than 90% of the class members). **Criterion-referenced** interpretation describes the specific performance that was demonstrated (e.g., typed 40 words per minute without error). When interpretations are confined to the attainment of a specific objective (e.g., capitalized all proper nouns), they are sometimes called *objective referenced*. This is a type of criterion-referenced interpretation, but it does not cover as broad a domain of tasks as that typically used in criterion referencing. These concepts are defined more specifically in the box "Terminology."

Current standards-based assessments provide a major example of criterion-referenced interpretations. Standards-based assessments are ones that are developed to be aligned with specific content standards and use a small number of levels of performance for reporting based on fixed performance standards. For example, the assessment results may be reported in terms of three to five categories of performance (e.g., partially proficient, proficient, and advanced performance levels). The categorization of a student as meeting, say, the proficient performance standard does not depend on a comparison of that student's performance to that of other students. Rather, the reference is only to the criterion or cut score established by the proficient performance standard. That is, a criterion-referenced interpretation is made of the performance on the standards-based assessment.

Norm-referenced interpretations depend on a comparison of a student's performance to that of other students whose performance defines the norms. The norms might be based on a local, state, or national group, depending on the use to be made of the results. Using national norms, for example, we might describe a student's performance on a vocabulary test as equaling or exceeding that of 76% of a national sample of sixth graders. Criterion-referenced interpretations can be made in various ways. For example, we can (a) describe the specific learning tasks a student is able to perform (e.g., counts from 1 to 100), (b) indicate the percentage of tasks a student performs correctly (e.g., spells 65% of the words in the word list), or (c) compare the test performance to a set performance standard and make a decision that the student meets or fails to meet a given standard (e.g., performed at the proficient level). Although a performance standard can be used in making one type of criterion-referenced interpretation, it is not an essential element of criterion-referenced assessment, as illustrated in the first two examples.

Although the term *percent* was used in illustrating both types of interpretation, it was used in a distinctly different way each time. The norm-referenced interpretation indicated the student's relative standing in a norm group by noting the percentage of students in the group who obtained the same or a lower score (called a percentile score). The criterion-referenced

TERMINOLOGY

Norm-referenced assessment: a test or other type of assessment designed to provide a measure of performance that is interpretable in terms of an individual's relative standing in some known group.

Criterion-referenced assessment: a test or other type of assessment designed to provide a measure of performance that is interpretable in terms of a clearly defined and delimited domain of learning tasks.

Other terms that are less often used but have meanings similar to criterion referenced: *standards based, objective referenced, content referenced, domain referenced*, and *universe referenced*.

interpretation focused on the percentage of items answered correctly (called a percentage-correct score). Although many types of scores are used in testing, the distinction between the percentile score and the percentage-correct score is a significant one because it illustrates the basic difference between a norm-referenced interpretation and a criterion-referenced interpretation.

Strictly speaking, "norm referenced" and "criterion referenced" refer only to the method of interpreting the results. However, these distinct types of interpretation are likely to be most meaningful and useful when tests (and other assessment instruments) are specifically designed for the type of interpretation to be made. Thus, it is legitimate to use the terms *criterion referenced* and *norm referenced* as broad categories for classifying tests and other assessment procedures.

Tests and assessments that are specifically built to maximize one type of interpretation are impossible to identify merely by examining the test itself (see the box "Comparison of Norm-Referenced Tests and Criterion-Referenced Tests"). It is in the construction, interpretation, and use of the tests and assessments that differences can be noted. An identifying feature of norm-referenced tests is the selection of items of average difficulty and the elimination of items that all students are likely to answer correctly. This procedure provides a wide spread of scores so that discrimination among students at various levels of achievement is possible. This is useful for decisions based on relative achievement, such as selection, grouping, and relative grading. By contrast, criterion-referenced tests include items that are directly relevant to the learning outcomes to be measured without regard to whether the items can be used to discriminate among students. No attempt is made to eliminate easy items or alter their difficulty. If the learning tasks are easy, then test items will be easy. The goal of the criterion-referenced test is to obtain a description of the specific knowledge and skills each student can demonstrate. This information is useful for planning both group and individual instruction.

These two types of assessments are best viewed as the ends of a continuum rather than as a clear-cut dichotomy. As shown in the following continuum, the criterion-referenced test emphasizes description of performance, and the norm-referenced test emphasizes discrimination among individuals.

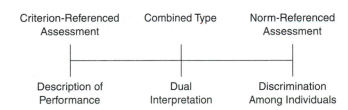

In an attempt to capitalize on the best features of both, test publishers have attempted to make their norm-referenced tests more descriptive, thus allowing for both norm-referenced and criterion-referenced interpretations. Similarly, test publishers have added norm-referenced interpretations to tests that were specifically built for criterion-referenced interpretation. The use of dual interpretation with published tests seems to be an increasing trend that will move many tests more toward the center of the continuum. Although this involves some compromises in test construction and some cautions in test interpretation, the increased versatility may contribute to more effective test use.

Comparison of Norm-Referenced Tests (NRTs) and Criterion-Referenced Tests (CRTs)*

Common Characteristics of NRTs and CRTs:

1. Both require specification of the achievement domain to be measured.
2. Both require a relevant and representative sample of test items.
3. Both use the same types of test items.
4. Both use the same rules for item writing (except for item difficulty).
5. Both are judged by the same qualities of goodness (validity and reliability).
6. Both are useful in educational assessment.

Differences Between NRTs and CRTs:

Remember, differences are only a matter of emphasis.

1. NRT: Typically covers a *large* domain of learning tasks, with just a few items measuring each specific task.

CRT: Typically focuses on a *delimited* domain of learning tasks, with a relatively large number of items measuring each specific task.

2. NRT: Emphasizes *discrimination* among individuals in terms of relative level of learning.

CRT: Emphasizes *description* of what learning tasks individuals can and cannot perform.

3. NRT: Favors items of average difficulty and typically omits very easy and very hard items.

CRT: Matches item difficulty to learning tasks, without altering item difficulty or omitting easy or hard items.

4. NRT: Interpretation requires a clearly defined group.

CRT: Interpretation requires a clearly defined and delimited achievement domain.

*When each is built to maximize its type of interpretation.

SUMMARY OF ASSESSMENT CATEGORIES

A summary of the basic ways of describing classroom tests and other assessment procedures is presented in Table 2.1. Further discussion of these assessment categories is encountered in later chapters.

Other Descriptive Terms

Some of the terms used to describe tests that are presented here as contrasting types are really the ends of a continuum (e.g., speed versus power tests).

Informal Versus Standardized Tests.   Informal tests are those constructed by classroom teachers, whereas those designed by test specialists and administered, scored, and interpreted under standard conditions are called standardized tests.

Table 2.1
Describing classroom assessment procedures

Basis for Classification	Type of Assessment	Function of the Assessment	Illustrative Instruments
	Maximum performance	Determines what individuals *can do* when performing at their best	Aptitude tests, achievement tests
Nature of assessment	Typical performance	Determines what individuals *will do* under natural conditions	Attitude, interest, and personality inventories; observational techniques; peer appraisal
	Fixed-choice test	Efficient measurement of knowledge and skills, indirect indicator	Standardized multiple-choice test
Form of assessment	Complex-performance assessment	Measurement of performance in contexts and on problems valued in their own right	Hands-on laboratory experiment, projects, essays, oral presentations
	Placement	Determines prerequisite skills, degree of mastery of course goals, and/or best mode of learning	Readiness tests, aptitude tests, pretests on course objectives, self-report inventories, observational techniques
	Formative	Determines learning progress, provides feedback to reinforce learning, and corrects learning errors	Teacher-made tests, custom-made tests from textbook publishers, observational techniques
	Diagnostic	Determines causes (intellectual, physical, emotional, environmental) of persistent learning difficulties	Published diagnostic tests, teacher-made diagnostic tests, observational techniques
Use in classroom instruction	Summative	Determines end-of-course achievement for assigning grades or certifying mastery of objectives	Teacher-made survey tests, performance rating scales, product scales
	Criterion referenced	Describes student performance according to a specified domain of clearly defined learning tasks (e.g., adds single-digit whole numbers)	Teacher-made tests, custom-made tests from test publishers, observational techniques
Method of interpreting results	Norm referenced	Describes student performance according to relative position in some known group (e.g., ranks 10th in a classroom group of 30)	Standardized aptitude and achievement tests, teacher-made survey tests, interest inventories, adjustment inventories

43

Individual Versus Group Tests. Some tests are administered on a one-to-one basis using careful oral questioning (e.g., individual intelligence test), whereas others can be administered to a group of individuals.

Mastery Versus Survey Tests. Some achievement tests measure the degree of mastery of a limited set of specific learning outcomes, whereas others measure a student's general level of achievement over a broad range of outcomes. Mastery tests typically use criterion-referenced interpretations, and survey tests tend to emphasize norm-referenced interpretations, but some criterion-referenced interpretations also are possible with carefully prepared survey tests.

Supply Versus Fixed-Response Tests. Some tests require examinees to supply the answer (e.g., essay test), whereas others require them to select one of two or more fixed-response options (e.g., multiple-choice test).

Speed Versus Power Tests. A speed test is designed to measure the number of items an individual can complete in a given time, whereas a power test is designed to measure level of performance under ample time conditions. Power tests usually have the items arranged in order of increasing difficulty.

Objective Versus Subjective Tests. An objective test is one on which equally competent examinees will obtain the same scores (e.g., multiple-choice test), whereas a subjective test is one in which the scores are influenced by the opinion or judgment of the person doing the scoring (e.g., essay test).

SUMMARY

Measurement and assessment play an important role in the instructional program of the school. They provide information that can be used in a variety of educational decisions. The main emphasis in classroom assessment, however, is on decisions concerning student learning and development.

From an instructional standpoint, assessment may be defined as a systematic process of determining the extent to which instructional objectives (i.e., intended learning outcomes) are achieved by students. The assessment process includes both measurement procedures (e.g., tests) and nonmeasurement procedures (e.g., informal observation) for describing changes in student performance as well as value judgments concerning the desirability of the changes.

The process of assessment is likely to be most effective when guided by a set of general principles. These principles emphasize the importance of (a) clearly specifying what is to be assessed, (b) selecting assessment procedures in terms of their relevance, (c) using a variety of assessment procedures, (d) being aware of their limitations, and (e) regarding assessment as a means to an end and not an end in itself.

The interrelated nature of teaching, learning, and assessment can be seen in the following sequential steps in the instructional process: (a) preparing instructional goals and objectives, (b) preassessing learners' needs, (c) providing relevant instruction (monitoring learning progress and diagnosing difficulties), (d) assessing the intended learning outcomes, and (e) using the assessment results to improve learning and instruction. In addition to the direct contribution that testing and assessment make to classroom instruction, they also play an important role in marking and reporting, curriculum development, educational and vocational guidance, and assessing the effectiveness of the school program.

The vast array of assessment procedures used in the school can be classified and described in many different ways. The following are especially useful designations for describing the various procedures.

Nature of the Assessment
1. Maximum performance (what a person can do)
2. Typical performance (what a person will do)

Format of Assessment
1. Selected-response test (student selects response to question from available options)
2. Complex-performance assessment (student constructs extended response or performs in response to complex task)

Use in Classroom Instruction
1. Placement assessment (measures entry behavior)
2. Formative assessment (monitors learning progress)
3. Diagnostic assessment (identifies causes of learning problems)
4. Summative assessment (measures end-of-course achievement)

Method of Interpreting the Results
1. Norm referenced (describes student performance in terms of the relative position held in some known group)
2. Criterion referenced (describes student performance in terms of a clearly defined and delimited domain of learning tasks)

Other terms used to describe tests and other assessment instruments include the following contrasting types.

Informal and standardized

Individual and group

Mastery and survey

Supply and fixed response

Speed and power

Objective and subjective

LEARNING EXERCISES

1. List several instructional decisions and explain how each can be improved by the use of tests and other types of assessments.
2. Describe the meaning of the following terms: *assessment, test, measurement.*
3. Why is it necessary to specify what is to be assessed before selecting or constructing an assessment instrument?

4. Give an example of a measure of maximum performance and a measure of typical performance. Of what value is this distinction?
5. What are some of the perceived advantages and disadvantages of fixed-choice tests relative to complex-performance assessments?
6. Classify each of the following by indicating whether it refers to placement assessment, formative

assessment, diagnostic assessment, or summative assessment.
   a. An end-of-course test used to assign grades
   b. A test of mathematics skills on the first day of algebra
   c. An assessment in science used to assess learning progress
   d. A device for observing and recording reading errors

7. List the similarities and differences between criterion-referenced assessment and norm-referenced assessment. For what purposes is each most useful?

8. Which of the following represents a criterion-referenced interpretation and which a norm-referenced interpretation?
   a. Mary's reading score placed her near the bottom of the class.
   b. Chan defined 90% of the science terms correctly.
   c. Mike can identify all the parts of a sentence.
   d. Katie surpassed 85% of the sixth graders on the mathematics test.

9. How would you distinguish between each of the following?
   a. Informal test and standardized test
   b. Individual test and group test
   c. Mastery test and survey test
   d. Supply test and fixed-response test
   e. Speed test and power test
   f. Objective test and subjective test

10. From your past school experiences, list examples of inadequate or inappropriate use of tests or other assessment instruments. For each example, describe how the action or situation should have been handled.

REFERENCES

Airasian, P. W., & Madaus, G. J. (1972). Functional types of student evaluation. *Measurement and Evaluation in Guidance, 4,* 221–233.

Cronbach, L. J. (1990). *Essentials of psychological testing* (5th ed.). New York: Harper & Row.

Resnick, L. B., & Resnick, D. P. (1992). Assessing the thinking curriculum: New tools for educational reform. In B. R. Gifford & M. C. O'Connor (Eds.), *Changing assessments: Alternative views of aptitude, achievement and instruction* (pp. 37–75). Boston: Kluwer Academic Publishers.

FURTHER READING

Bloom, B. S., Madaus, G. J., & Hastings, J. T. (1981). *Evaluation to improve learning.* New York: McGraw-Hill. Chapter 4, "Summative Evaluation"; Chapter 5, "Diagnostic Evaluation"; and Chapter 6, "Formative Evaluation" provide a comprehensive treatment of these evaluation types.

Gronlund, N. E. (2006). *Assessment of student achievement* (8th ed.). Boston: Allyn & Bacon. Chapter 1 provides a discussion of the relationship between instruction and assessment and the ways in which assessment can aid learning.

Popham, W. J. (2005). *Classroom assessment: What teachers need to know* (4th ed.). Boston: Allyn & Bacon. Chapter 1 describes what teachers need to know about assessment, and Chapter 5 discusses decisions about what and how to assess.

3

INSTRUCTIONAL GOALS AND OBJECTIVES: FOUNDATION FOR ASSESSMENT

What types of learning outcomes do you expect from your teaching? Knowledge? Understanding? Applications? Thinking skills? Problem-solving skills? Performance skills? Attitudes? Clearly, defining desired learning outcomes is the first step in good teaching. It is also essential to the assessment of student learning. Sound assessment requires relating the assessment procedures as directly as possible to intended learning outcomes.

Instructional goals and objectives play a key role in both the instructional process and the assessment process. They serve as guides for both teaching and learning, communicate the intent of the instruction to others, and provide guidelines for assessing student learning. These major purposes are illustrated in Figure 3.1.

Beginning in the late 1980s and continuing to the present, there were numerous attempts, as part of national and state educational reform efforts, to rethink the major goals of instruction. This rethinking was epitomized by publication of the *Curriculum and Evaluation Standards* by the National Council of Teachers of Mathematics (NCTM) (1989) and more recently updated in the form of the *Principles and Standards for School Mathematics* (NCTM, 2000). The NCTM standards have served as a model for other content areas working to establish new curriculum standards. With the encouragement and support of foundations and the federal government, national efforts to establish subject-matter standards were initiated in a variety of areas, including English, science, history, geography, social studies, civics, economics, foreign languages, physical education, and the arts. A key characteristic of these efforts is that they seek to establish more ambitious instructional goals for all students.

The NCTM standards illustrate what are called content standards in the federal Goals 2000: Educate America Act of 1994 and in the No Child Left Behind Act of 2001. The first two NCTM standards for grades K to 4 are shown in Figure 3.2. Although these brief

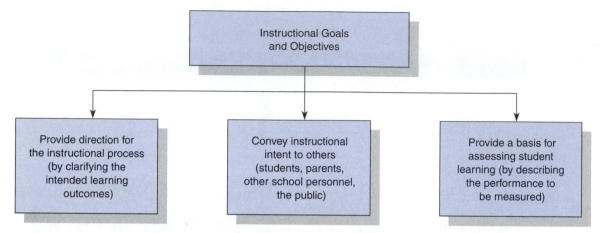

Figure 3.1
The purposes of instructional goals and objectives

NCTM Standard 1: Mathematics as Problem Soving

In Grades K–4, the study of mathematics should emphasize problem solving so that students can

- use problem-solving approaches to investigate and understand mathematical content;
- formulate problems from everyday and mathematical situations;
- develop and apply strategies to solve a wide variety of problems;
- verify and interpret results with respect to the original problem;
- acquire confidence in using mathematics meaningfully.

NCTM Standard 2: Mathematics and Communication

In Grades K–4 the study of mathematics should include numerous opportunities for communication so that students can

- relate physical materials, pictures, and diagrams to mathematical ideas;
- reflect on and clarify their thinking about mathematical ideas and situations;
- relate their everyday language to mathematical language and symbols;
- realize that representing, discussing, reading, writing, and listening to mathematics is a vital part of learning and using mathematics.

Source: Curriculum and Evaluation Standards (pp. 23 & 26) by National Council of Teachers of Mathematics, 1989. Reston, VA: National Council of Teachers of Mathematics Copyright 1989 by the National Council of Teachers of Mathematics. Reprinted by permission.

Figure 3.2
National Council of Teachers of Mathematics: Curriculum and evaluation standards

standards are described in more detail in the NCTM's publication, they are general descriptions of the knowledge, skills, and understandings that should be taught. They provide a broad framework from which more specific curriculum guidelines, instructional materials, and assessments may be developed.

A number of states and districts provide more detailed curriculum guidelines and associated instructional materials. Such guidelines and materials specify the types of performance students are expected to demonstrate at the end of the instructional sequence (e.g., unit or course). Describing intended learning outcomes in performance terms is the main function of properly stated instructional goals and objectives. This clarification of what students should be learning and how the learning is to be expressed not only aids the teacher but also helps others understand the focus of the instruction. Some states and districts are beginning to emphasize the importance of learning outcomes to the process of education by developing guidelines for outcomes-based education and tying graduation or grade retention requirements to the attainment of learning goals.

Examples of content standards in different subjects from five states are illustrated in Figure 3.3. The subject areas and grade ranges for state content standards vary from state

Colorado, Geography, Standard 4: "Students understand how economic, political, cultural, and social processes interact to shape patterns of human populations, interdependence, cooperation, and conflict. . . . In grades K–4, what students know and are able to do includes . . . identifying the causes of human migration" (*Colorado Model Content Standards for Geography*, Colorado Department of Education, Adopted, June 1995, Amended, November 1995; available: http://www.cde.state.co.us/download/pdf/geography.pdf).

New York State Standard 4: Science "students will understand and apply scientific concepts, principles, and theories pertaining to the physical setting and living environment and recognize the historical development of ideas in science" (Learning Standards of New York State; available: http://www.emsc.nyse.gov/ciai/pub/standards.pdf).

California Reading Comprehension Standard: "Read and orally respond to familiar stories and other texts by answering factual comprehension questions about cause-and-effect relationships. Read and orally respond to stories and texts from content areas by restating facts and details to clarify ideas" (*California English-Language Development Standards for California Public Schools*: *Kindergarten Through Grade Twelve,* July 1999; available: http://www.cde.ca.gov/cdepress/Eng-Lang-Dev-Stnd.pdf).

Florida Grades 6–8 Mathematics Standard 5: "The student understands and applies theories related to numbers. 1. Uses concepts about numbers, including primes, factors, and multiples, to build number sequences" (*Florida Sunshine Standards*; available: http://www.firn.edu/doe/curric/prek12/pdf/math6.pdf).

Virginia, Grade 3, History and Social Science Standards of Learning, Standard 3.1. "The student will explain how the contributions of ancient Greece and Rome have influenced the present world in terms of architecture, government (direct and representative democracy), and sports" (*History and Social Science Standards of Learning for Virginia Public Schools*, March 2001; available: http://www.pen.kqw.va.us/VDOE/superintendent/Sols/historysol2001.pdf).

Figure 3.3
Examples of state content standards statements

to state. In Colorado, for example, four separate sets of content standards were adopted for history, geography, civics, and economics. Some states, such as Virginia, have grade-level-specific standards, whereas other states have standards adopted for a range of grades, and a few states have grade-level-specific standards as well as standards covering a range of grades (e.g., Florida). The standards also vary from state to state in terms of their specificity and emphases within a content area. Links to content standards by subject area and by state are provided at *http://edstandards.org/standards.html.*

State content standards have been reviewed and graded (American Federation of Teachers, 2001; *Education Week*, 2006; Gross, 2005; and others). We do not attempt to evaluate the different perspectives brought to bear in the various reviews of state standards or the grades assigned to the standards by the reviewers. It is worth acknowledging, however, that the reviews have come to quite different conclusions about the state standards, in large part because the reviewers use different criteria for judging the standards. The reviewers differ not only in the importance given to the specificity and rigor of the standards but also in their views on the priority that should be given to basic skills and factual knowledge in comparison to applications of ideas to solve problems in contexts outside the classroom. The key point for present purposes, however, is that content standards can and should, if they are to be more than window dressing, influence the emphasis given to different topics within a content area and the assessments developed by teachers as well as those developed and required by states or districts.

Our interest in this book, of course, is in the usefulness of instructional goals objectives for assessing student learning. As noted in Chapter 2, effective assessment depends as much on a clear description of what is to be assessed as on a determination of how to assess. Thus, before we develop or select tests and other assessment instruments to measure student learning, we need to clearly specify the intended learning outcomes. That is the main function of well-stated instructional goals and objectives. State or district content standards provide a starting point, but given the general level at which most content standards are written, there is a need to elaborate the standards in order to clearly specify the learning outcomes in a form that can guide instruction and assessment in the classroom.

INSTRUCTIONAL OBJECTIVES AS LEARNING OUTCOMES*

Instructional goals and objectives are sometimes stated in terms of actions to be taken. Thus, we might have a statement such as this:

Demonstrate to students how to use the microscope.

Although this statement clearly indicates what the teaching activity is, it is less clear about intended learning outcomes and does not point explicitly to the type of student assessment that would be most appropriate. Literally, the objective will have been achieved when the demonstration has been completed—regardless if the students have learned anything. A better way to state objectives is in terms of what we expect students to be able to do at

---

* Some of the material in this chapter was adapted from N. E. Gronlund, *How to write and use instructional objectives*, 5th ed. (Upper Saddle River, NJ: Prentice Hall, 2000).

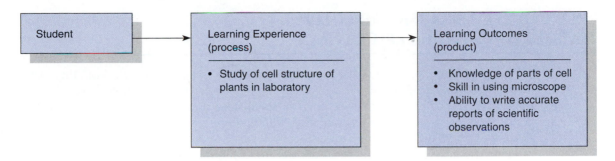

Figure 3.4
The relationship of learning experience to learning outcomes

the end of instruction. After demonstrating how to use the microscope, for example, we might expect students to be able to demonstrate skill in using the microscope to identify features of a cell.

A statement such as this directs attention to the students and to the types of performance they are expected to exhibit as a result of the instruction. Thus, our focus shifts from the teacher to the student and from the learning experiences to the learning outcomes. This shift in focus makes clear the intent of our instruction and sets the stage for assessing student learning. Well-stated outcomes make clear the types of student performance we are willing to accept as evidence that the instruction has been successful.

When viewing instructional objectives in terms of learning outcomes, it is important to keep in mind that we are concerned with the *products* of learning rather than with the *process* of learning. This is not meant to suggest that the process is unimportant. Quite the contrary, processes such as writing notes, outlining, drafting, and revision in developing a written essay may be quite important; but the long-term instructional objective concerns the product of the finished essay. Figure 3.4 makes three important points about the role of instructional objectives in teaching–learning situations.

First, objectives establish direction, and when they are stated in terms of learning outcomes, they go beyond knowledge of the specific course content. Note the distinction between "study of" and "knowledge of" cell structures. The content (study of cell structure) is more aptly listed under process because it is the vehicle through which objectives (knowledge of parts of cell and so on) are attained.

Second, consider the varying degrees of dependence that the products ("knowledge," "skill," and "ability") have on the course content. "Knowledge of parts of cell" is the most closely related to the specific content of a biology course. "Skill in using microscope" and "ability to write accurate reports of scientific observations" relate to a greater variety of course content that could be used to achieve the same objectives.

The third point illustrated by the diagram is the degree to which objectives vary in complexity. The first learning outcome, "knowledge of parts of cell," is specific, is easily attained, and can be measured readily by a short-answer or fixed-response paper-and-pencil test. The last learning outcome, "ability to write accurate reports of scientific observations," is rather general, is unlikely to be attained completely in a single course, and requires judgmental analysis of student performances.

FROM OVERLY SPECIFIC OBJECTIVES TO THE THINKING CURRICULUM

The predominant approach to the development and construction of tests from the 1920s through the 1980s relied on behavioral psychology. Behavioral psychology provided a framework to analyze learning outcomes in small steps and specific skills. Learning was conceptualized as being quite hierarchical, with higher-order skills dependent on a linear development based on a foundation of lower-level "essential skills." This decomposition of desired outcomes into small steps allowed for a high degree of specificity of learning outcomes (for an elaboration of these points, see Shepard, 1991, 2000).

Highly specific objectives enabled the construction of precise test objectives. When coupled with the notion of linear learning hierarchies, specific objectives provided a natural basis for developing "criterion-referenced mastery tests." The behavioral objectives used to construct mastery tests were typically concerned with relatively simple knowledge and skill outcomes. This made it possible to analyze each intended learning outcome in considerable detail and to describe the expected student performance in specific terms. The objective to "add whole numbers," for example, might be further defined by a list of specific tasks such as the following:

- Add two single-digit numbers with sums of 10 or less (2 + 5).
- Add two single-digit numbers with sums greater than 10 (6 + 8).
- Add three single-digit numbers with sums of 10 or less (2 + 4 + 3).
- Add three single-digit numbers with sums greater than 10 (7 + 5 + 9).
- Add two two-digit numbers without carrying (21 + 34).
- Add two two-digit numbers with simple carrying (36 + 27).
- Add two two-digit numbers with carrying into nine (57 + 48).
- Add two or more three-digit numbers with repeated carrying (687 + 839).

With mastery objectives such as these, it was frequently possible to specify a large representative sample of the specific responses expected of the students at the end of instruction. The learning tasks were then placed in sequential order so that they could be systematically taught and tested until mastery was achieved, as shown in Figure 3.5. This procedure of stating specific tasks and then teaching and testing them one by one has been used in individualized instruction, in training programs, and in areas of classroom instruction that stress simple learning outcomes (e.g., basic skills). The limited nature of the objectives and the detailed specification of the learning tasks enhance the use of criterion-referenced interpretation.

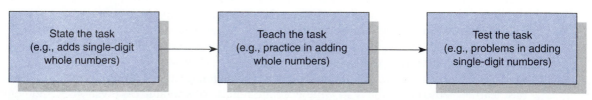

Figure 3.5
Learning tasks is sequential order

Although this approach to test specification and construction continues to be used by some, the learning theory on which it is based has been strongly challenged in recent years by researchers focusing on learning and cognitive development. Cognitive research has discredited the notion that basic skills must be learned before higher-level thinking, reasoning, and problem-solving skills can be learned. According to cognitive research and theory, effective learning even at the most elementary levels of reading and mathematics requires the active involvement of students in constructing meaning by thinking and reasoning (for a more complete discussion, see Resnick & Resnick, 1992).

This cognitive research perspective of learning has several implications for assessment that have been explored in some detail in a report of a committee of the National Academy of Sciences (Pellegrino, Chudowsky, & Glaser, 2001). First, the types of instructional objectives associated with the perspective are concerned with the more complex learning outcomes (e.g., understanding, problem solving, reasoning, thinking skills, application to authentic problem situations outside of school). Second, the perspective suggests the need for more comprehensive tasks that involve extended periods of time. Third, tasks need to be presented in a meaningful context; that is, they need to involve "authentic" problems.

Resnick and Resnick (1992) used an example from the assessment of writing to illustrate the distinction between the approaches to assessment that are compatible with the behavioral and cognitive perspectives. From either perspective, it could be readily agreed that the ability to edit one's own work is an important part of writing. An analysis of the specific skills involved might lead to the development of a test in which students were presented with written material and asked to identify errors and choose possible corrections. As Resnick and Resnick note, such a test might be useful for identifying copyediting skills but would not foster the skills involved in writing and revising one's own work because it would not involve actual "crafting [of] phrases and sentences to convey intended meaning" (Resnick & Resnick, 1992, p. 6). Thus, the cognitive perspective leads to the use of written essays where students write rough drafts, review their drafts, and revise.

The cognitive research perspective also has implications for assessments in other content areas. In reading, it encourages the use of authentic texts (e.g., complete short stories or informational pieces) rather than the use of short segments consisting of a paragraph or two written specifically for the test. In mathematics, it encourages the application of problems with real-world content (e.g., the collection and analysis of data to determine the best location of a store). In science, it encourages the use of performance-based tasks involving active experimentation and analysis of results. In social studies, it encourages the analysis of documents and the interpretation of historical events.

Shepard (2000) used an example problem of Thompson's (1995) to illustrate how even a simple mathematical question can probe a student's deep understanding of a concept. Thompson's illustrative problem was designed to assess understanding of simple fractions by elementary school children. A figure displayed for the problem showed a rectangle divided into five segments of equal size. Three of the five segments were shaded. A traditional paper-and-pencil test might simply ask what fraction of the rectangle is shaded. Although a correct answer of three fifths would provide some information, it would not, by itself, give much of an indication that the student had deep understanding of fractions. Additional questions are needed to probe the depth of the student's understanding. As discussed by Shepard (2000), Thompson explored the depth of understanding by asking questions such as "Can you see three fifths of something? Can you see five thirds of something? Can you see five thirds of three fifths?" An affirmative answer to any question was followed by a request for the student to show or explain how the student sees the particular quantity. Asking multiple questions on a single concept obviously is time consuming, particularly if the assessment is to cover a wide range of content in a short time, but such probing is necessary if the goal is the diagnosis of the depth of a student's understanding of a concept.

The previous description identifies two ends of a continuum running from highly specific objectives (e.g., add two-digit integers or identify details that are explicitly stated in text) to much more general learning goals (e.g., relate physical materials and diagrams to mathematical ideas or read complicated text with understanding). Part of the debate about content standards is related to the location of standards between the two ends of this continuum. In practice, neither extreme is apt to be entirely satisfactory as a guide to the development or selection of assessments. The specific discrete skills end of the continuum leads to an overemphasis on disconnected, low-level skills and factual knowledge. The broad cognitive process end often remains at too general a level to provide adequate guidance for the development or selection of assessments that will have desirable measurement properties. Thus, in practice, an intermediate framework is needed to guide the development of assessments.

Types of Learning Outcomes to Consider

Although the cognitive research perspective is useful in forcing attention on broader educational goals that need to be addressed in the development or selection of an assessment, those general goals need to be supplemented by more systematic thinking about the types of learning outcomes that would provide evidence that the goals are being achieved. It is useful, for this reason, to classify learning outcomes under a few general headings. Any such classification is necessarily arbitrary, but it serves several useful purposes. It indicates types of learning outcomes that should be considered, it provides a framework for classifying those outcomes, and it directs attention toward changes in student performance in a variety of areas.

The following list of outcomes delineates the major areas in which instructional objectives might be classified. The more specific areas under each type of outcome should not be regarded as exclusive; they are merely suggestive of categories to be considered. For a different set of categories, see the lists of outcomes in Appendix F.

1. Knowledge
    1.1 Terminology
    1.2 Specific facts
    1.3 Concepts and principles
    1.4 Methods and procedures
2. Understanding
    2.1 Concepts and principles
    2.2 Methods and procedures
    2.3 Written material, graphs, maps, and numerical data
    2.4 Problem situations
3. Application
    3.1 Factual information
    3.2 Concepts and principles

3.3 Methods and procedures
3.4 Problem-solving skills
4. Thinking skills
    4.1 Critical thinking
    4.2 Scientific thinking
5. General skills
    5.1 Laboratory skills
    5.2 Performance skills
    5.3 Communication skills
    5.4 Computational skills
    5.5 Social skills
6. Attitudes
    6.1 Social attitudes
    6.2 Scientific attitudes
7. Interests
    7.1 Personal interests
    7.2 Educational interests
    7.3 Vocational interests
8. Appreciations
    8.1 Literature, art, and music
    8.2 Social and scientific achievements
9. Adjustments
    9.1 Social adjustments
    9.2 Emotional adjustments

Taxonomy of Educational Objectives

A useful guide for developing a comprehensive list of instructional objectives is the *Taxonomy of Educational Objectives.* This detailed classification of objectives is similar in form to the classification system used for plants and animals. It attempts to identify and classify all possible educational outcomes. The system first divides objectives into the following three major areas.

1. **Cognitive Domain**: Knowledge outcomes and intellectual abilities and skills
2. **Affective Domain**: Attitudes, interests, appreciation, and modes of adjustment
3. **Psychomotor Domain**: Perceptual and motor skills

Each of the three domains is subdivided into categories and subcategories. The major categories in the cognitive domain, for example, are knowledge, comprehension, application, analysis, synthesis, and evaluation. These categories begin with relatively simple knowledge outcomes and proceed through increasingly complex levels of intellectual ability. This pattern of classification is characteristic of all three domains.

The *Taxonomy* is primarily useful in identifying the types of learning outcomes that should be considered when developing a comprehensive list of objectives for classroom instruction. One need not use the terminology of the taxonomies when stating learning outcomes, but a review of the various taxonomy categories will aid in the development of a more complete list. The broad range of learning outcomes covered in the *Taxonomy* provides assurance that important types of learning are not overlooked. Appendix G provides a detailed summary of the *Taxonomy* categories and a list of the original sources from which the summaries were derived. In addition to detailed descriptions of the categories in each domain, illustrative instructional objectives from a variety of content areas are presented, as are lists of verbs that are useful in stating objectives for student performance.

GUIDELINES

Begin with a Simple Framework

Starting with a simple framework (Knowledge, Understanding, Application, Analysis, Synthesis, Evaluation) will help move from factual information to more complex learning outcomes, as illustrated in the following examples.

K = Knowledge
U = Understanding
Ap = Application
An = Analysis
S = Synthesis
E = Evaluation

Each of these categories can be expanded with skills and affective outcomes as needed.

Reading

K: Knows vocabulary
U: Reads with comprehension
Ap: Reads to obtain information to solve a problem
An: Analyzes text and outlines arguments
S: Integrates the main ideas across two or more passages
E: Critiques the conclusions in a text and offers alternatives

Writing

K: Knows the mechanics of writing
U: Understands grammatical principles in writing
Ap: Writes to communicate for a specific purpose
An: Outlines essay before writing
S: Writes narrative essay
E: Critiques writings of others

Mathematics

K: Knows the number system and basic operations
U: Understands math concepts and processes
Ap: Uses mathematics to solve problems
An: Shows how to solve multistep problems
S: Derives proofs
E: Critiques proofs in geometry

Science

K: Knows terms and facts
U: Understands scientific principles
Ap: Applies principles to new situations
An: Analyzes chemical reactions
S: Conducts and reports experiments
E: Critiques scientific reports

Social Studies

K: Knows factual information about social issues
U: Understands causes of social issues
Ap: Applies critical-thinking skills to social issues
An: Analyzes events leading to social change
S: Writes speech on a social issue
E: Critiques essay on social change

Other Sources for Lists of Objectives

Illustrative instructional objectives for various grade levels and subject-matter areas may be obtained from the following sources.

1. Professional association standards: Although usually stated at a more general level than needed, the content standards of professional associations provide an excellent starting point for considering instructional objectives. A listing of some of the content standards of professional associations is provided in Appendix C.

2. State content standards: The content standards adopted by states also provide a good starting point for identifying instructional objectives. Although the content standards for the state or district in which a teacher is working obviously are most relevant, useful ideas may also be derived from standards of other states. For easy access to state content standards, see *http://www.ccsso.org/projects/State_Education_Indicators/ Key_State_Education_Policies/3160.cfm.*

3. Methods books: Most books on methods of teaching discuss objectives, present examples, and cite references to other sources of objectives in various instructional areas.

4. Yearbooks and subject-matter standards publications of educational organizations: The yearbooks (and other publications dealing with subject-matter standards) of organizations such as the National Council of Teachers of English, the National Council of Teachers of Mathematics, the National Council for the Social Studies, and the National Science Teachers Association provide an excellent resource.

5. Encyclopedia of Educational Research: This publication typically contains an article on each major teaching area, which includes references to sources of instructional objectives.

6. Curriculum frameworks and guides: Many local and state curriculum frameworks or guides contain lists of instructional objectives.

7. Test manuals. The manuals accompanying published tests frequently contain lists of objectives that were used in constructing the tests.

8. Banks of objectives: Some organizations and test publishers maintain various banks of objectives and relevant test items. See Appendix C for addresses of some objectives banks.

In using content standards objectives from these various sources, it is important that the ones selected be relevant to the local instructional program. Content standards and selected objectives will most likely need to be reworded. Many of them will not be stated as intended learning outcomes or in performance terms. Published content standards and lists of objectives are probably most useful for obtaining ideas concerning possible outcomes and for assessing the completeness of a prepared list.

Criteria for Selecting Appropriate Objectives

Our emphasis throughout this section has been on the role of the classroom teacher in the process of selecting instructional objectives. We have deliberately avoided discussions concerning which objectives should receive priority at various grade levels and in various subject-matter areas. This is a decision for school boards, administrators, curriculum committees, and individual teachers. Our aim has been to clarify how to identify those instructional objectives that will be most useful for teaching and assessment purposes.

In preparing a list of instructional objectives for a particular course, the teacher faces the problem of determining the adequacy of the final list of objectives. The following questions will serve as criteria for this purpose (see Figure 3.6).

1. Do the objectives include all important outcomes of the course? Knowledge objectives are seldom neglected. However, objectives in the area of understanding, application, thinking skills, attitudes, and the like tend to be slighted unless special efforts are made to consider them. Objectives derived mainly from the methods of instruction and the social experiences of the students are also easily overlooked.

2. Are the objectives in harmony with the content standards of the state or district and with general goals of the school? Where states or districts have adopted content standards, the objectives developed by individual teachers need to be consistent with those standards. The objectives developed by teachers must also be consistent with the general goals of the school in which they are used. For example, a teacher of third-grade social studies in Virginia would want to take into account the statement of the standard shown in Figure 3.3 that students "will explain how the contributions of ancient Greece and Rome have influenced the present world in terms of architecture, government (direct and representative democracy), and sports." Similarly, if independent thought, self-direction, and effectiveness of communication are highly valued in the school, then these outcomes should be reflected in the teachers' objectives. Objectives inconsistent with these valued outcomes should be omitted from the list. Part of the difficulty of applying this criterion is that the goals of the school are seldom explicitly stated.

3. Are the objectives in harmony with sound principles of learning? Because objectives indicate the desired outcomes of a series of learning experiences, they should be consistent with sound principles of learning. That is, they should (a) be appropriate to the age level and experiential background of the students (principle of readiness), (b) be related to the needs and interests of the students (principle of motivation), (c) reflect learning outcomes that are most permanent (principle of retention), and (d) include learning outcomes that are most generally applicable to various specific situations (principle of transfer).

4. Are the objectives realistic in terms of the abilities of the students and the time and facilities available? First attempts at identifying objectives for a particular course frequently result in an impressive but unattainable list of outcomes. Thus, the final list of objectives should be reviewed in light of the students' developmental levels, their beginning skills and understandings, the time available for achieving the objectives, and the adequacy of the instructional resources and equipment available. It is usually better to have a limited set of clearly defined, attainable objectives than a long list of nonfunctional goals.

Make Allowance for Unanticipated Learning Outcomes

No matter how carefully a set of instructional objectives has been selected for a course, there are likely to be some unanticipated effects of the instruction. These effects may be desirable or undesirable, and the majority of them are likely to fall into the affective area.

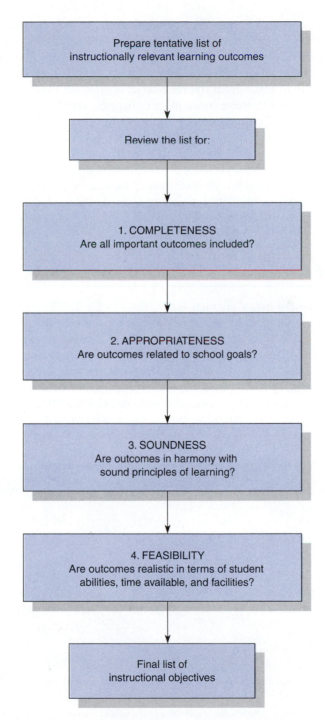

Figure 3.6
Summary of criteria for selecting the final list of objectives

For example, as a result of instruction, students may become more dependent or more independent, more conforming or more creative, more critical of printed material or less critical, more positive in their self-concept or more negative, and more interested in the subject or less interested. Outcomes of this nature are easily overlooked because they are more likely to result from the method of instruction than from the content of instruction.

In addition to these more global changes, specific classroom activities may create a need for focusing on outcomes that were not prespecified. An accident in the chemistry laboratory, for example, may indicate a need for special instruction in safety. Similarly, an unanticipated student interest in the metric system may create a need to modify instruction in a mathematics class, or an unforeseen international crisis may alter social studies instruction. Thus, although instructional objectives provide a useful guide for instruction, teachers must be flexible enough in their teaching and testing to allow for unplanned events and unanticipated learning outcomes.

METHOD OF STATING INSTRUCTIONAL OBJECTIVES

In preparing a list of instructional objectives for a course of study, we have two immediate goals in mind. One is to create as complete a list of objectives as possible. This is most likely to occur if we follow the procedures for selecting objectives described in the previous section. The other goal is to state the objectives so that they clearly indicate the learning outcomes that we expect from our instruction.

The task of stating instructional objectives can be simplified if we constantly keep in mind that we are listing intended outcomes of teaching–learning situations. We are not describing what we intend to do during instruction but are listing the expected results of that instruction. The point of orientation, then, is the student and the types of performance

GUIDELINES

Stating Objectives as Learning Outcomes

Don't state objectives in terms of the following:

1. Teacher performance (e.g., "Teach students key concepts.")
2. Learning process (e.g., "Student learns meaning of concepts.")
3. Course content (e.g., "Student studies geometric figures.")
4. Two objectives (e.g., "Student knows and understands concepts.")

State objectives in terms of student performance or the end of instruction:

1. "Knows the meaning of concepts."
   1.1 "Identifies a definition of the concept."
   1.2 "Identifies the concept that fits a given description."
   1.3 "Matches the concept to a picture" (e.g., geometric figures).
   1.4 "Differentiates between the concept and a second concept."
   1.5 "Applies the concept to an everyday situation."

that the student should demonstrate at the end of the teaching–learning experience. Stating objectives in terms of learning outcomes rather than the learning process is easier said than done. Most of us are so concerned with course content and the ongoing process in the classroom that we find it difficult to concentrate on the results of instruction. Although the very nature of teaching conditions us to focus our attention on the learning process, we can shift this focus if we continually ask ourselves, What should the students be able to do at the end of the course or unit of study that they could not do at the beginning? As we attempt to answer this question—always in terms of knowledge, understanding, skills, attitudes, and the like—we will find that the students' performance has, almost automatically, become the center of focus. We are then in a much better position to state our instructional objectives in terms of learning outcomes.

How to Obtain a Clear Statement of Instructional Objectives

A list of objectives for a course or unit of study should be detailed enough to convey the intent of the instruction yet general enough to serve as an effective overall guide in planning for teaching and assessment. You can do this most easily by defining your objectives in two steps: (1) stating the general objectives of instruction as intended learning outcomes, and (2) listing under each objective a sample of the specific types of performance that students should be able to demonstrate when they have achieved the objective (Gronlund, 2000). This procedure should result in statements of general objectives and specific learning outcomes such as the following:

1. Understands scientific principles
   1.1 Describes the principle in own words
   1.2 Identifies examples of the principle
   1.3 States tenable hypotheses based on the principle
   1.4 Uses the principle in solving novel problem
   1.5 Distinguishes between two given principles
   1.6 Explains the relationship between two given principles

The expected learning outcome is concerned with understanding, and the general objective starts right off with the verb *understands*. There is no need to add such repetitious material as "the students should be able to demonstrate that they understand." Keeping the statement free of unnecessary words and starting with a verb helps focus on the intended outcome.

There are several things to remember about the specific learning outcomes listed beneath the general objective. First, each statement begins with a verb. Here, however, the verbs are specific and indicate definite, observable responses, that is, ones that can be seen and assessed by an outside observer. These verbs—*describes, identifies, states, uses, distinguishes,* and *explains*—state specific learning outcomes in terms of observable student performance. See Appendix G for more verbs that state specific learning outcomes in the cognitive, affective, and psychomotor areas. Terms such as these clarify what the students will do to demonstrate their *understanding*. Vague terms, such as *realizes, sees,* and *believes* are less useful in defining objectives because they describe internal states that can be expressed by various types of overt behavior.

Second, the list of specific learning outcomes is merely a sample of the many specific ways that an **understanding of scientific principles** might be shown. A student who achieved this objective probably could demonstrate many other responses. Because it would be impractical to list all the specific types of performance that denote understanding, attempt to obtain a **representative sample**. This yields an operational definition of the general objective yet keeps the overall list of objectives and specific learning outcomes within manageable proportions.

Finally, note that the specific learning outcomes are free of specific course content. Rather than listing the scientific principles the students are to understand, they specify the types of student performance acceptable as evidence of understanding. Keeping the statements free of specific course content makes it possible to use the same list of learning outcomes with various units of study. Each unit of study will indicate the principles to be understood, and the list of specific learning outcomes will indicate how the students are expected to demonstrate their understanding. For example, if the unit were on force and motion, the previous list would be easily converted to that specific area science content (e.g., understands principles of force and motion: describes the principles of force and motion in own words, identifies examples of the principles of force and motion, and so on). Once developed, the instructional objectives can be readily converted into a table of specifications for an assessment. As we will see in Chapter 6, a table of specifications also is a convenient means of relating the learning outcomes to the various content areas for assessment purposes.

Stating the General Instructional Objectives

One problem in stating the general instructional objectives is selecting the proper level of generality. The objectives should be specific enough to provide direction for instruction but not so specific that instruction is reduced to training. When we state our major objectives in general terms, we provide for the integration of specific facts and skills into complex response patterns. General statements also give the teacher greater freedom in selecting the methods and materials of instruction. The "understanding of scientific principles," for example, may be achieved through lecture, discussion, demonstration, group problem-solving activity, laboratory work, or some combination of these methods. Similarly, the objective may be achieved through the use of different textbooks or various other types of instructional material. Stating the general objectives at this level provides a focus for instruction but does not restrict the teacher to a particular instructional method or a given set of instructional materials.

The following list of general instructional objectives shows the desired level of generality.

- Knows basic terminology
- Understands concepts
- Relates concepts to everyday observations
- Applies principles to new situations
- Interprets graphs
- Sings independently, on pitch and in rhythm
- Demonstrates skill in critical thinking
- Formulates a position on an issue
- Writes a well-organized theme
- Converses in a second language (e.g., Spanish)

- Appreciates poetry
- Demonstrates scientific attitude
- Evaluates an experiment's adequacy

The verbs at the beginning of each statement are general enough to encompass a range of specific learning outcomes. A sample of specific outcomes would need to be added before these general statements would be useful guides for teaching and assessment. Note that each statement contains a single objective (e.g., *not* "Knows and understands") and that each statement is relatively free of course content.

The degree of generality may, of course, vary somewhat with the period of instruction for which the list is being prepared. The objectives for a brief unit of instruction are likely to be more specific than those for an entire course of study. In either case, however, selecting 8 to 12 general instructional objectives will usually provide a list that is both manageable and suitable.

Stating the Specific Learning Outcomes

As stated earlier, each general instructional objective must be defined by a sample of specific learning outcomes to clarify how students can demonstrate that they have achieved the general objective. Unless the general objectives are further defined in this manner, they will not provide adequate direction for teaching or assessment.

Statements of specific learning outcomes for a general objective will be easier to write and will more clearly convey instructional intent if each statement begins with an action verb that indicates definite, observable responses (e.g., *identifies, solves, communicates*). Such statements specify the types of student performance acceptable as evidence that the general instructional objective has been achieved. This assumes, of course, that each specific learning outcome is directly relevant to the general objective it is defining. A statement such as "Writes the textbook definition of a principle" would be appropriate for listing under "Knows principles" but not under "Understands principles." For the latter objective, we would need a statement that goes beyond the recall of information because understanding implies some novelty in the response. Here, a statement such as "Explains the principle in own words" or "Applies the principle to solve an applied problem" would be more relevant.

A major problem in defining general instructional objectives is deciding how many specific learning outcomes to list under each objective. It is obvious that a fixed number cannot be specified. Simple knowledge and skill outcomes typically require fewer statements than complex ones. Because it is usually impossible or impractical to list all possible student responses for each general objective, the sample should be as representative as possible. In smost cases, there is not much advantage in listing more than seven or eight specific learning outcomes for each objective; four or five statements are probably more common. As a general guide, enough learning outcomes should be listed for each objective to show the typical performance of students who have satisfactorily achieved the objective.

The following general objectives and specific learning outcomes illustrate a satisfactory level of specificity for stating the intended learning outcomes.

1. Understands the meaning of concepts
    1.1 Explains the concept in own words
    1.2 Identifies the meaning of a concept in context

1.3 Differentiates between proper and improper instances of a concept
1.4 Distinguishes between two similar concepts on the basis of meaning
1.5 Uses a concept to explain an everyday event

2. Demonstrates skill in critical thinking
2.1 Distinguishes between fact and opinion
2.2 Distinguishes between relevant and irrelevant information
2.3 Identifies fallacious reasoning in written material
2.4 Identifies the limitations of given data
2.5 Formulates valid conclusions from given data
2.6 Identifies the assumptions underlying conclusions

In addition to illustrating the desired degree of specificity, these statements are good examples of content-free objectives. As noted earlier, both the general objectives and the specific learning outcomes should be kept free of specific content so that they can be used with various units of study. In stating our specific learning outcomes, we are attempting to describe what types of student performance represent each general objective—not what specific content the students are to learn.

Keeping the specific learning outcomes content free is, of course, a matter of degree. In some cases, all we can do is modify our statements so that they apply to a wider range of course material. The following statements illustrate ways to improve specific learning outcomes in this regard.

EXAMPLES

Poor: Distinguishes between a square and a rectangle
Better: Distinguishes among geometric shapes

Poor: Identifies relevant historical antecedents of the Louisiana Purchase
Better: Identifies relevant historical antecedents of a historical event

Poor: Describes the main characters in Toni Morrison's *Beloved*
Better: Describes the main characters in the story

If we used the first version of each of these specific learning outcomes, we would have to write new statements for each identification, comparison, or description we wanted our students to make. The better versions can be used with various areas of content, thus freeing us from the repetitious writing of objectives as new subject matter is considered. Specific learning outcomes should specify the *types of reactions* the students are to make to the content, not identify the content itself.

In some cases, it may be desirable or necessary to consult reference books and other relevant materials for the types of performance that might represent an objective. When defining such complex outcomes as critical thinking, literary appreciation, and scientific attitude, for example, a review of the literature can be very useful. Although you may not find a detailed list of the specific components of each outcome, even general descriptions of the concepts will aid in defining relevant types of performance. In any event, resist the temptation to omit complex outcomes simply because they are difficult to define.

Clarification of Verbs Used in Specific Learning Outcomes

Because the action verb is a key element in stating the specific learning outcomes, the selection and clarification of these verbs play an important role in obtaining a clearly defined set of instructional objectives. Ideally, we would like each verb (a) to convey clearly our instructional intent, and (b) to specify precisely the student performance we are willing to accept as evidence that the general objective has been attained. Some verbs convey instructional intent well (e.g., *identifies*); others are more effective at specifying the student responses to be observed (e.g., *labels, encircles, underlines*). When it is necessary to choose between these two types of verbs, it is best to select those that most clearly convey instructional intent and then, if necessary, clarify further the expected student responses in one of the following ways.

1. Add a third level of specificity to the list of objectives.
2. Define the action verbs used in the specific learning outcomes.
3. Use sample test items to illustrate the intended outcomes.

These procedures are probably most useful as guides to test construction and for communicating your intended learning outcomes to others.

The meaning of each specific learning outcome can be further clarified by listing tasks students are expected to perform to demonstrate achievement of the outcome. This would provide three levels for each instructional objective, as follows:

1. Comprehends the meaning of written material
   1.1 Identifies the main thought in a passage
       1.1.1 Underlines the topic sentence
       1.1.2 Selects the most appropriate title for the passage
       1.1.3 Writes the main theme of the passage

Adding the third level of specificity, might be useful for clarifying some learning outcomes. The specific tasks describe how students will indicate that they can "identify the main thought in a passage," but our intended outcome is still identifying the main thought. Underlining, selecting, and writing are simply responses we are willing to use as indicators of the "ability to identify." Thus, although the third level may be a desirable transition between specific learning outcomes and relevant test items, these specific responses are not instructional outcomes in their own right (i.e., we are not interested in teaching students how to underline, select, and write but how to identify). This third level of specificity highlights one of the advantages of using levels of objectives rather than a list of specific tasks to describe the intended outcomes of instruction. With levels, we are less likely to confuse the intended outcomes of instruction with the indicators of those outcomes.

Summary of Steps for Stating Instructional Objectives

The final list of objectives for a course or unit should include all important learning outcomes (e.g., knowledge, understanding, skills, attitude) and should clearly convey how students are expected to perform at the end of the learning experience. The following summary of steps (Gronlund, 2000) provides guidelines for obtaining a clear statement of instructional objectives.

I. Stating the general instructional objectives

1. State each general objective as an intended learning outcome (i.e., students' terminal performance).
2. Begin each general objective with a verb (e.g., *knows, applies, interprets*). Omit "The student should be able to . . ."
3. State each general objective to include only one general learning outcome (e.g., not "Knows and understands").
4. State each general objective at the proper level of generality (i.e., it should encompass a readily definable domain of responses). Eight to 12 general objectives will usually suffice.
5. Keep each general objective sufficiently free of course content so that it can be used with various units of study.
6. Minimize the overlap with other objectives.

II. Stating the specific learning outcomes

1. List beneath each general instructional objective a representative sample of specific learning outcomes that describe the terminal performance students are expected to demonstrate.
2. Begin each specific learning outcome with an action verb that specifies observable performance (e.g., *identifies, describes*).
3. Make sure that each specific learning outcome is relevant to the general objective it describes.
4. Include enough specific learning outcomes to describe adequately the performance of students who have attained the objective.
5. Keep the specific learning outcomes sufficiently free of course content so that the list can be used with various units of study.
6. Consult reference materials for the specific components of those complex outcomes that are difficult to define (e.g., critical thinking, scientific attitude, creativity).
7. Add a third level of specificity to the list of outcomes, if needed.

This procedure for stating objectives does not include the conditions under which the achievement of learning outcomes will be demonstrated (e.g., open book, diagrams will be provided) or the standards for evaluating performance (e.g., 90% correct). Although some teachers may want to add such information to each objective, there are advantages in stating the conditions and standards separately from the objectives. In many cases, the same conditions and standards apply to all objectives being assessed at a given time, and thus a statement such as the following may be sufficient for an entire set of objectives.

EXAMPLE   Student performance will be determined under closed-book conditions, but all needed formulas will be provided. Hand calculators may be used.

A statement such as this will prevent the repetitious writing of the same conditions and standards for each objective and also avoid rewriting the list of objectives each time the conditions or standards are changed. We may, for example, use the same objectives for different units of study (e.g., knows terms, understands principles, applies principles) but want to vary the conditions and standards to suit the nature and complexity of the material studied. We may also wish to modify the conditions or standards to match a particular group of students. Thus, limiting the statements of objectives to concise descriptions of desired student performance and stating the conditions and standards separately as needed seem to be desirable for most classroom instruction. The time saved from writing instructional objectives over and over can usually be well spent on other instructional activities.

SUMMARY

Instructional goals and objectives provide the foundation for both instruction and assessment of student learning. To achieve this purpose, they should not be so specific that they fractionalize learning and emphasize relatively simple knowledge and skill outcomes; nor should they be as broad and general as the goals described for state and national programs. For both instruction and assessment purposes, an intermediate framework is needed. We are describing one that is readily adaptable to the complex learning outcomes suggested by cognitive research.

Instructional objectives make clear what learning outcomes we expect from our teaching. They describe our instructional intent in terms of the types of performance students are expected to demonstrate as a result of instruction. A convenient means of preparing instructional objectives is to follow a two-step process: (1) State the general instructional objectives as intended learning outcomes, and (2) define each general objective with a list of specific learning outcomes that describe the observable responses the learners will be able to make when they have achieved the general objective.

When instructional objectives are viewed as learning outcomes and are defined in performance terms, numerous types of intended outcomes might be included. In addition to the more obvious knowledge outcomes, those in the areas of understanding, application, thinking skills, performance skills, attitudes, interests, appreciation, and adjustment should also be considered. Suggestions for objectives in these and other areas may be obtained from Appendix G, the *Taxonomy of Educational Objectives*, content standards of professional associations, state and district content standards, various published sources, and objectives banks that have been prepared for national distribution. External sources should be used as aids only. Instructional objectives usually are most relevant when teachers develop their own lists, as these take into account the unique features of the local school and community.

The adequacy of the list of objectives for a particular course can be judged by the extent to which it (a) includes all important outcomes of the course, (b) is in harmony with state or district content standards, (c) is consistent with the school's general goals, (d) is in harmony with sound principles of learning, and (e) is realistic in terms of the students' abilities and the time and facilities available.

No matter how comprehensive a set of instructional objectives may be, there are likely to be some unanticipated outcomes of instruction. Thus, teachers be alert to this possibility during instruction and take these unplanned effects into account when assessing the learning outcomes of a course.

The task of stating instructional objectives is simplified if we keep in mind that we are making a list of intended outcomes of instruction, stated in terms of the types of performance the students are expected to demonstrate at the end of the teaching–learning experience. The procedure for stating the objectives for a particular course includes the following steps.

1. State each general instructional objective as an intended learning outcome that encompasses a readily definable domain of student responses. Each general objective should begin with a verb (e.g., *knows, understands, applies*), contain only one general learning outcome, and be relatively content free. Typically, 8 to 12 general objectives will suffice.

2. List beneath each general instructional objective a representative sample of specific learning outcomes stated in terms of student performance. Each should begin with an action verb (e.g., *identifies, describes*), be relevant to the general objective, and be relatively free of course content so that it can be used with various units of study.

Instructional objectives will require the least rewriting and function most effectively if the conditions and standards of performance are stated separately.

LEARNING EXERCISES

1. What are some of the advantages of stating instructional objectives as learning outcomes?
2. Give examples of how ultimate objectives (e.g., good citizenship) might be stated as immediate objectives.
3. List multiple-course objectives (e.g., study skills) that might be emphasized in your teaching area.
4. Using the summary of steps for stating instructional objectives as a guide, restate each of the following as general instructional objectives.
   a. To learn the basic terms in the unit
   b. Be familiar with the laboratory procedures
   c. Can show how to write a well-organized paragraph
   d. Increases ability to read with comprehension
5. Using the summary of steps for stating instructional objectives as a guide, restate each of the following as specific learning outcomes.
   a. Sees the importance of following safety practices
   b. Realizes the correct way to spell technical terms
   c. Is aware of the proper use of laboratory equipment
   d. Learns the symbols on a weather map
6. List unplanned effects of instruction (i.e., unanticipated outcomes) that might occur in one of your teaching areas. Which ones would you include in your assessment of student learning? Why?
7. What arguments would you present for and against including the conditions of measurement and the desired standard of performance in each stated objective?
8. For a unit of instruction in one of your major teaching areas, prepare a list of general instructional objectives and specific learning outcomes following the procedures suggested in this chapter.

REFERENCES

American Federation of Teachers. (2001). *Making standards matter 2001.* Washington, DC: American Federation of Teachers. Available: *http://www.aft.org/pubs-reports/downloads/teachers/msm2001.pdf*

Education Week. (2006, January). Quality counts at 10: A decade of standards-based education. *Supplement to Education Week, 25,* 17.

Gronlund N. E. (2000). *How to write and use instructional objectives* (5th ed.). Upper Saddle River, NJ: Merrill/Prentice Hall.

Gross, P. R. (2005). *The state of state science standards 2005.* Washington, DC: Thomas B. Fordham Foundation.

National Council of Teachers of Mathematics. (1989). *Curriculum and evaluation standards for school mathematics.* Reston, VA: National Council of Teachers of Mathematics.

National Council of Teachers of Mathematics. (2000). *Principles and standards for school mathematics.* Reston, VA: National Council of Teachers of Mathematics.

Pellegrino, J., Chudowsky, N., & Glaser, R. (Eds.). (2001). *Knowing what students know: The science and design of educational assessment.* Washington, DC: National Academy Press.

Resnick, L. B., & Resnick, D. P. (1992). Assessing the thinking curriculum: New tools for educational reform. In B. R. Gifford & M. C. O'Connor (Eds.), *Changing assessments: Alternative views of aptitude, achievement, and instruction* (pp. 37–75). Boston: Kluwer Academic Publishers.

Shepard, L. A. (1991). Psychometricians' beliefs about learning. *Educational Researcher, 20*(7), 2–16.

Shepard, L. A. (2000). The role of assessment in a learning culture. *Educational Researcher, 29*(7), 4–14.

Thompson, P. W. (1995). Notation, convention, and quantity in elementary mathematics. In J. T. Sowder & B. P. Schapple (Eds.), *Providing a foundation for teaching mathematics in the middle grades* (pp. 199–221). New York: State University of New York Press.

FURTHER READING

Bloom, B. S., Madaus, G. J., & Hastings, J. T. (1981). *Evaluation to improve learning.* New York: McGraw-Hill. See appendix A for a condensed version of the *Taxonomy of Educational Objectives.*

Gronlund, N. E. (2004). *Writing instructional objectives in teaching and assessment* (7th ed.). Upper Saddle River, NJ: Pearson Merrill Prentice Hall. A brief guide describing the step-by-step procedures for stating instructional objectives as intended learning outcomes. Provides guidance for using them in teaching, testing, and assessment. Presents illustrations of instructional objectives and lists of action verbs. Includes chapters on the use of instructional objectives in achievement testing and in performance and affective assessment.

McMillan, J. H. (2001). *Classroom assessment: Principles and practice of effective instruction* (2nd ed.). Boston: Allyn & Bacon. Chapter 2, "Establishing Learning Targets," provides a discussion of the role of goals and objectives within the context of standards-based education to the establishment of learning targets to guide both instruction and assessment.

National Council of Teachers of Mathematics. (2000). *Principles and standards for school mathematics.* Reston, VA: Author. Available: http://standards.nctm.org/. Provides a statement of general principles intended to provide a foundation for school mathematics programs. Provides an excellent illustration of general statements of instructional goals, sometimes referred to as subject-matter standards, content standards, or curriculum standards. Includes both broad statements of standards and more specific statements of expectations for specific grade bands: prekindergarten through grade 2, grades 3 to 6, grades 6 to 8, and grades 9 to 12.

CHAPTER

4

VALIDITY

When constructing or selecting assessments, the most important questions are (a) to what extent will the interpretation of the scores be appropriate, meaningful, and useful for the intended application of the results? and (b) what are the consequences of the particular uses and interpretations that are made of the results?

Assessments take a wide variety of forms, ranging from the familiar multiple-choice or other types of fixed-response tests to extended observations of performance. They also serve a variety of uses in the school. For example, assessment results might be used to identify student strengths and weaknesses, to plan instructional activities, or to communicate progress to students and parents; achievement tests might be used for selection, placement, diagnosis, or certification; aptitude tests might be used for predicting success in future learning activities or occupations; and appraisals of personal–social development might be used to better understand learning problems or to evaluate the effects of a particular school program. Regardless of the type of assessment used or how the results are to be used, all assessments should possess certain characteristics. The most essential of these are *validity, reliability,* and *usability.*

You may wonder why *fairness* is not listed. Fairness certainly is an essential characteristic of a good assessment. We did not list it separately, however, because fairness is an essential part of the comprehensive view of validity that is presented in this chapter.

Validity is the adequacy and appropriateness of the interpretations and uses of assessment results. Clearly, use of an assessment that leads to unfair treatment of girls, or African Americans, or English-language learners would not be evaluated as either adequate or appropriate. Nor would the use of assessment results to make unfair interpretations about the "capacity" of a group of students to learn be considered either adequate or appropriate. In both cases, the lack of fairness would lead to a negative evaluation of the validity of the interpretation or use of assessment results.

An evaluation of the validity of the use and interpretation of an assessment can take many forms. For example, if an assessment is to be used to describe student achievement, then we should like to be able to interpret the scores as a relevant and representative sample of the achievement domain to be measured. If the results are to be used as a measure of students' understanding of mathematical concepts, then we should like our interpretations to be based on evidence that the scores actually reflect mathematical understanding and are not distorted by irrelevant factors, such as the reading demands of the tasks. If the results are to be used to predict students' success in some future activity, then we should like our interpretations to be based on as good an estimate of future success as possible. Basically, then, validity is always concerned with the specific use of assessment results and the soundness and fairness of our proposed interpretations of those results. As we will see later in this chapter, however, this does not mean that validation procedures can be matched to specific assessment uses on a one-to-one basis.

In recent years, our understanding of validation has also come to include an evaluation of the adequacy and appropriateness of the uses that are made of assessment results. This expanded view of validity leads to a focus on the consequences of particular uses of assessment results. For example, if a state- or district-mandated test led teachers to ignore important content not covered by the test, then that consequence should be taken into account in judging the validity of the test use. In evaluating consequences it is important to distinguish between those consequences that are due to the assessment procedures and those that are the result of social or educational policies (Messick, 1994). Both are relevant to an evaluation of the use of the assessment, but it is consequences tied directly to characteristics of the assessment (e.g., an overemphasis on drill and practice, because the test places an undue emphasis on factual knowledge at the expense of conceptual understanding or problem-solving applications) that are the primary concern in validation of a particular use of an assessment.

Reliability refers to the consistency of assessment results. If we obtain quite similar scores when the same assessment procedure is used with the same students on two different occasions, then we also can conclude that our results have a high degree of reliability from one occasion to another. Similarly, if different teachers independently rate student performances on the same assessment task and obtain similar ratings, we also can conclude that the results have a high degree of reliability from one rater to another. Like validity, reliability is intimately related to the type of interpretation to be made. For some uses, we may be interested in asking how reliable our assessment results are over a given period of time and, for others, how reliable they are over different samples of the same behavior. In all instances in which reliability is being determined, however, we are concerned with the *consistency* of the results rather than with the *appropriateness of the interpretations* made from the results (validity).

The relation between reliability and validity is sometimes confusing to persons who encounter these terms for the first time. Reliability (consistency) of measurement is needed to obtain valid results, but we can have reliability without validity. That is, we can have consistent measures that provide the wrong information or are interpreted inappropriately. The target-shooting illustration in Figure 4.1 depicts the concept that **reliability is a necessary but not sufficient condition for validity**.

In addition to providing results that possess a satisfactory degree of validity and reliability, an assessment procedure must meet certain practical requirements. It should be economical from the viewpoint of both time and money, it should be easily administered and scored, and it should produce results that can be accurately interpreted and applied

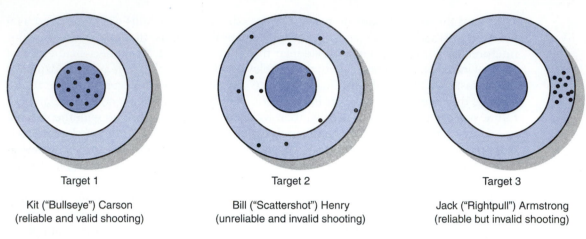

Target 1	Target 2	Target 3
Kit ("Bullseye") Carson (reliable and valid shooting)	Bill ("Scattershot") Henry (unreliable and invalid shooting)	Jack ("Rightpull") Armstrong (reliable but invalid shooting)

Figure 4.1
Reliability (consistency) is needed to obtain valid results (but one can be consistently "off target")

by available school personnel. These practical aspects of an assessment procedure all can be included under the heading of usability. The term **usability**, then, refers only to the *practicality* of the procedure and says nothing about the other qualities present.

NATURE OF VALIDITY

When using the term *validity* in relation to testing and assessment, keep the following cautions in mind.

1. Validity refers to the **appropriateness of the interpretation and use made of the results** of an assessment procedure for a given group of individuals, not to the procedure itself. We sometimes speak of the "validity of a test" for the sake of convenience, but it is more correct to speak of the validity of the interpretation and use to be made of the results.

2. Validity is a **matter of degree;** it does not exist on an all-or-none basis. Consequently, we should avoid thinking of assessment results as valid or invalid. Validity is best considered in terms of categories that specify degree, such as high validity, moderate validity, and low validity.

3. Validity is always **specific to some particular use or interpretation** for a specific population of test takers. No assessment is valid for all purposes. For example, the results of a mathematics test may have a high degree of validity for indicating computational skill, a low degree of validity for indicating mathematical reasoning, a moderate degree of validity for predicting success in future mathematics courses, and essentially no validity for predicting success in art or music. When indicating computational skill, the mathematics test may also have a high degree of validity for third- and fourth-grade students but a low degree of validity for second- or fifth-grade students. Thus, when appraising or describing validity, it is necessary to consider the specific interpretation or use to be made of the results. Assessment results are never just valid; they have a different degree of validity for each particular interpretation to be made.

4. Validity is a **unitary concept**. The conceptual nature of validity has typically been described for the testing profession in a set of standards prepared by a joint committee of members from three professional organizations that are especially concerned with educational and psychological testing and assessment. In the two most recent revisions of the *Standards for Educational and Psychological Testing* by the American Educational Research Association (AERA), American Psychological Association (APA), and National Council on Measurement in Education (NCME) (1999), the traditional view that there are several different types of validity has been discarded. Instead, validity is viewed as a unitary concept based on various kinds of evidence. We will refer to the 1999 AERA, APA, NCME standards simply as the *Standards*.

5. Validity involves an **overall evaluative judgment**. It requires an evaluation of the degree to which interpretations and uses of assessment results are justified by supporting evidence and in terms of the consequences of those interpretations and uses.

There are many ways of accumulating evidence to support or challenge the validity of an interpretation or use of assessment results. The *Standards* discuss five sources of evidence that are proposed for possible use in evaluating the validity of a specific use or interpretation. These sources of evidence are based on (a) test content, (b) response processes, (c) internal structure, (d) relations to other variables, and (e) consequences of testing. Thus, validation may include a consideration of the content measured, the ways in which students respond, the relationship of individual items to the test scores, the relationship of performance to other assessments, and the consequences of using and interpreting assessment results.

Traditionally, the ways of accumulating evidence have been grouped together in one of three categories (content-related, construct-related, and criterion-related evidence). Each type of evidence is an important consideration in arriving at an overall evaluation of the degree of validity of any given interpretation of scores on a test or other assessment procedure. Although the traditional methods of accumulating evidence include the first four sources of evidence in the *Standards* (mostly under the broad umbrella of construct validity), these traditional categories do not take into account that the consequences of uses and the interpretation of assessment results also influence validity. Hence, we will discuss four interrelated considerations—content, construct, assessment–criterion relationships, and consequences—in the evaluation of validity rather than a list of distinct validation methods.

MAJOR CONSIDERATIONS IN ASSESSMENT VALIDATION

Four major considerations for validation are briefly described in Table 4.1. The strongest case for validity can be made when evidence is obtained regarding all four considerations herein. That is, interpretations and uses of assessment results are likely to have greater validity when we have an understanding of (a) the assessment content and the specifications from which it was derived, (b) the nature of the characteristic(s) being measured, (c) the

Table 4.1
Major considerations in validation

Consideration	Procedure	Meaning
Content	Compare the assessment tasks to the specifications describing the task domain under consideration.	How well the sample of assessment tasks **represents** the domain of tasks to be measured and how it emphasizes the most important content.
Construct	Establish the meaning of the assessment results by controlling (or examining) the development of the assessment, evaluate the cognitive processes used by students to perform tasks, evaluate the relationships of the scores with other relevant measures, and experimentally determine what factors influence performance.	How well performance on the assessment can be interpreted as a meaningful measure of some characteristic or quality. For example, does the performance clearly imply that the student "understands" the relevant concept or principle intended to be used in responding to the task?
Assessment–criterion relationships	Compare assessment results with another measure of performance obtained at a later date (for prediction) or with another measure of performance obtained concurrently (for estimating present status).	How well performance on the assessment predicts future performance or **estimates** current performance on some valued measures other than the test itself (called a **criterion**).
Consequences	Evaluate the effects of use of assessment results on teachers and students. Both the intended positive effects (e.g., increased learning) and possible unintended negative effects (e.g., narrowing of instruction, drop out of school) need to be evaluated.	How well use of assessment results accomplishes intended purposes and avoids unintended effects.

relation of the assessment results to other significant measures, and (d) the consequences of the uses and interpretations of the results. However, for many uses of a test or an assessment, it is not practical or necessary to have evidence dealing with all four considerations. For example, it is not practical to expect that a teacher would provide evidence that a classroom assessment designed to measure student learning is related to other significant measures. In this case, the primary concern would be content, but some of the analyses of the meaning of the scores (construct considerations) and possible effects on student motivation and learning (consequence considerations) would be relevant.

Similarly, in using a scholastic aptitude test to predict future success in school, test–criterion relationships would be of major interest; but we would also be concerned about the appropriateness of the content, possible irrelevant factors (not part of the construct) that influence test performance (e.g., motivation, test anxiety, test-taking skills), and possible unintended consequences of using predictions. Thus, content, construct, and consequence considerations would be relevant. One consideration is likely to be of primary importance, but the other three are useful for a fuller understanding of the meaning of the assessment results and, therefore, contribute to the validation of our interpretations.

Although many other considerations are relevant to validity, our discussions of **content**, **construct**, **assessment–criterion relationships**, and **consequence** considerations will focus on those procedures that are most useful in practical educational settings.

CONTENT CONSIDERATIONS

Content considerations are of special importance when we wish to describe how an individual performs on a domain of tasks that the assessment is supposed to represent. We may, for example, expect students to be able to spell the 200 words on a given list. Because a 200-word spelling test is too time consuming, we may select a sample of 20 words to represent the total domain of 200 spelling words. If Margaret correctly spells 80% of these 20 words, we would like to be able to say that she can probably spell approximately 80% of the 200 words. Thus, we would like to be able to generalize from the student's performance on the **sample** of words in the test to the performance that the student would be expected to demonstrate on the domain of spelling words that the test represents.

The validity of the interpretation, in which a test score implies that the student can probably spell a given percentage of words in the whole domain, depends on considerations that go beyond the question of content. For example, construct considerations, such as the assumption that Margaret was trying to do her best, that she did not copy her neighbor's spelling words, and that she understood the teacher's pronunciation of the words, influence the validity of the interpretation that she can spell a given fraction of the words. Here, however, our concern is with the extent to which our 20-word test constituted a **representative sample** of the 200 words. In this instance, we can obtain a fairly representative sample of spelling words by simply starting with our 200-word list and selecting every 10th word. Having thus assured ourselves that we have a reasonably representative sample, we would have good support for the desired interpretation, in terms of content considerations. As we will see shortly, judging how adequately an assessment samples a given domain of achievement is usually much more complex than in this simple example, particularly when the learning outcomes involve more complex understandings or integrated performances.

The essence of the content consideration in validation, then, is determining the adequacy of the sampling of the content that the assessment results are interpreted to represent. More formally, **the goal in the consideration of content validation is to determine the extent to which a set of assessment tasks provides a relevant and representative sample of the domain of tasks about which interpretations of assessment results are made**. Focusing only on the issue of the adequacy of the sample from a content domain, of course, begs the question of priorities that should be given to different aspects of the content domain to be assessed. The definition of the domain to be assessed should derive directly from the identification of goals and objectives as discussed in Chapter 3. Emphasized in the quotes in the box "Defining the Content Domain of an Assessment," it is critical that the assessment begin with a content domain that reflects the important goals and objectives.

In classroom assessment, the domains of achievement tasks are determined by applicable content standards, the curriculum, and instruction. Assessment development involves (a) clearly specifying the domain of instructionally relevant tasks to be used to measure

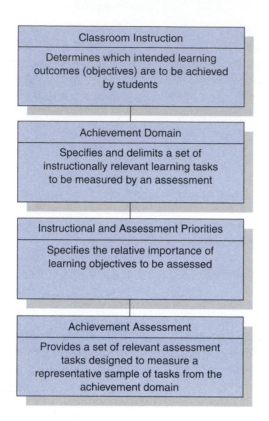

Figure 4.2
Content considerations in the assessment of classroom achievement

student achievement, (b) specifying the emphasis or relative importance according to the priority of goals and objectives, and (c) constructing or selecting a representative set of assessment tasks. Thus, to obtain a valid measure of learning outcomes, we proceed from the instruction (what has been taught) to the achievement domain (what is to be measured) to the priorities for measurement (what should be emphasized in the assessment) and finally to the assessment itself (a representative sample of relevant tasks). As shown in Figure 4.2, content considerations in validation require a judgment that all four are in close harmony.

Rigorous judgments regarding validity based on content considerations should not be confused with **face validity**, which refers only to the appearance of the assessment. Based on a superficial examination of the tasks, does the assessment appear to be a reasonable measure? A simple example can be used to draw a clear distinction between making validity claims based on rigorous consideration of content definitions and the adequacy of sampling of tasks and making claims based on face validity (i.e., on the basis of appearance). On an arithmetic test to a young child, we might phrase an item as follows: "If you had a 10-foot piece of *string* and you cut it in half, how long would the two pieces be?" If the test was to be given to carpenters, we would substitute the word *board* for *string* in this item. Similarly, for plumbers we would use the word *pipe* and for electricians the word *wire.* The problem remains the same, but by phrasing it in appropriate terms, it appears more relevant to the test taker (i.e., it has greater face validity). The validity of interpretations of the arithmetic test scores would not be determined by how the test

---

Defining the Content Domain of an Assessment

"Assessment activities should contribute to instructional improvement by focusing on instruction targets that are consistent with the goals of instructional activities" (Linn & Baker, 1996).

Science Standards: "Achievement data collected focus on the science content that is most important for students to learn"

(National Committee on Science Education Standards and Assessment, National Research Council, 1995, p. 79).

Mathematics Standards: "The mathematics standard: Assessment should reflect the mathematics that all students need to know and be able to do" (National Council of Teachers of Mathematics, 1995, p. 11).

---

looked, however, but by how well it sampled the domain of arithmetic tasks important to each group (i.e., children, carpenters, plumbers, and electricians). Thus, our arithmetic test may provide an adequate measure of content for one group but not another, even though the items were phrased in terms appropriate to each group. Although a test should look like an appropriate measure to obtain the cooperation of those taking the test, face validity should not be considered a substitute for more rigorous evaluation of content definitions and sampling adequacy.

Content Considerations in Assessment Development to Enhance Validity

Content issues are typically considered during the development of an assessment. It is primarily a matter of preparing detailed specifications and then constructing an assessment that meets these specifications. Although there are many ways of specifying what an assessment should measure, one widely used procedure in constructing achievement tests uses a two-way chart called a **table of specifications**. We will use a brief form of it here to help clarify the process of content validation in preparing classroom assessments. More elaborate tables of specifications and other types of specifications will be described and illustrated in Chapter 6.

Table of Specifications.   The learning outcomes of a course or curriculum may be broadly defined to include both subject-matter content and instructional objectives. The former is concerned with the topics to be learned and the latter with the types of performance students are expected to demonstrate (e.g., knows, comprehends, applies, analyzes, synthesizes, evaluates). Both of these aspects are of concern in defining content domain and ensuring adequate sampling from it. We should like any assessment of achievement that we construct to produce results that represent both the content areas and the objectives we wish to measure, and the table of specifications aids in obtaining a sample of tasks that represents both.

A table of specifications, in a very simple form, is presented in Table 4.2 to show how such a table is used in test development. The percentages in the table indicate the relative degree of emphasis that each content area and each instructional objective is to be given in the test. Thus, if a 50-item classroom test is to measure a representative

Table 4.2
Sample table of specifications

	Instructional Objectives						
Content Area	*Knows Concepts*	*Comprehends Concepts*	*Applies Concepts*	*Analyzes Concepts*	*Synthesizes Concepts*	*Evaluates Concepts*	*Total*
Air pressure	2	4	4	6	4	2	22
Air temperature	2	4	4	2	4	4	20
Humidity and precipitation	2	4	2	2	4	2	16
Wind	2	4	2	2	4	2	16
Clouds	2	4	2	2	4	0	14
Fronts	2	4	2	2	0	2	12
Total	12	24	16	16	20	12	100

sample of subject-matter content, then 22% of the items (i.e., 11 items) should be concerned with air pressure, 20% with air temperature, 16% with humidity and precipitation, 16% with the wind, 14% with the clouds, and 12% with fronts. Similarly, if the test is to measure a representative sample of the instructional objectives, then 12% of the items (i.e., 6 items) should measure knowledge of concepts, 24% should measure comprehension of concepts, 16% should measure application of concepts, 16% should measure analysis of concepts, 20% should measure synthesis of concepts, and 12% should measure evaluation of concepts. Thus, 52% of the items should measure the three lowest levels of Bloom's taxonomy and 48% of the items should measure the three highest levels of Bloom's taxonomy. This, of course, implies that the emphasis on knowledge, comprehension, application, analysis, synthesis, and evaluation for each content area will follow the percentages in the table of specifications. For example, 2% of the test items (i.e., a single item) concerned should measure knowledge of air pressure concepts, 4% should measure comprehension of air pressure concepts, 4% should measure application of air pressure concepts, 6% should measure analysis of air pressure concepts, 4% should measure synthesis of air pressure concepts, and 2% should measure evaluation of air pressure concepts.

As noted earlier, the specifications describing the achievement domain to be measured should be in harmony with what was taught. Thus, the weights assigned in this table reflect the emphasis that was given during instruction. For example, comprehension outcomes received more emphasis than either knowledge or application outcomes in the instruction, and synthesis outcomes received more emphasis than either analysis or evaluation outcomes. The weights assigned through the table show that 44% of the instruction should emphasize comprehension and synthesis. The table, then, indicates the sample of instructionally relevant learning tasks to be measured, and the more closely the test items correspond to the specified sample, the greater the likelihood of obtaining a valid measure of student learning.

The test items and other kinds of assessment tasks must function as intended if valid results are to be obtained. Test items and assessment tasks may function improperly if they contain inappropriate vocabulary, unclear directions, or some other defect. Similarly, tasks designed to measure comprehension and synthesis may measure only the simple recall of information if the solutions to the problems have been directly taught during instruction. In short, a host of factors can influence the intended function of the tasks and thus the validity of the assessment results. Much of what is written in this book concerning the construction of classroom assessments is directed toward producing valid measures of achievement.

Content Considerations in Test Selection

Evidence obtained from an analysis of content domain definition and content coverage (sampling adequacy) is also of concern when selecting published achievement tests. When test publishers prepare achievement tests for use in the schools, they pay special attention to content. Their test specifications, however, are based on what is commonly taught in many different schools. Thus, a published test may or may not fit a particular school situation. To determine whether it does, it is necessary to go beyond the title of the test and examine what the test actually measures. A careful consideration of what the test measures is a necessary step in adopting any test, because the *Standards* make it clear that the ultimate responsibility for test use and interpretation lies with the user (e.g., local educator) rather than the publisher. Thus, it is important to ask questions such as the following: How well is the test content aligned with the state or district content standards? How closely does the test content correspond to the course content and the curriculum and instructional goals in the local instructional program? Does the test provide a balanced measure of the intended learning outcomes? Are the most important objectives emphasized appropriately, or are some areas overemphasized and others neglected? A published test may provide more valid results for one school program than for another, depending on how closely the set of test tasks matches the achievement to be measured.

The same types of specifications used in preparing classroom assessments can be used in selecting published tests. The detailed descriptions of course content and instructional objectives and the relative emphasis to be given to each can help us determine which of several published tests is most relevant to our particular situation. It is simply a matter of examining the items in each test and comparing them to our test specifications. The test that provides the most balanced measure of the specified achievement domain is the one that will produce the most valid results. Many test publishers include a detailed description of their test specifications in the test manual. Although this makes it easier to judge the potential validity of the test results, there is no substitute for examining the test tasks themselves and judging how validly they measure the intended learning outcomes in the local instructional program.

Content Considerations in Other Areas

Although content considerations are of primary interest in assessing achievement, they are also of interest in other areas. For example, examining the content of a scholastic aptitude test aids in understanding the meaning of the scores and provides some evidence concerning the types of prediction for which it might be best suited. Similarly, when constructing or selecting an attitude scale, we are interested in how adequately the items cover those attitudinal topics included in the domain to be measured. In the same manner, an interest inventory should include samples of items that adequately represent those aspects of interest we wish to measure. In these and other situations, the content validation procedure is essentially the same as that in testing and assessment of achievement. It is a matter of analyzing the content and tasks included in the measuring instrument and the domain of outcomes to be measured and judging the degree of correspondence between them.

CONSTRUCT CONSIDERATIONS

Although we are considering them second, most measurement specialists would give highest priority to construct considerations in evaluating the validity of an interpretation or use of an assessment. We began with content considerations because the review of the content domain and sampling helps us determine how well test or assessment scores represent a given domain of tasks and is especially useful in both the preparation and the evaluation of all types of assessment of achievement. However, because we usually wish to interpret test and assessment results in terms of more general individual characteristics (e.g., reading comprehension, communication ability, understanding of scientific principles), we need to consider the construct that the assessment is intended to measure. These characteristics may be labeled in a variety of ways (e.g., skills, accomplishments, abilities, psychological traits, personal qualities), but regardless of the label, they involve some inference about a construct that goes beyond the factual statement that a student obtained a given score on a particular test or assessment. For example, rather than only stating that a student correctly solved 75% of the tasks on a particular mathematics test, we might want to infer that the student possesses a certain degree of mathematical reasoning ability. This provides a broad general description of student performance that has implications for many different uses.

Whenever we wish to interpret assessment results in terms of some individual characteristic (e.g., reading comprehension, mathematics problem-solving ability), we are concerned with a construct. A **construct** is an individual characteristic that we assume exists in order to explain some aspect of behavior. Mathematical reasoning is a construct, and so are reading comprehension, understanding of the principles of electricity, intelligence, creativity, and such personality characteristics as sociability, honesty, and anxiety. These are called constructs because they are theoretical constructions that are used to explain performance on an assessment. When we interpret assessment results as a measure of a particular construct, we are implying that there is such a construct, that it differs from other constructs, and that the results provide a measure of the construct that is little influenced by extraneous factors. Verifying such implications is the task of construct validation.

Construct validation may be defined as the process of determining the extent to which performance on an assessment can be interpreted in terms of one or more constructs. Although construct validation has been commonly associated with theory building and theory testing (Cronbach & Meehl, 1955), it also has implications for the practical use of assessment results. Whenever an assessment is to be interpreted as a measure of a particular construct, the various types of evidence useful for construct validation should be considered during its development or selection. This will almost certainly include consideration of content and may include consideration of assessment–criterion relationships, but a variety of other types of evidence is also relevant. The most appropriate types of evidence will be dictated by the particular construct to be measured.

Two questions are central to any construct validation: (1) Does the assessment adequately represent the intended construct? and (2) is performance influenced by factors that are ancillary or irrelevant to the construct? In the jargon of measurement specialists, these two questions are concerned with **construct underrepresentation** and **construct-irrelevant variance**. Both are stated in the negative. That is, validity is reduced to the degree that important aspects of the construct are underrepresented in the assessment. Validity is also reduced to the degree that performance is influenced by irrelevant factors such as skills that are ancillary to the intent of the assessment (e.g., reading speed on a reading comprehension test or punctuation on a test of understanding scientific principles).

Construct-irrelevant factors can lead to unfairness in the use and interpretation of assessment results. An assessment intended to measure understanding of mathematical concepts, for example, could lead to unfair inferences about the level of understanding of English-language learners because of the heavy reading demands of the assessment tasks, which are presented only in English.

In Chapter 3, a standard from the Colorado geography content standards was used as an illustration of state content standards. It will be repeated here to illustrate the important ideas of construct underrepresentation and construct-irrelevant variance. The standard is as follows:

> Students understand how economic, political, cultural, and social processes interact to shape patterns of human populations, interdependence, cooperation, and conflict. (*Colorado Model Content Standards for Geography,* Colorado Department of Education; adopted June 1995, amended November 1995)

The validity of an assessment of this standard would be undermined by construct underrepresentation if it dealt only with economic and political processes and their interactions. The cultural and social processes would be underrepresented (or not represented at all). The validity of the assessment would also be called into question because of construct-irrelevant variance if it were found that the major factors influencing student scores on the assessment were writing mechanics (e.g., grammar, punctuation, and spelling) of the essays written in response to the tasks. Although writing mechanics are skills that a teacher might want to assess, those skills are ancillary to determining whether a student has acquired the understanding that is the intent of the illustrative geography standard.

Although construct validation is often associated with tests and assessments used to measure theoretical psychological constructs such as anxiety or introversion, it should be clear from the previous example that considerations of construct underrepresentation and construct-irrelevant variance are equally applicable to both published and teacher-developed assessments used in the classroom.

Some aspects of construct underrepresentation were dealt with directly when considering the content basis of validity. For example, the validity assessment of a unit on weather that was supposed to be aligned with the table of specifications shown in Table 4.2 would be called into question if there were no tasks that required knowledge or understanding of clouds or if none of the higher cognitive levels (e.g., synthesis and evaluation) were needed to complete the unit. Construct considerations, however, also involve questions about student characteristics, such as understanding or problem-solving ability. This requires considering the possibility that a correct answer might simply reflect recall of an answer from a textbook or going through the motions of applying an algorithm to a problem rather than real understanding or problem-solving ability—both of which may require that the task be novel to the student.

In considering construct-irrelevant factors may undermine validity, it is useful to think about ancillary skills that may have an impact on performance on the assessment. On an assessment in mathematics or science, for example, reading ability is one obvious skill that may be ancillary to the intent of the assessment. Thus, it would be important to review the reading demands of the tasks to ensure that performance of some students was limited not by a lack of understanding of science principles or mathematical concepts but by reading difficulties. Such a review is likely to be particularly important for assessments involving English-language learners.

A wide range of construct-irrelevant factors may undermine validity. In addition to the influence of ancillary skills (e.g., reading on a science test), the test can interact with student characteristics such as test-wiseness, motivation, or anxiety. As a consequence, students who have low test-wiseness (or low motivation or high anxiety) might be expected to score lower that their true ability would indicate on a science test. Instruction can also introduce construct irrelevant factors when comparing two groups of students who have not had an equal opportunity to learn the material. For example, if one group of students has received instruction that emphasizes higher-order skills and another group of students received instruction that emphasized lower-level skills, then comparisons of the students' abilities on a test that measures higher-order skills would not lead to reasonable interpretations. In short, anything that affects performance on the assessment that is not the construct of interest introduces a potential source of construct-irrelevance, or invalidity.

Construct validation takes place primarily during the development and tryout of a test or an assessment and is based on an accumulation of evidence from varied sources. When selecting a published test that presumably measures a particular construct, such as mathematical reasoning or reading comprehension, the test manual should be examined to determine what evidence is presented to support the validity of the proposed interpretations.

An illustration of some types of evidence that might be used in the construct validation of an assessment of mathematical reasoning is shown in Figure 4.3. Although other types of studies could be added, this listing is sufficient to clarify the variety of types of evidence needed to support the claim that the assessment scores can be interpreted as measures of mathematical reasoning. Notice that considerations of both content and assessment–criterion relationships (considered in greater detail in the next section of this chapter) are included, along with other comparisons and correlations. No single type of evidence is sufficient, but the accumulation of various types of evidence helps describe what the assessment measures and how the scores relate to other significant variables. This clarifies the meaning of the assessment performance and aids in determining how validly mathematical reasoning is being measured.

In theory building and theory testing, the accumulation of evidence for construct validation may be endless. As new data are gathered, both the theory and the test or assessment are likely to be modified, and the testing of hypotheses continues. For the practical

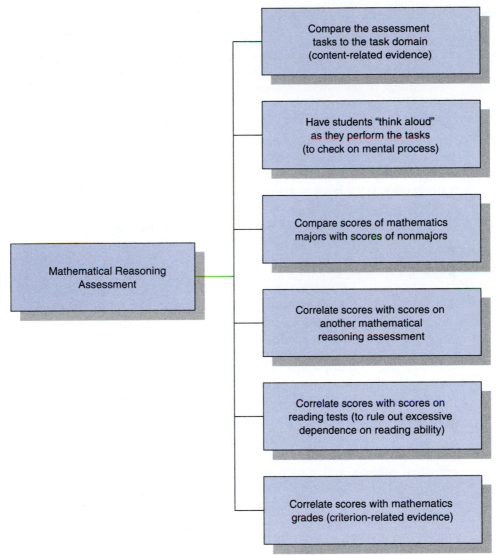

Figure 4.3
Types of evidence used in construct validation

use of test and assessment results, however, we need to employ a more restricted frame-work when considering construct validation. During the development and selection of tests and assessments, our focus should be on the types of evidence that it seems reasonable to obtain, giving special attention to those data that are most relevant to the types of interpretations to be made. We can thus increase our understanding of what the assessment measures and how validly it does so without becoming involved in an endless task of data gathering.

Methods Used in Construct Validation

Construct validation depends on logical inferences drawn from a variety of types of data. As noted earlier, analyses of content and criterion relationships provide partial support for our interpretations, but this must be supplemented by various studies that further clarify the meaning of the assessment results. Although it is impossible to describe all the specific procedures that might be used in construct validation, the following exemplify some of the more commonly used methods.

1. Defining the domain or tasks to be measured. The specifications should be so well defined that the meaning of the construct is clear and it is possible to judge the extent to which the assessment provides a relevant and representative measure of the task domain. If a single construct is being measured, then the tasks should evoke similar types of responses and be highly interrelated (also a content consideration).

2. Analyzing the response process required by the assessment tasks. The response process called forth by the assessment tasks can be determined both by examining the test tasks themselves and by administering the tasks to individual students and having them "think aloud" as they perform the tasks. Thus, examination of the items in a reading comprehension test may indicate that literal comprehension is emphasized, with relatively few items devoted to inferential comprehension. Similarly, a review of the requirements for performance of a laboratory task in science may reveal a substantial emphasis on accurate recording of results but too little emphasis on the conceptual integration of the laboratory results with theory or everyday experiences. Such judgments can be checked by administering the tasks to individual students and having them explain how they obtain their res-ponses. In the example in Figure 4.3, "thinking aloud" may verify that the tasks call for the intended reasoning process, or it may reveal that most problems can be solved by a simple trial-and-error procedure.

3. Comparing the scores of known groups. In some cases, it is possible to predict that scores will differ from one group to another. These may be age groups, trained and untrained, adjusted and maladjusted, and the like. For example, level of achievement generally increases with age (at least during childhood and adolescence). Also, it is reasonable to expect that performance on an assessment will differ for groups that have received different amounts of instruction in the subject matter of the assessment and that scores on adjustment inventories will discriminate between groups of adjusted and maladjusted individuals. Thus, a prediction of differences for a particular test or assessment can be checked against groups that are known to differ and the results used as partial support for construct validation.

4. Comparing scores before and after a particular learning experience or experimental treatment. We would like our assessments to be sensitive to some types of experiences and insensitive to others. Certainly, we would like assessments of student achievement in a given subject-matter area to improve during the course of instruction. On the other hand, we would not like them to be influenced by such factors as student anxiety. Thus, both a demonstration of increases in performance following instruction and a demonstration that performance was affected little by a treatment designed to reduce student anxiety would lend support to the construct validity of the assessment.

5. **Correlating the scores with other measures.** The scores of any particular assessment can be expected to correlate substantially with the scores of other measures of the same or a similar construct. (See the next section of this chapter and Appendix A for a discussion of correlation.) By the same token, lower correlations would be expected to be obtained with measures of a different ability or trait. For example, we would expect rather high correlation between two scholastic aptitude tests but much lower correlation between a scholastic and a musical aptitude test. Similarly, we would expect student performances on two assessments of writing to have substantially higher correlations with each other than either would have with an assessment in mathematics. Thus, for any given test or assessment, we would predict higher correlations with like tests and assessments and lower correlations with unlike tests and assessments. In addition, we might also predict that the assessment scores would correlate with various practical criteria. Scholastic aptitude scores, for example, should correlate satisfactorily with school grades, scores on performance in chemistry, and other measures of achievement in chemistry. This latter type of evidence is obtained by studies of assessment–criterion relationships. Our interest here, however, is not in the immediate problem of prediction, but in using these correlations to support the claim that the test measures scholastic aptitude or that the assessment measures understanding of chemical principles. As indicated earlier, construct validation depends on a wide array of evidence, including that provided by the other validation procedures.

Broadly conceived, construct validation is an attempt to account for the differences in assessment results. During the development of an assessment, an attempt is made to rule out extraneous factors that might distort the meaning of the scores, and follow-up studies are conducted to verify the success of these attempts. The aim is to clarify the meaning of student performance by identifying the nature and strength of all factors influencing the scores on the assessment.

Construct validation is important to all types of testing and assessment—achievement, aptitude, and personal–social development. Whether constructing or selecting an assessment, the meaning of the resulting scores depends on the care with which the assessment was constructed and the array of evidence supporting the types of interpretations to be made. Construct validation is emphasized in most recent discussions of validity in the technical and theoretical literature, in part because, as we have seen, it subsumes considerations of content and criterion relationships and in part because meaning is crucial in our uses and interpretations of the scores. The latter point was stressed by Messick (1989), who stated, "The meaning of the measure, and hence its construct validity, must always be pursued—not only to support test interpretation but also to justify test use" (p. 17).

ASSESSMENT–CRITERION RELATIONSHIPS

Although few teachers will conduct studies relating assessment results to other measures, it is important to understand the use of assessment–criterion relationships in evaluating validity. Understanding how assessment–criterion relationships are analyzed, for example, will help in evaluating the use of standardized tests to make predictions of student performance in other settings.

When test scores are to be used to predict future performance or to estimate current performance on some valued measure other than the test itself (called a **criterion**), we are especially concerned with evaluating the relationship between the test and the criterion. For example, reading readiness test scores might be used to **predict** students' future achievement in reading, or a test of dictionary skills might be used to **estimate** students' current skills in the actual use of the dictionary (as determined by observation). In the first example, we are interested in prediction and thus in the relationship between the two measures over time. This procedure for obtaining evidence of validity calls for a **predictive validation study**. In the second example, we are attempting to estimate present status, and thus we are interested in the relationship between two measures obtained concurrently. A high relationship in this case would show that the test of dictionary skills is a good indicator of actual skill in using a dictionary. This procedure for obtaining evidence of validity calls for a **concurrent validation study**. Both the predictive and the concurrent designs are subsumed under the more general category of criterion-related validation because the method of determining and expressing validity is the same in both cases. The major difference resides in the time period between the two obtained measures, as illustrated in Figure 4.4.

The focus of both types of studies shown in Figure 4.4 is on determining the extent to which test performance is related to some other valued measure of performance. As noted earlier, the second measure of performance (called a criterion) may be obtained at some future date (when we are interested in predicting future performance) or concurrently (when we are interested in estimating present performance). First, let us examine the use of test–criterion relationships from the standpoint of predicting success in some future activity.

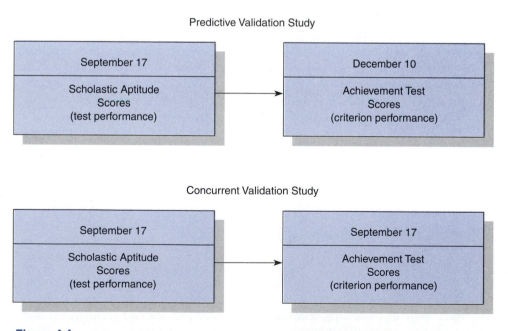

Figure 4.4
Studies of types of assessment–criterion relationships (based on time difference only)

Predicting Future Performance

Suppose that Mr. Tanaka, a junior high school teacher, wants to determine how well the scores from a scholastic aptitude test will predict success in his seventh-grade mathematics class. Because the scholastic aptitude test is administered to all students when they enter junior high school, these scores are readily available to Mr. Tanaka. His biggest problem is deciding on a criterion of successful achievement in mathematics. For lack of a better criterion, he decides to use a comprehensive departmental examination that is administered to all seventh-grade math sections at the end of the school year. It is now possible for Mr. Tanaka to determine how well the scholastic aptitude test scores predict success in his mathematics class by comparing the students' scholastic aptitude test scores with their scores on the departmental examination. Do those students who have high scholastic aptitude test scores also tend to have high scores on the departmental examination? Do those who have low scholastic aptitude test scores also tend to have low scores on the departmental examination? If this is the case, Mr. Tanaka is inclined to agree that the scholastic aptitude test scores tend to be reasonably accurate in predicting achievement in this mathematics class.

In our example, Mr. Tanaka merely inspected the scholastic aptitude and achievement test scores to determine the agreement between them. Although this may be a desirable preliminary step, it does not provide a precise notion of the degree of relationship between the aptitude test scores and the scores on the comprehensive departmental examination, nor does it provide a good way of communicating the results. The degree of relationship can be described more precisely by statistically correlating the two sets of scores. The resulting **correlation coefficient** provides a numerical summary of the degree of relationship between the two sets of scores. A correlation coefficient provides a concise, quantitative summary of the relationship for anyone who has learned to understand and interpret this statistical measure. Scores on the scholastic aptitude test also can be converted to predicted achievement scores by means of a **regression equation**.

Communication of the meaning of the relationship also can be facilitated by the use of a graphical presentation of the results in the form of a **scatter plot** or by the use of an **expectancy table**. The construction of scatter plots (also known as scattergrams or scatter diagrams) and the calculation and interpretation of correlation coefficients and regression equations are described and illustrated in Appendix A. In this chapter, we confine our discussion to the use and interpretation of these indicators of relationship within the context of criterion-related validation. The construction and interpretation of expectancy tables and regression equations also will be described here.

Correlation

To illustrate the use of correlation coefficients and scatter plots in studies of test–criterion relationships, let us consider the exact scores that Mr. Tanaka's students received on both the scholastic aptitude test (predictor) and the departmental examination in mathematics (criterion). This information is provided in the first two columns of Table 4.3. By inspecting these two columns of scores, we see that the high scores in column 1 tend to match the high scores in column 2. This comparison is difficult to make, however, because the sizes of the test scores in the two columns are different.

Table 4.3

Test scores and test-score ranks for 20 junior high school students

	1	2	3	4
Pupil	Fall Aptitude Score	Spring Mathematics Score	Aptitude Rank	Mathematics Rank
Sandra	119	77	1	3
Alex	118	76	2	4
Maria	116	72	3	6
Susan	115	67	4	8
Bill	112	82	5	1
Carl	109	63	6	10
Laura	108	60	7	12
Chang	106	78	8	2
Jane	105	69	9	7
Karl	104	49	10	18
Jim	102	48	11	19
Frank	100	58	12	14
Karen	98	56	13	16
Joan	97	57	14	15
Carlos	95	74	15	5
June	94	62	16	11
John	93	46	17	20
George	91	65	18	9
Alice	90	59	19	13
Martin	89	54	20	17

The agreement of the two sets of scores can be more easily seen if the test scores are converted to ranks. This has been done in columns 3 and 4 of Table 4.3. Note that the student who was first on the aptitude test ranked third on the departmental examination, the student who was second on the aptitude test ranked fourth on the departmental examination, and so on. Comparing the ranks of the students on the two tests, as indicated in columns 3 and 4 of Table 4.3, gives us a fairly good picture of the relationship between the two sets of scores. From this inspection, we know that students who had a high standing on the aptitude test also had a high standing on the departmental examination and that students who had a low standing on the aptitude test also had a low standing on the departmental examination. Our inspection of columns 3 and 4 also shows us, however, that the relationship between the students' ranks on the two tests is not perfect, as there is some shifting in rank from one test to another. Our problem now is how we can express the degree of relationship between these two sets of ranks in meaningful terms. This is where the scatter plot and the correlation coefficient become useful.

Figure 4.5
Scatter plot of test scores for
20 junior high school students
(scores shown in Table 4.3)

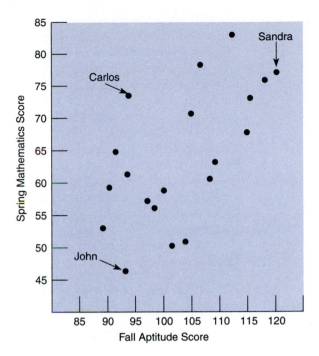

A scatter plot of the pairs of scores for the 20 students in Mr. Tanaka's class is shown in Figure 4.5. Each dot represents the two scores that were obtained by an individual student. The dots that correspond to the scores received by three of the students (Sandra, Carlos, and John) are labeled (see Appendix A for another example and details on the construction of a scatter plot). The scatter plot immediately shows us two important facts about the relationship between scores on the aptitude test administered in the fall and student performance on the comprehensive departmental examination in the spring. First, students such as Sandra, who score well above average in the fall, usually do better than average on the comprehensive examination in the spring, whereas most students who score well below average in the fall also score below average in the spring (e.g., John). Second, there are some notable exceptions. Carlos, for example, ranked 15th out of 20 on the fall aptitude test, but he obtained the fifth-highest score on the comprehensive examination in the spring. Although both facts (that there is a relationship and that it is imperfect) also could be seen from studying the scores in Table 4.3, the scatter plot provides an efficient summary and makes it clear that some of the exceptions to the statement that there is a relationship between the two sets of scores are substantial.

The relationship seen in Figure 4.5 still has not been quantified. For this, we need to obtain a correlation coefficient—a statistical summary of the relationship between the scores on the two tests. The correlation coefficient we will use is known as the **Pearson product-moment correlation coefficient** and is denoted by r. Procedures for calculating this coefficient are described in Appendix A. Here we will focus on its meaning.

When the procedures for calculating a product-moment correlation coefficient are applied to the scores for the 20 students in Mr. Tanaka's class, we find that $r = 0.58$. This correlation coefficient is a statistical summary of the degree of relationship between the two sets of scores in Mr. Tanaka's data. It indicates the extent to which the fall aptitude test scores (predictor) are predictive of the spring mathematics test scores (criterion). This type of correlation coefficient, called a **validity coefficient**, indicates the correlation between a test and a criterion measure. (A criterion-related validation study should be based on a larger number of cases than the 20 students used here, but we are simply explaining what a validity coefficient is and how to interpret it.) The validity coefficient is not a measure of the validity of the test use or interpretation by itself because, as has already been emphasized, content, construct, and consequences are also important to the overall evaluative judgment of validity.

How good is Mr. Tanaka's validity coefficient of 0.58? Should Mr. Tanaka be happy or disappointed with this finding? Is this aptitude test a good predictor of future performance in mathematics? Unfortunately, there are no simple and straightforward answers to such questions.

The following correlation coefficients indicate the extreme degree of relationship possible between variables:

1.00 = perfect positive relationship

0.00 = no relationship

−1.00 = perfect negative relationship

Because Mr. Tanaka's validity coefficient is 0.58, we know that the relationship is positive but substantially less than perfect. The closer a validity coefficient is to 1.00, the greater accuracy in predicting from one variable to another. A coefficient of −1.00 would also indicate perfect prediction from one variable to another, but in educational measurements we are most commonly concerned with positive relationships.

The three scatter plots in Figure 4.6 show in schematic form how Mr. Tanaka's validity coefficient of 0.58 compares with correlations of 0.00 and 1.00. Each dot on the scatter plot indicates an individual score's position on both the predictor and the criterion. Thus, with a correlation of 1.00, each individual falls at the same position on both measures, providing a perfect prediction. At the other extreme, with a correlation of 0.00, an individual's score on the predictor tells us nothing about the criterion score. At each score level on the predictor, some individuals have high criterion scores, some have low criterion scores, and others fall in between. There is simply no basis for predicting. The scatter plot for a correlation of about 0.60 indicates that high predictor scores tend to go with high criterion scores and that low predictor scores tend to go with low criterion scores, but the relationship is far from perfect. As the size of a correlation coefficient increases, the dots on a scatter plot move in the direction of the diagonal series of dots shown for a perfect positive correlation (1.00), indicating increased prediction efficiency.

Another way of evaluating Mr. Tanaka's validity coefficient of 0.58 is to compare it with the validity coefficients obtained from other methods of predicting performance in mathematics. If this validity coefficient is larger than those obtained with other prediction procedures, Mr. Tanaka will continue to use the scholastic aptitude test as the best means available to him for predicting his students' mathematics performance. Thus, validity coefficients are large or small only in relation to one another. When prediction is important, we will always consider more favorably the test with the largest validity coefficient. In this regard, however, even aptitude tests with rather low validity may be useful if they are the best predictors available and if the predictions they provide are better than chance.

Estimating Present Performance

Up to this point, we have emphasized the role of the test–criterion relationship in predicting future performance. Although this is probably its major use, at times we are interested in the relation of test performance to some other current measure of performance. In this case, we obtain both measures at approximately the same time and correlate the results. This is commonly done when a test is being considered as a replacement for a more time-consuming method of obtaining information. For example, Mrs. Valencia, a biology teacher, wondered if an objective test of study skills could be used in place of the elaborate observation and rating procedures she was currently using. She believed that if a test could be substituted for the more complex procedures, she would have much more time to devote to individual students during the supervised study period. An analysis of the specific student characteristics on which she rated the students' study skills indicated that many of the procedures could be stated in the form of objective test questions. Consequently, she developed an objective test of study skills that she administered to her students. To determine how adequately the test measured study skills, she correlated the test results with ratings of the students' study skills she obtained through arduous observation. The resulting correlation coefficient of 0.75 indicates considerable agreement between the test results and the criterion measure and validates Mrs. Valencia's test of study skills.

Several factors influence the size of correlation coefficients, including validity coefficients. Knowing these factors can help with the interpretation of a particular correlation coefficient—one we have computed ourselves or one found in a test manual. Basic factors to consider are shown in Figure 4.7. In general, larger correlation coefficients are

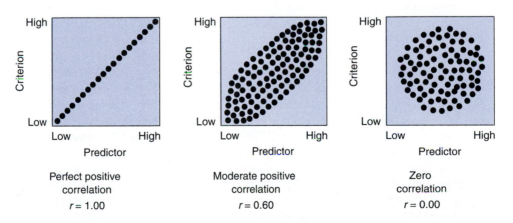

Figure 4.6
Scatter plots illustrating different degrees of positive relationship betweeen a predictor and a criterion

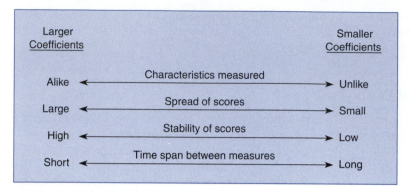

Figure 4.7
Basic factors influencing the size of correlation coefficients

obtained when the characteristics measured are more alike (e.g., correlating scores from two reading tests), the spread of scores is large, the stability of the scores is high, and the time span between measures is short. As we move along the continuum toward the other end of the scale on any of these factors, the correlation coefficients tend to become smaller. Thus, a small predictive validity coefficient might be explained, in part, by any one of the factors shown on the right side of Figure 4.7 or, more commonly, by some combination of them.

Expectancy Table

How well a test predicts future performance or estimates current performance on some criterion measure also can be shown by directly plotting the data in a twofold chart as shown in Figure 4.8. Here, Mr. Tanaka's data (from Table 4.3) have been tabulated by placing a tally showing each individual's standing on both the fall aptitude scores and the spring mathematics scores. For example, Sandra scored 119 on the fall aptitude test and 77 on the spring math test, so a tally representing her performance was placed in the upper-right-hand cell. The performance of all other students on the two tests was tallied in the same manner. Thus, each tally mark in Figure 4.8 represents how well each of Mr. Tanaka's 20 students performed on the fall and spring tests. The total number of students in each cell and in each column and row is also indicated.

The expectancy grid shown in Figure 4.8 can be used as an expectancy table simply by using the frequencies in each cell. The interpretation of such information is simple and direct. For example, of those students who scored above average on the fall aptitude test, none scored below 65 on the spring mathematics test, two of five scored between 65 and 74, and three of five scored between 75 and 84. Of those who scored below average on the fall aptitude test, none scored in the top category on the spring mathematics test, and four of five scored below 65. These interpretations are limited to the group tested, but from such results one might make predictions concerning future students. We can say, for example, that students who score above average on the fall aptitude test will probably score above average on the spring mathematics test. Other predictions can be made in the same way by noting

Fall Aptitude Scores	Spring Mathematics Scores				
	45–54	55–64	65–74	75–84	Totals
Above Average (over 110)			// 2	/// 3	5
Average (95–110)	// 2	州 5	// 2	/ 1	10
Below Average (below 95)	// 2	// 2	/ 1		5
Totals	4	7	5	4	20

Figure 4.8
Expectancy grid showing how scores on the fall aptitude test and spring mathematics test are tallied in appropriate cells (from data in Table 4.3)

the frequencies in each cell of the grid in Figure 4.8. More commonly, the figures in an expectancy table are expressed in percentages, which can be readily obtained from the grid by converting each cell frequency to a percentage of the total number of tallies in its row. This has been done for the data in Figure 4.8, and the results are presented in Table 4.4. The first row of the table shows that of the five students who scored above average on the fall aptitude test, 40% (two students) scored between 65 and 74 on the spring math test, and 60% (three students) scored between 75 and 84. The remaining rows should be read in a similar manner. The use of percentages makes the figures in each row and column comparable. Our predictions then can be made in standard terms (i.e., chances out of 100) for all score levels. Our interpretation is apt to be a little more clear if we say that Maria's chances of being in the top group on the criterion measure are 60 of 100 and that Jim's are only 10 of 100 than if we say that Maria's chances are 3 of 5 and Jim's are 1 of 10.

Expectancy tables take varied forms and may be used to show the relation between different types of measures. The number of categories used with the predictor, or criterion, may be as few as two or as many as seem desirable. Also, the predictor may be

Table 4.4
Expectancy table showing the relationship between fall aptitude scores and spring mathematics scores

Fall Aptitude Scores	Percentage in Each Score Group on Spring Mathematics Test			
	45–54	55–64	65–74	75–84
Above average (over 110)			40	60
Average (95–110)	20	50	20	10
Below average (below 95)	40	40	20	

Note: Data from Figure 4.8.

Table 4.5
Expectancy table for predicting college grade-point average from test scores

| Test Score | Probability of a Grade-Point Average of at Least | | |
	1.0 (D Avg.)	2.0 (C Avg.)	3.0 (B Avg.)
51–60	0.99+	0.93	0.72
41–50	0.98	0.80	0.53
31–40	0.91	0.68	0.35
21–30	0.75	0.53	0.22

any set of measures useful in predicting, and the criterion may be course grades, ratings, test scores, or whatever measure of success is relevant. For example, expectancy tables are frequently used in predicting the grade-point averages of college freshmen by combining data from high school grades and an admissions test such as the Scholastic Aptitude Test (SAT) or the American College Testing Program's ACT. An example of such an expectancy table is shown in Table 4.5. When interpreting expectancy tables based on a small number of cases, such as Mr. Tanaka's class of 20 students, our predictions should be regarded as highly tentative. Each percentage is based on so few students that we can expect large fluctuations in these figures from one group of students to another. It is frequently possible to increase the number of students represented in the table by combining test results from several classes. When we do this, our percentages are, of course, much more stable, and our predictions can be made with greater confidence. In any event, expectancy tables provide a simple and direct means of indicating the predictive value of test results.

Another commonly used approach to obtain predicted or estimated criterion performance from scores on an assessment is by means of regression equations. The use of regression equations to obtain estimates will not be developed here, but it is illustrated in Appendix A.

The "Criterion" Problem

In a criterion-related validation study, a major problem is obtaining a satisfactory criterion of success. Remember that Mr. Tanaka used a comprehensive departmental examination as the criterion of success in his seventh-grade mathematics class and that Mrs. Valencia used her own ratings of the students' study skills. In each instance, the criterion of success was only partially suitable as a basis for test validation. Mr. Tanaka recognized that the departmental examination did not measure all the important learning outcomes that he aimed at in teaching mathematics. There was not nearly enough emphasis on problem solving or mathematical reasoning, the interpretation of graphs and charts was sadly neglected, and, of course, the test did not evaluate the students' attitudes toward mathematics (which Mr. Tanaka considered to be extremely important). Likewise, Mrs. Valencia was well aware of the shortcomings of her rating of students' study skills. She sensed that some students "put on a show" when they knew they were being observed and that other students were probably overrated on study skills because of their high achievement in class work. Despite these recognized shortcomings, both Mr. Tanaka and Mrs. Valencia found it necessary to use these criterion measures because they were the best available.

The plights of Mr. Tanaka and Mrs. Valencia in finding a suitable criterion of success for test validation are not unusual. For most educational purposes, there is no entirely satisfactory criterion of success. Those used tend to be lacking in comprehensiveness and in most cases produce results that are less stable than those of the test being validated. The lack of a completely satisfactory criterion measure makes content and construct considerations all the more important.

CONSIDERATION OF CONSEQUENCES

Messick (1989, 1994) has argued persuasively that an overall judgment regarding the validity of particular uses and interpretations of assessment results requires an evaluation of the consequences of those uses and interpretations. Assessments are intended to contribute to improved student learning. The question is, Do they? And, if so, to what extent? What impact do assessments have on teaching? What are the possibly negative, unintended consequences of a particular use of assessment results?

The expansion of the concept of validity to include consideration of the consequences of use and interpretation of assessment results has been especially important in the recent movement toward more authentic, performance-based approaches to assessment. Several proponents of these alternative forms of assessment have argued that a heavy reliance on multiple-choice tests, especially in situations where students and teachers are being held accountable for results, has had unintended negative effects. They argue that the high stakes associated with test results lead teachers to focus narrowly on what is on the test while ignoring important parts of the curriculum not covered by the test.

In some instances, a single form of a standardized test—that is, a single set of multiple-choice questions—is used year after year in a state or school district. In such a situation, the narrowing may be worse than simply focusing on the domain of skills that the test is intended to measure. It may lead to teaching the specific content of the test items. Not only would this be an undesirable narrowing of what is taught, but also it would likely inflate test scores and change the meaning of the results, possibly changing the construct measured from problem solving to memorization ability.

Although the negative effects are most serious where high stakes are attached to the results obtained on a single test form used year after year, the concern about consequences is not limited to such situations. Distortions of instruction could be expected even if a new test form were used each year because of a lack of alignment of the test to the learning objectives emphasized in the curriculum. For example, a curriculum that emphasized problem solving and conceptual understanding could be undermined by holding teachers accountable for student scores on a test that emphasized low-level skills and factual knowledge. Drill and practice on the skills and facts emphasized on the test might raise scores but would not facilitate achievement of the primary learning goals.

Considerations of consequences are equally important for performance-based assessment. It is just as important to attend to both the intended positive effects and the possible unintended negative effects for performance-based assessments as it is for standardized, multiple-choice tests. For both types of assessment, consequences are directly related to the stakes that are attached to the results. As the stakes increase for teachers or students, so too should the demands for evidence regarding consequences of the uses and interpretations of results.

An adequate consideration of consequences needs to include both intended consequences (e.g., contributes to learning, increases student motivation) and unintended consequences (e.g., narrows the curriculum, increases the number of high school dropouts). Consequences are particularly important where assessment results are used to make high-stakes decisions regarding individuals (e.g., retention in grade, assignment to a remedial instructional program, or the award of a high school diploma).

The use of an assessment to retain students in grade is not recommended, but it is a way in which assessments are sometimes used and may be used to illustrate the impact of consequences on the overall validation. An analysis of consequences of the use of an assessment for retention in grade should seek evidence that students who are retained are generally better off than they would have been if they had not been retained. Such evidence might come from a comparison of the subsequent achievement and attitudes of students just below and just above the minimum score required for advancement in grade. A positive finding would require that students who were just below the cut score and therefore retained in grade eventually outperformed their counterparts who were just above the cut score and therefore promoted in grade. The opposite finding would provide evidence that the use of assessment to retain students had negative consequences and would contribute to a judgment that grade retention was not a valid use of this assessment. It would also be important to compare long-term results, such as dropout rates and eventual graduation rates. For a classroom assessment, studies of consequences obviously would be much less elaborate. Indeed, considerations of consequences generally would be limited to a logical analysis of likely effects.

Teachers have an excellent vantage point for considering the likely effects of assessments. First, they know the learning objectives that they are trying to help their students achieve. Second, they are quite familiar with instructional experiences that the students have had. Third, they have an opportunity to observe students while they are working on an assessment task and to talk to students about their performances. This firsthand awareness of learning objectives, instructional experiences, and students can be brought to bear on an analysis of the likely effects of assessments by systematically considering questions such as the following:

1. **Do the tasks match important learning objectives?**   WYTIWYG (What You Test Is What You Get) has become a popular slogan. Despite the fact that it is an oversimplification, it is a good reminder that assessments need to reflect major learning outcomes. Problem-solving skills and complex thinking skills requiring integration, evaluation, and synthesis of information are more likely to be fostered by assessments that require the application of such skills than by assessments that require students merely to repeat what the teacher has said or what is stated in the textbook.

2. **Is there reason to believe that students study harder in preparation for the assessment?**   Motivating student effort is a potentially important consequence of tests and assessments. The chances of achieving this goal are improved if students have a clear understanding of what to expect on the assessment, know how the results will be used, and believe that the assessment will be fair.

3. Does the assessment artificially constrain the focus of students' study?   If it is judged important, for example, to be sure that students can solve a particular type of mathematics problem, then it is reasonable to focus an assessment on that type of problem. However, much will be missed if such an approach is the only mode of assessment. In many cases, the identification of the nature of the problem may be at least as important as facility with application of a particular formula or algorithm. Assessments that focus only on the latter skills are not likely to facilitate development of problem identification skills.

4. Does the assessment encourage or discourage exploration and creative modes of expression?   Although it is important for students to know what to expect on an assessment and have a sense of what to do to prepare for it, care should be taken to avoid overly narrow and artificial constraints that will discourage students from exploring new ideas and concepts.

FACTORS INFLUENCING VALIDITY

Numerous factors tend to make assessment results invalid for their intended use. Some are rather obvious and easily avoided. No teacher would think of measuring knowledge of social studies with a mathematics assessment, nor would a teacher consider measuring problem-solving skills in third-grade mathematics with an assessment designed for seventh graders. In both instances, the assessment results would obviously be invalid. The factors influencing validity are of this same general nature but much more subtle in character. For example, a teacher may overload a social studies test with items concerning historical facts, and thus the scores are less valid as a measure of achievement in social studies. Or a third-grade teacher may select appropriate mathematical problems for an assessment but use vocabulary in the problems and directions that only the better readers are able to understand. The mathematics assessment then becomes, in part, a reading assessment and reduces the validity of the results for their intended use. These examples show some of the more subtle factors influencing validity to which the teacher should be alert, whether constructing classroom assessments or selecting published ones.

Factors in the Test or Assessment Itself

A careful examination of test items and assessment tasks will indicate whether the test or assessment appears to measure the subject-matter content and the mental functions that the teacher is interested in assessing. However, any of the following factors can prevent the test items or assessment tasks from functioning as intended and thereby lower the validity of the interpretations from the assessment results. The first five factors are equally applicable for assessments with tasks requiring extended student performances and traditional tests. The last five factors apply most directly to tests with fixed-choice or short-answer items that are scored right or wrong.

1. **Unclear directions:**   Directions that do not clearly indicate to the student how to respond to the tasks and how to record the responses tend to reduce validity.

2. **Reading vocabulary and sentence structure too difficult (construct-irrelevant variance):**   Vocabulary and sentence structure that are too complicated for the students taking the assessment result in the assessment's measuring reading comprehension and aspects of intelligence, which will distort the meaning of the assessment results.

3. **Ambiguity:**   Ambiguous statements in assessment tasks contribute to misinterpretations and confusion. Ambiguity sometimes confuses the better students more than it does the poor students.

4. **Inadequate time limits (construct-irrelevant variance):**   Time limits that do not provide students with enough time to consider the tasks and provide thoughtful responses can reduce the validity of interpretations of results. Rather than measuring what a student knows about a topic or is able to do given adequate time, the assessment may become a measure of the speed with which the student can respond. For some content (e.g., a typing test), speed may be important, but most assessments of achievement should minimize the effects of speed on student performance.

5. **Overemphasis of easy-to-assess aspects of domain at the expense of important but difficult-to-assess aspects (construct underrepresentation):**   It is easy to develop test questions that assess factual recall and generally harder to develop ones that tap conceptual understanding or higher-order thinking processes, such as the evaluation of competing positions or arguments. Hence, it is important to guard against underrepresentation of tasks getting at the important but more difficult-to-assess aspects of achievement.

6. **Test items inappropriate for the outcomes being measured:**   Attempting to measure understanding, thinking skills, and other complex types of achievement with test forms that are appropriate only for measuring factual knowledge will invalidate the results.

7. **Poorly constructed test items:**   Test items that unintentionally provide clues to the answer tend to measure the students' alertness in detecting clues as well as mastery of skills or knowledge the test is intended to measure.

8. **Test too short:**   A test is only a sample of the many questions that might be asked. If a test is too short to provide a representative sample of the performance we are interested in, then its validity will suffer accordingly.

9. **Improper arrangement of items:**   Test items are typically arranged in order of difficulty, with the easiest items first. Placing difficult items early in the test may cause students to spend too much time on these and prevent them from reaching items they could easily answer. Improper arrangement may also influence validity by having a detrimental effect on student motivation. This influence is likely to be strongest with young students.

10. **Identifiable pattern of answers:**   Placing correct answers in some systematic pattern (e.g., T, T, F, F or A, B, C, D, A, B, C, D) enables students to guess the answers to some items more easily, which lowers validity.

In short, any defect in the construction of the test or assessment that prevents it from functioning as intended will invalidate the interpretations to be drawn from the results. Much of what is written in the following chapters is directed toward helping teachers improve the validity of their interpretations of test scores and other assessment results.

Functioning of Tasks and Teaching Procedures

In assessing achievement, the ways in which tasks function cannot be determined merely by examining the form and content of the assessment. For example, the following task may appear to measure mathematical reasoning if examined without reference to what the students have been taught.

EXAMPLE   Ken learned that 60% of the graduates from his high school are admitted to community colleges, 30% are admitted to public 4-year colleges or universities, and 10% are admitted to private 4-year colleges or universities. Since these percentages add up to 100, Ken reasons that he is sure to be admitted to some college or university. Explain, possibly with the use of a diagram, what is wrong with Ken's reasoning.

However, if the teacher has taught the solution to this particular problem before giving the assessment, the task now will measure no more than memorized knowledge. Similarly, assessments of understanding, critical thinking, and other complex learning outcomes will provide valid measures in these areas only if the tasks function as intended. If the students have previously been taught the solutions to the particular problems included in the assessment or have been taught mechanical steps for obtaining the solutions, the assessment results cannot be considered valid indicators of the achievement of the more complex mental processes.

Factors in Administration and Scoring

The administration and scoring of an assessment may also introduce factors that have a detrimental effect on the validity of the interpretations from the results. In the case of teacher-made assessments, such factors as insufficient time, unfair aid to individual students who ask for help, cheating, and unreliable scoring of student performances tend to lower validity. In the case of published tests, failure to follow the standard directions and time limits, giving students unauthorized assistance, and errors in scoring similarly contribute to lower validity. For all types of assessments, adverse physical and psychological conditions at the time of the assessment may also have a negative effect.

Factors in Student Responses

In some instances, invalid interpretations are caused by personal factors influencing a student's response to the assessment situation rather than to any shortcomings in the test instrument or its administration. Some students may be bothered by emotional disturbances that interfere with their performance. Others may be frightened by the assessment situation and so are unable to respond normally, and still others may not be motivated to put forth their best effort. These and other factors that restrict and modify students' responses in the assessment situation obviously distort the results.

Nature of the Group and the Criterion

Validity is always specific to a particular group. A mathematics test based on story problems, for example, may measure reasoning ability in a group at an early stage of instruction and a combination of simple recall of information and computation skill in a more advanced group. Similarly, scores on a science assessment may be accounted for largely by reading comprehension in one group and by knowledge of facts in another. What an assessment measures may be influenced by such factors as age, gender, ability level, educational background, and cultural background. Thus, in appraising reports of validity included in test manuals or other sources, it is important to determine the nature of the validation group. How closely it compares in significant characteristics with the group of students we wish to assess determines how applicable the information is to our particular group.

As shown in Figure 4.7, correlations between a test and a criterion will be smaller when (a) the characteristics measured by the test and the criterion are less alike, (b) the spread of scores is smaller, (c) the stability of scores is lower, and (d) the time span between measures is longer. Of these factors, probably the most frequently overlooked is the nature of the criterion being predicted. This is unfortunate because knowing the specific nature of the criterion can help evaluate assessment–criterion correlations. For example, scores on a mathematics aptitude test are likely to provide a more accurate prediction of achievement in a science course in which quantitative problems are stressed than in one in which they play only a minor role. Likewise, we can expect scores on a critical-thinking test to correlate more highly with grades in social studies courses that emphasize critical thinking than in those that depend largely on the memorization of the factual information. These examples simply illustrate the general rule that assessment–criterion correlations are influenced by the similarity between the performance measured by the test and the performance represented in the criterion. Thus, both need to be examined carefully for a full understanding of the relationship.

Because validity information varies with the group tested and the composition of the criterion measures used, published validation data should be considered highly tentative. When possible, the validity of the test results should be checked in the specific local situation.

Teaching and Evaluating Assessments

As discussed earlier in this chapter, validity is the most important consideration in testing. Ultimately, the responsibility for interpreting and using test scores belongs to the user, who is frequently the teacher in the classroom. Although this chapter has given a broad range of validation strategies for teachers to use in evaluating tests, not all strategies will be used every time. The validation strategy that might be used in any given context will vary. Different strategies will be used with different types of tests (e.g., classroom tests vs. mandated tests, achievement vs. attitude) or different formats (e.g., open ended vs. multiple choice). In fact, the validation strategies may vary for each different use or interpretation of the same test. For example, a state-mandated assessment would require different validation strategies to show how well the content standards are being taught as opposed to making a decision about retaining students on a given grade level. Thus, teachers are left in a quandary about what to use from this chapter.

Although there is not a simple and straightforward choice on which validation strategies to use, experience with assessments will guide the questions to ask and the types of information to collect. Nevertheless, some minimal guidelines for evaluating assessments may be appropriate, and questions that should be asked for achievement tests are presented. Each of these guiding questions is intended to be used with any achievement test, but the method of accumulating validity evidence may vary for mandated standardized tests and classroom tests. The evidence collected might also be more systematic with some types of classroom assessments. For example, the evidence would not be as detailed for a weekly quiz as it would be for an end-of-the-semester final.

1. Does the content represent the construct?   Remember, *what you test is what you get.* The degree to which the content represents the construct should always be closely examined. In the case of state- or district-mandated assessments, studies should be completed and made available to teachers so that they understand the interpretations that can be made from student test scores. Teachers should request this information and examine the content standards, instructional objectives, or blueprints on which the test content is based. Even with weekly quizzes, teachers should pay close attention to the content. In the absence of formal data collection, teachers should be prepared to describe the content of their tests and be able to interpret test scores without generalizing beyond what is measured. Teachers may also be more systematic in their evaluation of the test content with tests that have greater impact than weekly quizzes. End-of-the-semester finals should be systematically examined on the basis of blueprints to make sure that they adequately sample the domain. In summary, teachers can examine content by understanding evidence collected by others (e.g., mandated standardized tests), by creating their own systematic evidence using blueprints (e.g., finals), or by a more informal examination of the assessment (e.g., weekly quizzes).

2. Will the test items elicit responses from the student that are consistent with the construct?   For mandated standardized tests and classroom assessments, understanding the student response processes is crucial to understanding the interpretations that can be made from test scores. Tests of reasoning or higher-order thinking should avoid using items that elicit rote responses. Even complex items, when practiced, can be answered on the basis of memory rather than problem-solving skills. On the other hand, basic measures of factual information should not include items that elicit complex responses. Teachers should examine the types of items used and understand student responses and how these responses are related to the interpretation and use of tests scores. If you are unclear about how to interpret student responses, interview the students shortly after test administration.

3. What are the consequences of using the assessment?   Any achievement test should be examined for the consequences on student motivation and learning. Even with classroom assessments, teachers should monitor the effect of the assessment on student learning and motivation. A test that leads to a narrow interpretation of the construct by measuring the content too narrowly or with limited response formats or that reduces student motivation to try to do well on the assessment is counterproductive to teaching, learning, and assessment. When these types of effects are observed, they should be taken into account in the interpretation of test scores. As much as possible, teachers should try to reduce these effects by strategies such as varying the formats of the assessment and creating assessments that engage students.

4. What is the relationship between the test scores and the criterion?   For state- and district-mandated standardized assessments, this type of evidence should be made available to teachers. The evidence would be reported in a number of ways as outlined in this chapter. With classroom assessments, teachers should plan studies to examine the relationship of some criterion with the achievement test. For finals or other important tests, teachers should look at the relationship of the assessment with criteria such as grades or their ratings of the students. To keep computations simple, teachers could routinely divide both the assessment and the criterion into a few groups (e.g., top, middle, and bottom third) and use simple approaches, such as an expectancy table. Expectancy tables will inform teachers about whether a test is consistent with their expectations or grades in the content area and thus lead to a better understanding of the interpretation of test scores. Even with weekly quizzes, teachers should informally examine who received high grades and who did not receive high grades. This logical analysis gives further evidence about how to interpret test scores.

In sum, teachers will have a vast array of options for examining the validity of the assessments that they use. When using required assessments from the district or state, the validation has often been completed, and the teacher's task is to examine the data to guide the appropriate uses and interpretations that can be made from the assessment. In contrast, teacher-made assessments will not automatically have data available to examine. Instead, teachers need to plan the validation studies within the limited time and resources available to them in their classrooms. As a result, the primary resources available for examining assessments are the teachers and their colleagues. Thus, the validation of an assessment in the classroom will rely heavily on teacher judgments with the cooperation of fellow teachers. The box "Checklist for Validation of Classroom Assessment" provides an example of the types of data that teachers might reasonably collect to examine the validity of an assessment for a particular use or interpretation. The checklist would provide a record of (a) reviews of the test by other teachers, (b) observations or interviews of students taking the test, and (c) potential consequences of the test.

SUMMARY

The most important quality to consider when constructing or selecting an assessment procedure is validity, which refers to the meaningfulness and appropriateness of the uses and interpretations to be made of assessment results. When assessing validity, keep in mind that validity is a quality of the interpretation of the results rather than of the assessment itself, that its presence is a matter of degree, that it is always specific to some particular interpretation or use, and that it is a unitary concept.

Although validity is a unitary concept, it involves the consideration of several kinds of evidence. Considerations of content, construct, assessment–criterion relationships, and consequences all can contribute to the meaning of a set of results; validity is strongest when evidence to support all four of these considerations is present.

An analysis of the content of an assessment should evaluate the appropriateness of the content domain and determine the extent to which the assessment tasks provide a relevant and representative sample of the domain of content under consideration. Content considerations are especially important when validating achievement testing or constructing classroom tests and assessments. Written specifications for the assessment should define a domain of instructionally relevant tasks, and then tasks that provide a representative sample of the domain should be constructed or selected. Content considerations are also important when selecting published achievement tests. Here the crucial question is how well the test measures the content and objectives of the local instructional program. The same types of test specifications used in constructing classroom tests can aid in selecting published tests.

Construct validation is the process of determining the extent to which performance on an assessment can be interpreted in terms of one or more construct. Construct validation typically includes consideration of content and may include assessment–criterion relationships as well as several other types of information. Critical concerns in construct validation include both the possibility that important aspects of the intended construct to be measured are left out or inadequately represented (i.e., construct underrepresentation) and the possibility that performance is influenced by factors that are irrelevant or ancillary to the intended construct (construct-irrelevant variance). The influence of construct-irrelevant factors on performance is of particular concern when it affects the fairness of interpretations or use of assessment results. The procedure is one of clarifying what is being measured and what factors influence the assessment results so that performance can be interpreted most meaningfully. This involves both logical analysis and various comparative and correlational studies. Although the accumulation of evidence could be endless, in practical situations we need to focus on the types of evidence that are reasonable to obtain and that are most relevant to the types of interpretations to be made. The more complete the evidence is, the more confident we can be concerning the meaning of the assessment results.

CHECKLIST

Checklist for Validation of Classroom Assessment

Assessment (Construct): _____

Use/Interpretation: _____

Teacher Reviews Completed:

    Instructional Objectives (IO)   _____

    Content Match to IO   _____

    Cognitive Level Match to IO   _____

    Scoring Criteria (rubrics, etc.)   _____

Reviews of Student Response Process:

    Observation during Assessment   _____

    Interview after Assessment   _____

Potential Consequences of Assessment. Describe: _____

Studies of the extent to which test performance is related to some other valued measure of performance (called a criterion) also contribute to the overall evaluation of the validity of an assessment, especially when the assessment is used as an indicator of likely performance in other settings (e.g., achieving good grades in college). This may involve studies of how well test scores predict future performance (predictive validation study) or estimate some current performance (concurrent validation study). These validity studies are typically reported by means of a correlation coefficient called a validity coefficient, by use of an expectancy table, or by solving a regression equation that converts test scores to estimated performance on the criterion. Assessment–criterion relationships are pertinent whenever test results are used to make predictions or substitute for assessment results obtained by more time-consuming methods, but they are of special significance in aptitude testing. Because the meaning of test scores is enhanced by knowing what other measures they relate to, assessment–criterion relationships are also used in construct validation.

Finally, the consequences of a particular use or interpretation of assessment results are important in arriving at an overall evaluative judgment of the validity of the assessment for that use or interpretation. The evaluation of consequences needs to attend to the anticipated positive effects of a particular use (e.g., enhancing student motivation). It is at least as important, however, to investigate plausible unintended consequences (e.g., increased anxiety, narrowing of instruction). The need of evidence regarding consequences increases as the stakes attached to the assessment results increase.

Many other factors tend to influence the validity of interpretations of tests and assessments. Some of these influences can be found in the test or assessment itself, some in the relationship of teaching to testing and assessment, some in the administration and scoring of the measure, some in the atypical responses of students to the assessment situation, and still others in the nature of the group assessed and in the composition of the criterion measures used. A major aim in the construction, selection, and use of tests and other assessment procedures is to control those factors that have an adverse effect on validity and to interpret the results in accordance with what validity information is available.

This discussion of factors influencing the validity of test and assessment results has shown how pervasive the concept of validity is. Ultimately, it is the users of tests and assessments who must make the final judgment concerning the validity of the uses and interpretations. Teachers need to become actively involved in examining and creating validity evidence to interpret and use tests in the teaching, learning, and assessment process.

LEARNING EXERCISES

1. If a fellow teacher told you that a particular reading test had high validity, what types of questions would you ask?

2. A high school science teacher prepared a set of assessment tasks to be used in all sections of biology without consulting the teachers of the other sections. What effect might this have on the assessment's validity? Why?

3. Compare the relative difficulty of determining validity for a norm-referenced survey test in social studies and an assessment of mathematical problem solving. For which one would a table of specifications be most useful? Why?

4. If you wanted to determine the validity of a published achievement test for use in a course you are teaching or plan to teach, what procedure would

you follow? Describe your procedure step by step and give reasons for each step.

5. What types of evidence might be useful in the construct validation of each of the following?
   a. An assessment of reading comprehension
   b. An assessment of mathematical reasoning
   c. A test of creativity

6. Consider a final examination that you might construct for a course that you have taught or would like to teach.
   a. Describe ways in which construct underrepresentation might undermine the validity of the examination.
   b. Describe ways that construct-irrelevant ancillary skills might influence performance and thereby undermine the validity of the examination.

7. Define a validity coefficient and list several factors that will influence its size.

8. Describe how to prepare an expectancy table. What is the advantage of an expectancy table over a validity coefficient for making predictions?

9. Describe a series of studies that would be useful in evaluating the consequences of a state-mandated high school graduation test.

10. Describe the steps you would follow to analyze the likely consequences of a series of assessments you developed to measure student progress in using mathematics to solve practical problems.

11. Study the validity sections of a test manual for a published achievement test and a scholastic aptitude test. How does the information differ for these two types of tests? Why?

12. Consult the validity section of the latest edition of *Standards for Educational and Psychological Testing* (see the references for this chapter) and review the types of information that test manuals should contain. Compare a recent test manual with the *Standards*.

13. List and briefly describe as many factors as you can think of that might lower the validity of a classroom assessment.

REFERENCES

American Educational Research Association, American Psychological Association, & National Council on Measurement in Education. (1999). *Standards for educational and psychological testing*. Washington, DC: American Educational Research Association.

Cronbach, L. J., & Meehl, P. E. (1955). Construct validity in psychological tests. *Psychological Bulletin, 52*, 281–302.

Linn, R. L., & Baker, E. L. (1996). Can performance-based assessments be psychometrically sound? In J. B. Baron & D. P. Wolf (Eds.), *Performance-based student assessment: Challenges and possibilities*. Ninety-fifth Yearbook of the National Society for the Study of Education, Part I (pp. 84–103). Chicago: University of Chicago Press.

Messick, S. (1989). Validity. In R. L. Linn (Ed.), *Educational measurement* (3rd ed.). Upper Saddle River, NJ: Merrill/Prentice Hall.

Messick, S. (1994). The interplay of evidence and consequences in the validation of performance assessments. *Educational Researcher, 23*, 13–23.

National Committee on Science Education Standards and Assessment, National Research Council. (1995). *National science education standards*. Washington, DC: National Academies Press. Available: http://newton.nap.edu/catalog/4962.html.

National Council of Teachers of Mathematics. (1995). *Assessment standards for school mathematics*. Reston, VA: Author.

FURTHER READING

American Educational Research Association, American Psychological Association, & National Council on Measurement in Education. (1999). *Standards for educational and psychological testing*. Washington, DC: American Educational Research Association. See Chapter 1 for general validity standards that are intended to apply to a full array of types of tests and test uses in settings outside of education as well as those in educational settings; and Chapter 13, which is explicitly directed toward the use and interpretation of tests and assessment in formal educational settings. Other chapters that are also relevant to validity considerations include Chapter 7, "Fairness in Testing and Test Use"; Chapter 9, "Testing Individuals of Diverse Linguistic Background"; and Chapter 10,

"Testing Individuals with Disabilities." These chapters provide detailed descriptions of basic validation procedures and the nature of validity information to be sought in test manuals.

Cronbach, L. J. (1990). *Essentials of psychological testing* (5th ed.). New York: Harper & Row. Chapter 5, "Validation," describes and illustrates the procedures of test validation.

Kane, M. T. (2006). Validation. In R. L. Brennan (Ed.), *Educational measurement,* (4th ed. pp. 17–64). Westport, CT: Greenwood Publishing Group ACE/Paeger series in higher education. Chapter 2 provides a comprehensive and contemporary discussion of validity.

Linn, R. L., Baker, E. L., & Dunbar, S. B. (1991). Complex, performance-based assessment: Expectations and validation criteria. *Educational Researcher, 20*(8), 15–21. Discusses some priorities in evaluating the validity of complex performance-based assessment.

Messick, S. (1989). Validity. In R. L. Linn (Ed.), *Educational measurement* (3rd ed.). Upper Saddle River, NJ: Merrill/Prentice Hall. Chapter 2 provides a comprehensive and theoretically sophisticated discussion of validity.

Shepard, L. A. (1993). Evaluating test validity. *Review of Research in Education, 19*, 405–450. Provides examples of applications of construct validity principles to the evaluation of test use.

5

RELIABILITY AND OTHER DESIRED CHARACTERISTICS

Next to validity, reliability is the most important characteristic of assessment results. Reliability (a) provides the consistency that makes validity possible and (b) indicates the degree to which various kinds of generalizations are justifiable. The practicality of the evaluation procedure is, of course, also of concern to the busy classroom teacher.

In Chapter 4, we emphasized that validity is the most important consideration in the selection and construction of assessment procedures. Fair use and interpretation of assessment results depends on validity. Thus, first and foremost, we want assessment results to serve the specific uses for which they are intended. Next in importance is reliability, and following that is a host of practical features that can be best classified under the heading "usability."

NATURE OF RELIABILITY

Reliability refers to the consistency of measurement, that is, how consistent test scores or other assessment results are from one measurement to another. Suppose, for instance, that Ms. Johnson has just given an achievement assessment to her students. How similar would the students' scores have been had she assessed them yesterday, or tomorrow, or next week? How would the scores have varied had she selected a different sample of tasks? How much would the scores have differed had a different teacher scored it? These are the types of questions with which reliability is concerned. Assessment results merely provide a limited measure of performance obtained at a particular time. Unless the measurement can be shown to be reasonably consistent (i.e., generalizable) over different occasions, different raters, or different samples of the same performance domain, we can have little confidence in the results.

We cannot expect assessment results to be perfectly consistent. Numerous factors other than the quality being measured may influence assessment results. If a single assessment is administered to the same group twice in close succession, some variation in scores can be expected because of temporary fluctuations in memory, attention, effort, fatigue, emotional strain, guessing, and the like. With a longer time between tests, additional variation in scores may be caused by intervening learning experiences, changes in health, forgetting, and less comparable assessment conditions. If essays or other types of student performances are evaluated by different raters, some variation in scores can be expected because of less-than-perfect agreement among raters. If we use a different sample of tasks in the second assessment, still another factor is likely to influence the results. Individuals may find one assessment easier than the other because it happens to contain more tasks on topics with which they are familiar. Such extraneous factors as these introduce a certain amount of measurement error into all assessment results. Methods of determining reliability are essentially means of determining how much measurement error is present under different conditions. In general, the more consistent our assessment results are from one measurement to another, the less error there will be and, consequently, the greater the reliability.

The meaning of reliability, as applied to testing and assessment, can be further clarified by noting the following general points.

1. Reliability refers to the results obtained with an assessment instrument and not to the instrument itself: Any particular instrument may have a number of different reliabilities, depending on the group involved and the situation in which it is used. Thus, it is more appropriate to speak of the reliability of the test scores or of the assessment results than of the test or the assessment.

2. An estimate of reliability always refers to a particular type of consistency: Assessment results are not reliable in general. They are reliable (or generalizable) over different periods of time, over different samples of tasks, over different raters, and the like. It is possible for assessment results to be consistent in one of these respects and not in another. The appropriate type of consistency in a particular case is dictated by the use to be made of the results. For example, if we wish to know what individuals will be like at some future time, constancy of scores over time will be important. On the other hand, if we want to measure an individual's current understanding of certain scientific principles, we are apt to be more interested in the consistency of performance across different tasks designed to allow students to apply those principles. Thus, for different interpretations, we need different analyses of consistency. Treating reliability as a general characteristic can lead to erroneous interpretations.

3. Reliability is a necessary but not sufficient condition for validity: An assessment that produces totally inconsistent results cannot possibly provide valid information about the performance being measured. On the other hand, highly consistent assessment results may be measuring the wrong thing or may be used in inappropriate ways. Thus, low reliability indicates that a low degree of validity is present, but high reliability does not ensure a high degree of validity. In short, reliability merely provides the consistency that makes validity possible.

4. Reliability is assessed primarily with statistical indices: The logical analysis of an assessment will provide little evidence concerning the reliability of the scores. To evaluate the consistency of scores assigned by different raters, two or more raters must score the same set of student performances. Similarly, an evaluation of the consistency of scores obtained in response to different forms of a test or different collections of performance-based assessment tasks requires the administration of both test forms or collections of tasks to an appropriate group of students. Whether the focus is on interrater consistency or the consistency across forms or collections of tasks, consistency may be expressed in terms of shifts in the relative standing of persons in the group or in terms of the amount of variation to be expected in an individual's score. Consistency in the first case is reported by means of a correlation coefficient called a reliability coefficient (see the "Terminology" box) and in the second case is reported by means of the standard error of measurement. Both methods of expressing reliability are widely used and should be understood by persons responsible for interpreting assessment results.

DETERMINING RELIABILITY BY CORRELATION METHODS

In determining reliability, it would be desirable to obtain two sets of measures under identical conditions and then compare the results. This procedure is impossible, of course, because the conditions under which assessment data are obtained can never be identical. As a substitute for this ideal procedure, several methods of estimating reliability have been introduced (American Educational Research Association, American Psychological Association, & National Council on Measurement in Education, 1999). The methods are similar in that all of them involve correlating two sets of scores, obtained either from the same assessment procedure or from equivalent forms of the same procedure. The correlation coefficient used to determine reliability is calculated and interpreted in the same manner as that used in determining statistical estimates of validity. The only difference between a validity coefficient and a reliability coefficient is that the former is based on agreement with an outside criterion and the latter on agreement between two sets of results from the same procedure.

TERMINOLOGY

Correlation coefficient: A statistic that indicates the degree of relationship between any two sets of scores obtained from the same group of individuals (e.g., correlation between height and weight).

Validity coefficient: A correlation coefficient that indicates the degree to which a measure predicts or estimates performance on some criterion measure (e.g.,

correlation between scholastic aptitude scores and grades in school).

Reliability coefficient: A correlation coefficient that indicates the degree of relationship between two sets of scores intended to be measures of the same characteristic (e.g., correlation between scores assigned by two different raters or scores obtained from administrations of two forms of a test).

The chief methods of estimating reliability are shown in Table 5.1. Note that different types of consistency are determined by the different methods: consistency over a period of time, over different forms of the assessment, within the assessment itself, and over different raters. The reliability coefficient resulting from each method must be interpreted according to the type of consistency being investigated. Each of these methods of estimating reliability is considered in further detail as we proceed.

Test–Retest Method

To estimate reliability by means of the test–retest method, the same assessment is administered twice to the same group of students with a given time interval between the two administrations (see Figure 5.1). The resulting assessment scores are correlated, and this correlation coefficient provides a measure of stability; that is, it indicates how stable the assessment results are over the given period of time. If the results are highly stable, then those students who are high on one administration of the assessment will tend to be high on the other administration, and the remaining students will tend to stay in their same relative positions on both administrations. Such stability is indicated by a large correlation coefficient. Recall from our previous discussion of correlation coefficients that a perfect positive relationship is indicated by 1.00 and no relationship by 0.00. Measures of stability in the 0.80 range are commonly reported for standardized tests of aptitude and achievement over occasions within the same year.

One important factor to keep in mind when interpreting measures of stability is the time interval between assessments. If the time interval is short, say, a day or two, the

Table 5.1
Methods of estimating reliability

Method	Type of Reliability Measure	Procedure
Test–retest	Measure of stability	Give the same test twice to the same group with some time interval between tests, from several minutes to several years
Equivalent-forms	Measure of equivalence	Give two forms of the test to the same group in close succession
Test–retest with equivalent-forms	Measure of stability and equivalence	Give two forms of the test to the same group with an increased time interval between forms
Split-half	Measure of internal consistency	Give test once; score two equivalent halves of test (e.g., odd items and even items); correct correlation between halves to fit whole test by Spearman–Brown formula
Coefficient alpha	Measure of internal consistency	Give test once; score test items and apply formula
Interrater	Measure of consistency of ratings	Give a set of student responses requiring judgmental scoring to two or more raters and have them independently score the responses

constancy of the results will be inflated because students will remember the tasks and their responses to them from the first assessment. If the time interval is long, say, about a year, the results will be influenced not only by the instability of the assessment procedure but also by actual changes in the students over that period of time. In general, the longer the interval between the first and second assessments, the more the results will be influenced by changes in the student characteristic being measured and the smaller the reliability coefficient will be.

The best time interval between assessment administrations will depend largely on the use to be made of the results. Because college admissions test scores may be submitted as part of an application to college several years after the test was taken, stability over several years is quite important. But stability over a long period is neither important nor desirable for an assessment of performance on a unit in a course that is focused on student understanding of certain concepts and readiness to move on to new material. Thus, for some decisions we are interested in reliability coefficients based on a long interval between test and retest; for others, reliability coefficients based on a short interval may be sufficient. The important thing is to seek evidence of stability that fits the particular interpretation to be made.

The test–retest method is unlikely to be relevant for teacher-constructed classroom tests because it is seldom possible or desirable to readminister the same assessment. In choosing standardized tests, however, stability is an important criterion. The test manual should provide evidence of stability, indicating the interval between tests and any unusual experiences the group members might have had between test administrations. Other things (such as validity) being equal, a test shown to possess the type of stability needed to make sound decisions is the best test.

Stability is also an important consideration when using assessment results from school records. When using any assessment result from permanent records, check the date of the assessment and any stability data available to determine whether the results are still dependable. If there is doubt and the decision is important, a reassessment is in order.

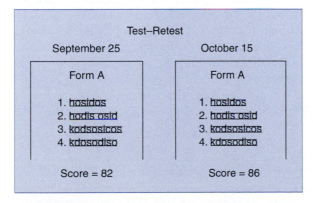

Figure 5.1
Test–retest method (using same test forms)

Equivalent-Forms Method

The equivalent-forms method for estimating reliability uses two different but equivalent forms of an assessment (also called parallel or alternate forms). Equivalent forms are built to the same set of specifications (e.g., test content and difficulty) but are constructed independently. The two forms of the assessment are administered to the same group of students in close succession, and the resulting assessment scores are correlated. This correlation coefficient provides a measure of the degree to which generalizations about student performance from one assessment to another are justified. Thus, it indicates the degree to which the two assessments are measuring the same aspects of behavior.

The equivalent-forms method tells us nothing about the long-term stability of the student characteristic being measured. Rather, it reflects short-term constancy of student performance and the extent to which the assessment represents an adequate sample of the characteristic being measured. In assessing achievement, for example, thousands of tasks might be presented in a particular assessment, but because of time limits and other restricting factors, only some of the possible tasks can be used. The tasks included in the assessment should provide an adequate sample of the possible tasks in the area. The easiest way to estimate whether an assessment measures an adequate sample of the content is to construct versions of the assessment that are intended to cover the same domain of content and student skills and correlate the results. A high correlation indicates that the two assessments are providing similar results and, therefore, are probably reliable samples of the general area of content being measured. Of course, both forms have to follow rigorous content sampling procedures as outlined in the test blueprint (see Chapter 4) since the correlation only represents equivalence without regard to the general content area.

The equivalent-forms method of estimating reliability is widely used in standardized testing because most standardized tests have two or more forms available. In fact, a teacher should be suspicious of any standardized test that has two forms available and does not provide information about equivalence. The comparability of the results of the two forms cannot be assumed unless such evidence is presented. The equivalent-forms method is sometimes used with an interval between the administration of the two forms of the test (see Figure 5.2). Under these test–retest conditions, the resulting reliability coefficient provides a measure of stability and equivalence. This is a more rigorous test of reliability than the test–retest method or equivalent-forms method with a short interval between forms, because the stability of the testing procedures, the constancy of the student characteristic being measured, and the representativeness of the sample of tasks included in the test all are taken into account. Consequently, this is generally recommended as the soundest procedure for estimating the reliability of test scores. As with the ordinary test–retest method, the reliability coefficient must be interpreted in light of the interval between the two forms of the test. For longer time periods, expect smaller reliability coefficients.

Split-Half Method

Reliability can also be estimated from a single administration of a single form of an assessment. The assessment is administered to a group of students in the usual manner and then is divided in half for scoring purposes. The split-half method is easy to implement with a traditional test or quiz consisting of, say, 10 or more items. To split the test into

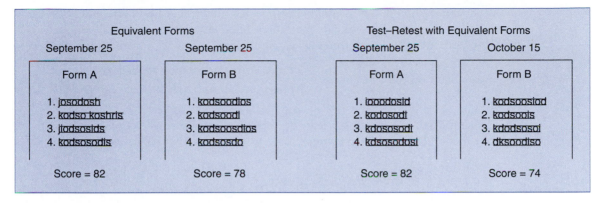

Figure 5.2
Equivalent-forms method (without and with a time interval)

halves that are equivalent, the usual procedure is to score the even-numbered and the odd-numbered tasks separately (see Figure 5.3). This produces two scores for each student that, when correlated, provide a measure of internal consistency. This coefficient indicates the degree to which consistent results are obtained from the two halves of the test and may be thought of as the "half-length test reliability estimate."

Although most often applied with traditional tests containing a sizable number of items, the split-half method is also applicable to assessments that consist of a smaller number of tasks each or that require a more extended period of time to complete. Some limited information can be obtained with as few as two tasks by correlating the scores obtained on one task with those obtained on another. Better information is provided as the number of tasks increases. With a small number of tasks, say, four to eight, it is better to divide the tasks into two sets that are judged to be most comparable to each other than to rely on the more mechanical odd–even method that is appropriate where a larger number of tasks or items is available.

Sum number of odd items correct	Sum number of even items correct	September 25 Test
Items 1 3 5 . . .	Items 2 4 6 . . .	1. nwso rho 2. nworh orh 3. Stopey 4. ta ta do 5. fsi ley 6. odd iteets
Odd score = 40	Even score = 42	Total score = 82

Figure 5.3
Odd–even scoring for use of split-half method (odd and even scores are then correlated)

As previously noted, the reliability coefficient is determined by correlating the scores of two half assessments. To estimate the scores' reliability based on the full-length assessment, the Spearman–Brown formula is usually applied.

$$\text{Realiability on full assessment} = \frac{2 \text{ times correlation between half assessments}}{1 \text{ plus correlation between half assessments}}$$

The simplicity of the formula can be seen in the following example, in which the correlation coefficient between scores on the assessment's two halves is 0.60.

$$\text{Reliability on full assessment} = \frac{(2)(0.60)}{(1 + 0.60)} = \frac{1.20}{1.60} = 0.75$$

This correlation coefficient of 0.75, then, estimates the reliability of a full assessment when the half assessments correlated at 0.60. The split-half method is similar to the equivalent-forms method in that it indicates the extent to which the sample of tasks is a dependable sample of the content being measured. A high correlation between scores on the two halves of an assessment denotes the equivalence of the two halves and consequently the adequacy of the sampling. Split-half reliabilities tend to be higher than equivalent-forms reliabilities because the split-half method is based on the administration of a single assessment. When two forms of an assessment are administered, even in close succession, more opportunity for inconsistency is introduced (e.g., differences from form to form in attention, speed of work, effort, fatigue, and assessment content). Because the equivalent-forms method takes into account more sources of inconsistency, it provides a more stringent evaluation of reliability.

Coefficient Alpha

Another method of estimating the reliability of assessment scores from a single administration is by means of formulas such as those developed by Kuder and Richardson and the generalized formula for coefficient alpha. As with the split-half method, these formulas provide an index of internal consistency but do not require splitting the assessment in half for scoring purposes. An early special case of coefficient alpha was called Kuder–Richardson Formula 20 (KR-20), and is applicable only in situations where student responses are scored dichotomously (zero or one) and therefore is most useful with traditional test items that are scored as right or wrong. The KR-20 is based on the proportion of persons passing each item and the standard deviation of the total scores. (A standard deviation is a measure of the spread of scores; see Appendix A.) The generalization of the KR-20 for assessments that have more than dichotomous, right–wrong scores (e.g., each task is scored on a 5-point scale), is called coefficient alpha. The computation of either KR-20 or coefficient alpha is rather cumbersome unless information is already available concerning the proportion passing or the standard deviations of scores for individual tasks; however, with the increasing availability of microcomputers and software for scoring and analyzing tests, it is now more feasible to obtain coefficient alpha estimates of reliability.

Here, our concern is with the interpretation of the coefficients rather than the calculations. Coefficient alpha estimates of reliability provide information about the degree to which the items or tasks in the assessment measure similar characteristics. For a test with relatively homogeneous content (e.g., a mathematics computation test), the reliability estimate generally will be similar to that provided by the split-half method. Indeed, coefficient alpha can be thought of as the average of all possible split-half coefficients for the groups tested. This is an advantage when considering an assessment with relatively homogeneous content, because the estimate does not depend on the way in which the items are assigned to the two half tests as in the split-half method. However, for assessments designed to measure more heterogeneous learning outcomes (e.g., an assessment covering ancient history, the Middle Ages, and modern history), coefficient alpha will usually be smaller than that provided by the split-half method, and the latter method is to be preferred.

The simplicity of applying the split-half method or the coefficient alpha method (i.e., only a single test administration) has led to their widespread use in determining reliability. Certain limitations, however, restrict their value. First, they are not appropriate for speeded assessments—for assessments with time limits that prevent students from attempting every task. If speed is a significant factor in the assessment, reliability estimates will be inflated to an unknown degree. This poses no great problem in estimating the reliability of results from teacher-made assessments because these are usually designed to allow students adequate time to complete all the tasks. In the case of standardized tests, however, time limits are seldom so liberal that all students complete the test. Thus, measures of internal consistency reported in test manuals should be interpreted with caution unless evidence is also presented that speed of work is a negligible factor. For speeded tests, reliability obtained by the test–retest or equivalent-forms method should be sought.

A second limitation of internal consistency procedures is that they do not indicate the constancy of student responses from day to day. In this regard, they are similar to the equivalent-forms method without a time interval. Only test–retest procedures indicate the extent to which test results are generalizable over different periods of time.

Interrater Consistency

Judgment is required in scoring student responses to many types of assessments. This is obvious in the case of essay exams, but judgment is also required in scoring responses to open-ended mathematics problems or laboratory exercises in science. When student work is judgmentally scored, it is reasonable to ask whether the same scores would be assigned by another equally qualified judge. Individual classroom teachers seldom have the luxury of having another teacher to independently score examples of student work from their classroom, but there is a growing need to evaluate interrater consistency as a result of the increasing numbers of state- and district-mandated assessments that must be judgmentally scored.

Estimation of interrater consistency is relatively straightforward. Two or more raters must independently score the performances obtained for an appropriately selected sample of students. Consistency can be evaluated by correlating the scores assigned by one judge with those assigned by another judge. Consistency can also be evaluated by computing the proportion of times that students' performances receive exactly the same scores from a pair of raters and the proportion that are within a single point of each other.

Suppose, for example, that two raters independently scored 50 student essays on a 6-point scale. The results of the ratings are summarized in Table 5.2. Rater 1 assigned a score of 6 to five of the essays. For those five essays, Rater 2 assigned a score of 6 to three of them and scores of 4 and 5 to the other two. Thus, each entry in a cell of Table 5.2 shows the number of essays that Rater 1 assigned the score associated with the row, while Rater 2 assigned the score associated with the column of the table.

The percentage of exact agreement is obtained by summing the counts where both raters assigned the same score (shown in boldface type), dividing that sum by the total number of essays, and multiplying the result by 100, as follows:

$$\text{Percentage exact agreement} = 100 * [(3 + 7 + 5 + 4 + 2 + 3)/50] = 48\%$$

The percentage of times that raters agreed to within 1 point (all the counts between the two diagonal lines) would be computed in a similar fashion. For this example, the percentage of agreement within 1 score point is 88% ($100 \times [44/50]$). One other indicator is the correlation between the two sets of scores, which, for the data in Table 5.2, is 0.80. The level of interrater consistency shown in Table 5.2 is high in comparison to levels of consistency generally achieved by independent raters. Even so, 6 of the 50 students would have their scores fluctuate by 2 points, depending on the person doing the scoring. One way to reduce the influence of raters is to have each performance independently scored by two or more raters and use the average rating. Double scoring is a common practice in situations where judgmentally scored performances have important consequences for individuals.

The percentage of agreement and correlation values indicates the degree to which the relative ordering of responses is consistent from one rater to another. It is possible, however, to have a high correlation and even a high percentage of agreement while still having important differences in the overall leniency of the two raters. Where there

Table 5.2
Scores assigned to 50 essays by two independent raters (Raters 1 and 2)

Total	Score	Scores Assigned by Rater 2						Row
		1	2	3	4	5	6	
Scores	6	0	0	0	1	1	**3**	5
Assigned	5	0	0	1	2	**2**	3	8
by	4	0	1	2	**4**	4	1	12
Rater 1	3	0	2	**5**	3	2	0	12
	2	1	**7**	1	0	0	0	9
	1	**3**	1	0	0	0	0	4
Column total		4	11	9	10	9	7	50

Note: Numbers in bold show the number of essays where the scores assigned by the raters were in exact agreement.

are disagreements, there is a strong tendency for one rater to consistently give a higher score than the other. Comparisons of the average score assigned by each rater provide a check on differences in leniency. For the example in Table 5.2, the average ratings assigned to the essays are reasonably similar (3.52 for Rater 1 and 3.60 for Rater 2). Thus, there is no cause for concern in this case. On the other hand, the results shown in Table 5.3 (which might have been obtained if Rater 1 had been paired with Rater 3 instead of Rater 2) clearly indicate that Rater 3 is much more lenient than Rater 1 despite the fact that the percentage of exact agreement and the percentage of agreement within 1 point are the same (48% and 88%, respectively) for the data in Table 5.3 as they are for the data in Table 5.2.

The evaluation of interrater consistency is important to ensure that some students do not receive high scores as the result of rater leniency while others receive low scores because their work was scored by a stringent rater. Average scores assigned by raters to a common set of responses, percentage of agreement, and the correlation between scores assigned by rater pairs contribute to an overall evaluation of the degree of consistency among different raters.

Achieving a high degree of interrater consistency requires the development of consensus among raters regarding the types of performances that are valued. Agreed-on scoring rubrics and training of raters to use those rubrics with examples of student work are generally required to achieve acceptable levels of interrater consistency and ensure that differences in the stringency of rating from one rater to another do not place some students at a disadvantage.

Achieving interrater consistency is important for judgmentally scored tasks, but it says nothing about other types of consistency. For example, a high degree of interrater consistency does not guarantee consistency of ratings across tasks. There are other methods of evaluating various types of consistency or generalizability (e.g., across raters, across

Table 5.3
Scores assigned to 50 essays by two independent raters (Raters 1 and 3)

Total	Score	Scores Assigned by Rater 3						Row
		1	2	3	4	5	6	
Scores	6	0	0	0	0	0	**5**	5
Assigned	5	0	0	0	0	**2**	6	8
by	4	0	0	0	**3**	5	4	12
Rater 1	3	0	0	**6**	4	2	0	12
	2	0	**5**	4	0	0	0	9
	1	**3**	1	0	0	0	0	4
Column total		3	6	10	7	9	15	50

Note: Numbers in bold show the number of essays where the scores assigned by the raters were in exact agreement.

tasks, and over time) simultaneously. Generalizability theory provides the foundation for those methods. That theory is beyond the scope of this book, but a good introduction is provided by Shavelson and Webb (1991).

Comparing Methods

As stated earlier, each of the methods of estimating reliability provides different information concerning the consistency of test results. A summary of this information is presented in Table 5.4, which shows that most methods are concerned with only one or two types of consistency. As its name suggests, the interrater method evaluates only the degree of consistency of scores assigned to the same performances by different raters. The test–retest method, without a time interval, takes into account only the consistency of the assessment procedure and the short-term constancy of the response. If a time interval is introduced between the assessments, the constancy of the characteristics of the student from day to day also will be included. However, neither of the test–retest procedures provides information concerning the consistency of results over different samples of tasks because both sets of scores are based on the same assessment.

The equivalent-forms method without a time interval, the split-half method, and the coefficient alpha method all take into account the consistency of assessment procedures and the consistency of results over different samples of tasks. Only the equivalent-forms method with an intervening time period between tests takes into account all three types of consistency, which is the reason that this measure of stability and equivalence is generally regarded as the most useful estimate of reliability.

Table 5.4
Type of consistency indicated by each of the methods for estimating reliability

Method of Estimating Reliability	Type of Consistency			
	Consistency of Testing Procedure	Constancy of Student Characteristics	Consistency Over Different Samples of Items	Consistency of Judgmental Scores
Test–retest (immediate)	X	*		
Test–retest (time interval)	X	X		
Equivalent-forms (immediate)	X	*	X	
Equivalent-forms (time interval)	X	X	X	
Split-half	X		X	
Coefficient alpha	X		X	
Interrater				X

Note: *Short-term constancy of response is reflected in immediate retest, but day-to-day stability is not shown.

STANDARD ERROR OF MEASUREMENT

If it were possible to assess a student over and over on the same assessment procedures, we would find that the scores would vary somewhat. The amount of variation in the scores would be directly related to the reliability of the assessment procedures. Low reliability would be indicated by large variations in the student's assessment results, and high reliability would be indicated by little variation from one assessment to another. Although it is impractical to administer the same set of assessment tasks many times to the same students, it is possible to estimate the amount of variation to be expected in the scores. This estimate is called the standard error of measurement.

Test manuals for published tests usually list the standard errors of measurement. Thus, all we need to do is take the standard error into account when interpreting individual test scores. For example, let us assume that we have just administered a standardized achievement test battery to a class of fourth-grade students and the results indicate that Mary Shea has a grade-equivalent (GE) score of 5.2 on the mathematics test. A GE score indicates the grade level that the average student has who has the same number of correct answers as Mary. (See Chapter 16 for a discussion of GE scores.) We find in the test manual that the standard error of measurement on the mathematics test is 0.4. What does the 0.4 tell us about Mary's mathematics achievement? In general, it indicates the amount of error that must be considered in interpreting Mary's score. More specifically, it provides the limits within which we can reasonably expect to find Mary's true mathematics achievement score. A true score is one that would be obtained if the test were perfectly reliable. If Mary Shea were tested repeatedly under identical conditions and there were no memory, learning, practice, or fatigue effects, 68% of her obtained scores would fall within one standard error (0.4) of her true score, 95% would fall within two standard errors (0.8), and 99.7% would fall within three standard errors (1.2) (see the box "Hypothetical Distribution Illustrating the Standard Error of Measurement").

For practical purposes, these limits may be applied to Mary's obtained score of 5.2 to give us the ranges shown in Table 5.5, within which we could be reasonably sure to find her true score.

Although Mary's score of 5.2 indicates that she did better on this particular test than the typical fourth-grade student, the range of scores shows that we cannot be certain that her true score is above that of the average fourth-grade student. One can be quite confident that her true score is somewhere between 4.4 and 6.0 because 95% of the observed scores fall within two standard errors of the true score. In interpreting individual test scores, however, the use of one standard error of measurement is more common. Thus, a range of 4.8 to 5.6 typically would be used to describe Mary's test performance.

Table 5.5
Standard error score bands

Number of Standard Errors Scores	Score Units to Apply to Mary's GE Score of 5.2	Range of
1	0.4	4.8–5.6
2	0.8	4.4–6.0
3	1.2	4.0–6.4

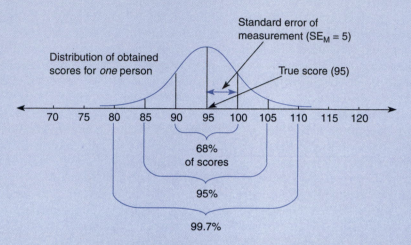

Hypothetical Distribution Illustrating the Standard Error of Measurement

Standard error of measurement ($SE_M = 5$)

Distribution of obtained scores for *one* person

True score (95)

70   75   80   85   90   95   100   105   110   115   120

68% of scores

95%

99.7%

Theoretical Explanation of the Standard Error of Measurement

1. It is assumed that each person has a *true score* on a particular test, a hypothetical value representing a score free of error (true score = 95 on the diagram).

2. If a person could be tested repeatedly (without memory, practice effects, or other changes), the average of the obtained scores would approximate the true score, and the obtained scores would be *approximately normally distributed* around the true score (see diagram and The Normal Curve and Standard Deviation section of Chapter 19).

3. From what is known about the normal distribution curve, approximately 68% of the obtained scores would fall within one standard error of measurement of the person's true score; approximately 95% of the

scores would fall within two standard errors; and approximately 99.7% of the scores would fall within three standard errors (see The Normal Curve and the Standard Deviation Unit in Chapter 19. The standard error of measurement is the standard deviation of the errors of measurement).

4. Although *the true score can never be known*, the standard error of measurement can be applied to a person's obtained score to set reasonable limits for locating the true score (e.g., an obtained score of 97 plus and minus 5 = 92 to 102).

5. These "reasonable limits" provide *confidence bands* for interpreting an obtained score. When the standard error of measurement is small, the confidence band is narrow (indicating high reliability), and thus we have greater confidence that the obtained score is near the true score.

The standard error of measurement shows why a test score should be interpreted as a band of scores (called a confidence band) rather than as a specific score. With a large standard error, the band of scores is wide, and we have less confidence in our obtained score. If the standard error is small, then the band of scores will be narrow, and we will have greater confidence that our obtained score is a dependable measure of the characteristic. Viewing an assessment score as a band of scores makes it possible to interpret and use assessment results more intelligently. Apparent differences in scores between individuals and for the same individual over a period of time often disappear when the standard error of measurement is considered. A teacher or counselor who is aware of the standard error of measurement realizes that it is impossible to be dogmatic in interpreting minor differences in assessment scores.

The relationship between the reliability coefficient and the standard error of measurement can be seen in Table 5.6, which presents the standard errors of measurement for various reliability coefficients and standard deviations. Notice that as the reliability coefficient increases for any given standard deviation, the standard error of measurement decreases. Thus, large reliability coefficients are associated with small measurement errors in specific test scores, and small reliability coefficients are associated with large measurement errors.

Table 5.6
Standard errors of measurement for given values of reliability coefficient and standard deviation

			Reliability Coefficient			
SD	*0.95*	*0.90*	*0.85*	*0.80*	*0.75*	*0.70*
30	6.7	9.5	11.6	13.4	15.0	16.4
28	6.3	8.9	10.8	12.5	14.0	15.3
26	5.8	8.2	10.1	11.6	13.0	14.2
24	5.4	7.6	9.3	10.7	12.0	13.1
22	4.9	7.0	8.5	9.8	11.0	12.0
20	4.5	6.3	7.7	8.9	10.0	11.0
18	4.0	5.7	7.0	8.0	9.0	9.9
16	3.6	5.1	6.2	7.2	8.0	8.8
14	3.1	4.4	5.4	6.3	7.0	7.7
12	2.7	3.8	4.6	5.4	6.0	6.6
10	2.2	3.2	3.9	4.5	5.0	5.5
8	1.8	2.5	3.1	3.6	4.0	4.4
6	1.3	1.9	2.3	2.7	3.0	3.3
4	0.9	1.3	1.5	1.8	2.0	2.2
2	0.4	0.6	0.8	0.9	1.0	1.1

Note: This table is based on the formula **SE** (Measurement) = $\mathbf{SD}\sqrt{(1-r)}$, where **SD** is the standard deviation of the assessment scores and *r* is the reliability coefficient.
Source: Reprinted from J. E. Doppelt, *How Accurate Is a Test Score?* Test Service Bulletin, no. 50 (New York: Psychological Corporation).

If the reliability of an assessment procedure and the standard deviation of the assessment scores are known, Table 5.6 can be used to estimate the standard error. In fact, this is the purpose for which the table was developed. All one needs to do to obtain an estimate of the standard error for a given assessment is to enter the column nearest to the reliability coefficient and the row nearest to the standard deviation and read the standard error of measurement from the cell for that row and column. For example, a reliability coefficient of 0.90 and a standard deviation of 16 would result in a standard error of 5.1, which is obtained by going down the 0.90 column to the row in which the standard deviation is 16. (See the "Guidelines" box.)

GUIDELINES

Practical Applications of the Standard Error of Measurement in Test Interpretation

A confidence band one standard error of measurement above and below the obtained score is commonly used in test profiles to aid in interpreting individual scores and in judging whether differences between scores are likely to be "real differences" or differences caused by chance.

1. **Interpreting an individual score.** The confidence band indicates "reasonable limits" within which to locate the true score (Mary's true math score probably falls somewhere between 4.8 and 5.6).

2. **Interpreting the difference between two scores from a test battery.** When the ends of the bands overlap, there is no "real difference" between scores (Mary's scores in reading and math show no meaningful difference).

3. **Interpreting the difference between the scores of two individuals on the same test.** When ends of bands do not overlap, there is a "real difference" between scores (Mary's reading score is higher than John's).

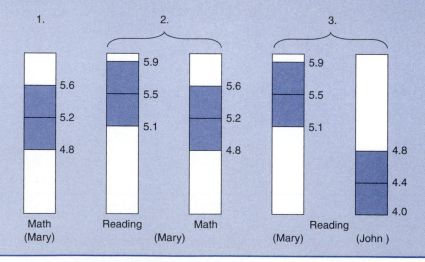

Keep several precautions in mind when using Table 5.6 to estimate the standard error of measurement. First, the reliability coefficient and standard deviation must be based on the same group of persons. Second, entering the table with the reliability coefficient and standard deviation nearest to those in the manual gives only an approximation of the standard error of measurement. Third, the table does not take into account the fact that the standard error of measurement varies slightly at different score levels. Within these limitations, however, Table 5.6 provides a simple and quick method for estimating the standard error of measurement and yields an approximation accurate enough for most practical applications of test results.

So far, we have discussed the standard error of measurement and its uses as if the magnitude of measurement errors were always the same regardless of the level of a person's score. Although this common practice works well most of the time, the assumption that the standard error of measurement is a constant throughout the score range does not hold up well for extremely high or extremely low scores. For example, if a multiple-choice test is much too difficult for a student, then that student's score is apt to be based almost entirely on the luck he or she has in guessing the correct answers. Likewise, an assessment requiring extended responses to problems that are far too difficult is apt to result in blank or off-task responses. In either case, the standard error for that student will be considerably larger than the standard error for students for whom the test difficulty is more appropriate.

Because the standard errors of measurement tend to be larger for very high and very low scores, some test publishers report standard errors of measurement separately for different ranges of scores. The procedures for estimating standard errors of measurement for different score levels are more complicated but really are no different, except that the numerical value of the standard error used would depend on an individual's test score. This additional information makes it possible to have more accurate score bands for people with extreme scores. Suppose, for example, that for a fourth-grade reading comprehension test, the test manual reported standard errors of measurement for various ranges of GE scores as shown in Table 5.7. From these results, we would recognize that scores indicating performance similar to that of the typical second- or seventh-grade student would be subject to much larger errors of measurement than scores similar to the typical fourth-grade student for whom the test was designed. The wide band for a student with

Table 5.7
Standard errors of measurement by score range

Grade Equivalent Score Range	Standard Error of Measurement
7.0–7.9	0.8
6.0–6.9	0.6
5.0–5.9	0.4
4.0–4.9	0.4
3.0–3.9	0.5
1.0–2.9	0.7

a score of, say, 7.1 (6.3–7.9) would warn us that although the student's performance is clearly well above that of the typical fourth-grade student, we cannot be very precise about how much higher.

The different standard errors by score level also help in selecting the level of a standardized test that will be most appropriate for a particular group of students. For example, if we know that most of the fourth-grade students in a school have scored far below the national average in earlier grades, then we would know that the fourth-grade level of the test is apt to be too difficult and will result in large standard errors of measurement. In this case, we could expect that using the level of the test designed for third-grade students would result in scores with smaller standard errors of measurement and, thus, provide more dependable results.

The standard error of measurement has two special advantages as a means of estimating reliability. First, the estimates are in the same units as the assessment scores. This makes it possible to indicate directly the margin of error to allow for when interpreting individual scores. Second, the standard error is likely to remain fairly constant from group to group. This is not true of the reliability coefficient, which is highly dependent on the spread of scores in the group assessed. Because the groups on which reliabilities are reported in test manuals will always differ somewhat from the group to be given the test, the greater constancy of the standard error of measurement has obvious practical value. The main difficulty encountered with the standard error occurs when we want to compare two assessments that use different types of scores. Here the reliability coefficient is the only suitable measure.

FACTORS INFLUENCING RELIABILITY MEASURES

Several factors have been shown to affect the conventional measures of reliability. If sound conclusions are to be drawn, these factors must be considered when interpreting reliability coefficients. We have already seen, for example, that speeded tests will produce a spuriously large reliability coefficient with the internal consistency methods of estimating reliability. We have also noted that test–retest reliability coefficients are influenced by the interval between assessments, with shorter intervals resulting in larger reliability coefficients. Although we might want to favor the assessment procedure with the largest reliability coefficient, we would not do so if we recognized that the reported coefficient was inflated by factors irrelevant to the consistency of the measurement procedure. Similarly, we might discount the difference between reliability coefficients reported for two different assessments if the conditions under which they were obtained favored the test with the larger reliability coefficient.

Consideration of the factors influencing reliability not only will help us interpret more wisely the reliability coefficients of standardized tests but also should aid us in constructing more reliable classroom assessments. Although teachers seldom find it profitable to calculate reliability coefficients for the assessments they construct, they should be cognizant of the factors influencing reliability to maximize the reliability of their own classroom assessments.

Number of Assessment Tasks

In general, the larger the number of tasks on an assessment, the higher its reliability will be. This is because a longer assessment will provide a more adequate sample of the behavior being measured, and the scores are apt to be less distorted by chance factors, such as special familiarity with a given task or lack of understanding of what is expected on a given task. Suppose that to measure spelling ability, we asked students to spell one word. The results would be patently unreliable. Students who were able to spell the word would be perfect spellers, and students who could not would be complete failures. If we happened to select a difficult word, most students would fail; if the word were an easy one, most students would appear to be perfect spellers. The fact that one word provides an unreliable estimate of a student's spelling ability is obvious. It should be equally apparent that as we add more spelling words to the list, we come closer and closer to a good estimate of each child's spelling ability. Scores based on a large number of spelling words thus are more apt to reflect real differences in spelling ability and therefore to be more stable. By increasing the size of the sample of spelling behavior, therefore, we increase the consistency of our measurement. A longer test also tends to lessen the influence of chance factors such as guessing. For example, on a 10-item true-and-false test, a student might know seven of the items and guess at the other three. A correct guess on all three items would result in a perfect score, and incorrect guesses on all three items would result in only seven correct. This represents a considerable variation in the test score resulting from guessing alone. However, if this same student were taking a test with 100 true-and-false items, the correct guesses would tend to be canceled by incorrect guesses, and the score would be a more dependable indication of actual knowledge.

The fact that a longer assessment tends to provide more reliable results was implied earlier in our discussion of the split-half method. You will recall that when scores from two halves of a test correlated at 0.60, the Spearman–Brown formula estimated the reliability of the scores for the full-length assessment to be 0.75. This is equivalent to estimating the increase in reliability to be expected when the number of assessment tasks is doubled.

The relationship of length to reliability poses a problem for assessments that require an extended time to complete, because the critical feature in the length–reliability relationship is the number of tasks, not the amount of assessment time. If each task requires a full class period or even longer to administer, then it is obvious that increases in the number of tasks have a high cost in terms of student time. Nonetheless, if consistency of performance across different tasks intended to assess a common domain of achievement is low, then multiple tasks will be required to achieve adequate levels of reliability.

There are at least two ways in which the extended time periods required for assessment results to achieve adequate reliability may be justified. First, greater time and expense may be justified when the assessment has major consequences for the individuals being assessed or for society (e.g., the licensing of physicians). Second, the devotion of extended periods of time to assessments is justified when the assessments are themselves considered good instructional activities that contribute not only to the measurement of achievement but also directly to student learning. The latter justification is likely to be more relevant for assessments in elementary and secondary schools than the former one.

There is one important reservation in evaluating the influence of the number of tasks on the reliability of the scores: The statements we have been making assume that the assessment will be lengthened by adding tasks of the same quality as those that are already part of the assessment. Adding 10 spelling words that are so easy that everyone will get them correct or adding 10 spelling words that are so difficult that no one will get them correct will not increase the reliability of the scores on a spelling test. In fact, there would be no influence on the reliability coefficient because such additions would not influence the standing of students relative to others in the group.

In constructing classroom tests or assigning assessment tasks, it is important to keep in mind the influence of the number of questions or tasks on reliability. If only a small number of questions or tasks can be used (because of time limits, the students' ages, or the extended time required to complete each task), then more frequent assessment may be used to obtain a dependable measure of achievement.

In using standardized tests, we should be wary of part scores based on relatively few items. Such scores are usually low in reliability and of little practical value even when the total test score is high in reliability. Before using such scores, the test manual should be checked for their reported reliabilities. If these are not reported or are very low, the part scores should be ignored, and only the total test score should be used.

Spread of Scores

As noted earlier, reliability coefficients are directly influenced by the spread of scores in the group assessed. Other things being equal, the larger the spread of scores, the higher the estimate of reliability will be. Because larger reliability coefficients result when individuals stay in the same relative position in a group from one assessment to another, it naturally follows that anything that reduces the possibility of shifting positions in the group also contributes to larger reliability coefficients. In this case, greater differences between the scores of individuals reduce the possibility of shifting positions. Stated another way, errors of measurement have less influence on the relative position of individuals when the differences among group members are large, that is, when there is a wide spread of scores.

This can be easily illustrated without recourse to statistics. Compare the two sets of scores shown in Table 5.8 in terms of the probability that the individuals will remain in the same relative position on a second administration of the assessment. Even a cursory inspection of these scores will show that the persons in Group B are more likely to shift positions on a second administration of the assessment. With a spread of only 10 points from the top score to the bottom score, radical shifts in position can result from changes of just a few points in the scores.

However, in Group A the scores of individuals could vary by several points on a second administration of the assessment, with very little shifting in the relative positions of the group members. The large spread of test scores in Group A makes shifts in relative position unlikely and thus gives us greater confidence that these differences among group members are real.

Objectivity

The objectivity of an assessment refers to the degree to which equally competent scorers obtain the same results. Most standardized tests of aptitude and achievement are high in

Table 5.8
Illustration of score spread

Group A	Group B
95	95
90	94
86	93
82	93
76	92
65	91
60	89
56	88
53	86
47	85

objectivity. The test items are of the objective type (e.g., multiple choice), and the resulting scores are not influenced by the scorers' judgment or opinion. In fact, such tests are usually constructed so that they can be accurately scored by trained clerks and scoring machines. When such highly objective procedures are used, the reliability of the test results is not affected by the scoring procedures.

However, for classroom assessments constructed by teachers or performance-based assessments mandated by states and districts, objectivity may play an important role in obtaining reliable measures of achievement. In essay testing and assessments requiring judgmental scoring, the results depend, to some extent, on the person doing the scoring. Different persons get different results, and even the same person may get different results at different times. Such inconsistency in scoring has an adverse effect on the reliability of the measures obtained, for the test scores now reflect the opinions and biases of the scorer as well as differences among students in the characteristic being measured.

The solution is *not* to use only objective tests or to abandon all methods of assessment that require judgmental scoring. This would have an adverse effect on validity, and, as noted earlier, validity is the most important characteristic of assessment results. A better solution is to select assessment procedures most appropriate for the learning goals being assessed and then make the assessment procedure as objective as possible. In the use of essay tests, for example, objectivity can be increased by careful phrasing of the questions and by a standard set of rules for scoring. Similarly, the objectivity in scoring of science exhibitions can be increased by establishing clear scoring criteria and carefully training raters. Such increased objectivity will contribute to greater reliability without sacrificing validity.

Methods of Estimating Reliability

When examining the reliability coefficients of standardized tests, it is important to consider the methods used to obtain the reliability estimates. In general, the size of the reliability coefficient is related to the method of estimating reliability.

1. Test–retest method	May be larger than with the split-half method if the time interval is short. Coefficients become smaller as the time interval between tests is increased.
2. Equivalent-forms method (without time interval)	Coefficients tend to be lower than with the split-half method or the test–retest method using a short time interval.
3. Equivalent-forms method (with time interval)	Coefficients become smaller as the time interval between tests is increased.
4. Split-half method (e.g., odd–even)	Provides an indication of the internal consistency of a test. Spuriously high estimates are produced for speeded tests.
5. Coefficient alpha	Typically provides reliability estimates that are smaller than those obtained by the split-half method when the two halves are carefully matched. These estimates are also inflated by speed.
6. Interrater method	Provides an indication of the degree to which similar scores are obtained regardless of who does the rating. Interrater consistency can be increased by using well-defined scoring rules and by careful training of raters.

The variation in the size of the reliability coefficient resulting from the method of estimating reliability is directly attributable to the type of consistency included in each method. Recall that the equivalent-forms method with an intervening time interval took into account the most sources of variation in the test scores and consequently is a more rigorous method of estimating reliability than test–retest, the use of equivalent forms without an intervening time interval, or internal consistency methods. Thus, smaller reliability coefficients can be expected with this method, and it is unfair to compare such reliability coefficients with those obtained by less stringent methods.

At the other extreme, the larger reliability coefficients typically reported for the split-half method must be accepted cautiously. If speed is an important factor in the testing, split-half reliability coefficients should be disregarded entirely, and other evidence of reliability should be sought.

RELIABILITY OF ASSESSMENTS EVALUATED IN TERMS OF A FIXED PERFORMANCE STANDARD

In a variety of situations the primary goal of an assessment is to determine whether performance meets a preestablished standard. Teachers may use preestablished standards to assign grades for a test, to make instructional decisions (e.g., review, relearn, or move on), or for placement at the beginning of the year. Criterion-referenced mastery tests are an example of an assessment that is widely used with a preestablished standard. Typically, such tests are designed to provide the basis for a decision regarding the mastery of a set of essential skills and therefore are frequently pitched at a relatively low level of performance. Comparing performance to a fixed standard rather than to the performance of other students, however, need not limit assessment to the testing of low-level skills and minimum levels of performance. Indeed, in recent years the emphasis has been on establishing high standards of performance for all students.

Regardless of the level of the standard, when we use assessments for the purpose of deciding whether performance meets an established standard, our desire for consistency of measurement is similar to that for norm-referenced tests. Thus, we would like an individual's performance to be consistent from (a) one rater to another; (b) one task to another, when all tasks measure the same learning outcome (internal consistency); (c) one time to another, when the learning outcomes are expected to have a reasonable degree of constancy (stability); and (d) one form of an assessment to another, when the forms are intended to measure the same sample of learning tasks (equivalence). However, the focus is more often on whether the performance meets the standard than on the actual score.

In addition, because of the specificity of mastery assessments and their close tie to instruction, they may have a narrower range of scores than is typically produced by norm-referenced measures. The focus on mastery decisions and the smaller variability in scores has led to different approaches in evaluating the reliability of mastery assessments.

Given the emphasis on whether a performance meets or fails to meet a standard, the most natural approach to reliability is to evaluate the consistency with which students are classified as performing above or below the standard. This type of reliability can be readily determined by computing the percentage of consistent decisions as the result of having performances evaluated by different raters or over two equivalent forms of an assessment. Although a number of more complicated approaches have been suggested, the simple calculation of the percentage of people who are consistently classified is the approach that is encouraged by the *Standards* (AERA, APA, & NCME, 1999) for tests that are used to make dichotomous decisions with regard to a standard. With only two categories, however, it becomes more important to take into account the level of agreement that would be expected by chance.

Let's assume that we have given two alternate assessments, each consisting of 10 open-ended mathematics tasks, to a classroom group of 30 students. Each task is scored on a 4-point scale (ranging from 0 for no response or a response that is off task to 3 for a solid solution to the problem with adequate justification). Thus, the range of possible scores on each assessment is from 0 to 30 for each alternate assessment. To meet the standard, a student must obtain a score of at least 20. All students obtaining a score of 20 or higher on both assessments are consistently classified as meeting the standard. All students obtaining a score of 19 or lower on both assessments are consistently classified as failing to meet the standard. The remaining students are classified as meeting the standard on one assessment and failing to meet it on the other one. If this latter group of reversals is relatively large, our assessment will obviously be inconsistent in classifying students. The data for such an analysis can be summarized in a two-by-two table like that in Figure 5.4.

		Assessment B	
		Fails to meet standard	Meets standard
Assessment A	Meets standard	2	20
	Fails to meet standard	7	1

Figure 5.4
A classification of 30 students with respect to a fixed performance standard

By using the information in Figure 5.4, we can compute a percentage of consistency using the following formula.

$$\% \text{ Consistency} = 100 \times \frac{\text{Meets standard on both forms} + \text{Fails to meet standard on both forms}}{\text{Total number in group}}$$

$$\% \text{ Consistency} = 100 \times \frac{20 + 7}{30} = 90\%$$

The 90% agreement should be compared to the agreement that would be expected by chance. The latter figure is computed by completing the following steps: (a) Multiply the proportion of students who meet the standard on Assessment A (22 of 30 = .733) by the proportion of students who meet it on Assessment B (21 of 30 = .700). This yields (.733 × .700 = .513). (b) Multiply the proportion of students who fail to meet the standard on Assessment A (8 of 30 = .267) times the corresponding figure for Assessment B (9 of 30 = .300). This yields (.267 × .300 = .080). (c) Sum the results of Steps 1 and 2 (.513 + .080 = .593). (d) Convert the result of Step 3 to a percentage by multiplying it by 100. This yields 59.3%, the level of agreement expected by chance given the passing rates on the two assessments. The observed percentage agreement of 90% compares favorably to that expected by chance.

Similar examples could be given for classifying students into more categories than mastery and nonmastery. On the other hand, the data presented in Table 5.3 and the computations for exact agreement are the extension of the dichotomous mastery–nonmastery data. As noted for the interrater example, one can report percentage exact agreement or percentage agreement within 1 score point. The percentage agreement expected by chance for exact agreement (or agreement within 1 score point) would be computed in the same way, and comparisons could be made between percentage agreement and percentage expected agreement by chance.

When using mastery testing in the classroom, comparing the percentage agreement with the percentage expected by chance is generally sufficient. However, standardized tests may report an index—Cohen's kappa—that accounts for the difference between the two numbers. Cohen's kappa is the proportion of agreement that is above and beyond what is expected by chance. The formula for Cohen's kappa is

Kappa = (percentage agreement−percentage agreement by chance)/(100% agreement by chance)

From the example for mastery–nonmastery, where the percentage agreement was 90 and the percent agreement by chance was 59.3,

$$\text{Kappa} = (90 - 59.3)/(100 - 59.3) = .754$$

Therefore, the test was consistent on about three fourths of the classifications above and beyond the 59.3% expected. For this index, any positive value is above and beyond what is expected. A value of zero would occur when the example had agreement at 59.3%. Hence, a test that is working at a chance level would have a value of zero even when there is substantial agreement. In the extreme, suppose that all students had reached mastery on two forms of the test. Then the previous computations would lead to an expectation of 100% agreement by chance, and Cohen's kappa would be equal to zero since the test had not done better than what was expected by chance. This provides an example of the problem with having no spread of scores. With a small spread of scores, kappa would be small even with a large percentage of agreement.

Although the percentage of agreement is conceptually simple and easy to compute, it does require two versions of the assessment. This is not a serious shortcoming, however, because assessments designed to determine whether students meet a standard should allow students who fail to meet the standard an opportunity to try again on an alternate set of assessment tasks. It is seldom wise to permit students who do not meet the performance standard on the first attempt to be reassessed with the identical set of tasks. Procedures have been developed to estimate decision consistency on the basis of the administration of a single test form or set of assessment tasks; however, those procedures are relatively complex and are beyond the scope of this textbook (Subkoviak, 1984). Suffice it to say that they are intended to provide approximations to the percentage of agreement based on equivalent forms from data available from the administration of a single set of assessment tasks.

How High Should Reliability Be?

The degree of reliability we demand in our educational assessments depends largely on the decision to be made. If we are going to use assessment results to decide whether to review certain areas of subject matter, we may be willing to use a teacher-made assessment of relatively low reliability. Our decision will be based on the scores of the total group, and variation in individual scores will not distort our decision too much. Even if we do err in our decision, no catastrophe will result. The worst that can happen is that the students will get an unnecessary review of material or will be deprived of a review that may be beneficial to them. On the other hand, if we are going to use an assessment to decide whether to award a high school diploma or a college scholarship, we should demand the most reliable measurement available. Such decisions have important consequences for the lives of the individuals involved.

It is not only the importance of a decision that matters, but also whether it is possible to confirm or reverse the judgment at a later time. Decision making in education is seldom

GUIDELINES

Reliability Demands and Nature of the Decision

High reliability is demanded when the
- Decision is important.
- Decision is final.
- Decision is irreversible.
- Decision is unconfirmable.
- Decision concerns individuals.
- Decision has lasting consequences.
    Example: Select or reject college applicants.

Low reliability is tolerable when the
- Decision is of minor importance.
- Decision making is in early stages.
- Decision is reversible.
- Decision is confirmable by other data.
- Decision concerns groups.
- Decision has temporary effects.
    Example: Whether to review a classroom lesson.

a single, final act. It tends to be sequential, starting with rather crude judgments and proceeding through a series of more refined judgments. In the early stages of decision making, low reliability might be quite tolerable because assessment results are used primarily as a guide to further information gathering. For example, on the basis of classroom assessments of questionable reliability, we might decide that some of our students are having such serious learning difficulties that they need special help. This decision can be confirmed or refuted by further assessment with more dependable measures. Opportunities for confirmation and reversal of judgments without serious consequences are almost always present in the early stages of educational decision making. Thus, the important thing when reliability is low or unknown is *not* to treat the scores as if they were highly accurate. Make tentative judgments, seek confirming data, and be willing to reverse decisions when wrong.

Thus, when we ask how high reliability should be, several considerations must be taken into account. How important is the decision? Is it one that can be confirmed or reversed at a later time? How far-reaching are the consequences of the action taken? For irreversible decisions that are apt to have great influence on the lives of individual students, we should make stringent demands on the reliability of the assessments we use. For lesser decisions, especially for those that can be later confirmed or reversed without serious consequences, we should be willing to settle for less reliable measures. Teacher-made tests commonly have reliabilities between 0.60 and 0.85, but they are useful for the types of instructional decisions typically made by teachers. Thus, the degree of reliability required depends largely on how confident we need to be about the decision being made. Greater confidence requires higher reliability (see the "Guidelines" box).

USABILITY

In selecting assessment procedures, practical considerations cannot be neglected. Assessments are usually administered and interpreted by teachers with only a minimum of training in measurement. The time available for assessment is almost always limited because assessment is in constant competition with other important activities for time in the school schedule. Likewise, the cost of assessment, although a minor consideration, is as carefully scrutinized by budget-conscious administrators as are other expenditures of school funds. These and other factors pertinent to the usability of assessment procedures must be taken into account when selecting assessment procedures. Such practical considerations are especially important when selecting published tests.

Ease of Administration

If the assessments are to be administered by teachers or others with limited training, ease of administration is an especially important quality to seek. For this purpose, directions should be simple and clear, subtests should be relatively few, and the time needed for administration of the assessment should not be too great. Administering a test with complicated directions and a number of subtests lasting but a few minutes each is a taxing chore for even an experienced examiner. For a person with little training and experience, such a situation is fraught with possibilities for errors in giving directions, timing, and other aspects of administration that are likely to affect results. Such errors of administration can, of course, have an adverse effect on the validity and reliability of the results.

Time Required for Administration

With time for assessment at a premium, we always favor the shorter assessment, other things being equal. But in this case, other things are seldom equal because reliability is directly related to the length of an assessment. If we attempt to cut down too much on the time allotted to assessment, we may reduce drastically the reliability of our scores. For example, tests designed to fit a normal class period usually produce total test scores of satisfactory reliability, but their part scores, obtained from the subtests, tend to be unreliable. If we want reliable measures in the areas covered by the subtests, we need to increase our testing time in each area. On the other hand, if we want a general measure in some area, such as verbal aptitude, we can obtain reliable results in 30 or 40 minutes, and there is little advantage in extending the testing time. A safe procedure is to allot as much time as is necessary to obtain valid and reliable results and no more. Between 20 and 60 minutes of testing time for each individual score yielded by a published test is probably a fairly good guide.

Ease of Interpretation and Application

In the final analysis, the success or failure of an assessment program is determined by the use made of the assessment results. If they are interpreted correctly and applied effectively, they will contribute to more intelligent educational decisions. On the other hand, if the assessment results are misinterpreted, misapplied, or not applied at all, they will be of little value and may actually be harmful to some individual or group.

Information concerning the interpretation and use of published test results is usually obtained directly from the test manual or related guides. Attention should be directed toward the clarity of score reports, the quality and relevance of norms, and the comprehensiveness of the suggestions for applying the results to educational problems. When the test results are to be presented to students or parents, ease of interpretation and application are especially important.

Availability of Equivalent or Comparable Forms

For many educational purposes, equivalent forms of the same test are often desirable. Equivalent forms of a test measure the same aspect of behavior by using test items that are alike in content, level of difficulty, and other characteristics. Thus, one form of the test can substitute for the other, making it possible to test students twice in rather close succession without their answers on the first testing influencing their performance on the second testing. The advantage of equivalent forms is readily seen in mastery testing, when we want to eliminate the factor of memory while retesting students on the same domain of achievement. Equivalent forms of a test also may be used to verify a questionable test score. For example, a teacher may believe that a scholastic aptitude or achievement test score is spuriously low for a given student and may easily check this by administering an equivalent form of the test.

Many tests also provide comparable forms. Published achievement tests, for example, are commonly arranged in a series that covers different grade levels. Although the content and level of difficulty vary, the tests at the different levels are made comparable by means of a common score scale. Thus, it is possible to compare measurements in grade 4 with measurements in grade 6 on a more advanced form of the test. Comparable forms are especially useful in measuring development.

Cost of Testing

The factor of cost has been left to the last because it is relatively unimportant in selecting published tests. The reason for discussing it at all is that it is sometimes given far more weight than it deserves. Testing is relatively inexpensive, and cost should not be a major consideration. In large-scale testing programs where small savings per student add up, using separate answer sheets, machine scoring, and reusable booklets will reduce the cost appreciably. But to select one test instead of another because the test booklets are a few cents cheaper is false economy. After all, validity and reliability are the important characteristics to look for, and a test lacking these qualities is too expensive at any price. The contribution that valid and reliable test scores can make to educational decisions means that such tests are always economical in the long run.

SUMMARY

Next to validity, reliability is the most important quality to seek in assessment results. Reliability refers to the consistency of scores and other assessment results from one assessment to another. In interpreting and using reliability information, it is important to remember that reliability estimates refer to the results of measurement, that different ways of estimating reliability indicate different types of consistency, that a reliable measure is not necessarily valid, and that reliability is strictly a statistical concept. Reliability estimates are typically reported in terms of a reliability coefficient or the standard error of measurement.

Reliability coefficients are determined by several different methods, and each provides a different measure of consistency. The interrater method requires that the same set of student performances be scored by two or more raters, and it provides an indication of the consistency of scoring across raters. The test–retest method involves giving the same assessment twice to the same group with an intervening interval, and the resulting coefficient provides a measure of stability. The length of the interval between assessments is determined largely by the use to be made of the results. We are interested primarily in reliability coefficients based on intervals comparable to the periods of time between when the assessment is given and when the scores will be used and interpreted. The equivalent-forms method involves giving two forms of an assessment to the same group in close succession or with an intervening time interval. The first assessment yields a measure of equivalence and the second a measure of stability and equivalence. The equivalent-forms method provides a rigorous evaluation of reliability because it includes multiple sources of variation in the assessment results. Reliability also can be estimated from a single administration of an assessment, either by correlating the scores on two halves of the assessment or by applying the coefficient alpha formula. Coefficient alpha provides a measure of internal consistency and is easy to apply. However, it is not applicable to speeded tests and provides no information concerning the stability of assessment scores from day to day.

The standard error of measurement indicates reliability in terms of the amount of variation to be expected in individual scores. It can be computed from the reliability coefficient and the standard deviation, but it is frequently reported directly in test manuals. The standard error is especially useful in interpreting test scores because it indicates the band of error (called a confidence band) surrounding each score. It also has the advantage of remaining fairly constant from one group to another.

Reliability estimates may vary in accordance with the length of the assessment, the spread of scores in the group assessed, the difficulty of the assessment tasks, the objectivity of the scoring, and the method of estimating reliability. These factors should be taken into account when appraising reliability information. The degree and type of reliability to be sought in a particular instance depend mainly on the decision being made. For tentative reversible decisions, low reliability may be tolerable; for final, irreversible decisions, we should make stringent demands on the reliability of our measures.

Conventional measures of reliability depend on scores throughout the range and are influenced by the variability among scores. In assessments designed to assess performance in terms of a fixed standard, the classification of students as meeting or failing to meet the standard is the primary concern. Hence, the consistency of classifications for equivalent assessments is most relevant, and the simple percentage of times that consistent decisions are made provides the information needed to evaluate reliability of the decision.

In addition to validity and reliability, it is also important to consider the usability of tests and other assessment procedures, including such practical features as ease of administration, time required, ease of interpretation and application, availability of equivalent or comparable forms, and cost of testing.

LEARNING EXERCISES

1. Define reliability and describe its importance in assessment.
2. Briefly describe the methods of estimating reliability. Can one method substitute for another? Why or why not?

3. Which method of estimating reliability provides the most useful information for each of the following? Why?
   a. Selecting a scholastic aptitude test for predicting future achievement

b. Reassessing students to determine standing relative to a fixed performance standard

c. Determining whether a test measures a homogeneous characteristic

d. Determining the degree to which essay scores obtained from different raters are affected by differences in the stringency of raters

4. What effect would the following most likely have on reliability?

a. Increasing the number of tasks in an assessment

b. Removing ambiguous tasks

c. Changing from a multiple-choice test to an essay test covering the same material

5. For which purpose is each of the following most useful? Why?

a. Reliability coefficient

b. Standard error of measurement

6. Using Table 5.6, determine the standard error of measurement for a set of scores with a standard deviation of 16 and a reliability coefficient of .85.

7. Study the reliability sections of test manuals for a few standardized achievement tests. What types of reliability data are reported? Are these types of data valuable in deciding whether to choose the tests?

8. In the reliability section of the *Standards for Educational and Psychological Testing* (see the references for this chapter), review the types of information that test manuals should contain and then compare a recent test manual with the *Standards*.

9. In reviewing the reliability data in a test manual, a teacher noted the following reliability coefficients: (a) correlation of Form A test scores over a 1-month interval = 0.90, (b) correlation of Form A with Form B scores over a 1-month interval = 0.85, and (c) correlation of scores based on two halves (odd–even) of Form A = 0.95. How would you account for these differences in reliability coefficients (assume that the groups tested were the same)? Which estimate of reliability provides the most useful information? Why?

10. List and briefly describe as many things as you can think of that might be done to increase the reliability of a classroom assessment.

REFERENCES

American Educational Research Association, American Psychological Association, & National Council on Measurement in Education. (1999). *Standards for educational and psychological testing.* Washington, DC: American Educational Research Association.

Shavelson, R. J., & Webb, N. M. (1991). *Generalizability theory: A primer.* Newbury Park, CA: Sage Publications.

Subkoviak, M. J. (1984). Estimating the reliability of mastery–nonmastery classifications. In R. A. Berk (Ed.), *A guide to criterion-referenced test construction* (pp. 267–291). Baltimore: Johns Hopkins University Press.

FURTHER READING

American Educational Research Association, American Psychological Association, & National Council on Measurement in Education. (1999). *Standards for educational and psychological testing.* Washington, DC: American Educational Research Association.

Anastasi, A., & Urbina, S. (1996). *Psychological testing* (7th ed.). New York: Macmillan. Chapter 5, "Reliability," describes the various types of reliability coefficients, the standard error of measurement, and the factors influencing reliability.

Cronbach, L. J. (1990). *Essentials of psychological testing* (5th ed.). New York: Harper & Row. Chapter 6, "How to Judge Tests," is an advanced treatment of reliability emphasizing the generalizability of test scores, methods of estimating error, and considerations in interpreting reliability estimates.

Feldt, L. S., & Brennan, R. L. (1989). Reliability. In R. L. Linn (Ed.), *Educational measurement* (3rd ed.). New York: Macmillan. Chapter 3 presents a comprehensive and technically advanced discussion of reliability.

Haertel, E. H. (2006). Reliability. In R. L. Brennan (Ed.), *Educational measurement* (4th ed. pp. 65–110). Westport, CT: Greenwood Publishing Group ACE/Paeger series in higher education. Chapter 3 provides a comprehensive and contemporary discussion of reliability and errors of measurement.

Shavelson, R. J., & Webb, N. M. (1991). *Generalizability theory: A primer*. Newbury Park, CA: Sage Publications. This primer provides an excellent introduction to generalizability, which is an expansion and integration of the reliability issues discussed in this chapter.

Traub, R. E. (1994). *Reliability for the social sciences: Theory and applications*. Thousand Oaks, CA: Sage Publications. This readable book provides broad coverage of the approaches to evaluating reliability in different situations.

CHAPTER

6

PLANNING CLASSROOM TESTS AND ASSESSMENTS

Classroom tests and assessments play a central role in the evaluation of student learning. They provide relevant measures of many important learning outcomes and indirect evidence concerning others. They make expected learning outcomes explicit to students and parents and show what types of performances are valued. The validity of the information they provide, however, depends on the care that goes into the planning and preparation of tests and assessments.

The main goal of classroom testing and assessment is to obtain valid, reliable, and useful information concerning student achievement. This requires determining what is to be measured and then defining it precisely so that tasks can be constructed that require the intended knowledge, skills, and understanding while minimizing the influence of irrelevant or ancillary skills. It also requires specifying the achievement domain in such a manner that the sample of items and assessment tasks will represent the total domain of achievement tasks giving appropriate emphasis to high-priority objectives. Satisfying these requirements provides the foundation for obtaining results that will be valid for the intended instructional uses.

The likelihood of preparing valid, reliable, and useful classroom tests and assessments is greatly enhanced if a series of steps like that shown in Figure 6.1 is followed.

Specific procedures for constructing each of the various types of test items are described in Chapters 7 through 9. Open-ended essay questions are discussed in Chapter 10 and other types of performance assessment tasks used for measuring complex achievement are described in Chapter 11. The systematic collection of student work into portfolios and the use of those portfolios for specific purposes are described in Chapter 12. Chapter 13 describes the use of observational techniques, peer appraisals, and self-report

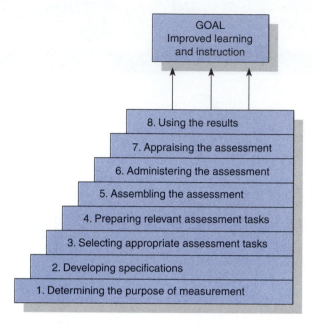

Figure 6.1
Basic steps in classroom testing and assessment

techniques to assess learning outcomes and student development. Chapter 14 is concerned with assembling, administering, and appraising classroom tests and assessments. Chapter 15, the last chapter in this section, describes approaches to grading and reporting.

THE PURPOSE OF CLASSROOM TESTING AND ASSESSMENT

Classroom tests and assessments can be used for a variety of instructional purposes. These can be best described in terms of their location in the instructional process, which closely parallels the types of assessment described in Chapter 3.

Pretesting

Tests and assessments may be given at the beginning of an instructional segment (e.g., unit or course) to determine (a) whether students have the prerequisite skills needed for the instruction (to determine readiness) or (b) to what extent students have already achieved the objectives of the planned instruction (to determine student placement or modification of instruction).

Readiness pretests are typically limited in scope. For example, a pretest in algebra might be confined to arithmetic operations and concepts, a pretest in physics might consist of basic physical concepts or prerequisite skills in algebra, and a pretest in beginning German might be limited to knowledge of English grammar. In addition to being confined to a limited domain, pretest items tend to have a relatively low level of difficulty. Published readiness tests are available at the primary school level in the basic skill areas, but most teachers must develop their own readiness pretests. These tests serve as a basis for remedial work or for adaptation of instructional plans.

Pretests for determining the extent to which students have already achieved the objectives of the planned instruction are no different from the tests used to measure the outcomes of instruction. Thus, a test designed to measure final achievement in a course or unit may be given at the beginning to measure entry performance on the objectives. In this case, the final test or assessment should, of course, not be the same test used in pretesting but an equivalent form of it.

Testing and Assessment During Instruction

Tests and assessments given during instruction provide the basis for formative assessment. They are used to monitor learning progress, detect misconceptions, encourage students to study, and provide feedback to students and teachers. Teachers commonly call these formative tests learning tests, practice tests, quizzes, unit tests, and the like. These tests and assessments typically cover some predefined segment of instruction (e.g., a chapter or particular set of skills) and thus encompass a rather limited sample of learning outcomes. The mix of types of test items and more complex performance assessment tasks needs to be selected with care to ensure that the full range of critical instructional objectives is assessed and to ensure that high-priority but possibly difficult-to-assess objectives are adequately represented in the assessment. Ideally, the tests and assessments will be constructed in such a way that corrective prescriptions can be given for learning objectives that are yet to be achieved. When most students fail a set of items or perform poorly on an extended performance task, a group review may be applicable. When a small number of students perform in ways that show a lack of understanding of critical concepts, alternative methods of study may be prescribed (e.g., special tutoring, reading assignments, practice exercises, and the like).

Persistent learning difficulties may require the use of diagnostic tests. For this type of testing, a number of test items are needed in each specific area, with some slight variation from item to item. In diagnosing students' difficulties in adding whole numbers, for example, it would be necessary to include addition problems containing various number combinations, some requiring carrying and some not, to pinpoint the specific types of errors being made. Diagnostic testing is a highly specialized area that has been somewhat neglected in educational measurement. There are some published diagnostic tests, but these are primarily in the basic skills area. In other areas, teachers have to depend more heavily on the diagnostic features of formative tests or prepare their own diagnostic tests and assessments.

End-of-Instruction Testing and Assessment

At the end of a segment of instruction (e.g., unit or course), our main interest is in measuring the extent to which the intended learning outcomes and performance standards have been achieved. Although these end-of-instruction tests and assessments are used

Table 6.1
The basic types of classroom tests and assessments

	Timing				
	Before Instruction		**During Instruction**		**End of Instruction**
Function	*Readiness*	*Placement*	*Formative*	*Diagnostic*	*Summative*
Focus of measurement	Prerequisite entry skills	Course or unit objectives	Predefined segment of instruction	Most common learning errors	Course or unit objectives
Nature of sample	Limited sample of selected skills	Broad sample of all objectives	Limited sample of learning tasks	Limited sample of specific errors	Broad sample of all objectives
Item difficulty	Typically has low level of difficulty	Typically has wide range of difficulty	Varies with the segment of instruction	Typically has low level of difficulty	Typically has wide range of difficulty
Time of administration	Beginning of course or unit	Beginning of course or unit	Periodically during instruction	As needed during instruction	End of course or unit
Use of results	Remedy entry deficiencies or assignment to learning group	Instructional planning and advanced placement	Improve and direct learning through ongoing feedback	Remedy errors related to persistent learning difficulties	Assign grades, certify accomplishment, or evaluate teaching

Source: Adapted from "Functional Types of Student Evaluation" by P. W. Airasian and G. F. Madaus, 1972, *Measurement and Evaluation in Guidance*, 4, pp. 221–233.

primarily for summative assessment (e.g., to certify accomplishment or assign grades), they can also serve other functions. End-of-unit tests can be used for feedback to students, encouraging students to undertake more challenging advanced work, assigning of remedial work, and assessing instruction as well as for grading purposes. In fact, they can serve the functions of both formative and summative assessment and in some cases serve as a pretest for the following unit (e.g., where the units are sequenced, as in math). End-of-course tests provide a broad survey of student learning over all the intended outcomes of a course. In addition to their use in grading, tests can also provide information for evaluating instructional effectiveness. A summary of the various types of classroom tests is presented in Table 6.1.

DEVELOPING SPECIFICATIONS FOR TESTS AND ASSESSMENTS

To ensure that classroom tests and assessments measure a representative sample of instructionally relevant tasks, it is important to develop specifications that can guide the selection of test items and assessment tasks. When preparing a brief learning test on a

limited area (e.g., spelling or capitalization), a simple listing of specific tasks, with an indication of the number of items measuring each task, may suffice. For most testing purposes,
however, more elaborate specifications are needed. One device that has been widely used
for this purpose is a two-way chart, called a table of specifications (or test blueprint).

Building a Table of Specifications

Building a table of specifications involves (a) preparing a list of instructional objectives,
(b) outlining the course content, and (c) preparing the two-way chart. These steps are
illustrated here for a weather unit in a middle school earth science class.

Preparing the List of Instructional Objectives.   Using the procedure for stating instructional
objectives described in Chapter 3, the following list of general objectives and specific
learning outcomes was prepared for the weather unit. Although the list is not exhaustive,
it illustrates both the method of stating the objectives and the desired amount of detail. If
this weather unit were being taught at a lower grade level, our objectives would be defined
by fewer and simpler specific learning outcomes; at a higher grade level, more complex
learning outcomes would be included.

Instructional Objectives for a Weather Unit

1. Knows basic terms
    1.1 Writes a definition of each term
    1.2. Identifies the term that represents each weather element
    1.3. Identifies the term that best fits a given weather description
    1.4. Matches the term to a picture of the concept
    1.5. Distinguishes between correct and incorrect uses of the term

2. Knows weather symbols
    2.1. Matches each symbol with the weather element it represents
    2.2. Draws the symbol for each weather element
    2.3. Identifies the meaning of each symbol

3. Knows specific facts
    3.1. Identifies the elements affecting weather
    3.2. Names the instrument used for measuring each weather element
    3.3. Identifies the unit of measurement used in reporting each weather element
    3.4. Distinguishes between correct and incorrect procedures for determining each
       weather element
    3.5. Matches the names of each cloud type with a description of its characteristics
    3.6. Identifies the weather conditions associated with each type of front

4. Understands the influence of factors on weather formation
    4.1. Describes the characteristics of a given weather condition
    4.2. Describes how clouds are formed
    4.3. Distinguishes between probable and improbable weather reports
    4.4. Identifies the factors causing a given weather change
    4.5. Predicts future weather from a change in conditions
    4.6. Explains how clouds affect weather and climate
    4.7. Delivers an oral weather report for another state to class

5. Interprets weather maps
    5.1. Describes the weather for a given locality
    5.2. Identifies the different types of fronts shown on a weather map
    5.3. Describes the weather conditions surrounding each front shown on a weather map
    5.4. Identifies the direction of movement for each front shown on a weather map
    5.5. Explains ways global patterns of atmospheric movement influence local weather
    5.6. Constructs a weather map using a written description of existing conditions

6. Measures relevant weather characteristics
    6.1. Measures and records changes in air pressure
    6.2. Measures and records direction and velocity of wind
    6.3. Measures relative humidity

The list of objectives is limited to those outcomes that can be measured by a classroom assessment. The form of the test question or assessment task may vary as a function of the outcome. Outcomes involving verbs such as *identifies, distinguishes,* or *matches* are effectively and efficiently measured by multiple-choice or other types of objective test items. Those involving verbs such as *names* or *draws* are readily measured by simple supply-type items where students are asked to "fill in the blank." Outcomes using verbs such as *describes* or *explains* can be measured by skillfully constructed objective items but are often more readily and better measured by essay questions. Those involving verbs such as *constructs, delivers,* or *measures* most clearly require performance assessment tasks. The listed objectives do not include affective outcomes (e.g., demonstrating scientific attitude). A more elaborate evaluation plan for a weather unit might contain a listing of all relevant outcomes with an indication of how each is to be assessed.

Outlining the Instructional Content.   The second step in preparing a table of specifications is to make an outline of the instructional content. The instructional objectives describe the types of performance the students are expected to demonstrate; the instructional content indicates the area in which each type of performance is to be shown. The amount of detail to include in the content outline is somewhat arbitrary, but the outline should be detailed enough to ensure an adequate sampling of content and proper interpretation of the results. The following list of topics and subtopics for a weather unit illustrates an adequate outline for test and assessment preparation.

Content Outline for a Weather Unit
A. Air pressure
    1. Measuring and reporting air pressure
    2. Factors affecting air pressure
    3. Relation to weather changes
B. Air temperature
    1. Measuring and reporting air temperature
    2. Factors affecting air temperature
    3. Relation to weather formations
C. Humidity and precipitation
    1. Measuring and reporting humidity
    2. Factors affecting humidity

   3. Forms of precipitation
   4. Measuring and reporting precipitation
 D. Wind
   1. Measurement of speed and direction
   2. Factors affecting speed and direction
   3. Symbols for reporting speed and direction
 E. Clouds
   1. Types of clouds
   2. Characteristics of cloud types
   3. Factors causing cloud formations
   4. Relation to weather conditions
   5. Symbols for cloud types
 F. Fronts
   1. Types of fronts
   2. Formation of fronts
   3. Weather related to fronts
   4. Symbols for fronts

Preparing the Two-Way Chart.   The final step in building a table of specifications is to prepare a two-way chart that relates the instructional objectives to the instructional content, thus specifying the nature of the sample of test items and assessment tasks. An example of the chart for our junior high weather unit is presented in Table 6.2. This table indicates both the total number of test items and assessment tasks and the percentage allotted to each objective and each area of content. For classroom testing, using the number of items may be sufficient, but the percentages are useful in determining the amount of emphasis to give to each area.

Table 6.2
Table of specifications for a weather unit in a middle school earth science class

Content	Knows — Basic Terms	Knows — Weather Symbols	Knows — Specific Facts	Understands — Influence of Each Factor on Weather Formation	Interprets — Weather Maps	Total Number of Items	Percentage of Items
Air pressure	1	1	1	3	3	9	15
Wind	1	1	1	10	2	15	25
Temperature	1	1	1	4	2	9	15
Humidity and precipitation	1	1	1	7	5	15	25
Clouds	2	2	2	6		12	20
Total number of items	6	6	6	30	12	60	
Percentage of items	10	10	10	50	20		100

Table 6.2 is limited to those objectives that can be measured with a classroom test with objective or restricted-response essay items. It excludes those objectives requiring performance (e.g., 4.7, an oral presentation; 5.6, constructing a weather map; and 6.1 through 6.3, using weather instruments). Thus, for comprehensive coverage, the classroom test would need to be supplemented by a set of performance assessment tasks. The relative weight to be given to the results of the performance assessments and the classroom test in the assignment of course grades should be determined in accordance with the relative importance of the objectives. It is critical that important objectives that cannot be assessed by the classroom test be identified so that plans for assessing the achievement of those objectives can be made. In this example, a simple list of five performance assessment tasks corresponding to instructional objectives 4.7, 5.6, 6.1, 6.2, and 6.3, together with a plan for the relative weight to be given to the scores on those tasks and the classroom test, would suffice.

Table 6.2 was prepared using the following steps.

1. List the general instructional objectives across the top of the table.
2. List the major content areas down the left side of the table.
3. Determine what proportion of the test items should be devoted to each objective and each content area.

The bottom row of Table 6.2 shows that 10% of the items are to be devoted to knowledge of basic terms, 10% to knowledge of weather symbols, 10% to knowledge of specific facts, 50% to understanding influence of weather factors, and 20% to interpretation of weather maps. Similarly, the column on the far right shows that 15% of the items are to be concerned with air pressure, 25% with wind, and so on down the column. Typically, these percentages are assigned first to indicate the relative emphasis to be given to each objective and each content area. The total number of items for each area is then determined. For example, because this is to be a 60-item test, 6 of the items (10%) are to measure knowledge of basic terms, and 9 of the items (15%) are concerned with air pressure. Thus, the total number of items is computed and listed across the bottom and down the right-hand side of the chart. These numbers are then used as a guide to assign test items to each cell. For example, 2 items (approximately 33% of 6) have been assigned to the cell in the lower-left-hand corner, indicating that the test will contain 2 items measuring knowledge of terms concerning clouds. The assignment of items to each cell is not strictly a matter of following the percentages, however. Some cells may be left blank, as shown in the chain, because items in those areas are inappropriate. Similarly, some cells may receive a larger number of items because they correspond to more important instructional objectives, and consequently the learning tasks for that cell may have received greater emphasis in teaching. In the example, 10 of the 60 items would be allocated to assessing a student's understanding of wind on weather formation, whereas only a single item would be included to measure knowledge of a specific fact about wind. Such a disproportionate allocation is appropriate if it is consistent with the intended and actual instructional priority given to understanding the influences of wind on weather formation. The table of specifications provides guidance in constructing the test. The actual test may deviate slightly from those specifications for specific cells, but the number of items in the cells of the table should approximate the desired distribution and should add up to the total number of items indicated for each column and row.

The final distribution of items in the table of specifications combined with performance assessments that are not part of the classroom tests should reflect the emphasis given during the instruction. Objectives considered more important by the teacher should be allotted more test items. This applies not only to the items within the classroom test but also to performance assessment tasks. The weight given to the performance of such assessment tasks should reflect the importance of the objective. Similarly, areas of content receiving more instruction time should be allocated more test items and assessment tasks. Although the decisions involved in making the table are somewhat arbitrary and the process is time consuming, the preparation of a table of test specifications, together with a listing of performance assessment tasks needed to supplement the test, is one of the best means for ensuring that the total set of test items and assessment tasks will measure a representative sample of instructionally relevant objectives. As noted in Chapter 4, this provides content-related evidence that the test will provide a valid measure of the intended learning outcomes. The effort that goes into developing specifications also makes it much easier to prepare the test once the plan is developed.

Other Examples of Specifications

Because of its broad coverage, a table of specifications is especially useful in constructing a test or assessment over a unit or course. Here the table ensures that each of the diverse types of learning outcomes will receive appropriate emphasis in the test. Whether a table of specifications is useful in constructing a test over a more limited area, however, depends on the scope of learning outcomes to be covered by the test. If the domain of tasks is very limited, such as "addition of fractions with the same denominator," a table of specifications might be unnecessary. Here we could simply list all, or nearly all, of the specific tasks encompassed by this learning outcome, as follows:

- Adds two fractions with same denominator where the answer is less than 1 (1/3 + 1/3).
- Adds two fractions with same denominator where the answer equals 1 (1/3 + 2/3).
- Adds two fractions with same denominator where the answer is greater than 1 (2/3 + 2/3).
- Adds two fractions with same denominator and reduces answer to lowest terms (4/6 + 4/6).
- Adds more than two fractions with same denominator and reduces answer (1/8 + 5/8 + 6/8).

A list of learning tasks such as this specifies quite clearly the precise nature of the performance involved in "the addition of fractions with the same denominator." We could obtain a fairly representative sample of such tasks by simply constructing five or more items for each task, using various number combinations.

If our mathematics test were to cover a slightly larger achievement domain, say, "addition of fractions," we might now find a table of specifications quite useful. An illustration of such a table for a 50-item test is shown in Table 6.3. The use of such a table does not mean, of course, that we should not make the type of detailed breakdown we did for

Table 6.3

Table of specifications for a 50-item test on addition of fractions

Content Area	Instructional Objectives			
	Adds Fractions	*Adds Fractions and Mixed Numbers*	*Adds Mixed Numbers*	*Total Items*
Denominators are alike	5	5	5	15
Denominators are unlike (with common factor)	5	5	5	15
Denominators are unlike (without common factor)	6	7	7	20
Total items	16	17	17	50

"addition of fractions with the same denominator." Such a detailed listing of tasks aids in teaching, in detecting learning errors, and in constructing test items. The table of specifications, however, supplements such lists by specifying the sample of tasks to be included in the test. As noted earlier, this provides greater assurance that the intended learning outcomes will be measured in a balanced manner.

A simple list such as that given for "addition of fractions with the same denominator" or specifications such as those in Table 6.3 can be readily constructed for the operational skills aspects of addition of fractions. It is often more difficult, however, to construct specifications that do justice to objectives of understanding concepts or the ability to apply the concepts in novel settings. This is made clear even with the relatively narrow topic of fractions by considering the National Council of Teachers of Mathematics (NCTM) Standard 12: Fractions and Decimals for Grades K–4. Among other things, that standard states that students should "develop concepts of fractions, mixed numbers, and decimals" and "apply fractions and decimals to problem situations" (NCTM, 1989).

Using Standard 12 as a statement of instructional goals for fractions, the assessment would clearly need to include tasks that measure students' conceptual understanding of fractions and their ability to apply fractions in novel problem situations. To ensure the inclusion of such tasks, understanding concepts and applications of fractions should be included in the table of specifications. Although the specifications in Table 6.3 might be appropriate for one segment of instruction, specifications similar to those in Table 6.4 might be more appropriate at another stage of instruction.

Because Table 6.4 is expressed in terms of the percentage of points associated with each combination of objectives and content area, a decision would need to be made about the total number of points. Because the points are to be obtained from a combination of a classroom test and a set of performance assessment tasks, additional specifications would also be needed to allocate the points to the different sources of information. A single performance assessment task involving relationships between decimals and fractions, for example, might be scored on a 5-point scale. Assuming a total

Table 6.4

Table of specifications for fractions and decimals showing targeted percentage of points from a combination of a classroom test and a set of performance assessment tasks

| Content Area | Instructional Objectives | | | |
	Procedural Skills	Understanding	Application	Total Percentage of Points
Simple fractions	5	10	5	20
Mixed numbers	5	15	10	30
Decimals	5	10	5	20
Decimal–fraction relationships	10	10	10	30
Total percentage of points	25	45	30	100

Table 6.5

List of reading comprehension skills and number of items for each specific skill

Reading Skill	Number of Items
Identifies details stated in a passage	10
Identifies the main idea of a passage	10
Identifies the sequence of actions or events	10
Identifies relationships expressed in a passage	10
Total number	50

of 100 points, that task would represent half the targeted total of 10 points for that cell. The other 5 points might then be allocated to five short-answer test items.

Using a One-Way Classification System

For tests in some areas, a one-way classification of items may be all that is needed. In planning for a reading test, for example, a list of the reading skills and the number of test items for measuring each skill may be sufficient for specifying what the test is to measure. The content (e.g., passages read) may vary from time to time, but the skill outcomes remain fairly constant. Thus, a master list of skills can be prepared for use with various types of reading material. An example of such a list is presented in Table 6.5.

It should be noted that each skill in Table 6.5 is stated in specific performance terms and that 10 items are used to measure each skill. This provides for criterion-referenced interpretation. Although the material to be read is not included in the specifications, it will, of course, need to be carefully selected in terms of interest and readability level. See the "Checklist" box.

CHECKLIST

Reviewing Specifications for Tests and Assessments

	Yes	No
1. Are the specifications in harmony with the purpose of the test or assessment?	____	____
2. Do the specifications indicate the nature and limits of the achievement domain?	____	____
3. Do the specifications indicate the types of learning outcomes to be measured?	____	____
4. Do the specifications indicate the sample of learning outcomes to be measured?	____	____
5. Is the number of test items of assessment tasks indicated for each subdivision?	____	____
6. Are the types of items and tasks to be used appropriate for the outcomes to be measured?	____	____
7. Is the distribution of items and tasks adequate for the types of interpretation to be made?	____	____
8. If sample items or tasks are included, do they illustrate the desired attributes?	____	____
9. Do the specifications, as a whole, indicate a representative sample of instructionally relevant tasks that fits the use to be made of the results?	____	____

SELECTING APPROPRIATE TYPES OF ITEMS AND ASSESSMENT TASKS

It is common to make a distinction between classroom tests that consist of objective test items and performance assessments that require students to construct responses (e.g., write an essay) or perform a particular task (e.g., measure air pressure). Objective test items are highly structured and require the students to supply a word or two or to select the correct answer from alternatives. They are called objective because they have a single right or best answer that can be determined in advance. Performance assessment tasks, such as essay questions, permit the student to organize and construct the answer in essay form. Other types of performance assessment tasks may require the student to use equipment, generate hypotheses, make observations, construct something (e.g., a model), or perform for an audience (e.g., give a speech). For most performance assessment tasks, there is not a single right or best response—there may be a variety of responses that are considered excellent. Problem identification may, in fact, be an important part of the task, and, of course, there may be multiple ways of structuring the problem and organizing a response. Expert judgment is required to score the performances. There is no conflict between these highly constrained objective items and the much less constrained performance assessment tasks. For some instructional purposes, objective items may be most efficient, whereas for others, performance assessments may prove most satisfactory. Each approach should be used where most appropriate, with appropriateness determined by the learning outcomes to be measured and by the advantages and limitations of each approach.

The Objective Test Item

Various forms and uses of objective items are discussed in greater detail in Chapters 7 to 9. Here we provide only a quick overview.

The great variety of different types of objective test items can be classified into those that require the student to supply the answer and those that require the student to select the answer from a given number of alternatives. These two general classes are commonly divided into basic types of objective test items, illustrated in the accompanying examples.

EXAMPLES **SUPPLY TYPES**

Short Answer

What is the name of the author of *Moby Dick? (Herman Melville)*
What is the formula for hydrochloric acid? (*HCl*)
What is the value of *X* in the equation $2X + 5 = 9$? (*2*)

Completion

Lines on a weather map joining points with the same barometric pressure are called_____.
   (*isobars*)

The formula for ordinary table salt is_____. (*NaCl*)
In the equation $2X + 5 = 9$, $X = .$_____(*2*)

SELECTION TYPES

Matching

(C)	1. And	A. Adjective
(D)	2. Dog	B. Adverb
(G)	3. Jump	C. Conjunction
(F)	4. She	D. Noun
(B)	5. Quickly	E. Preposition
		F. Pronoun
		G. Verb

True–False or Alternative Response

Ⓣ   F   A virus is the smallest known organism.

T   Ⓕ   An atom is the smallest particle of matter.

Yes   (No)   In the equation $2X + 5 = 9$; X equals 3.

(Yes)   No   Acid turns litmus paper red.

Multiple Choice

In the equation $2X + 5 = 9$, $2X$ means

    A   2 plus X.
    B   2 minus X.
    C   2 divided by X.
    Ⓓ   2 multiplied by X.

In which of the following sentences do the subject and verb disagree?

    A   When they win, they are happy.
    Ⓑ   Politics are hard to understand.
    C   The majority is always right.
    D   One or the other is to be elected.

In addition to these basic types of objective test items are numerous modifications and combinations of types. However, little is to be gained from listing all the possible variations, as many are unique to particular objectives or subject-matter areas. Some of the more common variations used to measure understanding, thinking skills, and other complex learning outcomes are illustrated later. An understanding of the principles of test construction and the principles that apply to each of the specific types of objective test items should enable teachers to make adaptations that best fit their particular purposes.

The various types of objective test items have one feature in common that distinguishes them from performance assessment tasks: They present students with a highly structured task that limits the type of response they can make. To obtain the correct answer, students must demonstrate the specific knowledge, understanding, or skill called for in the item; they are not free to redefine the problem or to organize and present the answer in their own words. They must select one of several alternative answers or supply the correct word, number, or symbol. This structuring of the problem and restriction on the method of responding contribute to objective scoring that is quick, easy, and accurate. On the negative side, this same structuring makes the objective test item inappropriate for measuring the ability to formulate problems and choose an approach to solving them or the ability to select, organize, and integrate ideas. To measure such outcomes, we must depend on performance assessment tasks. Performance assessment tasks are also needed to measure a student's ability to engage in hands-on activities, such as conducting an experiment, measuring precipitation, designing and conducting a survey, or creating an art object.

Because written essays are the most commonly used form of performance assessment tasks, it is worth focusing on essay questions before considering other types of performance assessment tasks. The essay question is commonly viewed as one item type. A useful classification, however, is one based on the amount of freedom of response the student is allowed. This includes extended-response essay questions, in which students are given almost complete freedom in making their responses, and restricted-response essay questions, in which the nature, length, or organization of the response is limited. These types of essay questions are illustrated as follows:

EXAMPLES **EXTENDED-RESPONSE ESSAY QUESTIONS**

Describe what you think the role of the federal government should be in maintaining a stable economy in the United States. Include specific policies and programs and give reasons for your proposals.

Explain how clouds are formed and how they affect weather and climate.

Predict the effects that an increase in interest rates would have on consumers, producers, and investors. Include an explanation of how your predictions follow from fundamental economic principles.

RESTRICTED-RESPONSE ESSAY QUESTIONS

State two advantages and two disadvantages of maintaining high tariffs on goods from other countries.

Name two types of clouds and describe the characteristics that distinguish them.

The percentage of the workforce that is unemployed increased following an increase in interest rates. Briefly explain the relationship.

Extended-response essay questions permit students to decide which facts they think are most pertinent, to select their own method of organization, and to write as much as seems necessary for a comprehensive answer. Thus, such questions tend to reveal the ability to evaluate ideas, to relate them coherently, and to express them succinctly. To a lesser extent, they also reflect individual differences in attitudes, values, and creative ability.

Although extended essay questions are valuable for measuring complex skills and understanding of concepts and principles, they have three weaknesses: (1) They are inefficient for measuring knowledge of factual material because the questions are so extensive that only a small sample of content can be included in any one assessment; (2) the scoring criteria are not as apparent to the student because it is not listed with the item; and (3) scoring is difficult and apt to be unreliable because the responses include an array of factual information of varying degrees of correctness, organized with varying degrees of coherence, and expressed with varying degrees of legibility and conciseness. Hence, extended essay questions are best used to assess more complex cognitive objectives involving application, evaluation, or the ability to express ideas in coherent, persuasive ways.

Restricted-response essay questions minimize some of the weaknesses of extended-response essay questions. Restricting the type of response makes it easier to measure knowledge of factual material, makes the scoring more clear to the student, and reduces somewhat the difficulty of the scoring. On the other hand, the more highly structured task presented by the restricted-response essay questions makes them less effective as a measure of the ability to select, organize, and integrate ideas. Furthermore, if the restrictions become too tight, the questions reduce to nothing more than a supply-type item.

Neither extended-response essay questions nor restricted-response essay questions can serve all purposes equally. The type of essay question to use in a particular situation depends primarily on the learning outcomes to be measured and, to a lesser extent, on such practical considerations as the difficulty of scoring.

Other Types of Performance Assessment

There are many other types of performance assessment tasks. Examples include oral presentations; construction of graphs, diagrams, or models; use of equipment or scientific instruments; typing; and playing a musical instrument. Tasks are selected so that the performance corresponds as closely as possible to an important instructional objective.

A distinction can be made between restricted-response performance tasks and extended-response performance tasks. These types are illustrated as follows:

EXAMPLES **EXTENDED-RESPONSE PERFORMANCE TASKS**

Prepare a weather report for another state and make an oral presentation of the report to the class using appropriate visual displays.

Take four strips of different-colored paper that are each 6 inches in length. Cut the white strip into two parts of equal length, the yellow strip into three parts of equal length, the green strip into four parts of equal length, and the blue strip into six parts of equal length. Compare the lengths when different numbers of pieces of strips are put together (e.g., two pieces of the yellow strip compared to three pieces of the blue strip) and describe the relationship between corresponding fractions (e.g., 2/3 and 3/6).

RESTRICTED-RESPONSE PERFORMANCE TASKS

Measure and record the relative humidity.

Take a number of 1-inch-square pieces of paper to use. Assuming each square represents the fraction 1/4, construct a whole. (Can be repeated using different fractions.)

The virtues and limitations of extended- and restricted-response performance tasks are much the same as those listed for extended- and restricted-response essay questions. The freedom provided by the extended-response performance task enables students to display such important skills as problem solving, planning, organization, integration, and creativity. Questions of this type also provide an opportunity to observe student performance in more realistic contexts than are possible with objective test items. On the other hand, they are time consuming to administer and difficult to score.

Restricted-response performance tasks are generally easier to score and require less time than extended-response performance tasks. However, they are generally less suited for measuring the higher-order skills measured by extended-response performance tasks.

Comparative Advantages of Objective Test Items and Performance Assessment Tasks

Both objective test items and performance assessment tasks can provide valuable evidence concerning student achievement. Each has advantages and limitations that make it more appropriate for some purposes than for others. A comparison of the relative merits of objective item tests and performance assessments is presented in Table 6.6. In considering the comparative advantages of objective-item tests and performance assessments, we must be careful not to fall into either/or thinking, that is, to use either objective items or performance assessment tasks. It is frequently better to use both, with each measuring the particular learning outcomes for which it is best suited. This should also have a desirable influence on student learning because in preparing for such tests students must attend to the specific types of learning outcomes measured by objective items as well as the synthesis and integrated performance outcomes measured by performance assessment tasks.

Selecting the Most Appropriate Types of Items and Tasks

A basic principle in selecting the type of test item and assessment task to use is to **select the item type that provides the most direct measure of the intended learning outcome**. If, for example, the intended learning outcome is writing, naming, listing, or speaking, the task should require the students to supply the answer. If the outcome involves the use of laboratory equipment to solve a problem, nothing short of an actual laboratory performance task will suffice. On the other hand, if the task calls for idntifying a correct answer, a selection-type item should be used. In those cases where the specific learning outcome does not make clear which item type to use, selection-type items would be favored because of the greater control over the student's response and the objectivity of the scoring. However, the intended learning outcome may also require more complex items or direct measures of performance. The following items were prepared for the weather unit discussed earlier. Note how each type of objective item provides a direct measure of the outcome it was designed to measure.

EXAMPLE   **SHORT-ANSWER ITEMS**

Specific Learning Outcome: Writes a definition of each term.

Directions: Write a one-sentence definition of each of the following terms.
   1. Weather
   2. Humidity
   3. Occluded front

Specific Learning Outcome: Names the instrument used for measuring each weather element.

   1. The instrument used to measure the amount of precipitation in a given locality is called a (an) _____.

Table 6.6

Comparative advantages of objective tests and performance assessments

	Objective Test	*Performance Assessment*
Learning outcomes measured	Is efficient for measuring knowledge of facts. Some types (e.g., multiple choice) can also measure understanding, thinking skills, and other complex outcomes. Inefficient or inappropriate for measuring ability to select and organize ideas, writing abilities, and some types of problem-solving skills.	Can measure understanding, thinking skills, and other complex learning outcomes (especially useful where originality of response is desired). Appropriate for measuring performance on tasks corresponding to important instructional objectives in realistic contexts. Is inefficient for measuring knowledge of facts.
Preparation of questions	A relatively large number of questions are needed for a test. Preparation is difficult and time consuming.	Only a few tasks are needed for an assessment.
Sampling of course content	Provides an extensive sampling of coursecontent because of the large number of questions that can be included in a test.	Sampling of course content is usually limited because of the small number of tasks that can be included in an assessment.
Control of student response	Complete structuring of task limits students to type of response called for. Prevents bluffing and avoids influence of writing skill, though selection-type items are subject to guessing.	Freedom to respond in own way enables students to display originality, and guessing is minimized.
Scoring	Objective scoring.	Judgmental scoring.
Influence on learning	Usually encourages student to develop a comprehensive knowledge of specific facts and the ability to make fine discriminations among them. Can encourage the development of understanding, thinking skills, and other complex outcomes if properly constructed.	Encourages students to concentrate on larger units of subject matter, with special emphasis on the ability to organize, integrate, and express ideas effectively.
Reliability	High reliability is possible and is typically obtained with well-constructed tests.	Reliability is typically low, primarilybecause of a limited sample of tasks and inconsistent scoring.

Specific Learning Outcome: Lists the characteristics of a given weather phenomenon.

   1. List three main characteristics of a hurricane.

Specific Learning Outcome: Measures relative humidity.

   1. Use the appropriate instrument to measure the relative humidity and record the value obtained.

MULTIPLE-CHOICE ITEMS

Specific Learning Outcome: Identifies the units of measurement used in reporting each weather element on a weather map.

   1. United States weather maps indicate air pressure in

A inches
B feet
Ⓒ pounds
D millibars

TRUE–FALSE ITEMS

Specific Learning Outcome: Distinguishes between correct and incorrect procedures for determining each weather element.

    T   Ⓕ   1.   Dew point is determined by cooling a sample of air until it is free of moisture.

    Ⓣ   F   2.   Ceiling is determined by using balloons that rise at known rates.

MATCHING ITEMS

Specific Learning Outcome: Matches each weather instrument to the weather element it measures.

Directions: On the line to the left of each weather element in Column A, write the letter of the weather instrument in Column B that is used for measuring it. Each instrument in Column B may be used once, more than once, or not at all.

Column A	*Column B*
(B) 1. Air pressure	A. Anemometer
(E) 2. Air temperature	B. Barometer
(C) 3. Humidity	C. Hygrometer
(A) 4. Wind velocity	D. Rain gauge
	E. Thermometer
	F. Wind vane

PERFORMANCE TASKS

Specific Learning Outcome: Measures and records changes in air pressure.

Directions: Measure the air pressure on 5 consecutive days at the same time of day and graph it to see the changes. Explain the reasons for the changes that occur.

In deciding which selection-type item to use, a common practice is to use the multiple-choice item if it will measure the learning outcome as directly as the other two types. The use of true–false items is typically most valuable in those special instances where there are only two possible alternatives (e.g., distinguishing between correct and incorrect procedures). The matching item is a specialized form of the multiple-choice item and should be used only where a series of homogeneous things are to be related (e.g., dates and events, authors and books, or instruments and uses). The multiple-choice item is favored for most other selection-type tasks because the use of four or five alternatives reduces the chances of guessing the answer and provides clues to students' misunderstandings. See Appendix G for other examples of how to relate test items to intended learning outcomes.

Whether a test item or an assessment task actually measures the particular performance called for by a specific learning outcome depends, of course, to a large extent on the skill with which the test item or assessment task is constructed. No amount of skill, however, will enable us to develop a valid test or assessment of achievement if the items or tasks selected for use are inappropriate for measuring the intended outcomes.

CONSIDERATIONS IN PREPARING RELEVANT TEST ITEMS AND ASSESSMENT TASKS

The construction of items and tasks should be preceded by a series of preliminary steps. First, the purpose of the test or assessment should be determined. Second, a set of specifications should be developed. Third, the most appropriate types of test items and performance assessment tasks should be selected. Finally, items and tasks should be constructed in accordance with the specifications developed during the preceding steps. The rules for constructing each type of objective item are discussed in Chapters 7 through 9, and rules for constructing performance assessments are discussed in Chapters 10 and 11. Here we focus on general considerations involved in preparing relevant objective items and assessment tasks.

Matching Items and Tasks to Intended Outcomes

Classroom tests and assessments are most likely to provide a valid measure of the instructional objectives if the test items and assessment tasks are designed to measure the performance defined by the specific learning outcomes. The process of matching test items and assessment tasks to the learning outcomes to be measured was illustrated earlier. Essentially, it involves fitting each item or task as closely as possible to the intended outcome, as follows:

EXAMPLE   *Specific Learning Outcome:*   Identifies the function of a given body structure.

Relevant Test Item:

What is the function of the kidneys?
- Ⓐ   Eliminate waste products
- B   Improve the circulation of blood
- C   Maintain respiration
- D   Stimulate digestion

Thus, the preparation of relevant test items and assessment tasks means analyzing the performance described in the specific learning outcome (i.e., "Identifies the function of . . . ") and constructing a test item or assessment task that calls forth that performance (i.e., "What is the function of . . . ?"). Note that the specific learning outcome defines the type of response the student is expected to make, but it does not indicate the specific course content (i.e., kidney) the student is to identify. Keeping the learning outcome free of specific course content makes it possible to key the intended response to various areas of content. For example, students could be asked to identify the function of the heart, the lungs, the muscles, or any other body structure pertinent to the course's content. The desired student performance stated in the specific learning outcome can be keyed to each specific area of content by means of the table of specifications.

In some cases, it may be desirable to prepare a general item pattern as an intermediate step between the specific learning outcome and the test item. A general item pattern for our illustrative test item would be as follows:

EXAMPLE   What is the function of . . . ?

An item pattern such as this could be completed adding the name of any body structure and using it as a short-answer question or by listing appropriate alternatives and using it as a multiple-choice item. Thus, using the item pattern as a guide, we could generate large numbers of relevant test items for this particular learning outcome. This procedure is especially useful when a file of test items is being prepared or when more than one form of the test is needed (e.g., pretesting, posttesting, and retesting).

When item patterns are used as a guide to test construction, they can be arranged by general type of learning outcome.

EXAMPLES **Knowledge Outcomes**

1. What is the name of . . . ?
2. What is the location of . . . ?
3. What are the characteristics of . . . ?
4. What is the function of . . . ?

Understanding Outcomes

1. What is the reason for . . . ?
2. What is the relationship between . . . ?
3. Which of these is an example of . . . ?
4. Which of these best summarizes . . . ?

Application Outcomes

1. What method would be best for . . . ?
2. What steps should be followed to construct . . . ?
3. Which of these indicates correct application of . . . ?
4. Which of these solutions is correct for . . . ?

Item patterns such as these should not, of course, be developed haphazardly. Rather, they should be derived from the specific learning outcomes they represent. Although it usually will not be possible to develop item patterns for all outcomes, listing them will help generate pools of relevant test items. The test construction time saved by using such a list can then be used to construct more effective items for those areas in which general item patterns are not feasible.

Obtaining a Representative Sample of Items and Tasks

A test or assessment, no matter how extensive, is almost always a sample of the many possible test items or tasks that could be included. We expect students to know thousands of facts, but we can test for only a limited number of them; we expect students to develop understanding applicable to innumerable situations, but we can test application to only a limited number of situations; and we expect students to develop thinking skills that will enable them to solve a variety of problems, but we can test their problem-solving ability with only a limited number of problems. In each area of content and for each specific learning outcome, then, we merely select a sample of student performance and accept it as evidence of achievement in that area. We assume that the students' responses to our selected set of items and tasks are typical of what their responses would be to other items and tasks drawn from the same area. This means, of course, that our limited samples must be selected in such a way that they provide as representative a sample as possible in each of the various areas for which the test or assessment is being developed.

Our sampling is most likely to be representative when the preparation of a test or assessment is guided by a carefully prepared set of specifications. Unless a table of specifications or some similar device is used as a guide in construction, there is a tendency to overload the test with items measuring knowledge of isolated facts and to neglect more complex learning outcomes. In social studies, for example, it is not uncommon to include a disproportionately large number of items that measure knowledge of names, dates, places, and the like. In science, defining terms and naming structures and functions are commonly overemphasized. In mathematics, computational skill is frequently the only learning outcome measured. In language arts and literature, the identification of parts of speech, literary characters, authors, and the like is frequently too prominent. These learning outcomes are stressed not because we think that knowledge of isolated facts is more important than understanding, applications, interpretations, and various thinking skills. Rather, they usually receive undue prominence because we find it easier to construct this kind of test item. Without a carefully developed test plan, ease of construction all too frequently becomes the dominant criterion in constructing test items. As a consequence, the test measures a limited and biased sample of learning tasks and neglects many learning outcomes of greater importance.

Supplementing objective test questions with performance assessment tasks is one means of ensuring that broader learning objectives are given proper attention. However, it is inefficient to rely only on performance assessments to measure more complex understandings. For this reason, it is important to find ways of constructing objective test items that do more than measure factual knowledge. One approach to this goal of measuring complex achievement is through the use of interpretive exercises. This approach is discussed in detail in Chapter 9.

Number of Items and Tasks.   The number of items and tasks is, of course, an important factor in obtaining a representative sample. The number of items and the number of performance tasks are determined when the set of specifications is built and depend on such factors as the purpose of measurement, the types of test items and assessment tasks used, the age of the students, and the level of reliability needed for effective use of the test or assessment results. Thus, an assessment over a third-grade social studies unit might contain 30 objective items, whereas a survey test over a 10th-grade social studies course might contain more than 100 objective items and several essay questions. Although there are no hard-and-fast rules for determining the number of items and tasks, an important consideration from a sampling standpoint is the number of items or tasks devoted to each specific area being measured. We want our tests and assessments to be long enough to provide an adequate sampling of each objective and each content area. As a rule of thumb, it is desirable when constructing a unit test to use at least 10 objective test items to measure each specific learning outcome. This number, however, might be lowered to as few as five if the task is extremely limited (e.g., "Adds two single-digit numbers" or "Capitalizes proper names") and the students are to supply the answers rather than to select them. For a survey test, where the sample of test items typically covers a broad area and emphasis is on the total score, using several objective test items for each specific learning outcome and 10 or more for each general objective probably would be sufficient.

Special problems of sampling arise when complex learning outcomes are being measured, because this requires more elaborate objective-type items (referred to as interpretive exercises) and performance assessment tasks. Both interpretive exercises and performance assessment tasks require considerable administration time, but a single test item or assessment task is still inadequate for measuring an intended outcome. One exercise calling for the interpretation of graphs, for example, is not sufficient to measure adequately the ability to interpret graphs. The nature of the data or the type of graph may be the most influential factor in determining whether it is interpreted properly. When several graphs are used, the effect of such factors is minimized, and we obtain a more representative sample of the ability to interpret graphs.

A similar situation occurs with the use of performance assessment tasks. The performance of any single task depends too heavily on the particular sample of information called for by the task, and thus the only feasible solution is to confine each assessment of complex outcomes to a rather limited area (e.g., graph interpretation or problem solving) and to assess more often. In any event, our aim should be to obtain as representative a sample of student performance as possible in each area to be assessed. Other things being equal, the greater the number of test items or assessment tasks, the greater the likelihood of an adequate sample and the more reliable the results.

Eliminating Irrelevant Barriers to the Performance

As was discussed in Chapter 4, the validity of the assessment may be undermined by the influence of construct-irrelevant factors or abilities that are ancillary to the intent of the assessment. Hence, care must be taken when constructing items or assessment tasks to eliminate any construct-irrelevant factors that might prevent students from performing their best. If students have achieved a particular learning outcome (e.g., knowledge of terms), we would want them to answer correctly those test items that measure the attainment of that learning outcome. We would be very unhappy (and so would they) if they answered such test items incorrectly merely because the sentence structure was too complex, the vocabulary too difficult, or the type of response called for unclear. These factors, which are extraneous to the central purpose of the measurement, limit and modify the students' responses and prevent them from showing their true levels of achievement. Such factors are as unfair as determining a person's running ability when an ankle is sprained. Although a measure of running ability would be obtained, the performance would be restricted by a factor we did not intend to include in our measurement.

One way to eliminate factors that are extraneous to the purpose of a measurement is to be certain that all students have the prerequisite skills and abilities needed to make the response. These have been called enabling behaviors because they enable the student to make the response but are not meant to be critical factors in the measurement. That is, they are a necessary but not sufficient condition for responding correctly or performing a task well. Probably the most important enabling behavior in objective testing is reading skill. In written performance assessments, skill in written expression is an additional factor to be considered. In measuring understanding, thinking skills, and other complex learning outcomes, knowledge of certain facts and simple computational skills also might be necessary prerequisites.

In constructing tests and assessments, then, we need to strive for items and tasks that measure achievement of the specific learning outcomes and not differences in ancillary abilities. Differences in reading ability, computational skill, communication skills, and the like should not influence the students' responses unless such outcomes are specifically being measured. The only functional difference between those students who perform well on a task and those who perform poorly should be the possession of the knowledge, understanding, or other learning outcome being measured by the task. All other differences are extraneous to the purpose of the task, and their influence should be eliminated or controlled for valid results.

A special problem in preventing extraneous factors from distorting our test and assessment results is avoiding ambiguity. Objective test items are especially subject to misinterpretation when long, complex sentences are used; when the vocabulary is unnecessarily difficult; and when words that lack precise meaning are used. Thus, from the viewpoint of both level of reading difficulty and preciseness of meaning, the antidote for ambiguity seems to be a careful choice of words and the use of brief, concise sentences. In some cases, ambiguity can be reduced by using pictures or other illustrative material in place of verbal descriptions. When this is done, the illustrative material must, of course, also be carefully checked to make sure it is clear and unambiguous.

Care should be taken to avoid any racial, ethnic, or gender bias in preparing the test items and performance assessment tasks. The vocabulary and task situations should be acceptable to various racial and ethnic groups and to both males and females and should be free of stereotyping. For example, in presenting characters in a story problem, a reading passage, or other test situation, minorities should not be portrayed in stereotypical fashion. Similarly, task situations should not always place males in such traditional roles as athlete, business executive, and professional person and females in such traditional roles as homemaker, teacher, and nurse. A balanced use of different roles for minorities and males and females is necessary if we are to avoid bias as a possible barrier to maximum performance. See the "Guidelines" box.

Avoiding Unintended Clues in Objective Test Items

Test items should be constructed so that students obtain the correct answer only if they have attained the desired learning outcome. In the preceding principle, we were concerned with those factors that prevent students from responding correctly even though they have attained the desired learning outcome. Here we are concerned with those factors that

---

GUIDELINES

Possible Barriers in Test Items and Assessment Tasks

- Ambiguous statements
- Excessive wordiness
- Difficult vocabulary
- Complex sentence structure
- Unclear instructions
- Unclear illustrative material
- Racial, ethnic, or gender bias

enable students to respond correctly even though they lack the necessary achievement. These are the clues, some rather obvious and some very subtle, that inadvertently creep into test items during construction. They lead the poor achiever to the correct answer and thereby prevent the items from functioning as intended. When test items are short-circuited in this manner, they provide invalid evidence of achievement. Note how *an* provides a clue to the following item.

EXAMPLE   A porpoise is an

    A. plant
    B. reptile
    Ⓒ animal
    D. bird

Such clues are not limited to selection-type items, as shown in the following supply-type item.

EXAMPLE   A piece of land that is completely surrounded by water is known as an _____.

The clue is much less obvious to the person constructing this test item than the clue in our first illustration. To the student taking the test, however, it is readily apparent. The two most plausible answers are *island* and *peninsula*. Because *peninsula* begins with a consonant sound and does not follow the article *an*, it is ruled out as a possibility. This does not imply, of course, that students need to know the rules for good grammatical structure in order to use clues; most clues are analyzed in terms of partial knowledge and hunches. *An peninsula* just does not sound right to the student, so the word *island* is used, and the correct answer is obtained.

Leads to the correct answer may also be provided by simple verbal associations. Note how the word *wind* in the following item provides a clue to the answer.

EXAMPLE   Which of the following instruments is used to determine the direction of the wind?

    A Anemometer
    B Barometer
    C Hygrometer
    Ⓓ Wind vane

Rather than lead the uninformed to the correct answer, such clues should lead the poor achiever away from the correct answer. In the following item, the same clue makes *wind vane* a plausible (but incorrect) answer for those students who have not learned the uses of the various weather instruments.

EXAMPLE   Which one of the following instruments is used to determine the speed of the wind?

    A Anemometer
    B Barometer
    C Hygrometer
    (D) Wind vane

Verbal clues need not be as obvious as these. In fact, the clues that appear in the final version of a test are usually rather subtle, as they are based on partial knowledge and verbal associations not readily apparent to the casual observer. For example, at first glance the following item appears to be free from clues.

EXAMPLE   Which one of the following is used to prevent polio?

    A Gamma globulin
    B Penicillin
    C Salk vaccine
    (D) Sulfa

An examination of this item, however, will indicate that the word *vaccine* provides a clue to the answer. All the student needs to know to answer the item correctly is that a vaccine is used to prevent disease. Because most students have been vaccinated at one time or another, they probably possess this partial knowledge needed to make the clue apparent to them. Some students also may have developed a verbal association between *Salk* and *polio* and respond correctly on that basis. In either case, partial knowledge can lead to the correct answer and prevent the item from functioning as intended.

Another type of subtle clue is one based on the words used to qualify statements. For example, true–false statements that include qualifiers such as *sometimes, usually, generally*, and the like are most often true, whereas statements containing absolutes such as *always, never, none*, and *only* are most often false. Such words have been called specific determiners. They are difficult to remove from true–false items because true statements generally must be qualified, and false statements frequently must be stated in absolute terms to make them clearly false.

Other common clues in selection-type items include (a) stating correct answers in textbook language or in greater detail than incorrect answers, (b) making correct answers longer than incorrect answers, and (c) placing the correct answers in some identifiable pattern (e.g., T, F, T, F). Some of these clues are more likely to be detected by low-achieving students who are desperately searching for some basis for answering. See the "Guidelines" box.

GUIDELINES

Common Clues in Test Items

- Grammatical inconsistencies
- Verbal associations
- Specific determiners (e.g., *always*)
- Phrasing of correct responses
- Length of correct responses
- Location of correct responses

General Suggestions for Writing Test Items and Assessment Tasks

In preparing a set of test items or assessment tasks, the following general rules apply to all types of items or tasks. The specific rules for writing each item or task type are described and illustrated in the following chapters.

1. Use your test and assessment specifications as a guide. The specifications describe the performance to be measured and the sample of learning outcomes to measure. Thus, they serve as an aid for selecting the types of items and tasks to prepare, for writing, and for determining how many items and tasks are needed for each subdomain of achievement.

2. Write more items and tasks than needed. Preparing more test items and assessment tasks than needed will permit the weaker items and tasks to be discarded during later review. It will also make it easier to match the final set of items and tasks to the specifications.

3. Write the items and tasks well in advance of the testing date. Setting the items and tasks aside for several days and then reviewing them with a fresh outlook will reveal any lack of clarity or ambiguity that was overlooked during their preparation. It is frequently surprising how many defects slipped through during the original writing.

4. Write each test item and assessment task so that the task to be performed is clearly defined and it calls forth the performance described in the intended learning outcome. Clarity is obtained by carefully formulating the question and instructions, using simple and direct language, using correct punctuation and grammar, and avoiding unnecessary wording. During both writing and review, compare the task students are asked to perform to the learning outcome the task is designed to measure to make sure the two match.

5. Write each item or task at an appropriate reading level. Keep the reading difficulty and vocabulary level as simple as possible to prevent these factors from distorting the results. Students' responses should be determined by the performance being measured, not by some factor the item or task was not designed to measure.

6. Write each item or task so that it does not provide help in responding to other items or tasks. Unless care is taken during writing, one item may provide information that is useful in answering another item. For example, a name, date, or fact inadvertently included in the stem of a multiple-choice item may be called for in a short-answer item in another part of the test.

7. Write each item so that the answer is one that would be agreed on by experts or, in the case of assessment tasks, the responses judged excellent would be agreed on by experts.   This rule is easy to satisfy when measuring factual knowledge but more difficult when measuring complex outcomes calling for the extended essays or other types of performance.

8. Whenever a test item or assessment task is revised, recheck its relevance.   When reviewing items or tasks for appropriateness, clarity, difficulty, and freedom from clues and bias, some revision is often needed. After revising an item or task, check to be sure that it still provides a relevant measure of the intended learning outcome. Even slight changes can sometimes modify the function of an item or a task.

Focusing on Improving Learning and Instruction

The ultimate purpose of testing and assessment is to improve student learning. As you construct classroom tests and assessments, keep in mind the extent to which it is likely to contribute, directly or indirectly, toward this end. Well-constructed classroom tests and assessments should increase both the quantity and the quality of student learning.

1. Tests and assessments can have a desirable influence on student learning if teachers pay attention to the breadth and depth of content and learning outcomes measured.   When we select a representative sample of content from all the areas covered in our instruction, we are emphasizing to the students that they must devote attention to all areas. They cannot neglect some aspects of the course and do well on the tests. By giving more weight to high-priority objectives that are emphasized in instruction, we also encourage at the same time a concentration of effort on those objectives thought to be most important. Similarly, when our tests measure a variety of types of learning outcomes, the students soon learn that a mass of memorized factual information is not sufficient. They must also learn to interpret and apply facts, develop deep conceptual understandings, draw conclusions, recognize assumptions, identify cause-and-effect relations, generate hypotheses, solve meaningful problems, and the like. This discourages the students from depending solely on memorization as a basis for learning and encourages them to develop the use of more complex mental processes.

2. Constructing tests and assessments that measure a variety of learning outcomes should also lead to improved teaching procedures and, thus, indirectly to improved student learning.   As we translate the various learning outcomes into test items and assessment tasks, we clarify our notion of understandings, thinking skills, and other complex learning outcomes. This clarification enables us to plan the learning experiences of students more effectively and increases the degree to which we emphasize understandings, thinking skills, and other complex learning outcomes in our teaching. A well-constructed test or assessment frequently leads to a review of teaching procedures and to the abandonment of those that encourage rote learning.

3. **Tests and assessments will contribute to improved teacher–student relations (with a beneficial effect on student learning) if students view the tests and assessments as fair and useful measures of their achievement.** We can make fairness apparent by including a representative sample of the learning outcomes that have been emphasized during instruction by writing clear directions, by making certain that the intent of each item or task is clear and that each item is free of any type of bias that would prevent a knowledgeable person from performing well, and by providing adequate time limits. Student recognition of usefulness, however, depends as much on what we do with the results of the test or assessment as on the characteristics of the instrument itself. We make the usefulness apparent by using the results as a basis for guiding and improving learning.

SUMMARY

Planning the classroom tests and assessments involves (a) determining the purpose of measurement, (b) developing a set of specifications, (c) selecting appropriate types of test items and assessment tasks, and (d) preparing a set of relevant items and tasks.

Classroom tests and assessments can be used for a variety of instructional purposes, best described in terms of their location in the instructional sequence. There are (a) pretests at the beginning of a course or unit to determine learning readiness, to aid in instructional planning, and to make advanced placements; (b) tests and assessments during instruction to improve and direct student learning and to identify and remedy learning errors; and (c) end-of-instruction tests and assessments used at the end of a course or unit to assign grades, certify accomplishment, or evaluate teaching. Each of these types of classroom testing and assessment places different demands on sampling of items and tasks and the type of interpretation used (i.e., criterion referenced or norm referenced).

A sample of student performance is more likely to be representative if a set of specifications is used in planning the test or assessment. Specifications define and delimit the achievement domain to be measured and describe the sample of test items and assessment tasks to be prepared. One form of specifications is a two-way chart called a table of specifications. Building the table involves (a) obtaining the list of instructional objectives, (b) outlining the course content, and (c) preparing the two-way chart that relates the instructional objectives to the course content and specifies the nature of the desired sample of items and tasks. Although a table of specifications is especially useful in preparing summative tests and assessments (because of the broad coverage), it is also useful in preparing some formative tests and assessments. In other cases, however, a test or assessment plan might be limited to a brief list of specific and precisely stated learning outcomes, or it might contain a comprehensive and detailed set of specifications with illustrative sample items or tasks.

The major categories of objective tests or performance assessments may be further subdivided into the following basic types of test items and assessment tasks.

Objective Test

A. Supply type
  1. Short answer
  2. Completion

B. Selection type
  1. True–false or alternative response
  2. Matching
  3. Multiple choice

Performance Assessment
A. Extended response
B. Restricted response

Objective tests present students with a highly structured task that limits their response to supplying a word, brief phrase, number, or symbol or to selecting the answer from among a given number of alternatives. Performance assessments permit students to respond by selecting, organizing, and presenting ideas or performing in a way they consider appropriate. Both objective tests and performance assessments serve useful purposes in measuring student achievement. The type to use in a particular situation is best determined by the learning outcomes to be measured and by the unique advantages and limitations of each approach. A good practice is to include both objective test items and performance assessment tasks in a comprehensive measurement of student achievement.

The preparation of a set of relevant test items and assessment tasks involves (a) matching the items and tasks to the learning outcomes as directly as possible, (b) obtaining a representative sample of all intended outcomes, (c) eliminating irrelevant barriers to the answer, (d) preventing unintended clues to the response, and (e) focusing on improving learning and instruction. The rules for constructing each type of objective test item and performance assessment task are described in the chapters that follow.

LEARNING EXERCISES

1. Describe the nature of a readiness pretest and how the results might be used in teaching.
2. Describe how formative tests and assessments and summative tests and assessments differ.
3. What are the advantages of using a two-way chart when preparing specifications for tests and assessments? For what type of testing and assessment is it most useful? Why?
4. Why is it important for classroom tests and assessments to measure a representative sample of intended learning outcomes?
5. What types of information should be considered during each of the following steps in constructing tests and assessments?
   a. Developing a set of specifications
   b. Selecting the types of test items and assessment tasks to use
   c. Writing the test items and assessment tasks

6. List several learning outcomes that are best measured with objective test items. List several that require the use of performance assessment tasks.
7. List as many specific factors as you can think of that might prevent some students from performing their best even though they possessed the knowledge and skills the item or task was designed to measure.
8. List as many specific factors as you can think of that would enable some students to answer an objective test item correctly even though they lacked the knowledge the item was designed to measure.
9. Assume that you are going to prepare a brief unit test for a unit of work in a course in your major teaching area. How would you proceed? How would your procedure differ if it were to be an end-of-course summative test or assessment?

REFERENCES

National Council of Teachers of Mathematics. (1989). *Curriculum and evaluation standards for school mathematics.* Reston, VA: National Council of Teachers of Mathematics.

FURTHER READING

Gronlund, N. E. (2005). *Assessment of student achievement* (8th ed.). Boston: Allyn & Bacon. Chapter 3 provides guidelines on planning achievement tests.

Millman, J., & Greene, J. (1989). The specification and development of tests of achievement and ability. In R. L. Linn (Ed.), *Educational measurement* (3rd ed.) New York: Macmillan. A comprehensive and advanced treatment of test development.

Popham, W. J. (2007). *Classroom assessment: What teachers need to know* (5th ed.). Boston: Allyn & Bacon. Chapter 5 discusses issues of what to assess and how to assess it.

7

CONSTRUCTING OBJECTIVE TEST ITEMS: SIMPLE FORMS

Each type of test item has its own unique characteristics, uses, advantages, limitations, and rules for construction. In this chapter, these characteristics are considered for objective test forms that typically measure relatively simple learning outcomes: (a) the short-answer item, (b) the true–false item, and (c) the matching exercise.

The preliminary test planning described in Chapter 6 provides a sound basis for developing classroom tests that can be used for a variety of instructional purposes. The test specifications clarify the sample of achievement to be measured, and the various considerations in test planning form a general framework within which to proceed. The next step is the actual construction of test items. This step is crucial because the validity of a classroom test is ultimately determined by the extent to which the performance to be measured is actually called forth by the test items. Selecting item types that are inappropriate for the learning outcomes to be measured, constructing items with technical defects, or unwittingly including irrelevant clues in the items can undermine all the careful planning that has gone on before.

The construction of good test items is an art. The skills it requires, however, are the same as those found in effective teaching. Needed are a thorough grasp of subject matter, a clear conception of the desired learning outcomes, a psychological understanding of students, sound judgment, persistence, and a touch of creativity. The only additional requisite for constructing good test items is the skillful application of an array of simple but important rules and suggestions. These techniques of test construction are the topic of this and the next two chapters. The rules for constructing test items, described in these chapters, are applicable to all types of classroom tests using supply-type or selection-type items. Guidelines for constructing assessments using essay questions or other types of performance assessments are provided in Chapters 10 and 11.

In this chapter, we limit our discussion to the simpler forms of objective test items: (a) short-answer items, (b) true–false or alternative-response items, and (c) matching exercises. These item types are treated together, as their use in classroom testing is restricted largely to the measurement of simple learning outcomes in the knowledge area. The discussion of each item type is followed by a checklist for reviewing the items.

SHORT-ANSWER ITEMS

The short-answer item and the completion item both are supply-type test items that can be answered by a word, phrase, number, or symbol. They are essentially the same, differing only in the method of presenting the problem. The short-answer item uses a direct question, whereas the completion item consists of an incomplete statement.

EXAMPLES   **Short Answer**

What is the name of the man who invented the steamboat? (<u>Robert Fulton</u>)

Completion

The name of the man who invented the steamboat is _____. (<u>Robert Fulton</u>)

Also included in this category are problems in arithmetic, mathematics, science, and other areas whose solution must be supplied by the student.

Uses of Short-Answer Items

The short-answer test item is suitable for measuring a wide variety of relatively simple learning outcomes. The following outcomes and test items illustrate some of its common uses.

EXAMPLES   **Knowledge of Terminology**

Lines on a weather map that join points of the same barometric pressure
are called _____. (<u>isobars</u>)

Knowledge of Specific Facts

A member of the United States Senate is elected to a term of _____ years. (<u>6</u>)

Knowledge of Principles

If the temperature of a gas is held constant while the pressure applied to it is increased, what will happen to its volume? (<u>It will decrease</u>)

Knowledge of Method or Procedure

What device is used to detect whether an electric charge is positive or negative? (<u>electroscope</u>)

Simple Interpretations of Data

How many syllables are there in the word *Argentina*? (<u>4</u>)
In the number 612, what value does the 6 represent? (<u>600</u>)
In the triangle below, what is the number of degrees in each angle? (<u>60</u>)

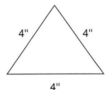

If an airplane flying northwest made a 180-degree turn, what direction would it be heading?
(<u>southeast</u>)

More complex interpretations can be made when the short-answer item is used to measure the ability to interpret diagrams, charts, graphs, and pictorial data.

Even more notable exceptions to the general rule that short-answer items are limited to measuring simple learning outcomes are found in the areas of mathematics and science, where the solutions to problems can be indicated by numbers or symbols. The following examples illustrate this use.

EXAMPLES **Ability to Solve Numerical Problems**

Milk sells for $.96 a quart and $3.68 a gallon. How many cents would you save on each quart of milk if you bought it by the gallon? (<u>4</u>)

Skill in Manipulating Mathematical Symbols

If $\dfrac{x}{b} = \dfrac{3}{b-1}$, then $x = ?$ $\dfrac{3b}{(b-1)}$

Ability to Complete and Balance Chemical Equations

$Mg + (2)\ HCl \rightarrow ?$ $(MgCl_2 + H_2)$

$(2)\ Al + (6)\ HCl \rightarrow ?$ $\overline{(2\ AlCl_3 + 3H_2)}$

For outcomes similar to those in these last examples, the short-answer item is clearly superior to items that require the student to select an answer. The performance described in the learning outcomes is identical with the performance called forth by the test items. To obtain correct answers, students must actually solve problems, manipulate mathematical symbols, and complete and balance equations.

Attempts are sometimes made to measure such problem-solving activities with selection-type test items, commonly resulting in test items that do not function as intended or that measure quite different learning outcomes. In the following multiple-choice items, for example, note how the division problem can be solved by working it backward (multiplying 2×43, or merely 2×3) and how in the second problem the value of x can be determined by substituting each of the alternative answers in the equation on a trial-and-error basis. Such problems obviously do not demand the problem-solving behavior we are attempting to measure.

EXAMPLES   **Supply-Type Items Superior to Multiple-Choice (see text):**

$$2\overline{)86} =$$

A	41
Ⓒ	43
D	44

(A) 41
(B) 42
Ⓒ 43
(D) 44

If $\dfrac{x}{4} + \dfrac{x}{16} = 10$, then x equals

(A) 16
(B) 24
Ⓒ 32
(D) 48

Similar difficulties are encountered when we substitute selection items measuring the ability to "recognize balanced chemical equations" for short-answer items measuring the ability to "complete and balance chemical equations." The selection task is a simple one requiring little more than a knowledge of mathematics, but the short-answer task requires extensive knowledge of chemical reactions and their resulting products.

For large-scale testing programs, it is possible to maintain some of the advantages of the supply-type item for mathematics problems that result in numerical answers while still retaining the efficiencies of machine scoring. The grid-in item, for example, was introduced on the Scholastic Assessment Test in the spring of 1994. This item type requires examinees to solve problems and enter their numerical responses in a grid (see example).

EXAMPLE   Five students get scores of 9, 7, 7, 5, and 4 on an eight-item quiz. What is the average score for these five students?

Grid-in problems requiring complex problem solving can be constructed, but the approach is likely to be useful only when a test is administered to a large number of students. For classroom use, short-answer problems and extended free-response assessment tasks of the type discussed in Chapters 10 and 11 are likely to provide more information about how students approach such problems and the nature of the difficulties they encounter.

In summary, if the short-answer test item is most effective for measuring a specific learning outcome, then it should be used. We should not discard it for selection-type items unless we are fairly certain that the same learning outcomes will be measured. For many of the simpler learning outcomes, such as knowledge of factual information, changing to some form of selection item will not decrease the validity of the measurement and will result in increased objectivity and ease of scoring. For some of the more complex learning outcomes, such as those in mathematics and science, however, discarding the short-answer test item may mean a change in the learning outcomes being measured and, hence, reduce the validity for the intended outcomes. In deciding whether to use short-answer items or some other item type, our best guide is to follow this principle: Each learning outcome should be measured as directly as possible, and the test-item type most appropriate for the purpose should be used.

Advantages and Limitations of Short-Answer Items

The short-answer test item is one of the easiest to construct, partly because of the relatively simple learning outcomes it usually measures. Except for the problem-solving outcomes measured in mathematics and science, the short-answer item is used almost exclusively to measure the recall of memorized information.

A more important advantage of the short-answer item is that the students must supply the answer. This reduces the possibility that the students will obtain the correct answer by guessing. They must either recall the information requested or make the necessary computations to solve the problem presented to them. Partial knowledge, which might enable them to choose the correct answer on a selection item, is insufficient for answering a short-answer test item correctly.

Two major limitations restrict the use of the short-answer test item. One—unsuitability for measuring complex learning outcomes—has already been mentioned. The other is the difficulty of scoring. Unless the question is carefully phrased, many answers of varying degrees of correctness must be considered for total or partial credit. For example, a question such as "Where was George Washington born?" could be answered by the name of the city, county, state, region, country, or continent. Although the teacher may have had the name of the state in mind when writing the question, the other answers cannot be dismissed as incorrect. Even when this problem is avoided, however, the scoring may be contaminated by the student's spelling ability. If full or partial credit is taken off for misspelled words, the students' test scores will reflect varying degrees of knowledge and spelling skill. If spelling is not counted in the scoring, the teacher must still decide whether misspelled words actually represent the correct answer. We all are familiar with misspellings so bad that it is difficult to determine what the student had in mind. The complications make scoring more time consuming and less objective than that obtained with selection-type items.

These limitations are less troublesome when the answer is to be expressed in numbers or symbols, as in physical science or mathematics. Here, more complex learning outcomes can be measured, spelling is not a problem, and it is usually easier to write test items for which there is only one correct response.

Suggestions for Constructing Short-Answer Items

The short-answer item is subject to a variety of defects, even though it is considered one of the easiest to construct. The following suggestions will help you avoid possible pitfalls and provide greater assurance that the items will function as intended.

1. **Word the item so that the required answer is both brief and specific.** As indicated earlier, the answer to an item should be a word, phrase, number, or symbol. This can be easily conveyed to the students through the directions at the beginning of the test and by proper phrasing of the question. More difficult is stating the question so that only one answer is correct.

EXAMPLES   *Poor:*   An animal that eats the flesh of other animals is (<u>carnivorous</u>).
             Better: An animal that eats the flesh of other animals is classified as (<u>carnivorous</u>).

The first version of this item is so indefinite that it could be completed with answers such as *the wolf, the lion,* or even *hungry.* Asking the students to classify this type of animal, as called for in the improved version, better structures the problem and defines the type of response required.

2. **Do not take statements directly from textbooks to use as a basis for short-answer items.** When taken out of context, textbook statements are frequently too general and ambiguous to serve as good short-answer items. Note the vagueness of the first version of the following test item, which was taken verbatim from a chemistry textbook.

EXAMPLES   *Poor:*   Chlorine is a (<u>halogen</u>).
                Better: Chlorine belongs to a group of elements that combine with metals to form salts. It
                             is therefore called a (<u>halogen</u>).

Students are most likely to respond to the first version of this test item with the word *gas* because that is the natural state of chlorine, and there is nothing in the statement to imply that the word *halogen* is wanted. The only students who are apt to supply the intended answer are those who memorized the textbook statements. The revised version measures factual knowledge that is not dependent on the phraseology of the textbook. Such items tend to discourage the students from developing little-understood verbal associations based on textbook language and encourage them to achieve the learning outcomes being measured. When items are not taken verbatim from another source, it also forces the item writer to carefully consider the importance of the word or phrase being omitted as well as the other words or phrases in the sentence that might provide a clue to the answer.

3. A direct question is generally more desirable than an incomplete statement. There are two advantages to the direct-question form. First, it is more natural to the students, as this is the usual method of phrasing questions in daily classroom discussions. This is especially important to elementary students when first exposed to short-answer tests. Second, the direct question is usually better structured and free of much of the ambiguity that creeps into items based on incomplete statements. Just the phrasing of a question requires us to decide what it is we want to know.

EXAMPLES   *Poor:*   John Glenn made his first orbital flight around the earth in _____. (<u>1962</u>)
                Better: When did John Glenn make his first orbital flight around the earth? _____. (<u>1962</u>)
                Best: In what year did John Glenn make his first orbital flight around the earth?
                             _____. (<u>1962</u>)

The first version of the item could, of course, be completed with *a space capsule, Friendship Seven, space,* and similar answers. Putting it in question form forces us to indicate whether it is the time, place, or method we are interested in knowing. The last version is a refinement that makes the question even more specific and that naturally evolves from a consideration of the ***when*** aspect of the previous question.

4. If the answer is to be expressed in numerical units, indicate the type of answer wanted. For computational problems, it is usually preferable to indicate the units in which the answer is to be expressed. This will clarify the problem and will simplify the scoring.

EXAMPLES   *Poor:*   If oranges weigh 5 2/3 oz. each, how much will a dozen oranges weigh?
                             (<u>4 lb. 4 oz.</u>)

                Better: If oranges weigh 5 2/3 oz. each, how much will a dozen oranges weigh? _____ lb.
                             _____ oz. (<u>4</u>) lb. (<u>4</u>) oz.

Unless the type of unit is specified, as in the revised version, correct answers will include *68 oz., 4 1/4 lb., 4.25 lb.,* and *4 lb. 4 oz.* This adds unnecessary confusion to the scoring.

When the problems do not come out even, it is also usually helpful to indicate the degree of precision expected in the answers. For example, specifying that the answers should be "carried out to two decimal places" or "rounded off to the nearest tenth of a percent" makes clear to the students how far to carry their calculations. This will ensure that they reach the degree of precision desired and also prevent them from wasting valuable testing time attempting to achieve a degree of precision not expected.

There are some instances, especially in science, when knowing the proper unit in which the answer is to be expressed and knowing the degree of precision to be expected are important aspects of the learning outcome to be measured. In such cases, the previous suggestions must, of course, be modified.

5. **Blanks for answers should be equal in length and in a column to the right of the question.** If blanks for answers are kept equal in length, the length of the blank space does not supply a clue to the answer. In the poor version of the following items, the lengths of the blanks restrict the possible answers the students need consider. For the first item they need a long word and for the second item a short one.

EXAMPLES   *Poor:*   What is the name of the part of speech that connects words, clauses, and sentences? _____ (<u>conjunction</u>)

What is the name of the part of speech that declares, asserts, or predicts something? _____ (<u>verb</u>)

Better: What is the name of the part of speech that connects words, clauses, and sentences? _____ (<u>conjunction</u>)

What is the name of the part of speech that declares, asserts, or predicts something? _____ (<u>verb</u>)

Placing the blanks in a column to the right of the question makes scoring quicker and more accurate. Avoid giving unintentional clues that the answer is a short or long word by making the blanks the same size and large enough for the longest response.

6. **When completion items are used, do not include too many blanks.** If a statement is too mutilated by blanks, the meaning will be lost, and the student will have to guess what the teacher had in mind. Although some mutilated statements seem to measure complex reasoning abilities, such responses are more appropriate as measures of intelligence than achievement.

EXAMPLES   *Poor:*   (<u>Warm-blooded</u>) animals that are born (<u>alive</u>) and (<u>suckle</u>) their young are called (<u>mammals</u>).
Better: Warm-blooded animals that are born alive and suckle their young are called (<u>mammals</u>).

CHECKLIST

Reviewing Short-Answer Items

	Yes	No
1. Is this the most appropriate type of item to use for the intended learning outcomes?	____	____
2. Can the items be answered with a number, symbol, word, or brief phrase?	____	____
3. Has textbook language been avoided?	____	____
4. Have the items been stated so that only one response is correct?	____	____
5. Are the answer blanks equal in length?	____	____
6. Are the answer blanks at the end of the items?	____	____
7. Are the items free of clues (such as *a* or *an*)?	____	____
8. Has the degree of precision been indicated for numerical answers?	____	____
9. Have the units been indicated when numerical answers are expressed in units?	____	____
10. Have the items been phrased so as to minimize spelling errors?	____	____
11. If revised, are the items still relevant to the intended learning outcomes?	____	____
12. Have the items been set aside for a time before reviewing them?	____	____

In the revised version, the blank is at the end of the statement so that the students are presented with a clearly defined problem before they come to the blank. See the "Checklist" box for a review of the guidelines for constructing short-answer tests.

TRUE–FALSE OR ALTERNATIVE-RESPONSE ITEMS

The alternative-response test item consists of a declarative statement that the student is asked to mark true or false, right or wrong, correct or incorrect, yes or no, fact or opinion, agree or disagree, or the like. In each case, there are only two possible answers. Because the true–false option is the most common, this item type is most frequently referred to as the true–false test item. Some of the variations, however, deviate considerably from the simple true–false pattern and have their own characteristics. For this reason, some prefer the more general category alternative-response item. Here we retain the more commonly used true–false designation.

Uses of True–False Items

Probably the most common use of the true–false item is in measuring the ability to identify the correctness of statements of fact, definitions of terms, statements of principles, and the like. For measuring such relatively simple learning outcomes, a single declarative statement is used with any one of several methods of responding.

Directions: Read each of the following statements. If the statement is true, circle the T. If the statement is false, circle the F.

(T)	F	1. The green coloring material in a plant leaf is called chlorophyll.
T	(F)	2. The corolla of a flower includes petals and sepals.
(T)	F	3. Photosynthesis is the process by which leaves make a plant's food.

Directions: Read each of the following questions. If the answer is yes, circle the Y. If the answer is no, circle the N.

(Y)	N	1. Is 50% of 38 more than 18?
Y	(N)	2. Is 50% of 4/10 equal to 2/5?
Y	(N)	3. If 60% of a number is 9, is the number smaller than 9?
(Y)	N	4. Is 25% of 44 less than 12?

One of the useful functions of the true–false item is in measuring the student's ability to distinguish fact from opinion. The following examples illustrate this use.

Directions: Read each of the following statements. If the statement is a fact, circle the F. If the statement is an opinion, circle the O.

(F)	O	1. The Constitution of the United States is the highest law of our country.
F	(O)	2. The First Amendment to the Constitution is the most important amendment.
(F)	O	3. The Fifth Amendment to the Constitution protects people from testifying against themselves.
F	(O)	4. Other countries should adopt a constitution like that of the United States.

Directions: Read each of the following statements. If the statement is true, circle the T. If the statement is false, circle the F. If the statement is an opinion, circle the O.

(T)	F	O	1. The earth is a planet.
T	(F)	O	2. The earth revolves around the moon.
T	F	(O)	3. There are intelligent life forms on planets orbiting some distant stars.

These items measure a learning outcome important to all subject-matter areas: If people are to think critically about a topic, they must first be able to distinguish fact from opinion.

All too frequently, true–false tests include numerous opinion statements to which the student is asked to respond true or false. This is extremely frustrating because there is no objective basis for determining whether a statement of opinion is true or false. The student must usually guess what opinion the teacher holds and mark the answers accordingly. This, of course, is undesirable from all standpoints—testing, teaching, and learning. It is much better to have the student identify statements of opinion as such. An alternative procedure is to attribute the opinion to some source, making it possible to mark the statements true or false and measuring knowledge concerning the beliefs held by an individual or the values supported by an organization or institution.

EXAMPLES   *Directions:* Read each of the following statements. If the statement is true, circle the T. If the statement is false, circle the F.

T   (F)   1. Franklin D. Roosevelt believed that labor unions interfered with the U.S. free-enterprise system.

T   (F)   2. The National Rifle Association favors strict gun control laws.

(T)   F   3. The National Education Association opposes the use of public funds for vouchers for students to attend private schools.

Items like these can become measures of understanding if the opinion statements attributed to an individual or group are new to the student. The task then becomes one of interpreting the beliefs held by the individual or group and applying them to the new situation.

Another aspect of understanding that can be measured by the true–false item is the ability to recognize cause-and-effect relationships. This type of item usually contains two true propositions in one statement, and the student is to judge whether the relationship between them is true or false.

EXAMPLES   *Directions:* In each of the following statements, both parts of the statement are true. You are to decide whether the second part explains why the first part is true. If it does, circle Yes. If it does not, circle No.

Yes   (No)   1. Leaves are essential *because* they shade the tree trunk.

Yes   (No)   2. Whales are mammals *because* they are large.

(Yes)   No   3. Some plants do not need sunlight *because* they get their food from other plants.

The true–false item also can be used to measure some simple aspects of logic, as illustrated by the following items that were developed for use in a science test.

EXAMPLES   *Directions:* Read each of the following statements. If the statement is true, circle the T; if it is false, circle the F. Also, if the converse of the statement is true, circle the CT; if the converse is false, circle the CF. Be sure to give two answers for each statement.

(T)   F   CT   (CF)   1. All trees are plants.

T   (F)   CT   (CF)   2. All parasites are animals.

T   (F)   (CT)   CF   3. All eight-legged animals are spiders.

(T)   F   (CT)   CF   4. No spiders are insects.

A common criticism of the true–false item is that a student may be able to recognize a false statement as incorrect but still not know what is correct. For example, when students answer the following item as false, it does not indicate whether they know what negatively charged particles of electricity are called; all the answer tells us is that they know they are not called neutrons.

EXAMPLE   T   Ⓕ   Negatively charged particles of electricity are called neutrons.

This is a rather crude measure of knowledge because there is an infinite number of things that negatively charged particles of electricity are *not* called. To overcome such difficulties, some teachers prefer to have the students change all false statements to true. When this is required, the part of the statement it is permissible to change should be indicated.

EXAMPLES   *Directions:* Read each of the following statements. If a statement is true, circle the T. If a statement is false, circle the F and change the underlined word to make the statement true. Place the new word in the blank space after the F.

    T Ⓕ   (electrons)   1. Particles of negatively charged electricity are called *neutrons*.

    Ⓣ F   _____   2. Mechanical energy is turned into electrical energy by means of the *generator*.

    T Ⓕ   (store)   3. An electric condenser is used to *generate* electricity.

Unless the key words to be changed are indicated, students are liable to rewrite the entire statement. In addition to the increase in scoring difficulty, this frequently leads to true statements that deviate considerably from the original intent of the item. A clever student may even change false statements to true by simply adding *not* in the appropriate place.

Advantages and Limitations of True–False Items

A major advantage of true–false items is that they are efficient. Students can typically respond to roughly three true–false items in the time it takes to respond to two multiple-choice items (Ebel & Frisbie, 1991).

Proponents of true–false items such as Ebel and Frisbie (1991) argue that verbal knowledge is central to educational achievement and that "all verbal knowledge can be expressed in propositions" which can be judged to be true or false (p. 135). They make a strong case that true–false items have utility for measuring a broad range of verbal knowledge.

One advantage cited frequently for true–false items is, unfortunately, more illusory than real: ease of construction. This has probably resulted from the common practice of taking statements from textbooks, changing half of them to false statements, and submitting the product to students as a true–false test. Such test items are often so obvious that everyone gets them correct or so ambiguous that even the better students are confused by them. In short, it is easy to construct *poor* true–false items. To construct unambiguous true–false items that measure significant learning outcomes, however, requires much skill.

A second advantage attributed to the true–false item is that a wide sampling of course material can be obtained. Certainly a student can respond to many test items in a short time, which makes it possible to cover a wide range of content, but some types of subject matter do not lend themselves to true–false types of items. True–false statements require course material that can be phrased so that the statements are true or false without qualification or exception. There are areas in which such absolutely true or false statements cannot be made. In some fields, such as the social sciences, practically all significant statements require some qualification. In some subject areas, only relatively trivial statements can be reduced to absolute terms.

One of the most serious limitations of the true–false item is in the types of learning outcomes that can be measured. True–false items are not especially useful beyond the knowledge area. The exceptions to this seem to be distinguishing between fact and opinion and identifying cause-and-effect relationships. These two outcomes are probably the most important measured by this type of item. Many of the learning outcomes measured by the true–false item can be measured more effectively by other forms of selection items, especially the multiple-choice form.

Another factor that limits the usefulness of the true–false item is its susceptibility to guessing. With only two alternatives, a student has a 50/50 chance of selecting the correct answer on the basis of chance alone, and because of the difficulty of constructing items that do not contain clues to the answer, the student's chances of guessing correctly are usually much greater than 50%. This disadvantage is offset, however, by the relatively large number of items that can be answered in a given period of time. Nevertheless, with a typical 100-item true–false test, it is not unusual to have the lowest score above 80. An indeterminate amount of knowledge is reflected in such a score: Many of the correct answers can be accounted for by chance or the presence of clues. A scoring formula utilizing a correction for guessing is frequently suggested as a solution for this problem. This formula compensates only chance guesses, however, and does not include those guided by clues. In addition, such a scoring formula favors individuals willing to take a chance. Even when warned that there will be a penalty for guessing, these individuals will continue to guess, using any clues available, and will do better than chance. Cautious students, on the other hand, will mark only those answers they are certain are correct and will omit many items they could have marked correctly using clues and partial information. Thus, the scores tend to reflect personality differences as well as knowledge of the subject.

The great likelihood of successful guessing on the true–false item has two implications that should be taken into account: (a) The reliability of each item is low, making it necessary to include many items in order to obtain a reliable measure of achievement; and (b) the diagnostic value of such a test is practically nil because analyzing a student's response to each item is meaningless.

One last caution that needs to be considered in the design of tests with true–false items is student response sets. As noted earlier, a response set is a consistent tendency to follow a certain pattern in responding to test items. In taking a true–false test, for example, some students will consistently mark "true" those items they do not know, and others will consistently mark them "false." Thus, if there is not a balance between true and false items, a given test will favor one response set over another and introduce an element into the test score that is irrelevant to the purpose of the test.

True–false items are most useful in situations in which there are only two possible alternatives (e.g., right, left; more, less; who, whom) and special uses such as distinguishing fact from opinion, cause from effect, superstition from scientific belief, relevant from irrelevant information, valid from invalid conclusions, and the like.

Suggestions for Constructing True–False Items

The main task in constructing true–false items is formulating statements free from ambiguity and irrelevant clues. This is extremely difficult, and the only guidance that can be given is a list of things to **avoid** when phrasing the statements.

1. **Avoid broad general statements if they are to be judged true or false.** Most broad generalizations are false unless qualified, and the use of qualifiers provides clues to the answer.

EXAMPLES   *Poor:*   T   (F)   The president of the United States is elected to that office.
                Poor: (T)   F   The president of the United States is usually elected to that office.

In this example, the first version is generally true but must be marked false because there are exceptions, such as when the vice president takes office in event of the president's death. In the second version, the qualifier **usually** makes the statement true but provides a definite clue. Words such as **usually, generally, often,** and **sometimes** are more likely to appear in true statements, and absolute terms such as **always, never, all, none,** and **only** are more apt to appear in false statements. Although the influence of such clues sometimes can be offset by balancing their use in true–false statements, the simplest solution seems to be to avoid the use of broad generalizations that are obviously false or must be qualified by specific determiners.

2. **Avoid trivial statements.** In an attempt to obtain statements that are unequivocally true or false, we sometimes inadvertently turn to specific statements of fact that fit this criterion beautifully but have little significance from a learning standpoint.

EXAMPLES   *Poor:*   (T)   F   Harry S. Truman was the thirty-third president of the United States.
                Poor: T   (F)   The United States declared war on Japan on December 7, 1941.

The first item calls for a relatively unimportant fact concerning Truman's tenure as president, and the second item expects the student to remember that the United States did not declare war until December 8. Such items cause students to direct their attention toward memorizing minutiae at the expense of more general knowledge and understanding.

3. **Avoid the use of negative statements, especially double negatives.** Students tend to overlook negative words such as **no** or **not,** and double negatives contribute to the statement's ambiguity. Note the ambiguity in this relatively simple statement, which uses two negatives.

EXAMPLES   *Poor:*   (T)   F   None of the steps in the experiment was unnecessary.
                Better: (T)   F   All of the steps in the experiment were necessary.

When a negative word must be used, it should be underlined or put in italics so that students do not overlook it.

4. Avoid long, complex sentences. As noted earlier, a test item should indicate whether a student has achieved the knowledge or understanding being measured. Long, complex sentences tend also to measure the extraneous factor of reading comprehension and therefore should be avoided in tests designed to measure achievement.

EXAMPLES   *Poor:*   Ⓣ   F   Despite the theoretical and experimental difficulties of
                                        determining the exact pH value of a solution, it is possible to
                                        determine whether a solution is acid by the red color formed
                                        on litmus paper when it is inserted into the solution.
            Better: Ⓣ   F   Litmus paper turns red in an acid solution.

As in the preceding example, it frequently is possible to shorten and simplify a statement by eliminating nonfunctional material and restating the main idea. If this is not possible, it may be necessary to change to another item form in order to avoid a complex sentence structure.

5. Avoid including two ideas in one statement, unless cause-and-effect relationships are being measured. Some difficulties arising from the inclusion of two ideas in one statement are apparent in the following example, which is one of many similar items a teacher actually used in a biology examination. In each instance, the students were asked to judge merely whether the statement was true or false.

EXAMPLE   *Poor:*   T   Ⓕ   A worm cannot see because it has simple eyes.

This item is keyed false because a worm does not have simple eyes. However, when this teacher asked a student why he marked it false, the student said, "Worms *can* see." This demonstrates that students can get items correct with erroneous information. This is so because the first proposition can be true or false, the second proposition can be true or false, and the relationship between them can be true or false. Thus, when students mark the item false, there is no way of determining to which of the three elements they are responding. The best solution to this dilemma seems to be to use only true propositions and to ask the students to judge the truth or falsity of the relationships between them. Such items also might, of course, be divided into two simple statements, each containing a single idea.

6. If opinion is used, attribute it to some source, unless the ability to identify opinion is being specifically measured. Statements of opinion cannot be marked true or false, and it is unfair to expect students to guess how the teacher will score such items or to respond to opinion statements as statements of fact. Knowing whether some significant individual or group supports or refutes a certain opinion, however, can be important from a learning standpoint.

| EXAMPLES | *Poor:* | T | Ⓕ | Adequate medical care can be best provided through socialized medicine. |
| | *Better:* | T | Ⓕ | The American Medical Association favors socialized medicine as the best means of providing adequate medical care. |

The first version cannot be answered true or false. It may serve a useful purpose in an attitude test, but there is no factual basis on which to decide the truth or falsity of the statement. The second version is clearly false.

7. **True statements and false statements should be approximately equal in length.** There is a natural tendency for true statements to be longer because such statements must be precisely phrased in order to be absolutely true. This can be overcome by lengthening the false statements through the use of qualifying phrases similar to those found in true statements. Thus, the length of the statement will be eliminated as a possible clue to the correct answer.

8. **The number of true statements and false statements should be approximately equal.** Constructing a test with an approximately equal number of true statements and false statements will prevent response sets from unduly inflating or deflating the students' scores. You will recall that some students consistently mark statements "true" when in doubt about an answer, whereas others consistently mark them "false." Neither response set should be favored by overloading the test with items of one type.

In honoring this suggestion, the words *approximately equal* should be given special attention. If a teacher consistently uses exactly the same number, this will provide a clue to the student who is unable to answer some of the test items. The best procedure seems to be to vary the percentage of true statements somewhere between 40% and 60%. Under no circumstances should the statements be all true or all false. Students who detect this as a possibility can obtain perfect scores on the basis of one guess.

See the "Checklist" box for questions to use in reviewing true–false items.

MATCHING EXERCISES

In its traditional form, the matching exercise consists of two parallel columns with each word, number, or symbol in one column being matched to a word, sentence, or phrase in the other column. The items in the column for which a match is sought are called premises, and the items in the column from which the selection is made are called responses. The basis for matching premises to responses is sometimes self-evident but more often must be explained in the directions. In any event, the student's task is to identify the pairs of items that are to be associated on the basis indicated. For example, the student may be asked to identify important historical events, as in the following illustration.

CHECKLIST

Reviewing True–False Items

	Yes	No
1. Is this the most appropriate type of item to use?	____	____
2. Can each statement be clearly judged true or false?	____	____
3. Have specific determiners (e.g., *usually, always*) been avoided?	____	____
4. Have trivial statements been avoided?	____	____
5. Have negative statements (especially double negatives) been avoided?	____	____
6. Have the items been stated in simple, clear language?	____	____
7. Are opinion statements attributed to some source?	____	____
8. Are the true and false items approximately equal in length?	____	____
9. Is there an approximately equal number of true and false items?	____	____
10. Has a detectable pattern of answers (e.g., T, F, T, F) been avoided?	____	____
11. If revised, are the items still relevant to the intended learning outcomes?	____	____
12. Have the items been set aside for a time before reviewing them?	____	____

EXAMPLE   *Directions:* On the line to the left of each United States space event in Column A, write the letter of the astronaut in Column B who achieved that honor. Each name in Column B may be used once, more than once, or not at all.

Column A	Column B
(G) 1. First United States astronaut to ride in a space capsule	A. Edwin Aldrin
	B. Neil Armstrong
(E) 2. First United States astronaut to orbit the earth	C. Frank Borman
	D. Scott Carpenter
(H) 3. First United States astronaut to walk in space	E. John Glenn
	F. Wally Schirra
(B) 4. First United States astronaut to step on the moon	G. Alan Shepard
	H. Edward White

This matching exercise illustrates an imperfect match; that is, there are more names in column B than are needed to match each event in column A. The directions also indicate that an item may be used once, more than once, or not at all. Both of these procedures prevent students from matching the final pair of items on the basis of elimination.

Two other factors are notable in our example. First, the items in the list of premises in Column A are homogeneous, as they all are concerned with important space events. Such homogeneity is necessary if a matching exercise is to function properly. Second, for each premise in Column A, there are several plausible responses in Column B. Thus, the incorrect responses serve as attractive choices for those students who are in doubt about the correct answers. Both factors tend to minimize the opportunity for successful guessing.

Uses of Matching Exercises

The typical matching exercise is limited to measuring factual information based on simple associations. Whenever learning outcomes emphasize the ability to identify the relationship between two things and a sufficient number of homogeneous premises and responses can be obtained, a matching exercise seems most appropriate. It is a compact and efficient method of measuring such simple knowledge outcomes. Examples of relationships considered important by teachers, in a variety of fields, include the following:

Persons . . . . Achievements

Dates. . . . . Historical Events

Terms . . . . Definitions

Rules. . . . . Examples

Symbols. . . . . Concepts

Authors . . . . Titles of Books

Foreign Words . . . . English Equivalents

Machines. . . . . Uses

Plants or Animals. . . . . Classification

Principles. . . . . Illustrations

Objects . . . . Names of Objects

Parts . . . . Functions

The matching exercise has also been used with pictorial materials in relating pictures and words or to identify positions on maps, charts, and diagrams. Regardless of the form of presentation, the student's task is essentially to relate two things that have some logical basis for association. This restricts the use of the matching exercise to a relatively small area of student achievement.

Advantages and Limitations of Matching Exercises

The major advantage of the matching exercise is its compact form, which makes it possible to measure a large amount of related factual material in a relatively short time. This is a mixed blessing, however, as it frequently leads to the excessive use of matching exercises and a corresponding overemphasis on the memorization of simple relationships.

Another advantage often cited for the matching exercise is ease of construction. Poor-matching items can be rapidly constructed, but good-matching items require a high degree of skill. The correct response for each premise must also serve as a plausible response for the other premises. Any lack of plausibility will reduce the number of possible choices and provide clues to the correct answer. The matching exercise tends to have more irrelevant clues than any other item type, with the possible exception of the true–false item.

The main limitations of the matching exercise are that it is restricted to the measurement of factual information based on rote learning and that it is highly susceptible to the presence of irrelevant clues. Another limitation, somewhat related, is the difficulty of finding homogeneous material that is significant from the viewpoint of our objectives and learning outcomes. For example, we might start out with a few great scientists and their achievements, which we feel all students should know. In order to construct a matching item, it becomes necessary to add the names and achievements of other, lesser-known scientists. Thus, we find ourselves measuring factual information that was not included in our original test plan and that is far less important than other aspects of knowledge we had intended to include. In short, less significant material is introduced into the test because enough significant, homogeneous material is unavailable. This is a common problem in constructing matching exercises and one not easily avoided. One solution is to begin with multiple-choice items, because each item can be directly related to a particular outcome, and to switch to the matching form only when homogeneous material makes the matching exercise a more efficient method of measuring the same achievement.

Suggestions for Constructing Matching Exercises

Although the matching exercise has only limited usefulness in classroom tests, whenever it is used, special efforts should be made to remove irrelevant clues and to arrange it so that the student can respond quickly and without confusion. The following suggestions are designed to guide such efforts.

1. Use only homogeneous material in a single matching exercise. This has been mentioned before and is repeated here for emphasis. It is without a doubt the most important rule of construction and yet the one most commonly violated. One reason for this is that homogeneity is a matter of degree, and what is homogeneous to one group may be heterogeneous to another. For example, let us assume that we are following the usual suggestion for obtaining homogeneity and develop a matching exercise that includes only men and their achievements. We might end up with a test exercise such as the following one.

EXAMPLE   *Directions:* On the line to the left of each achievement listed in Column A, write the letter of the man's name in Column B who is noted for that achievement. Each name in Column B may be used once, more than once, or not at all.

	Column A	*Column B*
(A)	1. Invented the telephone	A. Alexander Graham Bell
(B)	2. Discovered America	B. Christopher Columbus
(C)	3. First United States astronaut to orbit the earth	C. John Glenn
(F)	4. First president of the United States	D. Abraham Lincoln
		E. Ferdinand Magellan
		F. George Washington
		G. Eli Whitney

Although the matching exercise in our example may be homogeneous for most students in the primary grades, the discriminations called for are so gross that students above that level will see it as a heterogeneous collection of inventors, explorers, and presidents. Thus, to obtain homogeneity at higher grade levels, it is necessary to have only inventors and their inventions in one matching exercise, explorers and their discoveries in another, and presidents and their achievements in another. At a still higher level, it may be necessary to limit matching exercises still further, such as to inventors whose inventions are in the same field, in order to keep the material homogeneous and free from irrelevant clues. As we increase the level of discrimination called for in a matching exercise, significant homogeneous material becomes increasingly difficult to obtain. Take inventors, for example. How many significant inventions are there in any one area?

2. **Include an unequal number of responses and premises and instruct the student that responses may be used once, more than once, or not at all.** This will make all the responses eligible for selection for each premise and will decrease the likelihood of successful guessing. When an equal number of responses and premises are used and each response is used only once, the probability for guessing the remaining responses correctly is increased each time a correct answer is selected. The odds for correct guessing increase as the list of available responses decreases, and the final response, of course, can be selected entirely on the basis of this process of elimination. In most matching exercises, imperfect matching can be obtained by including more or fewer responses than premises. In either case, the directions should instruct the student that each response may be used once, more than once, or not at all.

3. **Keep the list of items to be matched brief and place the shorter responses on the right.** A brief list of items is advantageous to both the teacher and the student. From the teacher's standpoint, it is easier to maintain homogeneity in a brief list. In addition, there is a greater likelihood that the various learning outcomes and subject-matter topics will be measured in a balanced manner. Because each matching exercise must be based on homogeneous material, a long list will require excessive concentration in one area. From the students' viewpoint, a brief list enables them to read the responses rapidly and without confusion. Approximately four to seven items in each column seems best. There certainly should be no more than 10 items in either column.

Placing the shorter responses on the right also contributes to more efficient test taking, as it enables students to read the longer premise first and then to scan rapidly the list of responses.

4. **Arrange the list of responses in logical order, place words in alphabetical order, and numbers in sequence.** This will contribute to the ease with which the students can scan the responses in searching for the correct answers. It will also prevent them from detecting possible clues from the arrangement of the responses.

EXAMPLE   *Directions:* On the line to the left of each historical event in Column A, write the letter from Column B that identifies the time period when the event occurred. Each date in Column B may be used once, more than once, or not at all.

	Column A		*Column B*
(B)	1. Boston Tea Party	A.	1765–1769
(A)	2. Repeal of the Stamp Act	B.	1770–1774

<u>(E)</u> 3. Enactment of the Northwest Ordinance

<u>(C)</u> 4. Battle of Lexington

<u>(A)</u> 5. Enactment of Townshend Acts

<u>(B)</u> 6. First Continental Congress

<u>(E)</u> 7. United States Constitution drawn up

C. 1775–1779

D. 1780–1784

E. 1785–1789

This matching exercise also demonstrates the use of fewer responses than premises and the desirability of placing the shortest items on the right.

5. Indicate in the directions the basis for matching the responses and premises. Although the basis for matching is rather obvious in most matching exercises, there are advantages in clearly stating it. First, ambiguity and confusion will be avoided. Second, testing time will be saved because the student will not need to read through the entire list of premises and responses and then "reason out" the basis for matching.

Special care must be taken when stating directions for matching items. Directions that precisely indicate the basis for matching frequently become long and involved, placing a premium on reading comprehension. For younger students, it may be desirable to give oral directions, put an example on the blackboard, and have the students draw lines between the matched items rather than transfer letters.

6. Place all the items for one matching exercise on the same page. This will prevent the disturbance created by 30 or so students switching the pages of the test back and forth. It also will prevent them from missing the responses appearing on another page and generally adds to the speed and efficiency of test administration.

See the "Checklist" box for a review of all the construction guidelines given here.

CHECKLIST

Reviewing Matching Items

	Yes	No
1. Is this the most appropriate type of item to use?	____	____
2. Is the material in the two lists homogeneous?	____	____
3. Is the list of responses longer or shorter than the list of premises?	____	____
4. Are the responses brief and on the right-hand side?	____	____
5. Have the responses been placed in alphabetical or numerical order?	____	____
6. Do the directions indicate the basis for matching?	____	____
7. Do the directions indicate that each response may be used more than once?	____	____
8. Is all of each matching item on the same page?	____	____
9. If revised, are the items still relevant to the intended learning outcomes?	____	____
10. Have the items been set aside for a time before reviewing them?	____	____

SUMMARY

The construction of classroom tests, like other phases of teaching, is an art that must be learned. It is not enough to have a knowledge of subject matter, defined learning outcomes, or a psychological understanding of the students' mental processes, although all these are prerequisites. The ability to construct high-quality test items requires a knowledge of the principles and techniques of test construction and skill in their application.

In this chapter, we discussed techniques for constructing short-answer items, true–false or alternative-response items, and matching exercises. Although these simple forms of objective test items can be made suitable for measuring understanding, thinking skills, and other complex achievements, considerable skill in item construction is required to go beyond simple knowledge outcomes. Other types of items and tasks are generally more satisfactory for measuring higher-level skills. Thus, the primary use of these simple types of items is in measuring knowledge outcomes.

The short-answer item requires students to supply the appropriate word, phrase, number, or symbol to a direct question or incomplete statement. It can be used for measuring a variety of simple knowledge outcomes, but it is especially useful for measuring problem-solving ability in science and mathematics. The ease with which short-answer items can be constructed and their relative freedom from guessing favor their use. However, the areas in which they can be effectively used are restricted by the relatively simple learning outcomes measured and by the fact that the scoring can be contaminated by spelling errors. When short-answer items are used, the question must be stated clearly and concisely, be free from irrelevant clues, and require an answer that is both brief and definite. Problems requiring only a number or a symbol for an answer are particularly adaptable to the short-answer form.

The true–false item requires the student to select one of two possible answers. This item type is used for measuring knowledge outcomes when only two alternatives are possible or the ability to identify the correctness of statements of fact is important. It is also adaptable to measuring the ability to distinguish fact from opinion and the ability to recognize cause-and-effect relationships. The use of true–false items is limited by the difficulty of constructing clue-free items that measure significant learning outcomes, the susceptibility of this type to guessing, the low reliability of each item, and the general lack of diagnostic value. When the true–false item is used, special efforts must be made to formulate statements that are free from ambiguity, specific determiners, and clues.

The matching exercises consist of two parallel columns of phrases, words, numbers, or symbols that must be matched. Examples of items included in matching exercises are persons and achievements, dates and historical events, and terms and definitions. The nature of the matching exercise limits it to measuring the ability to identify the relationship between two things. For this restricted use, it is a compact item type that can be used to measure many relationships in a short time. Its limitations include the difficulty of removing irrelevant clues and the difficulty of finding significant homogeneous material. When homogeneous material is available, including more items in one column than in the other, arranging the shorter responses on the right and in logical order, and indicating clearly the basis for matching all will contribute to the effectiveness of the matching exercise.

LEARNING EXERCISES

1. Defend the statement "short-answer items should not be classified as objective items."
2. How would you handle the scoring of short-answer items when the answers were misspelled?
3. Marking a false statement false does not guarantee that the student knows what is true. How would you handle this problem?
4. You could expect 50 true–false items to have lower reliability than would 50 short-answer items. Why?
5. Under what conditions is it preferable to use a matching item rather than some other item type? When should matching items be avoided?
6. In an area in which you are teaching or plan to teach, construct five short-answer items, five true–false items, and one five-alternative matching exercise. State the objectives being measured by the items.

REFERENCE

Ebel, R. L., & Frisbie, D. A. (1991). *Essentials of educational measurement* (5th ed.). Englewood Cliffs, NJ: Prentice Hall.

FURTHER READING

Bloom, B. S., Madaus, G. F., & Hastings, J. T. (1981). *Evaluation to improve learning.* New York: McGraw-Hill. Chapter 7, "Item Writing and Item Selection," describes the various types of test items and suggestions for writing them. Includes numerous illustrative items and a summary checklist for item writing.

Ebel, R. L., & Frisbie, D. A. (1991). *Essentials of educational measurement* (5th ed.). Englewood Cliffs, NJ: Prentice Hall. In Chapter 8, "True–False Test Items," a strong case is made for their use, and their construction is described and illustrated.

Gronlund, N. E. (2005). *Assessment of student achievement* (8th ed.). Boston: Allyn & Bacon. Chapter 5, "Writing Selection Items: True–False, Matching, and Interpretive Exercises," describes true–false and matching item construction procedures and provides examples.

8

CONSTRUCTING OBJECTIVE TEST ITEMS: MULTIPLE-CHOICE FORMS

Objective test items are not limited to the measurement of simple learning outcomes. The multiple-choice item can measure both knowledge and understanding levels and is free of many of the limitations of other forms of objective items.

The multiple-choice item is generally recognized as the most widely applicable and useful type of objective test item. It can effectively measure many of the simple learning outcomes measured by the short-answer item, the true–false item, and the matching exercise. In addition, it can measure a variety of complex outcomes in the knowledge, understanding, and application areas. This flexibility, plus the higher-quality items usually found in the multiple-choice form, has led to its extensive use in achievement testing.

CHARACTERISTICS OF MULTIPLE-CHOICE ITEMS

A multiple-choice item consists of a problem and a list of suggested solutions. The problem may be stated as a direct question or an incomplete statement and is called the stem of the item. The list of suggested solutions may include words, numbers, symbols, or phrases and are called alternatives (also called choices or options). The student is typically requested to read the stem and the list of alternatives and to select the one correct, or best, alternative. The correct alternative in each item is called the answer, and the remaining alternatives are called distracters (also called decoys or foils). These incorrect alternatives receive their name from their intended function: to distract those students who are in doubt about the correct answer.

Whether to use a direct question or incomplete statement in the stem depends on several factors. The direct-question form is easier to write, is more natural for younger students, and is more likely to present a clearly formulated problem. On the other hand, the incomplete statement is more concise, and, if skillfully phrased, it too can present a well-defined problem. A common procedure is to start each stem as a direct question and shift to the incomplete-statement form only when the clarity of the problem can be retained and greater conciseness achieved.

EXAMPLES **Direct-Question Form**

In which one of the following cities is the capital of California?

    A   Los Angeles
    Ⓑ   Sacramento
    C   San Diego
    D   San Francisco

Incomplete-Statement Form

The capital of California is in

    A   Los Angeles.
    Ⓑ   Sacramento.
    C   San Diego.
    D   San Francisco.

In these examples, there is only one correct answer. The capital of California is in Sacramento and nowhere else. All other alternatives are wrong. For obvious reasons, this is known as the correct-answer type of multiple-choice item.

Not all knowledge can be stated so precisely that there is only one absolutely correct response. In fact, when we get beyond the simple aspects of knowledge, represented by questions of the **who, what, when,** and **where** variety, answers of varying degrees of acceptability are the rule rather than the exception. Questions of the **why** variety, for example, tend to reveal a number of possible reasons, some of which are better than the others. Likewise, questions of the **how** variety usually reveal several possible procedures, some of which are more desirable than the others. Measures of achievement in these areas, then, become a matter of selecting the best answer. This type is especially useful for measuring learning outcomes that require the understanding, application, or interpretation of factual information. Care must be taken, however, to be certain that the best answer is one agreed on by experts so that the answer can be defended as clearly best.

EXAMPLES **BEST-ANSWER TYPE**

Which one of the following factors contributed most to the selection of Sacramento as the capital of California?

    A   Central location
    Ⓑ   Good climate
    C   Good highways
    D   Large population

    (or)

Which one of the following factors is given most consideration when selecting a city for a state capital?

(A)   Location
B   Climate
C   Highways
D   Population

What is the most important purpose of city zoning laws?

A   Attract industry
B   Encourage the building of apartments
(C)   Protect property values
D   Provide school "safety zones"

The best-answer type of multiple-choice item tends to be more difficult than the correct-answer type. This is due partly to the finer discriminations called for and partly to the fact that such items are used to measure more complex learning.

USES OF MULTIPLE-CHOICE ITEMS

The multiple-choice item is the most versatile type of test item available. It can measure a variety of learning outcomes from simple to complex, and it is adaptable to most types of subject-matter content. It has such wide applicability and so many uses that many standardized tests use multiple-choice items exclusively. This practice is not recommended for classroom testing. Despite the wide applicability of the multiple-choice item, there are learning outcomes, such as the ability to organize and present ideas, that cannot be measured with any form of selection item. For such skills, some form of performance-based assessment is needed (see Chapters 10 and 11).

Because we cannot illustrate all the uses of the multiple-choice item, here we show only its use in measuring some of the more common learning outcomes in the knowledge, understanding, and application areas. The measurement of more complex outcomes, using modified forms of the multiple-choice item, are considered in the following chapter.

Measuring Knowledge Outcomes

Learning outcomes in the knowledge area are prominent in all school subjects, and multiple-choice items can measure such a variety of these outcomes that examples can be endless. Here we present the more typical uses of the multiple-choice form in measuring knowledge outcomes common to most school subjects.

Knowledge of Terminology.   A simple but basic learning outcome measured by the multiple-choice item is knowledge of terminology. For this purpose, students can be requested to show their knowledge of a particular term by selecting a word that has the same meaning as the given term or by choosing a definition of the term. Special uses of a term also can be measured by having students identify the meaning of the term when used in context.

EXAMPLES   Which one of the following words has the same meaning as the word *egress*?

    A   Depress
    B   Enter
    ©   Exit
    D   Regress

Which one of the following statements best defines the word *egress*?

    A   An expression of disapproval
    Ⓑ   An act of leaving an enclosed place
    C   Proceeding to a higher level
    D   Proceeding to a lower level

What is meant by the word *egress* in the following sentence: "The astronauts hope they can now make a safe egress"?

    A   Separation from the rocket
    B   Reentry into the earth's atmosphere
    C   Landing on the water
    Ⓓ   Escape from the space capsule

Knowledge of Specific Facts.   Another learning outcome basic to all school subjects is the knowledge of specific facts. It is important in its own right, and it provides a necessary basis for developing understanding, thinking skills, and other complex learning outcomes. Multiple-choice items designed to measure specific facts can take various forms, but questions of the **who, what, when,** and **where** variety are most common. These various types are illustrated in the following examples. Although based on the space program, similar questions could be written in many other subject areas.

EXAMPLES   Who was the first United States astronaut to orbit the earth in space?

    A   Scott Carpenter
    Ⓑ   John Glenn
    C   Virgil Grissom
    D   Alan Shepard

What was the name of the missile that launched the first United States astronaut into orbital flight around the earth?

    Ⓐ   *Atlas*
    B   *Mars*
    C   *Midas*
    D   *Polaris*

When did a United States astronaut first orbit the earth in space?

    A   1960
    B   1961
    ©   1962
    D   1963

Where did the *Friendship Seven* capsule land after the first United States orbital flight around the earth?

- (A)   Atlantic Ocean
- B   Caribbean Sea
- C   Gulf of Mexico
- D   Pacific Ocean

Knowledge of Principles.   Knowledge of principles is also an important learning outcome in most school subjects. Multiple-choice items can be constructed to measure knowledge of principles as easily as those designed to measure facts.

EXAMPLES   The principle of capillary action helps explain how fluids

- A   enter solutions of lower concentration.
- B   escape through small openings.
- C   pass through semipermeable membranes.
- (D)   rise in fine tubes.

Which one of the following principles of taxation is characteristic of the federal income tax?

- A   The benefits received by an individual should determine the amount of the tax.
- (B)   A tax should be based on an individual's ability to pay.
- C   All citizens should be required to pay the same amount of tax.
- D   The amount of tax an individual pays should be determined by the size of the federal budget.

Knowledge of Methods and Procedures.   Another common learning outcome readily acceptable to the multiple-choice format is knowledge of methods and procedures. This includes such diverse areas as knowledge of laboratory procedures; knowledge of methods underlying communication, computational, and performance skills; knowledge of methods used in problem solving; knowledge of governmental procedures; and knowledge of common social practices. In some cases, we might want to measure knowledge of procedures before we permit students to practice in a particular area (e.g., laboratory procedures). In other cases, knowledge of methods and procedures may be important learning outcomes in their own right (e.g., knowledge of governmental procedures). The following test items illustrate a few of these uses in different school subjects.

EXAMPLES   Which one of the following methods of locating a specimen under the microscope is most desirable?

- A   Start with the coarse adjustment up, and with your eye at the eyepiece, turn down the coarse adjustment.
- (B)   Start with the coarse adjustment down, and with your eye at the eyepiece, turn up the coarse adjustment.
- C   Start with the coarse adjustment in the center, and with your eye at the eyepiece, turn up and down until you locate the specimen.

To make treaties, the president of the United States must have the consent of the

    A   Cabinet.
    B   House of Representatives.
    Ⓒ   Senate.
    D   Supreme Court.

Alternating electric current is changed to direct current by means of a

    A   condenser.
    B   generator.
    Ⓒ   rectifier.
    D   transformer.

If you were making a scientific study of a problem, your first step should be to

    Ⓐ   collect information about the problem.
    B   develop hypotheses to be tested.
    C   design the experiment to be conducted.
    D   select scientific equipment.

We have merely scratched the surface with our examples of multiple-choice items measuring knowledge outcomes. As you develop items in the particular school subjects you teach, many other uses will occur to you.

Measuring Outcomes at the Understanding and Application Levels

Many teachers limit the use of multiple-choice items to the knowledge area because they believe that all objective-type items are restricted to the measurement of relatively simple learning outcomes. Although it is difficult to go beyond the knowledge level with most of the other types of objective items, the multiple-choice item is especially adaptable to the measurement of more complex learning outcomes. The examples that follow illustrate its use in measuring various aspects of understanding and application.

In reviewing the following items, it is important to keep in mind that such items measure learning outcomes beyond factual knowledge only if the applications and interpretations are new to the students. Any specific applications or interpretations of knowledge can, of course, be taught directly to students as any other fact is taught. When this is done, and the test items contain the same problem situations and solutions used in teaching, it is obvious that the students can be given credit for no more than the mere retention of factual knowledge. To measure understanding and application, an element of **novelty** must be included in the test items. For illustrative purposes, it is necessary to assume that such novelty exists in the examples that follow.

Ability to Identify Application of Facts and Principles.   A common method of determining whether students' learning has gone beyond the mere memorization of a fact or principle is to ask them to identify its correct application in a situation that is new to the student.

Application items measure understanding, but they also include the ability to transfer learning to situations that have not been previously studied. Thus, the items can be designed to measure understanding at a relatively high level.

EXAMPLES   Which one of the following is an example of a chemical element?

    A   Acid
    B   Sodium chloride
    Ⓒ   Oxygen
    D   Water

Directions: In each of the following sentences, circle the word that makes the sentence correct.

               that
1. This is the boy ⟨who⟩ asked the question.
              whom

          ⟨that⟩
2. This is the dog who he asked about.
          whom

Which one of the following best illustrates the principle of capillarity?

    Ⓐ   Fluid is carried through the stems of plants.
    B   Food is manufactured in the leaves of plants.
    C   The leaves of deciduous plants lose their green color in winter.
    D   Plants give off moisture through their stomata.

Pascal's law can be used to explain the operation of

    A   electric fans.
    Ⓑ   hydraulic brakes.
    C   levers.
    D   syringes.

Which one of the following best illustrates the law of diminishing returns?

    A   The demand for a farm product increased faster than the supply of the product.
    B   The population of a country increased faster than the means of subsistence.
    C   A machine decreased in utility as its parts became worn.
    Ⓓ   A factory doubled its labor force and increased production by 50%.

Ability to Interpret Cause-and-Effect Relationships.   Understanding can frequently be measured by asking students to interpret various relationships among facts. One of the most important relationships in this regard, and one common to most subject-matter areas, is the cause-and-effect relationship. Understanding of such relationships can be measured by presenting students with a specific cause-and-effect relationship and asking them to identify the reason that best accounts for it.

EXAMPLES   Bread will not become moldy as rapidly if placed in a refrigerator because

     (A)   cooling retards the growth of fungi.

     B   darkness retards the growth of mold.

     C   cooling prevents the bread from drying out so rapidly.

     D   mold requires both heat and light for best growth.

An increased quantity of carbon monoxide is produced when fuel is burned in a limited supply of oxygen because

     A   carbon reacts with carbon monoxide.

     (B)   carbon reacts with carbon dioxide.

     C   carbon monoxide is an effective reducing agent.

     D   greater oxidation takes place.

Investing money in common stock protects against loss of assets during inflation because common stock

     A   pays higher rates of interest during inflation.

     B   provides a steady but dependable income despite economic conditions.

     C   is protected by the Federal Reserve System.

     (D)   increases in value as the value of a business increases.

Ability to Justify Methods and Procedures.   Another phase of understanding important in various subject-matter areas concerns methods and procedures. A student might know the correct method or sequence of steps in carrying out a procedure without being able to explain why it is the best method or sequence of steps. At the understanding level, we are interested in the student's ability to justify the use of a particular method or procedure. This can be measured with multiple-choice items by asking the student to select the best of several possible explanations of a method or procedure.

EXAMPLES   Why is adequate lighting necessary in a balanced aquarium?

     A   Fish need light to see their food.

     B   Fish take in oxygen in the dark.

     (C)   Plants expel carbon dioxide in the dark.

     D   Plants grow too rapidly in the dark.

Why do farmers rotate their crops?

     (A)   To conserve the soil.

     B   To make marketing easier.

     C   To provide for strip cropping.

     D   It removes the brownish yellow color.

Although various aspects of understanding and application can be measured by single multiple-choice items, as shown in the preceding examples, a series of multiple-choice items based on a common set of data is even more adaptable to the measurement of complex achievement. Such items are illustrated in the next chapter.

ADVANTAGES AND LIMITATIONS
OF MULTIPLE-CHOICE ITEMS

The multiple-choice item is one of the most widely applicable test items for measuring achievement. It can effectively measure various types of knowledge and complex learning outcomes. In addition to this flexibility, it is free from some of the common shortcomings characteristic of the other item types. The ambiguity and vagueness that frequently are present in the short-answer item are avoided because the alternatives better structure the situation. In the following examples, note how the vague short-answer item becomes a clear-cut problem.

EXAMPLE

Poor: Lincoln was born in _____.
Better: Lincoln was born in

A   Indiana
B   Illinois
Ⓒ   Kentucky
D   Ohio

Your first reaction to the short-answer item might be, "Why not put it in question form to make it clearer?" But even if we ask, "In what state was Lincoln born?" answers such as "poverty" could not be ruled out. In addition to clarifying the specific type of response called for, the multiple-choice item relieves us of the problem of deciding how to score misspelled answers. Although we may be interested in having students spell the names of states correctly, this should be done in a separate spelling test rather than letting it contaminate our measures of achievement.

One advantage of the multiple-choice item over the true–false item is that students cannot receive credit for simply knowing that a statement is incorrect; they must also know what is correct. Note the difference in the following two items.

EXAMPLE

T   F   Lincoln was born in 1807.
Lincoln was born in

A   1805
B   1807
Ⓒ   1809
D   1811

In the true–false version, students will receive credit if they mark it false even if they think Lincoln was born in some year other than 1809. In fact, if a student thought he was born in 1909, it would be marked false, and the student would receive a 1-point credit for that response. Because marking statements false does not show that students know what is correct, the resulting scores tend to be inadequate measures of what students have learned. This problem is not encountered with multiple-choice items, however, because the students must select the correct answer to receive credit. Although the problem also could be resolved by having students change all false statements to true, that procedure is often cumbersome, especially when measuring complex learning outcomes.

Using the best-answer type of multiple-choice item also circumvents a difficulty associated with the true–false item—obtaining statements that are true or false without qualification. This makes it possible to measure learning outcomes in the numerous subject-matter areas in which solutions to problems are not absolutely true or false but vary in degree of appropriateness (e.g., best method, best reason, and best interpretation).

One other commonly cited advantage of the multiple-choice item over the true–false item is the greater reliability per item. Because the number of alternatives is increased from two to three, four, or five, the opportunity for guessing the correct answer is reduced, and the reliability is correspondingly increased. The effect of increasing the number of alternatives for each item is similar to that of increasing the length of the test. As was noted in Chapter 6, however, this advantage of the multiple-choice item is partially offset by the fact that roughly three true–false items can typically be responded to in the time it takes to respond to two multiple-choice items.

An advantage of the multiple-choice item over the matching exercise is that the need for homogeneous material is avoided. The matching exercise, which is essentially a modified form of the multiple-choice item, requires a series of related ideas to form the list of premises and alternative responses. In many content areas, it is difficult to obtain enough homogeneous material to prepare effective matching exercises. This problem is avoided with multiple-choice items, however, because each item measures a single idea. Thus, it is possible to measure one or many relationships in a given area when the multiple-choice item is used.

Two other desirable characteristics of the multiple-choice item are worthy of mention. First, it is relatively free from response sets. That is, students generally do not favor a particular alternative when they do not know the answer. Second, using a number of plausible alternatives makes the results amenable to diagnosis. The kind of incorrect alternatives students select provides clues to factual errors and misunderstandings that need correction.

It is easier to construct high-quality test items in multiple-choice form than in any of the other forms. This does not mean that good multiple-choice items can be constructed without effort, but for a given amount of effort, multiple-choice items will tend to be of a higher quality than short-answer, true–false, or matching-type items in the same area.

Despite its superiority in many respects to other simple forms of objective items, the multiple-choice item has limitations. First, as with all other paper-and-pencil tests, it is limited to learning outcomes at the verbal level. The problems presented to students are verbal problems, free from the many irrelevant factors present in natural situations. In addition, the applications students are asked to make are verbal applications, free from the personal commitment necessary for application in natural situations. In short, the multiple-choice item, like other paper-and-pencil tests, measures whether the student knows or understands what to do when confronted with a problem situation, but it cannot determine how the student actually will perform in that situation.

Second, as with other types of selection items, the multiple-choice item requires selection of the correct answer, and therefore it is not well adapted to measuring some problem-solving skills in mathematics and science or to measuring the ability to organize and present ideas.

Third, the multiple-choice item has a disadvantage not shared by the other item types: the difficulty of finding a sufficient number of incorrect but plausible distracters. This problem is especially acute at the early primary level because of the students' limited vocabulary and knowledge in any particular area. Even at this level, however, classroom teachers have been creative in adapting the multiple-choice item to the measurement of newly learned concepts (see Figure 8.1). As students move up through the grade levels and expand their vocabulary, knowledge, and understanding, plausible but incorrect answers become more available. It still takes a touch of creativity, however, to identify and state the most plausible distracters that will provide diagnostic information about misunderstandings and incorrect information. This is the task that separates a good test constructor from a poor one. Fortunately, the construction of such items gets easier with experience.

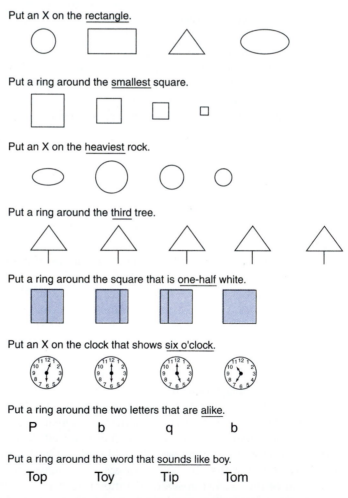

Figure 8.1
Illustrative multiple-choice items used at the early primary level (directions are given orally)

SUGGESTIONS FOR CONSTRUCTING MULTIPLE CHOICE ITEMS

The general applicability and the superior qualities of multiple-choice test items are realized most fully when care is taken in their construction. This involves formulating a clearly stated problem, identifying plausible alternatives, and removing irrelevant clues to the answer. The following suggestions provide more specific maxims for this purpose.

1. The stem of the item should be meaningful by itself and should present a definite problem. Often the stems of test items placed in multiple-choice form are incomplete statements that make little sense until all the alternatives have been read. These are not multiple-choice items but, rather, a collection of true–false statements placed in multiple-choice form. A properly constructed multiple-choice item presents a definite problem in the stem that is meaningful without the alternatives. Compare the stems in the two versions of the test item in the following example.

EXAMPLES   *Poor:*   South America

A   is a flat, arid country.
B   imports coffee from the United States.
C   has a larger population than the United States.
(D)   was settled mainly by colonists from Spain.

Better: Most of South America was settled by colonists from

A   England.
B   France.
C   Holland.
(D)   Spain.

Formulating a definite problem in the stem not only improves the stem of the item but also has a desirable effect on the alternatives. In the preceding example, the alternatives in the first version are concerned with widely dissimilar ideas. This heterogeneity is possible because of the stem's lack of structure. In the second version, the clearly formulated problem in the stem forces the alternatives to be more homogeneous.

A good check on the adequacy of the problem statement is to cover the alternatives and read the stem by itself. It should be complete enough to serve as a short-answer item. Starting each item stem as a direct question and shifting to the incomplete-statement form only when greater conciseness is possible is the most effective method for obtaining a clearly formulated problem.

2. The item stem should include as much of the item as possible and should be free of irrelevant material. This will increase the probability of a clearly stated problem in the stem and will reduce the reading time required. The following example illustrates how the conciseness of an item is increased by removing irrelevant material and including in the stem those words repeated in the alternatives. Notice that to obtain the conciseness of the final version, it is necessary to shift to the incomplete-statement form. The best version provides a slim-trim item that is easily read and focuses directly on the key element in the intended learning outcome.

EXAMPLES   *Poor:*   Most of South America was settled by colonists from Spain. How would you account for the large number of Spanish colonists settling there?

A   They were adventurous.
Ⓑ   They were in search of wealth.
C   They wanted lower taxes.
D   They were seeking religious freedom.

Better: Why did Spanish colonists settle most of South America?

A   They were adventurous.
Ⓑ   They were in search of wealth.
C   They wanted lower taxes.
D   They were seeking religious freedom.

Best: Spanish colonists settled most of South America in search of

A   adventure.
Ⓑ   wealth.
C   lower taxes.
D   religious freedom.

There are a few exceptions to this rule. In testing problem-solving ability, irrelevant material might be included in the stem of an item to determine whether students can identify and select the material that is relevant to the problem's solution. Similarly, repeating common words in the alternatives is sometimes necessary for grammatical consistency or greater clarity.

3. Use a negatively stated stem only when significant learning outcomes require it. Most problems can and should be stated in positive terms. This avoids the possibility of students' overlooking **no, not, least,** and similar words used in negative statements. In most instances, it also avoids measuring relatively insignificant learning outcomes. Knowing the least important method, the principle that does not apply, or the poorest reason are seldom important learning outcomes. We are usually interested in students' learning the most important method, the principle that does apply, and the best reason.

Teachers sometimes go to ridiculous extremes to use negatively stated items because they appear more difficult. The difficulty of such items, however, is in the lack of sentence clarity rather than in the difficulty of the concept being measured.

EXAMPLE   *Poor:*   Which one of the following states is not located north of the Mason-Dixon line?

A   Maine
B   New York
C   Pennsylvania
Ⓓ   Virginia

Better: Which one of the following states is located south of the Mason-Dixon line?

A   Maine
B   New York
C   Pennsylvania
Ⓓ   Virginia

Both versions of this item measure the same knowledge. But some students who can answer the second version correctly will select an incorrect alternative on the first version merely because the negative phrasing confuses them. Such items thus introduce factors that contribute to the invalidity of the test.

Although negatively stated items are generally to be avoided, there are occasions when they are useful, mainly in areas in which the wrong information or wrong procedure can have dire consequences. In the health area, for example, there are practices to be avoided because of their harmful nature. In shop and laboratory work, there are procedures that can damage equipment and result in bodily injury; and in driver training there are unsafe practices to be emphasized. When the avoidance of such potentially harmful practices is emphasized in teaching, it might well receive a corresponding emphasis in testing through the use of negatively stated items. When used, the negative aspects of the item should be made obvious.

EXAMPLES   *Poor:*   Which one of the following is not a safe driving practice on icy roads?

A   Accelerating slowly
Ⓑ   Jamming on the brakes
C   Holding the wheel firmly
D   Slowing down gradually

Better: All of the following are safe driving practices on icy roads

Except

A   accelerating slowly.
Ⓑ   jamming on the brakes.
C   holding the wheel firmly.
D   slowing down gradually.

In the first version of the item, the **not** is easily overlooked, in which case students would tend to select the first alternative and not read any further. In the second version, no student would probably overlook the negative element because it is placed at the end of the statement and is capitalized.

4. All the alternatives should be grammatically consistent with the stem of the item. In the following example, note how the better version results from a change in the alternatives in order to obtain grammatical consistency. This rule is not presented merely to perpetuate proper grammar usage, however; its main function is to prevent irrelevant clues from creeping in. All too frequently, the grammatical consistency of the correct answer is given attention but that of the distracters is neglected. As a result, some of the alternatives are grammatically inconsistent with the stem and are therefore obviously incorrect answers.

Poor: An electric transformer can be used

A   for storing electricity.
Ⓑ   to increase the voltage of alternating current.
C   it converts electrical energy into mechanical energy.
D   alternating current is changed to direct current.

Better: An electric transformer can be used to

A   store electricity.
Ⓑ   increase the voltage of alternating current.
C   convert electrical energy into mechanical energy.
D   change alternating current to direct current.

Similar difficulties arise from a lack of attention to verb tense, to the proper use of the articles *a* or *an,* and to other common sources of grammatical inconsistency. Because most of these errors are the result of carelessness, they can be detected easily by carefully reading each item before assembling them into a test. See the box "How Many Alternatives Should Be Used in Multiple-Choice Items?" for more guidelines on constructing multiple-choice assessments.

5. An item should contain only one correct or clearly best answer. Including more than one correct answer in a test item and asking students to select all the correct alternatives has two shortcomings. First, such items are usually no more than a collection of true–false items presented in multiple-choice format. They do not present a definite problem in the stem, and the selection of answers requires a mental response of *true* or *false* to each alternative rather than a comparison and selection of alternatives. Second, because the number of alternatives selected as correct answers varies from one student to another, satisfactory scoring methods are more cumbersome than most teachers are likely to want to use or have to explain to students.

Poor: The state of Michigan borders on

Ⓐ   Lake Huron.
B   Lake Ontario.
Ⓒ   Indiana.
D   Illinois.

Better: The state of Michigan borders on

A   Lake Huron.   Ⓣ   F
B   Lake Ontario.   T   Ⓕ
C   Indiana.   Ⓣ   F
D   Illinois.   T   Ⓕ

The second version of this item shows students what type of response is expected. They are to read each alternative and decide whether it is true or false. Thus, this is not a four-alternative, multiple-choice item but a series of four statements, each of which has two alternatives—true or false. This second version, which is called a cluster-type true–false item, not only identifies the mental process involved but also simplifies the scoring. Each statement in the cluster can be considered as 1 point and scored as any other true–false item is scored. In contrast, how would you score a student who selected alternatives A, B, and C in the first version? Would you give 2 points for the response because two answers were correctly identified? Would you give only 1 point because one incorrect alternative was also selected? Or would you give no points because the answer as a whole was not completely correct? How would you evaluate the lack of a response to alternative D? Assume that the student knew Illinois did not border on Michigan and therefore did not select it or assume that the student was uncertain and left it blank. Fairly complicated and cumbersome scoring rules are required to satisfactorily resolve these problems. Hence, multiple-choice items like the one in the first version should be avoided or converted to the true–false form.

There is another important facet of this rule concerning single-answer multiple-choice items: The answer must be agreed on by authorities in the area. The best-answer type of item is especially subject to variations of interpretation and disagreement concerning the correct answer. Care must be taken to make certain that the answer is clearly the best one. Frequently, rewording the problem in the stem will correct an otherwise faulty item.

In the first version of the following item, different alternatives could be defended as correct, depending on whether the **best** refers to cost, efficiency, cleanliness, or accessibility. The second version avoids this problem by making the criterion of **best** explicit.

EXAMPLE   *Poor:*   Which one of the following is the best source of heat for home use?

A   Coal
B   Electricity
C   Gas
D   Oil

Better: In the midwestern part of the United States, which one of the following is the most economical source of heat for home use?

(A)   Coal
B   Electricity
C   Gas
D   Oil

---

6. Items used to measure understanding should contain some novelty, but beware of too much. The construction of multiple-choice items that measure understanding requires a careful choice of situations and skillful phrasing. The situations must be new to the students but not too far removed from the examples used in class. If the test items contain problem situations identical with those used in class, the students can, of course, respond on the basis of memorized answers. On the other hand, if the problem situations contain too much novelty, some students may respond incorrectly merely because they lack necessary factual

How Many Alternatives Should Be Used in Multiple-Choice Items?

There is no magic number of alternatives to use in a multiple-choice item. Typically three, four, or five choices are used. Some favor five-choice items to reduce the chances of guessing the correct answer.

Number of Choices	Chances of a Correct Guess	Chance Score on 100-Item Test
Five-choice items	1 in 5	20
Four-choice items	1 in 4	25
Three-choice items	1 in 3	33

Reducing the chances of guessing the correct answers by adding alternatives enhances reliability and validity, but only if all the distracters are plausible and the items are well constructed. Our preference is for using four-choice items because, with reasonable effort, three good distracters usually can be obtained (a fourth distracter tends to be difficult to devise and is usually weaker than the others). For young students, three-choice items may be preferable in order to reduce the amount of reading. It should also be noted that there is a trade-off between the number of items and the number of choices per item. A 50-item test with three choices per item is likely to produce a more valid and reliable test than a 40-item test with five choices per item, especially if the fourth distractor is not very plausible for many of the items.

The number of alternatives can, of course, vary from item to item. You might use a five-choice item when four good distracters are available and a three-choice item when there are only two. Do not give up too soon on constructing distracters, however. It takes time and effort to generate several good ones.

information about the situations used. Asking students to apply the law of supply and demand to some phase of banking, for example, would be grossly unfair if they had not had a previous opportunity to study banking policies and practices. They may have a good understanding of the law of supply and demand but be unable to demonstrate this because of their unfamiliarity with the particular situation selected.

The problem of too much novelty usually can be avoided by selecting situations from the student's everyday experiences, by including in the stem of the item any factual information needed, and by phrasing the item so that the type of application or interpretation called for is clear.

7. All distracters should be plausible. The purpose of a distracter is to distract the uninformed from the correct answer. To the student who has not achieved the learning outcome being tested, the distracters should be at least as attractive as the correct answer and preferably more so. In a properly constructed multiple-choice item, each distracter will be selected by some students. If a distracter is not selected by anyone, it is not contributing to the functioning of the item and should be eliminated or revised.

One factor contributing to the plausibility of distracters is their homogeneity. If all the alternatives are homogeneous with regard to the knowledge being measured, then the distracters are more likely to function as intended. Whether alternatives appear homogeneous and distracters plausible, however, also depends on the students' age level. Note the difference in homogeneity in the following two items.

EXAMPLE

Poor: Who discovered the North Pole?

A   Christopher Columbus
B   Ferdinand Magellan
Ⓒ   Robert Peary
D   Marco Polo

Better: Who discovered the North Pole?

A   Roald Amundsen
B   Richard Byrd
Ⓒ   Robert Peary
D   Robert Scott

The first version would probably appear homogeneous to students at the primary level because all four choices are the names of well-known explorers. Students in higher grades, however, would eliminate alternatives A, B, and D as possible answers because they would know these men were not polar explorers. They might also recall that these men lived several hundred years before the North Pole was discovered. In either case, they could quickly obtain the correct answer by the process of elimination. The second version includes only the names of polar explorers, all of whom were active at approximately the same time. This homogeneity makes each alternative much more plausible and the elimination process much less effective. It also, of course, increases the item's level of difficulty. See the "Guidelines" box.

In selecting plausible distracters, the students' learning experiences must not be ignored. In the foregoing item, for example, the distracters in the second version would not be plausible to students if Robert Peary was the only polar explorer they had studied. Obviously, distracters must be familiar to students before they can serve as reasonable alternatives. Less obvious is the rich source of plausible distracters provided by the students' learning experiences. Common misconceptions, errors of judgment, and faulty reasoning that occur during the teaching–learning process provide the most plausible and educationally sound distracters available. One way to tap this supply is to keep a running record of such errors. A quicker method is to administer a short-answer test to students and tabulate the most common errors. This provides a series of incorrect responses that are especially plausible because they are in the students' own language.

8. **Verbal associations between the stem and the correct answer should be avoided.** Frequently a word in the correct answer will provide an irrelevant clue because it looks or sounds like a word in the stem of the item. Such verbal associations should never permit the student who lacks the necessary achievement to select the correct answer. However, words similar to those in the stem might be included in the distracters to increase their plausibility. Students who depend on rote memory and verbal associations will then be

GUIDELINES

Ways to Make Distracters Plausible

1. Use the students' most common errors.

2. Use important-sounding words (e.g., *significant, accurate*) that are relevant to the item stem. But do not overdo it!

3. Use words that have verbal associations with the item stem (e.g., *politician, political*).

4. Use textbook language or other phraseology that has the appearance of truth.

5. Use incorrect answers that are likely to result from student misunderstanding or carelessness (e.g., forgets to convert from feet to yards).

6. Use distracters that are homogeneous and similar in content to the correct answer (e.g., all are inventors).

7. Use distracters that are parallel in form and grammatically consistent with the item's stem.

8. Make the distracters similar to the correct answer in length, vocabulary, sentence structure, and complexity of thought.

CAUTION: Distracters should distract the uninformed, but they should not result in trick questions that mislead knowledgeable students (e.g., do *not* insert *not* in a correct answer to make it a distracter).

led away from, rather than to, the correct answer. The following item, taken from a fifth-grade test on a weather unit, shows the incorrect and correct use of verbal associations between the stem and the alternatives.

EXAMPLE

Poor: Which one of the following agencies should you contact to find out about a tornado warning in your locality?

A   State farm bureau
Ⓑ   Local radio station
C   United States Post Office
D   United States Weather Bureau

Better: Which one of the following agencies should you contact to find out about a tornado warning in your locality?

A   Local farm bureau
Ⓑ   Nearest radio station
C   Local post office
D   United States Weather Bureau

In the first version, the association between **locality** and **local** is an unnecessary clue. In the second version, this verbal association is used in two distracters to make them more attractive choices. If irrelevant verbal associations in the distracters are overused, however, students will soon catch on and avoid alternatives with pat verbal associations.

9. The relative length of the alternatives should not provide a clue to the answer. The best we can hope for in equalizing the length of a test item's alternatives is to make them approximately equal. Because the correct answer usually needs to be qualified, however, it tends to be longer than the distracters unless a special effort is made to control the length of the alternatives. If the correct answer cannot be shortened, then the distracters can be expanded to the desired length. Lengthening the distracters also is desirable for another reason. Added qualifiers and greater specificity frequently contribute to their plausibility. The correct answer should not be consistently longer, or consistently shorter, or consistently of medium length. The relative length of the correct answer should vary from one item to another in such a manner that no pattern is discernible to indicate the answer. This means, of course, that sometimes the correct answer will be the longest.

EXAMPLE   *Poor:*   What is the major purpose of the United Nations?

(A)   To maintain peace among the peoples of the world
B   To establish international law
C   To provide military control
D   To form new governments

Better: What is the major purpose of the United Nations?

(A)   To maintain peace among the peoples of the world
B   To develop a new system of international law
C   To provide military control of nations that have recently attained their independence
D   To establish and maintain democratic forms of government in newly formed nations

---

10. **The correct answer should appear in each of the alternative positions an approximately equal number of times but in random order.** Some teachers often bury the correct answer in the middle of the list of alternatives. As a consequence, the correct answer appears in the first and last positions far less often than it does in the middle positions. This, of course, provides an irrelevant clue to the alert student.

In placing the correct answer in each position approximately an equal number of times, care must be taken to avoid a regular pattern of responses. A random placement of correct answers can be attained with the use of any book. For each test item, open the book at an arbitrary position, note the number on the right-hand page, and place the correct answer for that test item as follows:

If Page Number Ends in	Place Correct Answer
1	First
3	Second
5	Third
7	Fourth
9	Fifth

11. Use sparingly special alternatives such as "none of the above" or "all of the above." The phrases "none of the above" or "all of the above" are sometimes added as the last alternative in multiple-choice items. This is done to force the student to consider all the alternatives carefully and to increase the difficulty of the items. All too frequently, however, these special alternatives are used inappropriately. In fact, there are relatively few situations in which their use is appropriate.

The use of "none of the above" is restricted to the correct-answer type of multiple-choice items and consequently to the measurement of factual knowledge to which absolute standards of correctness can be applied. It is inappropriate in best-answer types of items because the student is told to select the best of several alternatives of varying degrees of correctness.

Use of "none of the above" is frequently recommended for items measuring computational skill in mathematics and spelling ability, but these learning outcomes generally should not be measured by multiple-choice items, because they can be measured more effectively by short-answer items. When "none of the above" is used in such situations, the item may measure nothing more than a student's ability to recognize incorrect answers, a rather inadequate basis for judging computational skill or spelling ability.

The alternative "none of the above" should be used only when the measurement of significant learning outcomes requires it. As with negatively stated item stems, sometimes procedures or practices should be avoided for safety, health, or other reasons. When knowing what not to do is important, "none of the above" might be appropriately applied. When used for this purpose, it also must be used as an incorrect answer a proportionate number of times. See the box "Examples of Misuse of the Alternative 'None of the Above.'"

The use of "all of the above" is fraught with so many difficulties that it might best be discarded as a possible alternative. When used, some students will note that the first alternative is correct and select it without reading further. Other students will note that at least two of the alternatives are correct and thereby know that "all of the above" must be the answer. In the first instance, students mark the item incorrectly because they do not read all the alternatives, and in the second instance, students obtain the correct answer on the basis of partial knowledge. Both types of response prevent the item from functioning as intended.

12. Do not use multiple-choice items when other item types are more appropriate. When various item types can serve a purpose equally well, the multiple-choice item should be favored because of its many superior qualities. Sometimes, however, the multiple-choice form is inappropriate or less suitable than other item types. When there are only two possible responses (e.g., fact or opinion), the true–false item is more appropriate. When there are enough homogeneous items but few plausible distracters for each, a matching exercise might be more suitable. In certain problem-solving situations in mathematics and science, for example, supply types of short-answer items are clearly superior. The measurement of many complex achievement goals (such as organizing, integrating, and expressing ideas; the formulation and testing of hypotheses; or the construction of models, maps, or diagrams) requires the use of performance-based assessment tasks. Although we should take full advantage of the wide applicability of the multiple-choice form, we should not lose sight of a principle of test construction cited earlier— select the item type that measures the learning outcome. One of the primary criticisms of high-stakes assessments, an overreliance on multiple-choice items, is not

Examples of Misuse of the Alternative "None of the Above"

Which of the following is *not* an example of a mammal?

  Ⓐ Bird
  B. Dog
  C. Whale
  D. None of the above

(It would be easy to prove that D is *not* an example of a mammal.)

When the temperature drops, tire pressure tends to

  Ⓐ Decrease
  B. Increase
  C. Stay the same
  D. None of the above

(There may be something other than A, B, or C, but we cannot think of what it might be.)

United States federal law requires that first offenders must be fined or imprisoned if they possess

  A. Amphetamine
  B. Heroin
  C. Marijuana
  Ⓓ None of the above

(Sounds like a very unfair law. If you do not agree, read only the stem and answer D.)

CHECKLIST

Reviewing Multiple-Choice Items

	Yes	No
1. Is this the most appropriate type of item to use?	____	____
2. Does each item stem present a meaningful problem?	____	____
3. Are the item stems free of irrelevant material?	____	____
4. Are the item stems stated in positive terms (if possible)?	____	____
5. If used, has negative wording been given special emphasis (e.g., capitalized)?	____	____
6. Are the alternatives grammatically consistent with the item stem?	____	____
7. Are the alternative answers brief and free of unnecessary words?	____	____
8. Are the alternatives similar in length and form?	____	____
9. Is there only one correct or clearly best answer?	____	____
10. Are the distracters plausible to low achievers?	____	____
11. Are the items free of verbal clues to the answer?	____	____
12. Are verbal alternatives in alphabetical order?	____	____
13. Are numerical alternatives in numerical order?	____	____
14. Have *none of the above* and *all of the above* been avoided (or used sparingly and appropriately)?	____	____
15. If revised, are the items still relevant to the intended learning outcomes?	____	____
16. Have the items been set aside for a time before reviewing them?	____	____

really a criticism of multiple-choice items per se but a criticism of the lack of measurement of other types of learning outcomes that are better measured by other types of items. See the "Checklist" box.

SUMMARY

The multiple-choice item consists of a problem and a list of alternative solutions. The student responds by selecting the alternative that provides the correct or best solution to the problem. The incorrect alternatives are called distracters because their purpose is to distract the uninformed student from the correct response. The problem can be stated as a direct question or an incomplete statement. In either case, it should be a clearly formulated problem that is meaningful without reference to the list of alternatives.

The multiple-choice form is extremely flexible and can be used to measure a variety of learning outcomes at the knowledge and understanding levels. Knowledge outcomes concerned with vocabulary, facts, principles, and methods and procedures all can be measured with the multiple-choice item. Aspects of understanding, such as the application and interpretation of facts, principles, and methods, also can be measured with this item type. Other, more specific uses occur in particular school subjects.

The main advantage of the multiple-choice item is its wide applicability in the measurement of various phases of achievement. It is also free of many of the limitations of other forms of objective items. It tends to present a more well-defined problem than the short-answer item does, it avoids the need for homogeneous material required by the matching item, and it reduces the clues and susceptibility to guessing characteristic of the true–false item. In addition, the multiple-choice item is relatively free from response sets and is useful in diagnosis.

Its limitations are mainly that it is a selection type of paper-and-pencil test and measures problem-solving behavior at the verbal level only. Because it requires selection of the correct answer, it is inappropriate for measuring learning outcomes requiring the ability to recall, organize, synthesize, or evaluate ideas.

The construction of multiple-choice items involves defining the problem in the stem of the item, selecting one correct or best solution, identifying several plausible distracters, and avoiding irrelevant clues to the answer. Items used to measure learning outcomes at the understanding level must also include some (but beware of too much) novelty.

LEARNING EXERCISES

1. Describe the advantages of the multiple-choice item over each of the other objective-type items. What are the comparative disadvantages?
2. In an area in which you are teaching or plan to teach, construct one multiple-choice item in each of the following areas: knowledge, understanding, and application.
3. Make a checklist for evaluating the plausibility of distracters. Put the criteria in question form so that they can be answered with a simple *yes* or *no*.
4. How does a multiple-choice item designed to measure knowledge outcomes differ from one designed to measure understanding?
5. Describe the relative merits of using correct-answer and best-answer multiple-choice items. What types of learning outcomes are best measured by each type of multiple-choice item?

FURTHER READING

Bloom, B. S., Madaus, G. F., & Hastings, J. T. (1981). *Evaluation to improve learning.* New York: McGraw-Hill. Chapter 8, "Evaluation Techniques for Knowledge and Comprehension Objectives," and Chapter 9, "Evaluation Techniques for Application and Analysis Objectives," include numerous illustrations of modified forms of multiple-choice items.

Downing, S. M. (2006). Selected-response item formats in test development. In S. M. Downing & T. M. Haladyna (Eds.), *Handbook of test development* (pp. 287–301). Mahwah, NJ: Lawrence Erlbaum Associates, Publishers. Discusses the preparation of selected-response items and reviews research supporting the use of this item type.

Gronlund, N. E. (2005). *Assessment of student achievement* (8th ed.). Boston: Allyn & Bacon. Chapter 4, "Writing Selection Items: Multiple-Choice," describes and illustrates the use of multiple-choice items for measuring various types of outcomes. The chapter also provides a useful set of rules for writing multiple-choice items.

Haladyna, T. M., & Downing, S. M. (1989). A taxonomy of multiple-choice item-writing rules; and Validity of a taxonomy of multiple-choice item writing rules. *Applied Measurement in Education, 2,* 37–50, 51–78. The first of these two companion articles summarizes item-writing rules offered by a wide range of measurement textbooks and other references. The second article reviews results of theoretical and empirical studies that have investigated the validity of the rules.

9

MEASURING COMPLEX ACHIEVEMENT: THE INTERPRETIVE EXERCISE

Complex achievement includes those learning outcomes based on the higher mental processes, such as understanding, thinking skills, and various problem-solving abilities. Although some aspects of complex achievement require extended constructed responses and other types of performance assessment tasks, other aspects can be measured objectively.

We have already had some experience with measuring complex achievement, as this category encompasses all those learning outcomes requiring more than the mere retention of factual knowledge. The use of the short-answer item to measure problem-solving abilities in mathematics and science, the true–false item to measure the ability to recognize cause-and-effect relationships, and the multiple-choice item to measure various aspects of understanding and application all illustrate the measurement of complex achievement. These illustrations, however, were limited to the use of single, independent test items of the objective type. Greater range and flexibility in measuring complex achievement can be attained not only by moving to the extended response and other performance assessment tasks discussed in Chapters 10 and 11 but also by using more complex forms of objective test items.

A variety of learning outcomes are included in complex achievement. Following are typical examples.

- Ability to apply a principle
- Ability to interpret relationships
- Ability to recognize and state inferences
- Ability to recognize the relevance of information

- Ability to develop and recognize tenable hypotheses
- Ability to formulate and recognize valid conclusions
- Ability to recognize assumptions underlying conclusions
- Ability to recognize the limitations of data
- Ability to recognize and state significant problems
- Ability to design experimental procedures
- Ability to interpret charts, tables, and data
- Ability to evaluate arguments

These and similar learning outcomes have been classified under such categories as understanding, reasoning, critical thinking, scientific thinking, creative thinking, and problem solving. There is general agreement that learning outcomes based on higher-order thinking skills constitute some of the most significant outcomes of education. Given the importance of these complex learning outcomes, it is critical to use a full array of assessment techniques available for measuring those outcomes. The interpretive exercise provides one of those needed techniques. Used wisely, and supplemented by the techniques discussed in Chapters 10 and 11, the interpretive exercise can help ensure that complex learning outcomes are given adequate priority in classroom assessments.

NATURE OF THE INTERPRETIVE EXERCISE

An interpretive exercise (also called "classification exercise," "key-type item," or "master-list item") consists of a series of objective items based on a common set of stimuli. The stimuli may be in the form of written materials, tables, charts, graphs, maps, or pictures. The series of related test items may also take various forms but are most commonly multiple-choice or true–false items. Because all students are presented with a common set of stimuli, it is possible to measure a variety of complex learning outcomes. Students can be asked to identify relationships in data, to recognize valid conclusions, to appraise assumptions and inferences, to detect proper applications of data, and the like.

The common set of materials used in interpretive exercises ensures that all students will be confronted with the same task. It also makes it possible to control the amount of factual information given to them. We can give them as much or as little information as we think desirable in measuring their achievement of a learning outcome. In measuring their ability to interpret mathematical data, for example, we can include the formulas needed or require the students to supply them. In other areas, we can supply definitions of terms, meanings of symbols, and other facts or expect students to supply them. This flexibility makes it possible to measure various degrees of proficiency in any particular area.

FORMS AND USES OF THE INTERPRETIVE EXERCISE

As with other objective items, there are so many forms and uses of the interpretive exercise that it is impossible to illustrate all of them. Here we present examples of this item type as applied to the measurement of complex learning outcomes in a variety of school subjects at the elementary and secondary levels. Different types of introductory material and different methods of responding also will be used to illustrate the great flexibility of the interpretive exercise. The references at the end of this chapter offer additional illustrative exercises.

Ability to Recognize Inferences

In interpreting written material, it is frequently necessary to draw inferences from the facts given. The following exercise measures the extent to which students are able to recognize warranted and unwarranted inferences drawn from a passage.

EXAMPLE   *Directions:* Assuming that the information below is true, it is possible to establish other facts using the ones in this paragraph as a basis for reasoning. This is called drawing inferences. There is, of course, a limit to the number of kinds of facts which may be properly inferred from any statement.

By writing the proper symbol in the space provided, indicate that a statement is TRUE if it may be properly inferred from the information given in the paragraph. Indicate that it is UNTRUE if the information given in the paragraph implies that it is false. Indicate that NO INFERENCE can be drawn if the statement cannot be inferred one way or the other. Use only the information given in the paragraph as a basis for your responses. . . .

Use the following symbols in writing your answers:

   T—if the statement may be inferred as TRUE.
   F—if the statement may be inferred as UNTRUE.
   N—if NO INFERENCE can be drawn about it from the paragraph.

PARAGRAPH A

By the close of the thirteenth century there were several famous universities established in Europe, though of course they were very different from modern ones. One of the earliest to be founded was one of the most widely known. This was the University of Bologna, where students from all countries came who wished to have the best training in studying Roman law. Students especially interested in philosophy and theology went to the University of Paris. Those who wished to study medicine went to the Universities of Montpellier or Salerno.

QUESTIONS ON PARAGRAPH A

(T)   1. There were law suits between people occasionally in those days.
(N)   2. The professors were poorly paid.
(F)   3. In the Middle Ages people were not interested in getting education.
(T)   4. There were books in Europe at that time.
(N)   5. Most of the teaching in these medieval universities was very poor.
(N)   6. There was no place where students could go to study.
(F)   7. There were no doctors in Europe at this time.
(F)   8. There was no way to travel during the Middle Ages.
(T)   9. If a student wanted to be a priest, he would probably attend the University of Paris.

(N)   10. There were no universities in Europe before the thirteenth century.

(N)   11. There was only one language in Europe at this time.

Source: From "Selected Items for the Testing of Study Skills" by H. T. Morse and G. H. McCune, 1971, *Bulletin,* *15,* 66. Copyright 1971 by National Council for the Social Studies. Used by permission of the publisher.

Ability to Recognize Warranted and Unwarranted Generalizations

The ability to recognize the validity of generalizations is of central importance in the interpretation of data. At minimum, students should be able to determine which conclusions the data support, which the data refute, and which the data neither support nor refute. The data may be in the form of tables, charts, graphs, maps, or pictures, and the test items may be true–false or multiple-choice items. An illustration of recognizing the validity of generalizations is shown in the following example.

EXAMPLE   Percentage of population between the ages of 25 and 29 who have completed secondary and college (a bachelor's degree or higher education), by gender in 1980, 1985, 1990, 1995, 2000, and 2005

	Males		Females	
Year	High School	College	High School	College
1980	85.4	24.0	85.5	21.0
1985	85.9	23.1	86.4	21.3
1990	84.4	23.7	87.0	22.8
1995	86.3	24.5	87.4	24.9
2000	86.7	27.9	89.4	30.1
2005	84.9	25.3	87.3	32.0

Source: Data from "The Condition of Education: 2006," Washington, DC: National Center for Education Statistics, U. S. Department of Education, 2006.

Directions: The following statements refer to the data in the table above. Read each statement and mark your answer according to the following key.

Circle:

S if the statement is Supported by the data in the table.

R if the statement is Refuted by the data in the table.

N if the statement is Neither supported nor refuted by the data.

(S)   R   N   1. The discrepancy in percentage completion of higher education for males and females between the ages of 25 and 29 was smaller in 1995 than it was any of the other years shown in the table.

S   R   (N)   2. Since 2000, college admissions policies give preferential treatment to female applicants over male applicants.

S   R   (N)   3. It was more difficult to get into college in the 1980s and 1990s than it is today.

S   (R)   N   4. When males and females are combined, the percentage for young adults between the ages of 25 and 29 who have completed high school has increased every year over what it was 5 years earlier.

Ability to Recognize Assumptions

Another learning outcome pertinent to the interpretation of various types of information is the ability to identify unstated assumptions that are necessary to a conclusion or course of action. The following item illustrates this type of interpretive exercise.

EXAMPLE   Studies have shown that there is a relationship between vocabulary and crime. Crime rates are higher for people with poorly developed vocabularies, and crime rates are lower for people with well-developed vocabularies. Older studies have also shown that there is a positive relationship between the number of years of Latin studied and the size and preciseness of an individual's vocabulary. Conclusion: Crime rates can be lowered by reintroducing the study of Latin in the schools.

Which one of the following assumptions is necessary to reach such a conclusion?

A   Correlational methods were used to determine these relationships.
B   These reported relationships were statistically significant.
Ⓒ   Relationships such as these imply causation.
D   Latin scholars have a low crime rate.

Ability to Recognize the Relevance of Information

A learning outcome important to all subject-matter areas and that can be measured at all levels of instruction is the ability to recognize the relevance of information. The exercise presented here was prepared for third-grade students.

EXAMPLE   Bill lost his boot on the way to school. He wanted to put a notice on the bulletin board so that the other children could help him find it. Which of the following sentences tell something that would help children find the boot?

Directions: Circle *yes* if it would help. Circle *no* if it would not help.

ⓨ̲e̲s̲ no   1.   The boot was black.
yes ⓝ̲o̲   2.   It was very warm.
ⓨ̲e̲s̲ no   3.   It was for his right foot.
yes ⓝ̲o̲   4.   It was a Christmas present.
yes ⓝ̲o̲   5.   It was nice looking.
ⓨ̲e̲s̲ no   6.   It had a zipper.
ⓨ̲e̲s̲ no   7.   It had a gray lining.

Ability to Apply Principles

The application of principles may be shown in many different ways. In the following example, students are asked to identify principles that explain a situation and to recognize illustrations of a principle.

EXAMPLE   Mary Ann wanted her rose bush to grow faster, so she applied twice as much chemical fertilizer as was recommended and watered the bush every evening. About a month later she noticed that the rose bush was dying.

Directions: Which of the following principles is necessary in explaining why the rose bush is dying? If a principle is Necessary, circle **N**; if a principle is Unnecessary, circle **U**.

N   (U)   1. A chemical compound is changed into other compounds by taking up the elements of water.

(N)   U   2. Semipermeable membranes permit the passage of fluid.

N   (U)   3. Water condenses when cooled.

(N)   U   4. When two solutions of different concentration are separated by a porous partition, their concentration tends to equalize.

Use of Pictorial Materials

Pictorial materials can serve two useful purposes in interpretive exercises. First, they can help measure a variety of learning outcomes similar to those already discussed simply by replacing the written or tabular data with a pictorial presentation. This use is especially desirable with younger students and when ideas can be more clearly conveyed in pictorial form. Second, pictorial materials can also measure the ability to interpret graphs, cartoons, maps, and other pictorial materials. In many school subjects, these are important learning outcomes in their own right.

The following examples illustrate the use of pictorial materials.

EXAMPLE I

USE ORAL QUESTIONS

What clock shows the time that school starts?   (A) B   C   D

What clock shows the time closest to lunch time?   A   B (C) D

What clock shows half past the hour?   A (B) C   D

EXAMPLE II

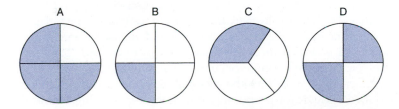

Use Oral Questions

What circle is 1/4 shaded?   A Ⓑ C D

What circle is 1/2 shaded?   A B C Ⓓ

What circle is *most* shaded?   Ⓐ B C D

What circle is *least* shaded?   A Ⓑ C D

EXAMPLE III

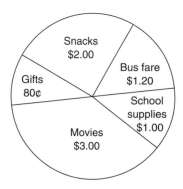

Above is a graph of Bill's weekly allowance distribution.

1. What is the ratio of the amount Bill spends for school supplies to the amount he spends for movies?

   A 7:2
   Ⓑ 1:3
   C 2:7
   D 3:1

2. What would be the best title for this graph?

   A Bill's weekly allowance
   B Bill's money graph
   Ⓒ Bill's weekly expenditures
   D Bill's money planning

These three examples were designed for use in lower grades. They illustrate the use of pictorial materials that can be drawn by the teacher and items that are useful for measuring rather simple interpretations of concepts and relationships.

Examples IV and V are interpretive exercises designed for higher grade levels. They are included here to illustrate the use of various types of pictorial materials, the measurement of different types of learning outcomes, and the use of both multiple-choice and true–false items. As noted in these examples, the pictures and diagrams used in an interpretive exercise frequently can be obtained from published sources. When this is done, care must be taken in reproducing the pictorial elements to make certain that they are clear and detailed enough for proper interpretation. It is also important, of course, to be aware of the copyright laws that govern the use of the material. However, there is seldom a problem in obtaining permission to reproduce copyrighted materials for classroom use.

Cartoons like the one in Example IV can be found in newspapers and news magazines. Then simply prepare questions that require the desired interpretations. Either true–false or multiple-choice items might be used with this type of exercise. It is important to select a cartoon that illustrates a concept or principle that is relevant to the learning outcomes to be measured. Interpretive exercises of this type are especially useful in social studies.

EXAMPLE IV

1. The cartoon illustrates which of the following characteristics of the party system in the United States?

   (A) Strong party discipline is often lacking.
   B The parties are responsive to the will of the voters
   C The parties are often more concerned with politics than with the national welfare.
   D Bipartisanship often exists in name only.

2. The situation shown in the cartoon is *least* likely to occur at which of the following times?

   A During the first session of a new Congress
   B During a political party convention
   C During a primary election campaign
   (D) During a presidential election campaign

EXAMPLE V TIMSS Average Fourth-Grade Mathmatics, score by Country. (From IEA's TIMSS 2003 International Report on Achievement in the Mathematics Cognitive Domains, Boston College.)

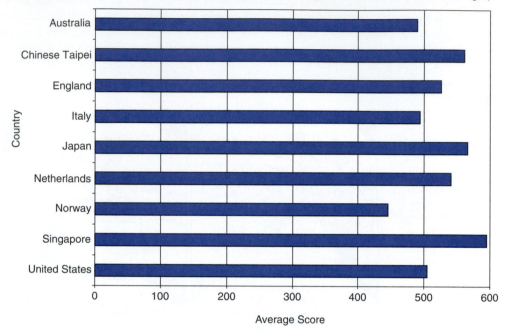

Directions: The following statements refer to the data in the chart above. Read each statement, and mark your answer according to the following key.

Circle:

    T—if the data in the chart are sufficient to make the statement True.
    F—if the data in the chart are sufficient to make the statement False.
    I—if the data in the chart are Insufficient to determine whether the statement is true or false.

  T (F) I   1. The average score is lower in the United States than in all but one of the other countries shown.

  (T) F I   2. The average score of days is higher in the three Asian countries than in any of the remaining six countries shown.

  T F (I)   3. Norwegian students spend fewer hours studying mathematics than students from any of the other countries shown.

A chart like that in Example V is typically easy to prepare but may sometimes be found in published sources. Maps and diagrams that contain data also make effective materials for interpretive exercises.

ADVANTAGES AND LIMITATIONS
OF INTERPRETIVE EXERCISES

The interpretive exercise has several advantages. First, the introductory material makes it possible to measure the ability to interpret written materials, charts, graphs, maps, pictures, and other communication media encountered in everyday situations. The rapid expansion of knowledge in every subject-matter area has made it impossible to learn all the important factual information in a given field, which has led to greater dependence on the internet, libraries, reference materials, self-study techniques, and interpretive skills. Second, the interpretive exercise makes it possible to measure more complex learning outcomes than can be measured with the single objective item. Some data are usually necessary if students are to demonstrate thinking and problem-solving skills, and the inclusion of such data is awkward in most kinds of test items. Third, by having a series of related test items based on a common set of data, greater depth and breadth can be obtained in the measurement of achievement skills. Fourth, the interpretive exercise minimizes the influence of irrelevant factual information on the measurement of complex learning outcomes. Students may be unable to demonstrate their understanding of a principle simply because they do not know some of the facts concerning the situation to which they are to be applied. This blocking of response, caused by a lack of detailed factual information not directly pertinent to the purpose of the measurement, can be largely eliminated with the interpretive exercise. In the introductory materials, we can give students the common background of information needed to demonstrate understanding, thinking skills, and problem-solving abilities.

The interpretive exercise is more structured than performance assessment tasks. Whether this is an advantage or disadvantage depends on the specific outcomes to be measured. Students are not free to redefine the problem or to demonstrate thinking skills at which they are most efficient on an interpretive exercise. The series of objective items forces them to use only the mental processes called for. This also makes it possible to measure separate aspects of problem-solving ability and to use objective scoring procedures. This structure has advantages for focusing the task on a specific outcome, such as the ability to identify assumptions underlying conclusions. For other types of outcomes, however, the structure may make it impossible to adequately assess the desired outcome. For example, an interpretive exercise would not be suitable for measuring whether students are able to generate the assumptions underlying a conclusion.

As with all forms of test items, the interpretive exercise has certain limitations. Probably the greatest limiting factor, and one that may have occurred to you as you reviewed the sample items, is the difficulty of construction. Selecting printed materials that are new to the students but relevant to the instructional outcomes requires considerable searching. When pertinent material is found, it usually must be edited and reworked to make it more suitable for testing purposes.

Next, test items must be constructed that demand the specific behaviors indicated in the learning outcomes being measured. The construction process is often circular (i.e., it goes back and forth between revising the introductory material and revising the test items until a satisfactory product is obtained). This entire procedure is time consuming and requires much greater skill than that needed to construct single objective test items. Three positive comments can be made regarding the difficulty of constructing interpretive exercises, however. First, more and more items of this type now appear in various subject-matter fields. The references at the end of this chapter contain numerous examples that may serve as guides to test construction.

Second, the greater instructional emphasis on complex learning outcomes resulting from the use of interpretive exercises offsets the additional effort required in test construction. Finally, the task becomes easier with practice and experience.

A second limitation, especially pertinent when the introductory material is in written form, is the heavy demand on reading skill. The poor reader is handicapped by both the difficulty of the reading material and the length of time it takes to read each test exercise. The first problem can be controlled somewhat by keeping the reading level low and the second by using brief passages. Both of these are only partial solutions, however, because the poor reader will still be at a decided disadvantage. In the primary grades and in classes that contain many poor readers, interpretive exercises might be better limited to the use of pictorial materials.

Compared to the extended essay questions and performance-based assessment tasks discussed in Chapters 10 and 11, the interpretive exercise has two shortcomings as a measure of complex achievement. First, it cannot measure a student's overall approach to problem solving. It is efficient for measuring specific aspects of the problem-solving process, but it does not indicate whether the student can integrate and use these skills when faced with a particular problem. Thus, it provides a diagnostic view of the students' problem-solving abilities in contrast with the holistic view of essay questions or other performance assessment tasks.

Second, because the interpretive exercise normally uses selection items, it is confined to learning outcomes at the recognition level. To measure the ability to define problems, to formulate hypotheses, to organize data, and to draw conclusions, performance assessment tasks must be used. Clearly, the interpretive exercise is not suitable for assessing a student's ability to communicate effectively in writing, perform an experiment, create a work of art, or make an oral presentation to a group. Essay questions and performance assessment tasks are needed for such outcomes. Nonetheless, the interpretive exercise is a valuable technique that can contribute to the valid measurement of complex outcomes.

SUGGESTIONS FOR CONSTRUCTING INTERPRETIVE EXERCISES

The two main tasks in constructing interpretive exercises are (1) selecting appropriate introductory material, and (2) constructing a series of dependent test items. In addition, care must be taken to construct test items that require analyzing the introductory material in terms of complex learning outcomes. The following suggestions will aid in constructing high-quality interpretive exercises.

1. **Select introductory material that is relevant to the objectives of the course.**   Interpretive exercises, like other testing procedures, should measure the achievement of specific instructional outcomes. Success in this regard depends to a large extent on the introductory material, as this provides the common basis for the test items. If the introductory material is too simple, then the exercise may become a measure of general information or simple reading skill. On the other hand, if the material is too complex or unrelated to instructional goals, then it may become a measure of general reasoning ability. Both extremes must be avoided. Ideally, the introductory material should be pertinent to the course content and complex enough to evoke the mental reactions specified in the course objectives.

The amount of emphasis given to the various interpretive skills in the course objectives is also important. Care must be taken not to overload the test with interpretive items in any particular area. The selection of introductory material should be guided by the emphasis to be given to the measurement of complex achievement and each type of interpretive skill.

2. Select introductory material that is appropriate to the students' curricular experience and reading level. Many complex learning outcomes can be measured with different types of introductory material. The ability to recognize the validity of conclusions, for example, can be measured with written materials, tables, charts, graphs, maps, or pictures. The type used should be familiar to the students so that the nature of the material does not prevent them from demonstrating their achievement of the complex learning outcomes. It would be unfair, for example, to ask students to recognize the validity of conclusions on the basis of data presented in graph form if they had not had experience in interpreting graphs similar to those used in the test. When various types of introductory material will serve a purpose equally well and all are familiar to the students, we favor material that places the least demand on reading skill. For elementary students, pictorial materials are definitely favored. For higher grade levels, pictorial materials and verbal materials with a low vocabulary load and simple sentences are preferred. Although general reading skill is necessary in all written tests, it can become prominent in interpretive exercises unless efforts are made to minimize its influence.

3. Select introductory material that is new to students. In order to measure complex learning outcomes, the introductory material must be new. Asking students to interpret materials identical to those used in instruction does not ensure that the exercise will measure anything other than rote memory. Too much novelty, however, must be avoided. Materials that are similar to those used in class but vary slightly in content or form are the most desirable. Such materials can be obtained by modifying selections from textbooks, newspapers, newsmagazines, and various reference materials pertinent to the course content.

4. Select introductory material that is brief but meaningful. Another method of minimizing the influence of general reading skill on the measurement of complex learning outcomes is to keep the introductory material as brief as possible. Digests of articles are frequently available and are good raw material for interpretive exercises. If digests are unavailable, the summary of an article or a key passage may be sufficient. In some cases, the relevant information is summarized better in a table, diagram, or picture. In striving for brief introductory material, be careful not to omit elements that are crucial to the interpretive skills being measured. The material also should, of course, be complete enough to be meaningful and interesting to the students.

5. Revise introductory material for clarity, conciseness, and greater interpretive value. Although some materials (e.g., graphs) can be used without revision, most selections require adaptation for testing purposes. Technical articles frequently contain long, detailed descriptions of events. On the other hand, news reports and digests of articles are brief but often present exaggerated reports of events to attract the reader's interest. Although such reports provide excellent material for measuring the ability to judge the relevance of arguments, the need for assumptions, the validity of conclusions, and the like, the material must usually be modified to be used effectively.

Revision of the introductory material and construction of the related test items tend to be interdependent procedures. Rewriting material often suggests questions to be used, and the construction of test questions often necessitates revisions of the material. In revising a description of an experiment, for example, assumptions, hypotheses, or conclusions explicitly stated in the description may be deleted and used as a basis for questions. Likewise, a question calling for application of the experimental findings may require the addition of new material to the selection. Thus, the revision of the introductory material and the construction of test items proceed in a circular fashion until a clear, concise interpretive exercise evolves.

6. Construct test items that require analysis and interpretation of the introductory material. There are two common errors in the construction of interpretive exercises that invalidate them as a measure of complex achievement. One is to include questions that are answered directly in the introductory material, that is, asking for factual information explicitly stated in the selection. Such questions measure reading and recall skills. The second error is to include questions that can be answered correctly without reading the introductory material, that is, requiring answers based on general information. These questions measure simple knowledge outcomes.

If the interpretive exercise is to function as intended, it should include only those test items that require students to read the introductory material and to make the desired interpretations. In some instances, the interpretations will require students to supply knowledge beyond that presented in the exercise. In others, the interpretations will be limited to the factual information provided. The emphasis on knowledge and interpretive skill will be determined by the learning outcomes being measured. Regardless of the emphasis, however, the test items should be dependent on the introductory material while at the same time calling forth mental reactions of a higher order than those related to reading comprehension.

7. Make the number of test items roughly proportional to the length of the introductory material. It is inefficient to have students analyze a long, complex selection of material and then answer only one or two questions about it. Although it is impossible to specify the exact number of questions that should accompany a given amount of material, the items presented earlier in this chapter show a desirable balance. Other things being equal, we always favor the interpretive exercise that has brief introductory material and a relatively large number of test items.

8. In constructing test items for an interpretive exercise, observe all pertinent suggestions for constructing objective items. The form of test item used in the interpretive exercise will determine the rules for construction. If multiple-choice or true–false items are used, the suggestions for constructing these item types should be followed. When modified forms are used, suggestions for constructing each of the various types of objective items should be reviewed for their applicability in construction. Freedom from irrelevant clues and technical defects is as important in interpretive exercises as it is in single, independent test items.

9. In constructing key-type test items, make the categories homogeneous and mutually exclusive. The key-type item, which is used frequently in interpretive exercises, is a modified multiple-choice form that uses a common set of alternatives. In this regard, it is also similar to the matching item and so should be constructed in the same way, with special attention devoted to the categories used in the key. All the categories in any one key should be homogeneous; that is, they all should be concerned with similar types of judgment. At the same time, there should be no overlapping of categories. Each alternative should provide a separate category so that there is a clear-cut system of classification and each item has only one correct answer.

EXAMPLE   The majority of medical researchers agree that exposure to secondhand cigarette smoke is detrimental to health. A number of cities have passed ordinances that prohibit smoking in public buildings. Despite an intensive educational campaign pointing out the dangers of secondhand smoke, many cities do not prohibit smoking in public buildings. Resolved: In the interests of national health, smoking should be prohibited in all public buildings in the United States.

Directions: Read each of the following statements carefully. In front of each statement mark

Key: **A** if the statement supports the resolution.
       B if the statement contradicts the resolution.
       C if the statement is a fact.
       D if the statement is an opinion.

_____1.   The amount of reduction in exposure to secondhand smoke in cities with ordinances prohibiting smoking in public buildings has not been studied.

(Similar items complete the exercise.)

In this example, the key includes two overlapping categories, one concerned with the relationship of each statement to the resolution and the other with the nature of the statement itself. This makes it impossible to have only one correct answer for each statement. Item 1, for example, would have to be marked category B because it contradicts the resolution and category C because it is a statement of fact.

The key could be improved by limiting the categories to the relevance of the statements to the resolutions, as illustrated in the following key.

EXAMPLE

Key: **A** if the statement supports the resolution.
       B if the statement contradicts the resolution.
       C if the statement neither supports nor contradicts the resolution.

If judging both the factual nature of a statement and its relevance is important, these two elements can be combined to form discrete categories as follows:

EXAMPLE

Key: **A** if it is a statement of fact that supports the resolution.
       B if it is a statement of opinion that supports the resolution.
       C if it is a statement of fact that contradicts the resolution.
       D if it is a statement of opinion that contradicts the resolution.

The main drawback to combining two types of judgment in one category is the greater complexity of the key. This is especially undesirable with younger students.

In mathematics, a key-type item that has been found to be quite efficient is the quantitative comparison item. The use of a fixed-response format for quantitative comparison items reduces the reading required and makes it possible for students to respond to a larger number of items in a given period of time.

EXAMPLE

Directions: Each of the following questions consists of two quantities, one in Column A and one in Column B. You are to compare the two quantities and choose:

Key: **A** if the quantity in Column A is greater.
        B if the quantity in Column B is greater.
        C if the two quantities are equal.
        D if the relationship cannot be determined from the information given.

Common Information: In a question, information concerning one or both of the quantities to be compared is centered above the two columns. A symbol that appears in both columns represents the same thing in Column A as it does in Column B.

				Column A	Column B
Ⓐ	B	C	D	1/3	.30
A	Ⓑ	C	D	4.9	25

Given that $X + Y = 5$ and $X - Y = 3$

				Column A	Column B
A	B	Ⓒ	D	$X^2 - Y^2$	15

Given that $X - 2Y = 20$

				Column A	Column B
A	B	C	Ⓓ	X	0

Source: ETS materials selected from GRE 1990–91 *Information Bulletin,* Princeton, NJ: Educational Testing Service, 1990, p. 37. Reprinted by permission of Educational Testing Service, the copyright owner.

---

10. In constructing key-type test items, develop standard key categories where applicable. Despite the usefulness of the interpretive exercise for measuring complex achievement, classroom teachers have not used it extensively, often because of the difficulty of construction. The popularity of the key-type item in interpretive exercises is probably because it uses a common set of alternatives. This makes it easier to construct than the regular multiple-choice form, which requires a different set of alternatives for each item.

It is often possible to simplify further the construction of key-type interpretive exercises by preparing key categories that can be reused with different content. For example, a learning outcome such as the ability to recognize assumptions might lead to the following key.

EXAMPLE

> Key: **A** an assumption that is necessary to make the conclusion valid.
>   **B** an assumption that would invalidate the conclusion.
>   **C** an assumption that has no bearing on the validity of the conclusion.

This key could be used with a brief description of a situation, a conclusion based on the situation, and a list of assumptions. Both the key and the form of the item could be used repeatedly, with only the content varying. Although selecting new content material is still a problem, the framework of the standard key categories simplifies the process.

Standard key categories, of course, cannot be used in all areas, and their use should not be permitted to determine which learning outcomes receive emphasis. Rather, the time and effort saved by such procedures should free the teacher to explore more creative applications of the interpretive exercise in other areas. See the "Checklist" box for reviewing interpretive exercises.

CHECKLIST

Reviewing Interpretive Exercises

	Yes	No
1. Is this the most appropriate item format to use?	___	___
2. Is the material to be interpreted relevant to the intended learning outcomes?	___	___
3. Is the material to be interpreted appropriate to the students' curricular experience and reading level?	___	___
4. Have pictorial materials been used whenever appropriate?	___	___
5. Does the material to be interpreted contain some novelty (to require interpretation)?	___	___
6. Is the material to be interpreted brief, clear, and meaningful?	___	___
7. Are the test items based directly on the introductory material (cannot be answered without it), and do they call for interpretation (not just recall or simple reading skills)?	___	___
8. Have reasonable numbers of test items been used in each interpretive exercise?	___	___
9. Do the test items meet the relevant criteria of effective item writing?	___	___
10. When key-type items are used, are the categories homogeneous and mutually exclusive?	___	___
11. If revised, are the interpretive exercises still relevant to the intended learning outcomes?	___	___
12. Have the interpretive exercises been set aside for a time before reviewing them?	___	___

SUMMARY

Complex achievement refers to those learning outcomes based on higher mental processes. Such outcomes are classified under various general headings, including understanding, reasoning, thinking, and problem solving. The attainment of goals in these areas can be measured by both objective and subjective means. The most commonly used objective item is the interpretive exercise.

The interpretive exercise consists of a series of objective questions based on written materials, tables, charts, graphs, maps, or pictures. The questions require students to demonstrate the specific interpretive skill being measured. For example, students might be asked to recognize assumptions, inferences, conclusions, relationships, applications, and the like. The structure of the interpretive exercise makes it possible to obtain independent measures of each aspect of thinking and problem solving. Although it is efficient for measuring such learning outcomes, it does not measure a student's ability to integrate and use these skills in a global attack on a problem. Thus, it is limited to a diagnostic analysis of problem-solving skills.

Probably the main reason for not using the interpretive exercise is the difficulty of construction. This process involves (a) selecting appropriate introductory material, (b) revising the material to fit the outcomes to be measured, and (c) constructing a series of dependent test items that call forth the desired behavior. Although these steps are admittedly time consuming, the rewards in improved teaching–learning practices seem to justify the time and effort.

LEARNING EXERCISES

1. What are the advantages of the interpretive exercise over the performance-based assessment for measuring complex achievement? What are the disadvantages?
2. For which types of learning outcomes is the interpretive exercise most likely to be appropriate? Why?
3. Discuss the relative merits of the interpretive exercise and the single-item multiple-choice question. For which situation would each be most useful? What are the limitations of each?
4. Construct one interpretive exercise for each of the following:
   a. Paragraph of written material
   b. Picture or cartoon
   c. Chart or graph
5. What steps would you follow in examining an interpretive exercise to determine whether it had been properly constructed?
6. What are some of the factors to consider when you are deciding whether to use interpretive exercises in a classroom test?

FURTHER READING

Educational Testing Service. (1973). *Multiple-choice questions: A close look*. Princeton, NJ: Author. Illustrates the use of the multiple-choice item for measuring complex achievement in a variety of fields. Maps, graphs, pictures, diagrams, and written materials are used. Each item is followed by a statistical and logical analysis of its effectiveness.

Gronlund, N. E. (2005). *Assessment of student achievement* (8th ed.). Boston: Allyn & Bacon. See Chapter 5, "Writing Selection Items: True–False, Matching, and Interpretive Exercises," for examples of interpretive exercises and their uses.

Mehrens, W. A., & Lehmann, I. J. (1991). *Measurement and evaluation in education and psychology* (4th ed.). New York: Holt, Rinehart & Winston. See Chapter 7, "Writing Objective Test Items: Multiple-Choice and Context-Dependent," for sample interpretive exercises and suggestions for construction.

Wesman, A. G. (1971). Writing the test item. In R. L. Thorndike (Ed.), *Educational measurement* (2nd ed.) (pp. 81–129). Washington, DC: American Council on Education. An extended treatment of the topic of item writing. See pages 120–128 for the construction of interpretive exercises.

10

MEASURING COMPLEX ACHIEVEMENT: ESSAY QUESTIONS

Some important learning outcomes may best be measured by the use of open-ended essay questions or other types of performance assessments. Essay questions provide the freedom of response that is needed to adequately assess the ability of students to formulate problems; organize, integrate, and evaluate ideas and information; and apply knowledge and skills.

Up to this point, our main concern has been with objective test items. We noted that such items can measure a variety of learning outcomes, from simple to complex, and that the interpretive exercise is especially useful for measuring complex achievement. Despite this wide applicability of objective-item types, there remain significant instructional outcomes for which no satisfactory objective measurements have been devised. These include such outcomes as the ability to recall, organize, and integrate ideas; the ability to express oneself in writing; and the ability to create rather than merely identify interpretations and applications of data. Such outcomes require less structuring of responses than objective test items, and it is in the measurement of these outcomes that written essays and other performance-based assessments are of greatest value.

In this chapter, we consider the most familiar form of performance-based assessment: the essay question. Other types of performance-based assessments (which include gathering information, making oral presentations, conducting experiments, repairing or manipulating equipment, and so on) are considered in Chapter 11. Purposeful collections of student work into portfolios, which may include a wide variety of different types of assessments (e.g., written essays and other types of performance assessments), are considered in Chapter 12. Teacher observations, peer appraisals, and self-reports are considered in Chapter 13.

FORMS AND USES OF ESSAY QUESTIONS

We focus our discussion of the essay question on its use in the measurement of complex achievement. We recognize, however, that many teachers use essay questions to measure knowledge of factual information. It certainly can be useful to ask students to generate, in their own words, the plot of a story, the causes of a historical event, or the steps in a scientific process, all of which may be provided by a text. Although measuring such knowledge of factual information with essay questions is useful and valid, it does not tap the full potential of essay questions.

The distinctive feature of essay questions is the freedom of response. Students are free to construct, relate, and present ideas in their own words. Although this freedom enhances the value of essay questions as a measure of complex achievement, it introduces scoring difficulties that make essays inefficient as a measure of factual knowledge. For most purposes, knowledge of factual information can be more efficiently measured by some type of objective item. Essay questions should be used primarily to measure those learning outcomes that are not readily measured by objective test items. The special features of essay questions can be utilized most fully when their shortcomings are offset by the need for such measurement. Learning outcomes concerned with the abilities to conceptualize, construct, organize, integrate, relate, and evaluate ideas require the freedom of response and the originality provided by essay questions. In addition, these outcomes are of such great educational significance that the expenditure of energy in the difficult and time-consuming task of evaluating the answers can be easily justified.

Essay tests and other performance-based assessments can also be justified on the grounds that the performances required correspond more closely to the larger instructional goals and objectives than discrete factual-knowledge questions. Indeed, the validity of measurement of complex achievement may be enhanced by the use of essay tests and other performance-based assessments. Furthermore, tests send a message of what it is important to learn and be able to do. Just consider how frequently teachers are asked the question, "Will this be on the test?" The form of the assessment provides a model. Thus, it is often argued that if you want students to be able to communicate in writing, then they not only need to be encouraged to write but also have to be required to do so when it counts.

As implied by the previous comments, essay assessments can be useful ways of assessing student understanding and ability to organize and apply information in a content area such as history, civics, literature, science, or mathematics. In any of these or other content areas, the essay assessment allows teachers to evaluate how well students can communicate ideas. Essay assessments are, of course, also widely used where the main focus is on evaluating student writing without regard to any particular subject-matter content. In the latter case, the emphasis is more likely to be on the form of the writing, distinguishing, for example, between narrative essays, expository essays, and persuasive essays. Essay assessments may also be used to focus teacher and student attention on the writing process itself through the use of various prewriting activities (e.g., discussion, listing and organizing ideas, constructing outlines, and clarification of audience) as well as the initial drafting and revision of essays.

The freedom of response provided by essay questions is not an all-or-nothing affair, but a matter of degree. At one extreme, the response is almost as restricted as that in the short-answer objective item, in which a sentence or two may be all that is required. At the other extreme, students are given almost complete freedom in constructing their responses. The written essay may be several pages in length. Where the emphasis is on the writing process itself, the essay responses may include prewriting responses such as notes, lists of ideas, and outlines as well as initial drafts and revisions. Although variations in freedom of response tend to fall along a continuum between these extremes, essay questions can be conveniently classified into two types: restricted-response questions and extended-response questions or assignments.

Restricted-Response Essay Questions

The restricted-response question usually limits both the content and the response. The content is usually restricted by the scope of the topic to be discussed. Limitations on the form of response are generally indicated in the question.

EXAMPLES   Describe two situations that demonstrate the application of the law of supply and demand. Do not use examples discussed in class.

State the main differences between the Vietnam War and previous wars in which the United States has participated.

Why is the barometer one of the most useful instruments for forecasting weather? Answer in a brief paragraph.

Write the verbal instructions you would give to a friend on the telephone so that the friend could draw a triangle on a piece of graph paper with sides that have relative lengths of 3, 4, and 5 units.

What is measured on an essay such as the one asking students to state the differences between the Vietnam War and previous wars depends on a student's previous instructional experiences. If the textbook or recent class presentations have explicitly discussed ways in which the Vietnam War was different from previous wars, then the students' task is simply to demonstrate an understanding of this material and to put it in their own words. That is, the essay question is simply a measure of comprehension. If the essay question presents students with their first opportunity to think about the Vietnam War in terms of differences from previous wars, however, then the essay requires analysis and higher-level thinking.

Another way of restricting responses in essay questions is to base the questions on specific problems. For this purpose, introductory material like that used in interpretive exercises can be presented. Such items differ from objective interpretive exercises only by the fact that essay questions are used instead of multiple-choice or true–false items.

EXAMPLE   There is a broad consensus among medical scientists that smoking is damaging to the health of both smokers and those who are exposed to cigarette smoke on a regular basis. Some cities have passed laws banning smoking inside all public buildings. Some people have argued against such regulations on the grounds that *smoking bans violate the freedom of choice of individual smokers*.

(A) Indicate whether you agree or disagree with the underlined part of the last statement.
(B) Support your position.

Because the restricted-response question is more structured than the extended-response essay considered next, it is most useful for measuring learning outcomes requiring the interpretation and application of data in a specific area. In fact, any of the learning outcomes measured by an objective interpretive exercise also can be measured by a restricted-response essay question. The difference is that the interpretive exercise requires students to select the answer, whereas the restricted-response question requires them to supply it. In some instances, the objective interpretive exercise is favored because of the ease and reliability of scoring. In other situations, the restricted-response essay question is better because of its more direct relevance to the learning outcome (e.g., the ability to formulate valid conclusions).

Although restricting students' responses to essay questions makes it possible to measure more specific learning outcomes, these same restrictions make them less valuable as a measure of those learning outcomes emphasizing integration, organization, and originality. Restricting the scope of the topic to be discussed and indicating the nature of the desired response limit the student's opportunity to demonstrate these behaviors. For higher-order learning outcomes, greater freedom of response is needed.

Extended-Response Essays

The extended-response question or assignment allows students to select any factual information that they think is pertinent, to organize the answer in accordance with their best judgment, and to integrate and evaluate ideas as they deem appropriate. This freedom enables them to demonstrate their ability to analyze problems, organize their ideas, describe in their own words, and/or develop a coherent argument. If analysis, organization, integration, creative expression, and evaluation skills are emphasized in the grading of the essays as well as in instruction, this form of assessment also makes clear the value that is placed on these higher-order skills. On the other hand, this same freedom that enables the demonstration of creative expression and other higher-order skills makes the extended-response question inefficient for measuring more specific learning outcomes and introduces scoring difficulties.

EXAMPLES   Imagine that you and a friend found a magic wand. Write a story about an adventure that you and your friend had with the magic wand.
Compare developments in international relations in the administrations of President William Clinton and President George W. Bush. Cite examples when possible.
Evaluate the significance of the sea captain's pursuit of the white whale in *Moby Dick*.
Describe the influence of Mendel's laws of heredity on the development of biology as a science.
Write a scientific evaluation of the Copernican theory of the solar system. Include scientific observations that support your statements.

The need to measure a student's global attack on a problem can be easily defended. The thinking and problem-solving skills measured by objective interpretive exercises and restricted-response essay questions seldom function in isolation. In a natural situation, they operate together in a manner that includes more than a sum of the skills involved. These skills interact with one another and with the knowledge and understanding the problem requires. Thus, it is not just the skills we are measuring but also how they function together.

Both teachers and test specialists agree that the extended-response question requires complex behaviors that cannot be measured by more objective means; but they often differ in their level of concern about the difficulty of scoring extended written responses in a way that can satisfactorily measure these behaviors. Test specialists point out that unless considerable attention is given to the choice of questions and to scoring procedures, the scoring may be too unreliable to yield defensible measurement. Nevertheless, many teachers continue to use the extended-response question to measure student achievement without adequate attention to the complexities involved in the construction and scoring of such questions. Neither a hard-line measurement position that rejects extended essays as an approach to measurement nor one that ignores the difficulties of scoring seems to contribute much to the valid measurement of student achievement. It seems more sensible to identify the complex skills we want to measure, formulate questions that elicit these skills, evaluate the results as reliably as we can, and then use these data as the best evidence we have available.

SUMMARY COMPARISON OF LEARNING OUTCOMES MEASURED

The restricted-response essay question can measure a variety of complex learning outcomes similar to those measured by the objective interpretive exercise. The main difference is that the interpretive exercise requires students to select the answer, and the restricted-response question requires the student to supply the answer. In comparison, extended-response essay assessments measure more general learning outcomes, such as the abilities to organize, integrate, evaluate, and express ideas. They may be used to measure writing skills as well as the understanding and ability to apply subject-matter content knowledge. A comparison of the types of complex learning outcomes measured by each of these types of assessment is presented in Table 10.1. The learning outcomes in the table, of course, merely suggest the types of learning outcomes that may be measured. With slight modifications, an infinite variety of outcomes can be stated in each area. The freedom of response to essay questions is a matter of degree, and thus the functions of the restricted-response question and the extended-response question often overlap.

ADVANTAGES AND LIMITATIONS OF ESSAY QUESTIONS

Advantages

A major advantage of the essay question is that it measures complex learning outcomes that cannot be measured by other means; but the use of essay questions does not guarantee the measurement of complex achievement. To do so, essay questions must be as carefully constructed as objective test items. The course objectives pertinent to complex achievement must be defined in terms of specific learning outcomes, and the essay questions must be phrased in a way that will require students to engage in the targeted thinking skills. When a table of specifications is used in planning for the assessment, it is simply a matter of constructing the questions in accordance with the specifications.

Table 10.1

Types of complex learning outcomes measured by essay questions and objective interpretive exercises

Type of Assessment Item	Examples of Complex Learning Outcomes That Can Be Measured
Objective interpretive exercises	Ability to— • identify cause-and-effect relationships • identify the application of principles • identify the relevance of arguments • identify tenable hypotheses • identify valid conclusions • identify unstated assumptions • identify the limitations of data • identify the adequacy of procedures (and similar outcomes based on the pupil's ability to *select* the answer)
Restricted-response essay questions	Ability to— • explain cause-and-effect relationships • describe applications of principles • present relevant arguments • formulate tenable hypotheses • formulate valid conclusions • state necessary assumptions • describe the limitations of data • explain methods and procedures (and similar outcomes based on the pupil's ability to *supply* the answer)
Extended-response essays	Ability to— • produce, organize, and express ideas • integrate learnings in different areas • create original forms (e.g., designing an experiment) • summarize (e.g., writing a summary of a story) • construct creative stories (e.g., narrative essays) • explain concepts or principles (e.g., expository essay) • persuade a reader (e.g., persuasive essay) (and similar outcomes based on a pupil's ability to write an essay for a given purpose)

A second advantage of the extended-response essay is its emphasis on the integration and application of thinking and problem-solving skills. Although objective items such as the interpretive exercise can be designed to measure various aspects of complex achievement, the ability to integrate and apply these skills in a general attack on a problem is best measured by extended-response essay questions.

Perhaps the most obvious advantage of essay assessments is that they enable the direct evaluation of writing skills. In some instances, the evaluation of specific writing skills may be combined with the assessment of subject-matter knowledge and understandings (e.g., communication of mathematical or scientific principles, ideas, and concepts). In other cases, the assessment of writing skills may be the sole or primary purpose (e.g., skill in developing characters in a narrative story or writing mechanics).

Another commonly cited advantage of the essay question is its ease of construction. This factor has led to the widespread use of essay questions by classroom teachers. In a matter of minutes, most teachers can formulate several essay questions, an attractive feature for the busy teacher. This apparent advantage can be very misleading, however. Constructing essay questions that require the conceptual understanding and thinking skills emphasized in a particular set of learning outcomes takes considerable thought and effort. When ease of construction is stressed, it usually refers to the common practice of dashing off questions with little regard for the course objectives. In such cases, there is some question whether ease of construction can be considered an advantage. In addition to the invalidity of the measurement, evaluating the answers to carelessly developed questions tends to be confusing. Moreover, valid scoring of responses to any essay question requires great care in the development and application of scoring rubrics, and providing written comments and suggestions on student essays that can help students improve their writing is both highly desirable and time consuming.

Finally, the potentially most important advantage of the essay question is its contribution to student learning. The contribution to learning can be direct. The process of preparing a response to an extended-response essay question, for example, may also be an effective learning exercise. The effects on learning can also be indirect. The model of what students are expected to do in response to essay questions often coincide with and encourage effective learning activities.

Limitations

The most commonly cited limitation of the essay question is the unreliability of the scoring. Over the years, various studies have shown that written essays are scored differently by different teachers and that even the same teachers score responses differently at different times. The poor reliability across scorers, however, is frequently the result of failure to identify clearly the learning outcomes being measured and the failure to establish well-defined scoring rubrics.

Evaluating essays without adequate attention to the learning outcomes being measured and the scoring rubrics to be used is like "three blind men appraising an elephant." One teacher stresses factual content; one, organization of ideas; and another, writing skill. With each teacher evaluating the degree to which different learning outcomes are achieved, it is not surprising that scoring diverges. Even variations in scoring by the same teacher can probably be explained to a large extent by inadequate attention to learning outcomes and scoring rubrics. When the evaluation of answers is not guided by clearly defined outcomes and scoring rubrics, it tends to be based on less stable, intuitive judgments. Although the judgmental scoring of essay responses will always have some degree of unreliability, scoring reliability can be greatly increased by clearly defining the outcomes to be measured, properly framing the questions, carefully following scoring rules, and obtaining practice in scoring.

A closely related limitation of essay questions is the amount of time required for scoring the responses. If the scoring is done conscientiously and helpful feedback is provided to students, even a small number of papers may require several hours of scoring time. If the classes are large and several extended-response essay questions are used, conscientious scoring becomes practically impossible. Ironically, most of the suggestions for improving the scoring of responses to essay questions require more time, not less, as might be hoped. The only practical solution is to reserve the use of extended-response essay questions for those learning outcomes that cannot be measured well objectively. With fewer essay questions to score in a given test, more time will be available for evaluating the answers.

Another shortcoming of essay questions is the limited sampling of content they provide. So few questions can be included in a given test that some areas are measured thoroughly while many others are neglected. This inadequate sampling makes essay questions especially inefficient for measuring knowledge of factual information. For such outcomes, we can use objective test items and reserve essay questions, especially extended-response questions, for measuring complex achievement. This does not eliminate the sampling problem, however, because we would also like an adequate sample of complex behaviors. When we use essay questions, we should try to obtain as representative a sample of learning outcomes as possible. One way of doing this is to accumulate evidence from a series of essay questions administered at different times throughout the school year. The collection of the results throughout the year into portfolios, as is described in Chapter 12, can serve other important evaluation and communication functions.

SUGGESTIONS FOR CONSTRUCTING ESSAY QUESTIONS

The improvement of the essay question as a measure of complex learning outcomes requires attention to two problems: (1) how to construct essay questions that call forth the desired student responses, and (2) how to score the answers so that achievement is reliably measured. Here we suggest ways of constructing essay questions, and in the next section we suggest ways of improving scoring, although these two procedures are interrelated.

1. **Restrict the use of essay questions to those learning outcomes that cannot be measured satisfactorily by objective items**. Other things being equal, objective measures have the advantage of efficiency and reliability. When objective items are inadequate for measuring the learning outcomes, however, the use of essay questions can be easily defended despite their limitations. Complex learning outcomes such as those pertaining

to the organization, integration, and expression of ideas will be neglected unless essay questions are used. By restricting the use of essay questions to these areas, the evaluation of student achievement can be most fully realized.

2. Construct questions that will call forth the skills specified in the learning standards. Like objective items, essay questions should measure the achievement of clearly defined content standards or instructional outcomes. If the ability to apply principles is being measured, for example, the questions should be phrased in such a manner that they require students to display their conceptual understanding or a particular skill. Essay questions should never be hurriedly constructed in the hope that they will measure broad, important (but unidentified) educational goals. Each essay question should be carefully designed to require students to demonstrate achievement defined in the desired learning outcomes. See the box "Types of Thought Questions and Sample Item Stems" for examples of the many types of questions that might be asked; the phrasing of any particular question will vary somewhat from one subject to another.

Constructing essay questions in accordance with particular learning outcomes is much easier with restricted-response questions than with extended-response questions. The restricted scope of the topic and the type of response expected make it possible to relate a restricted-response question directly to one or more of the outcomes. The extreme freedom of the extended-response question makes it difficult to present questions so that the student's responses will reflect the particular learning outcomes desired. This difficulty can be partially overcome by indicating the bases on which the answer will be evaluated.

EXAMPLE   Write a two-page statement defending the importance of conserving our natural resources. (Your answer will be evaluated in terms of its organization, its comprehensiveness, and the relevance of the arguments presented.)

Informing students that they should pay special attention to organization, comprehensiveness, and relevance of arguments defines the task, makes the scoring criteria explicit, and makes it possible to key the question to a particular set of learning outcomes. These directions alone will not, of course, ensure that the appropriate behaviors will be exhibited. It is only when the students have been taught the relevant skills and how to integrate them that such directions will serve their intended purpose.

3. Phrase the question so that the student's task is clearly defined.   The purpose a teacher had in mind when developing the question may not be conveyed to the student if the question contains ambiguous phrasing. Students interpret the question differently and give a hodgepodge of responses. Because it is impossible to determine which of the incorrect or off-target responses are due to misinterpretation and which to lack of achievement, the results are worse than worthless: They may actually be harmful if used to measure student progress toward instructional objectives.

One way to clarify the question is to make it as specific as possible. For the restricted-response question, this means rewriting it until the desired response is clearly defined.

Types of Thought Questions and Sample Item Stems

Comparing

Describe the similarities and differences between . . .
Compare the following two methods for . . .

Relating cause and effect

What are major causes of . . . ?
What would be the most likely effects of . . . ?

Justifying

Which of the following alternatives would you favor, and why?
Explain why you agree or disagree with the following statement.

Summarizing

State the main points included in . . .
Briefly summarize the contents of . . .

Generalizing

Formulate several valid generalizations from the following data.
State a set of principles that can explain the following events.

Inferring

In light of the facts presented, what is most likely to happen when . . . ?
How would Senator X be likely to react to the following issue?

Explaining

Why did the candle go out shortly after it was covered by the jar?
Explain what President Truman meant when he said, "If you can't stand the heat, get out of the kitchen."

Persuading

Write a letter to the principal to get approval for a class field trip to the state capital.
Why should the student newspaper be allowed to decide what should be printed without prior approval from teachers?

Classifying

Group the following items according to . . .
What do the following items have in common?

Creating

List as many ways as you can think of for . . .
Make up a story describing what would happen if . . .

Applying

Using the principle of . . . as a guide, describe how you would solve the following problem situation.
Describe a situation that illustrates the principle of . . .

(Continued)

(Continued)

Analyzing

Describe the reasoning errors in the following paragraph.
List and describe the main characteristics of . . .

Synthesizing

Describe a plan for proving that . . .
Write a well-organized report that shows . . .

Evaluating

Describe the strengths and weaknesses of . . .
Using the given criteria, write an evaluation of . . .

EXAMPLE   *Poor:*   Why do birds migrate?
               Better: State three hypotheses that might explain why birds migrate south in the fall. Indicate
               the most probable one and give reasons for your selection.

The improved version presents the students with a definite task. Although some students may not be able to give the correct answer, they all will certainly know what type of response is expected. Note also how easy it would be to relate such an item to a specific learning outcome, such as "the ability to formulate and defend tenable hypotheses."

When an extended-response question is desired, some limitation of the task may be possible, but care must be taken not to destroy the function of the question. If the question becomes too narrow, it will be less effective as a measure of the ability to select, organize, and integrate ideas and information. The best procedure for clarifying the extended-response question seems to be to give the student explicit directions concerning the type of response desired.

EXAMPLE   *Poor:*   Compare the Democratic and Republican parties.
               Better: Compare the current policies of the Democratic and Republican parties with regard
               to the role of government in private business. Support your statements with examples
               when possible. (Your answer should be confined to two pages. It will be evaluated in terms
               of the appropriateness of the facts and examples presented and the skill with which it is
               organized.)

The first version of the example offers no common basis for responding and, consequently, no frame of reference for evaluating the response. If students interpret the question differently, their responses will be organized differently, because organization is partly a function of the content being organized. Also, some students will narrow the problem before responding, thus giving themselves a much easier task than students who attempt to treat the broader aspects of the problem.

The improved version gives students a clearly defined task without destroying their freedom to respond in original ways. This is achieved both by specifying the scope of the question and by including directions concerning the type of response desired. See the box "The Importance of Writing Skill."

4. **Indicate an approximate time limit for each question.** Too often, essay questions place a premium on speed because inadequate attention is paid to reasonable time limits during the test's construction. As each question is constructed, the teacher should estimate the approximate time needed for a satisfactory response. In allotting response time, keep the slower students in mind. Most errors in allotting time needed are in giving too little time. It is better to use fewer questions and give more generous time limits than to put some students at a disadvantage.

The time limits allotted to each question should be indicated to the students so that they can pace their responses to each question and not be caught at the end of the testing time with "just one more question to go." If the assessment contains both objective and essay questions, the students should, of course, be told approximately how much time to spend on each part of the test. This may be done orally or included on the test form itself. In either case, care must be taken not to create overconcern about time. The adequacy of the time limits might very well be emphasized in the introductory remarks so as to allay any anxiety that might arise.

5. **Avoid the use of optional questions.** A fairly common practice when using essay questions is to give students more questions than they are expected to perform and then permit them to select a given number. For example, the teacher may include six essay questions in a test and direct the students to respond to any three of them. This practice is generally favored by students because they can select those questions they know most about. Except for the desirable effect on student morale, however, there is little to recommend the use of optional questions. If students answer different questions, it is obvious that they are taking different tests, and so the common basis for evaluating their achievement is lost. Each student is demonstrating the achievement of different learning outcomes. As noted earlier, even the ability to organize cannot be measured adequately

The Importance of Writing Skill

Performance on an essay test depends largely on writing ability. If students are to be able to demonstrate the achievement of higher-level learning outcomes, then they must be taught the thinking and writing skills needed to express themselves. This means teaching them how to select relevant ideas, compare and relate ideas, organize ideas, apply ideas, infer, analyze, evaluate, and write a well-constructed response that includes these elements. Asking students to "compare," "interpret," or "apply" has little meaning unless they have been taught how to do these things. This calls for direct teaching and practice in writing, in an atmosphere that is less stressful than an examination period. Use of analytic scoring criteria that give separate scores for characteristics such as the quality of ideas, use of examples, use of supporting evidence, and mechanics of writing such as grammar, punctuation, and spelling can improve scoring and, if communicated to students, can both guide their efforts in constructing essays and lead to improvements of specific writing skills.

CHECKLIST

Reviewing Essay Questions

	Yes	No
1. Is this the most appropriate type of task to use?	____	____
2. Are the questions designed to measure higher-level learning outcomes?	____	____
3. Are the questions relevant to the intended learning outcomes?	____	____
4. Does each question clearly indicate the response expected?	____	____
5. Are students told the bases on which their answers will be evaluated?	____	____
6. Are generous time limits provided for responding to the questions?	____	____
7. Are students told the time limits and/or point values for each question?	____	____
8. Are all students required to respond to the same questions?	____	____
9. If revised, are the questions still relevant to the intended learning outcomes?	____	____
10. Have the questions been set aside for a time before reviewing them?	____	____

---

without a common set of responses because organization is partly a function of the content being organized.

The use of optional questions might also influence the validity of the test results in another way. When students anticipate the use of optional questions, they can prepare responses on several topics in advance, commit them to memory, and then select questions to which the responses are most appropriate. During such advance preparation, it is also possible for them to get help in selecting and organizing their response. Needless to say, this provides a distorted measure of the student's achievement, and it also tends to have an undesirable influence on study habits, as intensive preparation in a relatively few areas is encouraged.

Of course, there are learning outcomes that involve in-depth study of topics that are shaped and defined by students. Evaluation of student work on topics of their own choosing is important for such learning outcomes. The assessment of such outcomes, however, is better approached through the assignment of projects than by an essay test. See the "Checklist" box to evaluate essay questions you construct.

SCORING CRITERIA

Clear specification of scoring criteria in advance of administering essay questions can contribute to improved reliability and validity of the assessment. Planning how responses will be scored will frequently lead to rethinking and clarification of the questions so that students have a clearer idea of what is expected. Informing students of the scoring criteria that will be used in evaluating their responses also can enhance the validity of the assessments because students are more likely to focus their efforts in the direction intended by the teacher.

After the assessment has been administered, it is often useful to do an initial review of the responses to a single question. Based on the initial review, a few exemplar or "anchor" responses may be identified that most clearly correspond to the levels of the scoring rubric. The comparability and fairness of scores assigned to student responses can be enhanced by comparing each response to the selected anchor responses.

It is important that scores or levels identified in a scoring rubric be descriptive and not merely judgmental in nature. It is better, for example, to define a level of the rubric as "writing is clear and thoughts are complete" than to only characterize the level as "excellent." Reliability, comparability, and fairness of scores are enhanced by clear descriptions.

Scoring Rubrics for Restricted-Response Essay Questions

In many instances, scoring guides for restricted-response essay questions are most readily constructed starting with the teacher writing an example of an expected response. If the student is asked to describe three factors that contributed to the start of the Civil War, for example, the teacher might construct a list of acceptable reasons and simply give the student 1 point for each of up to three reasons given from the list. In the example given earlier where students are asked to write a paragraph explaining why a barometer is one of the most useful instruments in forecasting weather, the teacher might list key ideas that would need to be there for the student to get full credit as well as the level of explanation that would be awarded partial credit.

Analytic Scoring Rubrics for Extended-Response Essays

Analytic scoring rubrics enable a teacher to focus on one characteristic of a response at a time. The separation of characteristics such as writing mechanics from the quality of the content of the essay can be especially useful. Separate scores for characteristics such as these provide the student with clearer feedback about the strengths and weaknesses of the response.

Analytic scores for writing skills may consist of just two broad categories such as rhetorical effectiveness and conventions or content quality and mechanics. Sometimes finer distinctions are useful. The scoring rubrics used by the state of Oregon for its statewide writing assessment consists of the following seven analytic dimensions.

1. Ideas and Content
2. Organization
3. Voice
4. Word Choice
5. Sentence Fluency
6. Conventions
7. Citing Sources

Scoring rubrics for 6-point ratings are available on-line at the Oregon Department of Education Web site at http://www.ode.state.or.us/teachlearn/testing/scoring/guides/2006-07/asmtwriscorguide0607eng.pdf. The analytic scoring rubrics are presented for the seven dimensions or "traits." The specification of a score of 6 on the Organization dimension is shown in the box showing a sample scoring rubric. Similar descriptions are given for score points of 1, 2, 3, 4, and 5 for this and the other six dimensions.

These lists, together with the actual descriptions of rubrics, may provide a useful starting point for constructing analytic scoring dimensions for use in the classroom. For any such list, decisions would need to be made about the number of score points to use and the criteria for determining the score level on each dimension. Scoring rubrics such as the one available on-line from the Oregon Department of Education illustrate ways in which the individual score points can be described.

Another example illustrating descriptions of score points on analytic dimensions is shown in Table 10.2. The examples in the table were adapted from work by Gearhart, Herman, Baker, and Whittaker (1994). Six scale points on four analytic scales and an overall general impression dimension are described. Scoring rubrics such as these are useful in scoring expository essays or descriptive summaries. Variations may be useful for other types of essays. For example, in scoring a persuasive essay, additional dimensions for rating the use of supporting evidence, distinguishing between fact and opinion, and determining the coherence of the argument may be desirable for giving students feedback on how to make their argument more effective.

Table 10.2
Example analytic scales for expository essays or descriptive summaries

Score	General Impression	Focus/ Organization	Language	Elaboration	Mechanics
6	Exceptional achievement	• Clearly stated main idea • Unified focus and organization • Effectively orients reader	• Specific and concrete • Details consistent with intent • Details create clear, vivid image	• Extended elaboration of one main point	• One or two minor errors • No major errors
5	Commendable achievement	• Stated or implied main idea • Focused and organized • Effectively orients reader	• Specific sensory details • Most details consistent with intent	• Full elaboration of one main point	• A few minor errors • No more than one major error
4	Adequate achievement	• Main idea present but may not maintain consistent focus	• Some specific details • Details usually clear	• Moderate elaboration of main point	• Some minor errors • One or two major errors

(Continued)

Table 10.2 (*Continued*)
Example analytic scales for expository essays or descriptive summaries

Score	General Impression	Focus/ Organization	Language	Elaboration	Mechanics
		• Some orientation of reader	• Generally clear images • Details usually clear		• Errors do not cause reader confusion
3	Some evidence of achievement	• Main idea not clear • Usually on topic, but with some digressions	• Few or inconsistent details • Some details, but all may not be appropriate	• Restricted elaboration of main point	• Some minor and some major errors • Some cause reader confusion
2	Limited evidence of achievement	• Vague indication of main idea or focus • Significant digression • No sense of closure	• Little concrete language • Simple or generic naming	• Limited elaboration of main point	• Many minor and major errors • Errors interfere with reader understanding
1	Minimal evidence of achievement	• No apparent main idea • No apparent plan or coherence	• No concrete language	• No elaboration of main point or central statement	• Many major errors causing reader confusion

Source: Adapted from Gearhart et al. (1994).

Holistic Scoring Rubrics for Extended-Response Essays

As the name suggests, holistic scoring rubrics yield a single overall score taking into account the entire response. Holistic scoring rubrics can generally be constructed more rapidly, and they generally can be used to score a set of essay responses more rapidly than analytic scoring rubrics. These advantages must be weighed against the major disadvantage that they do not provide students with feedback on specific aspects of the response that are strong and ones where improvement is needed. Of course, such feedback can be provided by marginal notes and comments that the teacher writes on the student's paper, but holistic scores alone provide less specific guidance to the student than analytic scores.

Example of the Oregon Department of Education Scoring Rubric to Be Considered a "6" on the Organization Dimension

"The organization enhances the central idea(s) and its development. The order and structure are compelling and move the reader through the text easily. The writing is characterized by

1. Effective, perhaps creative, sequencing and paragraph breaks: the organizational structure fits the topic, and the writing is easy to follow.
2. A strong, inviting beginning that draws the reader in and a strong, satisfying sense of resolution or closure.
3. Smooth, effective transitions among all elements (sentences, paragraphs, ideas).
4. Details that fit where placed."

Narrative essay rubrics for five analytic dimensions were developed by Gearhart, Herman, Baker, and Whittaker (1994) and used by primary classroom teachers in several studies (see Wolf & Gearhart, 1997). The five dimensions are as follows:

1. Theme, including considerations of degree to which it is explicit or implicit and the degree to which it is didactic or revealing
2. Character, including the degree to which the characters are flat and static or "round" and dynamic
3. Setting, including the degree to which the setting is simple or multifunctional and the degree to which it is merely part of the backdrop or essential to the story
4. Plot, including the degree to which the plot is simple or complex and the degree to which it is static or presents conflict
5. Communication, including the degree to which the story is context based or reader considerate and the degree to which it is literal or symbolic

For each of these dimensions, descriptions of six levels of performance are described (see Wolf & Gearhart, 1997; or see the home page for the Center for Research on Evaluation, Standards, and Student Testing [CRESST] at http://www.cse.ucla.edu).

It is also the case that the ease of construction of a set of labels (e.g., excellent, good, adequate, promising but has major shortcomings, weak, and inadequate) is no real advance of the traditional A, B, C, D, and F marks and provides little if any real guidance to the teacher in scoring or to the student in understanding what is expected. Such labels alone fall short of what is meant by a scoring rubric.

A holistic scoring rubric, like an analytic scoring rubric, needs to have the scores or labels elaborated by statements of the characteristics of the response that deserve the score of "excellent" or "promising but has major shortcomings." The National Assessment of Educational Progress (NAEP) writing assessment uses a 6-point holistic scoring rubric, shown in Table 10.3.

A sample CRESST scoring rubric for use in making holistic ratings of the quality of explanations is shown in Table 10.4.

Table 10.3

NAEP holistic scoring rubric for writing

Score	Description of Score Point
1	"*Response to topic* with little information pertinent to task."
2	"*Undeveloped response to the task* in which students began to respond, but did so in a very abbreviated, confusing, or disjointed manner."
3	"*Minimally developed:* a response in which student provided a response to the task that was brief, vague, and somewhat confusing."
4	*Developed:* "a response to the task that contained the necessary elements, but may have been unevenly developed or unelaborated."
5	*Elaborated:* "a well developed and detailed response that may have gone beyond the essential elements of the task."
6	*Extensively elaborated:* a response that shows "a high degree of control over the various elements of writing. Compared with papers given a rating of '5,' those rated '6' may have been similar in content, but they were better organized, more clearly written, and less flawed."

Source: Applebee, Langer, and Mullis (1994, p. 204).

Table 10.4

Example of CRESST scoring rubric for holistic rating of overall quality of an explanation, grade 10

Score	Description
5	The student is extremely knowledgeable about the topic.
This is the highest rating	The student demonstrates in-depth understanding of the relevant and important ideas.
	The student includes the important ideas related to topic and shows a depth of understanding of important relationships.
	The answer is fully developed and includes specific facts or examples.
	The answer is organized somewhat around big ideas, major concepts/principles in the field.
	The response is exemplary, detailed, and clear.
4	The student is knowledgeable about the topic.
	The student has a good understanding of the topic.
	The student includes some of the important ideas related to the topic.
	The student shows a good understanding of the important relationships.
	The answer demonstrates good development of ideas and includes adequate supporting facts or examples.
	The answer may demonstrate some organization around big ideas, major concepts/principles in the field.
	The response is good, has some detail, and is clear.

(Continued)

Table 10.4 (*Continued*)
Example of CRESST scoring rubric for holistic rating of overall quality of an explanation, grade 10

Score	Description
3 This is the middle score of the scale.	The student demonstrates some knowledge and understanding of the topic. The overall answer is OK but may show apparent gaps in his/her understanding and knowledge. The student includes some of the important ideas related to the topic. The student shows some (but limited) understanding of the relationships. The answer demonstrates satisfactory development of ideas and includes some supporting facts or examples. The response is satisfactory, containing some detail, but the answer may be vague or not well developed and may include misconceptions or some inaccurate information.
2	The student has little knowledge or understanding of the topic. The student may include an important idea, part of an idea, or a few facts but does not develop the ideas or deal with the relationships among the ideas. The response contains misconceptions, inaccurate, or irrelevant information. The student may rely heavily on the group activity. The response is poor and lacks clarity.
1	The student shows no knowledge or understanding of the topic. The student either: (1) writes about the topic using irrelevant or inaccurate information (2) recalls the steps of the Group Activity in Part II of the performance assessment, adding no new or relevant information and showing no understanding of how the activity relates to the general topic.
0	The student either: (1) left the answer blank (2) wrote about a different topic (3) wrote "I don't know."

Source: CRESST: http://www.cse.ucla.edu.

SUGGESTIONS FOR SCORING ESSAY QUESTIONS

Improving the reliability of scoring answers to essay questions begins long before the questions are administered. The first step is to decide what learning outcomes are to be measured. This is followed by phrasing the questions and the scoring rubrics in accordance with the learning outcomes and including explicit directions concerning the type of answers desired. Only when both the students and the teacher understand the task to be performed can reliable scoring be expected. No degree of proficiency in evaluating answers can compensate for poorly designed and phrased questions.

When the necessary preliminary steps have been taken in constructing essay questions, the following suggestions can be used effectively to increase the reliability of the scoring.

1. Prepare an outline of the expected answer in advance. This should contain the major points to be included, the characteristics of the answer (e.g., organization) to be evaluated, and the amount of credit to be allotted to each. For a restricted-response question calling for three hypotheses, for example, a list of acceptable hypotheses would be prepared, and a given number of scoring points would be assigned to each. For an extended-response question, the major points or aspects of the answer would be outlined. In addition, the relative amount of credit to be allowed for such characteristics as accuracy of the factual information, pertinence of examples, skill of organization, and effectiveness of presentation would be indicated.

Preparing a scoring rubric provides a common basis for evaluating the students' answers and increases the likelihood that our standards for each question will remain stable throughout the scoring. If prepared during the test's construction, such a scoring key also helps us phrase questions that clearly convey the types of answers expected. For a restricted-response essay question, a point might be assigned to each of two or three desired properties of the responses, and a point would be awarded to a student response for each of the desired properties it contained. For an extended-response essay question, a 5-point rating might be used. Five points would be awarded to a response that was well organized and clear and that displayed the type of analysis and reasoning sought by the question. Three points might be awarded for an answer that was clear and adequate but not very compelling. Answers that contained little accurate information and displayed inadequate reasoning might be awarded a single point.

2. Use the scoring rubric that is most appropriate. As discussed previously, two types of scoring rubrics, analytic and holistic, are commonly used with essay questions. Analytic rubrics focus attention on one characteristic at a time and are especially useful in providing students with specific feedback about aspects of their work. Holistic rubrics are likely to be more useful when the focus of the assessment is on overall content understanding than writing skill per se.

3. Decide how to handle factors that are irrelevant to the learning outcomes being measured. Several factors influence our evaluations of answers that are not directly pertinent to the purposes of the measurement. Prominent among these are legibility of handwriting, spelling, sentence structure, punctuation, and neatness. We should make an effort to keep such factors from influencing our judgment when evaluating the content of the answers. In some instances, such factors may, of course, be evaluated for their own sake. When this is done, you should obtain a separate score for written expression or for each of the specific factors. As far as possible, however, we should not let such factors contaminate the extent to which our scores reflect the achievement of other learning outcomes.

Another decision concerns the presence of irrelevant and inaccurate factual information in the response. Should you ignore it and score only that which is pertinent and correct? If you do, some students will write everything that occurs to them, knowing that you will sort it out and give them credit for anything correct. This discourages careful thinking and desirable evaluative abilities. On the other hand, if you reduce scores for irrelevant and inaccurate material, the question of how much to lower the score on a given paper is a troublesome one. Probably the best procedure is to decide in advance approximately how much the score on each question is to be lowered when the inclusion of irrelevant material is excessive. The students should then be warned that such a penalty will be imposed.

4. **Evaluate all responses to one question before going on to the next one.** One factor that contributes to unreliable scoring of essay questions is a shifting of standards from one paper to the next. A paper with average answers may appear to be of much higher quality when it follows a failing paper than when it follows a near-perfect one. One way to minimize this is to score all answers to the first question, reorder the papers to be evaluated, then score all answers to the second question and so on until all the questions have been scored. A more uniform standard can be maintained with this procedure because it is easier to remember the basis for judging each answer and because answers of various degrees of quality can be more easily compared. When the rating method is used and the responses are placed in several piles on the basis of each answer, shifting standards also can be checked by evaluating each answer a second time and reclassifying it if necessary.

Evaluating all answers to one question at a time helps counteract another type of error that creeps into the scoring of essay questions. When we evaluate all the answers of a single student, the first few answers create a general impression of the student's achievement that colors our judgment of the remaining answers. Thus, if the first answers are of high quality, we tend to overrate the following answers; if they are of low quality, we tend to underrate them. This "halo effect" is less likely when the answers for a given student are not evaluated in continuous sequence.

5. **When possible, evaluate the answers without looking at the student's name.** The general impression we form about each student during our teaching is also a source of bias in evaluating essay questions. It is not uncommon for a teacher to give a high score to a poorly written answer by rationalizing that "the student is really capable, even though she didn't express it clearly." A similar response by a student regarded less favorably will receive a much lower score, with the honest conviction that the student deserved the lower score. This halo effect is one of the most serious deterrents to reliable scoring by classroom teachers and is especially difficult to counteract. See the box "Bluffing: A Special Scoring Problem" for information about a scoring problem unique to essay questions.

When possible, the identity of the students should be concealed until all answers are scored. The simplest way to do this is to have the students put their names on the back of the papers. If a student's identity cannot be concealed because of familiar handwriting, the best we can do is make a conscious effort to eliminate any such bias from our judgment.

6. **If especially important decisions are to be based on the results, obtain two or more independent ratings.** Sometimes essay questions are included in assessments used to select students for awards, scholarships, special training, and the like. In such cases, two or more competent persons should score the responses independently, and their ratings should be compared. After any large discrepancies have been satisfactorily arbitrated (possibly by a third scorer), the independent ratings may be averaged for more reliable results.

SUMMARY

The essay question is especially useful for measuring those aspects of complex achievement that cannot be measured well by more objective means. These include (a) the ability to supply rather than merely identify interpretations and applications of data, and (b)

Bluffing: A Special Scoring Problem

It is possible for students to obtain higher scores on essay question responses than they deserve by means of clever bluffing. This is usually a combination of writing skill, general knowledge, and common "tricks of the trade." Following are some ways that students might attempt to influence the reader and, thus, inflate their grades.

1. Writing something for every question, even if it is only a restatement of the question (Students figure they might get some credit. Blank spaces get none.)
2. Stressing the importance of the topic covered by the question, especially when short on facts (e.g., "This battle played a significant role in the Civil War.")
3. Agreeing with the teacher's views whenever it seems appropriate (e.g., "The future of mankind depends on how well we conserve our natural resources.")
4. Being a name-dropper (e.g., "This is supported by the well-known

experiment by Smith." The reader assumes that the student knows Smith's "well-known" experiment.)
5. Writing on a related topic and fitting it to the question (e.g., Prepared to write on President Harry Truman but asked to write about General Douglas MacArthur, the student might start with, "Harry Truman was the president who fired General MacArthur." From then on, there is more about President Truman than General MacArthur.)
6. Writing in general terms that can fit many situations (e.g., In evaluating a short story, the student might say: "This was an interesting story. The characters were fairly well developed, but in some instances more detail would be welcome." This might be called the fortune-teller approach.)

Although bluffing cannot be completely eradicated, carefully phrasing the questions and following clearly defined scoring procedures can reduce it.

the ability to organize, integrate, and express ideas in a general attack on a problem. Outcomes of the first type are measured by restricted-response questions and outcomes of the second type by extended-response questions.

Although essay questions provide an effective means of measuring significant learning outcomes, they have certain limitations: (a) Scoring tends to be unreliable, (b) scoring is time consuming, and (c) only a limited sampling of achievement is obtained. Because of these shortcomings, essay questions, especially ones requiring extended responses, should be limited to assessing those outcomes that cannot be measured well by objective items.

The construction and scoring of essay questions are interrelated processes that require attention if a valid and reliable measure of achievement is to be obtained. Questions should be phrased so that they measure the attainment of definite learning outcomes and clearly convey to the students the type of response expected. To the extent possible, scoring criteria should be specified in advance. For restricted-response essay questions, scoring rubrics can usually be generated by outlining possible answers deserving full credit and indicating what aspects of the answers are required for different amounts of partial credit. For extended-response essays, a choice between analytic and holistic scoring rubrics should be made. Analytic scoring rubrics have the advantage of providing students with more specific feedback than holistic scoring rubrics. Holistic scoring rubrics can be developed and applied more rapidly and may correspond closely to grading decisions that need to be made. Available examples of both analytic and holistic scoring rubrics provide useful starting points for developing rubrics for classroom use.

Indicating an approximate time limit for each question and avoiding the use of optional questions also contribute to more valid results. Scoring procedures can be improved by (a) using a scoring rubric, (b) adapting the scoring method to the type of question used, (c) controlling the influence of irrelevant factors, (d) evaluating all answers to each question at one time, (e) evaluating without looking at the students' names, and (f) obtaining two or more independent ratings when important decisions are to be made.

LEARNING EXERCISES

1. In an area in which you are teaching or plan to teach, identify several learning outcomes that can be best measured with essay questions. For each learning outcome, construct two essay questions.
2. Criticize the following essay questions and restate them so that they meet the criteria of a good essay question.
   a. Discuss air transportation.
   b. Do you think the government should spend more on environmental protection?
   c. What is your attitude toward health care reform?
3. For each of the following, would it be more appropriate to use an extended-response question or a restricted-response question?

   a. Compare two periods in history.
   b. Describe the procedure for using a dictionary.
   c. Indicate the advantages of one procedure over another.
   d. Evaluate a short story.
4. Construct an analytic and a holistic scoring rubric for an extended-response essay question that might be used in the grade and content area of most interest to you.
5. What factors should be considered in deciding whether essay questions should be included in a classroom test? Which factors are most important?
6. Describe how essay tests might be used to facilitate learning. What types of learning are most likely to be enhanced?

REFERENCES

Applebee, A. N., Langer, J., & Mullis, I. V. S. (1994). *NAEP 1992 Writing Report Card.* Washington, DC: National Center for Education Statistics, GPO (065-000-00654-5).

Gearhart, M., Herman, J. L., Baker, E. L., & Whittaker, A. K. (1994). *Writing portfolios at the elementary level: A study of methods for writing assessment* (CSE Technical Report 337). Los Angeles: University of California, Center for Research on Evaluation, Standards, and Student Testing. Available: http://www.cse.ucla.edu.

Wolf, S. A., & Gearhart, M. (1997). New writing assessments: The challenge of changing teachers' beliefs about students as writers. *Theory Into Practice, 36,* 220–230. (Also available as CSE Technical Report 400). Los Angeles: University of California, Center for Research on Evaluation, Standards, and Student Testing. Available: http://www.cse.ucla.edu.

FURTHER READING

Gronlund, N. E. (2005). *Assessment of student achievement* (8th ed.). Boston: Allyn & Bacon. Chapter 6, "Writing Supply Items: Short Answer and Essay," discusses the construction and use of essay questions.

Herman, J. L., Aschbacher, P. R., & Winters, L. (1992). *A practical guide to alternative assessment.* Alexandria, VA: Association for Supervision and Curriculum Development. Presents examples of scoring rubrics and discusses approaches to developing essay assessments.

Regional Educational Laboratories. (1998). *Improving classroom assessment: A toolkit for professional developers.* Portland, OR: Regional Educational Laboratories, or available centrally from Northwest Regional Educational Laboratory. Includes samples of performance assessments and scoring rubrics.

Welch, C. (2006). Item and prompt development in performance testing. In S. M. Downing & T. M. Haladyna (Eds.), *Handbook of test development* (Chapter 13, pp. 303–327). Mahway, NJ: Lawrence Erlbaum. Provides guidance for improving the quality of essay prompts and gives examples of scoring rubrics.

11

MEASURING COMPLEX ACHIEVEMENT: PERFORMANCE-BASED ASSESSMENTS

Essay tests are the most common example of a performance-based assessment, but there are many others, including artistic productions, experiments in science, oral presentations, and the use of mathematics to solve real-world problems. The emphasis is on doing, not merely knowing—on process as well as product.

Essay tests are an example of one type of performance assessment, but there are many aspects of writing that are not tapped within the constraints of the normal essay test. Choosing a topic, identifying an audience, gathering information, preparing drafts, seeking critiques, and revising are all important aspects of writing that are not measured by the usual essay test. Moreover, writing is not the only type of performance outcome we need to assess. Many highly valued learning outcomes emphasize the actual performance of tasks in realistic settings. This is obvious in the case of art or music and for vocational or industrial education courses, such as auto repair, woodworking, or word processing. It is also true for mathematics, science, social studies, and foreign languages. In each case, performance-based assessments are needed to measure some of the desired learning outcomes.

For example, although knowledge of vocabulary and grammar in a foreign language can be measured with the various forms of paper-and-pencil tests, speaking skills cannot. Oral performance is required to assess a student's spoken communication skills in a foreign language. Similarly, the assessment of a student's ability to make observations, formulate hypotheses, collect data, and draw valid scientific conclusions may require the use of performance assessments. The use of mathematics to solve meaningful real-world problems and to communicate solutions to others may also be best assessed by the use of performance tasks in realistic settings.

Performance assessments provide a basis for teachers to evaluate both the effectiveness of the ***process*** or procedure used (e.g., approach to data collection or manipulation of instruments) and the ***product*** resulting from performance of a task (e.g., completed report of results or completed artwork). Unlike simple tests of factual knowledge, there is unlikely to be a single right or best answer. Rather, there may be multiple performances and problem solutions that would be judged to be excellent. Problem formulation, the organization of ideas, the integration of multiple types of evidence, and originality are all important aspects of performance that may not be adequately assessed by paper-and-pencil tests.

TYPES OF PERFORMANCE-BASED ASSESSMENT

Performance assessments are also sometimes referred to as "authentic assessments" or "alternative assessments," but the terms are not interchangeable. "Alternative assessment" highlights the contrast to traditional paper-and-pencil tests, whereas "authentic assessment" emphasizes the practical application of the tasks in real-world settings. We prefer the label "performance assessment" because it is more descriptive than "alternative assessment" and less pretentious than "authentic assessment."

Authenticity is a matter of degree. A highly authentic assessment of communication skills in German, for example, might involve listening to the verbal interactions of a student when visiting Germany; but such an assessment obviously would lack practicality for the teacher of a typical German class. Simulated spoken interactions between the teacher and a student or among students, although not quite as authentic, are much more practical. In either case, the focus of the assessment is on the student's performance in communicating in German.

Although authenticity is usually only approximated, it is an important goal of performance assessment. Providing realistic contexts can make problems more engaging for students and help the teacher evaluate whether a student who can solve a problem in one context can solve it in another. Hence, it is desirable to increase the authenticity of tasks to whatever extent possible.

Like essay questions, performance assessments should be used primarily to measure those learning outcomes that cannot be measured well by objective test items. Objective test items are generally more efficient and more reliable for measuring factual knowledge and the ability to solve well-structured problems (e.g., solve a quadratic equation). Performance assessments are better suited for applications with less-structured problems where problem identification; collection, organization, integration, and evaluation of information; and originality are emphasized (e.g., where is the best place to locate a restaurant?). They are also essential for learning outcomes that involve the creation of a product (e.g., a typed letter or a painting) or an oral or physical performance (e.g., the presentation of a speech, the repair of an engine, or the use of a scientific instrument).

Hands-on performance tasks that require students to manipulate objects, measure outcomes, and observe results of experimental manipulations are sometimes essential to capture the full array of skills needed to perform "authentic" tasks. This is obvious in the case of a driving test or a performance test for a dentist, but it may also be true in science and other areas. Research has shown that computer simulations of tasks in science sometimes may be good substitutes for actual hands-on performance of the task, but in other instances even high-fidelity simulations may have relatively poor relationships for hands-on performance. Poor relationships between simulations and actual hands-on performance occur most commonly when the manipulation of apparatus (e.g., mixing a compound or taking a measurement) is an integral part of the task.

Performance tasks can vary substantially in the degree to which performance is restricted. A word-processing test, for example, might be completely constrained with regard to format and content of a letter to be typed. The task of creating a sculpture might be almost completely unconstrained with regard to the approach a student might take or the nature of the product produced. Most performance tasks fall in between these extremes.

Restricted-Response Performance Tasks

A restricted-response performance task is usually relatively narrow in definition. The instructions are generally more focused than extended-response performance tasks, and the limitations on the types of performance expected are likely to be indicated.

Restricted-response performance tasks sometimes start with a simple multiple-choice or short-answer question, such as the one in Figure 11.1. Those questions are then extended by asking for an explanation of the answer and sometimes an explanation for why the other answers were not selected. Often, different answers in the first part of the task could be given full credit if the explanation provided sound reasoning to defend the choice.

EXAMPLES   Type a letter of application for a job.

Read aloud a section of a story.

Use various combinations of five straight pieces of plastic to construct as many different triangles as you can and record the perimeters of each.

Determine which of two liquids contains sugar and explain what results support your conclusion.

Construct graphs of the average amount of rainfall per month for two cities.

Request aloud directions to the train station in French.

Write the names of the countries in the appropriate areas of a blank map of Europe.

Sara knows that half the students in her class were invited to Kim's birthday party. Also, half were invited to Julie's party. Sara thinks that these figures add up to 100%, so she thinks she will surely be invited to one of the parties. Explain why Sara is wrong. If possible use a diagram in your explanation.*

*Adapted from a task used in the California Assessment program.

If the explanation parts of the task in Figure 11.1 were omitted, there would be no way to determine the basis for a student's choice of one of the three figures. Even if students selected the preferred choice (B), you would not know whether they did so for a sound reason or whether they simply guessed. Nor would you know whether they were attentive to the fact that graph C is impossible because it depicts 44 students when there were only 20 students in Mr. Pang's class.

There are 20 students in Mr. Pang's class. On Tuesday most of the students in the class said they had pockets in the clothes they were wearing.

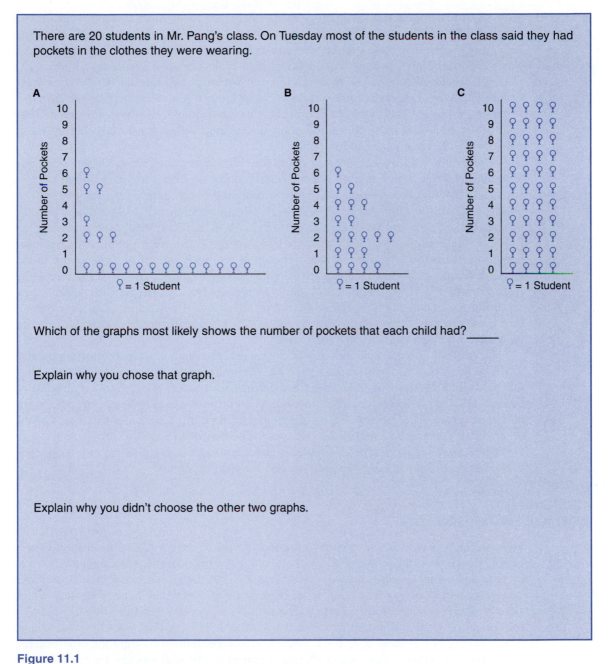

Which of the graphs most likely shows the number of pockets that each child had?_____

Explain why you chose that graph.

Explain why you didn't choose the other two graphs.

Figure 11.1

Example of stimulus material for a mathematics problem administered at grade 4 in the 1992 National Assessment of Educational progress

Source: NAEP 1992: Mathematics Report Card for the Nation and the States (p. 49) by I. V. S. Mullis, J. A. Dossey, E. H. Owen, and G. W. Phillips, 1993, Washington, DC: U.S. Department of Education. Report No. 23-ST02.

As is true of many tasks that are called performance assessment tasks, the example in Figure 11.1 is, of course, a type of essay question. No real manipulation or hands-on activity is involved. A task such as the one in the figure might readily be adapted to a classroom assessment activity that involved data collection and graphing. Children, for example, might each be asked to count the number of pockets in the clothes they were wearing. Those numbers could be reported, and each student could construct a graph. Separate graphs for boys and for girls in the classroom might also be constructed. They might then be asked to write a description of the graph they constructed before being presented with a task like that in Figure 11.1.

A variety of tasks may be used to assess the skills young students have at making and recording observations, summarizing the observations, and reaching conclusions. In one such task, students were instructed in how to find and count their pulse. They were then asked to count the number of pulses in each of four segments of 15 seconds where the teacher looked at a stopwatch and gave instructions to start and stop. After recording the four initial segments, students were told to jump up and down for 1 minute. After exercise, children were asked to count and record their pulse for four additional 15-second periods. Next, a second period of jumping for 2 minutes was required, followed by four more recordings of 15-second segments. Students were asked to construct a table and a graph reporting the results and describe what the results showed when the initial four recordings were compared to those following the first and second rounds of exercise. Finally, they were asked to explain what they observed.

The relative advantages and disadvantages of restricted performance tasks parallel those of restricted essay questions. They are generally more structured and require less time to administer than extended-response performance tasks. The shorter administration time makes it possible to administer more tasks and thereby gain broader coverage of the content domain. The greater degree of structure makes the task easier to score. On the other hand, the structure makes the tasks less valuable for measuring student skills, such as approaches to ill-structured problems, integration of information, and originality. Extended performance tasks are better suited for such outcomes.

Extended Performance Tasks

The extended performance task may require students to seek information from a variety of sources beyond those provided by the task itself. For example, students may need to use the library, make observations, collect and analyze data in an experiment, conduct a survey, or use a computer or other types of equipment. They may have to identify which aspects of the task are most relevant. The process or procedures that they use may be observed and be an important part of the assessment. The product that is produced may take a variety of forms, such as the construction and presentation of graphs or tables, the use of photographs or drawings, or the construction of physical models. Products may be developed over the course of several days and include opportunities for revision or modification. This freedom enables students to demonstrate their ability to select, organize, integrate, and evaluate information and ideas. The price of these gains includes the loss of efficiency, possible loss of breadth of coverage of the content domain, and greater difficulty in rating performance.

> Prepare and deliver a speech to persuade people to take actions to protect the environment.
>
> Hog is a game played with dice. The goal is to get the largest possible score. You may roll any number of dice out of a large cup. If none of the numbers is a 1, then the score for the roll is the sum of the numbers rolled. If a 1 is obtained on any of the dice, the score for the roll is zero. What number of dice do you think it best to roll? Defend your decision (Mathematical Sciences Education Board, 1993).
>
> Write a computer program in BASIC that will sort a list of words alphabetically.
>
> Design and carry out an investigation to estimate the acceleration, *a*, of a falling object such as a baseball. Describe the procedure used, present the data collected and analyzed, and state your conclusions.
>
> Read an abridged version of the Lincoln–Douglas debates. Imagine that you were living then and heard the debates. Write a letter to a friend explaining the historical issues addressed and their importance in terms of what you know about the problems facing the nation at the time of the debates (Baker, Aschbacher, Niemi, & Sato, 1992).

Performance assessments require students to demonstrate skills by actually performing. They involve doing rather than just knowing about, and there are sometimes important differences between the two. For example, a guitar player may know which frets to press the strings against for a particular chord without being able to perform the task smoothly to produce the desired sound. Similarly, a computer programmer may know the function of various needed commands without being able to produce a correctly working program to perform a specific task, or a science student may know the parts and functions of an instrument without being able to use it properly to obtain the information needed to solve a problem. Performance assessments are needed to observe and evaluate such skills. They also communicate the message that actual performance is important.

A performance assessment task used in the 1996 NAEP Science Assessment at grade 4 is shown in Figure 11.2. As can be seen, this task requires students to do simple manipulations, to measure and record the outcomes of placing the pencil and thumbtack in the different bottles of water, to draw conclusions about the "mystery water," and to make predictions about the effects of adding salt to a solution. In this example, the manipulations, observations, and measurements are relatively simple, but these basic skills are critical in many settings and are not well assessed in a purely paper-and-pencil assessment.

The effective use of performance assessments requires careful attention to task selection and to the ways performances will be scored. Care needs to be taken in the identification of the complex skills we want to measure, in the construction of tasks that will require students to demonstrate those skills, and in the evaluation of the resulting process and/or product. Without careful attention to these aspects of the assessment, it is unlikely that the effort will yield adequately reliable or valid measures of the complex skills that are being sought.

As the name suggests, performance assessments measure the ability of students to perform tasks that correspond to important instructional objectives. Restricted performance tasks generally focus on specific skills (e.g., reading a passage aloud). Extended performance tasks are more likely to involve problem solving and the integration of a variety of skills and understandings. A comparison of the types of complex learning outcomes measured by each of these types of performance tasks is presented in Table 11.1.

FLOATING PENCIL

Using a Pencil to Test Fresh and Salt Water

You have been given a bag with some things in it that you will work with during the next 20 minutes. Take all of the things out of the bag and put them on your desk. Now look at the picture below. Do you have everything that is shown in the picture? If you are missing anything, raise your hand and you will be given the things you need.

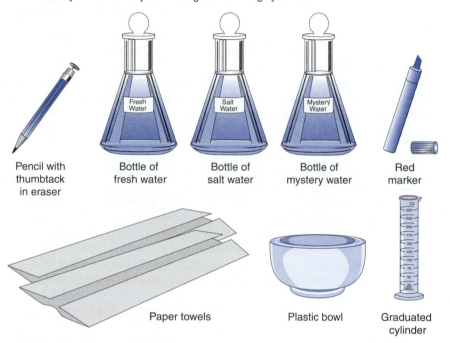

Figure 11.2

Example of hands-on science performance assessment task used at grade 4 in the 1996 National Assessment of Educational Progress

Source: From *NAEP 1996 Science: Report Card for the Nation and the States* by C. Y. O' Sullivan, C. M. Reese, and J. Mazzeo, 1997, Washington, DC: U.S. Department of Education.

ADVANTAGES AND LIMITATIONS OF PERFORMANCE ASSESSMENTS

Advantages

A major advantage of performance assessments is that they can clearly communicate instructional goals that involve complex performances in natural settings in and outside of school. By using tasks that require performances that correspond as closely as is feasible to major instructional objectives, they provide instructional targets and

Table 11.1
Types of performance tasks

Type of Task	Examples of Complex Learning Outcomes That Can Be Measured
Restricted-response performance task	Ability to • read aloud • ask directions in a foreign language • construct a graph • use a scientific instrument • type a letter
Extended-response performance task	Ability to • build a model • collect, analyze, and evaluate data • organize ideas, create visuals, and make an integrated oral presentation • create a painting or perform with a musical instrument • repair an engine • write a creative short story

thereby can encourage the development of complex understandings and skills. Often, performance assessment tasks are indistinguishable from good instructional activities.

A second advantage of performance assessments is that they can measure complex learning outcomes that cannot be measured by other means. As has already been stated, knowing how to do something is not the same as being able to do it, much less do it well. Thus, a paper-and-pencil test that measures what a student knows about effective public speaking, for example, does not provide a measure of the student's ability to deliver an effective speech.

A third advantage of performance assessments is that they provide a means of assessing **process** or procedure as well as the **product** that results from performing a task. For example, by observing students while they are conducting a laboratory experiment, strengths and weaknesses in the use of equipment and in technique can be assessed, as can success in completing the experiment and the strength of reasoning provided to support conclusions.

A fourth advantage of performance assessments is that they implement approaches that are suggested by modern learning theory. Rather than viewing students as recipients of discrete bits of knowledge, modern learning theory conceives of students as active participants in the construction of meaning. According to this view, new information must be actively transformed and integrated with a student's prior knowledge. High-quality performance-based assessments take student background knowledge into account and engage students in the active construction of meaning.

Limitations

The most commonly cited limitations of performance assessments parallel those cited for essay questions. Unreliability of ratings of performances across teachers or across time for the same teacher is clearly a limitation. Careful attention to the learning outcomes that the task is intended to assess and to the scoring rubrics that will be used in rating the performances is required both at the time tasks are developed and at the time performances are rated to minimize this limitation. Although the judgmental scoring of complex performances will always include some uncontrollable variations, the scoring reliability, the comparability of scores assigned to the performances of different students, and hence the fairness of the assessment can be greatly increased by clearly defining the outcomes to be measured, properly framing the tasks, and carefully defining and following rubrics for scoring performances.

Another limitation of extended performance assessments is their time-consuming nature. Because a substantial amount of time may be required to allow students to have an adequate opportunity to perform each task, relatively few extended performance assessments can be obtained within a reasonable amount of time. There is considerable evidence that performance on one task provides only a relatively weak basis for generalizing to performances on other tasks intended to assess common or related learning outcomes. Thus, solid generalization to a larger domain of outcomes requires the use of multiple tasks. Overcoming the limitation of weak generalization of performance across tasks requires the accumulation of information from performances on different tasks during the course of the year. Justification for the devotion of the required amount of instructional time to the assessments requires that the tasks provide students with good learning opportunities as well as assessment results.

SUGGESTIONS FOR CONSTRUCTING PERFORMANCE TASKS

The development of high-quality performance assessments that effectively measure complex learning outcomes requires attention to task development and to the ways in which performances are scored. We begin with a consideration of ways to improve the development of tasks and then suggest ways to improve scoring.

1. **Focus on learning outcomes that require complex cognitive skills and student performances**. It is important that tasks be interesting, but that is not sufficient. Tasks need to be developed or selected in light of important learning outcomes. Because performance-based tasks generally require a substantial investment of student time, they should be used primarily to assess learning outcomes that are not adequately measured by less time-consuming approaches.

2. **Select or develop tasks that represent both the content and the skills that are central to important learning outcomes**. Current conceptions of learning stress the interdependence of content and skills. Problem solving in one subject-matter area is not the same as it is in another area. Debating a political issue in social studies is different than debating the effectiveness of a piece of literature. In each case, the content and process are interdependent.

Thus, it is important to specify the range of content and resources students can use in performing a task. Past class assignments provide one natural basis for specifying content, but for many tasks it will be desirable to allow students the opportunity to do additional research to expand their knowledge base. In any event, the specification of assumed content understandings is critical to ensuring that a task functions as intended.

3. Minimize the dependence of task performance on skills that are irrelevant to the intended purpose of the assessment task. The key here is to focus on the intention of the assessment. Although both the ability to read complicated texts and the ability to communicate clearly are important learning outcomes, they are not necessarily the intent of a particular assessment. Reading ability, for example, might be irrelevant for an assessment that is intended to measure a student's ability to use mathematics to solve a practical problem (e.g., determine how much and what type of lumber to buy to build a clubhouse with specified features). However, if the task is presented in a way that requires substantial reading, then this factor may add to task difficulty for some students but not for others and thereby reduce the validity of the intended interpretation of the results. This irrelevant source of difficulty would also undermine the fairness of the assessment especially for students with learning disabilities or who are learning English as a second language. On the other hand, writing skills might be an intended part of a mathematics task where a goal of the assessment was to measure a student's ability to communicate mathematical reasoning and results.

4. Provide the necessary scaffolding for students to be able to understand the task and what is expected. Challenging tasks often involve ambiguities and require students to experiment, gather information, formulate hypotheses, and evaluate their own progress in solving a problem. However, problems cannot be solved in a vacuum. Students need to have the prior knowledge and skills required to address the problem. These prerequisites can be a natural outcome of prior instruction or may be built in to the task. Preassessment activities, for example, can be used not only to introduce a task but also to ensure that students have the prior knowledge essential for the task and are familiar with the materials or equipment that they need to use. It is important to ask: What prior knowledge and skills are assumed in order to perform the task?

5. Construct task directions so that the student's task is clearly indicated. Vague directions can lead to such a diverse array of performances that it becomes impossible to rate them in a fair or reliable fashion. By design, many performance-based tasks give students a substantial degree of freedom to explore, approach problems in different ways, and develop novel solutions. Such intended task characteristics, however, are not an excuse for vague directions. In the task shown in Figure 11.3, students need to experiment and decide on the placement of objects into categories on their own. They also have to construct an explanation for the classification they provide, but the task of using the magnet to test the items, the classification of objects into two categories, and the need to explain the difference between the objects in the two categories are made explicit.

6. Clearly communicate performance expectations in terms of the scoring rubrics by which the performances will be judged. Specifying the criteria to be used in rating performance helps clarify task expectations for a student. Explaining the criteria that will be used in rating performances not only provides students with guidance on how to focus their efforts but also helps convey priorities for learning outcomes.

Magnet

Task Descriptor

To use a magnet to identify magnetic and nonmagnetic items and then to explain the difference between them.

Equipment/Material

A magnet and the following seven objects: plastic button, iron or steel washer, steel paper clip, iron nail, glass marble, plastic rod, and copper coin.

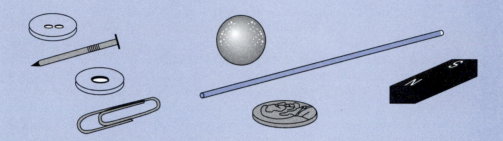

Student Instructions

Test the objects with the magnet and divide them into two groups. List the objects in the two groups and explain what makes the objects in the two groups different.

Scoring Scheme

Credit was given for grouping the objects correctly. Four categories of explanations were recorded: namely, that one group was made of iron or steel, that one group was attracted by the magnet, that one group was made of iron and steel and was attracted by the magnet, and any other explanation.

Figure 11.3
Example of performance assessment task in science

Source: Performance Assessment: An International Experiment by B.M. Sample, 1992, Princeton, NJ: Educational Testing Service, Report No. 22-Caep-06. Copyright 1992 by Educational Testing Service. Reprinted by permission.

Listing attributes such as appropriate symbol use, accuracy of information and scale, and ease with which the map can be read makes the rating criteria explicit. It also highlights the learning outcomes that are considered important for the task in the following example.

EXAMPLE   Construct a weather map. Your map will be evaluated for accuracy of information and scale, for appropriate use of symbols, and for the ease with which it can be read.

PERFORMANCE CRITERIA

Richard Stiggins (1987) has persuasively argued that the specification of performance criteria is the most important aspect of developing effective performance assessments. He suggests imagining the feedback that would be provided to a student who performed poorly before the task is administered. His rationale for focusing on the criteria to be used is straightforward: "If you do not have a clear sense of the key dimensions of sound performance—a vision of poor and outstanding performance—you can neither teach students to perform nor evaluate their performance."

The criteria to be used in judging student performance are critical for reliable, fair, and valid assessment, and the specification of the criteria should begin at the time the tasks are being selected or developed. Both the teacher and the student need to understand the criteria that will be used to judge performance. As was just noted, criteria help clarify the task expectations for students, and they communicate learning goals and standards. In addition, they guide the judgment process in ways that enhance reliability, fair treatment of each performance, and the validity of conclusions about each student's achievement.

The two main ways of guiding judgments of both the process used in performing a task and any product resulting from that performance are **scoring rubrics/rating scales** and **checklists**. We begin with scoring rubrics and rating scales and then turn to a consideration of checklists.

SCORING RUBRICS AND RATING SCALES

As was discussed in Chapter 10, a scoring rubric is a set of guidelines for the application of performance criteria to the responses and performance of students. A scoring rubric typically consists of verbal descriptions of performance or aspects of student responses that distinguish between advanced, proficient, partially proficient, and beginning levels of performance. Both analytic (Table 10.2) and holistic (Tables 10.3 and 10.4) scoring rubrics were illustrated in Chapter 10.

The analytic scoring rubric requires the identification of different dimensions or characteristics of performance that are rated separately. For example, a mathematics task might be rated in terms of the accuracy of the calculations and the clarity of the explanation. A written report on the results of a science experiment might be rated on factual accuracy, quality of analysis, and the degree to which conclusions were justified. A literary criticism might be rated for organization, quality of ideas, clarity of expression, and mechanics. An oral presentation might be rated both for the substantive quality of the report and for the effectiveness of the presentation.

A holistic rubric provides descriptions of different levels of overall performance. Holistic rubrics are efficient and correspond more directly to global judgments required in the assignment of grades, but they do not provide students with specific feedback about the strengths and weaknesses of their performance as is provided by analytic rubrics.

Rating scales are often limited to making quality judgments (e.g., excellent, good, fair, or poor) or scaled frequency judgments (e.g., always, frequently, sometimes, or never) for each level. As is illustrated in some of the following examples, however, the distinction between scoring rubrics and rating scales is often blurred by adding the descriptions of a rubric to the judgmental qualities of a rating scale.

As is illustrated in Figure 11.4, a scoring rubric may include a rating scale (excellent, good, and so on) but may also provide descriptions of characteristics or performance corresponding to each point on the scale. A scoring rubric makes explicit the criteria that are used to rate performance. Generic scoring rubrics are available that can be readily adapted for use in rating performance on a variety of tasks. Generic scoring rubrics, such as the one shown in Figure 11.4, provide a useful starting place for many assessments. The distinctions between the levels can be made more specific by considering the specific task and likely features that would distinguish between exemplary performance and competent performance or between satisfactory performance with minor flaws and performance that has serious flaws. For example, lists of minor and major flaws might be constructed for a specific task. In a similar fashion, common misconceptions that are anticipated in response to a particular task might be listed.

The number of levels and the verbal descriptions used to guide the scoring may vary from situation to situation. For the hands-on science task involving the floating pencil

Quality of Explanation

6 = Excellent explanation (complete, clear, unambiguous)
5 = Good explanation (reasonably clear and complete)
4 = Acceptable explanation (problem completed but may contain minor flaws in explanation)
3 = Needs improvement (on the right track but may contain serious flaws; demonstrates only partial understanding)
2 = Incorrect or inadequate explanation (shows lack of understanding of problem)
1 = Incorrect without attempt at explanation

Separate Ratings of Answer and Explanation

Answer
4 = Correct
3 = Almost correct or partially correct
2 = Incorrect but reasonable attempt
1 = Incorrect with no relationship to the problem
0 = No answer

Explanation
4 = Complete, clear, logical
3 = Essentially correct but incomplete or not entirely clear
2 = Vague or unclear but with redeeming features
1 = Irrelevant, incorrect, or no explanation

Figure 11.4
Examples of generalized scoring rubrics for mathematics problems

shown in Figure 11.2, for example, the separate scoring rubrics were used for each part of the response. For the part of the task where the student was supposed to identify the mystery water and explain how they could "tell what the mystery water is," student responses were scored using a rubric with three levels:

Complete: Student stated that "the mystery water was fresh water and gave a satisfactory explanation that referred to observations made doing the hands-on task" (O'Sullivan, Reese, & Mazzeo, 1997, p. 44).

Partial: Student stated that the water was fresh but did not support the choice with direct reference to observations from the hands-on task.

Incorrect: Student gave the wrong answer or gave contradictory explanation for the choice of the correct answer of fresh water.

EXAMPLE   **TASK**

First-grade children are asked to arrange four pictures of trees in the order of the seasons by pasting them in four boxes and printing the name of each season in the box.

SCORING RUBRIC

2 points: Student arranges the pictures in the right order, beginning with any season.
1 point: Student begins the task but does not complete arrangement.
0 points: Student does not respond appropriately.

Task and scoring guide adapted from part of a Utah State Office of Education set of assessment tasks called *Weathercaster's Helper* for first-grade students (Regional Educational Laboratories, 1998).

Scoring rubrics for hands-on tasks may include multiple dimensions, each of which focuses on a particular aspect of the process of carrying out the task. For example, in an elementary school science task used by Shavelson, Baxter, and Pine (1991) and Shavelson, Baxter, and Gao (1993), students were asked to determine which of several paper towels absorbed the most water. The scoring rubric records the method used to get the towel wet, the saturation of each towel, the procedure used to measure the amount of water absorbed, the care in measurement, and the accuracy of the result.

Rating scales provide a flexible way of converting information about one or more characteristics of a performance (e.g., overall quality, adequacy of measurement, and appropriateness of summary of results). Typically, a rating scale consists of a set of characteristics or qualities to be judged and some type of scale for indicating the degree to which each attribute is present. The rating form itself is merely a reporting device. Its value in appraising the learning and development of students depends largely on the care with which it is prepared and the appropriateness with which it is used. As with other assessment instruments, it should be constructed in accordance with the learning outcomes to be assessed, and its use should be confined to those areas in which there is a sufficient opportunity to make the necessary observations. If these two principles are properly applied, a rating scale will serve several important assessment functions: (a) It will direct observation toward specific aspects of performance, (b) it will provide a common frame of reference for rating the performance of all students on the same set of characteristics, and (c) it will provide a convenient method for recording the observer's judgments.

Types of Rating Scales

Rating scales may take many forms, but most of them belong to one of the types described next. Each type is illustrated by using two dimensions from a scale for rating contributions to class discussion.

Numerical Rating Scale.   One of the simplest types of rating scales is that in which the rater checks or circles a number to indicate the degree to which a characteristic is present. Typically, each of a series of numbers is given a verbal description that remains constant from one characteristic to another. In some cases, it is merely indicated that the largest number is high, one is low, and the other numbers represent intermediate values.

The numerical rating scale is useful when the characteristics or qualities to be rated can be classified into a limited number of categories and there is general agreement concerning the category represented by each number. As commonly used, however, the numbers are only vaguely defined, so the interpretation and use of the scale vary.

EXAMPLE   *Directions:* Indicate the degree to which this student contributes to a group problem-solving task by circling the appropriate number. The numbers represent the following values: 4—consistently appropriate and effective; 3—generally appropriate and effective; 2—needs improvement, may wander from topic; and 1—unsatisfactory (disruptive or off topic).

   1. To what extent does the student participate in group discussions?

        1   2   3   4

   2. To what extent are the comments related to the topic under discussion?

        1   2   3   4

Graphic Rating Scale.   The distinguishing feature of the graphic rating scale is that each characteristic is followed by a horizontal line. The rating is made by placing a check on the line. A set of categories identifies specific positions along the line, but the rater is free to check between these points.

EXAMPLE

Directions: Indicate the degree to which this student contributes to a group problem-solving task by placing an *X* anywhere along the horizontal line under each item.

   1. To what extent does the student participate in group discussion?

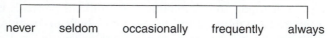

   2. To what extent are the comments related to the topic under discussion?

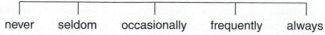

The scale shown in this example uses the same set of categories for each characteristic and is commonly referred to as a **constant-alternatives scale.** When these categories vary from one characteristic to another, the scale is called, quite logically, a **changing-alternatives scale.**

Although the line in the graphic rating scale makes it possible to rate at intermediate points, using single words to identify the categories has no great advantage over the use of numbers. There is little agreement among raters concerning the meaning of such terms as *seldom, occasionally,* and *frequently.* What is needed are descriptions of performances that indicate more specifically how students behave who possess various degrees of the characteristic being rated.

Descriptive Graphic Rating Scale.   The descriptive graphic rating scale uses descriptive phrases to identify the points on a graphic scale. The descriptions are thumbnail sketches of how students behave at different steps along the scale. In some scales, only the center and end positions are defined. In others, a descriptive phrase is placed beneath each point. A space for comments is also frequently provided to enable the rater to clarify the rating.

EXAMPLE   *Directions:* Make your ratings on each of the following characteristics by placing an *X* anywhere along the horizontal line under each item. In the space for comments, include anything that helps clarify your rating.

1. To what extent does the student participate in group discussions?

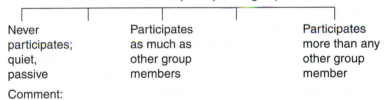

Never
participates;
quiet,
passive

Participates
as much as
other group
members

Participates
more than any
other group
member

Comment:

2. To what extent are the comments related to the topic under discussion?

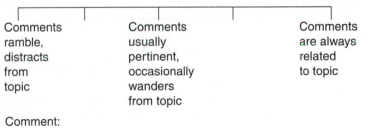

Comments
ramble,
distracts
from
topic

Comments
usually
pertinent,
occasionally
wanders
from topic

Comments
are always
related
to topic

Comment:

The descriptive graphic rating scale is generally the most satisfactory for school use. It explains to both the teacher and the student the types of performance that represent different degrees of progress toward desired learning outcomes. In well-written rubrics, the top level of description actually is the desired learning outcome or at least communicates what good work is intended to look like. The more specific performance descriptions also contribute to greater objectivity and accuracy during the rating process. To aid scoring, numbers also may be added to each position on the scale.

Uses of Rating Scales

Rating scales can be used to assess a wide variety of learning outcomes and aspects of development. As a matter of convenience, these uses may be classified into two assessment areas: (1) process or procedure, and (2) product.

Process or Procedure Assessment.   In many areas, achievement is expressed specifically through the student's performance. Examples include the ability to give a speech, manipulate laboratory equipment, work effectively in a group, sing, play a musical instrument, and perform various physical feats. Such activities do not result in a product that can be assessed, and short-answer or fixed-response tests are generally inadequate. Consequently, the process or procedures used in the performance itself must be observed and judged.

Rating scales are especially useful in assessing process or procedures because they focus on the same aspects of performance in all students and have a common scale on which to record our judgments. If the rating form has been prepared in terms of specific learning outcomes, it also serves as an excellent teaching device. The dimensions and behavior descriptions used in the scale show the student the type of performance desired.

Two items from a typical rating scale for assessing a speech are presented in Figure 11.5. The first part of the form is devoted to the content of the speech and how well it is organized. The second part is concerned with aspects of delivery, such as gestures, posture, appearance, eye contact, voice, and enunciation. In developing such a scale, a teacher must, of course, include those characteristics that are most appropriate for the type of speaking ability to be assessed and for the age level of the student to be judged.

Product Assessment.   When student performance results in some type of product, it is frequently more desirable to judge the product than the process or procedures. The ability to write a theme, for example, is best assessed by judging the quality of the theme itself. Little is to be learned by observing the student's performance. In some areas, however, such as word processing, conducting work in the laboratory, and woodworking, it might be most desirable to rate procedures during the early phase of learning and products later, after the basic skills have been mastered. In any event, product rating can provide assessment information in many areas. In addition to those already mentioned, it is useful in assessing such things as handwriting, drawings, maps, graphs, notebooks, term papers, book reports, results of laboratory experiments, and objects made in vocational courses.

A rating scale serves somewhat the same purpose in product assessment than it does in process assessment. It helps us judge the products of all students in terms of the same characteristics, and it emphasizes to the students those qualities desired in a superior product.

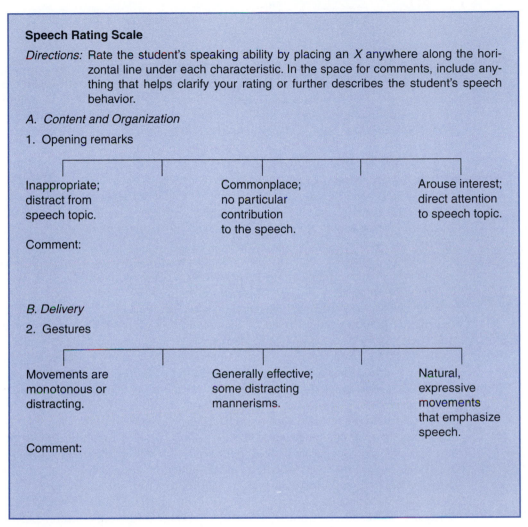

Figure 11.5
Sample items from speech rating scale

Common Errors in Rating

Certain types of errors occur so often in ratings that special efforts are needed to counteract them. These include (a) personal bias, (b) halo effect, and (c) logical errors.

Personal bias errors occur when there is a general tendency to rate all individuals at approximately the same position on the scale. Some raters tend to use the high end of the scale only, which is referred to as the **generosity error.** Occurring less frequently (but persistently for some raters) is the **severity error,** in which the lower end of the scale is favored. A third type of constant response is shown by the rater who avoids both extremes of the scale and tends to rate everyone as average. This is called the **central tendency error.**

It also occurs much less often than the generosity error, but it tends to be a fixed-response style for some raters.

The tendency of a rater to favor a certain position on the scale has two undesirable results. First, it puts in doubt a single rating of an individual. A high or low rating might reflect the personal outlook of the rater rather than the actual performance or personal characteristics of the person rated. Second, favoring a certain position on the scale limits the range of any individual's ratings. Therefore, even if we make allowances for a teacher's general tendency to rate students high, the ratings for different students may be so close together that they fail to provide reliable discriminations.

The **halo effect** is an error that occurs when a rater's general impression of a person influences the rating of individual characteristics. If the rater has a favorable attitude toward the person being rated, then there will be a tendency to give high ratings on all traits; but if the rater's attitude is unfavorable, the ratings will be low. This differs from the generosity and severity errors, in which the rater tends to rate everyone high or everyone low.

Because the halo effect causes a student to receive similar ratings on all characteristics, it tends to obscure strengths and weaknesses on different traits. This obviously limits the value of the ratings.

Teachers need to guard against the possibility that their ratings might be distorted because of preconceptions based on inappropriate factors such as gender, race, ethnicity, and social background. Halo effects leading to lowered ratings of all performances of some students as the result of such preconceptions are of particular concern. Concealing the identity of the student where feasible when rating products of performance is one good safeguard against halo effects. Awareness of our own personal preferences and prejudices is also important.

A **logical error** results when two characteristics are rated as more alike or less alike than they actually are because of the rater's beliefs concerning their relationship. In rating achievement, for example, teachers tend to overrate the achievement of students identified by aptitude tests as gifted because they expect achievement and giftedness to go together. Similarly, teachers who hold the common but false belief that gifted students have poor social adjustment will tend to underrate them on social characteristics. These errors result not from biases toward certain students or certain positions on the rating scale but from the rater's assumption of a more direct relationship among traits than actually exists.

The various types of errors that appear in ratings are rather disconcerting to the classroom teacher who must depend on rating scales for assessing certain aspects of learning and development. Fortunately, however, the errors can be markedly reduced by proper design and use.

Principles of Effective Rating

The improvement of ratings requires careful attention to selection of the characteristics to be rated, design of the rating form, and conditions under which the ratings are obtained. The following principles summarize the most important considerations in these areas. Because the descriptive graphic rating scale is the most generally useful form for school purposes, the principles are directed toward the construction and use of this type of rating scale.

1. Characteristics should be educationally significant. Rating scales, like other assessment instruments, must be in harmony with the school's objectives and desired learning outcomes. Thus, when constructing or selecting a rating scale, the best guide for determining what characteristics are most significant is the list of intended learning outcomes. When these have been clearly stated in performance terms, it is often simply a matter of selecting those that can be most effectively assessed by ratings and then modifying the statements to fit the rating format (see the "Guidelines" box).

GUIDELINES

Preparing Rating Scales

The same basic principle guiding the construction of test items should be followed in preparing rating scales. That is, the instrument should be designed to measure the student performance described in the instructional objectives. Let us assume, for example, that a science teacher has listed the following outcomes as evidence of skill in one phase of laboratory performance.

Demonstrates Effective Use of Laboratory Equipment

1. Selects proper equipment for a given experiment.
2. Sets up equipment quickly and correctly.
3. Manipulates equipment as needed during the experiment.
4. Measures accurately with each measuring device.
5. Follows safety rules when using equipment.
6. Cleans and returns equipment to its proper place.
7. Interprets the results of the experiment appropriately.
8. Integrates results with other knowledge in drawing conclusions.

This list of intended outcomes can then serve as the basis for preparing a rating scale to assess skill in using laboratory equipment. Each item in the list becomes an item in the rating form by simply adding some basis for recording degrees of effectiveness, as follows:

Selecting Laboratory Equipment

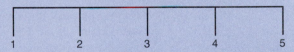

| 1 | 2 | 3 | 4 | 5 |

| Cannot select equipment without help | Inconsistent in selecting proper equipment | Consistently selects proper equipment |

The same procedure is followed when rating an educational product (e.g., theme, graph, painting, or shop and home economics projects). The characteristics of a good product are listed, and these then become the items in the rating scale. The instrument itself is simply a convenient form for recording observations and judgments concerning the extent to which students are meeting the criteria specified in the objectives.

2. Identify the learning outcomes that the task is intended to assess. The intent of the assessment is critical for determining those characteristics of performance that should determine the ratings. Clear identification of the learning outcomes helps establish priorities for rating, distinguish levels of performance in terms of learning outcomes, and reduce dependence on factors that are irrelevant to the intent of the assessment. When there are multiple learning outcomes associated with the task, separate ratings corresponding to each outcome may be desirable and can enhance the value of the formative feedback that is provided to students.

3. Characteristics should be directly observable. There are two considerations involved in direct observation. First, the characteristics should be limited to those that occur in school situations so the teacher has an opportunity to observe them. Second, they should be characteristics that are clearly visible to an observer. Overt behaviors, such as participation in classroom discussion, clear enunciation, and use of facts to support an argument, can be readily observed and reliably rated. However, less tangible types of behavior, such as interest in history, attitude toward literature, and amount of effort expended in library research, tend to be unreliably rated because their presence must be inferred from outward signs that are indefinite, variable, and easily faked. When possible, we should confine our ratings to those characteristics that can be observed and judged directly.

4. Characteristics and points on the scale should be clearly defined. Many rating errors arise from the use of vague characterizations and inadequate identification of the scale points. The brief descriptions used with the descriptive graphic rating scale help overcome this weakness. They explain both the points on the scale and each characteristic being rated. When it is infeasible or inconvenient to use a descriptive scale, as on the back of a school report card, a separate sheet of instructions can be used to provide the desired descriptions.

5. Select the type of scoring rubric that is most appropriate for the task and the purpose of the assessment. With a holistic rubric, each performance is given a single rating or score, usually on a scale with 4 to 6 points, based on an overall judgment of the quality of the performance in comparison to the criteria specified in the scoring rubric. Holistic rubrics are efficient and translate easily into grades. As already noted, however, analytic scoring rubrics have more diagnostic value because they focus attention on those aspects of performance where improvement is needed. For analytic scores to be of diagnostic value, the characteristics or dimensions being rated must be sufficiently distinct to allow each to be reliably rated and not simply be redundant reflections of the same global impression of the performance.

6. Between three and seven rating positions should be provided. The exact number of points to be designated on a particular scale is determined largely by the judgments to be made. In areas permitting only crude judgments, fewer scale positions are needed. There is usually no advantage in going beyond the 7-point scale. Only rarely can we make finer discriminations than this, and we can provide for those few situations by allowing the rater to mark between points.

7. Rate performances of all students on one task before going on to the next one. The advantages of rating all performances on one task before starting another task parallel those described for scoring all answers to an essay question before going on to the next question. It is easier to keep the scoring criteria clearly in mind and to apply them more uniformly when considering only a single task at a time than it is when going from task to task for each student. It also reduces the likelihood that judgments of performance on one task will be contaminated by judgments of a student's performance on a preceding task. When responses of a single student to several tasks are considered one after another, there is a strong tendency for the performance on early tasks to create an expectation for performance on later tasks. Those expectations can result in more lenient or more stringent ratings of performance than would otherwise be given.

By rating one task at a time for all students before going to the next task, it is also possible to change the order in which student performances are rated. Thus, a student is not rated first or last on all tasks or right after another student who has exceptionally good performance or exceptionally bad performance on all tasks.

8. When possible, rate performances without knowledge of the student's name. This suggestion is the same as the one given for scoring answers to essay questions. Obviously, it is not possible for all types of performance (e.g., an oral presentation), but it is good practice when possible. It is a practice that enhances the fairness of ratings because it reduces the chances that ratings will be influenced by a halo effect rather than only by the actual performance of a student.

9. When results from a performance assessment are likely to have long-term consequences for students, ratings from several observers should be combined. The pooled ratings of several teachers will generally yield a more reliable description of student performance than that obtained from any one teacher. In averaging ratings, the personal biases of individual raters tend to cancel out one another, but there is still a need to be alert for biases that may be shared due to similarity of background and experiences of teachers doing the rating.

CHECKLISTS

A checklist is similar in appearance and use to the rating scale. The basic difference between them is in the type of judgment needed. On a rating scale, one can indicate the degree to which a characteristic is present or the frequency with which a behavior occurs. The checklist, on the other hand, calls for a simple yes–no judgment. It is basically a method of recording whether a characteristic is present or absent or whether an action was or was not taken. Obviously, a checklist should not be used when degree or frequency of occurrence is an important aspect of the appraisal.

The checklist is especially useful at the primary level, where much of the classroom assessment depends on observation rather than testing. A simple checklist for assessing the mastery of mathematics skills at the beginning primary level is shown in Figure 11.6. If the intended learning outcomes are stated as specifically as this for each learning area, a checklist can be prepared by simply adding a place to check yes or no. As with the rating scales, the stated learning outcomes specify the performance to be assessed, and the checklist is merely a convenient means of recording judgments.

Checklists are also useful in assessing those performance skills that can be divided into a series of specific actions. An example of such a checklist for the proper application

Mathematics Skills Checklist

Primary Level

Directions: Circle YES or NO to indicate whether skill has been demonstrated.

YES	NO	1. Identifies numerals 0 to 10.
YES	NO	2. Counts to 10.
YES	NO	3. Groups objects into sets of 1 to 10.
YES	NO	4. Identifies basic geometric shapes (circle, square, rectangle, triangle).
YES	NO	5. Identifies coins (penny, nickel, dime).
YES	NO	6. Compares objects and identifies bigger–smaller, longer–shorter, heavier–lighter.
YES	NO	7. States ordinals for a series of 10 objects (1st, 2nd, 3rd, etc.).
YES	NO	8. Copies numerals 1 to 10.
YES	NO	9. Tells time to the half hour.
YES	NO	10. Identifies one-half of an area.

Figure 11.6

Checklist for evaluating student's mastery of begining skills in mathematics

of varnish is shown in Figure 11.7. The performance has been subdivided into a series of observable steps, and the observer simply checks whether each step was satisfactorily completed. The checklist in Figure 11.7 includes mostly those actions that are desired in a good performance. In some cases, it may be useful to add those actions that represent common errors so that they can be checked if they occur. In Figure 11.7, for example, we might add after Item 4, "Does **not** stir varnish before using." Because stirring paint is a necessary step when painting, some students might incorrectly carry over this action when using varnish. If the checklist is to be used by students, the incorrect actions should, of course, be clearly identified as such.

The following steps summarize the development of a checklist for assessing a procedure consisting of a series of sequential steps.

1. Identify each of the specific actions desired in the performance.
2. Add to the list those actions that represent common errors (if they are useful in the assessment, are limited in number, and can be clearly stated).
3. Arrange the desired actions (and likely errors, if used) in the approximate order in which they are expected to occur.
4. Provide a simple procedure for checking each action as it occurs (or for numbering the actions in sequence, if appropriate).

In addition to its use in assessment of process, the checklist can also be used to assess products. For this purpose, the form usually contains a list of characteristics that the finished product should possess. In assessing the product, the teacher simply checks whether each characteristic is present or absent. Before using a checklist for product assessment, you should decide whether the quality of the product can be adequately described by merely noting the presence or absence of each characteristic. If quality is

Directions: On the space in front of each item, place a plus (+) sign if performance was satisfactory, place a minus (−) sign if it was unsatisfactory.

_____ 1. Sands and prepares surface properly.
_____ 2. Wipes dust from surface with appropriate cloth.
_____ 3. Selects appropriate brush.
_____ 4. Selects varnish and checks varnish flow.
_____ 5. Pours needed amount of varnish into clean container.
_____ 6. Puts brush properly into varnish (1/3 of bristle length).
_____ 7. Wipes excess varnish from brush on inside edge of container.
_____ 8. Applies varnish to surface with smooth strokes.
_____ 9. Works from center of surface toward the edges.
_____ 10. Brushes with the grain of the wood.
_____ 11. Uses light strokes to smooth the varnish.
_____ 12. Checks surface for completeness.
_____ 13. Cleans brush with appropriate cleaner.
_____ 14. Does *not* pour excess varnish back into can.
_____ 15. Cleans work area.

Figure 11.7
Checklist for evaluating the proper application of varnish

Source: N. E. Gronlund, *Stating Objectives for Classroom Instruction,* 3rd ed. Copyright 1985, Prentice Hall, New Jersey. Used by permission.

more precisely indicated by noting the degree to which each characteristic is present, a rating scale should be used instead of a checklist.

In the area of personal–social development, the checklist can be a convenient method of recording evidence of growth toward specific learning outcomes. Typically, the form lists the behaviors that have been identified as representative of the outcomes to be assessed. In the area of work habits, for example, a primary teacher might list the following behaviors (to be marked yes or no):

- Follows directions
- Seeks help when needed
- Works cooperatively with others
- Waits turn in using materials
- Shares materials with others
- Tries new activities
- Completes started tasks
- Returns equipment to proper place
- Cleans work space

Although such items can be used in checklist form if only a crude appraisal is desired, they can also be used in rating scale form by recording the frequency of occurrence (e.g., always, sometimes, never).

Although we have described the individual use of checklists, rating scales, and anecdotal records (see Chapter 13), they are often used in combination when assessing student performance (see Table 11.2).

Table 11.2
Combining techniques to assess laboratory performance in science

Types of Proficiency	Examples of Performance to Be Assessed	Assessment Techniques
Knowledge of experimental procedures	Describes relevant procedures Identifies equipment and uses Criticizes defective experiments	Paper-and-pencil testing Laboratory identification tests
Skill in designing an experiment	Plans and designs an experiment to be performed	Performance assessment with focus on product (checklist)
Skill in conducting the experiment	Selects equipment Sets up equipment Conducts experiment	Performance assessment with focus on process (rating scale)
Skill in observing and recording	Describes procedures used Reports proper measurements Organizes and records results	Performance assessment (analysis of report)
Skill in interpreting results	Identifies significant relationships Identifies weaknesses in data States valid conclusions	Performance assessment and oral questioning
Work habits	Manipulates equipment effectively Completes work promptly Cleans work space	Performance assessment with focus on process (checklist)

STUDENT PARTICIPATION IN RATING

In this chapter, we have limited our discussion to rating scales and checklists used by the teacher. We purposely omitted those checklists and rating scales used as self-report techniques by students because these will be considered in the following chapter. Before closing our discussion here, however, we should point out that most of the devices used for recording the teacher's observations also can be used by students to judge their own progress. From an instructional standpoint, it is often useful to have students rate themselves (or their products) and then compare the ratings with those of the teacher. If this comparison is made during an individual conference, the teacher can explore with each student the reasons for the ratings and discuss any marked discrepancies between the two sets.

Self-rating by a student and a follow-up conference with the teacher can have many benefits. It should help the student (a) understand better the instructional objectives, (b) recognize the progress being made toward the objectives, (c) diagnose more effectively particular strengths and weaknesses, and (d) develop increased skill in self-assessment. Of special value to the teacher is the additional insight gained.

Student participation need not be limited to the use of the assessment instruments. It is also useful to have students help develop the instruments. Through class discussion, for example, they can help identify the qualities desired in a good speech or a well-written report. A list of these suggestions can then be used as a basis for constructing a rating scale or checklist. Involving students in the development of assessment devices has special instructional values. First, it directs learning by causing the students to think more carefully about the qualities to strive for in a performance or product. Second, it has a motivating effect because students tend to put forth most effort when working toward goals they have helped define.

SUMMARY

Performance tasks provide a means of assessing a variety of student skills that cannot be measured by objective tests. To name just a few of the possibilities in addition to written responses, the performances may include oral communication; the construction of models, graphs, diagrams, or maps; or the use of tools and equipment (computers, or scientific or musical instruments). Unlike objective items, both the **process** and the **product** resulting from the performance can be assessed. Because they are time consuming both for students to do and for teachers to rate, the emphasis on performance assessment should be on measuring complex achievement that cannot be measured well by objective tests.

Restricted-response tasks are more structured and require less time to administer than extended-response tasks. These features facilitate reliability and wider coverage of a content domain. Extended-response tasks are best suited to the measurement of more complex learning outcomes, such as gathering, organizing, synthesizing, evaluating, and presenting information.

Extended performance tasks underscore the importance attached to effective performance and provide an effective means of measuring significant learning outcomes. They are the only feasible approach for measuring some important learning outcomes, they allow for the assessment of process as well as product, and their emphasis on the engagement of students in the active construction of meaning is consistent with modern learning theory. Their limitations are due mainly to the unreliability of judgmental ratings and to the time-consuming nature of the tasks and rating. Careful attention to rating criteria is critical for minimizing the unreliability due to scoring. Because of the limited generalizability of performance across tasks designed to measure the same or similar learning outcomes, it is important to base decisions on evidence accumulated from several tasks.

Rating methods are a systematic procedure for obtaining and recording the observers' judgments. Of the several types of rating scales available, the descriptive graphic scale seems to be the best for school use. In rating procedures, products, and various aspects of personal–social development, certain types of errors commonly occur. These include personal bias, halo effect, and logical errors. The control of such errors is a major consideration in constructing and using rating scales. Effective ratings result when we (a) select educationally significant characteristics, (b) identify the learning outcomes that the task is intended to assess, (c) limit ratings to directly observable behavior, (d) define clearly the characteristics and the points on the scale, (e) select the most appropriate rating procedure, (f) limit the number of points on the scale, (g) rate performances of all students on one task before going on to the next ones, (h) rate performances without knowledge of the student's name when possible, and (i) combine ratings from several raters when results may have long-term consequences for students.

Checklists perform somewhat the same functions as rating scales. They are used in assessing both process and products where assessment is limited to a simple present–absent judgment.

Having students help construct and use rating devices has special values from the standpoint of learning and aids in the development of self-assessment skills.

LEARNING EXERCISES

1. In an area in which you are teaching or plan to teach, identify several learning outcomes that can be best measured with performance-based assessment tasks. For each learning outcome, construct two tasks.
2. What factors should be considered in deciding whether extended performance assessment tasks are to be included in a classroom assessment? Which of the factors are most important?
3. Describe how performance assessments might be used to facilitate learning. What types of learning are most likely to be enhanced?
4. Construct a rating scale for one of the following that would be useful for assessing the effectiveness of the performance.
   a. Giving an oral report
   b. Working in the laboratory
   c. Participating in group work
   d. Playing some type of game
   e. Demonstrating a skill
5. Construct a rating scale or checklist for one of the following that would be useful for assessing the product.
   a. Constructing a map, chart, or graph
   b. Writing a personal or business letter
   c. Writing a theme, poem, or short story
   d. Making a drawing or painting
   e. Making a product in home economics
   f. Making a product in industrial education
6. Prepare a checklist for assessing the ability to drive an automobile. Would a rating scale be better for this purpose? What are the relative advantages of each?
7. List some of the areas of assessment in which product scales might be used for rating.

REFERENCES

Baker, E. L., Aschbacher, P. R., Niemi, D., & Sato, E. (1992). *CRESST performance assessment models: Assessing content area explanations.* Los Angeles: University of California Center for Research on Evaluation, Standards, and Student Testing.

Mathematical Sciences Education Board. (1993). *Measuring up: Prototypes for mathematics assessment.* Washington, DC: National Academy Press. See pages 141–155 for a discussion of this game and related assessment questions.

O'Sullivan, C. Y., Reese, C. M., & Mazzeo, J. (1997). *NAEP 1996 Science Report Card for the Nation and the States.* Washington, DC: National Center for Education Statistics. Available: http://www.ed.gov/NCES/naep

Regional Educational Laboratories. (1998). *Improving classroom assessment: A toolkit for professional developers.* Portland, OR: Regional Educational Laboratories or available centrally from Northwest Regional Educational Laboratory. Available: http:/www.nwrel.org. Includes samples of performance assessments and scoring rubrics.

Shavelson, R. J., Baxter, G. P., & Gao, X. (1993). Sampling variability of performance assessments. *Journal of Educational Measurement, 30,* 215–232.

Shavelson, R. J., Baxter, G. P., & Pine, J. (1991). Performance assessment in science. *Applied Measurement in Education, 4,* 347–362.

Stiggins, R. J. (1987). Design and development of performance assessments. *Educational Measurement: Issues and Practice, 6*(3), 33–42. Part of an instructional series of the National Council on Measurement in Education. It presents helpful guidelines for the construction of performance assessments.

FURTHER READING

Educational Testing Service. (1993). *Performance assessment sampler: A workbook.* Princeton, NJ: Educational Testing Service. This workbook presents examples of performance assessments in various subjects, with examples of student responses and scores assigned.

Gronlund, N. E. (2005). *Assessment of student achievement* (8th ed.). Boston: Allyn & Bacon. Chapter 7, "Traditional Performance Assessments of Skills and Products," and Chapter 8, "Expanded Performance Assessments," discuss the construction and use of various types of performance assessments.

Hart, D. (1994). *Authentic assessment: A handbook for educators.* Menlo Park, CA: Addison-Wesley. Provides a variety of examples of performance-based assessments and arguments for the importance of this approach to assessment.

Herman, J. L., Aschbacher, P. R., & Winters, L. (1992). *A practical guide to alternative assessment.* Alexandria, VA: Association for Supervision and Curriculum Development. In addition to providing examples of performance assessments and guidelines for rating, the book presents a model for linking assessment and instruction.

Lane, S., & Stone, C. (2006). Performance assessment. In R. L Brennan (Ed.), *Educational measurement* (4th ed.) (pp. 387–433). Westport, CT: American Council on Education/ Praeger. Provides a detailed discussion of the types and uses of performance assessments and examples of holistic and analytic scoring rubrics.

Mullis, I. V. S., Dossey, J. A., Owen, E. H., & Phillips, G. W. (1993). *NAEP 1992: Mathematics Report Card for the Nation and the States* (Report No. 23-STO2). Washington, DC: U.S. Department of Education.

Welch, C. (2006). Item and prompt development in performance testing. In S. M Downing & T. M Haladyna (Eds.). *Handbook of Test development* (Chapter 13, pp. 303-327). Mahway, NJ: Lawrence Erlbaum. Provides guidance for improving the quality of performance assessments and gives examples of scoring rubrics.

12

PORTFOLIOS

Systematic collections of student work into portfolios can serve a variety of instructional and assessment purposes. The value of portfolios depends heavily on clarity of purpose, the guidelines for inclusion of materials, and the criteria to be used in evaluating portfolios.

Portfolios of work have been used as the basis for assessment with increasing frequency in the past 20 years. They have been defined and used by individual classroom teachers for use in their day-to-day instruction and assessment of student progress. They have also been used as the basis for determining grades and for reporting student achievement and progress to parents. Portfolios of work may span more than a single school year and provide information to teachers about student achievement as students move from one grade to the next. Sometimes portfolios have been adopted as an approach to assessment by entire schools. In some instances, such as the case of Central Park East Secondary School described later in this chapter, they have become a primary basis for satisfying requirements for graduation from high school. They have sometimes been used by high school graduates as part of their applications to college or submitted to employers when applying for jobs. There are even examples of district- and statewide adoptions of portfolios as a means of assessment for purposes of school or system accountability.

Although the focus in this chapter is on portfolios of student work, it is worth noting that portfolios of work have also been used in college admissions, student evaluation in higher education, job employment, and the evaluation of teaching. The National Board of Professional Teaching Standards (NBPTS), for example, bases its decisions about the certification of accomplished teachers primarily on portfolios of work that teachers applying for NBPTS certification prepare during a school year. Those portfolios contain videotapes showing a teacher interacting with students in the classroom, examples of problems assigned to students, samples of student work in response to those assignments, and teacher commentary on the portfolio entries.

At an earlier career stage, teachers in some states are now required to submit portfolios that include videotapes of their teaching and other examples of their work as teachers as part of their initial certification. Some highly regarded teacher preparation programs have made substantial use of portfolios of teaching in their preservice teacher preparation and evaluation of student teachers. Because of the widespread interest in portfolios as a means of assessing teaching performance, a number of states have joined together in a project called the Interstate New Teacher Assessment and Support Consortium (INTASC) to develop a common, portfolio-based teacher assessment system. Like the NBPTS assessment system for accomplished teachers, the INTASC portfolios include videotapes of teaching, examples of student work, teacher feedback on that work, and teacher commentary and reflections on their teaching.

The INTASC and NBPTS portfolios are more elaborate and expensive to construct and to score than portfolios of student work that a teacher would have students construct. The stakes associated with the decisions that are based on the portfolio assessments are also quite different for the teacher certification examples than for a third-grade teacher, for example, who uses student portfolios of writing to plan instruction and provide helpful feedback to students on their work. When compared to the latter use of a portfolio of student work, however, the teacher certification examples illustrate that portfolios come in many different forms, including electronic or digital, and may be used for many different purposes. In a summary of testing for employment, credentialing, and higher education, Sackett, Schmitt, Ellingson, and Kabin (2001) point out that ethnic differences are reduced when using portfolios and other more realistic assessments instead of traditional tests. Presumably, the reduced gap between ethnic groups is due to the ability of portfolios to reflect more than cognitive abilities and skills, such as effort or persistence.

WHAT QUALIFIES AS A PORTFOLIO OF STUDENT WORK?

It has long been common to collect student work in folders. A student portfolio is also a collection of pieces of student work, but it differs from a folder of work in several important ways. A portfolio is a collection of student work selected to serve a particular purpose, such as the documentation of student growth. Unlike some folders of work, a portfolio does not contain all the work a student does. Instead, a portfolio may contain examples of "best" works or examples from each of several categories of work (e.g., a book review, a letter to a friend, a creative short story, and a persuasive essay). Pieces of work for a portfolio must be selected with care to serve the intended purposes of the portfolio.

A student portfolio is a **purposeful collection** of pieces of student work. Portfolios are sometimes described as portraits of a person's accomplishments. Using this metaphor, a student portfolio is usually a self-portrait, but one that often has benefited from guidance and feedback from a teacher and sometimes from other students. With the flexibility of student portfolios, teaching, learning, and assessment are often enmeshed in a single activity. Although the use of portfolios can be time consuming and require substantial effort on the part of students and teachers, the benefits to instruction and learning as well as assessment can make it worth the time and energy.

POTENTIAL STRENGTHS AND WEAKNESSES OF PORTFOLIOS

Portfolios are believed to have a number of potential strengths (see the box "Potential Strengths of Portfolios"). The ease with which portfolios can be integrated with instruction has made them particularly appealing to teachers. Portfolios also foster student skills in evaluating their own work. Self-evaluation is a critical skill in developing independent learning ability and one that is often emphasized and reinforced by asking students to include some form of self-evaluation and thoughtful reflection on each entry in their portfolios.

Communicating with parents about student progress is an important and challenging goal for any teacher. Thoughtfully selected collections of student work in portfolios can provide parents with concrete examples of what students are accomplishing. They can also provide the focus for discussion among teachers, students, and parents. Sometimes students are asked to take the lead in conferences with parents, and using the portfolio to shape the discussion can have positive effects for both parents and students. Moreover, three-way conferences involving teachers, students, and parents with students taking the lead in explaining their portfolios to parents can give teachers an unusual opportunity to see how students and parents interact about the work.

Realizing these potential strengths and others listed in the box depends heavily on the effort that goes into clarifying the purposes to be served by portfolios. It depends on the quality of the guidelines for determining what should be included in portfolios and the criteria for evaluating them. Of course, achieving these valued results also depends on the actual uses that are made of portfolios.

Although the potential strengths of portfolios make them attractive both as aids in instruction and as assessment devices, portfolios also have weaknesses. They can be quite

---

Potential Strengths of Portfolios

Because portfolios consist of products of classroom instruction, they can be readily integrated with instruction.

Portfolios provide students with opportunity to show what they can do.

Portfolios can encourage students to become reflective learners and to develop skills in evaluating the strengths and weaknesses of their work.

Portfolios can help students take responsibility for setting goals and evaluating their progress.

Portfolios can provide teachers and students with opportunities to collaborate and reflect on student progress.

Portfolios can be an effective way of communicating with parents by showing concrete examples of student work and demonstrations of progress.

Portfolios can provide a mechanism for student-centered and student-directed conferences with parents.

Portfolios can give parents concrete examples of a student's development over time as well as their current skills.

time consuming to assemble. The investment of student time in constructing portfolios may be well spent, but teachers need to guard against any tendency for the portfolio demands to foster busywork that contributes neither to student learning nor to better assessment.

Portfolios are time consuming for teachers as well as students. Although students can benefit from the process of constructing a portfolio, they need to have constructive feedback from teachers on the work included in their portfolios and on the portfolios as a whole. They also need guidance about how best to construct a portfolio for a specific purpose and audience. Considerable thought, preparation, and experience is needed to ensure that the benefits of portfolios justify this investment in time by both students and teachers.

Another potential weakness of portfolios arises when they are used as the basis for summative evaluation, such as the assignment of course grades, the certification of achievement, or in school, district, or state accountability systems. For several reasons, ratings of portfolios tend to have relatively low reliability. Part of the poor reliability comes from the difficulty of establishing clear scoring criteria for the large and often diverse sets of materials that may be included. Poor reliability is also due, in part, to a lack of standardization that leads to limited comparability of portfolio entries that different students choose to include. Unfortunately, attempts to deal with these two problems by formulas that convert ratings of individual entries into an overall portfolio rating and by increased standardization and rigid rules for what students must include in their portfolios may undermine the validity and utility of portfolios for their intended purposes.

Perhaps the biggest obstacle to realizing the potential value of effective portfolio use is not a weakness per se but the naive perception that portfolios can be easily created. Because teachers and students are accustomed to keeping work in folders or files, it seems but a simple step to call the folder a portfolio. Unorganized collections of work in folders will not accomplish the goals implicit in the strengths listed in the box. Nonetheless, considerable evidence from surveys, interviews, and teachers' observations shows that far too frequently so-called portfolios are indistinguishable from unorganized collections of work in folders with inadequate specifications of purposes, guidelines for construction, or evaluation criteria.

Careful planning is required to capitalize on the potential strengths of portfolios and minimize their weaknesses. In addition, teachers need to be prepared to commit the time and effort required for implementing the plan and using the results. There are a number of steps in defining, implementing, and using portfolios. The box "Key Steps in Defining, Implementing, and Using Portfolios" lists five of the key steps in the process, starting with the specification of purpose. All five steps are important, but clarity of purpose provides a critical foundation on which to base the other steps.

PURPOSE OF PORTFOLIOS

As with other forms of assessment, the first question to be answered in designing a portfolio is: What is the purpose of the portfolio? Without a clear understanding of purpose, portfolios are likely to be indistinguishable from unorganized collections of materials. Students need guidance in deciding what should and should not be included in a portfolio. They need to understand the purpose and develop skills in distinguishing between samples of their work that best serve the intended purpose and ones that are irrelevant to the purpose or that may even undermine it.

Just as a photographer might select one set of photographs for use in a photography class focusing on light and composition, and quite a different set for a job interview, the selection of pieces of work for a portfolio should be guided by the purpose. Because of the variety of purposes for creating student portfolios, the entries may be quite varied. For example, the purpose of a portfolio might be to display evidence about student growth in writing during the school year. For the purpose of documenting growth, the portfolio obviously must include pieces of work that span a period of time. If the period of interest is the school year, then the collection needs to include examples of student writing completed at the beginning of the year as well as ones completed at intermediate times and toward the end of the year. In contrast, a portfolio that is intended to provide evidence for certifying student achievement might include only examples of the student's recently completed best works.

Arter, Spandel, and Culham (1995) argued that there are fundamentally two global purposes for creating portfolios of student work: student assessment and instruction. These two global purposes need not be mutually exclusive. Indeed, as has been noted in previous chapters, good assessment is an integral part of effective instruction. The emphasis, however, is likely to be different when the primary purpose is assessment than when the sole purpose is instruction.

When the primary purpose is enhancing student learning by having pupils evaluate their own work, for example, there may be little if any concern about the comparability of selections of work from one student to the next. The emphasis is more appropriately placed on teaching students how to make wise choices of the pieces of work to be included and in providing them with examples of how to reflect on the quality of that work. The fact that Donna chooses to include a short story she wrote while Ricardo chooses a book review for his portfolio is of less concern than the basis each student had for choosing the work and their reflections on the work. On the other hand, if the purpose of the portfolio is to provide a partial basis for determining a student's grade, then comparability of the type of work included in the portfolio may be quite important. In the latter case, the teacher may want to specify that all students should include both a short story and a book review that they wrote.

Although the relative emphasis on instruction and assessment is one way of distinguishing the different purposes of portfolios, it is not the only dimension of importance. Other authors have distinguished between portfolios that are intended to display **current accomplishments** and ones intended to demonstrate **progress.** Within either of these general purposes, distinctions can be made between portfolios that contain only examples of "best work," which are commonly called **showcase** portfolios, and portfolios that document a range of accomplishments, which are commonly called **documentation** portfolios. Showcase portfolios often include only completed products, though this is not necessarily the case. The key feature is that students believe that the work included shows them at their best. Portfolios that emphasize documentation, on the other hand, are generally more comprehensive than a showcase portfolio and may include examples of work that a student considers below par as well as examples that are exemplary. Thus, documentation portfolios would place more emphasis on "typical work."

Another way in which portfolios may be distinguished is the degree to which a portfolio is a dynamically evolving collection of work or a finished collection. Finished portfolios are more likely to be used for summative evaluation purposes, whereas working portfolios, which contain examples of work as it evolves, are more useful for the formative evaluation that guides student learning on a day-to-day basis. Working portfolios often include student questions as well as notes, outlines, initial drafts, revised drafts, the final product, and self-evaluations of the work.

The four characteristics just described as if they were dichotomies—(1) instruction and assessment, (2) current accomplishments and progress, (3) showcase and documentation, and (4) finished and working portfolios—are best thought of as dimensions or continua. The purpose may involve varying degrees of the poles of each continuum. That is, the poles represent relative emphases rather than sharp dichotomies. For example, although the emphasis may be on documentation, there is no implication that there should be an exhaustive inclusion of all work products. Indeed, you would usually want to encourage students to be selective and include examples of work that they believe is high quality (best work). However, with the emphasis on documentation, you would also expect students to include portfolio entries that document work in areas that may not be areas of strength or that they are not particularly proud of and those would not be included in a showcase portfolio.

Recognizing that there are gradations between the poles of the four dimensions and that most portfolios involve a combination of the extremes, it is still useful to highlight aspects of each characteristic.

Instructional Purposes

A variety of distinctions may be made within each of the two global purposes of portfolios identified by Arter and her colleagues (1995). For example, when the primary purpose of a portfolio is instruction, the portfolio might be used as a means of helping students develop and refine self-evaluation skills. Learning to evaluate one's own work is an

Four Dimensions Distinguishing the Purposes of Portfolios

Instruction	←	→	Assessment
Current Accomplishments	←	→	Progress
Best Work Showcase	←	→	Documentation
Finished	←	→	Working

important instructional goal for all students. Skills in self-evaluation are critical for student development as independent learners.

As is true of other important instructional goals, self-evaluation skills require practice and feedback. Well-designed portfolios of student work often include not only examples of student work that the student selects but also self-reflection and commentary on the work. The combination of selected work and self-reflection can provide the teacher with both information about the student's achievement and a window on the student's self-evaluation skills. The portfolio can also be the focus of discussion between a teacher and a student about performance expectations and criteria of excellence, thereby helping the student internalize standards to be used in the evaluation of his or her own work.

Portfolios can also be used as the focus of student-directed conferences with parents and teachers. When a student presents and explains the examples of work in the portfolio to his or her parents, both the teacher and the parents have an opportunity to gain a better understanding of the student's thought processes and awareness of standards for judging the quality of the work. The teacher can then use this understanding of the student to plan and implement future instruction and interventions.

Another important instructional use of a portfolio is in teaching students to communicate with different audiences. For a portfolio designed to be used as the focus of a student-directed conference with parents, the intended audience is obviously the student's parents. Students might be encouraged to think about examples of work that would let their parents see what they have learned. For high school students, potentially important audiences in addition to teachers and parents include employers and colleges. Other students may also be an important audience for the portfolio as a whole or for selected entries in the portfolio. For example, an entry in the portfolio might include an oral presentation to the class. The artifacts that might be included in the physical portfolio could be exhibits or copies of overhead slides that the student prepared for use in the presentation, an outline or notes prepared for the presentation, the student's self-evaluation, and evaluations provided by other students. The entry might also include an audio recording or even a videotape of the presentation.

Assessment Purposes

When the emphasis of a portfolio is on assessment, it is important to distinguish between the **formative** and **summative** roles of assessment. Portfolios of work collected over the course of a semester or a school year can be particularly effective for purposes of formative evaluation of student progress. A simple comparison of essays written in September, November, and February, for example, can provide a teacher with concrete examples of areas where the student has shown considerable progress (e.g., organization and voice) and areas where there has been little improvement (e.g., grammar and punctuation).

A portfolio of work might also be used as a basis for certifying accomplishment. If portfolios are to be used as the basis of assigning grades or certifying accomplishments, then students should be given clear specifications of the contents of the portfolio and the scoring criteria that will be used.

At some high schools, a portfolio of work may provide the primary documentation used to determine the award of diplomas. Central Park East Secondary School in New York

City provides one of the best-known examples of the use of a graduation portfolio. As will be seen, considerable effort has to go into the development of guidelines for portfolios and to the criteria used for judging their quality when they are used for such a high-stakes purpose as high school graduation.

In some states and districts, portfolios are used as part of the system accountability requirements. For example, in Kentucky and Vermont, the state assessment system has included an evaluation of portfolios of student writing. At the district level, Pittsburgh provides a highly regarded example of the use of portfolios of student work as part of system accountability. Such large-scale uses of portfolios for assessment require a higher degree of uniformity of the portfolios and more refined scoring systems than are needed for portfolios designed and used by classroom teachers. Nonetheless, experience with such systems provides useful information for teachers when planning their own portfolios or when working to develop a schoolwide portfolio system. We will return to these examples when considering guidelines for portfolios.

Current Accomplishments and Progress

The distinction between portfolios that emphasize current accomplishments and ones that focus on progress are fairly self-evident. When the focus is on accomplishments, portfolios usually are limited to finished work and may cover only a relatively brief period of time. When the focus is on demonstrating growth and development, the time frame is generally longer. A possibly less obvious distinction is that a portfolio focusing on progress will often include multiple versions of a single piece of work. For example, a writing project might include an initial outline, notes taken while doing background reading for the project, a first draft, a self-evaluation of that draft as well as comments from the teacher or from other students on the draft, possibly a second draft with comments, and a final version of the report or essay.

Showcase and Documentation Portfolios

Showcase portfolios usually should contain student-selected entries. That does not mean that students should not have the benefit of the reactions of other students or of teacher advice on how to select and evaluate the entries of a showcase portfolio; but an important goal of a showcase portfolio is for students to learn to identify work that best demonstrates what they know and can do with a specific purpose and audience in mind. The documentation portfolio, on the other hand, usually is intended to provide evidence about breadth as well as depth of learning. Thus, it needs to be more inclusive and not be limited to areas of special strength for a student.

Finished and Working Portfolios

The label *finished* may be an overstatement. It simply implies that the work is completed for use with a particular audience. A job application portfolio, for example, is obviously finished as far as the prospective employer is concerned at the time it is submitted. On the other hand, it might be refined before it is submitted as part of another job application. As the name suggests, the intent of a working portfolio is one that is expected to evolve and should not be held up to the summative evaluation standards that may be appropriate for a finished portfolio. Working portfolios are often used to document day-to-day activities and are most useful for formative evaluation purposes. The working portfolio can provide the teacher with timely information about day-to-day progress and be a means of providing students with formative feedback for use in refining or revising their work. It is critical that students not be penalized for expressing ideas that may be incorrect or that display a lack of understanding in working portfolios. The working portfolio is most useful when students are encouraged to express themselves freely and are given timely feedback on their work. Thus, there are obviously work implications for the teacher, ones that should not be entered into lightly at the peak of enthusiasm about the use of working portfolios.

GUIDELINES FOR PORTFOLIO ENTRIES

The full purpose of a particular portfolio will be a combination of the four dimensions just discussed. Clearly specifying that purpose to students provides the foundation for developing portfolios. Alone, however, the purpose will not give students sufficient guidance. The purpose needs to be accompanied by clear guidelines for the construction of portfolios.

The guidelines need to be specific enough so that students know what is expected without being overly constraining. One of the appeals of a portfolio is its flexibility. Too much specification can stifle student creativity and thwart the goals of self-reflection and being responsible for their own learning. On the other hand, too little specificity leaves students in the dark about what is considered an appropriate entry. When portfolios are used for summative evaluation purposes, the lack of specificity is likely to be a source of unfairness. Students who choose to pursue an activity that is not valued in the criteria used for evaluation or that does not provide the opportunity to display valued skills may be put at a disadvantage in comparison to students who choose other activities.

At a minimum, guidelines should specify (a) the uses that will be made of the portfolio, (b) who will have access to it, (c) what types of work are appropriate to include, and (d) what criteria will be used in evaluating the work. For example, if the portfolio is to be used as the basis for student-directed conferences with parents, students obviously should know that their parents are an important audience. Students need to know if the portfolios are supposed to contain only finished work or if they are supposed to include illustrations of the process of planning, beginning and intermediate stages of the work, and the final product. They need to know the range of acceptable entries. For example, are tape recordings, models, or videos appropriate to include? Or should the portfolio be limited to paper-and-pencil entries?

Although the physical form of a portfolio is secondary to the purpose, there are practical issues concerning storage and philosophical issues regarding the degree to which various media other than paper and pencil should be encouraged or allowed to be part of the portfolio. Concerns for equal access to the means to create videotapes or computer presentations, for example, are important considerations in this regard. These concerns interact with purpose. Unequal access to resources is generally of greatest concern when portfolios are used for summative evaluation purposes, such as the assignment of grades or to determine awards or other types of honors, because the differences in access to resources may lead to real or perceived unfairness.

Another critical guideline concerns the role of collaboration with others in doing the work. Frequently, portfolios include examples of both independent work and work that is done collaboratively by small groups of students. For some entries, it may be appropriate to include the suggestions of peers or of parents that are used to revise the entry. The guidelines need to be explicit about the ground rules for working independently or obtaining various kinds of assistance from others. The ground rules may be constant for all entries in a portfolio or may vary from one entry to another, but in either case they need to be clearly stated.

The guidelines should define the time line for the portfolio as well as the minimum and possibly the maximum number of entries. The variety of entries in terms of both form (e.g., letter, narrative essay, book review, or persuasive essay) and content (e.g., topics or historical periods) should be specified in the guidelines, making a clear distinction between required and optional entries.

The guidelines may also specify the physical structure of the portfolio (e.g., a binder or a computer disc) and its contents. For example, guidelines might specify that the portfolio include a table of contents, a cover sheet describing each entry, and a self-reflection on each entry. Increased access to and use of computers has led to increased use of electronic portfolios or for parts of the portfolio to be kept and stored electronically. Indeed, it is increasingly likely that students use computers when they type an essay or report in the first place. With a scanner, even handwritten essays and many figures can also be incorporated into an electronic portfolio. Students with access to the internet may readily download a wide array of materials that can be used to illustrate aspects of works.

Students also must be informed about how the evaluation of the portfolio will influence their grades. Both entry-specific criteria in the form of scoring rubrics or checklists and criteria for combining entry-by-entry evaluations into an overall evaluation of the complete portfolio need to be included in the guidelines.

An Example of a Graduation Portfolio

Darling-Hammond, Ancess, and Falk (1995) provide a detailed description of the Central Park East graduation portfolio. The portfolio is the culmination of a student's last 2 or 3 years of work in the Senior Institute, which is a division of the school corresponding to the junior and senior years of high school. The graduation portfolios completed during the 2 or possibly 3 years a student is in the Senior Institute has requirements in 14 categories. These 14 categories are listed in Table 12.1 along with a brief description of each portfolio entry.

Note that the portfolio entries in Table 12.1 are broadly defined. They include not only written materials, but possibly a variety of forms of oral presentations such as a speech, a debate, or a play. Works of art and various types of exhibits such as a science demonstration or a model may also be included. Audiotapes, videotapes, and computer discs may also be used as part of a portfolio entry.

Table 12.1
Required categories of work in the Central Park East Secondary School graduation portfolios

1. Postgraduate Plan	Must describe their purpose for earning a diploma and their short- and long-term career and life plans. Includes indicators of progress such as letters of reference.
2. Autobiography	Written, oral, or other forms (e.g., photos or audiotape of interview of grandparent) may be used to examine family history, student beliefs, and values.
3. School/Community Service and Internship	A formal résumé of their past work and employment experiences, including evidence of accomplishments and what they have learned.
4. Ethics and Social Issues	Demonstration of ability to see multiple perspectives and reason with evidence about social and moral issues using a variety of forms (e.g., an editorial, drama, or debate).
5. Fine Arts and Aesthetics	A performance or exhibition of work in any one of the arts (e.g., dance, sculpture, or music) along with evidence of understanding of an aesthetic area of study.
6. Mass Media	Demonstration of understanding of different forms of mass media and their influence on people and their perspectives.
7. Practical Skills	Evidence of the development of skills in one or more areas, such as technology, health, and citizenship.
8. Geography	Evidence includes performance on a faculty-designed test and a student-designed project (e.g., the construction of map).
9. Second Language or Dual Language	Must demonstrate competence to read and write and to listen and speak in a language other than English.
10. Science and Technology	Must include both traditional evidence (e.g., examinations and projects) as well as the use of scientific methods and understanding of the roles of science in modern world.
11. Mathematics	Evidence includes performance on faculty-designed tests and projects demonstrating conceptual understanding and applications.
12. Literature	Must include list of texts read demonstrating a wide range of genres as well as student essays about literary works or figures.
13. History	Evidence includes performance on state- or faculty-designed tests as well as historical projects demonstrating understanding of history and its relevance for current issues.
14. Physical Challenge	Must document participation in team or individual sport or activity.

Source: Based on Darling-Hammond et al. (1995, pp. 34–36).

Examples of Statewide and Districtwide Portfolio Guidelines

Vermont was the first state to introduce portfolios as the primary state assessment. Portfolios in mathematics and writing were collected statewide for students in grades 4 and 8. The mathematics portfolios required students and teachers to pick five to seven "best"

> ## Criteria Used for Rating Mathematics Portfolios in Vermont
>
> **Four Aspects of Problem Solving**
>
> - Understanding the problem
> - How you solved the problem
> - Why—decisions along the way
> - So what—outcomes of activities
>
> **Three Aspects of Communication**
>
> - Mathematical language
> - Mathematical representation
> - Presentation
>
> *Note:* For details of 4-point scoring rubrics and examples, see Stecher and Mitchell (1995).

pieces of work. The portfolios were sent to a central location where they were rated by volunteer teachers on a 4-point scale for each of seven different dimensions. Four of the dimensions were related to aspects of problem solving; the other three dealt with aspects of communication (see the box "Criteria Used for Rating Mathematics Portfolios in Vermont").

The Vermont writing portfolios had great specificity in the required contents. At grade 4, for example, a student's portfolio was supposed to include the following (Koretz, Stecher, Klein, & McCaffrey, 1994a, p. 4):

1. Table of contents
2. Single best piece, which is selected by the student, and can come from any class and need not address an academic subject
3. Letter explaining the composition and selection of the best piece
4. Poem, short story, or personal narration
5. Personal response to a book, event, current issue, mathematics problem, or scientific phenomenon
6. Prose piece from any subject area other than English or language arts

The writing portfolios were scored in two parts: (1) the best piece, and (2) the rest of the portfolio. Four-point rating scales were used for each of five dimensions (purpose, organization, details, voice/tone, and usage/grammar/mechanics) when rating the best piece and the rest of the writing portfolio.

Evaluations of the Vermont portfolios supported two major conclusions. First, on the positive side, the use of portfolios was found to have positive effects on classroom practice. This conclusion was supported by teacher reports of how the work on portfolios affected their day-to-day instructional practices and by independent observations. The professional development gained through teachers working together on the scoring and sharing thoughts on what constitutes exemplary student work was also seen as a major benefit of the effort. Second, on the negative side, there was relatively poor interrater reliability in the central scoring process. Thus, the evaluation by Koretz and his colleagues was mixed, concluding on the one hand that the reliability was inadequate for accountability purposes but that on the other hand the effects on instruction were generally positive (Koretz, Stecher, Klein, & McCaffrey, 1994b).

Another example of a major effort in using portfolios for large-scale assessment comes from Pittsburgh. The Pittsburgh Public School District undertook a districtwide effort to evaluate student writing in grades 6 through 12 using portfolios. The portfolios were created by having students select four examples of their work using a set of district guidelines. For each example, students were required to include drafts as well as the final version of the writing. They also were required to include a written reflection on the entry and to answer several questions about it and their experience in writing it. Guidelines for selecting the four pieces of writing specified that they should include (a) a piece that the student considered to be "important," (b) a piece that the student considered to be "satisfying," (c) a piece that the student considered to be "unsatisfying," and (d) a "free pick." Students were also required to complete a table of contents, a writing inventory about their experience as a writer, and a "final reflection" in which they were asked to review their writings and "describe changes in their writing and in themselves as writers" (LeMahieu, Gitomer, & Eresh, 1995, p. 12).

All students were expected to complete a writing portfolio using the previously mentioned guidelines. A random sample of 1,250 portfolios was scored along the three major dimensions shown in Table 12.2 using a 6-point scale ranging from "inadequate" to "outstanding" performance for each dimension. Considerable developmental work with teachers and administrators before the districtwide applications went into identifying the

Table 12.2
Dimensions and elements of the Pittsburgh writing portfolio scoring rubric

1. Accomplishment in Writing

    - Meeting worthwhile challenges
    - Establishing and maintaining purpose
    - Use of the techniques and choice of the genre
    - Control of conventions, vocabulary and sentence structure
    - Awareness of the needs of the audience (organization, development, use of detail)
    - Use of language, sound, images, tone, voice
    - Humor, metaphor, playfulness

2. Use of Processes and Strategies of Writing

    - Effective use of prewriting strategies
    - Use of drafts to discover and shape ideas
    - Use of conferencing opportunities to refine writing (peers, adults, readers)
    - Effective use of revision (reshaping, refocusing, refining)

3. Growth, Development, and Engagement as a Writer

    - Evidence of investment in writing tasks
    - Increased engagement with writing
    - Development of sense of self as a writer
    - Evolution of personal criteria and standards for writing
    - Ability to see the strengths and needs in one's writing
    - Demonstration of risk-taking and innovation in interpreting writing tasks
    - Use of writing for varied purposes, genres, and audiences
    - Progress from early to late pieces, growth, development

Source: LeMahieu et al. (1995). Used by permission.

elements (shown as bullets in Table 12.2) that contributed to the definition of varying degrees of adequacy of the performance on each of the three dimensions.

The portfolios were judged by a relatively small cadre of teachers (12 raters for the middle school portfolios and 13 raters for the high school portfolios) who were trained and calibrated using preselected portfolios as benchmarks or anchors for the scale points on the three dimensions. All portfolios were independently scored by two of the trained raters, and an arbitration process with a third reader was used in cases where differences in scores assigned by the two raters were greater than 1 point. Otherwise, the score for the portfolio was the average of the two independent ratings.

The rating process for the 1,250 portfolios took a total of 815 person-hours over the period of a week. Clearly, this was no trivial undertaking to score the random sample of 8% of the students in the district. The results, however, were exceptional. Relatively high interrater reliability was achieved (reliability coefficients between .74 to .80 for the three dimensions for high school and .84 to .87 for middle school portfolios). The title of the article about the Pittsburgh experience sums up a major conclusion of the effort: "Portfolios in Large-Scale Assessment: Difficult but Not Impossible" (LeMahieu et al., 1995). Like Koretz and his colleagues (1995), LeMahieu and associates also conclude that the portfolio effort had positive effects on instruction. The difference is that they showed that—with sufficient planning, specification of portfolio guidelines, refinement of scoring procedures, and rater training— it is also possible to achieve acceptable levels of reliability for the portfolio ratings.

Examples of Classroom Portfolio Guidelines

Classroom uses of portfolios for assessing student work need not be as comprehensive as a high school graduation portfolio or as tightly defined as a portfolio used in a statewide or districtwide assessment to report on the progress of schools, districts, and the state. It is nonetheless critical for the classroom teacher to be clear on the purpose, the expectations for what should be included in the portfolio, the responsibilities of students for selecting and evaluating their work, and the criteria that will be used in evaluating the work. Sometimes, as in the following example, broad guidelines are available from the state or district to help teachers in implementing a portfolio. Such guidelines can be adapted by each teacher to provide students with more specific instructions for completing their portfolios.

An Example of a High School Science Portfolio.   The California Golden State Exam (GSE) science portfolio consisted of a collection of student work based on a year of study in a high school course in biology, chemistry, or second-year coordinated science. Evaluations of portfolios are combined with other sections of the GSE in the subject area to award recognition to students for their performance on the GSE. The California Department of Education's "Golden State Examination Science Portfolio: A Guide to Teachers" (available at http://www.nwrel.org/assessment/toolkit98/folio.html) provides sample activities and explicates scoring guides for the entries. Sample activities include the following:

1. A problem-solving investigation, such as
   - a student-generated laboratory investigation (e.g., determine the effectiveness of household cleaning fluids for controlling the growth of bacteria—idea contributed to guidelines by Kasey Smith-Penner, Sequoia High School, Redwood City),

- a field experience (e.g., conduct a study of aspects of soil, flora, fauna, or climate on a 1-meter plot of land and relate it to environmental issues in the community—idea contributed to guidelines by Joe Mahood, Aragon High School, San Mateo), or
- a research investigation (e.g., predict the risk of developing an ailment such as cancer or AIDS in student's community—idea contributed to guidelines by Netta Freeman, Paduca High School, Tilghham, Kentucky).

2. A creative expression entry displaying a scientific result or finding, for example,

- games,
- video,
- art, or
- poetry.

3. An example of growth through writing, illustrating relevant findings or issues in science, using, for example,

- current events or
- original stories.

4. GSE self-reflection sheet, requiring students to

- identify the scientific concept for the entry,
- explain why the entry is an excellent way to show the concept, and
- describe how the entry shows the concept.

An Example of a Primary School Mathematics Portfolio. Leon Paulson developed guidelines for the Multnomah (Oregon) Educational Service District to help give teachers ideas about the development and use of mathematics portfolios for students in the primary grades (Paulson, 1994). His "Portfolio Guidelines in Primary Math" are available at http://www.nwrel.org/assessment/toolkit98/primary.html. Some of the kinds of things Paulson's guidelines encourage teachers to have students include in their portfolios are the following:

- Use of manipulatives—documented for portfolio where feasible by drawings or photographs
- Use of technology—computer and calculators with written or recorded oral statements about results
- Use of group work to solve problems—might include teacher observations or recorded student interactions and statements about individual contributions
- Use of real-world examples—examples of applications of mathematics outside class with written or recorded oral statements about examples
- Use of interdisciplinary problems—examples of mathematics, graphs, and charts from other subject areas
- Use of journals and class publications—keep a mathematics journal in portfolios

Writing Portfolios. In a content area such as writing, it is natural to ask: What is the difference between a traditional writing assessment and a writing portfolio assessment? The answer, of course, depends on what sort of "traditional writing assessment" and what sort of "writing portfolio assessment" you are talking about. Answers given to this question by Gearhart, Herman, Baker, and Whittaker (1992) for their study of writing portfolios provide a list of differences that are likely to be applicable in varying degrees in comparing writing portfolios to writing assessments where students are given a prompt and asked to write an essay in a set period of time, such as a single class period. Gearhart and her colleagues noted that the writing portfolios that they developed and analyzed differed from such traditional writing assessments in the following five ways.

1. Portfolios contained samples of classroom writing that occurred in a wide range of conditions and that might address a variety of topics rather than responses to prompts under standardized conditions and time limits.
2. Portfolios contained multiple and varied forms of writing samples obtained in varied contexts over a period of time rather than responses to a single or limited number of prompts at a single point in time.
3. Portfolios included considerable variation in the types or genres of writing tasks (e.g., narratives, summaries, or letters) rather than a task from a single genre.
4. Portfolios gave more of a window into the writing process by the inclusion of drafts and repeated revisions rather than only a single draft of an essay.
5. Portfolios contained a variety of supplemental materials, such as notes, student reflections on the writing experience, self-evaluations, and evaluations by others (e.g., teacher, peer, and/or parents), rather than only the written response to a prompt.

All these factors contribute to the richness of the information that a well-planned and well-implemented portfolio assessment can provide. These factors also complicate the challenges of rating the work or using it as the basis of assigning grades. For example, if the portfolio is intended to assess student progress, then the wide variation in types and genres of writing makes comparison extremely difficult. Based on work with writing portfolios in Hawaii, for example, Baker and Linn (1992) found it almost impossible to achieve consistent ratings of progress when "comparing an October folk tale with a December fantasy, a January haiku, a March whale report, a May letter to a pen pal, and a June summary of a field trip" (p. 12). Though still a challenge, it is much easier to evaluate progress by comparing performance within a single genre (e.g., narrative essays) over time.

In addition to the five differences noted by Gearhart and her colleagues (1992), portfolios also differ from traditional essay or performance assessments in that they may include work that has a substantial collaborative component. Including collaborative assessment tasks in a portfolio may enrich the learning, but it raises questions that need to be considered when the work becomes part of the evaluation of an individual student's work: How should the groups be formed—by student choice or by teacher assignment? How much does it matter if the groups are homogeneous or heterogeneous in achievement? Whose work is it, and what specializations may have evolved for the group?

Many examples of portfolios can be found on the internet. A quick search will often lead to good examples in specific content areas. However, portfolios are best when adapted to the local context, and the internet examples should be used only as a starting point for planning and implementing portfolios.

GUIDELINES AND STUDENTS' ROLE IN SELECTION OF PORTFOLIO ENTRIES AND SELF-EVALUATION

Much of the strength of a portfolio depends on students' involvement in the selection of work to include and on their reflections on that work. Hence, it is important to have students involved in the selection of portfolio entries. This does not mean that students can simply include anything they choose. Rather, teachers need to give students clear guidelines for selecting pieces of work. Those guidelines should be based on the purpose of the portfolio and the learning goals that the teacher is trying to foster.

If the goal in a science class is that students should "know and be able to use the experimental method," then the guidelines should ensure that students not only describe the experimental method or respond to questions in an assignment about it but also apply the method to answer a specific question. Guidelines for the portfolio entry might specify that the entry include a description of the problem, a statement of the hypothesis to be tested, the design and data collection procedures to be used, the data collected, the analysis of results, and a statement of conclusions. The guidelines might suggest a range of appropriate problems for experimentation or provide a list of example problems. The student would still have considerable latitude, however, in the choice of the particular problem, in determining the details of the experimental design, in planning the analyses, and in interpreting the data.

In a Spanish-language class, students might be asked to include tape recordings of their conversation with a speaker whose first language is Spanish, an essay written in Spanish, and a translation of a letter from Spanish to English. In each of these categories, the range of topics as well as other characteristics, such as a minimum duration of the recorded conversation or the type of letter, might be specified. The key is to provide students with latitude for exercising their creativity and gaining experience in setting goals, planning, and conducting the work while achieving specific instructional objectives.

In both the science experiment example and the Spanish class example, students have substantial room to define and shape the details of portfolio entries, as well as clear guidelines on the nature of the work to be included. A review of an experiment conducted by someone else or the summary of what is known about a topic clearly would not qualify as an example of a student's use of the experimental method. Similarly, a tape recording of a student reading a passage from a Spanish-language magazine would not meet the requirement for a tape-recorded conversation with a person whose first language is Spanish.

To help students reflect on their choice of entries for a portfolio, it is useful not only to have guidelines specifying requirements but also to have students complete a brief form with each entry. An example of such a form is shown in Figure 12.1. In addition to identifying the entry with the student's name and a brief description, the form provides encouragement for students to think about why the particular entry was selected and what they consider its salient features. By including a place for teacher comments on the same form, the cover sheet provides a lasting record in the portfolio of the feedback provided to the student.

A separate form, as shown in Figure 12.2, may provide more explicit guidelines on student reflections on the entry and their self-evaluation of its strengths and weaknesses.

Student Name: _____   Date: _____

Description of Entry:

Student Comments:

I chose this item for my portfolio because:

Please notice:

Other Comments:

Teacher Comments:

Teacher Name: _____   Date: _____

Strong points of entry:

Some things to consider or areas needing work are:

Other Comments:

Figure 12.1
Sample cover sheet for portfolio entry

Student Name: _____   Date: _____

Description of Entry:

Self-Evaluation of Entry:

What I tried to accomplish:

What I did:

What I learned:

What I am proud of about this entry:

What I need to work on or would do differently next time:

Teacher Comments:

Teacher Name: _____   Date: _____

Figure 12.2
Sample self-reflection and evaluation form

The prompts on the form are intended to encourage students to think about what they planned to do and what they actually did, and to evaluate the strong and weak points of the entry. By asking students to say what they might do differently next time, students are encouraged to think about how their work might be improved.

EVALUATION CRITERIA

To specify evaluation criteria, a teacher must be clear in his or her mind about the instructional goals for individual portfolio entries and for the portfolio as a whole. If the instructional goals are not clear already to the teacher, efforts to specify evaluation criteria will either force reconsideration and clarification of goals or risk being irrelevant or even counterproductive. The evaluation criteria should clarify instructional goals not only for the teacher but for students and parents as well.

The clear specification of evaluation criteria enhances fairness. As with any other type of assessment, students need to know what is expected and how their work will be evaluated if a portfolio assessment is to be fair to students in reality and to be so perceived by students and parents. Of course, evaluation criteria are also important to help teachers be consistent and unbiased in scoring portfolios of different students.

The place to start in developing evaluation criteria for portfolios is with the specified purpose or purposes of the portfolio. Analytic scoring rubrics on individual portfolios are useful for formative evaluation purposes. Holistic scoring rubrics may be more appropriate for summative evaluations. The formative–summative distinction is also useful in determining the emphasis of evaluation rubrics for individual portfolio entries and ones designed for evaluating the complete portfolio.

The evaluation criteria for individual entries may be specified using the various types of scoring rubrics and rating scales discussed in Chapters 10 and 11. The narrative scoring rubric used by Wolf and Gearhart (1997) that was discussed in Chapter 10, for example, might be used as the basis for evaluating narrative essays included in an English/language arts portfolio. Accordingly, both the student and the teacher might judge each narrative essay entry in terms of the effectiveness of the development of the essay theme, the characters, the setting, and the plot as well as how effectively the essay communicates.

The sample items of a rating scale for a speech shown in Figure 11.5 in Chapter 11 might be used for rating a videotape of a student presentation. Those items might be completed by the teacher, the student whose presentation was videotaped, and by other students.

Scoring rubrics used at Central Park East Secondary School for evaluating portfolio entries define 4-point scales on each of five dimensions of performance: (1) viewpoint, (2) connections, (3) evidence, (4) voice, and (5) conventions. Viewpoint concerns the degree to which the entry demonstrates a wide knowledge base while maintaining a clear focus. To obtain a score of 4 on the viewpoint dimension, the entry must clearly display an in-depth understanding of ideas and issues and persuasively present a coherent position while acknowledging other views as appropriate.

The connections rubric distinguishes between well-organized and interconnected entries with a clear beginning and end, and ones that do not clearly connect the parts into a coherent whole. The evidence rubric provides the basis for evaluating the degree to which evidence is used to support arguments and conclusions in a credible and convincing way. The voice dimension is used to evaluate the degree to which the entry is engaging for the intended audience. The overall appearance, format, and appropriate use of sentence structure, grammar, and the mechanics of punctuation and spelling are evaluated by the conventions scoring rubric (for a more complete description, see Darling-Hammond et al., 1995, pp. 36–39).

Guidelines to help teachers implement the portfolio requirements in their classrooms for the California Golden State Exam included descriptions of the score points for each type of entry. Six score levels are defined for each type of portfolio entry, ranging from inadequate performance (1) to exceptional performance (6). An example of one of the descriptions of a score of 5 for the problem-solving investigation is given in the box "Problem-Solving Investigation: Score Level 5."

In addition to evaluation criteria for individual entries, criteria may also be specified for evaluating the structure of the portfolio and for the overall evaluation of the entire collection. The evaluation of structure may include ratings of the organization, the appearance, and the quality of self-reflections.

An overall evaluation of the portfolio that cuts across entries is especially useful for portfolios intended to assess student progress. Specific ratings might be provided on dimensions such as those shown in Table 12.3. Each of the rating scales in the table emphasizes comparisons among portfolio items that were added to the portfolio at different times during the year.

When judgmental scoring is required of assessments for purposes of grading or other summative evaluations, it is good practice to conceal the identity of the student. This can sometimes be accomplished on essay examinations by scoring one item at a time and shuffling the order of the examinations after completing the scoring of each item. With projects or extended reports, it is usually more difficult to conceal the student's identity while grading the work, but it may be possible in some instances by instructing students to put their names only on a cover page or at the end of the work. Such procedures, though seldom foolproof, can also be used when evaluating individual portfolio entries. For global ratings of the portfolio as a whole, however, it is nearly impossible to conceal the student's identity from the teacher when he or she is evaluating the portfolio. Thus, other approaches are needed to guard against unintended biases that arise when a teacher

Problem-Solving Investigation: Score Level 5

"Student work and self-reflection show the student's strong skill in experimental design. Observations and data analysis indicate very good knowledge of the scientific ideas presented. Analyses and conclusions are supported by observations and data and show a high level of reasoning. The entry includes strong evidence that the student worked cooperatively with others. The self-reflection sheet clearly identifies how working with others improved the student's understanding of the scientific ideas presented. The student makes generally valid applications to real-world situations. All aspects of the task and analysis are complete. Written expression is very good and contributes to clear and coherent communication" (California Department of Education, 1994).

Table 12.3
Overall ratings of mathematics portfolio

Development of Mathematics Understanding	Unsatisfactory Progress			Outstanding Progress	
• Progress from early to late problem sets	1	2	3	4	5
• Improvement in ability to formulate and solve problems	1	2	3	4	5
• Reduction in errors in computation	1	2	3	4	5
• Increased ability to make connections	1	2	3	4	5
• Improvement in ability to communicate mathematical results to others	1	2	3	4	5
• Increased ability to estimate and to check solutions for reasonableness	1	2	3	4	5
• Increased skills in using charts and graphs	1	2	3	4	5

gives the benefit of the doubt because the teacher "knows" that the student "understands the material based on other observations" or rates the work of a student who rarely does good work more harshly because of this preconception.

One useful safeguard against unintended biases that arise in ratings of portfolios from knowledge of the student's identity is to rescore a portfolio after setting it aside for a period of time and to compare the two sets of scores. Where teachers from different classes collaborate on assessments, it may also be possible to exchange some portfolios so that each teacher scores the portfolios of some of the students from the other class. Comparing the scores assigned to your own students with the scores assigned by another teacher can be useful not only in guarding against unintended scoring biases but also in refining scoring rubrics and enhancing reliability of scoring. Obviously, it is not always possible to have portfolios independently scored by another teacher. Where it is feasible, however, it can be the basis for fruitful discussions between the teachers regarding instructional goals, the adequacy of the evidence collected in the portfolio to evaluate the achievement of those goals, and the evaluation criteria that are used.

When portfolios are used on a schoolwide, districtwide, or statewide basis as part of an accountability system, a more formal scoring process should be employed. Teachers may be brought together and trained to use common scoring criteria. Benchmark or anchor papers for each entry may be identified and used to elaborate the meaning of scoring rubrics and to train teachers to use common scoring standards. Independent audit procedures may also be used where a random sample of portfolios is selected for rescoring at a central site. Although such a training and scoring enterprise requires substantial time and resources, teachers in locations where this is done have frequently reported that the experience is one of the best professional development activities with which they have been involved.

USING PORTFOLIOS IN INSTRUCTION AND COMMUNICATION

Most appropriate uses are, of course, either the explicit or the implicit focus of the purposes for which portfolios are introduced. Thus, we have already said quite a bit about the primary uses of portfolios for purposes of instruction and assessment. Here we need only add a few specific points about the relationship of portfolios to instruction and elaborate on the idea of using portfolios to communicate to others outside the classroom, especially parents or guardians.

A salient feature of portfolios is the dynamic way in which they evolve over days, weeks, and months. As students work on individual entries, teachers have many opportunities to examine the work and discuss ideas on possible next steps with students. Observations of portfolios in progress provide teachers with a basis for ongoing planning and formative evaluation.

Portfolios also provide an excellent means of communicating with parents. The products and student self-reflections can provide parents with a window into the classroom. It gives them a more intimate basis for seeing aspects of their children's experiences in school. As was previously noted, portfolios can also be used as a vehicle for student-directed conferences of students, parents, and teachers. The specifics of the portfolio provide a framework for meaningful three-way discussions of the student's achievements, progress, and areas to work on next. Parents' comments on the specific entries and overall portfolio can also contribute to and become part of the portfolios.

SUMMARY

Portfolios come in many different varieties and can serve an equally wide array of purposes. What distinguishes a portfolio of student work from merely a file where student work is collected and stored is that a portfolio is a purposeful collection of student work. Clear definition of purpose is one of the most important steps in planning the uses of portfolios. Clarity of purpose provides the foundation for determining the contents of a portfolio, how entries will be selected, and how the portfolio will be evaluated.

The two primary purposes for using portfolios in the classroom are instruction and assessment. Although most portfolios serve some mix of these two purposes, it is critical that the relative emphasis be clarified before work begins on the construction of portfolios. As with other assessments, it is important to distinguish between using the portfolio for purposes of formative or summative evaluation. The formative uses are readily compatible with portfolios that are intended to be used primarily as an instructional tool. Summative evaluation uses, such as grades and the award of honors, may also contribute to learning, but issues of comparability from student to student and fairness constrain the freedom with which portfolios can be constructed.

Portfolio purposes can also be distinguished in terms of the emphasis placed on current achievement or progress over time, the use of portfolios as a showcase of best work or for purposes of documentation, and whether they are finished or working portfolios.

Guidelines should provide students with a sound understanding of what is expected and a reasonable basis for selecting entries. These guidelines obviously need to be congruent with the purposes. They must be specific enough so that students know what they need to do but not so specific that they stifle the creativity and freedom of choice that is reasonable within the constraints of the portfolio's purpose.

Guidelines should specify the contents, types, and minimum number of entries that students are expected to include. The guidelines should be clear about intended audiences and about who has access to the portfolio. Requirements for self-reflection and self-evaluation of both the entries and the portfolio as a whole should be stated in the guidelines. Finally, guidelines should clarify the evaluation criteria that will be used in judging entries and portfolios as a whole.

As is true of any instructional assessment tool, portfolios have both strengths and weaknesses. Some of the most important strengths are the ease with which they can be integrated with classroom instruction; their value in encouraging students to develop self-evaluation skills, take responsibility for their own learning, and become reflective learners; and their effectiveness in communicating with parents and other audiences outside the classroom. Two frequently cited weaknesses or drawbacks are that portfolios are labor intensive for the teacher—requiring considerable time in planning, monitoring, and providing feedback to students—and that they are difficult to score reliably.

LEARNING EXERCISES

1. Suppose you were designing a portfolio for this measurement class.
   a. What are two purposes that might be served by a portfolio for this class?
   b. In what ways would the portfolio need to be different for these two purposes?
   c. Specify guidelines for inclusion of six entries in the portfolio.
   d. Describe scoring guidelines for one of the six entries and for obtaining an overall portfolio score.
   e. Discuss the advantages and disadvantages of using a portfolio for the two purposes you identified.
2. Devise a portfolio to use in assessing student progress and communicating that progress to parents that would be used by students in a subject area and grade level that you would like to teach. Address issues of purpose, audience, who will have access to the portfolio, guidelines for the contents of the portfolio, the appropriate role of collaboration on entries, student self-evaluations and reflections on their work, and the scoring criteria that will be used.
3. Obtain, if possible, examples of one or more student portfolios and guidelines used by the student's teacher to specify how students should construct their portfolios. Review and evaluate the portfolio of work using either the evaluation criteria provided by the teacher or, if there are none, criteria that you specify. Analyze the strengths and weaknesses of the portfolio guidelines.

REFERENCES

Arter, J., Spandel, V., & Culham, R. (1995). *Portfolios for assessment and instruction. ERIC Digest.* Available: http://ericae.net/db/edo/ED388890._htm. Provides framework for development and use of portfolios in instruction and assessment.

Baker, E. L., & Linn, R. L. (1992). *Writing portfolios: Potential for large-scale assessment* (Final Report). Los Angeles: University of California, Center for Research on Evaluation, Standards, and Student Testing. Describes a large-scale application of portfolio assessment.

California Department of Education. (1994). *Golden State Examination science portfolio: A guide to teachers*. Sacramento: California Department of Education. Available: http://www.nwrel.org/assessment/toolkit98/folio.html.

Darling-Hammond, L., Ancess, J., & Falk, B. (1995). *Authentic assessment in action: Studies of schools and students at work*. New York: Teachers College Press. Presents examples of uses of portfolios and performance assessments in school settings.

Gearhart, M., Herman, J. L., Baker, E. L., & Whittaker, A. K. (1992). *Writing portfolios at the elementary level: A study of methods for writing assessment* (CSE Technical Report 337). Los Angeles: University of California, Center for Research on Evaluation, Standards, and Student Testing. Available: http://www.cse.ucla.edu. Provides examples of scoring rubrics.

Koretz, D., Stecher, B., Klein, S., & McCaffrey, D. (1994a). *The evolution of a portfolio program: The impact and quality of the Vermont program in the second year* (CSE Technical Report 385). Los Angeles: University of California, Center for Research on Evaluation, Standards, and Student Testing. Available: http://www.cse.ucla.edu. Describes the Vermont experience with portfolios.

Koretz, D., Stecher, B., Klein, S., & McCaffrey, D. (1994b). The Vermont portfolio assessment program: Findings and implications. *Educational Measurement: Issues and Practice, 13*(3), 5–16.

LeMahieu, P. G., Gitomer, D. H., & Eresh, J. (1995). Portfolios in large-scale assessment: Difficult but not impossible. *Educational Measurement: Issues and Practice, 14*(3), 11–28. Describes the use of portfolios in Pittsburgh.

Paulson, L. (1994). *Portfolio guidelines in primary math*. Portland, OR: Multnomah County Educational Service District.

Sackett, P. R., Schmitt, N., Ellingson, J. E., & Kabin, M. B. (2001). High-stakes testing in employment, credentialing, and higher education: Prospects in a post-affirmative-action world. *American Psychologist, 56*(4), 302–318.

Stecher, B., & Mitchell, K. J. (1995). *Portfolio-driven reform: Vermont teachers' understanding of mathematical problem solving and related changes in classroom practice* (CSE Technical Report 400). Los Angeles: University of California, Center for Research on Evaluation, Standards, and Student Testing. Available: http://www.cse.ucla.edu.

Wolf, S. A., & Gearhart, M. (1997). New writing assessments: The challenge of changing teachers' beliefs about students as writers. *Theory into Practice, 36*, 220–230. (Also available as CSE Technical Report 400. Los Angeles: University of California, Center for Research on Evaluation, Standards, and Student Testing. Available: http://www.cse.ucla.edu)

FURTHER READING

Gronlund, N. E. (2005). *Assessment of student achievement* (8th ed.). Boston: Allyn & Bacon. Chapter 9 provides practical guidance on the use of portfolio assessment.

Johnson, B. (1996). *Performance assessment handbook: Volume 1: Portfolios and socratic seminars*. Princeton, NJ: Eye on Education. Illustrates the use of portfolios in practice.

Popham, W. J. (2007). *Classroom assessment: What teachers need to know* (5th ed.). Boston: Allyn & Bacon. Chapter 9, "Portfolio Assessment," describes the key ingredients of portfolio assessment and discusses the pros and cons of this type of assessment.

Tierney, R. J., Carter, M. A., & Desai, L. E. (1991). *Portfolio assessment in the reading-writing classroom*. Norwood, MA: Cristopher-Gordon Publishers.

Valencia, S. W., & Calfee, R. (1991). The development and use of literacy portfolios for students, classes, and teachers. *Applied Measurement in Education, 4*, 333–345.

13

ASSESSMENT PROCEDURES: OBSERVATIONAL TECHNIQUES, PEER APPRAISAL, AND SELF-REPORT

Direct observation is the best means we have for assessing some aspects of learning and development. The use of anecdotal records can turn informal teacher observations into a systematic source of information about student development. Judgments and reports made by students themselves are also a valuable source of information in many areas of learning and development. Peer judgments are especially useful in assessing personal–social development, and self-report methods provide a fuller understanding of students' needs, problems, adjustments, interests, and attitudes.

Many outcomes in the cognitive domain, such as those pertaining to knowledge, understanding, and thinking skills, can be measured by paper-and-pencil tests or performance-based assessments. However, there also are many important learning outcomes that require informal observation of natural interactions in the classroom, on the playground, or in the lunchroom. In this chapter, we focus on procedures for observing and recording student performances in natural settings throughout the school year. These techniques are also useful for assessing important noncognitive outcomes, such as attitudes, appreciations, and personal–social development. We also describe procedures for complementing teacher observations of student development with judgments and reports from students. Both peer reports and self-reports are the best sources of information about some aspects of personal–social development and can provide valuable supplements to teacher observations in other areas.

Although we have included this chapter in Part II of this book, the uses of some of the information that can be collected by techniques discussed in this chapter often do not differ from the information gained through the types of tests and assessments discussed in Chapters 6 through 12. Some of the informal observations may contribute, along with information obtained through more formal assessment procedures, to the evaluation of student progress and grading. Much of the information, however, will be more useful in attempting to understand student attitudes and interests and the dynamics of the classroom than for evaluating cognitive outcomes. Such information can be useful in considering what approaches will be most likely to be benefical to individual students and what arrangements and group interactions are likely to be helpful in enhancing the learning of all students.

Learning outcomes in skill areas and behavioral changes in personal–social development are especially difficult to assess with paper-and-pencil tests. A list of such outcomes, with representative types of student behavior, is presented in Table 13.1. This list is by no means complete, but it is comprehensive enough to show the great need to supplement paper-and-pencil testing with other methods of assessment. Performance-based tasks of the type discussed in Chapter 11 are well suited for the types of skills illustrated at the top of the table. The other outcomes in the table, however, require the use of informal observation techniques throughout the school year. The use of the observational and recording techniques described in this chapter can improve the assessment of all these outcomes.

Learning outcomes and aspects of development such as those in Table 13.1 can generally be assessed by (a) observing students as they perform and describing or judging that behavior (assessing interactions with other students), (b) asking their peers about them (assessing social relationships), and (c) questioning them directly (assessing expressed interests). Although these observational techniques, peer appraisals, and self-report methods are more subjective than we would like and their use frequently requires more time and effort than typical assessment procedures, they are the best means available for assessing a variety of important behaviors. Our choice is simple: Either we use these techniques to assess each learning outcome and aspect of development as directly and validly as possible, or we neglect learning outcomes that cannot be measured by paper-and-pencil tests.

In this chapter, we describe the use of anecdotal records to systematically accumulate information from a teacher's informal observations. We then describe the use of peer appraisals and self-report techniques to supplement and complement teacher observations.

ANECDOTAL RECORDS

Teachers' daily observations give them a wealth of information concerning the learning and development of their students. For example, a third-grade teacher notices during oral reading that Mike mispronounces several simple words, that Maria sits staring out the window, and that Carl keeps interrupting the reading with irrelevant questions. Similarly, a high school chemistry teacher notices during a laboratory period that Bill is slow and inefficient in setting up his equipment, that Juan finishes his experiments early and helps others, and that Sandy handles the chemicals in a careless and dangerous manner despite repeated warnings. Such daily incidents and events have special significance for assessing

Table 13.1
Outcomes requiring assessment procedures beyond the typical paper-and-pencil tests

Outcome	Representative Behaviors
Skills	Speaking, listening, oral reading, performing laboratory experiments, drawing, playing a musical instrument, dancing, gymnastics, work skills, study skills, and social skills
Work habits	Effectiveness in planning, use of time, use of equipment, and use of resources; demonstration of such traits as initiative, creativity, persistence, and dependability
Social attitudes	Concern for the welfare of others, respect for rules/laws, respect for the property of others, sensitivity to social issues, concern for social institutions, and desire to work toward social improvement
Scientific attitudes	Open-mindedness, willingness to suspend judgment, sensitivity to cause-and-effect relations, and an inquiring mind
Academic self-concept	Expressed as self-perceptions as a learner in particular subjects (e.g., math or reading) and, in general, a willingness to attempt new problems
Interests	Expressed feelings toward various educational, mechanical, aesthetic, scientific, social, recreational, and vocational activities
Appreciations	Feeling of satisfaction and enjoyment expressed toward nature, music, art, literature, physical skill, and outstanding social contributions
Social adjustments	Relationship to peers, reaction to praise and criticism, reaction to authority, emotional stability, and social adaptability

student learning and development. They enable us to determine how a student typically performs or behaves in a variety of situations. In some instances, this information supplements and verifies data obtained by more objective methods; but in other cases, it is the only means we have for assessing desired outcomes.

Impressions gained through observation are apt to provide an incomplete and biased picture, however, unless we keep an accurate record of our observations. A simple and convenient method of doing this is through anecdotal records. Such records reduce problems caused by selective memory and can be useful not only in planning ways to interact more effectively with individual students but also in preparing for parent–teacher conferences. The specific examples recorded on anecdotal records can provide a more effective basis for communication with parents than mere generalities.

Anecdotal records are factual descriptions of the meaningful incidents and events that the teacher has observed. Each incident should be written down shortly after it happens. The descriptions may be recorded on separate cards like the one shown in Figure 13.1 or as running accounts, one for each student, on separate pages in a notebook. A good anecdotal record keeps the objective description of an incident separate from any interpretation of the behavior's meaning. For some purposes, it is also useful to keep an additional space for recommendations concerning ways to improve the student's learning or adjustment. Such recommendations are seldom made, however, until several anecdotes have been recorded.

Class __4th Grade__   Pupil __Mary Johnson__
Date __4/25/94__   Place __Classroom__

Incident

Shortly before class was about to start, Mary showed me a poem that she had written about "spring." It was a delightful poem, and I asked her if she wanted to read it to the class. She bowed her head and then nodded yes. She read the poem in a low voice, constantly looked down at the paper, moved her right foot back and forth, and pulled on the collar of her blouse. When she finished, Steve (in the back row) said, "I couldn't hear it. Will you read it again—louder?" Mary said "no" and sat down.

Interpretation

Mary enjoys writing stories and poems, and they reflect considerable creative ability. However, she seems very shy and nervous in performing before a group. Her refusal to read the poem again seemed to be due to her nervousness.

Figure 13.1
Anecdotal record form

Uses of Anecdotal Records

The use of anecdotal records has frequently been limited to the area of social adjustment. Although they are especially appropriate for this type of reporting, this is a needless limitation. Anecdotal records can be used for obtaining data pertinent to a variety of learning outcomes and to many aspects of personal and social development. The potential usefulness of the anecdotal method is revealed in the various areas of learning outcomes presented earlier in this chapter (see Table 13.1); you will see that many of the behaviors listed there can be appraised by means of direct observation.

The problem in using anecdotal records is not so much what *can* be assessed as what *should* be assessed with this method. It is obvious that we cannot observe and report on all aspects of student behavior no matter how useful such records might be. Thus, we must be selective in our observations.

What Behaviors to Observe and Record

In general, our objectives and desired outcomes will guide us in determining what behaviors are most worth noting. We must also be alert to those unusual and exceptional incidents that contribute to a better understanding of each student's unique pattern of behavior. Within this general framework are certain steps we can take to control our observations so that a realistic system of recording can be developed.

1. Confining our observations to those areas of behavior that cannot be assessed by other means
2. Limiting our observations of all students at any given time to only a few types of behavior
3. Restricting the use of extensive observations of behavior to those few students who are most in need of special help

There is no advantage in using anecdotal records to derive evidence of learning in areas in which more objective and practical methods are available. Knowledge, understanding, and various aspects of thinking skill can usually be assessed by paper-and-pencil tests. Many learning outcomes of other types that are well suited to the use of performance-based assessment tasks, such as the ability to give a speech, operate a microscope, or write a theme, are most effectively assessed by rating methods or product assessment. Records of actual behavior are best used to assess how a student typically behaves in a natural setting. How does David approach a problem? How persistent is Rachel in carrying out a task? How willing is Steve to listen to the ideas of others? What contributions does Kwang make to class activities? How willing is Kristen to participate in games with other children on the playground? What type of books does Brooke select from the library? A student's verbal comments and actions in various natural situations reveal certain clues to attitudes, interests, appreciations, habits, and social adjustment patterns that cannot be discovered by any other means. These are the types of behavior on which we should focus when keeping anecdotal records.

The best we can hope to get from anecdotal records is a fairly representative sample of student behavior in the different areas for which we want information. This usually can be obtained more easily if we concentrate our observations on a few areas at a time. For example, an elementary teacher might pay particular attention to reading interests during the free reading period, to signs of appreciation during music and art, and to patterns of social interactions during recess. Similarly, a high school science teacher might concentrate on incidents reflecting scientific attitude during certain class discussions and laboratory periods and on work habits and laboratory skills during others. In some cases, the activity itself will indicate the types of observation most fruitful to focus on, whereas in others the emphasis at any given time may need to be determined. Despite the concentration of attention on certain areas at a particular time, however, we should always be alert to other incidents and events that have special significance for understanding a student's learning and development.

In addition to recording some information on all students, at times we need more comprehensive information regarding a relative few. The child struggling to learn to read, the socially rejected child, the disruptive child, and the child with a learning disability are typical of those needing special attention. More extensive observations of such students are helpful in understanding their difficulties and in planning effective instructional strategies. The most complete and useful information is obtained when we concentrate our observations on one or two students at a time. During such observations it also may be necessary to restrict our record keeping on other students.

Some teachers become discouraged when they first use anecdotal records because they attempt to do too much. Limiting observations and reports to specific types of behavior, to specific students, or both is frequently necessary to make the procedure feasible. It is much better to have a clearly delimited and workable observational plan than to end up with an incomplete and atypical collection of unrelated incidents.

Advantages and Limitations of Anecdotal Records

Probably the most important advantage of anecdotal records is that they depict actual behavior in natural situations. The old adage that "actions speak louder than words" has a direct application here. A student may show good knowledge of health practices but violate them in everyday situations, may profess great interest in science but approach laboratory work in a haphazard and uninterested fashion, or may express great concern for the welfare of others but behave in a selfish manner. Records of actual behavior provide a check on other assessment methods and also enable us to determine the extent of change in the student's typical patterns of behavior.

In addition to compiling descriptions of the most characteristic behavior of a student, anecdotal records facilitate gathering evidence on events that are exceptional but significant. Typical examples are the quiet student who speaks in class for the first time, the hostile student who makes a friendly gesture, the extreme conformist who shows a sign of originality, and the apathetic student who shows a spark of interest. These individually significant behaviors are apt to be excluded by other assessment techniques. They are also likely to be overlooked by teachers unless a concerted effort is made to observe such incidents. Keeping anecdotal records makes us more diligent in observation and increases our awareness of such behaviors.

Anecdotal records can be used with very young students and with students who have limited basic communication skills. They are especially valuable in situations where paper-and-pencil tests, performance assessments, self-report techniques, and peer appraisals are likely to be impractical or of limited use. Observational records of younger students are of value for still another reason. Because young children tend to be more spontaneous and uninhibited in their actions, their behavior is often easier to observe and interpret.

One limitation of anecdotal records is the amount of time required to maintain an adequate system of records. Though this can be offset somewhat by limiting observations and reports, as suggested earlier, record keeping is still a time-consuming task. If teachers keep anecdotal records for their own use only, then they can work out a realistic plan by starting with a few anecdotes each day and gradually increasing it to a reasonable number. If the entire staff uses anecdotal records, then it is good to have all teachers record as many anecdotes as is practical for a period of a few weeks followed by a staff meeting to discuss the recorded anecdotes and to decide what constitutes a reasonable number. It is generally unwise to set a specific number that must be recorded each week, but an approximate minimum can serve as a general guide.

Another serious limitation of anecdotal records is the difficulty of being objective when observing and reporting student behavior. Ideally, we would like a series of verbal snapshots that accurately represent the student's actual behavior. This goal is seldom attained, however, for teachers' own biases, hopes, and preconceived notions inevitably enter into their observations and reports. For example, they will tend to notice more desirable qualities in those students they like best and more undesirable qualities in those they like least. If they are assessing the effectiveness of a new teaching technique in which they have great faith, they may notice positive results and ignore the negative. If they believe that boys are less coordinated than girls, they will tend to perceive their performance skills as being of lower quality. Training in observation and reporting can reduce such distortions to a minimum, but they cannot be eradicated entirely. In striving to eliminate distortions, it is particularly important that teachers be self-reflective about possible biases in their observations as the result of stereotypes and preconceptions about children on the basis of gender, race, ethnicity, or socioeconomic background. They must be on guard against self-fulfilling prophecies, especially in cases where immediate impressions lead to low expectations for individual students.

A related difficulty is obtaining an adequate sample of behavior. When participating in class discussion, some students may be so tense and anxious that they appear cold and unfriendly toward others and their ideas seem disorganized. When observed in less formal settings, however, such as in the laboratory or on the playground, their behavior might be quite different. Similarly, a student may appear highly motivated and interested in mathematics class but bored and uninterested during English literature; or a student may be attentive and inquisitive in science one day and apathetic the next. Everyone's behavior fluctuates somewhat from situation to situation and from one time to another. Therefore, to gain a reliable picture of a typical pattern of behavior, we need to observe students over a period of time and in a variety of situations. This also implies that general interpretations and recommendations concerning a student's adjustment should be delayed until a fairly adequate sample of behavior is obtained.

Effective Use of Anecdotal Records

In the previous chapters, we stated or implied a number of ways to improve procedures for observing and reporting student behavior. These and other points are listed here as suggestions for the effective use of anecdotal records.

1. Determine in advance what to observe, but be alert for unusual behavior. We are more apt to select and record meaningful incidents if we review objectives and outcomes and decide which behaviors require assessment by direct observation, that is, those that cannot be effectively assessed by other means. We can further focus our observations by looking for just a few types of behavior at any given time. Although such directed observations are valuable for obtaining evidence of student learning, there is always the danger that unique incidents that have special value for understanding a student's development will be overlooked. Consequently, we must be flexible enough to notice and report any unusual behavior in the event that it may be significant.

2. Analyze observational records for possible sources of bias. We should carefully review our initial impressions of each student. We need to consider the possibility that they are influenced by stereotypes based on gender, race, or ethnicity. We can minimize bias by reflecting on these and other factors that may bias our observations. Distinguishing between what is actually observed and the interpretation of that observation can be especially useful in that regard. We should consider, for example, how the same recorded observation might have led to a different interpretation if it had been another student. Different interpretations of the same recorded observation may, of course, be appropriate if they are based on knowledge of different patterns of behavior for two students; but variation in interpretation should not be a consequence of preconceptions based on gender, race, ethnicity, or social background.

3. Observe and record enough of the situation to make the behavior meaningful. It is difficult to interpret behavior apart from the situation in which it occurred. An aggressive action, such as pushing another child, might reflect good-natured fun, an attempt to get attention, a response to direct provocation, or a sign of extreme hostility. Clues to the meaning of behavior frequently can be obtained by directing attention to the actions of the other students involved and the particular setting in which the behavior took place.

The record, therefore, should contain a rich enough description of those conditions that seem necessary for understanding the student's behavior.

4. Make a record of the incident as soon after the observation as possible. In most cases, it is infeasible to write a description of an incident when it occurs. However, the longer we delay in recording observations, the greater the likelihood that important details will be forgotten. Try to make a few brief notes at opportune times following behavioral incidents and complete the records as soon as possible after the incident.

5. Limit each anecdote to a brief description of a single incident. Brief and concise descriptions take less time to write and less time to read and are more easily summarized. Just enough detail should be included to make the description meaningful and accurate. Limiting each description to a single incident also simplifies the task of writing, using, and interpreting the records (see the "Guidelines" box).

6. Keep the factual description of the incident and your interpretation of it separate. The description of an incident should be as accurate and objective as you can make it. This means stating exactly what happened in clear, nonjudgmental words. Avoid such terms as *unhappy, shy, hostile, sad, ambitious, persistent,* and the like. If used at all, reserve such words for the separate section in which you give your tentative interpretations of the incident. There is no need to interpret each incident, but when interpretations are given, they should be kept separate and labeled as such.

7. Record both positive and negative behavioral incidents. Teachers are often more apt to notice those behaviors that disturb them personally and that interfere with the process in the classroom. The result is that anecdotal records frequently contain a disproportionate number of the incidents that indicate the lack of learning or development. For assessment purposes, it is equally important to record the less dramatic incidents that provide clues concerning the growth that is taking place. Thus, a conscious effort should be made to observe and record subtle positive behaviors as well as the more obvious negative reactions.

8. Collect a number of anecdotes on a student before drawing inferences concerning typical behavior. A single behavioral incident is seldom very meaningful in understanding a student's behavior. We all have our moments of peak performance and extreme error proneness, elation and despair, and confidence and self-doubt. It is only after observing a student a number of times in a variety of settings that the basic pattern of behavior begins to emerge. Consequently, we should generally delay making any judgments concerning learning or development until we have a sufficient sample of behavior to provide a reliable picture of how the student typically behaves in different situations.

9. Obtain practice in writing anecdotal records. At first, most teachers have considerable difficulty selecting significant incidents, observing them accurately, and describing them objectively. It is wise to start by recording just a few records each day rather than attempting too much. It might be wise to start by observing students' study habits during recess or during a study period, as this will allow sufficient time to observe and record significant behavior. A review of the usefulness of records kept over a period of a month or two can help hone the skills distinguishing between incidents that yield useful information and ones that do not. A review can also help in refining the nature and efficiency of the notes that are recorded.

GUIDELINES

Writing Anecdotal Records

- Write brief, specific descriptions.
- Include a concise description of what the student said or did and the situation in which it occurred. (Example: On the playground today, Debbie and Kim were choosing sides for softball. Michelle said, "I want to be on Debbie's team and play first base, or I won't play.")
- Do not write generalized descriptive anecdotes. These describe the behavior in general terms, as being typical of the student. (Example: On the playground today, Michelle again showed that she always wants her own way.)
- Do not write evaluative anecdotes. These judge the behavior as acceptable or unacceptable, good or bad. (Example: Michelle was selfish and disruptive on the playground today.)
- Do not write interpretive anecdotes. These explain the reasons for the behavior, usually in terms of a single general cause. (Example: Michelle can't play well with others because she is an overprotected, only child.)

STUDENT JUDGMENTS AND REPORTS

Teachers' observations and judgments of student behavior are of special value in those areas in which the behavior is readily observable and the teachers have special competence to judge. In assessing the ability to conduct and interpret experimental data, the effectiveness of an essay, or the quality of handwriting, for example, the teacher is unquestionably in the best position to make the judgment. The procedure or the product resulting from the procedure can be directly observed, and the teacher's knowledge in the area contributes to the validity and reliability of the judgments. In certain areas of student development, however, the teacher's assessment of behavior is apt to be inadequate unless observations are supplemented and complemented by the students' judgments and reports.

Various aspects of personal–social development can be more effectively assessed by including peer ratings and other peer appraisal methods in the assessment program. In the realms of leadership ability, concern for others, effectiveness in group work, and social acceptability, for example, students often know better than the teacher one another's strengths and weaknesses. The intimate interactions that occur among peers are seldom fully visible to an outside observer. Some differences between teacher judgment and peer judgment also can be expected because each is using different standards. Children's criteria of social acceptability, for example, are apt to be quite different from teachers' criteria.

Self-report techniques are also a valuable adjunct to the teacher's observations of behavior. A complete picture of students' adjustments, interests, and attitudes cannot be obtained without reports from them. Their expressed feelings and beliefs in these areas are at least as important as evidence obtained from observing their behavior. Although expressed feelings and observable behavior do not always completely agree, the self-report provides valuable evidence concerning the students' perceptions of themselves and how they want others to view them. In fact, a discrepancy between reported feelings and actual behavior is, in itself, significant assessment information.

Though peer appraisal and self-report techniques are useful for understanding students better and guiding their learning, development, and adjustment, the results should not be used for marking and reporting or in any manner that interferes with honest responses. The students must be convinced that it is in their own best interests to respond as accurately and frankly as possible. Teachers who have good relations with their students and who have consistently emphasized the positive values of the assessment information should have no difficulty obtaining the students' cooperation in these techniques. When only group results are needed, the students can, of course, respond anonymously.

PEER APPRAISAL

In some instances, it is possible to have students rate their peers on the same rating device used by the teacher. At the conclusion of a student's oral report before the class, for example, the other students could rate the performance on a standard rating form. The average of these ratings is a good indication of how the group felt about the student's performance. Except for oral reports, speeches, demonstrations, and similar situations in which one individual performs at a time, however, the usual rating procedures are seldom feasible with students. If we ask students to rate their classmates on a series of personal–social characteristics, each student will be required to fill out 30 or more rating forms. This becomes so cumbersome and time consuming that we can hardly expect the ratings to be diligently made. When peer ratings and other methods of peer appraisal are used, we must depend on greatly simplified procedures. Some of the techniques are so simple that they can be used effectively with students at the primary school level. The guess-who technique is an example of this type of measure.

Guess-Who Technique

One of the simplest methods of obtaining peer judgments is by means of the guess-who technique. With this procedure, each student is presented with a series of brief behavior descriptions and asked to name those students who best fit each description. The descriptions may be limited to positive characteristics, or they may also include negative behaviors. The following items, taken from a form for assessing sociability, are typical of the types of positive and negative descriptions used.

1. Here is someone who is always friendly.
2. Here is someone who is never friendly.

Some teachers prefer to use only the positive behavior descriptions because of the possible harmful effects of negative nominations on group morale. Teachers must make this decision for themselves, however, because they are the only ones who can determine what the effects might be on their students. When good relations have been established among students and between teacher and students, this is not likely to be a problem.

When in doubt, however, it is usually better to sacrifice part of the assessment data than to disrupt the morale of the class.

In naming persons for each behavior description, the students are usually permitted to name as few or as many as they wish. Directions and sample items from a form for assessing concern for others are shown in Figure 13.2. The directions and behavior descriptions must, of course, be adapted to the students' age level. With very young students, the technique can be presented as a guessing game, with the items stated as follows: "Here is someone who talks a lot—guess who?" When the technique is used with older students, the guess-who aspect is dropped, and the students are merely told to write the names of those who best fit each behavior description.

The guess-who technique is based on the nomination method of obtaining peer ratings and is scored by simply counting the number of mentions each student receives on each description. If both positive and negative descriptions are used, such as friendly and unfriendly, the number of negative mentions on each characteristic is subtracted from the number of positive mentions. For example, 12 mentions as being friendly and 2 mentions of being unfriendly would result in a score of 10 on friendliness. The pattern of scores indicates each student's reputation in the peer group. This may not completely

---

Directions: Listed below are descriptions of what some students in this room are like. Read the descriptions and write the names of the students who *best fit* each description. You may write the names of anyone in this room, including those who are absent. Your choices will not be seen by anyone else. Give first name and initial of last name.

Remember!

1. Write the names of students in this room who best fit each description.
2. Write as many names as you wish for each description.
3. The same person may fit more than one description.
4. You should write the first name and initial of last name.
5. Your choices will *not be seen* by anyone except you and me (_teacher's name_).

Write the names below each description.

1. Here is someone who enjoys working and playing with others.

2. Here is someone who is willing to share materials with others.

3. Here is someone who is willing to help others with their schoolwork.

4. Here is someone who makes sure others are not left out of games.

5. Here is someone who encourages others to do well.

6. Here is someone who is kind to others who have a problem.

Figure 13.2
Guess-who form for assessing stuent's "concern for others"

1. Who is best able to state the problem clearly?

2. Who asks the best questions?

3. Who is most willing to seek more information?

4. Who comes up with the best suggestions?

5. Who is most willing to consider the different solutions?

6. Who comes up with the most complete plan?

Figure 13.3
Guess-who items for evaluating problem solving

agree with the teacher's impressions of the student, but it is significant information concerning personal–social development. In fact, one of the great values of this type of peer appraisal is that it makes the teacher aware of feelings and attitudes among students that were undetectable through direct observation.

This nominating method can be used to assess any aspect of personal–social development that students have had an adequate opportunity to observe. It is especially valuable for appraising personality characteristics, character traits, and social skills, but it is not limited to these areas. It is also useful in such areas as creativity, critical thinking, and problem solving. As with other assessment techniques, the items used in any particular guess-who form should be derived directly from the objectives to be assessed.

The items shown in Figure 13.3 were used to assess problem solving at the elementary school level and were derived directly from the stated objectives. More elaborate statements would, of course, be used at higher grade levels.

The main advantage of the guess-who technique is its usability. It can be administered in a relatively few minutes to students of all age levels, and scoring is a simple matter of counting the number of nominations received. Its main limitation is the lack of information it provides on the shy, withdrawn student. Such students are frequently overlooked when nomination methods are used. In effect, they have no reputation in their peer group and are simply ignored during the rating process.

SELF-REPORT TECHNIQUES

The oldest and best-known method of obtaining information directly from an individual is the personal interview. The face-to-face contact has several advantages as a self-report procedure. First, it is flexible. Interviewers can clarify questions, pursue promising lines of inquiry, and give the interviewees an opportunity to qualify or expand on their answers. Second, interviewers can observe interviewees, noting the amount of feeling attached to their answers, the topics on which they seem to be evasive, and the areas in which they are most expansive. Third, the interview makes possible not only collecting information from interviewees but also sharing information with them and, as in the counseling interview, using the face-to-face contact as a basis for therapy.

The personal interview would be an almost ideal method of obtaining self-report information from students except for two serious problems. It is extremely time consuming, and the information gained is not standard from one person to another. Therefore, in the interests of both feasibility and greater comparability of results, the self-report inventory or questionnaire is commonly used in place of the personal interview. An inventory consists of a standard set of questions pertaining to some particular area of behavior, administered and scored under standard conditions. It is a sort of standardized, written interview that enables the collection of a large amount of information quickly and that provides an objective summary of the data collected.

The effective use of self-report inventories assumes that individuals are both willing and able to report accurately. Responses can usually be easily faked if individuals want to present a distorted picture of themselves. Even when they want to be truthful, their recollections of past events may be inaccurate and their self-perceptions biased. These limitations can be partly offset by using self-report inventories only when students have little reason for faking, by emphasizing the value of frank responses for self-understanding and self-improvement, and by taking into account the possible presence of distortion when interpreting the results. When these inventories are used for assessing affective behavior in the classroom, it may be wise to have the students respond anonymously.

ATTITUDE MEASUREMENT

One of the areas in which self-report inventories are very useful in the classroom is attitude measurement. In some instances, attitudes may be important instructional outcomes in their own right (e.g., scientific attitude). In other cases, we may wish to obtain measures of students' attitudes toward certain classroom activities, the textbook, laboratory experiences, or our own instruction so that needed adjustments can be made. Some information concerning attitudes can, of course, be discovered by observation, but a more complete assessment requires that observation be supplemented by reports of the students' feelings and opinions.

A simple self-report device for measuring attitude is listing the activities or statements the students are expected to respond to and then devising some simple means of responding. The teacher-made form for measuring attitude toward mathematics activities at the lower primary level shown in Figure 13.4 illustrates this type of self-report form. The directions can be given orally and repeated for each activity as follows: "Put an X in the box under the face that tells how you feel about counting."

Another simple and widely used self-report method for measuring attitude is to list clearly favorable or unfavorable attitude statements and to ask the students to respond to each statement on the following 5-point scale: *strongly agree (SA), agree (A), undecided (U), disagree (D)*, and *strongly disagree (SD)*. This is called a *Likert scale,* named after its originator, and it is easily constructed and scored. The construction involves the following steps.

Things We Do	I like a lot 😊	It's OK 😐	Don't like it 🙁
Counting			
Adding			
Subtracting			
Story problems			
Math games			
Drawing shapes			
Measuring			
Telling time			
Making change			

Figure 13.4
Teacher-made form for measuring attitude toward mathematics activities at the lower primary level

1. Write a series of statements expressing positive and negative opinions toward some attitude object. For example, in preparing a scale to measure attitude toward school, a number of items such as the following might be written.
   • School is exciting.
   • School is a waste of time.
   To get a measure of student self-concept in mathematics, items such as the following might be used:
   • I am good at solving mathematics problems.
   • I usually cannot solve a new mathematics problem.
   A good pool of such items can be obtained by having the students in your class each write several positive and negative statements.

2. Select the best statements (at least 10), with a balance of positive and negative opinions and edit as needed.

3. List the statements, mixing up the positive and negative, and put the letters of the 5-point scale *(SA, A, U, D, SD)* to the left of each statement for easy marking. For students at the elementary level, it might be best to list the 5 points in multiple-choice fashion with the words written out (e.g., *strongly agree*).

4. Add the directions telling students how to mark their answers and include a key at the top of the page if letters are used for each statement *(SA, A, U, D, SD)*.

5. Some prefer to drop the *undecided* category so that respondents will be forced to show agreement or disagreement. Others have expanded the scale by adding the categories *slightly agree* and *slightly disagree*. Although such changes might be useful for some purposes, the 5-point scale is quite satisfactory for most uses.

A Likert scale for measuring attitude toward a science course is shown in Figure 13.5. By lengthening the instrument and preparing separate scales, it is possible to obtain a more detailed measure of attitude toward specific parts of the course (e.g., textbook, visual aids, tests, or laboratory work). Our example here simply shows the procedure and format.

The scoring of a Likert scale is based on assigning weights from 1 to 5 for each position on the scale. Favorable statements such as item 1 in Figure 13.5 are weighted 5, 4, 3, 2, 1, going from *SA* to *SD*. Unfavorable statements such as item 2 in Figure 13.5 have these weights reversed. Thus, they are weighted 1, 2, 3, 4, 5, going from *SA* to *SD*. An individual's total score on this type of scale is the sum of the scores on all items, with the higher score indicating a more favorable attitude.

In using attitude scales such as the one in Figure 13.5, it is usually best to ask for anonymous responses. This will indicate how the students in class feel about the course and, if separate scales are used, how they view the various activities in it. Such information is useful in making course revisions, and anonymous responses provide greater assurance that the replies will reflect the students' real feelings.

In interpreting the results of attitude scales, it is important to keep in mind that these are verbal expressions of feelings and opinions that individuals are willing to report. Good rapport with the students and a sincere belief on their part that frank responses are in their own best interests will help produce valid responses. Even under the most ideal conditions, however, it is wise to supplement attitudes determined by self-report methods with evidence from other sources. For example, if students have reported a favorable attitude toward other ethnic groups, guess-who data can be used to determine how

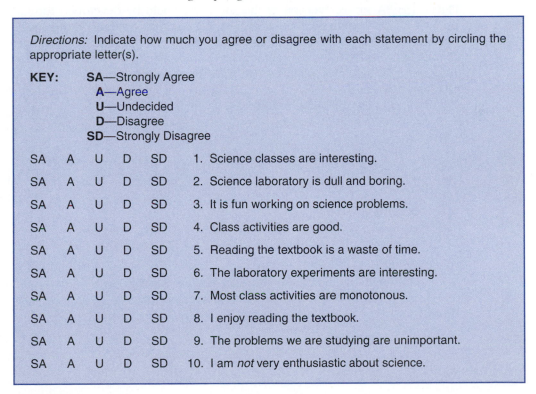

Figure 13.5
Illustrative Likert scale for measuring attitude toward a science course

frequently members of those groups are chosen for classroom activities. Similarly, if favorable attitudes toward students with disabilities are reported, this might be checked by observing how the students interact with students with disabilities in the classroom.

Published Attitude Scales

Numerous published attitude scales are available for school use. An example is the Estes Attitude Scales (grades 3 through 12), designed to measure attitude toward school subjects. At the secondary level, the scales measure attitude toward English, mathematics, reading, science, and social studies. Specialized scales for topics such as attitudes toward computers are also available. See the ERIC/ETS Test Locator Web site at http://ericae.net/testcol.htm to locate published attitude scales.

INTEREST INVENTORIES

As with attitude measurement, information about students' interests can be gathered from simple self-report devices prepared by the teacher. An interest inventory for reading, for example, might be no more than a list of types of books with the students asked to mark whether they like or dislike each type. An example of such an inventory is shown in Figure 13.6. A simpler version of this inventory could be developed for students at the primary level by using broader categories (e.g., animals, people, and places).

Various methods of responding can be used with informal interest inventories. The simple like–dislike response method can be expanded to more points, such as *like, indifferent, dislike* or *strongly like, like, indifferent, dislike, strongly dislike.* When there are relatively few items to respond to, the students can rank them in order from *like most* to *like least,* as in the following example.

Rank	Type of Reading
_____	Fiction
_____	Nonfiction
_____	Poetry
_____	Drama

A simple paired-comparison procedure also might be used to find out the students' reading preferences when there are relatively few items to respond to. Using these same four items, for example, we would have six pairs as follows:

_____ Fiction		_____ Drama	
_____ Nonfiction		_____ Drama	
_____ Fiction		_____ Nonfiction	
_____ Poetry		_____ Drama	
_____ Nonfiction		_____ Poetry	
_____ Poetry		_____ Fiction	

Reading Interest Inventory

Directions: For each type of book listed below, circle L if you *like* reading that type of book and circle D if you *dislike* reading that type. List any other types of books you like to read on the lines below.

L D 1. Adventure	L D 10. Mystery
L D 2. Animal	L D 11. Politics
L D 3. Art	L D 12. Psychology
L D 4. Biography	L D 13. Romance
L D 5. Boating	L D 14. Science
L D 6. Car racing	L D 15. Science fiction
L D 7. History	L D 16. Sociology
L D 8. Hobbies	L D 17. Sports
L D 9. Music	L D 18. Western

List any others here _____   _____   _____

_____   _____   _____   _____

Figure 13.6
Illustrative inventory for surveying reading interets

The students are instructed to mark the type of reading that they most prefer in each pair. A simple tally of the number of marks for each type of reading will indicate the students' relative preference.

Using any of the preceding response methods, we can obtain an interest score for each individual student, or we can combine the results for the entire class. Although students can fake responses to informal interest inventories, they seldom do. There are no right or wrong answers, and the results are usually used to plan classroom activities or to develop individual learning programs. In contrast with attitude scales, there is little reason to fear that one's responses to the inventory will influence grades.

Published Interest Inventories

There are a number of published interest inventories, but most of them have been designed for use in educational and vocational guidance. In some cases, however, the results can be used in planning more effective classroom instruction. Low interest scores in art and music, for example, might suggest that special activities are needed in these areas. Similarly, when a number of students have low interest scores in such areas as computation and science, a review of classroom activities and materials may be helpful. As with informal interest inventories, an individual's pattern of interests also may be useful in selecting reading material and planning individual learning programs.

One interest inventory that has been widely used at the high school and college levels is the Strong Interest Inventory (formerly known as the Strong-Campbell Interest

Inventory). This inventory consists of 291 items that are 5-point Likert scales measuring interest in occupations, work and leisure activities, and educational subjects The main part of the Strong Interest Inventory is scored and interpreted in terms of the similarity between an individual's expressed interests and those of persons engaged in particular occupations. The answers are placed on answer sheets or it can be taken on the Internet (available at http://www.cpp.com/products/strong/index.asp). The results are printed out on a profile that contains 244 occupational scales, 30 basic interest scales, and 6 personal style scales.

Another interest inventory that is often used in high schools is the Self-Directed Search (SDS) Career Explorer developed by John Holland and Amy Powell (available at http://www.self-directed-search.com/). The SDS Career Explorer is designed for use by middle school and high school students. Results are reported using a three-letter code developed by Holland to highlight the three of six possible general occupational themes that are of greatest interest according to the student's responses. The six dimensions are called *(R) realistic, (I) investigative, (A) artistic, (S) social, (E) enterprising,* and *(C) conventional.* For example, a student with highest scores on the realistic, enterprising, and investigative dimensions would have the *REI* letter code. Occupations where people frequently have a given three-letter code can be identified.

As with other self-report techniques, responses to published interest inventories can be easily faked. This is seldom a problem, however, where the emphasis is on self-understanding and educational and vocational planning. Students are anxious to find out about their interests, and the inventories consist of items that tend to be psychologically nonthreatening.

The instability of students' interests during elementary and high school years suggests that we should use interest inventories with extreme caution at these levels. Interests typically are not stable until approximately age 17. This does not mean that we must wait until this age to measure interests but that our interpretations must be highly tentative. In one sense, the instability of interests among children and adolescents is highly encouraging, for it indicates that our efforts to broaden and develop interests through school activities have some chance of succeeding. It is mainly when we are attempting to use them in career planning that stability poses a serious problem. For vocational decisions, we should rely most heavily on interest measures obtained during the last 2 years of high school and later.

Another precaution to keep in mind is not to confuse interest scores with measures of ability. A strong interest in science, for example, may or may not be accompanied by the verbal and numerical abilities needed to pursue successfully a course of study or a career in science. A scientific interest may be satisfied by collecting butterflies or by discovering a cure for cancer. Interest measures merely indicate whether an individual is apt to find satisfaction in a particular type of activity. Measures of ability determine the level of activity at which the individual can expect to function effectively.

PERSONALITY MEASURES

Classroom assessments of students' personality characteristics and adjustment problems are probably best made through the use of anecdotal records, rating scales, and other observational and peer appraisal techniques. However, there are two types of personality measures that classroom teachers should know about: personality inventories and projective techniques. These are briefly described for general information only. Using them effectively requires special training in counseling or clinical psychology.

Personality Inventories

The typical personality inventory presents students with a series of questions like those used in a psychiatric screening interview. For example, an inventory might include items such as the following:

> Do you daydream often?
> Are you frequently depressed?
> Do you have difficulty making friends?
> Do you usually feel tired?

Responses to such questions are commonly indicated by circling *yes, no,* or *?* (for uncertain). In some instances, a forced-choice procedure is used where the items are paired and the respondent must indicate which of the two statements is more characteristic of self.

Personality inventories vary considerably in the type of score provided. Some provide a single adjustment score, whereas others have separate scores for particular adjustment areas (e.g., health, social, or emotional) or for specific personality traits (e.g., self-confidence, sociability, or ascendancy). In general, research has not supported the validity of separate scores for assessing adjustment by means of inventories. Even using the total score for distinguishing between adjusted and maladjusted individuals is open to question.

All the limitations of the self-report technique tend to be accentuated in the personality inventory. First, the replies can be easily faked, and the threatening nature of many of the questions encourages presenting a distorted picture. Some inventories have "control keys" to detect faking, and others reduce faking by means of the forced-choice procedure, but it cannot be entirely eliminated. Second, in addition to honesty, accurate responses require good self-insight, but this is the very characteristic that poorly adjusted individuals are apt to lack, as they are prone to excessive use of adjustment mechanisms that tend to distort their perceptions of themselves and their relations with others. Finally, the ambiguity of the items is also likely to distort the results. Such questions as "Are you frequently depressed?" do not mean the same thing to all individuals. Although some ambiguity may be desirable in these inventories (as we are seeking perceptions rather than facts), words such as *frequently* have such a broad range of meanings that error is likely to be introduced. In addition to these technical shortcomings, there is the invasion-of-privacy issue. Congressional investigators, parents, and others have raised the question of the school's right to ask students such personal questions. Primarily because of the invasion-of-privacy issue, the routine use of personality and adjustment inventories in schools has declined to near zero.

Psychologically trained counselors may find personality inventories useful for beginning counseling interviews. The client can be asked to fill out the inventory early in the counseling session, and the response to individual items can serve as a starting point for discussion. Even if the responses are not completely frank or insightful, this can be dealt with in the counseling sessions. When used in this way, the inventory serves as an icebreaker. Invasion of privacy is not an issue here because the client has voluntarily sought out a relationship in which revelation of inner feelings is a known requisite for obtaining help.

Projective Techniques

Projective techniques are another method of assessing personal–social adjustment with which the classroom teacher should be familiar. Because they generally require clinical training to administer and interpret, it is not expected that teachers will use them directly. It is more than likely, however, that they will encounter some clinical reports of students that contain interpretations of projective test results.

In contrast with the highly structured personality inventory, projective techniques provide almost complete freedom of response. Typically, individuals are presented with a series of ambiguous forms or pictures and asked to describe what they see. Their responses are then analyzed to determine what content and structure they have "projected" onto the ambiguous stimuli.

Two of the best-known projective techniques are the Rorschach inkblot test and the Thematic Apperception Test (TAT). The Rorschach test consists of 10 inkblot figures on cards, and the TAT includes a series of pictures. These tests are usually administered to one individual at a time, and the individual's responses are recorded during the testing. Analysis of the results requires both systematic scoring and impressionistic interpretation, with emphasis on the total personality pattern revealed. Projective techniques are used primarily as part of a complete clinical study of those individuals who are experiencing adjustment difficulties.

SUMMARY

Observational techniques are especially useful in assessing performance skills and certain aspects of personal–social development. In addition, observation supplements and complements paper-and-pencil testing and performance-based assessments by indicating how students typically behave in natural situations.

The least structured observational technique is the anecdotal record: This is simply a method of recording factual descriptions of student behavior. To make anecdotal record keeping feasible, it is desirable to restrict observations at any given time to a few types of behavior or to a few students. Anecdotal records have the advantages of (a) describing behavior in natural settings, (b) highlighting evidence of exceptional behavior apt to be overlooked by other techniques, and (c) being usable with the very young. Their limitations are (a) the time and effort required to maintain an adequate record system, (b) the difficulty of writing objective descriptions of behavior, and (c) the problem of obtaining an adequate sample of behavior. These disadvantages can be minimized by following specific procedures for observing and recording the behavioral incidents. Suggestions for improving anecdotal records include (a) determining in advance what to observe, (b) analyzing observational records for possible sources of bias, (c) describing the setting in which the behavior occurred, (d) making the record as soon as possible after observing the behavior, (e) confining each anecdote to a single incident, (f) separating factual description from interpretation, (g) recording both positive and negative incidents, (h) collecting a number of anecdotes before drawing inferences, and (i) obtaining practice in observing and recording student behavior.

In some areas of learning and development, it is desirable to supplement the teacher's observations with information obtained directly from the students. We can ask the students to rate or judge their peers and to report on their own feelings, thoughts, and past behavior. Several peer appraisal methods and self-report techniques have been developed for this purpose.

Peer appraisal is especially useful in assessing personality characteristics, social relations skills, and other forms of typical behavior. The give-and-take of social interaction in the peer group provides students with a unique opportunity to observe and judge the behavior of their fellow students. Because these peer ratings are based on experiences that are seldom fully visible to adult observers, they are an important adjunct to teachers' observations.

Peer appraisal methods include the guess-who technique. This technique for obtaining peer ratings requires students to name those classmates who best fit each of a series of behavior descriptions. The number of nominations students receive on each characteristic indicates their reputation in the peer group. This nominating procedure can be used to assess any aspect of behavior that is observable to fellow students. The results can be used to rearrange groups, to improve the social adjustment of individual students, and to assess the influence of school practices on students' social relations.

Self-report techniques are used to obtain information that is inaccessible by other means, including reports on the student's attitudes, interests, and personal feelings. Such information can be obtained by means of a personal interview, but a self-report inventory is more commonly used. The inventory is a sort of standardized written interview that produces comparable results from one person to another. The effective use of self-report techniques assumes that the respondent is both willing and able to report accurately. Thus, special efforts must be made to ensure these conditions.

Attitude scales can be used to gather information concerning students' feelings and opinions toward various classroom activities, situations, groups, and special events. Interest inventories contribute to a better understanding of students' preferences and are useful in educational and vocational planning. Personality inventories and projective techniques aid in assessing students' personal–social adjustment but are not recommended for use by the classroom teacher.

Both peer ratings and self-report inventories can provide useful information for understanding students better and for guiding their learning, development, and adjustment. These purposes are best served, however, when this information is combined with test results, observational data, and other information concerning the students.

LEARNING EXERCISES

1. Observe a child at play and write an anecdotal record. Give both your descriptive account of the child's behavior and your interpretation of the behavior, but place these under separate headings.
2. What are the advantages and disadvantages of using observational techniques for assessing student learning?
3. Briefly describe the steps you would follow if you were going to have students help assess the effectiveness of their class discussion.
4. What types of behavior are best assessed by peer appraisal? What are some of the necessary precautions in using peer appraisal methods?
5. List several positive and negative statements that might be used on a guess-who form for assessing ability to work effectively in a group.
6. Describe the advantages and limitations of self-report inventories. What can be done to increase the validity of the results?
7. Write several statements that might be useful in a Likert-type attitude scale for assessing students' attitudes toward homework.
8. What are the advantages and disadvantages of using each of the following for assessing attitudes toward school?
   a. Attitude scale
   b. Teacher observation
   c. Guess-who technique
9. Why have so few interest inventories been developed for use at the elementary level? How might interest inventories contribute to the instructional program?
10. What types of peer appraisal and self-report methods might be used to determine whether ability grouping adversely affects student development? How would you develop each instrument?

FURTHER READING

Anastasi, A., & Urbina, S. (1997). *Psychological testing* (7th ed.). New York: Macmillan. Chapter 17, "Self-Report Inventories," and Chapter 18, "Measuring Interests, Values, and Attitudes," discuss the development and use of inventories and describe widely used instruments.

Boehm, A. E., & Weinberg, R. A. (1996). *The classroom observer: A guide to developing observation skills* (3rd ed.). New York: Teachers College Press. A brief guide to help preservice and in-service teachers make systematic observations of classroom situations and individual students at the preschool and grade school levels.

Cohen, D. H., Stern, V., & Balaban, N. (1996). *Observing and recording the behavior of young children* (4th ed.). New York: Teachers College Press. Describes methods of studying children in various classroom situations. Includes numerous checklists and examples for preschool and primary levels.

Cronbach, L. J. (1990). *Essentials of psychological testing* (4th ed.). New York: Harper & Row. See Chapter 12, "Interest Inventories"; Chapter 13, "General Problems in Studying Personality"; and Chapter 14, "Personality

Measurement Through Self-Report," for a comprehensive discussion of self-report measures, their validity, and the ethical issues involved.

Ebel, R. L., & Frisbie, D. A. (1991). *Essentials of educational measurement* (5th ed.). Englewood Cliffs, NJ: Prentice Hall. Chapter 14, "Nontest and Informal Evaluation Methods," describes the use of observational techniques and rating scales.

Harmon, L. W. (1992). Interest measurement. In M. C. Alkin, (Ed.), *Encyclopedia of educational research* (6th ed., vol. 2). New York: Macmillan. Provides an overview of the measurement of interests and the use of interest measurement in education.

Kifer, E. (1992). Attitude measurement. In M. C. Alkin (Ed.), *Encyclopedia of educational research* (6th ed., vol. 1). New York: Macmillan. Describes the techniques of attitude measurement and discusses the validity and reliability of attitude measures.

Krug, S. E. (1992). Personality measurement. In M. C. Alkin (Ed.), *Encyclopedia of educational research* (6th ed., vol. 3). New York: Macmillan. Provides an introduction to personality measurement.

Mehrens, W. A., & Lehmann, I. J. (1987). *Using standardized tests in education* (4th ed.). New York:

Longman. See Chapter 9, "Interest, Personality, and Attitude Inventories," for a discussion of the problems of using self-report inventories and a description of representative instruments.

Mueller, D. J. (1986). *Measuring social attitudes: A handbook for researchers and practitioners.* New York: Teachers College Press. Describes and illustrates various methods of attitude scale construction. Includes an annotated bibliography of various sources of attitude scales.

14

ASSEMBLING, ADMINISTERING, AND APPRAISING CLASSROOM TESTS AND ASSESSMENTS

Care in preparing an assessment plan and constructing relevant test items and assessment tasks should be followed by similar care in reviewing and editing the items and tasks, preparing clear directions, and administering and appraising the results. Classroom assessments also can be improved by using simple methods to analyze student responses and by building a file of effective items and tasks.

Effective classroom assessment begins with an assessment plan that specifically describes the instructional objectives and content to be measured and the relative emphasis to be given to each intended learning outcome. This is followed by the selection of the most appropriate item and task formats (e.g., multiple choice, essay, or hands-on performance assessment) and the preparation of items and tasks that are relevant to the learning outcomes specified in the plan. These steps have received considerable attention in the preceding chapters because they are crucial to the validity of the assessment. The only way we can ensure that a classroom test will serve its intended purpose is to identify the learning outcomes we want to measure and then to construct test items and assessment tasks that call forth the specific performance described in the learning outcomes. We must also assemble the items and tasks, prepare directions, administer the instrument, score the student responses, and interpret and appraise the results.

Our goal throughout the preparation and use of classroom tests and assessments is to obtain valid evidence of student learning. In the final analysis, valid measurement of achievement is the product of a systematically controlled series of steps, beginning with the identification of instructional objectives and ending with the scoring and interpretation of results. Although validity is built in during the construction of the items and tasks, systematic procedures of assembly, administration, and scoring will provide greater assurance that the items and tasks will function as intended. Appraising the test items and assessment tasks after they have been administered can also help improve their quality. Procedures for analyzing student responses provide information for evaluating the effectiveness of each item or task and for detecting weaknesses that should be corrected. This information is useful when reviewing the results with students, and it is indispensable when building a file of high-quality items and tasks for future use.

Performance-based assessments typically involve a relatively small number of tasks because each task requires a substantial amount of time. Thus, some of the issues addressed in this chapter apply more to classroom tests that involve a substantial number of items and/or restricted response tasks. For example, if a single extended-response, performance-based task is to be administered, the issues of test assembly and some aspects of item analysis are not relevant. Hence, in this chapter we focus on classroom tests with a substantial number of items and make note where the same or related considerations apply to performance-based assessments.

ASSEMBLING THE CLASSROOM TEST

The preparation of items for use in a test is greatly facilitated if the items are properly recorded, if they are written at least several days before they are to be used, and if extra items are constructed.

Recording Test Items

When constructing the test items, it is desirable to write each one in a form that makes it possible to easily address and retrieve individual items. The items may be written into a word-processing program or onto index cards. In addition to the test item, the item record should contain information concerning the instructional objective, the specific learning outcome, and the content measured by the item. A space should also be reserved for item-analysis information to allow room to record the data each time the item is used. An example of this type of informational record is presented later in the chapter in relationship to the discussion of item analysis (Figure 14.2).

Item records, whether in the form of separate sheets in a standard word-processing system or physical cards, provide flexibility. As the items are reviewed and edited, they can be eliminated, added, or revised with little difficulty. The same holds true when arranging the items for the test: They can be arranged and rearranged merely by sorting the records. The flexibility of this recording system also makes it easy to add the items to a computer item bank. Specialized software for item writing and item banks is available, but functions of maintaining a bank of items can also be readily handled by a standard word-processing system.

Reviewing Test Items and Assessment Tasks

No matter how carefully items or tasks have been prepared, defects inadvertently creep in during construction. As we concentrate on the clarity and conciseness of a question, a verbal clue slips in unnoticed. As we attempt to construct more challenging items, we unwittingly introduce some ambiguity. As we rework a multiple-choice item to make the incorrect choices more plausible, the behavior called forth by the item is unintentionally modified. As we attempt to increase the authenticity of a task for problems faced outside the classroom, we introduce unintended reliance on access to resources that put students from families with limited resources at an unfair disadvantage. In short, we focus so closely on some aspects of item or task construction that we overlook others. This results in an accumulation of unwanted errors that may distort the function of the item or task. Such technical defects can be most easily detected by (a) reviewing the items and tasks after they have been set aside for a few days, and (b) asking a fellow teacher to review and criticize them.

In reviewing test items and tasks, we should try to view them from the student's perspective as well as from that of the teacher. From these two vantage points, each item or task should be read carefully and its effectiveness judged. The following questions will help you analyze the quality of each item or task.

1. Is the format appropriate for the learning outcome being measured? If the learning outcome calls for the definition of a term, for example, then a supply-type item (e.g., short-answer item) would be appropriate and a selection-type item (e.g., multiple choice) would be clearly inappropriate. If the learning outcome calls for the ability to collect, organize, integrate, and present information in the form of a coherent argument, then nothing short of a performance-based task will suffice. On the other hand, if the intended outcome was simply the identification of the correct definition, then a selection-type item would be adequate. Thus, the first step is to check whether the format is suitable for the type of student performance described in the testing and assessment plan. The action verb in the statement of each specific learning outcome (e.g., *defines, describes, identifies*) indicates which item format is more appropriate.

2. Does the knowledge, understanding, or thinking skill called forth by the item or task match the specific learning outcome and subject-matter content being measured? When a table of specifications has been used as a basis for constructing items and tasks, this is merely a matter of checking to see whether the item or task is still relevant to the same cell in the table. If, for example, an item's functioning content has shifted during construction, the item should be either modified so that it serves its original purpose or reclassified in light of the new purpose. In any case, the response called forth by an item or task should agree with the purpose for which it is to be used.

3. Is the point of the item or task clear? A careful review of items and tasks often reveals ambiguity, inappropriate vocabulary, and awkward sentence structure that were overlooked during their construction. Returning to items and tasks after they have been set aside for a few days provides a fresh outlook that makes such defects more apparent. The difficulty of the vocabulary and the complexity of the sentence structure must, of course, be judged in terms of the students' maturity level. At all levels, however, ambiguity should be removed. In its final form, each item or task should be so clearly worded that all students understand its meaning. The quality of student responses should be determined solely by whether they possess the knowledge, understanding, or skill being measured.

4. Is the item or task free from excessive verbiage? Often, items become excessively wordy because of awkward sentence structure or the inclusion of nonfunctional material. Some teachers justify the use of an item by including a statement or two concerning the problem's importance. Others expand a simple question into an elaborate story situation to make the item more interesting. Although adding such nonfunctional material may be useful in some instances, items and tasks are generally more effective when the problem is stated as concisely as possible. When reviewing items, the content of each item should be analyzed to determine the functional elements leading to the correct response. If there are any elements that the students may disregard entirely and still respond correctly, they probably should be removed. See the "Guidelines" box.

5. **Does the item have an answer that would be agreed on by experts? How well would experts agree about the degree of excellence of task performances?** This is seldom a problem with factual material, which usually can be judged as correct or incorrect. It is more of a problem with selection-type items that ask for the best reason, the best method, or the best interpretation. The problem is greatest with tasks requiring extended performances where qualified judges may differ in their evaluation of performances. If experts agree on the best response, fine, but do not include items that require students to endorse someone's unsupported opinion (even if it happens to be yours), and do not evaluate performances on tasks simply in terms of your personal preferences.

6. Is the item or task free from technical errors and irrelevant clues? The checklists for reviewing each of the item types, presented in Chapters 7 through 11, list points to consider in searching out technical errors and irrelevant clues. As noted earlier, an irrelevant clue for a selection-type item is any element that leads the poor achiever to the correct answer and thereby prevents the item from functioning as intended. These include (a) grammatical inconsistencies, (b) verbal associations, (c) specific determiners (e.g., words such as *always* and *never*), and (d) some mechanical features, such as correct statements tending to be longer than incorrect ones. Most of these clues can be removed merely by trying to detect them during the item review. They somehow seem more obvious after the items have been set aside for a while.

7. Is the item or task free from racial, ethnic, and gender bias? A final check should be made to make certain that the vocabulary and problem situation in each item or task would be acceptable to the members of all groups and would have a similar meaning to them. An effort should be made to remove any type of stereotyping, such as always portraying minorities in subservient roles, women in homemaking roles, and the like. A judicious and balanced use of different roles for minorities and males and females should contribute to more effective assessment.

When possible, it can be useful to get fellow teachers to review your test items and assessment tasks. With right–wrong or best-answer items, they should be asked to read each item, indicate the answer, and note any technical defects. If an answer does not agree with the key, it may be because the question is ambiguous. Asking another teacher to "think out loud" when deciding on the answer will usually reveal the misinterpretation of the question and the source of the ambiguity. For performance tasks requiring extended

GUIDELINES

Reviewing and Revising Test Items

1. Matching the learning outcome.
Specific Learning Outcome: Identifies the use of weather instruments.
Item: Describe how the hygrometer works.
Improved: The hygrometer is used to measure
A. Air pressure.
*B. Humidity.
C. Rainfall.
D. Wind velocity.

2. Clarifying the point of the item and the desired response.
Item: Earthquakes are detected by
_____ .

Improved: Earthquakes are detected by an instrument called a(n)
_____ (seismograph).

3. Removing excessive verbiage from multiple-choice stems.
Item: In which one of the following regions of the United States can we expect annual rainfall to be the greatest?
Improved: In which region of the Uniited States is yearly rainfall greatest?
A. Midwest
B. New England
*C. Pacific Northwest
D. Southwest

4. Removing excessive verbiage from multiple-choice alternatives.
Item: In which direction do tornadoes move?
*A. They move toward the Northeast.
B. They move toward the Northwest.
C. They move toward the Southeast.
D. They move toward the Southwest.
Improved: Tornadoes move toward the
*A. Northeast.
B. Northwest.
C. Southeast.
D. Southwest.

5. Keeping the reading level low.
Item: *T F There is a dearth of information concerning the possibility that life exists on Mars.
Improved: *T F There is a lack of information concerning life on Mars.

6. Removing verbal clues.
Item: Evaporation is shown by water changing to
A. Dew.
B. Ice.
*C. Water vapor.
Improved: Evaporation is shown by water changing to
A. Dew.
B. Ice.
*C. Steam.

responses, reviewers identify the nature of the performances that they would expect and the qualities they would look for in evaluating the performances as well as possible defects in the task itself. This is how other persons can be most useful. Reviewers will be less helpful in evaluating the types of responses called forth by the items because this requires a knowledge of what the students have been taught. Only the teacher who prepared the item or task knows for sure whether it is likely to measure understanding or merely the recall of a previously learned response.

When items or tasks have been revised and those to be included in the test or assessment have been tentatively selected, ask the following questions.

1. Does the set of items and tasks measure a representative sample of the learning outcomes and course content included in the assessment plan?
2. Are there enough items or tasks for each interpretation to be made?
3. Is the difficulty of the items and tasks appropriate for the measurement purpose and for the students for whom the test or assessment is intended?
4. Are the test items free from overlapping so that the information in one does not provide a clue to the answer in another?

The first question can be answered by comparing the final selection of items and tasks with the table of specifications or other assessment plan. Answers to the last three are determined by reviewing the items and tasks in each content area and as a total set. Affirmative answers to these questions mean the items and tasks are ready to be assembled for administration. See the box "Review of Test Items Selected from Item Banks" for guidelines on selecting items from published sources.

Arranging Items in the Test

There are various methods of grouping items in an achievement test, and the method will vary somewhat depending on the use of the results. For most classroom purposes, the items can be arranged by a systematic consideration of (a) the types of items used, (b) the learning outcomes measured, (c) the difficulty of the items, and (d) the subject matter measured.

First, the items should be arranged in sections by item type. That is, all true–false items should be grouped together, then all matching items, then all multiple-choice items, and so on. This arrangement requires the fewest sets of directions, it is the easiest for the students because they can retain the same mental set throughout each section, and it greatly facilitates scoring. When two or more item types are included in a test, there is also some advantage in keeping the simpler item types together and placing the more complex ones in the test, as follows:

1. True–false or alternative-response items
2. Matching items
3. Short-answer items
4. Multiple-choice items
5. Interpretive exercises
6. Restricted-response essay questions
7. Restricted-response performance tasks

Extended-response essay questions and performance tasks usually take enough time that they would be administered alone. If combined with some of the other types of items and tasks listed previously, the extended-response tasks should come last. It is not expected that all item types will appear in the same test. Seldom are more than a few types used, but this is the general order.

Arranging the sections of the test in this order produces a sequence that roughly approximates the complexity of the learning outcomes measured, ranging from the simple to the complex. It is then merely a matter of grouping the items within each item type. For this purpose, items that measure similar outcomes should be placed together and then

---

Review of Test Items Selected from Item Banks

Test items selected from workbooks, teacher guides, instructor manuals, and item banks are seldom appropriate for use without modification. Thus, before they are used in a classroom test, they should be screened and modified to fit the local instructional program. Both the checklists for reviewing test items and tasks, presented in Chapters 7 through 11, and the list of review questions in this chapter are guides for this purpose. Our aim when selecting items for classroom use should be the same as when constructing them. We want the items to be both technically sound and relevant to what has been taught during the instruction.

---

arranged in order of ascending difficulty. For example, the items in the multiple-choice section might be arranged in the following order: (a) knowledge of terms, (b) knowledge of specific facts, (c) knowledge of principles, and (d) application of principles. Keeping together items that measure similar outcomes is especially helpful in determining the types of learning outcomes causing students the greatest difficulty.

If, for any reason, it is not feasible to group the items by the learning outcomes measured, then it is still desirable to arrange them in order of increasing difficulty. Beginning with the easiest items and proceeding gradually to the most difficult has a motivating effect on students. Also, encountering difficult items early in the test often causes students to spend a disproportionate amount of time on such items. If the test is long, they may be forced to omit later questions that they could easily have answered.

With the items classified by item type, the sections of the test and the items within each section can be arranged in order of increasing difficulty. Some shifts in the first four item types may be warranted by the difficulty of the items used, but the interpretive exercises and essay items certainly should be last.

In constructing classroom achievement tests, there is little to be gained by grouping test items according to content. When it appears desirable to do so, such as in separating historical periods, these divisions should be kept to a minimum.

Extended-response essay questions, by their very nature, require separate administration. Performance-based tasks or oral presentations requiring extended time or access to such resources as the library, laboratory equipment, or a computer for construction of a response also obviously need to be assigned as separate units rather than as part of a classroom test.

To summarize, the most effective method for organizing items in the typical classroom test is to (a) form sections by item type, (b) group the items within each section by the learning outcomes measured, and (c) arrange both the sections and the items within sections in an ascending order of difficulty. Use subject-matter groupings only when needed for some specific purpose.

Preparing Directions for the Test or Assessment

Teachers sometimes devote considerable time and attention to the construction and assembly of test items or a challenging performance-based assessment and then dash off directions with very little thought. In fact, many teachers include no written directions with their tests, assuming either that the items are self-explanatory or that the students are conditioned to answering the types of items used in the test. Some teachers also use oral directions, but they frequently leave much to be desired. Whether written, oral, or both, the directions should include at least the following points (see Gronlund, 2005).

1. Purpose of the test or assessment
2. Time allowed for completing the test or performing the task
3. Directions for responding
4. How to record the answers
5. What to do about guessing for selection-type test items
6. The basis for scoring open-ended or extended responses

The amount of detail for each of these points depends mainly on the students' age level, the comprehensiveness of the test or assessment, the complexity of the items or tasks, and the students' experience with the testing or assessment procedure used. Using new item types and separate answer sheets, for example, requires much more detailed directions than do familiar items requiring students merely to circle or underline the answer.

Purpose of the Test or Assessment.   The purpose of the test or assessment is usually indicated when the test is announced or at the beginning of the semester when the evaluation procedures are described as a part of the general orientation to the course. Should there be any doubt whether the purpose is clear to all students, however, it could be explained again at the time of testing or assessment. This is usually done orally. The only time a statement of the purpose of the test or assessment needs to be included in the written directions is when it is to be administered to several sections taught by different teachers. Then a written statement of purpose ensures greater uniformity.

Time Allowed for Completing the Test or Performing the Task.   It is helpful to tell the students how much time they will have for the whole test or performance task and how to distribute their time among the parts. When essay questions are included, it is also good to indicate approximately how much time should be allotted to each question. This enables the students to use their time most effectively and prevents less able students from spending too much time on questions that are particularly difficult for them.

Classroom tests or assessments of achievement should generally have liberal time allowances. With a few exceptions, such as measures of fluency or special computational skills, speed is not important. Our main concern is the level of achievement each student has attained. Were it not for practical considerations like the length of class periods and the pressure of other school activities, there would be no need for any time limits with most classroom achievement tests or assessment tasks.

Judging the amount of time that students will need to complete a given test or assessment task is not simple. It depends on the types of items and tasks used, the age and ability of the students, and the complexity of the learning outcomes measured. As a rough guide, the average high school student should be able to answer two true–false items, one multiple-choice item, or one short-answer item per minute of testing time. Interpretive test items take much more time; the exact amount depends on the length and complexity of the introductory materials. The time required for essay questions and other performance-based assessment tasks can vary anywhere from a few minutes each to several class periods. Also, elementary school students generally require more time per item than high school students, and reading skill is an important determiner of the amount of time needed by a specific group. Experienced teachers familiar with the ability and work habits of a given group of students are in the best position to judge time allotments. It is better to err in the direction of allotting too much time than to deprive some of the slower students from demonstrating their maximum levels of achievement.

Directions for Responding.   The directions for each section of the test should indicate the basis for selecting or supplying the answers. With true–false, matching, and multiple-choice items, this part of the directions can be relatively simple. For example, the statement, "Select the choice that best completes the statement or answers the question" might be sufficient for multiple-choice items. When interpretive exercises are used, however, more detailed directions are necessary because the basis for the response is much more complex. The directions must clearly indicate the type of interpretation expected. As stated in Chapter 9, each interpretive exercise usually requires its own directions.

It is sometimes good to include sample test items correctly marked so that students can check their understanding of the basis for answering. This practice is especially helpful to elementary school students and to students at other levels when complex item types are used.

As noted earlier, essay questions and other performance-based assessment tasks frequently require special directions concerning the type of response expected. If the selection and organization of ideas are emphasized, for example, this should be indicated to the students so that they have a more adequate basis for responding.

Procedure for Recording Answers.   Answers may be recorded on the test form itself or on separate answer sheets. If the test is short, the number of students taking the test is small, or the students are relatively young, then answers are generally recorded directly on the test paper. For most other situations, separate answer sheets are preferred because they reduce the time needed for scoring, and they make it possible to use the test papers over again. The latter feature is especially useful when the test is to be given to students in different sections of the same course.

Directions for recording the answer on the test paper itself can be relatively simple. With selection items, it is merely a matter of instructing the students to circle, underline, or check the letter indicating the correct answer. For students in the primary grades, it is usually better to ask them to mark the answer directly by drawing a line under it. With supply items, the directions should indicate where to put the answer and the units in which it is to be expressed if the answer is numerical.

Separate answer sheets are easily constructed, and the directions for their use can be placed on the test paper or on the answer sheet itself. A common type of teacher-made sheet is shown in Figure 14.1. The directions on this sheet are rather general, as they must cover instructions for recording various types of answers. Students are instructed to cross out rather than circle the letters indicating the correct answers to facilitate scoring with a stencil key. Circled letters cannot be readily seen through holes in a stencil.

Special answer sheets for machine scoring can be used with classroom tests, but there is no advantage in using them unless machine scoring facilities are readily available and the number of papers to be scored warrants the expense. When machine scoring is used, special directions should be obtained from the company supplying the scoring service.

Course _____   Name _____

Section _____   Date _____

Test _____   Score: Part I _____

Part II _____

Total _____

Directions: Read all directions on the test paper carefully and follow them exactly. For each test item, indicate your answer on this sheet by crossing out the appropriate letter (X) or filling in the appropriate blank. Be sure that the number on the answer sheet is the same as the number of the test item your are answering.

True–False		**Multiple-Choice**		**Short Answer**	
Item	*Answer*	*Item*	*Answer*	*Item*	*Answer*
1	T F	21	A B C D E	41	_____
2	T F	22	A B C D E	42	_____
3	T F	23	A B C D E	43	_____
4	T F	24	A B C D E	44	_____

Figure 14.1
Top portion of a teacher-made answer sheet

What to Do About Guessing for Selection-Type Items.   When selection-type items are used, the directions should tell students what to do when they are uncertain of the answer. Should they guess or omit the item? If no instructions are given on this point, the bold students will guess freely, whereas others will answer only those items of which they are fairly certain. The bold students will select some correct answers just by lucky guesses, and thus their scores will be higher than they should be. On the other hand, if the students are instructed "Do not guess" or "Answer only those items of which you are certain," the more timid students will omit many items they could answer correctly. Such students are not very certain about anything, which prevents them from responding even when they are reasonably sure of the answers. With these directions, the bold students will continue to guess, although possibly not quite so wildly.

As Cronbach (1990) pointed out, the tendency to guess or not to guess when in doubt about an item is determined by personality factors and cannot be entirely eliminated by directions that caution against guessing or that promise penalties to those who do guess. The only way to eliminate variations in the tendency to guess is to instruct students to answer every item. When this is done, no student is given a special advantage, and it is unnecessary to correct for guessing in the scoring. Directions such as the following are usually sufficient to communicate this to the students: "Because your score is the number right, be sure to answer every item."

Some teachers object to such directions on the grounds that encouraging guessing is undesirable from an educational standpoint. Most responses to doubtful items are not wild guesses, however, but are guided by some information and understanding. In this respect, they are not too different from the informed guesses we make when we predict weather, judge the possible consequences of a decision, or choose one course of action over another. Problem solving always involves a certain amount of this type of informed guessing.

A more defensible objection to directions that encourage guessing is that the chance errors introduced into the test scores lower the accuracy of measurement. Although this is certainly objectionable, it probably has less influence on the validity of the results than does the systematic advantage given to the bold guessers by the "do not guess" directions.

For liberally timed classroom tests, the "answer every item" directions are favored. For speed tests and when teachers want to discourage guessing, however, directions such as the following are a good compromise: "Answer all items for which you can find some reasonable basis for answering, even though you are not completely sure of the answer. Do not guess wildly, though, because there will be a correction for guessing."

The Basis for Scoring Open-Ended or Extended Responses.   For tasks requiring extended or open-ended written responses, it is important to tell students the basis for scoring. If there are several essay questions, for example, the number of points possible for the response to each question should be indicated. The importance attached to factors such as factual accuracy, organization, comprehensiveness, persuasiveness, and originality can be indicated. Students should also be informed if their responses will be graded for mechanics (see the "Guidelines" box).

GUIDELINES

Helping Students Prepare for Tests Assessments

General Preparation

1. Suggest ways of studying.
2. Give practice tasks like those to be used.
3. Teach test-taking skills.
4. Teach how to write well-organized essay answers.
5. Stress the value of tests and assessments for improving learning.

Preparation for Each Test or Assessment

1. Announce in advance when the test or assessment will be given.
2. Describe the conditions of administration (e.g., 1-hour closed book).
3. Describe the length and the types of items or tasks to be used (20 multiple-choice, three essay items, or one extended-response performance task).
4. Describe the content and type of performance to be covered (a table of specifications is useful for this).
5. Describe how the test or assessment will be scored and how the results will be used.
6. Give the students sample items and tasks similar to those to be used (use a short practice test or present items orally and discuss responses).
7. Relieve anxiety by using a positive approach in describing the test or assessment and its usefulness.

Reproducing the Test

In preparing the test materials for reproduction, it is important that the items be spaced and arranged so that they can be read, answered, and scored with the least amount of difficulty. Cramming too many test items onto a page is poor economy. What little paper is saved will not make up for the time and confusion that results during the administration and scoring of the test.

All test items should have generous borders. Multiple-choice items should have the alternatives listed in a vertical column beneath the stem of the item rather than across the page. Items should not be split, with parts of the item on two different pages. With interpretive exercises, the introductory materials can sometimes be placed on a facing page or separate sheet, with all the items referring to it on a single page.

Unless a separate answer sheet is used, the space for answering should be down one side of the page, preferably the left. The most convenient method of response is circling the letter of the correct answer. With this arrangement, scoring is simply a matter of placing a strip scoring key beside the column of answers.

Test items should be numbered consecutively throughout the test. Each test item will need to be identified during discussion of the test and for other purposes, such as item analysis. When separate answer sheets are used, consecutive numbering is, of course, indispensable.

It is desirable to proofread the entire test or assessment before it is administered. Charts, graphs, and other pictorial material must be checked to ensure that the reproduction has been accurate and the details are clear.

ADMINISTERING AND SCORING CLASSROOM TESTS AND ASSESSMENTS

The same care that went into the preparation of the test or assessment should be carried over into its administration and scoring. Here we are concerned with (a) providing optimum conditions for obtaining the students' responses, and (b) selecting convenient and accurate procedures for scoring the results.

Administration

The guiding principle in administering any classroom test or assessment is that all students must be given a fair chance to demonstrate their achievement of the learning outcomes being measured. This means a physical and psychological environment conducive to their best efforts and the control of factors that might interfere with valid measurement.

Physical conditions such as adequate work space, quiet, proper light and ventilation, and comfortable temperature are sufficiently familiar to teachers to warrant little attention here. Of greater importance but frequently neglected are the psychological conditions influencing results. Students will not perform at their best if they are tense and anxious during testing. The following may create excessive test anxiety.

1. Threatening students with tests if they do not behave
2. Warning students to do their best "because this test is important"
3. Telling students they must work fast in order to finish on time
4. Threatening dire consequences if they fail

The antidote to test anxiety is to convey to the students, by both word and deed, that the test and assessment results are to be used to help them improve their learning. They also should be reassured that the time limits are adequate to allow them to complete the test or assessment tasks. This, of course, assumes that the test and assessment results will be used to improve learning and that the time limits are adequate.

The time of testing can also influence the results. If tests are administered just before the "big game" or the "big dance," the results may not be representative. Furthermore, for some students, fatigue, the onset of illness, or worry about a particular problem may prevent maximum performance. Arranging the time of testing accordingly and permitting its postponement when appropriate can enhance the validity of results.

Actual administration is relatively simple because a properly prepared test or assessment is practically self-administering. Oral directions, if used, should be presented clearly. Any sample problems or illustrations put on the board should be kept brief and simple. Beyond this, suggestions for administration consist mainly of things to avoid.

1. **Do not talk unnecessarily before letting students start working.** When a teacher announces that there will be "a full 40 minutes" to complete the test and then talks for the first 10 minutes, students feel that they are being unfairly deprived of testing time. Besides, just before a test is no time to make assignments, admonish the class, or introduce next week's topic. Students are mentally set for the test and will ignore anything not pertaining to the test for fear it will hinder their recall of information needed to answer the questions. Thus, the well-intentioned remarks merely increase anxiety toward the test and create hostility toward the teacher.

2. **Keep interruptions to a minimum.** At times, a student will ask to have an ambiguous item clarified, and it may be beneficial to explain the item to the entire group at the same time. Such interruptions are necessary but should be kept to a minimum. All other distractions outside and inside the classroom should, of course, also be eliminated when possible. It is sometimes helpful to hang a "Do not disturb—TESTING" sign outside the door.

3. **Avoid giving hints to students who ask about individual items.** If the item is ambiguous, it should be clarified for the entire group, as indicated earlier. If it is not ambiguous, refrain from helping the student answer it. Refraining from giving hints to students who ask for help is especially difficult for beginning teachers; but giving unfair aid to some students (the bold, the apple polishers, and so on) decreases the validity of the results and lowers class morale.

4. **Discourage cheating, if necessary.** When there is good teacher–student rapport and the students view tests as helpful rather than harmful, cheating is usually not a problem. Under other conditions, however, it might be necessary to discourage cheating by special seating arrangements and careful supervision. Receiving unauthorized help from other students during a test has the same deleterious effect on validity and class morale as does receiving special hints from the teacher. We are interested in students doing their best; but

GUIDELINES

Steps to Prevent Cheating

1. Take special precautions to keep the test secure during preparation, storage, and administration.
2. Have students clear off the tops of their desks (for adequate work space and to prevent use of notes).
3. If scratch paper is used (e.g., for math problems), have it turned in with the test.
4. Proctor the testing session carefully (e.g., walk around the room periodically and observe how the students are doing).
5. Use special seating arrangements, if possible (e.g., leave an empty row of seats between students).
6. Use two forms of the test and give a different form to each row of students (for this purpose, use the same test but simply rearrange the order of the items for the second form).
7. Prepare tests that students will view as relevant, fair, and useful.
8. Create and maintain a positive attitude concerning the value of tests for improving learning.

for valid results, their scores must be based on their own unaided efforts. See the "Guidelines" box.

Scoring the Test

Procedures for scoring performance-based assessments were described in Chapter 11. Here we discuss scoring objective items.

If the students' answers are recorded on the test paper itself, a scoring key can be made by marking the correct answers on a blank copy of the test. Scoring then is simply a matter of comparing the columns of answers on this master copy with the columns of answers on each student's paper. A strip key, which consists merely of strips of paper on which the columns of answers are recorded, may also be used if more convenient. These can easily be prepared by cutting the columns of answers from the master copy of the test and mounting them on strips of cardboard cut from manila folders.

When separate answer sheets are used, a scoring stencil is most convenient. This is a blank answer sheet with holes punched where the correct answers should appear. The stencil is laid over each answer sheet, and the number of marks appearing through the holes are counted. When this type of scoring procedure is used, each test paper should also be scanned to make certain that only one answer was marked for each item. Any item containing more than one answer should be eliminated from the scoring.

As each test paper is scored, mark each item that is answered incorrectly. With multiple-choice items, a good practice is to draw a red line through the correct answer of the missed items rather than through the student's wrong answers. This will indicate to the student those items missed and at the same time will indicate the correct answers. Time will be saved and confusion avoided during discussion of the test. Marking the correct answers of missed items is especially simple with a scoring stencil. When no mark appears through a hole in the stencil, a red line is drawn across the hole.

In scoring objective tests, each correct answer is usually counted as 1 point because an arbitrary weighing of items makes little difference in the students' final scores. If some items are counted as 2 points, some 1 point, and some 0.5 point, the scoring will be more complicated without any accompanying benefits. Scores based on such weightings will be similar to the simpler procedure of counting each item as 1 point. When a test consists of a combination of objective items and a few more time-consuming essay questions, however, more than a single point is needed to distinguish several levels of response and to reflect the disproportionate time devoted to each of the essay questions.

When students are told to answer every item on the test, a student's score is simply the number of items answered correctly. There is no need to consider wrong answers or to correct for guessing. When all students answer every item on a test, the rank of the students' scores will be the same whether the number right or a correction for guessing is used.

See the box "Correction for Guessing" for a simple formula that is sometimes used. The formula is based on the questionable assumption that students either know the answer or guess it at random. It is not needed when students are allowed sufficient time to respond to all the items on the test. Thus, it is recommended that it *not* be used with the ordinary classroom test. The only exception is when the test is speeded to the extent that students complete different numbers of items. Here its use is defensible because students can increase their scores appreciably by rapidly (and blindly) guessing at the remaining untried items just before the testing period ends.

Correction for Guessing

Correcting for guessing is usually done when students do not have sufficient time to complete all items on the test and when they have been instructed that there will be a penalty for guessing. The most common formula used for this purpose is the following:

$$\text{Score} = \text{Right} - \text{Wrong}/(n - 1)$$

In this formula, n is the number of alternatives for an item. Thus, the formula applies to various selection-type items as follows:

True–False Items

$$\text{Score} = \text{Right} - \text{Wrong}/(2 - 1)$$

(or)

$$\text{Score} = \text{Right} - \text{Wrong}$$

Multiple-Choice Items

$$\text{Score} = \text{Right} - \text{Wrong}$$

Three alternatives	Score = Right − Wrong/2
Four alternatives	Score = Right − Wrong/3
Five alternatives	Score = Right − Wrong/4

APPRAISING CLASSROOM TESTS AND ASSESSMENTS

Before a classroom test or assessment has been administered, it should be evaluated according to the points discussed earlier. The most important of these points are listed in the checklist "Evaluating the Classroom Assessment." Most of these questions also apply to a performance-based assessment. A *yes* response to each of these questions indicates that the test or the assessment has been carefully prepared and will probably function effectively.

After a test or assessment has been scored and the students have discussed the results, it is often simply discarded. Except for the students' criticism during class discussion, which helps identify some of the defective items or ambiguities in a task, the teacher has little evidence concerning the quality of the test or assessment that was used. Much of the careful planning and hard work that went into the preparation of the test or assessment is wasted. A better procedure is to appraise the effectiveness of the test items and assessment tasks and to build a file of high-quality items and tasks for future use.

Determining Item and Task Effectiveness

The effectiveness of each test item can be determined by analyzing student responses to it. Item analysis is generally associated with a norm-referenced perspective. This is natural because the results of an item analysis can be used to select items of desired difficulty that best discriminate between high- and low-achieving students. Selection on these grounds is not relevant from a criterion-referenced perspective. From both perspectives, however, the results of an item analysis can be useful in identifying faulty items and can provide information about student misconceptions and topics that need additional work.

Item analysis is usually designed to answer questions such as the following:

1. Did the item function as intended?
2. Was the test item of appropriate difficulty?
3. Was the test item free of irrelevant clues and other defects?
4. Were the distracters effective (in multiple-choice items)?

Answers to all but the second question are relevant in constructing future tests based on either a norm-referenced or a criterion-referenced perspective. The answer to the second question is relevant only when planning future norm-referenced tests; however, it is relevant in instructional planning regardless of perspective.

Answers to such questions are of obvious value in selecting or revising items for future use. The benefits of item analysis are not limited to the improvement of individual test items, however. There are a number of fringe benefits of special value to classroom teachers. The most important of these are the following:

1. **Item-analysis data provide a basis for efficient class discussion of the test results**. Knowing how effectively each item or task functioned in measuring achievement makes it possible to confine the discussion to those areas most helpful to students. Misinformation and misunderstandings reflected in the choice of particular distracters on multiple-choice problems or frequently repeated errors on performance tasks can be corrected, thereby enhancing the instructional value of the assessment. Item analysis will also expose

CHECKLIST

Evaluating the Classroom Assessment

Adequacy of Assessment Plan

	Yes	No
1. Does the assessment plan adequately describe the instructional objectives and the content to be measured?	____	____
2. Does the assessment plan clearly indicate the relative emphasis to be given to each objective and each content area?	____	____

Adequacy of Test Items and Assessment Tasks

	Yes	No
3. Is the format of each item and task suitable for the learning outcome being measured (*appropriateness*)?	____	____
4. Does each item or task require pupils to demonstrate the performance described in the specific learning outcome it measures (*relevance*)?	____	____
5. Does each item or task present a clear and definite task to be performed (*clarity*)?	____	____
6. Is each item or task presented in simple, readable language and free from excessive verbiage (*conciseness*)?	____	____
7. Does each item or task provide an appropriate challenge (*ideal difficulty*)?	____	____
8. Does each item or task have an answer that would be agreed upon by experts (*correctness*)?	____	____
9. Is there a clear basis for awarding partial credit on items or tasks with multiple points (*scoring rubric*)?	____	____
10. Is each item or task free from technical errors and irrelevant clues (*technical soundness*)?	____	____
11. Is each test item free from racial, ethnic, and gender bias (*cultural fairness*)?	____	____
12. Is each test item independent of the other items in the test (*independence*)?	____	____
13. Is there an adequate number of test items for each learning outcome (*sample adequacy*)?	____	____

Adequacy of Test Format and Directions

	Yes	No
14. Are test items of the same type grouped together in the test (or within sections of the test)?	____	____

	Yes	No
15. Are the test items arranged from easy to more difficult within sections of the test and the test as a whole?	____	____
16. Are the test items numbered in sequence?	____	____
17. Is the answer space clearly indicated (on the test itself or on a separate answer sheet), and is each answer space related to its corresponding test item?	____	____
18. Are the correct answers distributed in such a way that there is no detectable pattern?	____	____
19. Is the test material well spaced, legible, and free of typographical errors?	____	____
20. Are there directions for each section of the test and the test as a whole?	____	____
21. Are the directions clear and concise?	____	____

technical defects in items and tasks. It can also suggest needed changes in scoring rubrics. During discussion, defective items can be pointed out to students, saving much time and heated discussion concerning the unfairness of these items. If an item is ambiguous and two answers can be defended equally well, both answers should be counted correct and the scoring adjusted accordingly.

2. **Item-analysis data provide a basis for remedial work.** Although discussing the test results in class can clarify and correct many specific points, item analysis frequently brings to light general areas of weakness requiring more extended attention. It is often informative to compare actual student performance on a task to the performance expected based on the teacher's notion of how challenging the task would be for students. Performance that is much worse than expected may suggest the need to revisit particular critical concepts or topics. In a mathematics test, for example, item analysis may reveal that the students are fairly proficient in mathematics skills but are having difficulty with problems requiring the application of these skills. In other subjects, item analysis may indicate a general weakness in knowledge of technical vocabulary, in an understanding of principles, or in the ability to interpret data. Such information makes it possible to focus remedial work directly on the particular areas of weakness.

3. **Item-analysis data provide a basis for the general improvement of classroom instruction.** In addition to the preceding uses, item-analysis data can assist in evaluating appropriateness of the learning outcomes and course content for the particular students being taught. For example, material that is consistently too simple or too difficult might suggest curriculum revisions or shifts in teaching emphasis. Similarly, errors in student thinking that persistently appear in item-analysis data might direct attention to the need for more effective teaching procedures. In these and similar ways, item-analysis data can reveal instructional weaknesses and clues for improvement.

4. **Item-analysis procedures provide a basis for increased skill in test construction.** Item analysis reveals ambiguities, clues, ineffective distracters, and other technical defects that were missed during the test's preparation. This information is used directly in revising the test items for future use. In addition to the improvement of the specific items, however, we derive benefits from the procedure itself. As we analyze students' responses to items, we become increasingly aware of technical defects and what causes them. When revising the items, we gain experience in rewording statements so that they are clear, rewriting distracters so that they are more plausible, and modifying items so that they are at a more appropriate level of difficulty. As a consequence, our general test construction skills improve.

Simplified Item-Analysis Procedures

A simplified form of item analysis is all that is necessary or warranted for classroom tests. Because most classroom groups consist of 20 to 40 students, an especially useful procedure is to compare the responses of the 10 highest-scoring students with the responses of the 10 lowest-scoring students. As we will see later, keeping the upper and lower groups at 10 students each simplifies the interpretation of the results. It also is a reasonable number for analysis in groups of 20 to 40 students. For example, with a small classroom group, like that of 20 or fewer students, it is best to use the upper and lower halves to obtain dependable data, whereas with a larger group, like that of 40 students, use of the upper and lower 25% is quite satisfactory. For more refined analysis, the upper and lower 27% is often recommended, and most statistical guides are based on that percentage.

To illustrate the method of item analysis, suppose that we have just finished scoring 32 test papers for a sixth-grade science unit on weather. Our item analysis might then proceed as follows:

1. Rank the 32 test papers in order from the highest to the lowest score.
2. Select the 10 papers within the highest total scores and the 10 papers with the lowest total scores.
3. Put aside the middle 12 papers, as they will not be used in the analysis.
4. For each test item, tabulate the number of students in the upper and lower groups who selected each alternative. This tabulation can be made directly on the test paper or on the test item record, as shown in Figure 14.2.
5. Compute the difficulty of each item (percentage of students who got the item right).
6. Compute the discriminating power of each item (difference between the number of students in the upper and lower groups who got the item right).
7. Evaluate the effectiveness of distracters in each item (attractiveness of the incorrect alternatives).

The first steps of this procedure are merely a convenient tabulation of student responses from which we can readily determine item difficulty, item discriminating power, and the effectiveness of each distracter. This latter information can frequently be obtained simply by inspecting the item-analysis data. Note that in Figure 14.2, for example, when the item was used in the spring of 2006, eight students in the upper group and four students in the lower group selected the correct alternative, B. Thus, 12 of the 20 students

COURSE ___Science___   UNIT ___Weather___

OBJECTIVE ___Identifies use of instruments___

ITEM

Which of the following is most useful in weather forecasting?

  A. Anemometer
*B. Barometer
  C. Thermometer
  D. Rain gauge

Item-Analysis Data

| | | Frequencies | | | | | | Indices | |
Dates Used	Pupils	A	(B)	C	D	E	Omits	Difficulty	Discrimination
4/25/06	Upper 10	1	8	0	1		0		
	Lower 10	2	4	1	3		0	60%	.40
4/30/08	Upper 10	0	10	0	0		0		
	Lower 10	1	3	2	2		1	65%	.70
	Upper 10								
	Lower 10								
	Upper 10								
	Lower 10								

Comment:

Figure 14.2
Test item record with item-analysis data

(difficulty = 60%) got the item right, indicating that the item has a moderate difficulty. When the same item was used in 2008, the difficulty was similar (65%) based on 10 students in the upper group and 3 in the lower group for a total of 13 of 20 who selected the correct option (B).

Because more students in the upper group than in the lower group got the item right, it is discriminating positively in both years. That is, it is distinguishing between high and low achievers (as determined by the total test score). The .40 for the 2006 administration equals the difference in the proportion of students in the upper and lower groups who answered the item correctly (8/10 − 4/10 or .8 −.4). In 2008, the discrimination of the items was higher than in 2006 (.70 = 1.00 − .30, the proportions in the upper and lower groups answering the item correctly in 2008). Finally, because all the alternatives were selected by some of the students in the lower group, the distracters (alternatives A, C, and D) appear to be operating effectively.

From a norm-referenced perspective, the fact that in 2008 all 10 students with the highest test scores but only 3 of the 10 with the lowest scores answered the item correctly makes this item a good candidate for use in the future because it helps discriminate between high- and low-achieving students. Although this would not be a basis for selecting an item for a criterion-referenced test, it does provide an indication that the item is keyed correctly and that it is not being misinterpreted by the higher-achieving students. It also provides an indication that some students do not understand the uses of instruments listed.

Although item analysis by inspection will reveal the general effectiveness of a test item and is satisfactory for most classroom purposes, it is sometimes useful to obtain a more precise estimate of item difficulty and discriminating power. This can be done by applying relatively simple formulas to the item-analysis data.

Computing Item Difficulty.   The difficulty of a test item that is scored right or wrong is indicated by the percentage of students who get the item right. Hence, we can compute item difficulty (P) by means of the following formula, in which R equals the number of students who got the item right and T equals the total number of students who tried the item:

$$P = 100R/T$$

Applying this formula to the item-analysis data in Figure 14.2, our index of item difficulty is 65% for the April 30, 2008, test as follows:

$$P = 100 * 13/20 = 65\%$$

In computing item difficulty from item-analysis data, our calculation is based on the upper and lower groups only. We assume that the responses of students in the middle group follow essentially the same pattern. This estimate of difficulty is sufficiently accurate for classroom use and is easily obtained because the needed figures can be taken directly from the item-analysis data.

Note that because our item analysis is based on 10 in the upper group and 10 in the lower group, all we need to do to obtain item difficulty is to divide the number getting it right by 2 (13/2 = 6.5), move the decimal point one place to the right (65), and add the percent sign (65%). In other words, 13 of 20 is the same as 6.5 of 10, which is 65%. In April 2006, when 12 students got the item right, item difficulty was 6 of 10 (12/2 = 6), or 60%. This may seem a bit confusing at first, but once you grasp the idea, you can compute item difficulty very quickly. As noted earlier, the ease of interpreting item statistics is one of the advantages of using 10 in each group. If more (or fewer) than 10 are used, the formula for computing item difficulty is the same, but it is much more difficult to compute the results mentally.

Similar calculations are used for a task scored 0, 1, 2, or 3 to get the overall mean for the students in the upper and lower groups combined. That is, the average would simply be the sum of the means for the upper and lower groups divided by 2.

Computing Item Discriminating Power.   As we have already stated, an item discriminates positively if more students in the upper group than the lower group get the item right. Positive discrimination indicates that the item is discriminating in the same direction as the total test score. Because we assume that the total test score reflects achievement of desired objectives, we would like all our test items to show positive discrimination.

The discriminating power of an achievement test item refers to the degree to which it discriminates between students with high and low achievement. Item-discriminating power (D) can be obtained by subtracting the number of students in the lower group who get the item right (RL) from the number of students in the upper group who get the item right (RU) and dividing by one half the total number of students included in the item analysis $(.5T)$. Summarized in formula form, it is as follows:

$$D = (RU - RL)/(.5T)$$

Applying this formula to the item-analysis data for April 2008 in Figure 14.2, we obtain an index of discriminating power of .70 as follows:

$$D = (10 - 3)/10 = .70$$

This indicates approximately average discriminating power. An item with maximum positive discriminating power is one in which all students in the upper group get the item right and all the students in the lower group get the item wrong. This results in an index of 1.00, as follows:

$$D = (10 - 0)/10 = 1.00$$

An item with no discriminating power is one in which an equal number of students in both the upper and the lower groups get the item right. This results in an index of .00, as follows:

$$D = (10 - 10)/10 = .00$$

When our item analysis is based on 10 in the upper group and 10 in the lower group, the index of discriminating power, like item difficulty, can be computed easily and quickly. All we need to do is subtract the number in the lower group who get it right from the number in the upper group who get it right $(10 - 3 = 7)$, move the decimal point one place to the left $(.7)$, and add a zero after it $(.70)$. With 10 in each group, the index of discrimination is essentially the difference between the number getting it right in the two groups with the decimal point moved one place to the left. The zero is added simply because the index of discrimination is usually carried to two decimal places. With more than 10 in each group, we could not make these simple mental calculations but would have to resort to use of the formula.

Evaluating the Effectiveness of Distracters.   How well each distracter is operating can be determined by inspection, so there is no need to calculate an index of effectiveness, although the formula for discriminating power can be used for this purpose. In general, a good distracter attracts more students from the lower group than the upper group. Thus, it should discriminate between the upper and lower groups in a manner opposite to that of the correct alternative. An examination of the following item-analysis data will illustrate the ease with which the effectiveness of distracters can be determined by inspection. Alternative A is the correct answer:

Alternatives	(A)	B	C	D	Omits
Upper 10	5	4	0	1	0
Lower 10	3	2	0	5	0

First, note that the item discriminates positively because five in the upper group and three in the lower group got the item right. The index of discriminating power is fairly low, however (D = .20), and this may be partly due to the ineffectiveness of some of the distracters. Alternative B is a poor distracter because it attracts more students from the upper group than from the lower group. This is most likely due to some ambiguity in the statement of the item. Alternative C is evidently not a plausible distracter because it attracted no one. Alternative D is functioning as intended, for it attracts a larger proportion of students from the lower group. Thus, the discriminating power of this item can probably be improved by removing any ambiguity in the statement of the item and revising or replacing alternatives B and C. The specific changes must, of course, be based on an inspection of the test item itself; item-analysis data merely indicate poorly functioning items, not the cause of the poor functioning.

In some cases, an examination of the test item will reveal no obvious error in the structure of the item and it may be best to try it with a second group. The number of cases involved is so small that considerable variation in student response can be expected from one group to another. A casual comment by the teacher or some other classroom event may cause students to select or reject a particular alternative.

Recording Item-Analysis Data on the Test Paper.   There is some advantage in recording item-analysis data directly on the test paper that was used as a scoring key, as shown in Figure 14.3, and making the calculations mentally. These mental calculations for the two items in Figure 14.3 are summarized in Figure 14.4. Thus, during discussion of the test results, you can quickly judge the difficulty and discriminating power of each item and the effectiveness of the distracters. This will help determine how much discussion to devote to any particular item, the types of misconceptions students may have (by the distracters selected), and which items are so defective that they might be discounted. See "Item Analysis by Computer" for a look at another way to analyze test items.

Cautions in Interpreting Item-Analysis Results

Item analysis is a quick, simple technique for appraising the effectiveness of individual test items. The information from such an analysis is limited in many ways, however, and must be interpreted accordingly. Observe the following major cautions.

1. **Item discriminating power does not indicate item validity.** In our description of item analysis, we used the total test score as a basis for selecting the upper group (high achievers) and the lower group (low achievers). This is the most common procedure because comparable measures of achievement are usually not available. Ideally, we would examine each test item in relation to some independent measure of achievement. However, the best measure of the particular achievement we are interested in assessing is usually the total score on the achievement test we have constructed because each classroom test

WEATHER UNIT

Name _____ Date_____

Directions. This test will measure what you have learned during the unit on weather. There are 40 objective questions in the test. You will have the entire class period to complete it.

For each question there are several possible answers. Select the *best* answer and indicate it by encircling the letter of your answer.

Your score will be the number of questions answered correctly so *be sure to answer every question.*

KNOWLEDGE OF FACTS

U	L	
		1. Which of these instruments is used to measure humidity?
0	1	A. Anemometer
0	1	B. Barometer
10	8	C. Hygrometer
0	0	D. Thermometer

U	L	
		2. What does the Beaufort scale indicate on a weather map?
1	2	A. Air pressure
0	1	B. Air temperature
0	1	C. Precipitation
9	6	D. Wind velocity

Figure 14.3
Sample test scoring key with item-analysis data added (U = Upper 10 pupils, L = Lower 10 pupils)

Item Difficulty Index

Steps (using numbers to left of answer)	Item 1	Item 2
1. Add U + L and divide by 2.	18/2 = 9	15/2 = 7.5
2. Move decimal point one to the right.	90	75
3. Add the percent sign.	90%	75%

Item Discrimination Index

Steps (using numbers to left of answer)	Item 1	Item 2
1. Subtract U − L.	10 − 8 = 2	9 − 6 = 3
2. Move decimal point one place to the left.	.2	.3
3. Add a zero after the number.	.20	.30

Figure 14.4
Illustrative item-analysis calculations from data in Figure 14.3

is related to specific instructional objectives and course content. Even standardized tests in the same content area are usually inadequate as independent criteria because they are aimed at more general objectives than those measured by a classroom test in a particular course.

Using the total score from our classroom test as a basis for selecting high and low achievers is perfectly legitimate as long as we remember that we are using an internal criterion. In doing so, our item analysis offers evidence concerning the internal consistency of the test rather than its validity. That is, we are determining how effectively each test item is measuring whatever the whole test is measuring. Such item-analysis data can be interpreted as evidence of item validity only when the validity of the total test has been proven or can be legitimately assumed. This is seldom possible with classroom tests, so we must be satisfied with a more limited interpretation of our item-analysis data.

2. A low index of discriminating power does not necessarily indicate a defective item. Items that discriminate poorly between high and low achievers should be examined for the possible presence of ambiguity, clues, and other technical defects. If none is found and the items measure an important learning outcome, they should be retained for future use. Any item that discriminates in a positive direction can contribute to the measurement of student achievement, and low indexes of discrimination are frequently obtained for reasons other than technical defects.

Classroom achievement tests are usually designed to measure several different types of learning outcomes (knowledge, understanding, application, and so on). When this is the case, test items that represent an area receiving relatively little emphasis will tend to have poor discriminating power. For example, if a test has 40 items measuring knowledge of facts and 10 items measuring understanding, the latter items can be expected to have low indexes of discrimination, because the items measuring understanding have less representation in the total test score and there is typically a low correlation between measures of knowledge and measures of understanding. Low indexes of discrimination here merely indicate that these items are measuring something different from what the major part of the test is measuring. Removing such items from the test would make it a more homogeneous measure of knowledge outcomes, but it would also damage the test's validity because it would no longer measure learning outcomes in the understanding area. Because most classroom tests measure a variety of types of learning outcomes, low positive indexes of discrimination are the rule rather than the exception.

Another factor that influences discriminating power is the difficulty of the item. Those items at the 50% level of difficulty make maximum discriminating power possible because only at this level of difficulty can all students in the upper half of the group get the item right and all students in the lower half get it wrong. The 50% level of difficulty does not guarantee maximum discriminating power but merely makes it possible. If half the students in the upper group and half the students in the lower group got the item right, the level of difficulty would still be 50%, but the index of discrimination would be zero. As we move away from the 50% level of difficulty toward easier or more difficult items, the index of discriminating power becomes smaller. Thus, items that are very easy or very difficult have low indexes of discriminating power. Sometimes it is necessary or desirable to retain such items, however, in order to measure a representative sample of learning outcomes and course content. To summarize, a low index of discriminating power should alert us to the possible presence of technical defects in a test item but should not cause us to discard an otherwise worthwhile item. A well-constructed achievement test will, of necessity, contain items with low discriminating power; to discard them would result in a less, rather than more, valid test.

3. Item-analysis data from small samples are highly tentative. Item-analysis procedures focus our attention so directly on a test item's difficulty and discriminating power that we are commonly misled into believing that these are fixed, unchanging characteristics. This, of course, is not true. Item-analysis data will vary from one group to another, depending

Item Analysis by Computer

Many schools now have computers (or have access to them) that can both score and analyze tests. The computer printout will provide item-analysis information, a reliability coefficient, standard error of measurement for the test, and various other types of information concerning the performance of the individuals tested and the characteristics of the test. The nature of the information depends on the sophistication of the computer and the program that is used.

When item analysis is done by computer, the scores of the entire group are usually used rather than just the scores of the upper and lower groups. The total set of scores might be divided into two, three, four, or five levels, depending on the size of the group and the types of analyses. Item-analysis data on a computer printout based on 50 pupils might appear as follows, for each item.

Item-Response Pattern

Item 1	A	B	(C)	D	E	Omit	Total	Item Statistics
Upper 30%	1	1	12	1	0	0	15	Difficulty 60%
Middle 40%	2	2	12	3	1	0	20	Discrimination .40
Lower 30%	2	3	6	3	1	0	15	
Total	5	6	30	7	2	0	50	

The item-response data indicate how many pupils, at each level, selected the correct answer (C) and how many selected each of the distracters. The item statistics at the right indicate the index of difficulty and the index of discrimination for this item. Some computer programs report only the item statistics, but the item-response pattern is especially valuable for evaluating the effectiveness of the distracters and planning for item revision. Alternative E, for example, should be examined to determine whether it can be replaced by a more effective distracter because it is rarely selected.

The following Web sites provide information about two of the many item-analysis computer programs that are available.

ITEMAN at
http://www.assess.com
Remark Products at
http://www.gravie.com/remark/

on the students' level of ability, educational background, and type of instruction they have had. Add to this the small number of students available for analyzing the items in our classroom tests, and the tentative nature of our item-analysis data becomes readily apparent. If just a few students change their responses, our indexes of difficulty and discriminating power can be increased or decreased by a considerable amount.

The tentative nature of item-analysis data should discourage us from making fine distinctions among items on the basis of indexes of difficulty and discriminating power. If an item is discriminating in a positive direction, all the alternatives are functioning effectively, and it has no apparent defects, then it can be considered satisfactory from a technical standpoint. The important question then is **not** how high the index of discriminating power is but whether the item measures an important learning outcome. In the final analysis, the worth of an achievement test item must be based on logical rather than statistical considerations.

When used with norm-referenced classroom tests, item analysis provides us with a general appraisal of the functional effectiveness of the test items, a means for detecting defects, and a method for identifying instructional weaknesses. For these purposes, the tentative nature of item-analysis data is relatively unimportant. When we record indexes of item difficulty or discriminating power on item records for future use, we should interpret them as rough approximations only. As such, they are still superior to our unaided estimates of item difficulty and discriminating power.

Application of Item-Analysis Principles with Performance-Based Assessments

Item-analysis procedures have somewhat limited applicability with performance-based assessments, primarily because such assessments generally contain a relatively small number of tasks. If the assessment has several tasks, however, the general principles can be readily adapted for use. One necessary modification results from the fact that scores on performance-based tasks almost always involve more than a simple 0 or 1. For example, each task might have possible scores of 0, 1, 2, 3, or 4. Still, a comparison of the individual task scores for the 10 highest and 10 lowest scoring students can be useful.

Suppose, for example, that a performance assessment consisted of five separate tasks, each of which had possible scores ranging from a low of 0 for no response or a response that was unrelated to the task, to a 4 for a complete and well-elaborated response. Possible total scores for the set of five tasks would range from 0 to 20. As before, the total scores would be ranked to identify the 10 highest and the 10 lowest scores. The individual task scores for these two groups of students would then be summarized as illustrated in Figure 14.5. The 10 highest-achieving students generally have higher scores on each item than the 10 lowest-achieving students. The higher average score on Task 1 for the upper 10 students than for the lower 10 indicates that the task discriminates between these two groups. The equal means on Task 2 for the two groups of students indicate that the latter task does not discriminate.

A couple of possible reasons for results such as those shown in Figure 14.5 need to be considered. It is possible that Task 2 simply has less similarity than Task 1 to the remaining tasks; that is, it calls for different skills and abilities than the other four tasks. It

Task 1						
Score	0	1	2	3	4	Average
Upper 10	0	0	1	4	5	3.4
Lower 10	1	3	4	2	0	1.7
Task 2						
Score	0	1	2	3	4	Average
Upper 10	2	2	3	1	1	1.5
Lower 10	3	2	2	3	0	1.5

Figure 14.5
Illustrative analysis of scores on two tasks

may be that the type of performance expected on Task 2 is ambiguous. If careful review of the task in comparison to the other four tasks leads to the first conclusion, then there is no need to revise or discard the task. If a review leads to the second conclusion, however, then the task would need to be either discarded or revised to clarify what is intended.

BUILDING A FILE OF EFFECTIVE ITEMS AND TASKS

A file of effective items and tasks can be built and maintained easily if items and tasks are recorded on records like the one shown in Figure 14.2. By indicating on the record both the objective and the content area being measured, it is possible to file the records under both headings. Course content can be used as major categories, with the objectives forming the subcategories. For example, the item in Figure 14.2 measures knowledge of weather instruments, so it is placed in the first category under weather instruments as follows:

Weather Instruments

Knowledge

Understanding

Application

This type of filing system makes it possible to select items or tasks in accordance with any table of specifications in the particular area covered by the file. See the box "Item Banking by Computer" for a description of another way to build an assessment bank.

Building a file of effective items and tasks is a little like building a bank account. The first several years are concerned mainly with making deposits; withdrawals must be delayed until a sufficient reserve is accumulated. Thus, items and tasks are recorded on records as they are constructed; information from analyses of student responses is added after the items and tasks have been used, and then the effective items and tasks are deposited in the file. At first, it seems to be additional work, with very little return. However, in a few years, it is possible to start using some of the items and tasks from the file and supplementing these with newly constructed items and tasks. As the file grows, it becomes possible to select the majority of the items and tasks from the file for any given test or assessment without repeating them too frequently. To prevent using a test item or assessment task too often, record the date it is used.

A file of effective items and tasks assumes increasing importance as we shift from test items that measure knowledge of facts to items and tasks that measure understanding, application, and thinking skills. Items and tasks in these areas are difficult and time consuming to construct. With all the other demands on our time, it is nearly impossible to construct effective test items or assessment tasks in these areas each time we prepare a new test or assessment. We have two alternatives: Either we neglect the measurement of learning outcomes in these areas (which, unfortunately, has been the practice), or we slowly build a file of effective items and tasks in these areas. If quality of student learning is our major concern, the choice is obvious.

SUMMARY

Some of the topics considered in this chapter are more relevant to traditional classroom tests involving right–wrong or single-best-answer items than to complex, performance-based tasks involving extended responses and more complicated scoring procedures. Test assembly and item analysis, for example, are more relevant for a classroom test containing many items than for a performance assessment involving a single task for a class period. At a conceptual level, however, the general principles considered in this chapter apply to complex performance-based assessments as well as to classroom tests involving only objective items.

The same care that goes into the construction of individual test items and assessment tasks should be carried over into the final stages of development and use. Attending to

Item Banking by Computer

Some schools use computers to maintain systematic item files (or item pools) for each of the various subjects and grade levels. The items are coded and stored by the test builder for easy retrieval. The code includes such things as instructional level, subject area, instructional objective, content topic, and item statistics (e.g., difficulty and discrimination indexes). This makes it possible to select items and build a test that matches a particular set of test specifications. The coded information concerning each item also aids in arranging the items in the test (e.g., by objective or order of difficulty).

The computer will print out these custom-designed tests and will also score, report, and analyze them. For examples and additional information, see the following Web sites:

Assessment System Corporation

http://www.assess.com

ERIC Clearinghouse on Assessment and Evaluation

http://ericae.net

Computer item banks are like any other item pool—you get out only what you put in. If you store ineffective items, you will get back ineffective items. Thus, item banking by computer requires careful screening of the items before they are entered.

the procedures for assembling, administering, scoring, and appraising the results will increase assurance that results are valid.

The preliminary steps in preparing the test will be simpler if items are recorded on cards. This facilitates the task of editing and arranging the items. Editing includes checking each item to make certain that its format is appropriate, that it is relevant to the specific learning outcome it measures, and that it is free from ambiguity, irrelevant clues, and nonfunctioning material. The final group of items selected for the test also should be checked against the table of specifications or other test plan to ensure that a representative sample of the learning outcomes and course content is being measured. In arranging the items in the test, all items of one type should be placed together in a separate section. The items within each section should be organized by the learning outcome measured and then placed in order of ascending difficulty.

The directions for the test or assessment should clearly convey the purpose of the measurement, the time allowed to finish, the basis for responding, and the procedure for recording the responses. The directions should indicate what to do about guessing for selection-type items. For performance-based tasks, the directions should describe the scoring procedure.

The procedures for administering the test or assessment should give all students a fair chance to demonstrate their achievement. Both the physical and the psychological atmosphere should be conducive to maximum performance. Unnecessary interruptions and unfair aid from other students or the teacher should be avoided.

Scoring the test can be facilitated by a scoring key or scoring stencil if separate answer sheets are used. Counting each right answer as 1 point is usually satisfactory. A correction for guessing is unnecessary on a typical classroom test for which students have sufficient time. Because assumptions underlying the use of correction-for-guessing formulas are debatable, it is recommended that they be used only with speeded tests. For most classroom tests, it is satisfactory to tell students to answer every question and then simply count the number of correct answers.

After the test has been scored, you should appraise the effectiveness of each item by means of item analysis. Use simple statistical procedures for determining the index of item difficulty (percentage of students who got the item right), item-discriminating power (the difference between high and low achievers), and the effectiveness of each distracter (degree to which it attracts more low achievers than high achievers). Item-analysis indexes can be computed quickly and easily if the data are based on the 10 highest-scoring and 10 lowest-scoring students (for class sizes ranging from 20 to 40 students). Because criterion-referenced mastery tests are designed to describe the learning tasks that students can perform rather than to discriminate among students, traditional indexes of item analysis are not used to select items for future tests—but they are relevant for detecting faulty items and for planning instruction. The results of item analysis are valuable in discussing the test with students, in planning remedial work, in improving teaching and testing skills, and in selecting and revising items for future use. Item-analysis data must always be interpreted cautiously because of their limited and tentative nature.

Building a file of effective test items and assessment tasks involves recording the items or tasks, adding information from analyses of student responses, and filing the records by both the content area and the objective that the item or task measures. Such a file is especially valuable in areas of complex achievement, when the construction of test items and assessment tasks is difficult and time consuming. When enough high-quality items and tasks have been assembled, the burden of preparing tests and assessments is considerably lightened. Computer item banking makes the task even easier and is available in many schools.

LEARNING EXERCISES

1. What are the advantages of recording items during test construction?
2. List as many things as you can think of that might prevent a test item or assessment task from functioning as intended. Compare your list with the checklist on pages 352–353.
3. In what ways might poorly arranged items in a test adversely influence the validity of test results? What arrangement is best for valid results? Why?
4. What factors should be included in the general directions for a comprehensive departmental examination? How would the directions for a teacher's unit test differ?
5. What special precautions might be taken to avoid ambiguity, irrelevant clues, and other errors in objective test items?
6. Under what conditions should a correction for guessing be used to score a test?
7. If item-analysis data showed that an item was answered correctly by 7 of 10 students in the upper group and 3 of 10 students in the lower group, what would be the index of item difficulty? What would be the index of discriminating power? Would this item be considered effective or ineffective? Why?
8. How can you increase the discriminating power of a norm-referenced test?

REFERENCES

Cronbach, L. J. (1990). *Essentials of psychological testing* (5th ed.). New York: Harper & Row.

Gronlund, N. E. (2005). *Assessment of student achievement* (8th ed.). Boston: Allyn & Bacon.

FURTHER READING

Anastasi, A., & Urbina, S. (1997). *Psychological testing* (7th ed.). New York: Macmillan. Chapter 8, "Item Analysis," describes item-analysis procedures for norm-referenced tests with a brief introduction to item-response theory.

Baker, F. A. (1989). Computer technology in test construction and processing. In R. L. Linn (Ed.), *Educational measurement* (3rd ed.). New York: Macmillan. Describes the use of microcomputers for item writing, item banking, test construction, scoring, and reporting.

Crocker, L. (1992). Item analysis. In M. C. Alkin (Ed.), *Encyclopedia of educational research* (6th ed., vol. 1). New York: Macmillan. Provides an overview of item-analysis procedures and uses of the results.

Ebel, R. L., & Frisbie, D. A. (1991). *Essentials of educational measurement* (5th ed.). Englewood Cliffs, NJ: Prentice Hall. Chapter 13, "Using Item Analysis to Evaluate and Improve Test Quality," describes item analysis and illustrates its use in item revision.

Mehrens, W. A., & Lehmann, I. J. (1991). *Measurement and evaluation in education and psychology* (4th ed.). New York: Holt, Rinehart & Winston. Chapter 8, "Assembling, Reproducing, Administering, Scoring, and Analyzing Classroom Achievement Tests," presents a discussion of topics like those covered in this chapter.

15

GRADING AND REPORTING

Grading and reporting student progress is one of the more frustrating aspects of teaching—there are so many factors to consider and so many decisions to be made. This chapter removes some of the complexity by describing the various types of grading and reporting systems and providing guidelines for their effective use.

The task of reporting student progress cannot be separated from the procedures used in assessing student learning and development. If instructional objectives have been clearly defined in performance terms and relevant tests and other assessment procedures have been properly used, grading and reporting become a matter of summarizing the results and presenting them in understandable form. The task is still a perplexing one, however, because the evidence of learning and development must be presented on a very brief report form that is understandable to a variety of users (e.g., students, parents, teachers, counselors, and administrators).

As we discussed in Chapter 12, the systematic collection of student work into a portfolio can provide an effective means of reporting student progress. In most schools, however, teachers are required to submit a grade that provides the overall summary of student achievement for the semester or school year. Reporting student progress becomes especially difficult when the vast array of assessment data must be summarized as a single letter grade (e.g., A, B, C, D, F) or numerical value. Should the assigned grade represent achievement only, or should effort and work habits be included? How should the various aspects of achievement (e.g., tests, daily assignments, reports, lab work, and responses to oral questioning) be weighted and combined? Should the achievement be judged in relation to other students, some absolute standard, or the individual's learning potential? What distribution of grades (i.e., A, B, C, D, F) should be used, and how should this be determined? How can student work be displayed to illustrate progress, strengths, and weaknesses to students and parents? There are no simple answers to these questions.

School or state policies may provide guidelines for answering some of these questions. For example, it may be specified that grades are to be based solely on student achievement.

Verbal labels such as "excellent," "proficient," or "above average" may be associated with the grade. Guidelines may also specify a standards-based or comparative orientation. But the specifics of deciding how to implement performance standards, when a performance meets a proficiency standard, and how to combine the information obtained from classroom observations, homework assignments, tests, assessments, and projects of various types still must be addressed by individual teachers.

Even when schools or states provide guidelines for assigning grades, specific implementation practices vary from school to school and from teacher to teacher within the same school. Many schools have circumvented the problems of using a single letter grade by supplementing it with a more elaborate reporting system. Some of these systems will be described here, but first let us consider some of the functions served by a grading and reporting system.

FUNCTIONS OF GRADING AND REPORTING SYSTEMS

School grading and reporting systems are designed to serve a variety of functions in the school. These include instructional uses, reports to parents, and administrative and guidance uses.

Instructional Uses

The focus of the grading and reporting system should be the improvement of student learning and development. This is most likely to occur when the report (a) clarifies the instructional objectives, (b) indicates the student's strengths and weaknesses in learning, (c) provides information concerning the student's personal–social development, and (d) contributes to the student's motivation. These functions require a much more comprehensive report than the single letter grade.

The improvement of student learning is probably best achieved by the day-to-day assessments of learning and the feedback from tests and other assessment procedures. A portfolio of work designed to display progress can show the strides that have been made during the year with concrete examples. However, students and parents also seem to need a periodic summary of their learning progress. They find it difficult to integrate test scores, ratings, and other assessment results into a summary of how they are doing. A well-designed report form, together with a portfolio of student work that contains carefully selected examples, can provide this systematic summary of learning progress. If they are sufficiently detailed, the report and portfolio of work can pinpoint strengths and weaknesses in learning with implications for corrective action. They also can help communicate desired learning outcomes.

Periodic progress reports can contribute to student motivation by providing short-term goals and knowledge of results. Both are essential features of effective learning. How motivating the reports are likely to be, however, depends on the nature of the report and how it is used. If a single letter grade is used and students are threatened with low grades unless they study harder, the results are likely to have a negative impact. However, if a comprehensive report of learning strengths and weaknesses is used and the report is presented as an opportunity to check on progress, motivation toward improved learning is likely to result.

As was discussed in Chapter 12, involvement of students in the selection of examples of work to include in a portfolio can encourage reflection on standards of performance. Asking students to select their best piece of writing and to explain why they chose that piece encourages self-reflection and self-evaluation. The inclusion of examples that show early efforts, teacher feedback, and final products can illustrate progress and help students internalize performance standards.

Well-designed progress reports can also aid in evaluating instructional procedures by identifying areas needing revision. When a majority of students have reports showing poor learning progress in a particular area, there may be a need to modify the instructional objectives or the classroom activities. In other cases, the reports may indicate that some special instructional activities would be beneficial for small groups or individuals.

Reports to Parents/Guardians

Informing parents (or guardians) of their children's school progress is a basic function of a grading and reporting system. These reports should help parents understand the objectives of the school and how well their children are achieving the intended learning outcomes of their particular program. This information is important from several viewpoints. First, by knowing what the school is attempting to do, parents are better able to cooperate with the school in promoting their children's learning and development. Second, information concerning their children's successes, failures, and special problems enables parents to give them the emotional support and encouragement needed. Third, knowing their children's strengths and weaknesses in learning provides a basis for helping them make more sound educational and vocational plans. To serve these purposes adequately, the reports and portfolios of student work should contain as much information and detail as parents can comprehend and use. At the elementary level, the report form is frequently supplemented by parent–teacher conferences.

Administrative and Guidance Uses

Grades and progress reports serve a number of administrative functions. They are used for determining promotion and graduation, awarding honors, determining athletic eligibility, and reporting to other schools and prospective employers. For most administrative purposes, a single letter grade is typically required. Such grades have appeal, in part, because they are compact and can be easily recorded and averaged.

There is little doubt that the convenience of the single letter grade in administrative work has been a major factor in retarding the development of more comprehensive and useful progress reports. This need not be the case, however. When a new reporting system is being developed, it is possible to retain the use of letter grades for administrative purposes and supplement them with the type of information needed by students, parents, teachers, and counselors. At the high school level, the retention of letter grades is almost mandatory because most college admission offices insist on them.

Counselors use reports on student achievement and development, along with other information, to help students make realistic educational and vocational plans. Reports that include ratings on personal and social characteristics are also useful in helping students with adjustment problems. These guidance functions are best served by a reporting system that is both comprehensive and detailed.

In summary, the diverse functions to be served by a grading and reporting system indicate that more elaborate reports are needed than the traditional single letter grade. This does not mean that letter grades should be discarded. They are convenient, easily averaged, useful for administrative functions, and required for college admissions. Instead, letter grades should be supplemented by the type of information needed by the various users of the reports. When this is done, the letter grade can be retained as a pure measure of achievement, and such factors as effort, attitude, work habits, and personal–social characteristics can be reported separately.

TYPES OF GRADING AND REPORTING SYSTEMS

Throughout the history of education, letter grades have been the primary method of reporting student progress in school. Various studies have indicated that approximately 50% to 90% of all schools use letter grades. In some cases, especially at the elementary level, the report form also includes a series of work habits and personal–social characteristics to be checked by the teacher. Various attempts have been made to replace or improve the traditional report form. The modifications typically represent some type of compromise between the need for detailed information and the need for simplicity and conciseness.

Traditional Letter-Grade System

The traditional use of the letter-grade system is to assign a single letter grade (e.g., A, B, C, D, F) for each subject. In some cases a single number (e.g., 5, 4, 3, 2, 1 or 100, 95, 90) is used instead of a letter, but the grading system is essentially the same. This system is concise and convenient, the grades are easily averaged, and they are useful in predicting future achievement, but they have the following shortcomings when used as the sole method of reporting.

1. They typically are a combination of achievement, effort, work habits, and good behavior.
2. The proportion of students assigned each letter grade varies from teacher to teacher.
3. They do not indicate a student's specific strengths and weaknesses in learning.

These limitations of the single letter grade make them difficult to interpret and use. A grade of C, for example, may represent good achievement but poor work habits and disruptive behavior or poor achievement accompanied by attentiveness, strong effort, and good behavior. In reacting to criticisms that the letter-grade system fosters unfair competition among students, some schools have reduced the number of grades to two (e.g., S = satisfactory, U = unsatisfactory) or three (e.g., by adding H = honors). Standards-based efforts have also led to the use of a small number of categories corresponding to the performance standards for which a variety of labels are used in different states and districts (e.g., advanced, proficient, partially proficient, not yet partially proficient; distinguished, proficient, apprentice, novice; exceptional, proficient, basic, below basic). A smaller number of categories (e.g., satisfactory–unsatisfactory, proficient–not proficient), of course, provide even less information than the traditional letter-grade system.

Pass–Fail System

A two-category system (e.g., satisfactory–unsatisfactory, pass–fail) has been used in some elementary schools for many years. More recently, it has also been used in some high schools and colleges. At these levels, it typically serves as an option to the traditional letter grade in a limited number of courses. It permits students to take some courses, usually elective courses, under a pass–fail option that is not included in their grade-point average. The intent is to encourage students to explore new areas, even those for which they are not fully prepared. It also permits students to focus on those aspects of a course that relate most directly to their major field of study and to neglect those areas of little interest or relevance. Removing the fear of a lower grade-point average gives students greater freedom to select their learning experiences.

Like any two-category system, the pass–fail option is easy to use, but it offers less information than the traditional (A, B, C, D, F) system. It provides no indication of the level of learning, and thus its value for describing present performance or predicting future achievement is lost. Also, study effort is frequently directed toward merely passing rather than a higher level of achievement. Despite its shortcomings, however, the pass–fail option can serve the purposes for which it is intended if its use is restricted to a small number of courses.

A pass–no grade grading system is often used for courses taught under a pure mastery learning approach. Here, where students are expected to demonstrate mastery of all course objectives before receiving credit for a course, a simple *pass* is all that is needed to indicate mastery. The practice of assigning a letter grade of A to all students who complete a course under mastery conditions, as is sometimes done, simply adds greater confusion to the meaning of letter grades. When the pass–no grade system is used, nothing is recorded on a student's school record until mastery of the course is demonstrated. The mastery learning approach presupposes that each student will be given as much time as needed to attain mastery of the course objectives. Thus, the school record remains a blank until the course is successfully completed.

Checklists of Objectives

To provide more informative progress reports, some schools have replaced or supplemented the traditional grading system with a list of objectives to be checked or rated. These reports, which are most common at the elementary school level, typically include ratings of progress toward the major objectives in each subject-matter area. The following statements for reading and arithmetic illustrate the nature of these reports:

Reading

1. Reads with understanding
2. Works out meaning and use of new words

3. Reads well to others
4. Reads independently for pleasure

Arithmetic

1. Uses fundamental processes
2. Solves problems involving reasoning
3. Is accurate in work
4. Works at a satisfactory rate

The symbols used to rate students on each of these major objectives vary considerably. In some schools, the traditional A, B, C, D, F lettering system is retained, but more commonly there is a shift to fewer symbols, such as O (outstanding), S (satisfactory), and N (needs improvement) or P (proficient), PP (practically proficient), and N (needs improvement).

The checklist form of reporting has the obvious advantage of providing a detailed analysis of the student's strengths and weaknesses so that constructive action can be taken to help improve learning. It also provides students, parents, and others with a frequent reminder of the objectives of the school. The main difficulties encountered with such reports are in keeping the list of statements down to a workable number and in stating them in such simple and concise terms that they are readily understood by all users of the reports. These difficulties are probably best overcome by obtaining the cooperation of parents and students during the development of the report form.

Letters to Parents/Guardians

Some schools have turned to the use of letters to provide for greater flexibility in reporting student progress to parents (or guardians). Letters make it possible to report on the unique strengths, weaknesses, and learning needs of each student and to suggest specific plans for improvement. In addition, the report can include as much detail as is needed to make clear the student's progress in all areas of development.

Although letters to parents might provide a good supplement to other types of reports, their usefulness as the sole method of reporting progress is limited by the following factors.

1. Comprehensive and thoughtful written reports require an excessive amount of time and skill.
2. Descriptions of a student's learning weaknesses are easily misinterpreted by parents.
3. Letters fail to provide a systematic and cumulative record of student progress toward the objectives of the school.

The flexibility of this method, which is one of its major strengths, limits its usefulness in maintaining systematic records. Because different aspects of development are likely to be stressed from one report to another, the continuity in reporting is lost.

When used in connection with a more formal reporting system, the informal letter can serve a useful role in clarifying specific points in the report and in elaborating on various aspects of student development. Letters can also be an effective supplement to a portfolio of student work by providing an overview of the portfolio entries and calling attention to particular things that the parent might consider in reviewing the portfolio. In general, letters probably should be restricted to this supplementary role, however, and be used only as needed for clarification. See the box "Tactful Remarks for Reporting to Parents" for some extreme examples that illustrate the touchiness of reporting to parents.

Portfolios of Student Work

Portfolios of student work were discussed in greater detail in Chapter 12. As we noted there, a carefully constructed portfolio can be an effective means of showing student progress, illustrating strengths, and identifying areas where greater effort is needed. The process of identifying products for the portfolio and commenting on the entries can help students gain a better understanding of expectations and standards of excellence. The portfolio is also an effective means of making grades and other summary reports more concrete for parents and guardians by illustrating both progress and current levels of student achievement.

An effective portfolio is more than simply a file into which student work products are placed. It is a purposefully selected collection of work that often contains commentary on the entries by both students and teachers. The entries in the portfolio need to be selected to illustrate the range of student work (e.g., types of writing, types of mathematical problems, or results of laboratory experiments). The entries also need to be selected to illustrate progress during the year (e.g., products from different parts of the school year) and, in some cases, progress from early to later stages of completing a project (e.g., drafts, revisions, and final versions of a project).

Parent–Teacher Conferences

To overcome the limited information provided by the traditional report card and to establish better cooperation between teachers and parents (or guardians), some schools

---

Tactful Remarks for Reporting to Parents

A teacher listed tactful ways of reporting to parents concerning their children's misbehavior in school. It included items such as the following:

- **Lying:** "Presents interesting oral reports but has difficulty in differentiating between factual and imaginary material."
- **Cheating:** "Uses all available resources in obtaining answers but needs help in determining when it is appropriate and inappropriate to get assistance from other students."

- **Bullying:** "Has leadership qualities but needs to redirect them into more constructive activities."
- **Laziness:** "Works on school tasks when given ample supervision but needs to develop independent work habits."

Caution: Although tact is desirable, it should not be an excuse for obscuring the message.

use regularly scheduled parent–teacher conferences. This reporting method is most widely used at the elementary level, with its greatest use in the primary grades.

The parent–teacher conference is a flexible procedure that provides for two-way communication between home and school. Besides receiving a report from the teacher, parents have an opportunity to present information concerning the student's out-of-school life. The conference permits teachers and parents to ask questions, discuss their common concerns in helping the student, and cooperatively plan a program for improving the student's learning and development. The give-and-take in such a conference makes it possible to avoid or overcome any misunderstandings concerning the student's progress.

Structuring a conference around a portfolio of student work can greatly facilitate communication between a teacher and parent by using explicit examples of accomplishments and progress. As was discussed in Chapter 12, portfolios can also provide a useful basis for a three-way conference of student, parent, and teacher.

The parent–teacher conference is an extremely useful tool, but it shares two important limitations with the informal letter: (a) It requires a substantial amount of time and skill, and (b) it does not provide a systematic record of student progress. In addition, some parents (or guardians) are unwilling or unable to come for conferences. Thus, it is most useful as a supplementary method of reporting.

MULTIPLE GRADING AND REPORTING SYSTEMS

Schools have used traditional letter grades (A, B, C, D, F) to report student progress for more than 80 years despite efforts to replace them with a more meaningful report. Their continued use indicates that they are serving some useful functions in the school (e.g., administrative). They are a simple and convenient means of maintaining permanent school records. Thus, rather than replace letter (or number) grades, it seems more sensible to try to improve the letter-grade system and supplement it with more detailed and meaningful reports of student learning progress. Some schools already use multiple grading and reporting systems.

The typical multiple reporting system retains the use of traditional grading (letter grades or numbers) and supplements the grades with checklists of objectives. In some cases, two grades are assigned to each subject: one for achievement and the other for effort, improvement, or growth. An example of a high school report form used for multiple grading is shown in Figure 15.1 The report form in the figure uses separate grades for achievement, effort, and ratings on two lists of objectives. On the left side is a list of common school objectives appearing on all the report forms. The list of objectives on the right side is of those pertaining to the particular subject being graded, in this case social studies. This report form makes it possible to assign an achievement grade that solely measures achievement because effort and other personal characteristics are graded separately. It also informs both the student and parents of the progress being made toward the school's objectives and each subject's objectives. This report form was developed by

PROGRESS REPORT
University of Illinois High School
Urbana, Illinois

SOCIAL STUDIES

_____ 1st quarter–November _____ 3rd quarter–April

_____ Semester–February _____ Final Report–June

RATING SCALE: + Outstanding S–Satisfactory U–Unsatisfactory O–Inadequate basis for judgment

S	+	U	O	Respects rights, opinions, and abilities of others
S	+	U	O	Accepts responsibility for group's progress
S	+	U	O	Is careful with property
S	+	U	O	Uses time to advantage
S	+	U	O	Is attentive
S	+	U	O	Makes regular preparations as directed

+ S U O Evidences independent thought and originality
+ S U O Seeks more than superficial knowledge
+ S U O Evidences growth in orderly and constructive group discussion
+ S U O Keeps informed on current affairs
+ S U O Discriminates in the selection and use of social studies materials
+ S U O Demonstrates growth in the skills of critical thinking
+ S U O Places people and events in their chronological and cultural setting
+ S U O Demonstrates social responsibility

ACHIEVEMENT

The grade is a measure of achievement with respect to what is expected of a student of this class in this school and in relation to what is expected in the next higher course in this subject.

_____ 5 excellent   _____ 2 passing, but weak
_____ 4 very good   _____ 1 failing
_____ 3 creditable   _____ 0 inadequate basis for judgment

EFFORT

The grade below is an estimate, based on evidence available to the teacher, of the individual student's effort.

_____ 5 excellent   _____ 2 weak
_____ 4 very good   _____ 1 very weak
_____ 3 creditable   _____ 0 inadequate basis for judgment

COMMENTS:

Teacher: _____

Figure 15.1
A comprehensive report form that combines dual grading and checklists of objectives

375

committees of students, parents, teachers, and other school personnel and thus reflects the types of information these groups considered most useful.

Guidelines for Developing a Multiple Grading and Reporting System

No grading and reporting system is likely to be equally satisfactory in all schools. Each school system must develop methods that fit its particular needs and circumstances. The following principles for devising a multiple grading and reporting system are guidelines for this purpose.

1. **The development of the grading and reporting system should be guided by the functions to be served.** The type of information most needed by the report's users should be included. This typically requires a study of the functions for which the reports are to be used by students, parents, teachers, counselors, and administrators. Although it is seldom possible to meet all their needs, a satisfactory compromise is more likely if they are known. It is helpful to supplement letter grades in each subject with separate reports on course objectives, effort, personal and social characteristics, and work habits. The letter grade should be retained as a pure measure of achievement, and any grades for improvement, effort, or growth should be made separately.

2. **The grading and reporting system should be developed cooperatively by parents, students, and school personnel.** School reports are apt to be most useful when all users have some voice in their development. This is usually done by organizing a committee consisting of representatives of parent groups, student organizations, elementary and secondary school teachers, counselors, and administrators. Ideas and suggestions are fed into the committee through the representatives, and the members carry back to their own respective groups, for modification and final approval, the committee's tentative plans. This cooperative participation not only will result in a more adequate reporting system but also increases the likelihood that the reports will be understood by those for whom they are intended.

3. **The grading and reporting system should be based on a clear statement of educational objectives.** The same objectives that have guided instruction and assessment should serve as a basis for grading and reporting. Some of these will be general school objectives, and others will be unique to particular courses or areas of study. Nevertheless, when devising a reporting system, the first question should be, How can we best report student progress toward these particular objectives? The final report form will be limited and modified by a number of practical considerations, but the central focus should be on the objectives of the school and course and the types of performance that represent the achievement of these objectives.

4. **The grading and reporting system should be consistent with school standards.** Schools and districts that are implementing content and performance standards need to review grading policies in light of those standards. The grading system needs to be aligned with the performance standards if it is to support rather than undermine the implementation of those standards. Use of the same categories for grades and performance standards is one obvious step. There is also a need, however, to align the performances that students are expected to achieve with the verbal descriptions of the performance standards.

5. The grading and reporting system should be based on adequate assessment. Teachers should not be expected to report on aspects of student performance when evidence is lacking or is unreliable. By the same token, including items on a report form assumes that the performance will be assessed as objectively as possible. Ratings on such items as critical thinking, for example, should be the product of testing, assessment, and controlled observation rather than snap judgments or hazy recollections of incidental happenings. Therefore, in planning a grading and reporting system, it is necessary to take into account the types of assessment data needed. The items included in the final report form should be those on which teachers can obtain reasonably reliable and valid information. The validity and reliability of the grade is directly determined by the reliability and validity of the items constituting the grade as well as having a reasonable number of items to determine the grade.

6. The grading and reporting system should be detailed enough to be diagnostic and yet compact enough to be practical. For guiding students' learning and development, we should present as comprehensive a picture of their strengths and weaknesses as possible. This desire for detail, however, must be balanced by such practical demands as (a) a reasonable amount of time required to prepare and use the reports; (b) reports that are understandable to students, parents, school and college or university personnel, and employers; and (c) reports that are easily summarized for school records. As noted earlier, a compromise between comprehensiveness and practicality is probably best obtained by supplementing the letter-grade system with more detailed reports on other aspects of student development.

7. The grading and reporting system should provide for parent–teacher conferences as needed. At the elementary school level, regularly scheduled conferences with parents might constitute part of the reporting system. At the high school level, such conferences are typically arranged as needed to deal with specific problems. At both levels, however, such conferences should supplement a more formal report form rather than replace it. A uniform method of reporting student progress is needed for school records, and this is difficult to obtain from conference notes.

In summary, a multiple grading and reporting system takes into account the varied needs of students, parents, teachers, and other school personnel. The letter-grade system (A, B, C, D, F) provides a simplified method of keeping a record of student achievement. The checklist of objectives provides a detailed report of student strengths and weaknesses in learning and development. The carefully constructed portfolio provides concrete examples of both progress and level of achievement. The parent–teacher conference helps maintain cooperation between home and school. When letter grades are supplemented by these other methods of reporting, the grades become more meaningful. Rather than being a conglomerate of achievement, effort, improvement, and personal behavior, letter grades can be confined to measuring achievement only. Multiple grading makes this possible by reporting separately on the other aspects of student development.

ASSIGNING LETTER GRADES

Because most schools use the A, B, C, D, F grading system, most teachers will be faced with the problem of assigning letter grades. This involves questions such as the following:

1. What should be included in a letter grade?
2. How should achievement data be combined in assigning letter grades?
3. What frame of reference should be used in grading?
4. How should the distribution of letter grades be determined?

Each of these issues is discussed in turn.

Determining What to Include in a Grade

As noted earlier, letter grades are likely to be most meaningful and useful when they represent achievement only. If they are contaminated by such extraneous factors as effort, amount of work completed (rather than quality of the work), personal conduct, and so on, their interpretation will become hopelessly confused. When letter grades combine various aspects of student development, they lose their meaningfulness as a measure of achievement and suppress other important aspects of development. A letter grade of B, for example, may represent average achievement with outstanding effort and excellent conduct or high achievement with little effort and some disciplinary infractions. Only by making the letter grade as pure a measure of achievement as possible and reporting on these other aspects separately can we hope to improve our descriptions of student learning and development.

Teachers often are comfortable with the notion that grades should be based strictly on achievement for students that they judge to be highly able; but they believe that effort should be considered along with achievement for students whom they judge to be less able (Stiggins, Frisbie, & Griswold, 1989). Although this position seems reasonable on the surface, it has some major drawbacks: (a) It is difficult, if not impossible, for a teacher to adequately assess a student's effort or potential; (b) it is difficult to distinguish between aptitude and achievement even with the most sophisticated measures, as both depend on student learning; and (c) using different bases of grading for different students sends a mixed message and may be unfair to students who are perceived as being more able than they are.

If letter grades are to be valid indicators of achievement, they must be based on valid measures of achievement. This involves the process described earlier in this book—defining the course objectives as intended learning outcomes and developing or selecting tests and assessments that measure these outcomes most directly. How much emphasis should be given to tests, ratings of performances, written reports, and other measures of achievement in the letter grades is determined by the nature of the course and the objectives being stressed. Thus, a grade in English might be determined largely by tests and writing projects, a grade in science by tests and assessments of laboratory performance, and a grade in music by tests and ratings on performance skills. The types of assessment data to include in a course grade and the relative emphasis to be given to each type of evidence are determined primarily by examining the instructional objectives.

Other things being equal, the more important an objective is, the greater the weight it should receive in the course grade. In the final analysis, letter grades should reflect the extent to which students have achieved the learning outcomes specified in the course objectives, and these should be weighted according to their relative importance.

Combining Data in Assigning Grades

When the aspects of achievement (e.g., tests, written reports, or performance ratings) to be included in a letter grade and the emphasis to be given to each aspect have been decided, the next step is to combine the various elements so that each element receives its intended weight. If we decide, for example, that the final examination should count 40%, the midterm 30%, laboratory performance 20%, and written reports 10%, then we will want our course grades to reflect these emphases. A typical procedure is to combine the elements into a composite score by assigning appropriate weights to each element and then use these composite scores as a basis for grading.

Combining data into a composite score to produce the desired weighting is not as simple as it may appear at first glance. This can be illustrated by a simple example. Let us assume that we want to combine scores on a final examination and a term report and that we want them to be given equal weight. Our range of scores on the two measures is as follows:

Range of Scores

Final examination	80 to 100
Term report	10 to 50

In practice, we would want to combine more than two assessment results before assigning grades, but the use of just two elements is sufficient for illustration. Because the two sets of scores are to be given equal weight, we may be inclined simply to add together the final examination score and the term report score for each student. We can check on the effectiveness of this procedure by comparing the composite score of a student who is highest on the final examination and lowest on the term report (100 + 10 = 110) with a student who is lowest on the final examination and highest on the term report (80 + 50 = 130). It is obvious from this comparison that simply adding together the two scores will not give them equal representation.

Another common but erroneous method of equating scores is to make the maximum possible scores the same for both sets of scores. For our scores, this would mean multiplying the scores on the term report by 2, so that the top score on both measures would equal 100. Applying this procedure to the same two extreme cases we considered earlier, our first student would have a score of 120 (100 + 20) and our second student a score of 180 (80 + 100). It is obvious that this procedure does not equate the scores. In fact, there is now an even larger difference between the two composite scores, because the influence each component has on the composite score depends on the variability, or spread, of scores, not on the total number of points. Thus, to properly weight the components in a composite score, the variability of the scores must be taken into account.

The range of scores in our example provides a measure of score variability, or spread, and this can be used to give the two sets of scores comparable weight. We can give the final examination and the term report equal weight in the composite score by using a multiplier that makes the two ranges equal. Because the final examination scores have a range of 20 (100 – 80) and the term report scores a range of 40 (50 – 10), we would need to multiply each final examination score by 2 to obtain the desired equal weight. Note that this weighting is the reverse of the incorrect weighting procedure based on making the maximum possible scores equal. We can check on the effectiveness of this procedure by using the same two cases we considered earlier. The student highest on the final examination and lowest on the term report would now have a score of 210 (200 + 10), and the student lowest on the final examination and highest on the term report would also have a score of 210 (160 + 50). Our check shows that the procedure gives the two sets of scores equal weight in the composite score. If we wanted our final examination to count twice as much as the term report, it would be necessary to multiply each final examination score by 4 rather than by 2.

A more refined weighting system can be obtained by using the standard deviation as the measure of variability. For teachers with access to computers, this is a simple matter of converting scores on each test or assessment to T-scores (see Chapter 19). The T-scores can then be multiplied by whatever weights are desired and summed to yield a composite

Using T-Scores to Compute Composite Scores

Assessment Component	Mean	Standard Deviation	Desired Weight	$T = 50 + 10\ [(X - M)/S]$
Midterm (X1)	30	10	20%	$T1 = 50 + 10\ [(X1 - 30)/10]$
Project (X2)	20	4	40%	$T2 = 50 + 10\ [(X2 - 20)/4]$
Final (X3)	65	20	40%	$T3 = 50 + 10\ [(X3 - 65)/20]$

	Raw Scores			T-Scores			Weighted Composite
Students	X1	X2	X3	T1	T2	T3	.2T1 + .4T2 + .4T3
Bob	20	16	55	40	40	45	42
Carla	20	18	45	40	45	40	42
Casey	40	24	85	60	60	60	60
Eva	30	20	95	50	50	65	56

X = raw score, M = mean, S = standard deviation

Note that Bob and Carla have the same weighted composite T-score and that Casey has a slightly higher weighted composite T-score than Eva. If the difference in standard deviations had been ignored and the same weights were applied to raw scores, the weighted composite raw scores would give Bob a higher score (32.4) than Carla (29.2) because he had his best performance on the component with the largest standard deviation, whereas she had her best performance on the component with the smallest standard deviation. Consider why Casey's weighted composite raw score (51.6) is slightly lower than Eva's (52), but their T-scores show the opposite pattern.

score for which grades are assigned (see the box "Using T-Scores to Compute Composite Scores"). Using T-scores or other ways of converting scores to account for differences in standard deviations can easily be accomplished with a personal computer and specialized software described later in this chapter that is designed for purposes of grading. However, the range is satisfactory for most classroom purposes.

Selecting the Proper Frame of Reference for Grading

Letter grades are typically assigned on the basis of one of the following frames of reference:

1. Performance in relation to other group members (relative grading)
2. Performance in relation to specified standards (absolute grading)
3. Performance in relation to learning ability or amount of improvement

Assigning grades on a relative basis involves comparing a student's performance with that of a reference group, typically one's classmates. With this system, the grade is determined by the student's relative ranking in the total group rather than by some absolute standard of achievement. Because the grading is based on relative performance, the grade is influenced by both the student's performance and the performance of the group. Thus, one will fare much better, gradewise, in a low-achieving group than in a high-achieving group.

Although relative grading has the disadvantage of a shifting frame of reference (i.e., grades depend on the group's ability), it is widely used in the schools because much of classroom testing is norm referenced. That is, the tests are designed to rank students in order of achievement rather than to describe achievement in absolute terms. Although position in the group is the key element in a relative system of grading, the actual grades assigned are also likely to be influenced to some extent by achievement expectations the teacher has acquired from teaching other groups. Thus, a high-achieving group of students is likely to receive a larger proportion of good grades than a low-achieving group.

The disadvantages of relative grading are particularly evident in high school, where higher-achieving students may enroll in more challenging advanced or honors courses. Achievement slightly below the class average in an advanced or honors course may actually be equal to or better than that of the highest-ranking student in another, less demanding course in the same subject. It is both misleading and unfair to give the former student a C while the latter student receives an A. Some states have given formal recognition to the more demanding nature of honors courses. Rather than converting letter grades of A, B, C, and D to numerical values of 4, 3, 2, and 1, respectively, for computing grade-point averages, as would be done for a typical course, honors course grades would be converted to values of 5, 4, 3, and 2. Another approach with relative grading that gives appropriate recognition to student self-selection and the more demanding nature of advanced and honors courses is simply to give a larger percentage of As and Bs in those courses than in typical courses.

Assigning grades on an absolute basis involves comparing a student's performance to specified standards set by the teacher, preferably in reference to agreed-on performance standards for the school and/or district. These standards may be concerned with the degree of mastery to be achieved by students and may be specified as (a) tasks to be performed (e.g., type 40 words per minute without error) or (b) the percentage of correct answers to be obtained on a test designed to measure a clearly defined set of learning tasks. In recent years, school, district, or even state performance standards have been adopted and are intended to guide the absolute judgments about whether a student's record of performance meets the established standards.

With a standards-based system, letter grades are assigned on the basis of an absolute standard of performance rather than a relative one. If all students demonstrate a high level of mastery consistent with the established performance standards, then all will receive high grades.

The absolute grading required for a standard-based reporting system is much more complex than it first appears. To use absolute level of achievement as a basis for grading requires that (a) the domain of learning tasks be clearly defined, (b) the standards of performance be clearly specified and justified, and (c) the measures of student achievement be criterion referenced. These conditions are difficult to meet except in a mastery learning situation. When complete mastery is the goal, the learning tasks tend to be more limited and easily defined. In addition, percentage-correct scores, which are widely used in setting absolute standards, are most meaningful in mastery learning because they indicate how far a student is from complete mastery. All too frequently, schools use absolute grading based on percentage-correct scores (e.g., A = 95–100, B = 85–94, C = 75–84, D = 65–74, F = below 65), but the domain of learning tasks has not been clearly defined, and the standards have been set in a completely arbitrary manner. To fit the grading system, teachers attempt to build norm-referenced tests with scores in the 60 to 100 range. If the test turns out to be too difficult or too easy, they adjust the scores to fit the absolute grading scale. But such grades are difficult to interpret because they represent an adjusted level of performance, often with an ill-defined adjustment procedure, on some ill-defined conglomerate of learning tasks.

Although reporting student performance in relation to learning ability or amount of improvement shown is fairly widespread at the elementary school level, it is inconsistent with a standards-based system of evaluating and reporting student performance. Moreover, grading in relationship to student ability or in terms of student improvement is fraught with difficulties. Making reliable estimates of learning ability, with or without tests, is a formidable task because judgments or measurements of ability are likely to be contaminated by achievement to some unknown degree. Similarly, improvement (i.e., growth in achievement) over short spans of time is extremely difficult to estimate reliably with classroom measures of achievement. Thus, the lack of reliability in judging achievement in relation to ability and in judging degree of improvement will result in grades of low dependability. If used at all (e.g., to motivate low-ability students), such grades should be supplementary. In dual grading, for example, one letter grade might indicate level of achievement (relative or absolute), and the second letter grade might be used to represent achievement in relation to ability or the degree of improvement shown since the last grading period.

Determining the Distribution of Grades

As noted in the previous section, there are two ways of assigning letter grades to measure the level of student achievement: the relative grading system based on relative level of achievement and the absolute grading system based on absolute level of achievement.

Relative Grading.   The assignment of relative grades is essentially a matter of ranking the students in order of overall achievement and assigning letter grades on the basis of each student's rank in the group. This ranking might be limited to a single classroom group or might be based on the combined distributions of several classroom groups taking the same course. In any event, before letter grades can be assigned, the proportion of As, Bs, Cs, Ds, and Fs to be used must be determined.

Although clearly inconsistent with current efforts to introduce and use standards-based grading and reporting systems, one method of grading that has been widely used in the past and is still used in some schools is to assign grades on the basis of the normal curve. Grading on the normal curve results in an equal percentage of As and Fs and Bs and Ds. Thus, regardless of the group's level of ability, the proportion of high grades is balanced by an equal proportion of low grades. Such grading is seldom defensible for classroom groups because (a) the groups are usually too small to yield a normal distribution and (b) classroom assessment instruments are usually not designed to yield normally distributed scores. It is only when a course or combined courses have a relatively large and unselected group of students that grading on the normal curve might be defended. Even, then, however, one might ask whether the decision concerning the distribution of grades should be left to a statistical model (e.g., normal curve) or should be made on a more rational basis.

If "grading on the curve" is to be used, the most sensible approach in determining the distribution of letter grades to be used in a school is to have the school staff set general guidelines for the approximate distribution of grades. This might involve separate distributions for introductory and advanced courses, for gifted and remedial classes, and the like. In any event, the distributions should be flexible enough to allow for variation in the performance of students from one course to another and from one time to another in the same course. Indicating ranges rather than fixed percentages of students who should receive each letter grade offers this flexibility. Thus, a suggested distribution for an introductory course might be stated as follows:

A = 10% to 20% of the students

B = 20% to 30% of the students

C = 30% to 50% of the students

D = 10% to 20% of the students

F = 0% to 10% of the students

These percentage ranges are presented for illustrative purposes only; there is no simple or scientific means of determining what these ranges should be for a given situation. The decision must be made by the local school staff, taking into account the school's philosophy, the student population, and the purposes of the grades. All staff members must understand the basis for assigning grades, and this basis must be clearly communicated to users of the grades.

In setting an approximate distribution of grades for teachers to follow, the distribution should provide for the possibility of *no* failing grades. Whether students pass or fail a course should be based on their absolute level of learning rather than their relative position in some group. If all low-ranking students have mastered enough of the material to succeed at the next-higher level of instruction, they all probably should pass. On the other hand, if some have not mastered the minimum essentials needed at the next-higher level, these students probably should fail. Whether minimum performance has been attained can be determined by reviewing the low-ranking students' performance on tests and other assessment instruments or by administering a special mastery test on the course's minimum essentials. Thus, even when grading is done on a relative basis, the pass–fail decision must be based on an absolute standard of achievement if it is to be educationally sound.

Absolute Grading.   If the course's objectives have been clearly specified and the standards for mastery appropriately set, the letter grades in an absolute system may be defined as the degree to which the objectives have been attained, as follows:

A = Outstanding. Student has mastered all the course's major and minor instructional goals.

B = Very good. Student has mastered all the course's major instructional goals and most of the minor ones.

C = Satisfactory. Student has mastered all the course's major instructional goals but just a few of the minor ones.

D = Very weak. Student has mastered just a few of the course's major and minor instructional goals and barely has the essentials needed for the next highest level of instruction. Remedial work would be desirable.

F = Unsatisfactory. Student has not mastered any of the course's major instructional goals and lacks the essentials needed for the next highest level of instruction. Remedial work is needed.

If the tests and other assessment instruments have been designed to yield scores in terms of the percentage of correct answers, absolute grading then might be defined as follows:

A = 95% to 100% correct

B = 85% to 94% correct

C = 75% to 84% correct

D = 65% to 74% correct

F = below 65% correct

It should be emphasized, however, that it is a nontrivial task to design a test such that these ranges or any other prespecified ranges will correspond to the intended standards of performance for those grades.

As noted earlier, defining letter grades in this manner is defensible only if the necessary conditions of an absolute grading system have been met. Using percentage-correct scores when the measuring instruments are based on some undefined hodgepodge of learning tasks produces uninterpretable grades.

With absolute grading systems such as these, the distribution of grades is not predetermined. If all students demonstrate a high level of mastery, all will receive high grades. If some students demonstrate a low level of performance, they will receive low grades. See the "Guidelines" box.

The absolute grading system for reporting on student progress seldom uses letter grades alone. A comprehensive report generally includes a checklist of objectives to inform both student and parent which objectives have been mastered and which have not been mastered by the end of each grading period. In some standards-based programs, letter grades (or numbers) are assigned to each objective or benchmark associated with a content standard to indicate the level of proficiency that has been achieved. An example of such a report form, designed for use in a middle school, is shown in Figure 15.2. This form is designed for reporting on benchmarks at the middle school level associated with one of the six Colorado Model Content Standards for Mathematics. A numerical rating is assigned to each objective as follows:

Has Acquired Proficiency

4 = Skill well developed, good proficiency

3 = Skill developed satisfactorily, proficiency could be improved

2 = Basic skill developed, low proficiency, needs additional work

Not Acquired

1 = Basic skill not acquired

As with other types of absolute grading, the number of 1s, 2s, 3s, and 4s to be assigned to each benchmark associated with the standard is not predetermined but depends entirely

GUIDELINES

Effective Grading

1. Describe your grading procedures to students at the beginning of instruction.
2. Make clear to students that the course grade will be based on achievement only.
3. Explain how other elements (effort, work habits, and personal–social characteristics) will be reported.
4. Relate the grading procedures to the intended learning outcomes (i.e., instructional goals and objectives).
5. Obtain valid evidence (e.g., tests, assessments, reports, or ratings) as a basis for assigning grades.
6. Take precautions to prevent cheating on tests and assessments.
7. Return and review all test and assessment results as soon as possible.
8. Properly weight the various types of achievement included in the grade.
9. Do not lower an achievement grade for tardiness, weak effort, or misbehavior.
10. Be fair. Avoid bias, and when in doubt (as with a borderline score), review the evidence. If still in doubt, assign the higher grade.

Example Content Standard for Middle School Mathematics

Colorado Model Content Standards for Mathematics: Standard 2

"Students use algebraic methods to explore, model, and describe patterns and functions involving numbers, shapes, data, and graphs in problem-solving situations and communicate the reasoning used in solving these problems" (see http://www.cde.state.co.us/download/pdf/math.pdf).

Middle School Reported Proficiencies

	Achievement of Benchmark			
	4	3	2	1
1. Representing patterns and relationships in tables and graphs	___	___	___	___
2. Analyzing patterns and relationships using standard algebraic notation	___	___	___	___
3. Describing patterns using variables, equations, and expressions	___	___	___	___
4. Analyzing functional relationships between variables	___	___	___	___
5. Using functional relationships to explain how change in one variable results in change in another	___	___	___	___
6. Using and distinguishing between linear and nonlinear functions	___	___	___	___
7. Solving simple linear equations using a variety of methods	___	___	___	___
8. Using a calculator to solve problems	___	___	___	___
9. Using a computer to solve problems	___	___	___	___

Figure 15.2

Illustrative report form used for reporting benchmarks intended to be consistent with content standard

on the absolute level of performance achieved by each student. If all students achieve good proficiency on a particular objective, all will receive 4s on that benchmark.

RECORD-KEEPING AND GRADING SOFTWARE

Gradebooks have been a familiar part of teaching for many decades. Although that is as true in the 21st century as it was at the start of the 20th, the form of the gradebook has undergone substantial change as electronic gradebooks replace or supplement the familiar notebook-style paper gradebook.

Although any simple spreadsheet can be used as a gradebook, a host of specialized software is available that is designed to facilitate the common tasks of recording and combining grades. Most computer gradebook software is based on an underlying spreadsheet design. The software may have templates to aid in data entry and simple procedures for specifying rules for combining grades from several sources, such as home-work, tests, assessments, and projects. The software also provides various options for printing, reporting, and summarizing results. Sometimes the gradebook software may be linked to software designed to perform other functions, such as test construction, item banking, test administration, or keeping attendance.

A listing of a few examples of gradebook software programs is provided in the box "Examples of Gradebook Computer Software." The list is not exhaustive but provides a range of examples. Because existing software is constantly being updated and new software is added on a regular basis, a search of the Internet is a good way to bring such a list up to date and learn about new options. A brief overview written by Sherril Steele-Carlin is available on the Education World Web site at http://www.education-world.com/a_tech/tech031.shtml.

CONDUCTING PARENT–TEACHER CONFERENCES

Regardless of the type of grading and reporting system used in the school, the parent–teacher conference is an important supplement to the written report of student progress. The face-to-face conference makes it possible to share information with parents (or guardians), to overcome any misunderstanding between home and school, and to plan cooperatively a program of maximum benefit to the student. At the elementary school level, where parent–teacher cooperation is particularly important, conferences with parents are regularly scheduled. At the secondary level, the parent–teacher conference is typically used only when some special problem situation arises.

Examples of Gradebook Computer Software

Software	Company	Web site
1st Class GradeBook	1st Class Software	http://www.1st-class-software.com
Class Mate Grading	4th Street	http://www.classmategrading.com
GradeGenie™ Software	Kilowatt Software	http://www.kilowattsoftware.com/GradeGeniepage.htm
Class Action Gradebook	CalEd Software	http://www.classactiongradebook.com
MyGradeBook	Pearson Education	http://www.mygradebook.com/default.cfm
Grade Machine®	Misty City Software	http://www.mistycity.com

Conferences with parents are most likely to be productive when they are preceded by careful planning and the teacher has skill in conducting such conferences. Many schools offer in-service training for teachers to help them develop effective conference techniques. Typically, such training includes knowledge of how to conduct a parent–teacher conference and role playing to practice the use of conference skills. The following points provide helpful reminders when preparing for and conducting parent–teacher conferences.

1. Make plans for the conference. Determine ahead of time the goals of the conference. Your main purpose may be to inform parents of their student's progress, but you may also want to obtain information from parents, make suggestions for home study, or discuss how to solve a particular problem. It is helpful to review the student's record, organize the information you are going to present, and make a list of points you want to cover and questions you plan to ask. Portfolios can provide a good basis for highlighting topics for discussion, but only if the entries are carefully selected and reviewed.

2. Begin the conference in a positive manner. Starting the conference by making a positive statement about the student sets the tone for the meeting. Saying something like "Kimberly really enjoys helping others," "Ruben is an expert on dinosaurs," or "Marie is always smiling" tends to create a cooperative and friendly atmosphere. Once established, this positive attitude should be maintained throughout the conference.

3. Present the student's strong points before describing areas needing improvement. It is helpful to present examples of the student's work when discussing the student's performance. A brief review of portfolio entries before the conference is useful in identifying appropriate examples. The work examples help keep the focus on what the student can do and what he or she has yet to learn. Showing a mathematics test to a parent is much more effective than simply saying the student "does addition problems well but has difficulty with division problems" or "is good with simple computation but needs help with story problems." Similarly, showing examples of an essay written in September alongside one written the following February makes the statement that the student's writing "has shown great improvement" much more concrete.

4. Encourage parents to participate and share information. Although as a teacher you are in charge of the conference, you must be willing to listen to parents and share information rather than "talk at" them. They may have questions and concerns about the school and about their child's behavior that need to be brought out before constructive, cooperative action can be taken.

5. Plan a course of action cooperatively. The discussion should lead to what steps can be taken by the teacher and the parent to help the student. A brief summary at the end of the conference should review the points discussed and the action to be taken at home and school.

6. End the conference with a positive comment. At the end of the conference, thank the parents for coming and say something positive about the student, such as "Noah has a good sense of humor, and I enjoy having him in class." Any such statement should, of course, fit the student and not be a vague generality that is used repeatedly.

7. Use good human relations skills during the conference. Some of these skills can be summarized by the following **do's** and **don'ts.**

Do's
- Be friendly and informal.
- Be positive in your approach.
- Be willing to explain in understandable terms.
- Be willing to listen.
- Be willing to accept parents' feelings.
- Be careful about giving advice.

Don'ts
- Don't argue or get angry.
- Don't ask embarrassing questions.
- Don't talk about other students, teachers, or parents.
- Don't bluff if you don't know an answer.
- Don't reject parents' suggestions.
- Don't be a know-it-all, with pat answers.

Although one cannot expect to conduct an effective conference by reading about how to do it, these points serve as a helpful reminder of things to do and to avoid when preparing for a conference.

REPORTING STANDARDIZED TEST RESULTS TO PARENTS

Standardized test results are sometimes reported to parents during a parent–teacher conference. Although parents may have a legal right to all information the school has concerning their children, it should be presented to them in an understandable and usable form. This means avoiding technical jargon and presenting test results to parents in language that is meaningful to them. There also will be less chance of misunderstanding and more chance of being viewed in proper perspective if the test results are presented as part of the total pattern of information about the student.

In preparing to report to parents, review the test results and decide when and how they will be introduced into the conference. The meaningful communication of test results to parents includes the following:

1. Describing what the test measures
2. Explaining the meaning of test scores
3. Clarifying the accuracy of test scores
4. Discussing the use of test results

The amount of detail you give in each of these areas will, of course, depend on the time available for the conference and the parents' depth of understanding of the test results. In general, it is best to keep the explanations brief and simple. Do not overwhelm parents with more test information than they can grasp in the short span of time that is typically available for presenting test information.

Describing What the Test Measures

In reporting on the results of an aptitude or learning ability test, saying something like "This test measures skills and abilities useful in school learning" may be sufficient. If the test contains several scores (e.g., verbal, quantitative, and nonverbal), each section of the test may be described in similarly general terms. Test manuals usually contain general descriptions of the tests and subtests that can be used to explain the test to parents. The following list of things to avoid should help prevent misinterpretation.

1. Do not refer to aptitude or learning ability tests as intelligence tests. The term *intelligence* is emotionally charged and often misunderstood.
2. Do not describe aptitude or learning ability tests as measures of fixed abilities. They are not! They measure learned abilities.
3. Do not say, "These test scores predict how well your child will do in school." They won't! Predictions for individuals are hazardous at best, and many factors determine school success. It is better to say something like "Students with scores like these usually do well in school" or, for low scores, " . . . usually find learning difficult."

Achievement tests are easily described in terms of the test content, and the names of the subtests usually indicate what the test measures. To say that a reading test measures "vocabulary and reading comprehension" or that a math test measures "computation and problem solving" is frequently sufficient. In some cases, it may be desirable to describe the test results by objective or item clusters, and these are typically identified on the student's individual report form. When narrative report forms are used, the test content is included as part of the narrative report.

Interpretations of vocational interest inventories, personality inventories, and other guidance-oriented assessment devices are best interpreted by the school counselor or other guidance personnel. Parents should be referred to the appropriate staff member if they have questions about scores on these instruments.

Explaining the Meaning of Test Scores

More detailed discussion of standardized tests and the meaning of various types of scores are provided in Chapters 16 through 19. In this section, we simply provide a broad overview of issues in explaining standardized test results to parents. In making norm-referenced interpretations of test scores, both the meaning of the score and the nature of the norm group should be explained to parents, both simply and understandably. Percentile ranks, grade-equivalent scores, and stanines are widely used in reporting to parents because they are easy to explain and misinterpretations are less likely to occur. Saying something like the following will usually suffice with these scores.

Figure 15.3 shows the relation of stanines, percentile ranks, and broad verbal descriptions that can be used in reporting to parents.

It is wise to report all test results in terms of the same type of score (e.g., percentile ranks, grade equivalents, or stanines). This makes it easier to explain the scores to parents and makes comparisons among tests more understandable.

Although parents are interested in how their child's test performance compares with that of other children, they also want to know what the child has learned and has yet to

EXAMPLES   *Interpreting percentile ranks:* "On the reading vocabulary test, Mary scored higher than 85% of a national group of fourth-grade students." (It might also be necessary to point out that the 85% refers not to the percentage of items answered correctly but only to the percentage of students scoring lower.)

Interpreting grade-equivalent scores: "On the reading vocabulary test, Mary scored as well as the typical student in a national group did in the spring of the fifth grade. That is well above the national average for fourth-grade students. The score does not necessarily mean that Mary can do all aspects of fifth-grade work, however, only that she does fourth-grade work better than most in the fourth grade and about as well as the typical fifth-grade student."

Interpreting stanines: "On a scale of 1 to 9, on which the average score is 5, Mary received a score of 7 on the reading vocabulary test, when compared with a national group of fourth-grade students." (In some cases it may be desirable to use verbal descriptions such as *above average* [7, 8, 9], *average* [4, 5, 6], or *below average* [1, 2, 3] in place of numbers.)

learn. This type of criterion-referenced interpretation is more readily understood by parents and is typically reported in terms of relative degree of mastery. If you use percentage-correct scores, you may want to distinguish between percentile scores and percentage-correct scores. If you use mastery–nonmastery designations, describe the standard of mastery and explain how it was determined.

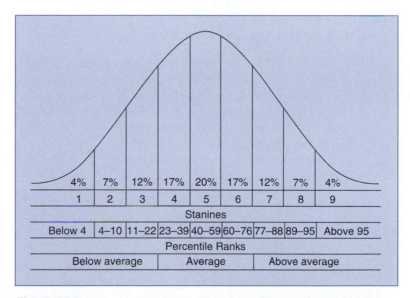

Figure 15.3
Relation of stanines, percentile ranks, and broad verbal descriptions in a normal distribution

Clarifying the Accuracy of Test Scores

It is important to communicate to parents that all test scores contain some error. This can be done most easily if confidence bands (i.e., error bands) are used in interpreting test scores. Profiles using percentile rank frequently include confidence bands. If these are not available, percentile ranks should be interpreted as estimates that may vary up or down by several points on retesting.

Stanines contain broad units that allow for measurement error. Because each stanine is at least half a standard deviation wide, a difference of two stanines usually represents a significant difference in test performance.

Thus, if we had scores such as these,

Mathematics	8
Reading	6
Science	5

we could make the following interpretation: "Performance is higher in mathematics than reading and science, but there is no real difference in performance between reading and science." Parents should be told that a difference of 1 stanine is so small that it can be accounted for by errors of measurement alone.

When interpreting test results by objective or by item cluster, attention should be paid to the number of items on which each interpretation is based. If the number of items is small (say less than 10), make only tentative interpretations and explain to the parents that these are simply clues to be verified by further study. When combined with the results of teacher-made tests and other classroom work, more dependable interpretations may be possible. It is always good practice to interpret test scores to parents in light of the other available data concerning the student.

Discussing the Use of Test Results

The interpretation of test results should be accompanied by an explanation of how the test results are to be used in the instructional program and a discussion of what action should be taken by both teacher and parent to improve the student's learning and development. This discussion, of course, should not be limited to the test results but should be based on all the evidence concerning the student's learning and development. The value of test scores becomes clearer to parents when they are coordinated with all the other information about the student and when they are seen as contributing to plans for constructive action.

SUMMARY

School grades and progress reports serve various functions in the school. They provide information that is helpful to students, parents, and school personnel. Students find them useful as summary appraisals of learning progress that serve somewhat the same functions as other assessment results. Parents, teachers, and counselors use the information in guiding learning and development and in helping students make realistic future plans.

Administrators use the information to determine promotion, athletic eligibility, honors, and graduation. The reports also provide a basis for reporting to other schools, to colleges and universities, and to prospective employers.

The diverse functions of progress reports make it difficult to find a universally satisfactory reporting method. Some of the methods that have been tried include (a) the traditional grading system (e.g., A, B, C, D, F), (b) the pass–fail system, (c) checklists of objectives, (d) informal letters, (e) portfolios of selected examples of student work, and (f) parent–teacher conferences. Each method has rather severe limitations when used alone. Probably the best reporting system combines a concise grade for administrative functions with a more detailed report and portfolio for teaching and guidance purposes. In any event, some combination of methods seems most appropriate.

The letter-grade system of grading (A, B, C, D, F) continues to be the most widely used system at both the elementary and secondary levels despite attempts to replace it with a more meaningful report. This is probably because such grades are easily assigned and averaged and serve many useful administrative functions. Thus, it seems sensible to retain letter grades as a pure measure of achievement and to supplement them with more detailed and meaningful reports of learning progress. Such a multiple grading and reporting system should be developed cooperatively by parents, students, teachers, and other school personnel. Efforts should be made to develop a system that is in harmony with the functions to be served, the school's objectives, and the assessment data available. Ideally, the report form should be as comprehensive and detailed as is practical and should be supplemented by parent–teacher conferences as needed.

Whether or not a multiple grading and reporting system is used in a school, most teachers will be responsible for assigning letter grades to students. This involves such considerations as determining what to include in the letter grade, how to combine the various achievement data into a composite, what frame of reference to use, and what distribution of letter grades to use. The letter grade is most likely to provide a meaningful measure of achievement when (a) it reflects the extent to which students have attained the learning outcomes specified in the instructional goals and objectives, (b) it is based on valid measures of achievement, and (c) each component of achievement is weighted in terms of its relative importance. Assigning weights to each component requires that the variability (i.e., spread) of scores be taken into account.

Letter grades may be used to indicate a student's relative level of achievement or absolute level of achievement. When assigning relative grades, the normal curve is seldom an appropriate model for determining the distribution of grades. A more sensible approach is to have the school staff set up suggested distributions of grades that take into account the school's philosophy, the student population, the nature of the course (e.g., whether it is an advanced or honors course), and the purposes to be served by the grades. Attention should be given to ensuring that the grades are aligned with and contribute to performance standards adopted by the school or district. In absolute grading, the letter grades represent the degree to which the performance standards have been achieved. With this system, no predetermined distribution of letter grades is specified. If all students achieve a high degree of proficiency, all will receive high grades.

Even when students are assigned grades on a relative basis, the pass–fail decision should be based on a student's absolute level of achievement. The important consideration is whether the student has the minimum knowledge and skills needed to succeed at the next-highest level of instruction.

Letter grades are sometimes assigned on the basis of performance in relation to learning ability or amount of improvement. The problems of adequately judging learning ability apart from achievement and of reliably measuring learning gain over short spans of time restrict the use of these grading methods. If used at all (e.g., for motivation purposes), such grades should supplement grades based on the student's relative or absolute level of achievement.

Parent–teacher conferences are an important method of sharing information with parents. Such conferences should supplement the more formal written report of student progress, however, rather than replace it. Effective conferences with parents require careful planning and sound conference techniques. Portfolios of student work can help make both student progress and level of achievement concrete for parents. Because reports of standardized test results also may be expected to be part of some conferences, teachers should know how to report test results to parents. Although guidelines are useful in preparing for conferences with parents, in-service training is usually needed to develop adequate conference skills.

LEARNING EXERCISES

1. What are the advantages and limitations of each of the following grading systems?
   a. Letter-grade system (A, B, C, D, F)
   b. Pass–fail system
   c. A standards-based reporting system (e.g., advanced, proficient, partially proficient, and unsatisfactory)
   d. Checklist of objectives

2. What types of information are most useful in a grading and reporting system designed to support the instructional program of the school? Why?

3. What are the advantages and limitations of a multiple grading and reporting system?

4. What are some of the uses of portfolios of student work? How are portfolios different than simple files of student work?

5. If you were to help set up a grading and reporting system for the level at which you plan to teach, what types of grades and reports would you want included? Why?

6. What procedures are involved in using an absolute basis for grading? What are some of the problems in using this system?

7. What are the advantages and limitations of assigning grades on a relative basis?

8. Describe the procedure for combining two test scores into a composite score where one of the scores is given twice the weight of the other.

9. List as many ways as you can think of for improving grading and reporting in the school.

10. What factors should be considered when deciding whether to pass or fail a student? Do you think the decision should be based on a relative standard or an absolute standard? Why?

11. What types of information should you have at hand during the parent–teacher conference? How would you explain to parents that their child was performing poorly in school? Describe the general approach that you would use in explaining test scores to parents.

REFERENCES

Stiggins, R. J., Frisbie, D. A., & Griswold, P. A. (1989). Inside high school grading practices: Building a research agenda. *Educational Measurement: Issues and Practice, 8*(2), 5–14.

FURTHER READING

Airasian, P. W. (2004). *Classroom assessment* (5th ed.). New York: McGraw-Hill. The chapter on grading provides a discussion of grading and gives examples of report cards.

Arter, J. R., & Spandel, V. (1992). Using portfolios of student work in instruction and assessment. *Educational Measurement: Issues and Practice, 11*(1), 36–44. Describes characteristics of portfolios and provides suggestions on their design. The article is part of an instructional module series of the National Council on Measurement in Education.

Gronlund, N. E. (2005). *Assessment of student achievement* (8th ed.). Boston: Allyn & Bacon. Chapter 10, "Grading and Reporting," discusses the selection of the basis for grades as well as straightforward examples of combining results to determine grades.

Macmillan, J. H. (2006). *Classroom assessment: Principles and practice for effective instruction* (4th ed.). Boston: Allyn & Bacon. Chapter 11, "Grading and Reporting Student Performance," describes the functions and types of grades as well as ways of combining results from different assessments into grades. Also discusses reporting to parents and provides a list of computer software packages in Appendix C.

Ory, J. C., & Ryan, K. E. (1993). *Tips for improving testing and grading.* Newbury Park, CA: Sage Publications. Chapter 7, "Assigning Grades," discusses the purposes of grading and provides suggestions for developing and implementing a grading strategy.

Popham, W. J. (2007). *Classroom assessment: What teachers need to know* (5th ed.). Boston: Allyn & Bacon. Chapter 15, "Evaluating, Teaching and Grading Students," includes a discussion of electronic record keeping and grading.

Terwilliger, J. S. (1989). Classroom standard-setting and grading practices. *Educational Measurement: Issues and Practice, 8*(2), 15–19. Presents a model of grading that combines features of normative and absolute grading approaches.

CHAPTER

16

ACHIEVEMENT TESTS

There are hundreds of published achievement tests available for use. Some consist of a battery of tests, whereas others measure an individual subject or skill; some provide a general survey of learning outcomes, whereas others provide descriptive and diagnostic information. Some are off-the-shelf published tests; some are customized to specifications of state assessment programs. Becoming familiar with these basic types of achievement tests and principles of selection and use should provide helpful guidelines for effective achievement testing.

Achievement testing plays an important role in the school program, and published achievement tests are widely used at both the elementary and secondary school levels. Most published achievement tests are called standardized achievement tests. These typically are norm-referenced tests that measure the students' level of achievement in various content and skill areas by comparing their test performance with the performance of other students in some general reference group (e.g., a nationwide sample of students at the same grade level). Quite a few criterion-referenced achievement tests also have been published.

In recent years, a number of states and districts have introduced their own testing and assessment systems or have contracted with publishers to develop assessments to their specifications. The tests and assessments developed under contract are frequently customized with the intent of aligning with a state or district's content standards. Those customized tests may include elements of a published test but are usually supplemented to cover the content specified in the standards. Many of these assessments have included open-ended performance assessment tasks. Test publishers also market writing assessments and other types of open-ended performance assessments as supplements to their standardized tests. Nevertheless, standardized tests are still widely used either as part of a broader assessment system or alone, in part because they provide an efficient and relatively inexpensive means of measuring broad achievement goals. Hence, it is important to understand the strengths and weaknesses of these tests.

Although norm-referenced achievement tests, criterion-referenced achievement tests, and tests customized to specific content standards can be considered distinct test types, test publishers often attempt to incorporate elements of each in the same test. For example, most newly developed standardized achievement tests provide for both norm-referenced interpretation and interpretation by objective or skill area. Some of the customized tests developed for states not only report results in terms of specified performance standards but also provide normative interpretations of results. Caution is needed when interpreting by objective or specific content standard, however, because standardized tests usually cover such a broad area of achievement that there may be relatively few items for each objective or skill being measured. On the other hand, some criterion-referenced achievement tests provide norms for further interpretation.

Few teachers have the chance to make decisions to purchase a particular standardized test or to shape the requirements of a customized test developed under a state or district contract. Teachers may have an opportunity to be involved in committees that review off-the-shelf tests for district purchase or committees that review proposals from potential contractors to construct tests customized to content standards. Furthermore, almost all teachers are expected to administer the tests and participate in the use and interpretation of the results. Thus, it is important to understand the strengths and weaknesses of these instruments and to know how to interpret the results that they provide.

We begin by examining the characteristics of norm-referenced standardized achievement tests and showing how they compare with teacher-made achievement tests. We then discuss the major types of published achievement tests used in schools. Although we give examples of some of the more widely used tests, there are many other published achievement tests of high quality. We hope that the tests referred to here will simply serve as a starting point for exploring the many achievement tests available. At minimum, you should become familiar with some of the better published tests in your teaching area. See Appendix F for a selected list of published tests.

CHARACTERISTICS OF STANDARDIZED ACHIEVEMENT TESTS

A standardized achievement test has certain distinctive features, including a fixed set of test items designed to measure a clearly defined achievement domain, specific directions for administering and scoring the test, and norms based on representative groups of individuals like those for whom the test was designed. Standard content and procedure make it possible to give an identical test to individuals in different places at different times. The norms enable us to compare an individual's test score with those of known groups who also have taken the test. Thus, test norms provide a standard frame of reference for determining an individual's relative level of test performance on a particular test and for comparing test performance on several different tests (provided that all were standardized on the same group).

Equivalent forms are included in many standardized achievement tests, which make it possible to repeat the test without fear that the test takers will remember the answers from the first testing. Because equivalent forms of a test are built according to the same specifications, they measure the same domain of achievement with different sets of test items. They therefore can be used interchangeably for such purposes as measuring educational growth, checking on questionable test results from an earlier testing, and the like.

Comparable forms are also included in some standardized tests. These are forms that measure the same aspects of behavior but at different grade levels. For example, one form will cover grade 1, another form will cover grades 2 and 3, while other forms will cover grades 4 to 6, 7 to 9, and 10 to 12. Such forms are especially useful for maintaining continuity of measurement in a schoolwide testing program or for studying long-term trends in educational growth.

The characteristics of a carefully constructed standardized achievement test include the following:

1. The test items are of a high technical quality. They have been developed by educational and test specialists, tried out experimentally (pretested), and selected on the basis of difficulty, discriminating power, and relationship to a clearly defined and rigid set of specifications (see the box "How Publishers Select Test Items").

2. Directions for administering and scoring are so precisely stated that the procedures are standard for different users of the test.

3. Norms based on national samples of students in the grades where the test is intended for use are provided as aids in interpreting the test scores. Separate norms are usually provided for different parts of the school year (e.g., fall or spring). Norms for regions, states, or special groups, such as private schools, also might be supplied.

4. Equivalent and comparable forms of the test are usually provided, as is information concerning the degree to which the forms are comparable.

5. A test manual and other accessory materials are included as guides for administering and scoring the test, evaluating its technical qualities, and interpreting and using the results.

Despite the common characteristics of standardized tests, no two are exactly alike. Each test measures somewhat different aspects of content and skill. Also, there is wide variation in the completeness and quality of materials from one test to another. To further complicate test selection, some tests with similar titles measure objectives that differ markedly. Thus, the intelligent selection of standardized achievement tests from among the hundreds of tests available in each area requires studying the test content and the test materials in light of the objectives to be measured and the uses to be made of the results.

STANDARDIZED TESTS VERSUS INFORMAL CLASSROOM TESTS

Standardized achievement tests and carefully constructed classroom tests are similar in many ways. Both are based on a table of specifications, and both provide clear directions to the students. The main differences between the two types are (a) the nature of the learning outcomes and content measured, (b) the quality of the test items, (c) the reliability

How Publishers Select Test Items

Iowa Tests of Basic Skills, Levels 9–14: Selection Process for Test Questions

1. **Research**: Writing teams study curriculum guides, textbooks, latest professional literature and research to identify the skills to be tested and new ways of testing these skills.

2. **Writing**: Four times as many test questions are produced as will eventually be used.

3. **Editing for Tryouts**: Questions are checked for length, reading level, vocabulary, art, and space requirements; and changed or dropped as necessary.

4. **Editing after Tryouts**: Iowa Testing Program tries out questions on school population of over 300,000. Each question is tried out on at least 200 students. Those questions that do not measure well (almost half) are dropped.

5. **Author Reviews**: Test authors review questions' relationship to skills categories, review balance between skills categories, and check for freedom from bias, eliminating where necessary.

6. **Publisher Reviews**: Test editors review questions for all factors, especially balance (geographical, urban/rural, sex, race, etc.) and recommend further changes, which are made.

7. **Independent Reviews**: National team of professionals, representing five ethnic and racial groups, review questions for all factors, particularly cultural fairness. More changes are made following their recommendations.

8. **Final Editing for Standardization**: Editors and authors make final reviews for all factors, and final choice of questions is made for national norming.

of the tests, (d) the procedures for administering and scoring, and (e) the interpretation of scores. Comparative advantages of standardized and informal classroom tests of achievement are shown in Table 16.1. A review of the comparative advantages of the two types of tests indicates that each is superior for certain purposes and inferior for others. The broader coverage of the standardized test, its more rigidly controlled procedures of administering and scoring, and the availability of norms for evaluating scores make it especially useful for the following instructional purposes.

1. Evaluating students' general educational skill development in those learning outcomes common to many courses of study

Table 16.1

Comparative advantages of standardized and informal classroom tests of achievement

Property	Standardized Achievement Tests	Informal Achievement Tests
Learning outcomes and content measured	Measure outcomes and content common to majority of U.S. schools. Test of basic skills and complex outcomes adaptable to many local situations; content-oriented tests do not reflect emphasis or timeliness of local curriculum.	Well adapted to outcomes and content of local curriculum. Flexibility affords continuous adaptation of measurement to new materials and changes in procedure. Adaptable to various-size work units. Too often neglect complex learning outcomes.
Quality of test items	General quality of items high. Written by specialists, pretested, and selected on basis of effectiveness.	Quality of items is unknown unless test item file is maintained and used. Quality typically lower than standardized because of teacher's limited time and lack of opportunity to pretest items.
Reliability	Reliability high, commonly between .80 and .95; frequently around .90.	Reliability usually unknown; can be high if carefully constructed.
Administration and scoring	Procedures *standardized;* specific instructions provided.	Uniform procedures favored but may be flexible.
Interpretation	Scores can be compared with those of norm groups. Test manual and other guides aid interpretation and use.	Score comparisons and interpretations limited to local school situation; can be interpreted in light of known instructional history.

2. Evaluating student progress during the school year or over a period of years

3. Determining students' relative strengths and weaknesses in broad subject or skill areas

4. Comparing students' general level of achievement with their scholastic aptitude

The standardized test's inflexibility makes it less valuable for those purposes for which the informal classroom test is so admirably suited.

1. Evaluating the learning outcomes and content unique to a particular class or school

2. Evaluating students' day-to-day progress and their achievement on work units of varying sizes

3. Evaluating knowledge of current developments in rapidly changing content areas, such as science and social studies

The complementary functions of the two types of tests indicate that both can contribute to a sound instructional program. Each provides a specific type of information regarding the students' educational progress. In both cases, however, the value of the information depends on the extent to which the tests are related to the instructional objectives of the school and the ways in which the results are used. Standardized achievement tests, like informal classroom tests, can serve the many worthwhile instructional purposes attributed to them only when they measure the particular outcomes and content deemed important by those responsible for the instructional program. In addition, the test results must be used appropriately.

Much of the criticism of standardized tests can be related to misuses of results. Too often standardized tests are expected to serve functions for which they were never intended or for which they are poorly suited. Rigid tracking of students based only on standardized test results, for example, places too much reliance on a single source of information and frequently results in inferior instructional opportunities for students placed in the lower tracks. Overemphasis on test results as a primary means of teacher accountability can also lead to distortions of instruction by narrowing the curriculum to the content of the standardized tests at the expense of other important instructional goals that are not measured by the test.

STANDARDIZED ACHIEVEMENT TEST BATTERIES

Standardized achievement tests are frequently used in the form of survey test batteries. A battery consists of a series of individual tests all standardized on the same national sample of students. This makes it possible to compare test scores on the separate tests and thus determine the students' relative strengths and weaknesses in the different areas covered by the test. With an elementary school test battery, for example, it is possible to determine that a student is strong in language skills but weak in mathematics skills, good in reading but less proficient in spelling, and so on. Such comparisons are not possible with separate tests that have been standardized on different groups of students because the base for comparison is not uniform.

The most widely used test batteries are published by three test publishers: CTB/McGraw-Hill, Harcourt Educational Measurement, and Riverside Publishing Company. Each of these publishers offers an array of tests and assessments in addition to their major achievement test batteries. Some of those services are associated with the main achievement test batteries. Examples include aptitude tests normed together with the achievement test battery, a variety of supplements including written essay and other types of performance assessments, and a wide range of scoring and reporting services. Information is readily available on the range of products and services in the publishers' catalogs and Web sites (see the box "Web Sites of Achievement Test Publishers").

One limitation of test batteries is that all parts of the battery are usually not equally appropriate for measuring a particular school's objectives. When a test battery is constructed, it is based on the objectives and the content considered important by the specialists building the test. Although a particular school's goals probably will agree with some sections of the battery, it is fairly certain that they will not agree with all sections. Variations in subject-matter content from one curriculum to another and differences in grade placement of instructional materials make it unlikely that the various sections of a test battery will be uniformly applicable to the instructional program of any given school. This limitation is especially pronounced in content-oriented test batteries. It is less important in batteries designed to measure general educational development.

Web Sites of Achievement Test Publishers

CTB/McGraw-Hill

   Acuity
   TerraNova
   TerraNova CTBS
   TerraNova Performance Assessments
   TerraNova Algebra Assessment System
   California Achievement Tests (CAT)

   http://www.ctb.com

Riverside Publishing

   Iowa Tests of Basic Skills (ITBS)
   Iowa Tests of Educational Development (ITED)

Woodcock-Johnson III

   http://www.riverpub.com

Harcourt Assessment

   Metropolitan Achievement Tests (MAT)
   Metropolitan Performance Assessment
   Metropolitan Readiness Tests
   Stanford Achievement Test Series (Stanford)
   Stanford Open-Ended Assessments
   Stanford Reading First

   http://www.harcourtassessment.com

Achievement batteries are used most often at the elementary school level. Most schools use an achievement battery in grades 3 through 6, and many also use a battery in grades 1 and 2. This extensive usage is understandable because there is considerable uniformity in the learning outcomes sought.

Elementary school batteries usually include sections on reading, language, and mathematics. To allow for increasing difficulty and for varying emphasis from one grade level to another, a series of comparable forms has been developed to cover the various grade levels. Each form in the series covers one or two grades at the primary level and two or more grades beyond grade 4. The skills in an achievement battery are measured by a number of subtests. Although the names of the subtests vary somewhat from one test publisher to another and the batteries at the primary level usually contain fewer subtests, there is considerable uniformity in the outcomes measured by the various basic skill batteries. The content areas included in an achievement test battery vary depending on the option selected (e.g., basic battery or comprehensive battery) and the publisher. For example, the multiple-choice *Stanford 10 (Stanford Achievement Test Series, Edition 10) Complete Battery* includes Reading, Lexile Measure, Mathematics, Language, Spelling, Listening, Science, and Social Science, whereas the *Abbreviated Battery* offers a shorter version of all subtests except Listening. Open-ended assessments can be added to supplement the multiple-choice battery in Reading, Mathematics, Science, Social Studies, and Language. Reading assessments now extend to early childhood with the Reading First requirements of No Child Left Behind.

Within major content areas such as reading or mathematics, publishers also offer results for various subtests. The following examples of subtests are illustrative of those used in each basic skill area.

Reading

- Decoding skills (discrimination, analysis)
- Vocabulary (meaning of words)
- Comprehension (meaning of paragraphs and other written material)

Language

- Mechanics (capitalization, punctuation)
- Expression (correctness, effectiveness)
- Spelling (from dictation or identifying misspelled words)

Mathematics

- Computation (fundamental operations)
- Concept (meaning of concepts)
- Problem solving (solving story problems)

In addition to the traditional basic skills, some achievement batteries at the elementary school level include tests in listening comprehension. For example, the *Listening Assessment* for the *ITBS* is an optional supplement to the *Iowa Tests of Basic Skills* that may be administered independently. Complete batteries offered by the publishers also include tests in the content areas of science and social studies. The major batteries also offer writing supplements requiring students to write essays in response to standard prompts (e.g., the *Constructed-Response Supplement to the Iowa Tests,* the *Stanford Writing Assessment Program,* and the *TerraNova Performance Assessments*). For these batteries, it is usually possible also to obtain a separate partial battery limited to the measurement of basic skills. Batteries confined to the basic skills are generally preferred because content-oriented tests become outdated more quickly and are seldom well suited to the objectives of the local instructional program.

Achievement batteries are less widely used at the high school level. The wide diversity of course offerings and the variations in course content within the same subject area have made it difficult to find a common core on which to base the tests. Most high school batteries focus on the same basic skills of reading, mathematics, language, and study skills that are covered by the elementary batteries (with the optional science and social studies tests). This provides for the continuous measurement of the basic skills throughout all grade levels.

Some high school batteries, such as the *Iowa Tests of Educational Development,* were designed to measure general educational development in intellectual skills and abilities that are not dependent on any particular series of courses. Instead, they assess analytical and evaluative skills that are needed in everyday life. The complete battery contains the following nine tests.

- *Vocabulary*
- *Reading Comprehension*
- *Language: Revising Written Materials*
- *Spelling*
- *Mathematics: Concepts and Problem Solving*
- *Computation*

- *Analysis of Social Studies Materials*
- *Analysis of Science Materials*
- *Sources of Information*

Interpretive-type exercises are used throughout the test battery. Sample items representing two of the tests are shown in Figure 16.1. In both tests, Part 1 focuses on understandings and thinking skills gained from the content area, and Part 2 stresses the ability to analyze and evaluate various types of material.

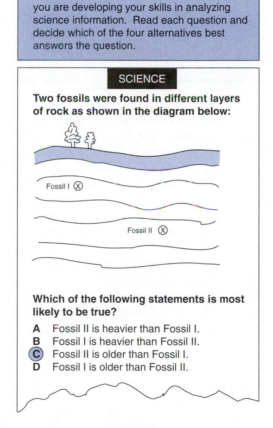

Figure 16.1

Sample items like those in the *Iowa Tests of Educational Development*

Table 16.2
Representative list of achievement batteries

	Achievement Grade Levels Covered Batteries													
	K	1	2	3	4	5	6	7	8	9	10	11	12	13
California Achievement Tests	X	X	X	X	X	X	X	X	X	X	X	X	X	
TerraNova CTBS	X	X	X	X	X	X	X	X	X	X	X	X	X	
Iowa Tests of Basic Skills	X	X	X	X	X	X	X	X	X	X	X	X	X	
Metropolitan Achievement Tests	X	X	X	X	X	X	X	X	X	X	X	X	X	
Stanford Achievement Test Series	X	X	X	X	X	X	X	X	X	X	X	X	X	X
Iowa Tests of Educational Development										X	X	X	X	

A list of widely used achievement batteries is shown in Table 16.2. The grade range covered by each test series is indicated in the table. In some of the test series (e.g., *Stanford*), the tests at various levels have different names, but they are all part of a coordinated series that provides for continuous assessment throughout the grade range. Also, the *Iowa Tests of Educational Development (ITED)* may be used in conjunction with the *Iowa Tests of Basic Skills* to form a coordinated program covering grades K to 12. Although the batteries of tests designed to measure the basic skills are all somewhat similar in terms of the areas of skill covered, they vary considerably in terms of the nature of the test materials used and the specific abilities measured within each skill area. Therefore, in selecting an achievement battery, it is important to appraise carefully the specific test items to be certain that the abilities measured are relevant to the learning outcomes stressed in the school program. Any achievement battery will, of course, measure only some of the important outcomes of the school program. Other tests and assessment procedures will be needed for comprehensive coverage of a school's objectives.

Supplements to Standardized Tests

Some test publishers provide performance assessments as supplements to their standardized tests. The most common form of supplement is a direct writing assessment. The *Stanford Writing Assessment Program,* for example, includes standard prompts that are designed to elicit written responses in four different modes of writing: (a) *Descriptive:* Students are asked to write about a place or thing based on their own experiences. (b) *Narrative:* The prompt presents a brief scenario, and students are asked to write a story. (c) *Expository:* Students are asked to state an opinion or position regarding a topic and defend it. (d) *Persuasive:* Students are asked to write about an issue from their own point of view in a way that would persuade a particular audience. A central scoring service provides both holistic scores for the overall quality of the essay and analytical scores for writing mechanics, sentence formation, and usage.

Diagnostic Batteries for Instructional Use

Achievement test batteries traditionally were designed as survey tests. That is, they provided a general, overall measure of the various areas of the curriculum. Typically, however, there were too few items measuring each skill to provide much help in making instructional decisions unless the content area is narrowly defined. The results might indicate that a student's performance was low in reading or mathematics, for example, but were of limited value for identifying the specific areas of strength and weakness. The few items in each area served as indicators of achievement, but they were insufficient for describing what individual students had learned, what they had yet to learn, and the types of errors they were making.

Test publishers have taken steps to make the test results of achievement batteries more useful to classroom teachers. Some test batteries, for example, consist of an integrated series of survey tests and group-administered diagnostic tests covering the same areas of basic skills. The survey battery provides information about the students' relative performance in each of the areas, and the diagnostic tests in reading, mathematics, and language provide a more detailed description of the students' strengths and weaknesses in each skill area. This is accomplished in part by including a larger number of items in the diagnostic tests within a single content area such as reading, using more subtests, and providing for criterion-referenced interpretation. In addition to the direct interpretation of strengths and weaknesses by subscores and instructional objectives, several special features were built into the *Metropolitan Achievement Tests* to aid instructional decisions.

1. An instructional reading level can be determined by comparing the criterion-referenced reading comprehension score to graded basal readers.
2. An instructional mathematics level can be determined by comparing criterion-referenced mathematics scores to graded levels of mathematics books.
3. Various comparisons between mathematics scores can be made to determine whether low problem-solving performance is due to lack of computational skills, low reading ability, or carelessness.
4. A research skills score is obtained from items embedded in various subject-matter tests.
5. A higher-order thinking skills score is obtained from critical-thinking items used in several subject-matter tests.
6. Specific information is provided for instructional planning for those students needing remediation as well as for those performing at or above average levels.

Similar diagnostic batteries in reading and mathematics are provided as separate components of the *Stanford Achievement Tests,* the *California Achievement Tests,* and the *TerraNova CTBS*. This two-component system of survey and diagnostic tests, which are statistically linked, provides a sound approach for meeting both administrative and instructional needs. The survey tests provide a general measure of achievement for comparisons among schools, and the diagnostic tests provide a more detailed measure of achievement for assessing the learning of individual students.

GUIDELINES

Selecting Achievement Batteries

1. Achievement batteries that focus on the basic skills measure important outcomes of the elementary school program, but these constitute only a portion of the outcomes of a modern curriculum.
2. At the high school level, basic skill batteries may serve both as learning readiness tests and as measures of learning outcomes in remedial basic skills programs. However, they provide only a limited measure of the many intended outcomes of the secondary school program.
3. Content-oriented tests in basic achievement batteries have broad coverage but limited sampling in each content area and may tend to become more quickly outdated than basic skills tests.
4. Achievement batteries differ in their emphasis on the various areas of basic skills, the different areas of content, and the specific types of learning outcomes measured. Thus, the selection of a battery should be based on its relevance to the school's objectives.
5. Diagnostic batteries should contain a sufficient number of test items for each type of interpretation to be made.

Although some achievement test batteries do not have a separate series of diagnostic tests, they typically aid instructional use by providing for analysis of results by objective, by specific skill area, or both. Whenever achievement test batteries (or any other test) provide for interpretation by objective or specific skill, it is important to note the number of test items involved. It is not uncommon to base interpretation on as few as two or three test items. A lucky guess or careless error may be the deciding factor in determining whether success or failure is indicated. In such cases, it would be wiser to base instructional decisions on larger item clusters formed by combining items measuring similar objectives or skills.

Group-administered survey and diagnostic batteries are useful for identifying students who could benefit from remedial teaching and individual help. More serious learning problems, however, typically require the use of individually administered diagnostic tests and a careful study of the student's total development. The diagnosis and remediation of severe learning disabilities are best left to the skilled clinician. See the "Guidelines" box.

ACHIEVEMENT TESTS IN SPECIFIC AREAS

In addition to achievement batteries, there are literally hundreds of separate tests designed to measure achievement in specific areas. The majority of these can be classified as tests of course content or reading tests of the general survey type. Tests also have been developed for use in determining learning readiness.

A separate test has certain advantages over a test battery. First, it is easier to select a test that fits the instructional objectives of a particular area. The difficulty of relating an entire battery of tests to instructional objectives was pointed out earlier. Second, a separate test is usually longer than a battery's subtests. This provides a more adequate sample of performance and more reliable part scores for instructional and diagnostic purposes. Third, the separate test's flexibility makes it easier to adapt to classroom instruction. Teachers can administer separate tests when they best fit their instructional needs rather than following the rigid schedule of the school testing program.

One disadvantage of separate tests is that each one is usually standardized on a different group of students. Because norm groups are not comparable, relative achievement of students in different areas cannot be compared. For example, it is not possible to determine whether a student has achieved more in science than in mathematics or in social studies than in English if the tests were not standardized on the same representative group of students.

Separate Content-Oriented Tests

There are many achievement tests at the secondary level designed to measure the outcomes of specific courses. In fact, there are over 100 separate tests in each of the major content areas of English, mathematics, science, and social studies. There are also separate tests in foreign language, business, and fine arts but not as many as those designed for the basic courses. All these tests of specific course content are intended as end-of-course tests and thus are used primarily to measure the students' final levels of achievement. Although the tests vary in quality, many of them require students to demonstrate understanding and application as well as knowledge of factual information. See the "Guidelines" box for selection criteria. For a complete listing of the separate tests available for use in schools, consult the catalogs of the test publishers in Appendix E. For critical reviews of the tests, see the latest *Mental Measurements Yearbook*.

Because of its flexibility and timeliness, an informal teacher-made test is frequently better suited to the measurement of instructional objectives in a particular course than a standardized achievement test. However, when carefully selected according to course content and learning outcomes, the standardized test can serve as a valuable check on the teacher's informal classroom tests.

Reading Tests

One of the most widely used tests at all levels of instruction is the reading test. It occupies a prominent position in achievement test batteries and receives special emphasis in tests of general educational development. In addition, there are well over 100 separate tests of reading ability.

Many reading tests are of the survey type, designed to measure a student's general level of reading ability. Such tests commonly measure vocabulary, reading comprehension, and rate of reading. The following list of reading skills is typical of those that reading survey tests attempt to measure.

- Identifies the meaning of given words
- Identifies the meaning of words when used in context

GUIDELINES

Selecting Separate Tests in Specific Content Areas

1. Because separate tests are content oriented, the date of construction is especially important. Developments in some content areas, such as science and social studies, take place at such a rapid rate that some are soon out of date.

2. In addition to timeliness of test content, attention should be directed toward its appropriateness for the particular course in which it is to be used. Because a standardized test includes only the content common to many school systems, it may lack comprehensiveness and at the same time include questions on material that has not been covered in the local instructional program.

3. Many content-oriented tests emphasize the measurement of knowledge outcomes, although there are a number of exceptions. Standardized tests of specific knowledge are seldom as relevant and useful as well-constructed teacher-made tests in the same area.

4. When a content-oriented test measures a variety of learning outcomes beyond those of specific knowledge (e.g., understanding, application, interpretation), it is important that the learning outcomes measured by the test complement those emphasized in the local instructional program.

- Identifies details directly stated in a passage or selection
- Identifies ideas implied in a passage or selection
- Identifies relationships (e.g., time, cause and effect) in a passage or selection
- Identifies the main thought or purpose of a passage or selection
- Identifies inferences drawn from a passage or selection
- Identifies conclusions drawn from a passage or selection
- Identifies the writer's tone, mood, and intent

Reading tests differ greatly in the extent to which they cover these skills and in the degree of emphasis given to each. Some tests focus on the lower levels of comprehension (e.g., identifying directly stated details), whereas others stress the more complex interpretive skills (e.g., identifying relationships, inferences, and conclusions). Moreover, the last two reading skills in this list are more likely to be found in reading tests for high school than elementary school.

Reading tests also differ widely in the material to be read by the student. Some tests use short passages of a sentence or two, whereas others use extended passages. Some use stories only, and others use stories, letters, poems, and scientific articles. Still another source of difference among reading tests is the extensiveness with which each type of reading material and each reading skill is sampled. One test, for example, may have a relatively large number of test items measuring the ability to draw conclusions from scientific articles, whereas another test has just a few such items. These differences highlight the importance of defining what reading abilities are to be measured before selecting a test.

Reading tests may be selected for any of the following uses: (a) to evaluate the effectiveness of reading instruction, (b) to identify those students needing remedial work in reading, (c) to predict success in subject-matter courses, (d) to determine whether poor reading ability can account for low scores on scholastic aptitude tests, and (e) to help locate the causes of learning problems. Although a single reading test may not serve all these uses equally well, how the results are to be used is an important consideration in test selection. The ideal reading test for a particular program is the one that best measures the instructional objectives and most effectively fulfills the uses to which the results will be put. See the "Guidelines" box for help in selecting reading tests and Appendix F for a list of reading tests.

Readiness Tests

Some tests have been designed to determine student readiness for learning school tasks. At the elementary level, reading readiness tests are probably the most familiar, but other types of tests are also used. Although readiness tests are essentially specialized scholastic aptitude tests, they are considered here because their test items are drawn from specific achievement areas. This gives them the advantage of providing diagnostic as well as predictive information. Thus, in addition to predicting learning success in a particular achievement area, test performance can provide information concerning the specific skills that students need to improve if their learning is to be effective.

GUIDELINES

Selecting Reading Tests

1. No two reading tests are exactly alike. Although reading survey tests usually measure vocabulary, reading comprehension, and rate of reading, they differ in the material that the reader is expected to comprehend, in the specific reading skills tested, and in the adequacy with which each skill is measured.

2. Reading survey tests measure only some of the outcomes of reading instruction. The mechanics of reading (e.g., perceptual skills and word analysis) are typically measured by diagnostic reading tests. Some specialized reading skills (e.g., reading maps, graphs, and charts) are more commonly measured by tests of study skills. Attitude toward reading and interest in reading, both of which are extremely important outcomes of reading instruction, must be determined by observation or other means.

3. Reading tests can serve many purposes in the school program. Thus, in addition to matching the objectives of instruction, test selection should take into account all the possible uses to be made of the results.

In the 1980s, many school districts started making wider use of early school readiness tests, not for the instructional planning purposes that the tests are intended to serve but for screening children before they are allowed to start kindergarten or first grade. That is, children with low scores are often forced to delay starting kindergarten for a year, are retained a second year in kindergarten, or are placed for a year in a transitional class before starting the first grade. Unfortunately, none of the available readiness tests has sufficiently high predictive validity to support this type of use. They are more appropriately used to make instructional decisions regarding skills a child needs to develop.

Early School Readiness and Achievement Tests.   Several tests have been developed to measure those basic concepts and skills considered essential for effective learning in the early school years. The tests are intended to be useful in instructional planning. The tests are usually designed for preschool use (kindergarten or sooner) but also can be used in the early primary grades. A typical example is the *Boehm Test of Basic Concepts—Revised*. This test is based on a selection of verbal concepts (e.g., *biggest, nearest, several*) that are needed to understand oral communication and to profit most from school experiences. The test items are read to the students, and they answer by placing an X on the pictures designed to measure the concepts.

Reading Readiness Tests.   Tests of reading readiness are used at the kindergarten and first-grade level to help identify skills that have been mastered and those that need to be learned and to help plan beginning reading instruction. The following functions are commonly measured by reading readiness tests.

1. **Visual discrimination**: Identifying similarities and differences in words, letters, numbers, geometric figures, or pictures
2. **Auditory discrimination**: Identifying similarities and differences in spoken words or sounds
3. **Verbal comprehension**: Demonstrating or understanding the meaning of words, sentences, and directions
4. **Recognition of letters, words, and numbers**: Identifying letters of the alphabet, words, and numerals
5. **Recognition of words in sample lessons**: Identifying words that have been taught in sample lessons
6. **Memory**: Reproducing a geometric figure, following instructions, or selecting a picture from memory
7. **Drawing or copying**: Demonstrating skill in drawing or copying geometric forms, objects, letters, or numbers

Not all reading readiness tests provide comprehensive coverage of these areas. Some tests cover only a few readiness skills, whereas others include tasks from four or five of the areas. Thus, as in all types of testing, the first step is to decide what is to be measured. In this particular case, it means deciding what reading readiness skills are most relevant to the reading program. A clear description of the skills to be measured is a prerequisite to valid test selection and use. See the "Guidelines" box for selecting readiness tests.

A typical example of a widely used readiness test is the *Metropolitan Readiness Test*. It is available in two levels: Level 1 is used up to the middle of kindergarten, and Level 2

GUIDELINES

Selecting Readiness Tests

1. Because these tests are predictive instruments, the test manual should be examined concerning the effectiveness with which they predict success in the given area. Validity coefficients should be at least as high as those obtained with general scholastic aptitude tests and preferably higher.

2. In addition to their predictive value, these tests also have some general diagnostic value. Thus, the test's content should be evaluated in light of the type of readiness information desired and the uses to be made of the results.

3. These tests provide just a fraction of the information needed to determine readiness for learning in a given area. The pupil's social and emotional adjustment, past achievement in the area, motivation to learn, and cultural background also must be taken into account.

4. Readiness tests do not have sufficient predictive validity to be used alone to screen children out of Kindergarten or delay entry into first grade.

is used in the second half of kindergarten and the first half of first grade. *The Metropolitan Readiness Test, Version 6* measures readiness in the following three areas:

1. Emerging literacy concepts in an authentic context
2. Developing language/literacy concepts
3. Developing quantitative/mathematics concepts

Readiness for beginning reading involves more than the skills measured by readiness tests. Such factors as mental ability, physical development, experiential background, social and emotional adjustment, and desire to read also must be considered. The readiness test focuses on important prerequisite skills, but test performance must be interpreted in light of the student's total readiness for learning.

CUSTOMIZED ACHIEVEMENT TESTS

Banks of objectives and related test items are maintained by most large test publishers and by some other organizations. These item banks are used for computer generation of customized tests. In some cases, the tests are prepared by the test publisher. In others, the publisher will sell or lease computer software that includes banks of items keyed to objectives and a program for constructing and printing locally prepared customized tests.

When using publisher-prepared customized achievement tests, the test user typically selects the objectives to be measured from an objective catalog and specifies the number of items to be used for measuring each objective. The test publisher then assembles and prints the test by taking from the item banks those items that measure the selected objectives. Scoring and reporting services are also available from the publisher for these tests.

Customized tests prepared by test publishers or prepared locally are especially useful for classroom testing because they can be designed to yield measurements of the specific knowledge and skills covered in the instructional program. Locally controlled micro-computer systems have the added advantage of being able to prepare tests as needed, without the time lag created when ordering customized tests from the publisher. In addition, a computer system makes it easy to add locally prepared objectives and test items to the bank. In using customized tests, however they are prepared, it is important to select the objectives carefully and to include enough items for each instructional objective or skill cluster to provide for reliable interpretations. It is also necessary, of course, to make certain that the individual items are relevant to the instructional objectives they are to measure.

Information concerning customized test development and microcomputer software can be obtained from test publishers' catalogs. See Appendix E for test publishers' addresses and a list of banks of items keyed to objectives that are available for school use.

INDIVIDUAL ACHIEVEMENT TESTS

Because of the increased number of students with disabilities in the regular classroom, it would seem desirable for classroom teachers to become familiar with some of the individual tests that are available for measuring achievement. These tests are administered to one student at a time and the questions are typically answered orally or by pointing, although some writing may be required. Some of the tests provide for norm-referenced interpretation, some use criterion-referenced interpretation, and still others provide for both types of interpretation. Typical examples of individual achievement tests include the following:

- *Basic Achievement Skills Individual Screener* (grade 1 to adult)
- *Peabody Individual Achievement Test—Revised* (K to adult)
- *KeyMath Diagnostic Arithmetic Test—Revised* (K to grade 6)
- *Woodcock Reading Mastery Tests—Revised* (K to adult)

Each of these tests can be administered in 30 to 60 minutes, with much of the scoring completed during the administration. Other individual achievement tests can be obtained from test publishers' catalogs (see Appendix E). For reviews of these and other achievement tests discussed in this chapter, see the latest *Mental Measurements Yearbook,* as described in Chapter 18.

SUMMARY

Standardized achievement tests measure the common objectives of a wide variety of schools, have standard procedures for administration and scoring, and provide norms for interpreting the scores. A test manual and other accessory materials are typically provided to aid in the administration of the test and the interpretation and use of the results. The test items are generally of high quality because they have been prepared by specialists, pretested, and selected on the basis of their effectiveness and their relevance to a rigid set of specifications.

Despite their high technical quality, standardized achievement tests complement rather than replace teachers' informal classroom tests. They are especially useful for measuring general educational development, determining student progress from one year to the next, grouping students, diagnosing learning difficulties, and comparing achievement with learning ability. They are of less value for measuring learning outcomes unique to a particular course, the day-to-day progress of students, and knowledge of current developments in rapidly changing fields. These purposes are more effectively served by informal classroom tests.

Achievement test batteries are widely used at the elementary school level. They cover the basic skills (i.e., reading, language, mathematics, and study skills), and some batteries also include sections on listening comprehension, science, and social studies. Test batteries are less widely used at the high school level because of the difficulty of identifying a common core of content. Batteries at this level are confined to the basic skills, to content included in the basic high school subjects, or to measures of general educational development. The main advantage of a test battery is that a student's strengths and weaknesses in different areas can be determined. Most test batteries provide for both norm-referenced interpretation and interpretation by objective or skill area. The complete test battery seldom fits all the instructional objectives of the school, however, and this must be taken into account when one is interpreting the results.

Some test publishers offer open-ended assessment exercises to supplement their standardized tests. Writing supplements are the most common addition, but sets of open-ended assessment tasks are also offered in different content areas. Typically, the responses can be scored locally or by means of a central scoring service. When the central scoring option is used, the scores can be compared to national norms.

The instructional use of achievement batteries has been enhanced by the publishing of sets of diagnostic batteries that are statistically linked to the survey batteries. The larger number of items and subtests in the diagnostic batteries makes it possible to obtain a more detailed description of each student's strengths and weaknesses in learning.

In addition to achievement test batteries, there are many separate published tests designed to measure achievement in specific areas. These include tests on course content, reading tests, and readiness tests. Although these can be more readily adapted to the instructional program than complete batteries, the following cautions should be kept in mind during their selection and use: (a) Published tests with similar titles may differ radically in terms of the type of test content and in terms of the emphasis given to the various skills measured; (b) published tests measure only a portion of the knowledge, skills, and abilities needed to evaluate, predict, or diagnose learning progress; and (c) published tests are effective to the extent that they measure the instructional objectives and serve the intended uses of the particular school program in which they are administered.

To more adequately meet the needs of classroom teachers for individualized instruction and mastery learning, test publishers are now making available customized achievement tests. Some publishers also provide item banks and software programs that enable schools to produce their own customized tests with microcomputers. These customized achievement tests measure student mastery of locally selected instructional objectives and thus describe what learning tasks a student can and cannot perform in the local instructional program. The interpretations must be made with great caution, however, because there are frequently a small number of test items measuring each objective or skill.

There are now many students with handicaps in regular classrooms. In testing these students, an individual achievement test may be more appropriate. These are administered on a one-to-one basis, and the questions are typically answered orally or by pointing. There are a number of such tests available for school use.

LEARNING EXERCISES

1. What are the similarities and differences in the making of a classroom test and a standardized test of achievement? How are the uses of the two tests likely to differ?

2. What are the advantages of using an achievement battery rather than separate achievement tests? What are the disadvantages?

3. Describe how a survey achievement battery and a related diagnostic battery differ in makeup and use.

4. If possible, study the manual of an achievement test battery. Review the information on how it was constructed. How complete is the information?

5. Examine two standardized achievement tests in an area you are teaching or plan to teach. How do the tests differ in terms of the learning outcomes and content each measures? What types of interpretations are suggested?

6. What are the advantages of using school readiness tests? What are some possible disadvantages?

7. For what situations might you use a customized achievement test instead of a standardized test?

8. What are the advantages of providing both norm-referenced interpretations and objective-referenced interpretations of published achievement tests? What are some of the cautions to be observed in making both types of interpretation for the same test?

FURTHER READING

Anastasi, A., & Urbina, S. (1997). *Psychological testing* (7th ed.). New York: Macmillan. Chapter 14, "Educational Testing," describes common types of achievement tests used in education with illustrative test items.

Ebel, R. L., & Frisbie, D. A. (1991). *Essentials of educational measurement* (5th ed.). Englewood Cliffs, NJ: Prentice Hall. Chapter 16, "The Nature of Standardized Tests," describes the characteristic features of standardized tests.

Linn, R. L. (1992). Achievement testing. In M. C. Alkin (Ed.), *Encyclopedia of educational research* (6th ed., vol. 1). New York: Macmillan. Provides a discussion of contemporary issues in achievement testing.

Mehrens, W. A., & Lehmann, I. J. (1991). *Using standardized tests in education* (4th ed.). New York: Holt, Rinehart & Winston. Chapter 8, "Standardized Achievement Tests," describes various types of achievement tests used in the schools and the uses of achievement test results.

Shepard, L. A. (1990). Readiness testing in local schools: An analysis of backdoor policy. *Politics of Education Association Yearbook*, 159–179.

17

APTITUDE TESTS

Aptitude tests are designed to predict future performance in some activity. Those used in schools range from traditional scholastic aptitude tests to more comprehensive differential aptitude tests. Attempts have also been made to develop special culture-fair tests. In this chapter, typical examples of aptitude tests used in schools are discussed and illustrated.

Aptitude tests can provide information that is useful in determining learning readiness, individualizing instruction, organizing classroom groups, identifying underachievers, diagnosing learning problems, and helping students with their educational and vocational plans. Although the results of achievement tests are also useful for these purposes, aptitude tests make a special contribution.

To avoid misinterpretations and misuses it is important to understand the limitations as well as the strengths of aptitude tests. Contrary to popular belief, aptitude tests do ***not*** measure a fixed capacity. Rather, they provide an indication of present level of learned abilities and can be useful in predicting future performance. Performance on aptitude tests is influenced by previous learning experiences, but it is less directly dependent on specific courses of instruction than is performance on achievement tests.

ACHIEVEMENT AND APTITUDE TESTS

Before we discuss the various types of aptitude tests, we consider some similarities and differences between achievement tests and aptitude tests. A common distinction is that achievement tests measure what a student has learned and that aptitude tests measure the ability to learn new tasks. Although this appears to be a clear distinction, it oversimplifies the problem and hides important similarities and differences. Actually, both measure what a student has learned, and both are useful for predicting success in learning new tasks. The main differences lie in (a) the types of learning measured by each test and (b) the types of prediction for which each test is most useful.

Types of Learning Measured: The Ability Spectrum

The various types of learning measured by achievement and aptitude tests can be best depicted if they are arranged along a continuum, as shown in Table 17.1. In this spectrum of ability tests, achievement tests fall at Levels A and B, and aptitude tests fall at Levels C, D, and E. The spectrum classifies the various types of tests according to the degree to which the test content depends on specific learning experiences. At one extreme (Level A) is the content-oriented achievement test that measures knowledge of specific course content. At the other extreme (Level E) is the culture-oriented nonverbal aptitude test that measures a type of learning not influenced much by typical school experiences. Thus, as we move through the different levels of the spectrum from A to E, the test content becomes less dependent on any particular set of learning experiences.

The closer in the spectrum, the more nearly alike will be the types of learning measured. Achievement tests designed to measure general educational development (Level B) and scholastic aptitude tests based on school-learned abilities (Level C), for example, both measure somewhat similar abilities and can be expected to correlate highly. Likewise, the farther apart two tests are in the spectrum, the less they will have in common and the lower the correlation will be between them. This information is useful in selecting and using aptitude tests. For instance, we can expect aptitude tests at Levels C and D to provide a better prediction of school achievement than those at Level E. On the other hand, if we are primarily interested in identifying students with undeveloped learning potential, tests at Level E will be more useful. When using this spectrum, however, remember that these are merely convenient categories for classifying the different types of ability tests and that some tests will cover two or more categories. Several wide-spectrum

Table 17.1

Spectrum of ability tests according to types of learning measured

Level	General Test Type	Types of Learning Measured
A	Content-oriented achievement tests	Knowledge of subject matter in courses such as social studies, English, mathematics, and science
B	Tests of general educational development	Basic skills and complex learning outcomes common to many courses, such as the application of principles and interpretation of data
C	School-oriented aptitude tests	Verbal and quantitative problem-solving abilities and writing skills similar to those learned in school, such as vocabulary, reading, and mathematical reasoning
D	Culture-oriented verbal aptitude tests	Verbal, numerical, and general problem-solving abilities derived more from the general culture than from common school experiences
E	Culture-oriented nonverbal aptitude tests	Abstract reasoning abilities based on figure analogies, figure classification, and other nonverbal tasks unrelated to school experience

Source: From L. J. Cronbach, *Essentials of Psychological Testing*, 4th ed. Boston: Allyn & Bacon. Copyright © 1984 by Allyn & Bacon, a Pearson Education Company. Reprinted by permission of the publisher.

scholastic aptitude tests, for example, include a range of test content covering Levels C, D, and E in a single test score.

Types of Predictions Made with Achievement and Aptitude Tests

Achievement and aptitude tests also can be distinguished according to the types of predictions for which each is most useful. Because past achievement is frequently the best predictor of future achievement, both types of achievement tests (Levels A and B) are useful in predicting future learning. In general, the content-oriented achievement test (Level A) can predict how well a student will learn new knowledge in the same content area, but it is of less value in predicting future learning in other areas. For example, a test of first-semester English will be a good predictor of second-semester English but not of second-semester mathematics, science, or social studies. In other words, its value as a predictor of future learning depends largely on the relationship between the content being measured and the content in the future learning situation. Tests measuring general educational development (Level B) are much more effective predictors of future achievement than are content-oriented tests because they measure intellectual skills and abilities common to a variety of content areas.

If achievement tests are such good predictors of future learning, then why do we use aptitude tests (Levels C to E) in schools? There are several good reasons. First, an aptitude test can be administered in a relatively short time (some as short as 20 minutes), whereas a comprehensive battery of achievement tests takes several hours. Second, aptitude tests can be used with students of more widely varying educational backgrounds. Because the type of learning measured is common to most students, an individual is less apt to be penalized because of specific weaknesses in past instruction. Third, aptitude tests can be used before a student has had any training in a particular area. For example, success in a French course cannot be predicted by an achievement test in French until the person has had some instruction in it. Another reason applies more to the culture-oriented aptitude test (Levels D and E). Because these measures of aptitude are least influenced by school-learned abilities, they can be used to distinguish low achievers working up to their ability from those with the potential for higher achievement. Identifying such underachievers with aptitude tests that depend heavily on school-learned abilities (Level C) is possible but less effective because the achievement skills required to respond to the test are those in which the underachiever is most apt to be weak.

In summary, both achievement tests and aptitude tests measure learned abilities, but achievement tests measure those that are more directly dependent on specific school experiences, whereas aptitude tests measure those based on a wide range of both in-school and out-of-school experiences. This is a matter of degree, however, and it is possible to arrange both types of tests on a continuum, ranging from the measurement of specific course content (Level A) to the measurement of more broadly based abilities (Levels D and E). Achievement tests and aptitude tests become very much alike near the center of the continuum (Levels B and C). Achievement and aptitude tests are also similar in that both are useful for predicting future achievement. In general, aptitude tests are a more convenient measure and one that predicts over a wide range of future experiences. As with types of learning outcomes measured, these differences are less pronounced near the center of the continuum.

SCHOLASTIC APTITUDE AND LEARNING ABILITY

Tests designed to measure learning ability traditionally have been called "intelligence tests." This terminology is still used for some individually administered tests and for some group tests, but its use is declining. There are a number of reasons for this: (a) Many people have come to associate the concept ***intelligence*** with inherited capacity; (b) there is increasing controversy over the meaning of intelligence and the factors that should be included in the concept; and (c) tests in this area have been increasingly used for predicting achievement and describing learning abilities. In place of the term *intelligence tests* have come such terms as *learning ability tests, school ability tests, cognitive ability tests,* and *scholastic aptitude tests.* All these terms emphasize the fact that these tests measure developed abilities useful in learning and not innate capacity or undeveloped potential.

Students' scores on scholastic aptitude tests or ability tests are best interpreted as a measure of present learning ability. Test performance is influenced by such factors as inherited characteristics, experiential background, motivation, particular skills (e.g., reading and test taking), attention, persistence, self-confidence, and emotional adjustment. All these factors are part of an individual's present ability to perform and, as such, affect both test scores and school achievement. Many of these factors can be modified by educational experiences, however, and therefore both learning ability and school achievement can be improved. It is when we misinterpret the test scores as unmodifiable measures of learning potential that we are apt to misuse the results.

GROUP TESTS OF LEARNING ABILITY

The majority of tests of learning ability administered in the schools are group tests. These are tests that, like standardized achievement tests, can be administered to many students at one time by persons with relatively little training in test administration. Some group tests yield a single score; others yield two or more scores based on measures of separate aspects of ability. Here we briefly describe and illustrate the various types of group tests. Critical reviews of these and other ability tests can be found in the *Mental Measurements Yearbooks.*

Single-Score Tests

Tests that yield a single score are sometimes designed to measure students' general learning ability. Typically, such a variety of types of items is included in the test that no particular ability or skill receives undue emphasis in the total score. Thus, the specific aspects of ability (such as verbal, numerical, and abstract reasoning) are blended together into one global measure of ability. These are sometimes called wide-spectrum tests and cover Levels C through E in the spectrum of abilities described earlier (see Table 17.1).

The single-score test based on a mixture of general verbal and nonverbal items is less common than it once was. Even one of the most widely used tests of this type, the *Otis–Lennon School Ability Test (OLSAT™),* has moved away from a single score. The fifth and earlier editions of the *OLSAT* reported a single general score. The sixth edition, published in 1989, the seventh edition, published in 1996, and the eighth edition, published in 2006, report separate verbal and nonverbal scores as well as a total score.

It is now more common for single-score tests to focus on verbal abilities. Like the *Boehm Test of Basic Concepts, 3rd Edition,* that was discussed in Chapter 16, single ability tests are typically used to measure readiness for school learning and to predict success in future schoolwork. They are highly verbal in nature, and this, of course, contributes to their predictive value because school learning is largely verbal. There are exceptions, however, to this general emphasis on verbal abilities. The *Matrix Analogies Test—Short Form,* for example, is a test of nonverbal reasoning that presents abstract designs with missing elements or matrices containing a progression of elements. Students are asked to select the missing element or the next element in the progression.

Whether a test contains a mixture of verbal and nonverbal items or focuses on only one of these abilities, single-score tests do not provide for differential prediction for various types of schoolwork. They are intended only as a general measure of current learning readiness. Thus, a low score will indicate a lack of readiness to perform well on school tasks but will reveal neither the nature nor the cause of the poor performance. Single-score ability tests provide a quick, effective, general measure of present learning ability.

Tests Yielding Separate Scores

A number of tests of learning ability yield two or more part scores as well as the total score. Some tests, like the *Otis–Lennon School Ability Test, Eighth Edition* (Grades K–12) (*OLSAT™8*), have both verbal and nonverbal scores as well as a total score. The nonverbal score provides a check on the verbal score for those students who have limited verbal skills (e.g., poor readers). Other tests provide verbal and quantitative scores. The purpose of these is to obtain differential prediction of school success between courses emphasizing verbal concepts and those emphasizing mathematical concepts. Predictive studies indicate that verbal scores tend to be the best predictor of success in most courses, however, so interpretations concerning differential prediction must be cautiously made. A relatively large difference between verbal and quantitative scores is needed before it is meaningful. The test manual will indicate what size score difference is significant.

When administered with an associated achievement test battery, ability tests such as the *OLSAT* can be used to obtain "achievement/ability comparisons." For example, the *OLSAT™8* was normed with the *Stanford 10* achievement tests. If both the *OLSAT™8* and the *Stanford 10* are administered, achievement/ability comparison scores can be obtained that describe a student's achievement in relation to the achievement of other students with the same ability as measured by the *OLSAT.*

The *Cognitive Abilities Test* (*CogAT®*) (Grades K–12) provides a measure of three types of reasoning ability important in school learning. It provides scores for each of three different test batteries: verbal, quantitative, and nonverbal. The test includes three primary levels for testing in kindergarten through grade 2 and eight higher levels for use in grades 3 through 12. These later eight levels are published in a single multilevel booklet that contains all three batteries. With the multilevel format, the items in each subtest are arranged in order of increasing difficulty, and the examinees start and stop at different places, depending on their grade level. If the assigned level is inappropriate for a particular group (e.g., extremely good or poor readers), it is simply a matter of shifting to a higher or lower level within the test.

The primary levels of the *Cognitive Abilities Test, Form 6* include the following six tests.

Verbal Battery

Oral Vocabulary. Mark a picture that illustrates a word or phrase read aloud (e.g., "the one that is round").

Verbal Reasoning. Mark a picture that belongs with three other pictures that are alike in some way (e.g., all are toys).

Quantitative Battery

Quantitative Concepts. Mark a picture illustrating a concept (e.g., half a pie).

Relational Concepts. Mark a picture illustrating a relation (e.g., tallest tree).

Nonverbal Battery

Matrices. Mark the figure that completes a four-cell matrix containing three geometric figures and one empty cell.

Figure Classification. Mark the figure that belongs with three other figures that are alike in some way (e.g., all are triangles).

Tests at the primary level are all administered with oral directions, and a predetermined pattern of testing is followed. The order alternates tests from different batteries to maintain interest and attention. Time limits are suggested, but they are power tests, not speed tests. The test administrator reads the instructions for each item and allows sufficient time for all children to try the item. No reading is involved.

The multilevel edition for grades 3 to 12 contains three tests in each of the three batteries: verbal, quantitative, and nonverbal. The three tests in the verbal battery are illustrated by the sample items shown in Figure 17.1. The items in all three tests include verbal tasks that have not been directly taught in school but require the use of verbal concepts that have been learned both in and out of school. The instructions for our illustrative items are very abbreviated.

The quantitative battery contains three tests that require students to solve quantitative tasks that have not been directly taught in school. The sample items in Figure 17.2 illustrate the nature of these tests. Like the verbal battery, the emphasis is on reasoning abilities that require the use of concepts that have been learned both in and out of school.

The nonverbal battery consists of three tests using geometric shapes and figures, as illustrated in Figure 17.3. The concepts needed to solve the problems in these items are learned primarily from experiences out of school. Because the tests use neither words nor numbers, the nonverbal battery provides a poorer prediction of school success than the other two batteries. However, the nonverbal tests provide a more accurate measure of the reasoning abilities of poor readers and those deficient in language skills.

Verbal Classification

Directions: In each question there are three words in dark type. These three words are alike in some way. Decide how they are alike. Then choose the word from the answer choices that goes with the first three words.

tea   cocoa   milk

A bread   B coffee   C cookie   D cup   E drink

Sentence Completion

Directions: Each question has a sentence with one word left out. Choose the word from the answer choices that best completes the sentence.

In school Mario _____ reading the best.

A hated   B felt   C heard   D forgot   E liked

Verbal Analogies

Directions: For each question there are three words in dark type. The first two words go together in some way. The third word goes with one of the answer choices in the same way. Choose the word from the answer choices that goes with the third word.

good → bad : best →

A average   B worst   C better   D friend   E perfect

Figure 17.1

Sample items from the verbal battery of the *Cognitive Abilities Test, Multilevel Edition*

The scores on all batteries of the *Cognitive Abilities Test* are expressed as a standard age score (SAS) that has a mean of 100 and a standard deviation of 16. Separate verbal, quantitative, and nonverbal scores are reported, but no total score is reported for the combined batteries. It was believed that a total score could be misleading where skill development in the three areas was very uneven. For instructional purposes, it is better to

Quantitative Relations

Directions: In each question, there are two things to compare. You have to decide if one is bigger than the other or if they are equal.

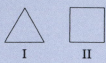

I   II

A   I has more sides than II.
B   I has fewer sides than II.
C   I has the same number of sides as II.

Number Series

Directions: Each question shows a series of numbers. You have to figure out the rule used to arrange the numbers. Then decide which number should come next in the series.

$$80 \quad 70 \quad 60 \quad 50 \quad 40 \longrightarrow$$

A 10   B 20   C 30   D 40   E 50

Equation Building

Directions: For each question, you are given some numbers and signs. You can make different equations or number sentences by combining all of the numbers and signs. You are to make an equation that will give you one of the answer choices for the solution.

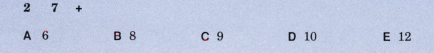

2   7   +

A 6   B 8   C 9   D 10   E 12

Figure 17.2
Sample items from the quantitative battery of the *Cognitive Abilities Test, Multilevel Edition*

(Copyright © 1993 by The Riverside Publishing Company. Sample items from the *Cognitive Abilities Test™ (CogAT®)*. Reproduced by permission of The Riverside Publishing Company. No part of this work may be reproduced or transmitted in any form or by any means, electronic or mechanical, including photocopying and recording or by any information storage or retrieval system without the proper written permission of The Riverside Publishing Company unless such copying is expressly permitted by federal copyright law. Address inquiries to Contracts and Permissions Department, The Riverside Publishing Company, 425 Spring Lake Drive, Itasca, Illinois 60143-2079.)

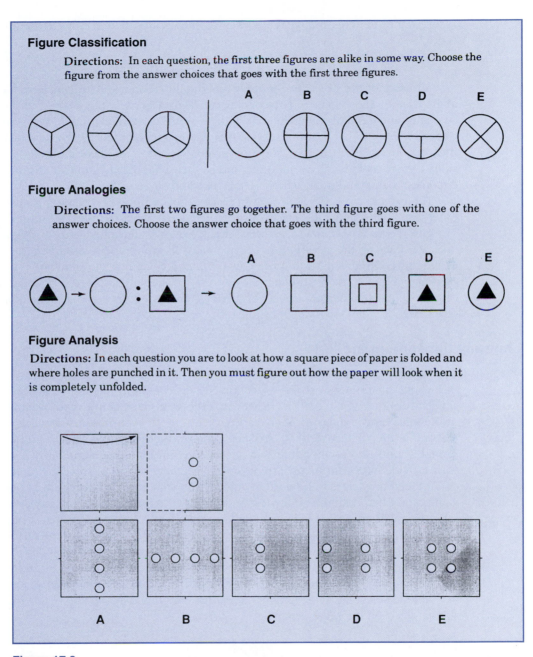

Figure 17.3

Sample items from the nonverbal battery of the *Cognitive Abilities Test, Multilevel Edition*

focus on the strengths and weaknesses in cognitive skills than to conceal them with a total score.

In keeping with the current trend in ability testing, the authors make explicit that this test measures developed abilities that are modifiable by experience.

All users of the *Cognitive Abilities Test* should recognize that it measures developed abilities, not innate abilities. The cognitive skills measured by the test reflect the cognitive strategies and general cognitive control processes that an individual has developed, from experience both in and out of school, that enable him or her to learn new tasks or solve problems when instruction is absent or incomplete. Research has clearly shown that these skills change as individuals get older and as their experiences both in and out of school become broader and more varied (Thorndike and Hagen, 1993).

The use of standard age scores, in place of the outmoded deviation IQ used in some older tests, helps avoid the many misinterpretations associated with IQ scores.

The *Cognitive Abilities Test* was described and illustrated in considerable detail because it shows the variety of item types used in group ability tests and includes some of the current trends in testing (e.g., use of a multilevel format, elimination of the terms *intelligence* and *IQ scores*, and emphasis on power rather than speed of work). There are, of course, many other good tests of learning ability. See Appendix F for representative examples.

Choosing the Appropriate Test

The decision as to which type of test to select depends largely on the use to be made of the results. If the test is to be used only for an overall prediction of school success, a single-score test would suffice. However, if we want to obtain a more accurate measure of the reasoning abilities of poor readers or want to detect students weak in quantitative reasoning, then a test yielding separate scores would be favored. The single-score test provides a quick, easy-to-administer, global measure of reasoning ability, but multiscore tests provide information concerning several separate types of reasoning ability.

If the ability test is to be used in conjunction with an achievement test battery, then it is important that both the ability test and the achievement battery be standardized on the same population. This makes it possible to compare directly the two sets of scores and thus obtain a more complete description of educational progress and the factors affecting it. Most publishers of achievement test batteries publish a corresponding ability test, covering the same grade levels, and administer both to the same standardization groups. A list of such ability and achievement tests is presented in Table 17.2. In some cases, it may be desirable to select the achievement battery first and then use the ability test that has been standardized on the same groups.

INDIVIDUAL TESTS

Learning abilities are also measured by individual tests. These are typically called intelligence tests or intelligence scales, but a broader interpretation is more defensible. Like the group tests, they measure present abilities that have been acquired through both in-school and out-of-school experiences.

Table 17.2

Representative ability tests and corresponding achievement batteries standardized on the same populations

Ability Test	Grade Levels	Achievement Batteries
Otis–Lennon School Ability Test (OLSAT)	1–12	Metropolitan Achievement Tests Stanford Achievement Test Series
Cognitive Abilities Test (CogAT)	K–12	Iowa Tests of Basic Skills (K–9) Iowa Tests of Educational Development (9–12)
Tests of Cognitive Skills	2–12	California Achievement Tests (K–12) TerraNova: Comprehensive Tests of Basic Skills (K–12)

Individual tests are administered to one examinee at a time in a face-to-face situation. The problems are presented orally by the examiner, and the examinee responds by pointing, giving an oral answer, or performing some manipulative task. The administration of individual tests requires extensive training. This is typically obtained in a special course in individual testing. A basic part of the course is extensive practice in test administration under supervision. No one should attempt to use individual tests without this special training.

Group tests provide a satisfactory estimate of learning abilities for the majority of students. However, individual tests have some special advantages over a group test. Because the individual test is administered to one student at a time, it is possible to control more carefully such factors as motivation and to assess more accurately the extent to which disabling behaviors are influencing the score. The influence of reading skill is deemphasized because the tasks are presented orally to the student. In addition, clinical insights concerning the student's method of attacking problems and persistence in solving them are more readily obtained with individual testing. These advantages make the individual test especially useful for testing young children, for retesting students whose scores on group tests are questionable, and for testing students with special problems. For example, in planning individualized programs for students with mental handicaps, the more dependable and informative individual measure of ability is preferred.

The two most highly regarded individual tests for use with school children are the *Stanford–Binet Intelligence Scale* and the *Wechsler Intelligence Scales*. Each of these is briefly described. Although teachers would not be expected to administer such tests, some familiarity with the testing procedures should contribute to more effective interpretation and use of the test scores.

Stanford–Binet Scale, Fifth Edition

The fifth edition of the *Stanford–Binet Scale* changed considerably from earlier editions. In the former editions (from 1908 on), the tests were arranged by age levels, and the examiner presented a variety of item types as he or she moved from one age level to the next. The resulting measure of ability was expressed as a mental age that was then converted to a deviation IQ with a mean of 100 and a standard deviation of 16. The deviation IQ represented a highly verbal measure of general ability.

In the fifth edition, the organization of the tests includes five factors by two domains. That is, each of the factors includes a nonverbal and a verbal domain. The five factors being measured are Fluid Reasoning, Knowledge, Quantitative Reasoning, Visual-Spatial Processing, and Working Memory. The 10 subtests include many of the item types of earlier editions but provide broader coverage of the nonverbal domain, which is more valuable for evaluating learner disabilities and individuals with limited English.

The *Stanford–Binet* includes standard scores, percentile ranks, grade equivalents, and change-sensitive scores. Intelligence Scores (Full Scale, Abbreviated, Nonverbal, and Verbal) have a mean of 100 with a standard deviation of 15. Scores on the same scale can also be obtained for each of the five factor scores (Fluid Reasoning, Knowledge, Quantitative Reasoning, Visual-Spatial Processing, and Working Memory). The 10 subtest scores have a mean of 10 and a standard deviation of 3.

The *Stanford–Binet* also reports validity studies that show its usefulness for identifying disabilities. Specific studies have been completed for identifying individuals who are learning disabled, gifted, mentally retarded, ADHD, speech and language delayed, traumatic brain injured, or autistic.

Wechsler Scales

The *Wechsler Scales* include three tests that collectively cover all ages, from age 3 through adult:

1. *Wechsler Preschool and Primary Scale of Intelligence*™—*Third Edition* (2002) (*WPPSI-III*®) (ages 2.5–7.25)
2. *Wechsler Intelligence Scale for Children*®—*Fourth Edition* (2003) (*WISC-IV*®) (ages 6–16)
3. *Wechsler Adult Intelligence Scale*®—*Third Edition* (1997) (*WAIS-III*®) (ages 16–adult)

The *Wechsler* tests report a full-scale IQ and from two to six factor or index scores that are the sum of multiple subtests. Although the factors and subtests vary slightly from one level to another, the following factors and subtests from the *WISC-IV* exemplify the test content in the *Wechsler Scales*. The sample questions in parentheses were not taken from the *WISC-IV* but are similar to items in the *WISC-IV*.

Verbal Comprehension

1. **Similarities:** Explain in what way a series of paired things are alike (e.g., apple and orange).
2. **Vocabulary:** Tell the meaning of words from a master list of 32, arranged in order of increasing difficulty.
3. **Comprehension:** Answer questions requiring commonsense comprehension (e.g., "Why should people tell the truth?").

Information (supplementary): Answer questions based on general information (e.g., "How many legs does a cat have?"). May be included in the Verbal Comprehension scale.

Word Reasoning (supplementary): Identifies an underlying concept given successive clues. May be included in the Verbal Comprehension scale.

Perceptual Reasoning

4. **Block Design:** Arrange sets of blocks (colored red and white) so that they match pictures of designs on examiner's cards.
5. **Picture Concepts:** From two or three rows of concepts, the pair that go together are selected (e.g., pictures include two animals, a pencil, and a toy).
6. **Matrix Reasoning:** Fill in a grid with the graphic that completes the matrix.

Picture Completion (supplementary): Tell what part is missing in incomplete pictures. May be included in Perceptual Reasoning scale.

Working Memory

7. **Digit Span:** Repeat a series of digits forward and backward after hearing them once (e.g., 493).
8. **Letter-Number Sequencing:** Presented with a mixed sequence of letters and numbers, the child repeats the numbers first in numerical order followed by the letters in alphabetical order (e.g., F83A).

Arithmetic (supplementary): Solve problems similar to those used in school (e.g., "If two pencils cost a nickel, how many could you buy for a quarter?"). May be included in the Working Memory scale.

Processing Speed

9. **Coding:** Match numbers and symbols by referring to a simple code that is kept in front of the examinee.
10. **Symbol Search:** Locate a designated symbol.

Cancellation (supplementary): Remove a nonanimal object from a series of random and structured animal target forms. May be included in the Processing Speed scale.

Each subtest in the *WISC-IV* is administered and scored separately. The tests are administered by alternating between the verbal and performance scales to maintain greater interest and attention. The raw scores on the individual tests are converted to scaled scores with a mean of 10 and a standard deviation of 3. They are then combined to produce a factor score and a total IQ. The factor scores and the total IQ are deviation IQs with a mean of 100 and a standard deviation of 15.

The three *Wechsler Scales* are similar in test content and organization, and all three provide the same deviation IQs for the factor scores and the total scales. Like the *Stanford–Binet*, a number of abbreviated scales also can be used for various screening purposes.

Both the *Stanford–Binet* and the *Wechsler Scales* have been widely used for the individual testing of school children. Both yield highly reliable results (.90+ for the full-scale scores) when administered by competent examiners, and they are probably equally good for predicting success in school.

CAUTIONS IN INTERPRETING AND USING LEARNING ABILITY SCORES

Keep in mind the following cautions when interpreting and using learning ability tests.

1. Allow for normal variation in the test scores. Learning ability or scholastic aptitude tests are some of our most reliable psychological tests. A reliability coefficient of .90 (which is typical), however, results in a standard error of measurement of approximately 5 points (SD = 15). Thus, a score of 100 should be interpreted as a band of scores ranging from 95 to 105 rather than as a precise point. When scores from different tests are compared, we can expect differences larger than 5 points because the tests measure different aspects of ability, and are standardized on different populations. The largest variations in scores can be found at the elementary school levels because abilities are less stable during their formation and testing conditions are more difficult to control with elementary students.

2. Seek the causes of low scores. The scores on learning ability tests are based on the use of concepts acquired from both in-school and out-of-school experiences. Thus, inadequate motivation to do school tasks, a language handicap, or a barren home environment can prevent the learning of concepts required in the test. Similarly, poor reading ability, lack of test-taking skills, anxiety, and low self-esteem can lower scores by adversely influencing test performance. Many of these factors can be detected by simply looking for possible causes of low scores. Following up low scores on a group test with an individual test is also helpful. This reduces the influence of reading ability and provides for more careful observation of test-taking skills, language skills, motivation, and other relevant personal characteristics.

3. Verify test results by comparison with other information. More effective interpretation of learning ability test scores is likely to result when test performance is checked against teachers' observations, achievement test scores, and other evidence of learning and development. Discrepancies between the test scores and other information may suggest retesting or clarify the nature of the factors influencing test performance.

4. Use the test results to improve learning. Learning ability tests provide a fairly good prediction of school success. Correlations between these test scores and school marks typically fall between .40 and .60. When correlated with scores on achievement test batteries, correlations of .60 to .80 are common. Unfortunately, the relationship between learning ability test scores and achievement is all too frequently used as a rationalization for inadequate school performance. For example, we might hear comments such as, "These students aren't doing well in school because of their poor learning ability." Instead, teachers should alter the instruction for these children, slow the pace, introduce programs that build up their verbal and quantitative concepts, and provide more direction and practice in problem solving. The same factors that lower school achievement (e.g., poor verbal and quantitative development) also lower scores on learning ability tests, and both types of performance are modifiable. Thus, learning ability scores can be used, in conjunction with other information, to facilitate plans for improved learning rather than as an excuse for lack of school success.

5. Be cautious in identifying students as underachievers. Comparing a student's scores on a learning ability test and an achievement test and labeling the student as an underachiever if the achievement test scores are lower is fraught with difficulties. Because both are measuring developed abilities, these discrepancies typically can be accounted for by such factors as the measurement error in both tests, the differences in content measured by the two tests, and variations in attitude and attention during test taking. If the two tests are normed on different populations, another basis for deviation is introduced. Discrepancies between learning ability and achievement test scores simply reflect the fact that the correlation between them is far from perfect. The safest procedure is to consider only very large discrepancies as possible signs of underachievement and then confirm these judgments by examining other types of information.

CULTURE-FAIR TESTING

Because all tests are measures of learned abilities, special problems arise when testing the aptitudes of individuals from different cultures and subcultures. Numerous cultural differences are likely to influence test performance. In addition to the more obvious one of language, there are such differences as motivation, attitude toward testing, competitiveness, speed, practice in test taking, and opportunity to learn the knowledges and skills measured by the test. Culture-fair testing is an attempt to obtain a measure of ability that is relatively free of all or most of these differences. Although various approaches have been used to accomplish this, the following procedures are typical: (a) The test materials are primarily nonverbal and include diagrams or pictures familiar to the various cultural groups for whom the test is intended. Sometimes translated verbal tests are used. (b) Attempts are made to use materials and methods that are interesting to the examinees in order to encourage motivation. (c) Liberal time limits are typically provided to deemphasize speed as a factor. (d) The test procedures are kept simple in order to rule out differences in test-taking experience. (e) Test content is based on those intellectual skills common to the cultural groups being tested. Of course, culture-fair testing is an ideal, not a reality. Most attempts to remove cultural influences from tests have fallen short of their goal.

One of the best-known tests in this area is R. B. Cattell's *Culture-Fair Intelligence Tests*. These short, nonverbal tests use pictures and diagrams common to many cultures. There are three scales available for different age levels. Scale 1 is for ages 4 to 8. It includes eight subtests, four of which must be administered individually. Scales 2 and 3 (age 8–adult) each contain four subtests, involving the following perceptual tasks (see sample items in Figure 17.4).

1. **Series:** Select the item that comes next in a series.
2. **Classification:** Select the item that does not belong with the others.
3. **Matrices:** Select the item that completes a matrix.
4. **Conditions:** Match the conditions in a sample design by placing a dot in the appropriate place on one of several alternate designs. In the item in Figure 17.4, the dot must be in the circle but not in the small square.

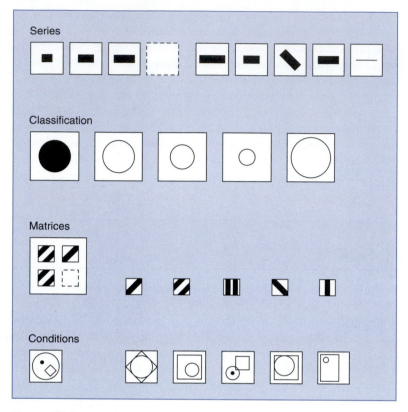

Figure 17.4
Sample items from the *Culture-Fair Intelligence Tests*

(Copyright © 1949, 1960 by the Institute of Personality and Ability Testing, Inc., Champaign, Illinois, USA. All rights reserved. Reproduced from *Culture Fair Scale 2, Test A* by R. B. Cattell and A. K. S. Cattell.)

Scales 2 and 3 can be administered individually or as group tests. They have been given to individuals in a number of countries with mixed results. In general, test performance tended to differ most where the cultural differences were greatest. When used in schools in the United States, the *Culture-Fair Intelligence Tests* can be expected to produce results similar to those of the *Nonverbal Battery of the Cognitive Abilities Test*.

DIFFERENTIAL APTITUDE TESTING

The work of Guilford (1967) had an important influence in moving testing from the measurement of a limited number of general mental abilities to the measurement of numerous specific abilities. On the basis of years of research, using the method of factor analysis, he proposed a three-dimensional model to provide a complete "structure of intellect." His theoretical model is shown in Figure 17.5. The model contains 120 cells

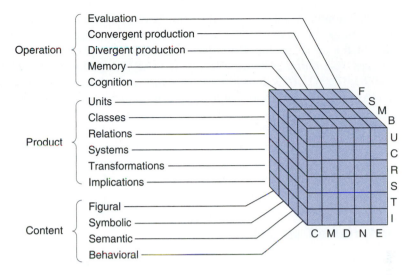

Figure 17.5
Guilford's structure of intellect model

(From J. P. Guilford, *The Nature of Human Intelligence*. New York: McGraw-Hill, 1967. Reproduced by permission.)

(5 × 6 × 4), and each cell represents an ability that can be described by (a) what the person does (operation), (b) the nature of the material on which the operation is performed (content), and (c) the type of outcome or product involved (product). For example, a test based on figure analogies, like that in the nonverbal battery of *Cognitive Abilities Test* (see Figure 17.3), would be classified in the Cognition–Figural–Relations cell because it calls for the recognition of figure relations. Similarly, a test using verbal analogies, such as those in the verbal battery of *Cognitive Abilities Test* (see Figure 17. 1), would be classified in the Cognition–Semantic–Relations cell because it calls for the recognition of the relations between word meanings.

Tests have not been developed for each of the cells in the structure of intellect, but the model has served as a guide to Guilford and his coworkers in their search for specific abilities. Although it was assumed that someday there will be tests for all 120 cells, many of the distinctions between cells are so minor that they are unlikely to be reliably measured or be of practical importance. Broader dimensions that would span several cells are generally of greater utility in practical applications.

The experimental search for multiple abilities by Guilford and others, combined with the increasing emphasis on educational and vocational guidance since World War II, has resulted in a number of multiaptitude batteries. Although such batteries are intended primarily for guidance purposes, they also can be useful in individualizing instruction and in planning courses that utilize a broader range of human abilities. As noted earlier, school learning is largely verbal learning regardless of the name of the course. The differential testing of abilities provides an opportunity to develop learning experiences that take advantage of each individual's total pattern of aptitudes.

Multiaptitude batteries that measure both educational and vocational aptitudes have been designed primarily for the high school level and beyond. Among the most widely used tests of this type are the *Differential Aptitude Tests (DAT™) (grades 8–12)*, the *Armed Services Vocational Aptitude Battery (ASVAB)*, and the *General Aptitude Test Battery (GATB)*. The *ASVAB* is used in screening and counseling enlisted personnel for the military services. It is also made available for use in high school counseling programs. The *GATB* was developed by the federal government for use in offices of the United States Employment Service (USES). It can be given in high schools, however, by special arrangement with USES. The *GATB* contains more vocationally oriented tests than the *DAT™* or *ASVAB*.

Here we describe the *DAT™* in order to illustrate the nature and content of multiaptitude batteries. Information concerning other batteries available for use in the schools can be obtained from the *Mental Measurements Yearbooks*.

Differential Aptitude Tests (DAT™)

The first edition of the *DAT™* battery was published shortly after World War II (1947) by the Psychological Corporation. The most recent version, the fifth edition, was published in 1990. The fifth edition includes eight tests, each measuring a separate set of abilities. Although some of the tests measure abilities specific enough to fit a particular cell in Guilford's model (see Figure 17.5), most measure a composite of abilities that have been found useful in educational and vocational guidance. The eight tests are Verbal Reasoning (VR), Numerical Reasoning (NR), Abstract Reasoning (AR), Perceptual Speed and Accuracy (PSA), Mechanical Reasoning (MR), Space Relations (SR), Spelling (S), and Language Usage (LU). In addition to separate scores for each of these tests, a combined Verbal Reasoning and Numerical Reasoning score (VR + NR) provides an index of scholastic aptitude.

The Verbal Reasoning and Numerical Reasoning subtests are also available for administration alone in what is called the partial battery. Sample items from the eight tests are shown in Figure 17.6. Using a battery of aptitude tests like the *DAT™* has several advantages over using a series of separate tests covering the same areas. First, because all tests have been standardized on the same population, it is possible to compare a student's strengths and weaknesses on the various measures of aptitude. Second, because all tests are built for the same population of users, they are matched in difficulty and appropriateness for the grade levels for which they are intended. Separate tests covering the same areas are apt to range widely in difficulty, especially the vocational tests. Third, using a common test format and uniform testing procedures for all tests simplifies test administration.

The tests in the *DAT™* tend to be internally consistent (split-half reliabilities average about .90), and the intercorrelations between tests are low enough (average about .50) to indicate that each test measures a relatively independent ability. The evidence of differential prediction, however, is rather disappointing. One might expect the Verbal Reasoning scores to best predict English achievement, the Numerical Reasoning scores to best predict mathematics and science achievement, the Space Relations scores to best predict achievement in mechanical drawing, and so on. A review of the extensive data presented in the test manual, however, reveals only slight differences in prediction from one area to another. The best predictor of school marks in all courses turned out to be the general ability measure, VR + NR.

Verbal Reasoning* (25 min.)

Measures the ability to see relationships among words; may be useful in predicting success in business, law, education, journalism, and the sciences.

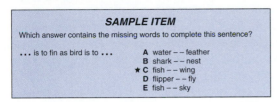

SAMPLE ITEM

Which answer contains the missing words to complete this sentence?

... is to fin as bird is to ...

- **A** water – – feather
- **B** shark – – nest
- ★ **C** fish – – wing
- **D** flipper – – fly
- **E** fish – – sky

Numerical Reasoning* (30 min.)

Measures the ability to perform mathematical reasoning tasks; important in jobs such as bookkeeping, lab work, carpentry, and toolmaking.

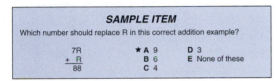

SAMPLE ITEM

Which number should replace R in this correct addition example?

```
  7R
+ R
───
 88
```

- ★ **A** 9
- **B** 6
- **C** 4
- **D** 3
- **E** None of these

Abstract Reasoning (20 min.)

A nonverbal measure of the ability to reason using geometric shapes or designs; important in fields such as computer programming, drafting and vehicle repair.

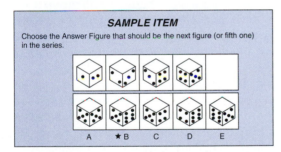

SAMPLE ITEM

Choose the Answer Figure that should be the next figure (or fifth one) in the series.

A ★B C D E

Perceptual Speed and Accuracy (6 min.)

Measures the ability to compare and mark written lists quickly and accurately; helps predict success in performing routine clerical tasks.

SAMPLE ITEM

Look at the underlined combination of letters or numbers and find the same one on the answer sheet. Then fill in the circle under it.

1 XY Xy XX YX Yy
2 6g 6G G6 Gg g6
3 nm mn mm nn nv
4 Db BD Bd Bb BB

* Also available in the DAT *Partial Battery*

Mechanical Reasoning (25 min.)

Understanding basic mechanical principles of machinery, tools, and motion is important for occupations such as carpentry, mechanics, engineering, and machine operations.

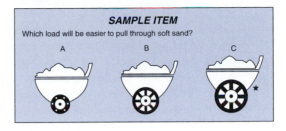

SAMPLE ITEM

Which load will be easier to pull through soft sand?

A   B   C

Space Relations (25 min.)

Measures the ability to visualize a three-dimensional object from a two-dimensional pattern, and to visualize how this object would look if rotated in space; important in drafting, architecture, design, carpentry, and dentistry.

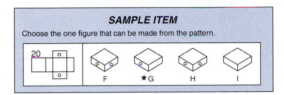

SAMPLE ITEM

Choose the one figure that can be made from the pattern.

F ★G H I

Spelling (10 min.)

Measures one's ability to spell common English words; a useful skill in many academic and vocational pursuits.

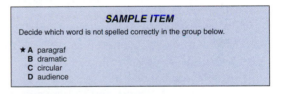

SAMPLE ITEM

Decide which word is not spelled correctly in the group below.

- ★ **A** paragraf
- **B** dramatic
- **C** circular
- **D** audience

Language Usage (15 min.)

Measures the ability to detect errors in grammar, punctuation, and capitalization; needed in most jobs requiring a college degree.

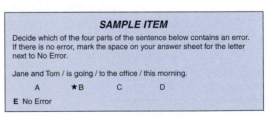

SAMPLE ITEM

Decide which of the four parts of the sentence below contains an error. If there is no error, mark the space on your answer sheet for the letter next to No Error.

Jane and Tom / is going / to the office / this morning.

    A   ★B   C   D

E No Error

Figure 17.6

Sample items from the *Differential Aptitude Tests* (DAT™), *Fifth Edition*

SUMMARY

Standardized aptitude tests are designed to predict future performance in some activity, such as school learning. Like achievement tests, aptitude tests measure learned abilities. They differ from achievement tests, however, in that the test content is broader in scope, and test performance is less dependent on any specific set of learning experiences. This makes it possible to use the tests with students of varying educational backgrounds and to predict performance over a wide range of learning activities.

Group tests of learning ability (or scholastic aptitude) may yield a single score, separate verbal and nonverbal scores, separate verbal and quantitative scores, or several scores based on a series of specific aptitudes. The single-score test is designed to measure general learning ability only. In tests using verbal and nonverbal scores, the nonverbal score serves as a check on the learning ability of the poor reader. Tests with separate verbal and quantitative scores are used primarily for differential prediction. Which type of test to choose depends largely on the type of information desired and the use for which it is intended. For straightforward prediction of school success, a single-score test may suffice, but for helping students with learning problems and educational choices, tests with two or more scores are desirable.

Individual tests of learning ability deemphasize reading skill and provide more carefully controlled testing conditions. Thus, the individual test is especially valuable for testing young children and for checking on questionable scores obtained with group tests. Although extensive training and experience are required to administer individual tests, classroom teachers will likely encounter the scores on school records. It is therefore desirable to know the nature of the test content and the types of scores that are commonly used.

Most group and individual tests of learning ability report test performance in terms of standard scores with a mean of 100 and a standard deviation of 15. In interpreting and using the scores, it is important to allow for normal variation due to error, to seek causes of low scores, to verify the scores by comparison to other information, to use the results to improve learning, and to interpret underachievement cautiously.

Various attempts have been made to develop culture-fair tests by using nonverbal materials that are interesting and common to many cultures and by using simple procedures and liberal time limits. Although the instruments have not lived up to expectations, they have helped clarify the problems involved.

Comprehensive aptitude batteries, such as the *Differential Aptitude Tests* (*DAT*™), have also been developed for school use. These tests include reasoning ability tests as well as vocationally oriented tests.

LEARNING EXERCISES

1. List the similarities and differences between achievement tests and aptitude tests.
2. What are the relative advantages and disadvantages of using group tests of learning ability rather than individual tests?
3. What are the main factors that might account for a difference in scores between two different group tests of learning ability?
4. List the similarities and differences between the *Stanford–Binet Scale* and the *Wechsler Scales*.

5. What cautions are necessary in interpreting and using group ability tests?
6. A student from a culturally different home received a verbal score of 80 and a nonverbal score of 90 on the *Otis–Lennon School Ability Test*. What additional information would help you interpret the scores? If you could have the student take another test, what type of test would you want him or her to take? Why?

7. What tests in the *Differential Aptitude Tests* are most similar to the *Cognitive Abilities Test*?
8. What are the advantages of using the *Differential Aptitude Tests* instead of a group test like the *Cognitive Abilities Test*? What are the disadvantages?

REFERENCES

Cronbach, L. J. (1984). *Essentials of psychological testing* (4th ed.). Boston: Allyn & Bacon.

Guilford, J. P. (1967). *The nature of human intelligence.* New York: McGraw-Hill.

Thorndike, R. L., & Hagen, E. (1993). *Cognitive Abilities Test.* Itasca, IL: Riverside Publishing Company.

FURTHER READING

Anastasi, A., & Urbina, S. (1997). *Psychological testing* (7th ed.). New York: Macmillan. Includes descriptions of widely used individual, group, and multiple aptitude tests.

Pellegrino, J. (1992). Intelligence and aptitude testing. In M. C. Alkin (Ed.), *Encyclopedia of educational research* (6th ed., vol. II). New York: Macmillan. Provides an overview of contemporary issues in intelligence and aptitude testing.

Salvia, J., & Ysseldyke, J. (2004). *Assessment: In special and inclusive education* (9th ed.). Boston: Houghton Mifflin. See descriptions of group and individual ability tests and difficulties of using them in current practice.

Sattler, J. M. (1988). *Assessment of children* (3rd ed.). San Diego: Jerome M. Sattler. Chapters 6 to 11 describe the administration and interpretation of the *Stanford–Binet* and the *Wechsler Scales.*

Thorndike, R. M., Cunningham, G. K., Thorndike, R. L., & Hagen, E. P. (1991). *Measurement and evaluation in psychology and education* (5th ed.). New York: Macmillan. Chapter 12, "Aptitude Tests," gives examples from several aptitude tests, including illustrative items from the *Wechsler Intelligence Scale for Children—Revised* and the *General Aptitude Test Battery.*

TEST SELECTION, ADMINISTRATION, AND USE

Published tests play an important role in the instructional program of the school. They supplement and complement informal classroom tests and aid in many instructional decisions. The task for schools is to locate and select those tests that are most suitable, administer and score them under carefully controlled conditions, and make effective use of the results.

There are many published tests available for school use. The two types of most value to the instructional program of the school are the achievement tests and aptitude tests discussed in the last two chapters. There are hundreds of tests of each type, so great care is needed in selecting those tests that are most relevant to the objectives of the school program and most appropriate for the uses to be made of the results.

Some published tests are selected by individual teachers, but more frequently the tests are selected in accordance with the district or state testing program. Some states or districts may require the administration of an off-the-shelf published test, while others, particularly in the case of states, may require the administration of a test that has been developed or customized by a publisher to align with the state's content standards. Even when the adoption or development is controlled by the state or district, teachers still should have a voice in the selection process, either through direct service on a test committee or through departmental and general staff meetings.

In this chapter, our focus is on published tests, but many of the principles discussed apply equally well to either off-the-shelf published tests or to assessments that are specially developed or customized to meet state content standards. For example, the *Code of Fair Testing Practices in Education* and the *Standards for Educational and Psychological Testing* are applicable in either type of situation and can provide help in test selection or in the development or review of customized assessments.

It is important that teachers participate actively in the selection of published tests and in the development or review of assessments customized to state or district content standards. Their participation provides greater assurance that the tests are aligned with the objectives of the instructional program and that the results will serve the various instructional uses for which they are intended. Although published tests can serve a variety of administrative and guidance functions, of central concern to any testing program is the effective use of tests in the instructional program.

In addition to familiarity with the procedures for selecting tests, teachers must also know the procedures for administering tests (see Appendix D, especially standard 3). In some schools, teachers participate directly in these functions, whereas in others, special personnel is used. In either case, however, the teacher's understanding of the procedures contributes to more effective interpretation and use of test results.

OBTAINING INFORMATION ABOUT PUBLISHED TESTS

There are many available resources that are useful for locating and evaluating published tests in specific areas (see Table 18.1). These will aid in selecting tests that are most suitable and that are technically sound.

Table 18.1
Sources for locating and evaluating published tests

Publisher	Sources	Test Descriptions	Technical Information	Test Reviews
Buros Institute of Mental Measurements	*Mental Measurements Yearbooks, Tests in Print*	X X	X	XX
Educational Testing Service	Test Collection, *News on Tests*	X X (N)		X (S)
(See publishers in Appendix C)	Test Publishers' catalogs	X (N)		
American Educational Research Association	*Standards for Educational and Psychological Testing*		XX	
(Varies)	Test Manuals	XX	XX	
(See list in Appendix B)	Professional Journals	X (N)	X (S)	X (S)
(Varies)	Measurement Textbooks	X (S)	X (S)	X (S)

Note: XX = most useful, X = useful, X (N) = useful for new tests, X (S) = useful for some tests.

Buros Institute of Mental Measurements Guides

A basic source of information about tests is the *Mental Measurements Yearbook,* first published in 1938. The *Yearbook* was started and edited by Oscar K. Buros for many years and is now published by the Buros Institute of Mental Measurements of the University of Nebraska–Lincoln. The *Yearbooks* are published periodically but on no definite schedule. Each *Yearbook* typically includes the following types of material:

1. Descriptive information concerning each test
2. Critical reviews written by test specialists for the *Yearbook*
3. Excerpts from test reviews published in professional journals
4. Comprehensive bibliographies for many specific tests
5. Listing of measurement books and book reviews

The test reviews in the *Yearbooks* provide especially valuable information for evaluating the quality of published tests. Each test is typically reviewed by two or more specialists qualified by training and experience to evaluate the test. The reviewers often point out test weaknesses as well as any exaggerated claims made by test publishers. They also indicate the strengths of a test and the uses for which it is best suited.

Another useful Buros Institute guide for locating tests and information about tests is *Tests in Print.* This publication includes a descriptive listing of published tests, with extensive bibliographies for some. Although test reviews are not included, each is indexed to those editions of the *Yearbooks* that contain reviews of the test.

As aids for locating tests for a particular use, *Tests in Print* provides an excellent guide to available tests, and the *Yearbooks* provide the information needed to evaluate them. The cross-references to the *Yearbooks* in *Tests in Print* make it possible to locate numerous reviews for each test.

Tests in Print has been published less frequently than the *Yearbooks* and in the event a recent edition is not available, tests can be located by going directly to the *Yearbooks.* They are fully indexed and contain descriptions of the tests as well as the test reviews. The *Yearbooks* can also be used, of course, for evaluating tests that have been located through test publishers' catalogs or other sources.

The Buros Institute of Mental Measurements also provides test information through a *Yearbooks* database. This computer database is updated monthly and thus provides the most recent information available (see the box "*Mental Measurements Yearbooks and On-line Computer Service*").

Mental Measurements Yearbooks and On-Line Computer Service

The Buros Institute of Mental Measurements (University of Nebraska–Lincoln) produces a database that is part of the on-line computer service available. The *Mental Measurements Yearbooks* include reviews of over 2,000 tests. It includes the reviews from the Buros Institute's 10th through 15th *Mental Measurements Yearbooks* and is updated every 6 months. For further information on the on-line access to *Yearbook* reviews, go to **http://www.unl.edu/buros/.**

Educational Testing Service (ETS) Test Collection

The Educational Testing Service (Princeton, New Jersey) developed a Test Collection that contains information about thousands of tests. The ETS Test Collection database is now available through a joint project of ETS and the ERIC Clearinghouse on Assessment and Evaluation. The database contains information on over 10,000 tests and research instruments. The database entries include information about the title, author, publication date and source, as well as an abstract that describes the test and intended uses and intended population (e.g., age and grade level). A subset of the collection is available for purchase on microfiche from the test collection. For further information, go to *http://ericae.net/testcol.htm#ETSTF*.

Test Publishers' Catalogs

Recent information concerning tests available for school use also can be obtained from test publishers' catalogs. These usually contain brief descriptions of each test, including possible uses of the test, cost, administration time, and similar information. If a publisher's claims for its tests are checked by independent reviews such as those presented in the *Mental Measurements Yearbooks,* test catalogs provide a good source of information. They are especially useful for locating new tests and recent editions of earlier tests. A brief list of test publishers who will send catalogs on request is included in Appendix E.

Testing Standards

An especially useful aid in evaluating and using published tests is the *Standards for Educational and Psychological Testing* (American Educational Research Association, American Psychological Association, & National Council on Measurement in Education, 1999). The *Standards* include recommendations intended for both test publishers and test users. Part I contains standards for test construction, evaluation, and documentation (validity, reliability, test development, norming, scaling, and related issues). Part II provides standards on fairness in testing (general issues, diverse linguistic backgrounds, and disabilities). Part III covers standards for the use of tests in various situations (clinical, educational, counseling, employment, professional licensure, and program evaluation). Each standard is followed by a comment used to clarify or justify the recommendation or to describe the conditions under which the standard would apply (see the box "Illustrative Test Standard from the 'Validity' Section").

A review of the standards in Part I provides a good background for selecting and evaluating tests, and the specific recommendations in Parts II and III provide excellent guidelines for effective test use.

Code of Fair Testing Practices in Education

The *Code of Fair Testing Practices in Education* was prepared by a Joint Committee on Testing Practices, a group that was formed in cooperation with several professional associations. The *Code* is intended to apply to a wide range of published tests and tests used in formal administrations that may be developed and required by school districts or

Illustrative Test Standard from the "Validity" Section

Standard 1.1

A rationale should be presented for each recommended interpretation and use of test scores, together with a comprehensive summary of the evidence and theory bearing on the intended use or interpretation.

Comment

The rationale should indicate what propositions are necessary to investigate the intended interpretation. The comprehensive summary should combine logical analysis with empirical evidence to provide support for the test rationale. Evidence may come from studies conducted locally, in the setting where the test is to be used; from specific prior studies; or from comprehensive statistical syntheses of available studies meeting clearly specified criteria. No type of evidence is inherently preferable to others; rather, the quality and relevance of the evidence to the intended test use determine the value of a particular kind of evidence. A presentation of empirical evidence on any point should give due weight to all relevant findings in the scientific literature, including those inconsistent with the intended interpretation or use. Test developers have the responsibility to provide support for their own recommendations, but test users are responsible for evaluating the quality of the validity evidence provided and its relevance to the local situation.

Source: Standards for Educational and Psychological Testing by American Educational Research Association, American Psychological Association, and National Council on Measurement in Education, 1999, Washington, DC. Copyright 1999 by American Educational Research Association.

states. The code is not intended to apply to tests developed by individual teachers for use in their own classrooms.

The *Code* is intended for two primary audiences: test users and test developers. Test users are defined as "people who select tests, commission test development services, or make decisions on the basis of test scores." The *Code* presents standards in four areas: (a) developing and selecting appropriate tests, (b) administering and scoring tests, (c) reporting and interpreting test results, and (d) informing test takers. Each of these sections of the *Code* is discussed in subsequent sections of this chapter and in Chapter 19.

Other Sources of Test Information

Test reviews and information concerning the nature and use of particular tests can frequently be found in professional journals (see list in Appendix B). Journal articles can be most easily located through the use of such bibliographic sources as the *Current Index to Journals in Education,* the *Education Index,* and *Psychological Abstracts.* In using these guides, it is usually necessary to search under many different headings, such as aptitude testing, achievement testing, psychological tests, reading tests, tests and scales, and testing programs. In locating information on tests in a specific content area, it also may be necessary to look under that subject in a specific content area (e.g., English or science). Test reviews in professional journals can be most easily located by a computerized literature search.

Some textbooks in educational and psychological measurement include descriptions and evaluations of widely used tests and contain selected lists of tests in an appendix. Also, some textbooks in particular areas (e.g., reading or special education) describe tests that are especially useful in those areas. Although textbooks provide descriptive information concerning representative tests, this is useful mainly for orientation to the field of testing. Test selection for a particular situation includes a study of the situation to determine testing needs, searching for possible tests, consulting test reviews, and examining the test manuals and other test materials of the most likely prospects.

SELECTING APPROPRIATE TESTS

Published tests play an important role in the educational program of the school and therefore should be selected with utmost care. When carefully selected and appropriately used, they can make a valuable contribution to instructional planning and student learning. On the other hand, hastily or casually selected tests seldom are in harmony with the objectives of the instructional program and thus may provide inadequate or inappropriate information on which to base educational decisions. Even when selected with care, however, the value of the information depends on the way in which it is used. Misinterpretations (e.g., assuming that performance on an aptitude test is an indication of innate capacity) and misuses (e.g., placement of students in remedial programs based solely on low test performance) can have serious negative consequences. The following sequence of steps provides general guidelines for a systematic approach to test selection. Issues regarding the use and interpretation of results are considered in a subsequent section of this chapter.

Defining Testing Needs

The first task in selecting published tests is to define specifically the purpose of testing and the type of information being sought through testing. As is emphasized by the first standard for test users in the *Code of Fair Testing Practices in Education* (see Table 18.2), it is critical that purpose be clearly defined and that the test match the purpose. In selecting achievement tests, for example, it is insufficient to search for a test to evaluate "achievement in social studies" or to measure "reading comprehension." There are numerous tests in any given content area, and each measures somewhat different aspects of knowledge, understanding, and skill. To make a proper selection, we must first identify the objectives and specific learning outcomes of our instructional program. This is necessary in choosing relevant tests, whether selecting a single test for a particular course or a battery of tests for a schoolwide testing program.

Clarifying the type of information needed is equally necessary in selecting aptitude tests. It makes a difference whether we are going to use the results for determining reading readiness, for grouping students, for vocational planning, or for predicting success in science and mathematics courses. Each function requires different information and consequently a different type of aptitude measure. Thus, selection must be preceded by an analysis of the intended use of the results and the type of test data most appropriate for each use.

Table 18.2
Standards for developing/selecting appropriate tests

Test Developers	Test Users
Test developers should provide the information and supporting evidence that test users need to select appropriate tests.	**Test users should select tests that meet the intended purpose and that are appropriate for the intended testtakers.**
A-1. Provide evidence of what the test measures, the recommended uses, the intended test takers, and the strengths and limitations of the test, including the level of precision of the test scores.	A-1. Define the purpose for testing, the content and skills to be tested, and the intended test takers. Select and use the most appropriate test based on a thorough review of available information.
A-2. Describe how the content and skills to be tested were selected and how the tests were developed.	A-2. Review and select tests based on the appropriateness of test content, skills tested, and complete content coverage for the intended purpose of testing.
A-3. Communicate information about a test's characteristics at a level of detail appropriate to the intended test users.	A-3. Review materials provided by test developers and select tests for which clear, accurate, and to information is provided.
A-4. Provide guidance on the levels of skills, knowledge, and training necessary for appropriate review, selection, and administration of tests.	A-4. Select tests through a process that includes persons with appropriate knowledge, skills, and training.
A-5. Provide evidence that the technical quality, including reliability and validity, of the test meets its intended purposes.	A-5. Evaluate evidence of the technical quality of the test provided by the test developer and any independent reviewers.
A-6. Provide to qualified test users representative samples of test questions or practice tests, directions, answer sheets, manuals, and score reports.	A-6. Evaluate representative samples of test questions or practice tests, directions, answer sheets, manuals, and score reports before selecting a test.
A-7. Avoid potentially offensive content or language when developing test questions and related materials.	A-7. Evaluate procedures and materials used by test developers, as well as the resulting test, to ensure that potentially offensive content or language is avoided.
A-8. Make appropriate modified forms of tests or administration procedures available for test takers with disabilities who need special accommodations.	A-8. Select tests with appropriately modified forms or administration procedures for test takers with disabilities who need special accommodations.
A-9. Obtain and provide evidence on the performance of test takers of diverse subgroups, making significant efforts to obtain sample sizes that are adequate for subgroup analyses. Evaluate the evidence to ensure that differences in performance are related to the skills being assessed.	A-9. Evaluate the available evidence on the performance of test takers of diverse subgroups. Determine to the extent feasible which performance differences may have been caused by factors unrelated to the skills being assessed.

Source: Code of Fair Testing Practices in Education, 2004, Washington, DC: Joint Committee on Testing Practices. (Mailing address: Joint Committee on Testing Practices, American Psychological Association, 750 First Street, NE, Washington, DC 20002-4242)

Narrowing the Choice

The need for published tests is usually considered in relation to the total measurement program. This makes it possible to choose tests that supplement and complement the other means of assessing students. It is desirable to choose a test of general educational development, for example, if certain learning outcomes in the knowledge area already are being adequately measured by informal classroom tests and assessments. Similarly, if a scholastic aptitude test is to be used at a particular grade level for identifying students needing extra help in learning to read, it is best to replace the aptitude test with a diagnostic reading test. Such decisions can be made only when the need for testing is viewed in terms of the total measurement program.

Other factors in the school situation also help narrow the choice. If, for instance, the school lacks a person with the training and experience required to administer individual tests, only group tests should be considered. If the tests are to be administered by teachers without experience in test administration, tests with simple directions are best. If the same type of achievement battery is desired for both the elementary and the high school level, only those batteries with tests at all grade levels need to be examined. Considerations such as these offer additional criteria for determining the types of tests to seek.

Although reputable test publishers work hard to eliminate materials that are offensive to different groups of test takers, avoid stereotypes, and in other ways make the material as fair as possible for test takers of different races, gender, or ethnic backgrounds, it is also important that test users review potential tests for possible sources of unfairness. Useful guidelines in this regard from the *Code of Fair Testing Practices in Education* are reproduced in Table 18.3.

Locating Suitable Tests

When the needs for testing have been identified, a list of possible tests can be compiled from test publishers' catalogs and the most recent edition of the *Mental Measurements Yearbook*. The reviews in these guides are sufficiently detailed to weed out those tests that are clearly inappropriate or that have obvious technical weaknesses. Further evaluative information also can be found in other sources, such as those described earlier.

Obtaining Specimen Sets

When the list of tests has been reduced to a reasonable number, specimen sets should be obtained so that test manuals and the test items themselves can be evaluated. Test publishers generally supply specimen sets for each test they publish.

These can be purchased at relatively low cost and include a test manual, a test booklet, and scoring keys. Many universities, colleges, and large school systems maintain a file of such specimen sets.

Table 18.3
Standards for administering and scoring tests

Test Developers	*Test Users*
Test developers should explain how to administer and score tests correctly and fairly.	**Test users should administer and score tests correctly and fairly.**
B-1. Provide clear descriptions of detailed procedures for administering tests in a standardized manner.	B-1. Follow established procedures for administering tests in a standardized manner.
B-2. Provide guidelines on reasonable procedures for assessing persons with disabilities who need special accommodations or those with diverse linguistic backgrounds.	B-2. Provide and document appropriate procedures for test takers with disabilities who need special accommodations or those with diverse linguistic backgrounds. Some accommodations may be required by law or regulation.
B-3. Provide information to test takers or test users on test question formats and procedures for answering test questions, including information on the use of any needed materials and equipment.	B-3. Provide test takers with an opportunity to become familiar with test question formats and any materials or equipment that may be used during testing.
B-4. Establish and implement procedures to ensure the security of testing materials during all phases of test development, administration, scoring, and reporting.	B-4. Protect the security of test materials, including respecting copyrights and eliminating opportunities for test takers to obtain scores by fraudulent means.
B-5. Provide procedures, materials, and guidelines for scoring the tests, and for monitoring the accuracy of the scoring process. If scoring the test is the responsibility of the test developer, provide adequate training for scorers.	B-5. If test scoring is the responsibility of the test user, provide adequate training to scorers and ensure and monitor the accuracy of the scoring process.
B-6. Correct errors that affect the interpretation of the scores and communicate the corrected results promptly.	B-6. Correct errors that affect the interpretation of the scores and communicate the corrected results promptly.
B-7. Develop and implement procedures for ensuring the confidentiality of scores.	B-7. Develop and implement procedures for ensuring the confidentiality of scores.

Source: Code of Fair Testing Practices in Education, 2004, Washington, DC: Joint Committee on Testing Practices. (Mailing address: Joint Committee on Testing Practices, American Psychological Association, 750 First Street, NE, Washington, DC 20002-4242).

Reviewing Test Materials

The test manual (sometimes accompanied by a technical manual and related aids) usually provides the most complete information for judging the appropriateness and the technical qualities of a test. A good test manual includes the following types of information.

1. Uses for which the test is recommended
2. Qualifications needed to administer and interpret the test
3. Evidence of validity for each recommended use

4. Evidence of reliability for recommended uses and an indication of equivalence for any equivalent forms provided
5. Directions for administering and scoring the test
6. Adequate norms (including a description of the procedures used in obtaining them) or other bases for interpreting the scores

Some test manuals (or supplements to the manuals) also contain suggestions and guides for interpreting and using the results. These are especially helpful for determining the functions for which the test is best suited.

In addition to reviewing the test manual, it is also wise to study the individual test items. The best method of doing this is to try to answer each item as if you were taking the test. For achievement tests, it is also helpful to classify the items by means of a previously prepared table of specifications or other test plan. Although the process is time consuming, there is no better means of determining how appropriate a test is for measuring the knowledge, skills, and understanding emphasized in the instructional program.

Using a Test Evaluation Form

Gathering information about specific tests is made easier if a test evaluation form is used. This provides a convenient means of recording significant data, it increases the likelihood that pertinent information will not be overlooked, and it provides for a summary comparison of each test's strengths and weaknesses (see the box "Test Evaluation Form").

Test Evaluation Form

Test title _____   Authors _____
Publisher _____   Publication date _____
Purpose of test _____
For grades (ages) _____   Forms _____
Scores available _____   Types of scoring _____
Administration time _____   Cost _____

Technical Features

  Validity: Nature of evidence
  Reliability: Nature of evidence (stability, internal consistency, equivalence). Standard error of measurement (size, type)
  Norms: Type, adequacy, and appropriateness to local situation. Criterion-referenced interpretation: Describe (if available)

Practical Features

  Ease of administration (procedure and timing)

Ease of scoring and interpretation
Adequacy of test manual and accessory materials

General Evaluation

Comments of reviewers (see *Mental Measurements Yearbooks*)
Summary of strengths
Summary of weaknesses
Recommendations concerning local use

Although a test evaluation form provides a useful summary of information concerning tests, no test should be selected on the basis of this information alone. How well a test fits the school program and the particular uses for which it is being considered are always the main considerations.

ADMINISTERING PUBLISHED TESTS

Most group tests of achievement and scholastic aptitude can be successfully administered by any conscientious teacher. The main requirement is that the testing procedures prescribed in the test manual be rigorously followed. To do this, it is necessary to shift from being a teacher and helper to being an impartial test examiner who will not deviate from the test directions.

Teachers sometimes wonder why it is important to follow the test procedures so closely. What harm is there in helping students if they do not understand particular questions? Why not give the students a little more time if they are almost finished? Aren't some of the directions nit-picking, anyway? The answer is:

A published test must be administered under standard conditions if the results are to be meaningfully interpreted.

When a published, norm-referenced test is given to a national sample of students to establish norms, it is administered in exact accordance with the procedures prescribed in the test manual. Unless teachers adhere strictly to the same procedures, the standard conditions of measurement will be violated, and the test norms cannot legitimately be used to interpret scores. Although not all published criterion-referenced tests have norms, the interpretation of the results according to an absolute standard (e.g., mastery–nonmastery) also depends on controlled conditions of administration. In short, when we alter the procedures for administering a published test, we lose the basis for a meaningful interpretation of the scores.

Test Administration

The administration of group tests is relatively simple: (a) Motivate students to do their best, (b) follow the directions closely, (c) keep time accurately, (d) record any significant events that might influence test scores, and (e) collect the materials promptly.

1. Motivate the students. In testing, our goal should be to obtain maximum performance within the standard conditions set forth in the testing procedures. We want all students to earn as high a score as they are capable of achieving. This obviously means that they must be motivated to put forth their best effort. Although some students will respond to any test as a challenge to their ability, others will not work seriously at the task unless they are convinced that the test results will be beneficial to them. In school testing, we can stimulate students to put forth their best effort by convincing them that the test results will be used primarily to help them improve their learning. We can also explain to them the value of the test results for understanding themselves better and for planning their future. But these need to be more than hollow promises. Test results must be used in such a way that these benefits are clearly evident to the students.

Before administering a particular test, the teacher should explain to students the purpose of the test and the uses to be made of the results (see Table 18.4). At this time, the teacher should emphasize the advantages of obtaining a score that represents the students' best efforts but should not make the students overly anxious. Verbal reassurance that the size of the score is not as important as the fact that it represents one's best effort is usually helpful. The judicious use of humor can also offset test anxiety. The most effective remedy, however, is a positive attitude toward test results. When the students are convinced that valid test scores are beneficial to their own welfare, both their test anxiety and motivation tend to become minor problems.

With the recent growth in statewide testing, student motivation on standardized tests has been a major concern for teachers, schools, and parents. Many schools have begun to use external motivation techniques that include posters, pep rallies, and the like; however, internal motivation of students (i.e., motivating students to perform well because they understand the importance of the test and they want to do well) is the

Table 18.4
Standards for informing test takers

Under some circumstances, test developers have direct communication with the test takers and/or control of the tests, testing process, and test results. In other circumstances the test users have these responsibilities.

Test developers or test users should inform test takers about the nature of the test, test taker rights and responsibilities, the appropriate use of scores, and procedures for resolving challenges to scores.

D-1. Inform test takers in advance of the test administration about the coverage of the test, the types of question formats, the directions, and appropriate test-taking strategies. Make such information available to all test takers.

D-2. When a test is optional, provide test takers or their parents/guardians with information to help them judge whether a test should be taken—including indications of any consequences that may result from not taking the test (e.g., not being eligible to compete for a particular scholarship)—and whether there is an available alternative to the test.

D-3. Provide test takers or their parents/guardians with information about rights test takers may have to obtain copies of tests and completed answer sheets, to retake tests, to have tests rescored, or to have scores declared invalid.

D-4. Provide test takers or their parents/guardians with information about responsibilities test takers have, such as being aware of the intended purpose and uses of the test, performing at capacity, following directions, and not disclosing test items or interfering with other test takers.

D-5. Inform test takers or their parents/guardians how long scores will be kept on file and indicate to whom, under what circumstances, and in what manner test scores and related information will or will not be released. Protect test scores from unauthorized release and access.

D-6. Describe procedures for investigating and resolving circumstances that might result in canceling or withholding scores, such as failure to adhere to specified testing procedures.

D-7. Describe procedures that test takers, parents/guardians, and other interested parties may use to obtain more information about the test, register complaints, and have problems resolved.

Source: Code of Fair Testing Practices in Education, 2004, Washington, DC: Joint Committee on Testing Practices. (Mailing address: Joint Committee on Testing Practices, American Psychological Association, 750 First Street, NE, Washington, DC 20002-4242)

more effective method for achieving good results. Therefore, students must recognize the importance of the test and remain confident in their ability to perform their best.

2. Follow directions strictly. The importance of following the directions given in the test manual cannot be overemphasized. Unless the test is administered in exact accordance with the standard directions, the test results will contain an indeterminate amount of error and thereby prevent proper interpretation and use. The test directions should be read word for word in a loud, clear voice. They should never be paraphrased, recited from memory, or modified in any way. The oral reading of directions will usually be more effective if the directions have been practiced beforehand.

After the directions have been read and during the testing period, some students are likely to ask questions. It is usually permissible to clarify the directions and to answer questions concerning mechanics (e.g., how to record the answer), but the test manual must be your guide. If it is permissible to clarify the directions, you should not change or modify the directions in any way during your explanation. Some teachers find it hard to refrain from helping students who are having difficulty answering items on a published test. When questioned about a particular test item, they are tempted to say, "You remember, we discussed that last week," or give similar hints to the students. This merely distorts the results. When asked about a particular test item during testing, the teacher should quietly tell the student, "I'm sorry, but I cannot help you. Do the best you can."

3. Keep time accurately. If a series of short subtests must be timed separately, it is desirable to use a stopwatch when giving the test. For most other purposes, a watch with a second hand is satisfactory. To ensure accurate timing, keep a written record of the starting and stopping times, the exact hour, minute, and second as follows:

	Hour	Minute	Second
Starting Time	2	10	0
Time Allowed		12	
Stopping Time	2	22	0

4. Record significant events. The students should be carefully observed during testing and a record made of any unusual behavior or event that might influence the test scores. If, for example, a student appears overly tense and anxious, sits staring out of the window for a time, or seems to be marking answers randomly without reading the questions, a description of the behavior should be recorded. Similarly, if there are interruptions during the testing (despite your careful planning), a record should be made of the type and length of the interruption and whether it did or did not alter the testing conditions. A record of unusual student behavior and significant events provides valuable information for determining whether test scores are representative of the students' best efforts and whether standard conditions have been maintained during testing. Questionable test scores should, of course, be rechecked by administering a second form of the test.

5. Collect test materials promptly. When the test has ended, all test materials should be collected promptly so that students cannot work beyond the time limits and so that all materials can be accounted for and secured.

For those responsible for the testing program, from the ordering of the tests to their administration, the box "Test Giver's Checklist" summarizes the points that need to be considered.

Improving Students' Test-Taking Skills

Our suggestions for test administration, as summarized in the "Test Giver's Checklist," emphasize the importance of establishing the most suitable environment for the test taker

---

Test Giver's Checklist

1. Order and check test materials well in advance of the testing date.
   a. Were correct forms of the test sent?
   b. Is there the right number of tests and answer sheets?
   c. Have all needed materials been assembled (pencils, watch, etc.)?
   d. Have all test materials been securely stored until the testing date?

2. Select a suitable location for testing.
   a. Is there adequate work space?
   b. Is the lighting, heat, and ventilation satisfactory?
   c. Is the room in a quiet location?
   d. Is the seating arrangement satisfactory?

3. Take steps to prevent distractions.
   a. Will a "Testing in Progress" sign be posted on the door?
   b. Will all needed materials be on hand before starting?
   c. Have arrangements been made to terminate distractions (e.g., bells)?
   d. Has the test been scheduled to avoid major school events?

4. Study the test materials and practice giving the test.
   a. Did you carefully read the test manual?
   b. Did you take the test yourself?
   c. Did you practice reading the directions?
   d. Did you anticipate questions students might ask?

5. Motivate the students.
   a. Was the purpose of the test explained to the students?
   b. Were the students told how the results would be used?
   c. Were the students encouraged to put forth their best effort?
   d. Has care been taken not to create test anxiety?
   e. Is the student adequately prepared to take the test?

6. Follow test directions strictly and keep time accurately.
   a. Did you read the test directions word for word?
   b. Did you refrain from helping students (except with mechanics)?
   c. Did you make a written record of starting and stopping times?
   d. Did you stick to the exact time schedule?

7. Record significant events.
   a. Did students do anything that might affect the test results?
   b. Were there any interruptions that might affect the scores?

8. Collect the test materials promptly when the testing has ended.
   a. Were all test materials collected immediately?
   b. Were the collected materials counted, checked, and secured?

and using methods that motivate the students to put forth their best efforts. Despite these procedures, however, some students might not perform at the level of which they are capable because they lack skill in test taking. It has been suggested by Sarnacki (1979) that all students be given training in test-taking skills to prevent such deficiencies from lowering their test scores. This seems to be a sensible suggestion and one that could be easily handled in the regular classroom or through the use of programmed materials. Among the skills important in test taking are the following:

1. Listening to or reading directions carefully
2. Listening to or reading test items carefully
3. Setting a pace that will allow time to complete the test
4. Bypassing difficult items and returning to them later
5. Making informed guesses rather than omitting items
6. Eliminating as many alternatives as possible on multiple-choice items before guessing
7. Following directions carefully in marking the answer sheet (e.g., darken the entire space)
8. Checking to be sure the item number and answer number match when marking an answer
9. Checking to be sure that the appropriate response was marked on the answer sheet
10. Going back and checking the answers if time permits

Test-taking skills such as these can be easily mastered, but students need practice to develop them. Fortunately, many test publishers now provide practice tests that can be given before the regular test. This is of some help, but special training in test taking will provide even greater assurance that a student's test scores are not depressed by deficiencies in test-taking skills.

Unsound and Unethical Test Preparation Practices

Although it is important to take steps such as those discussed here to help students be ready to do their best when taking tests, it is easy to go overboard. Especially in high-stakes testing situations, where teachers are under great pressure to get their students to score high, it is natural to focus more and more attention on the contents of the test. Unfortunately, this can lead to poor instructional practices and inflated test scores.

In some schools, teachers devote the majority of their instructional time for several weeks to practice for the high-stakes test. Such practice ignores important learning objectives that are not on the test and is not even a sound pedagogical approach for the objectives that are covered by the test. Moreover, when the practice materials match the actual test too closely, the result can be improved test scores without improved achievement. As a consequence, the scores give an inflated impression of the students' overall achievement.

Occasionally, the actual items that appear on a test become the focus of instruction. Providing practice on the actual test items before administration of a standardized test invalidates the results. It is an unethical practice.

USING RESULTS OF PUBLISHED TESTS

Published achievement and learning ability tests can serve many different purposes in the school's educational program. Here we describe briefly some of the possible uses and misuses of published tests that are of special interest to teachers.

Possible Uses of Published Tests

If they are selected and used with discretion, published tests of achievement and ability can play an important role in the school's evaluation program. Tests should be selected in accordance with the school's objectives and the purposes for which the results are to be used. When selected in this manner, they can contribute to more effective educational decisions in a number of areas.

Instructional Planning.   Published tests of achievement and learning ability can aid instructional planning in a particular school or course in the following ways.

1. Identifying the level and range of ability among students. Among other things, instructional plans must take into account the students' learning ability and their present levels of achievement. Published tests can provide objective evidence on both of these points.

2. Identifying areas of instruction needing greater emphasis. If the published tests have been selected in accordance with the school's objectives, instructional weaknesses will be revealed by those areas of the test in which the students do poorly. Published tests are especially helpful in appraising strengths and weaknesses in learning (see Table 18.5).

Table 18.5
Percentage of teachers using standardized achievement test results in various ways

Teachers Were Asked to Indicate Which of These Uses They Made	*Percentage Reporting Each Use*
Diagnosing strengths and weaknesses	74
Measuring student "growth"	66
Individual student evaluation	65
Instructional planning	52
Class evaluation	45
Reporting to parents	42
Evaluation of teaching methods	37
Reporting to students	24

Source: Adapted from "Attitudes Toward Standardized Tests: Students, Teachers, and Measurement Specialists" by J. P. Stetz and M. D. Beck, *NCME Measurement in Education* (Washington, DC: National Council on Measurement in Education, 12 [1], 1981).

Note: Based on a survey of 3,306 teachers, grades K through 12.

3. Identifying discrepancies between learning ability and achievement. Although differences between learning ability and achievement must be interpreted with caution, large discrepancies can aid in identifying students who may be underachieving. In this as well as other areas, however, the results of published tests should be verified by other available evidence.

4. Diagnosing learning errors and planning remedial instruction. Published diagnostic tests are especially useful for pinpointing the learning errors that are handicapping a student's learning progress. Published tests provide a more systematic approach than informal methods, and the manuals typically provide suggestions for remediation. Unfortunately, these tests are limited almost entirely to the basic skills of reading and mathematics.

5. Clarifying and selecting instructional objectives. The use of published tests aids in the clarification and selection of objectives in several ways. First, selecting the tests forces us to identify and state our objectives as clearly as possible. Second, an examination of the items in published tests tells us how different objectives function in testing. As we go back and forth (during test selection) between our objectives and the items in the tests under consideration, what a particular objective looks like in operational terms becomes clearer. Third, the results of published tests provide evidence that helps in selecting objectives at a particular grade level or in a particular course. If fall test results indicate that students in the sixth grade are weak in study skills, for example, sixth-grade teachers may want to include an objective in this area, even though they had not originally planned to devote much attention to study skills. Similarly, published test results might indicate that a particular objective is unnecessary because it has been satisfactorily achieved at an earlier grade level.

Individualizing Instruction.   In any classroom, there are substantial individual differences in aptitude and achievement. Thus, it is necessary to study the strengths and weaknesses of each student in class so that instruction can be adapted as much as possible to individual learning needs. For this purpose (a) scholastic aptitude tests provide clues concerning learning ability, (b) reading tests indicate the difficulty of material the student can read and understand, (c) norm-referenced achievement tests point out general areas of strength and weakness, (d) criterion-referenced achievement tests describe how well specific tasks are being mastered, and (e) diagnostic tests aid in detecting and overcoming specific learning errors.

Criterion-referenced tests are especially well adapted to individualizing instruction because each set of test items is keyed to a specific objective. This makes it possible for a student to proceed through a given learning sequence by demonstrating mastery of the objectives one by one. Many publishers also provide references to books and other learning aids to guide the individual study of students who have failed to master a particular objective.

Identifying the Needs of Exceptional Children.   Some students deviate so markedly from students at their grade or age level that special instructional programs are needed. The gifted, mentally retarded, emotionally disturbed, and physically handicapped and similar exceptional children fall into this category. For this student, published tests are helpful in identifying problems of learning and development so that special provisions can be made for meeting exceptional needs. This use of tests is growing in importance now that inclusion and mainstreaming (placing children with handicapping conditions in the least-restrictive environment) have increased the number of exceptional children in regular classrooms. Mainstreaming and inclusion emphasize the importance of each handicapped student having a detailed individualized educational program.

Monitoring of Educational Progress over Extended Periods.   Published tests are especially useful in measuring learning progress over a given number of years. Comparable forms make it possible to measure the same learning outcomes annually and thus obtain a long-range picture of the students' educational development. Teacher-made tests are not as useful for this purpose because of the lack of uniformity from one year to the next.

In using published tests as a basis for determining students' educational development, care must be taken not to overgeneralize from the results. Tests that yield comparable measures of general educational progress throughout the school years must, of necessity, be confined to learning that is continuously developing and that is common to diverse curricula. In the main, this means the basic skills and critical abilities used in the interpretation and application of ideas that cut across subject-matter lines. Although these are significant learning outcomes, they are only a partial indication of total educational development. Knowledge and understanding of specific content, skills unique to each subject field, attitudes and appreciation, and similar learning outcomes that cannot be measured by survey tests of educational development are equally important.

Providing Parents with an Independent Source of Information.   Teacher reports regarding student achievement and grades assigned provide parents with the most important information about the educational progress of their children. Standardized test results, however, are a useful supplement to teacher reports. They have the advantage of being independent of teacher opinions. Normative information also provides a comparison against a wider context than that provided by an individual classroom or school.

Helping Students Make Educational and Vocational Choices.   At the high school level, published test results can contribute to more intelligent educational and vocational decisions. In deciding which curriculum to pursue, which courses to take, whether to plan for college, or which occupations to consider, students can be aided greatly by knowing their aptitudes and their strengths and weaknesses in achievement. Published tests are especially useful in educational and vocational planning because they indicate to students how they compare with persons beyond the local school situation. This is important because these are the persons with whom they will be competing after leaving high school.

Supplementary Uses.   In addition to the preceding uses of published tests, all of which are directly concerned with improving students' instruction and guidance, there are a number of supplementary uses to which they can be put, including (a) placing students transferred from other schools, (b) appraising the general effectiveness of the school program in developing basic skills, (c) identifying areas in the educational program in which supervisory aid and in-service training can be used most effectively, (d) evaluating new educational programs, (e) providing evidence for interpreting the school program to the public, and (f) gathering information for reports to other schools, colleges, and prospective employers. When published test results are presented to individuals and groups outside the school, it should be emphasized that these tests measure only some of the objectives of the school program.

Misuses of Published Tests

Published tests can be misused in any of the preceding areas if (a) there is inadequate attention to the educational objectives being measured, (b) there is a failure to recognize the limited position of tests in the total assessment program, (c) there is unquestioning faith in the test results, or (d) the group tested is markedly different from the group for whom the test was intended. These factors contribute to the misapplication and misinterpretation of published test results in any situation. In addition, three misuses warrant special attention.

Assignment of Course Grades.   Some teachers use the scores from published tests as a basis for assigning course grades. This is undesirable for at least two reasons: (1) Published tests are seldom closely related to the instructional objectives of a particular course, and (2) they measure only a portion of the desired learning outcomes emphasized in instruction. Using these tests for grading purposes tends to overemphasize a limited number of ill-fitting objectives. In addition to the unfairness to the student, this practice encourages both teachers and students to neglect those objectives that are not measured by the tests.

In borderline cases, especially when promotion or retention is being decided, published test results can be a valuable supplement. Knowing a student's scholastic aptitude and general level of educational development contributes to a more intelligent decision concerning the best grade placement. Except for such special uses, however, published tests should play a minor role, if any, in determining course grades.

Assignment of Remedial Track or Retention in Grade Solely on the Basis of a Test Score. Although test results can contribute to informed decisions regarding student placement in special programs, they are not adequate for such decisions when used in isolation. Information about a student's background and prior learning experiences needs to be considered. Teacher observations of classroom behavior and performance are also relevant considerations. Moreover, there should be compelling reasons to believe that students placed in special instructional programs or required to repeat a grade will be likely to learn more than they would in a normal class and sequence. It should be noted that research suggests remedial tracks frequently **do not** lead to improved learning and that students who are retained in grade seldom benefit more than they would if promoted (Shepard & Smith, 1989).

Evaluation of Teaching Effectiveness.   In some schools, teacher effectiveness is judged by the scores students make on published tests. This is an extremely unfair practice because so many factors other than teaching effectiveness influence test scores. Many of these, such as the class's level of ability, the students' cultural background, the students' educational experiences, and the relative difficulty of learning different course materials, cannot be controlled or equated with sufficient accuracy to justify inferring that the results are solely, or even largely, based on the teacher's efforts. Even if such factors could be controlled, published test results would be a poor criterion of teaching success because they are not closely related to the instructional objectives of particular courses and they measure only a portion of the learning outcomes teachers strive for in their instruction. At most, they should play only a minor role in teacher evaluation.

An especially undesirable side effect of using published tests as the sole or main measure of teaching effectiveness is that some teachers will obtain copies of the test and start teaching students the answers to specific test items. Although this unprofessional practice may begin with a few unethical teachers, subtle pressures (to avoid looking ineffective by comparison) soon cause the practice to spread. Such "teaching for the test," of course, not only distorts the measures of teaching effectiveness but also invalidates the test scores for other school uses.

SUMMARY

Teachers should know how to locate, select, administer, interpret, and use published tests. This contributes to more effective use of the test results in the instructional program. One of the most useful sources for locating and evaluating tests is provided by the Buros Institute for Mental Measurements (*Mental Measurements Yearbooks* and *Tests in Print*). Both sets of publications provide comprehensive coverage of available tests. Other sources include the ETS Test Collection, *News on Tests,* test publishers' catalogs, and various professional journals and textbooks. The *Standards* helps determine what to look for in evaluating a test, the test manual provides useful information for the evaluation, and the *Yearbooks* provide critical reviews by measurement experts.

To ensure that the most appropriate tests are selected, a systematic procedure should be followed. This includes (a) defining the specific type of testing information needed, (b) appraising the role of published tests in relation to other measurement procedures and to the practical constraints of the school situation, (c) locating suitable tests through the various guides and test publishers' catalogs, (d) obtaining specimen sets of those tests that seem most appropriate, (e) reviewing the test materials in light of their intended uses, and (f) summarizing the data and making a final selection. A summary of data concerning each test under consideration is simplified if a standard evaluation form is used when compiling the information.

Administration of published tests involves careful preparation beforehand and strict adherence to the set procedures during testing. In preparing for testing, (a) order and check the materials well in advance, (b) select a suitable location for testing, (c) make provisions to prevent distractions, and (d) practice administering the test. During test administration, (a) closely follow the directions and time limits, (b) encourage the students to do their best, and (c) keep a record of any event during the testing period that might affect the test scores. Test results are more likely to be valid if questionable scores are checked by administering a second form of the test and students are given training in test-taking skills.

Published test results can serve a number of useful purposes in the school. They can aid in instructional planning, individualizing instruction, identifying the needs of exceptional children, monitoring educational progress over extended periods, reporting to parents, making educational and vocational decisions, and appraising and reporting on the effectiveness of the school program. In general, they should not be used for assigning course grades, as the sole basis for assignment to remedial programs or retention in grade, or as the sole or main basis for evaluating teaching effectiveness. Published tests are not closely enough related to the instructional objectives of particular courses, and they measure too limited a sampling of the intended learning outcomes to be useful for these purposes. Using published test results to judge a teacher's effectiveness may lead to "teaching for the test" and invalidate the test scores for other school uses.

LEARNING EXERCISES

1. List the steps you would follow in locating and selecting the most recent suitable test in one of your teaching areas.
2. What types of information would you expect to find in each of the following: (a) *Mental Measurements Yearbooks,* (b) *Tests in Print,* and (c) a test manual?
3. Why is it important to follow the directions strictly when administering a published test?
4. Describe some of the ways published tests might be used for instructional planning in one of your teaching areas.
5. Consult a test publisher's catalog and read the descriptions of one achievement test and one scholastic aptitude test. What type of information is provided?
6. Consult the latest *Mental Measurements Yearbook* and study the reviews for one achievement battery, one reading test, and one scholastic aptitude test. What strengths and weaknesses do the reviewers emphasize?
7. Consult the *Standards for Educational and Psychological Testing* and review the types of validity and reliability information that test manuals should contain. Compare a recent test manual against the *Standards* and evaluate its strengths and weaknesses.
8. Why should published achievement tests not be used as the main basis for assigning course grades, retention in grade, or determining teaching effectiveness?

REFERENCES

American Educational Research Association, American Psychological Association, & National Council on Measurement in Education. (1999). *Standards for educational and psychological testing.* Washington, DC: Author.

Sarnacki, R. E. (1979, Spring). An examination of test-wiseness in the cognitive domain. *Review of Educational Research, 49,* 252–279.

Shepard, L. A., & Smith, M. L. (Eds.). (1989). *Flunking grades: Research and policies on retention.* New York: Falmer Press.

FURTHER READING

American Educational Research Association, American Psychological Association, & National Council on Measurement in Education. (1999). *Standards for educational and psychological testing.* Washington, DC: Author.

Anastasi, A., & Urbina, S. (1997). *Psychological testing* (7th ed.). New York: Macmillan. For an orientation to psychological testing see Chapter 1, "Functions and Origins of Psychological Testing"; Chapter 2, "Nature and Use of Psychological Tests"; and Chapter 3, "Social and Ethical Considerations in Testing."

Murphy, L. L., Plake, B. S., Impara, J. C., & Spies, R. A. (Eds.). (2002). *Tests in print VI.* Lincoln, NE: Buros Institute of Mental Measurements. Includes brief descriptions of published tests, references on specific tests, and a directory of test publishers with an index to their tests. The test entries are cross-referenced to reviews in the *Mental Measurements Yearbooks.*

Plake, B. S., Impara, J. C., & Spies, R. A. (Eds.). (2003). *The fifteenth mental measurements yearbook.* Lincoln, NE: Buros Institute for Mental Measurements. Provides test descriptions, critical reviews by measurement specialists, and references.

Salvia, J., & Ysseldyke, J. (2004). *Assessment: In special and inclusive education* (9th ed.). Boston: Houghton Mifflin. For an orientation to the selection, administration, and use of tests with elementary and secondary students with special problems, the entire book should be reviewed. Written for beginners.

Thorndike, R. M. (1996). *Measurement and evaluation in psychology and education* (6th ed.). New York: Macmillan. Chapter 10, "Sources of Information about Tests," and Appendix 4, "Commercially Available Psychological and Educational Tests and Inventories," provide a discussion of sources of information about a wide range of tests and a brief description of some of the more widely used ones.

19

INTERPRETING TEST SCORES AND NORMS

T est results can be interpreted in terms of the types of tasks that can be performed (criterion reference or standards based) or the relative position held in some reference group (norm reference). Both types of interpretation are useful. The first describes what a person can do, and the second describes how the performance compares with that of others. Standardized tests traditionally emphasized norm-referenced interpretation, but many now include both types of information. Interpreting test scores with the aid of norms requires an understanding of the various methods of expressing test scores and a clear grasp of the nature of the norm group. Criterion-referenced or standards-based interpretations require analysis by content cluster or content and performance standards.

Test interpretation would be greatly simplified if we could express test scores on scales like those used in physical measurement. We know, for example, that "5 feet" means the same height whether we are talking about the height of a boy or a picket fence, that a 200-pound football player weighs exactly twice as much as a 100-pound cross-country runner, and that 8 minutes is exactly one third as long as 24 minutes, whether we are timing a standardized test or a basketball game. This ability to compare measurements from one situation to another and to speak in terms of "twice as much as" or "one third as long as" is possible because these physical measures are based on scales that have a true zero point and equal units.

The **true zero point** (i.e., the point at which there is no height at all or no weight at all) indicates precisely where measurement begins. The equal units (e.g., feet, pounds, or minutes) provide uniform meaning from one situation to another and from one part of the scale to another. Ten pounds indicates the same weight to a doctor, a grocer, a farmer, or a homemaker. The difference between 15 and 25 pounds is exactly the same as the difference between 160 and 170 pounds.

Unfortunately, the properties of physical measuring scales with which we all are so familiar are generally lacking in educational measurement. A student who receives a score of zero on a history test does not have zero knowledge of history; there are probably many simple questions that could be answered correctly but were not included in the test. A true zero point in achievement, where there is no achievement at all, cannot be clearly established. Even if it could, it would be impractical to start from that point each time we tested. What we do in actual practice is assume a certain amount of basic knowledge and measure from there. This arbitrary starting point, however, prevents us from saying that a zero score indicates no achievement at all or that a score of 100 represents twice the achievement of a score of 50. Because we are never certain how far the zero score on our test is from the true zero point (i.e., the point of no achievement at all), test scores cannot be interpreted in the same way as physical measurements. We can speak of more or less of a given characteristic but not twice as much as or half as much as.

The interpretation of test results is additionally handicapped by the inequality of our units of measurement. Sixty items correct on a simple vocabulary test does not have the same meaning as 60 items correct on a more difficult one, nor does either of the scores represent the same level of achievement as 60 items correct on a test of mathematics, science, or study skills. Test items simply do not represent equal units such as feet, pounds, and minutes.

To overcome this lack of a definite frame of reference in educational measurement, a variety of methods of expressing test scores have been devised. As we will see shortly, the methods vary considerably in the extent to which they provide satisfactory units of measurement. Much of our difficulty in the interpretation and use of test results is because we have so many different scoring systems—each with its own peculiar characteristics and limitations.

It is important that teachers understand the various types of score reports not only for their own use but also so that they can help parents understand the appropriate interpretations of the scores. As indicated in the discussion following standard 3 of the "Standards for Teacher Competence in Educational Assessment of Students," teachers "should be able to interpret commonly reported scores: [such as] percentile ranks, percentile band scores, standard scores, and grade equivalents" (see Appendix C).

METHODS OF INTERPRETING TEST SCORES

Raw Scores

If a student responds correctly to 65 items on an objective test in which each correct item counts as 1 point, the raw score will be 65. Thus, a **raw score** is simply the number of points received on a test when the test has been scored according to the directions. It does not make any difference whether each item is counted as 1 point, whether the items are weighted in some way, or whether a correction for guessing is applied; the resulting point score is still known as a raw score. We all are familiar with raw scores from our many years of taking classroom tests.

Although a raw score is a numerical summary of a student's test performance, it is not very meaningful without further information. If we are told that Michael Adams answered

35 items correctly on a mathematics test and therefore has a raw score of 35, our response is likely to be a question: "What does a 35 mean?" or "Is that a good score?" We might also have a list of more specific questions: "How many items were on the test?" "What kinds of arithmetic problems (e.g., addition of integers, multiplication of fractions, story problems) were presented?" "How difficult was the test?" "How does a score of 35 compare with the scores received by other students in Michael's class?"

Answers to these or similar questions are needed to make any raw score meaningful. We can provide meaning to a raw score by converting it into a description of the specific tasks that the student can perform (criterion-referenced interpretation) or comparison of that performance to specified performance standards (e.g., if the proficient performance standard corresponded to a raw score of 34 and the advanced performance standard corresponded to a raw score of 40, then Michael's 35 would be called proficient). Alternatively, we can provide meaning by converting a raw score into some type of derived score that indicates the student's relative position in a clearly defined reference group (norm-referenced interpretation). Questions such as the one about the specific kind of mathematics problems that are on the test are directed at a desire for criterion-referenced and standards-based interpretations, while those such as the one asking for a comparison with the performance of other students are directed at the desire for norm-referenced interpretations. Often both types of interpretation are appropriate and useful.

Criterion-Referenced and Standards-Based Interpretations

Criterion-referenced test interpretation permits us to describe an individual's test performance without referring to the performance of others. Thus, we might describe student performance in terms of the speed with which a task is performed (e.g., types 40 words per minute without error), the precision with which a task is performed (e.g., measures the length of a line within one-sixteenth of an inch), or the percentage of items correct on some clearly defined set of learning tasks (e.g., identifies the meaning of 80% of the terms used to describe fractions). Performance standards specify levels of performance that students are expected to achieve for the performance to be considered "partially proficient," "proficient," or "advanced" and thereby provide a basis for defining the level of performance that is judged to be adequate or exemplary.

The percentage-correct score is widely used in criterion-referenced test interpretation. Standards for judging whether a student has mastered each of the instructional objectives or achievement domains measured by a criterion-referenced test are frequently set in these terms. The key, however, is in providing a clear description of what a student can and cannot do rather than in the use of a percentage-correct score. Knowing, for example, that Michael Adams's raw score of 35 corresponds to a percentage-correct score of 70 because there were 50 items on the mathematics test provides little help in understanding the meaning of the score. We still need to have a clear description of the domain of mathematics items that the test represents in order to make a criterion-referenced interpretation of his score. We may also want to have prespecified performance standards in determining the adequacy of Michael's score.

Criterion-referenced and standards-based interpretations of test results are most meaningful when the test has been specifically designed for this purpose (see Chapter 16).

This typically involves designing a test that measures a set of clearly stated learning tasks. Enough items are used for each interpretation to make it possible to describe test performance in terms of a student's mastery or nonmastery of the tasks. The value of these descriptions of test performance is enhanced by the fact that the domain of measured achievement is delimited and clearly specified, the test items are selected on the basis of their relevance to the domain being measured, and there are enough test items to make dependable judgments concerning the types of tasks a student can and cannot perform.

Criterion-Referenced Interpretation of Standardized Tests.   Although standardized tests are frequently designed for norm-referenced interpretations, it is possible to attach criterion-referenced meaning to the test results. This simply involves analyzing each student's test responses by item content and summarizing the results with descriptive statements (e.g., Michael solved all the addition problems involving no carrying but solved only two of the five problems requiring carrying). Some test publishers aid this type of interpretation by (a) providing the list of objectives measured by the test, with each item keyed to the appropriate objective, and (b) arranging the items into larger homogeneous content clusters for easy analysis.

Later in this chapter, we describe and illustrate how criterion-referenced interpretations have been added to the norm-referenced interpretations of standardized tests. Because these tests are usually designed for norm-referenced testing, however, the criterion-referenced interpretations must be made with considerable caution (see the "Guidelines" box).

GUIDELINES

Making Criterion-Referenced Interpretations of Standardized Tests

1. Are the achievement domains (objectives or content clusters) homogeneous, delimited, and clearly specified? If not, avoid specific descriptive statements.

2. Are there enough items (say 10) for each type of interpretation? If not, make tentative judgments and/or combine items into larger content clusters for interpretation.

3. In constructing the test, were the easy items omitted to increase discrimination among individuals? If so, remember that the descriptions of what low achievers can do will be severely limited.

4. Does the test use selection-type items only? If so, keep in mind that a proportion of correct answers may be based on guessing (this is especially crucial when only a few items are used to measure a specific content domain).

5. Do the test items provide a directly relevant measure of the objectives? If not, base interpretation on what the items actually measured (e.g., "ability to identify misspelled words" rather than "ability to spell"—they are related but are not the same process).

Grouping items in standardized tests by objective and by larger content clusters enhances the instructional use of the results, but criterion-referenced interpretations must be made cautiously.

Expectancy Tables.   The use of expectancy tables, as discussed in Chapters 4, also falls within the province of criterion-referenced interpretation. The expectancy table makes it possible to interpret raw scores in terms of expected performance on some measure other than the test itself. As illustrated in Chapters 4, the scores on an aptitude test can be used to predict the probability of earning a particular letter grade (A, B, C, D, F) in a course. Similarly, expectancy tables can be used to predict the probability of success in a training program, on a job, or in any other situation of interest. The use of an expectancy table makes it possible to interpret a raw score simply and directly without the aid of test norms.

Norm-Referenced Interpretation

Norm-referenced test interpretation tells us how an individual compares with other persons who have taken the same test. The simplest type of comparison, one that is used in classroom testing, is to rank the scores from highest to lowest and to note where an individual's score falls. Noting whether a particular score is third from the top, about average, or one of the lowest scores in class provides a meaningful report to teacher and student alike. If a student's test score is third from the top in a classroom group of 30 students, then it is a high score, whether it represents 90% of the items correct or 60% correct. The fact that a test is relatively easy or difficult for the students does not alter our interpretation of test scores in terms of relative performance. All that is required is a sufficient spread of test scores to provide a reliable ranking.

Derived Scores.   Although the simple ranking of raw scores may be useful for reporting the results of a classroom test, it is of limited value beyond the immediate situation because the meaning of a given rank depends on the composition of the group and on the number of group members. To obtain a more general framework for norm-referenced interpretation, raw scores are converted into some type of derived score. A derived score is a numerical report of test performance on a score scale that has well-defined characteristics and yields normative meaning. The most common types of derived scores are grade equivalents, percentile ranks, and standard scores. Grade-equivalent scores, which are sometimes described as an example of a developmental score scale, report test performance in terms of the grade group in which an individual's raw score is just average. Percentile ranks and standard scores indicate the individual's relative standing within some particular group (see Table 19.1). Converting raw scores to derived scores is simple with standardized tests. Frequently, the test publisher performs the conversions before reporting the scores. If not, however, all we need to do is consult the table of norms in the test manual and select the derived score that corresponds to the individual's raw score. Some derived scores are so easily computed that we can also develop local norms if desired.

There are, as we will see, a variety of ways of expressing standard scores (e.g., T-scores, normal-curve equivalent scores, and standard age scores), but they are based on a common logic. They differ only in terms of the numerical values used and whether they are based on a normal distribution. There are also a number of approaches other than grade equivalents (e.g., age equivalents or publisher-specific extended score scales) to the definition of a developmental score scale. However, grade equivalents are by far the most common for educational achievement tests.

Table 19.1
Most common types of test norms

Type of Test Norm	Name of Derived Score	Meaning in Terms of Test Performance
Grade norms	Grade equivalents	Grade group in which student's raw score is average
Percentile norms	Percentile ranks (or percentile scores)	Percentage of students in the reference group who fall below student's raw score
Standard score norms	Standard scores	Distance of student's raw score above or below the mean of the reference group in terms of standard deviation units

Norms.   Tables of norms in test manuals merely present scores earned by students in clearly defined reference groups. The raw scores and derived scores are presented in parallel columns so that the conversion to derived scores can be easily made. These scores do not represent especially good or desirable performance but, rather, normal or typical performance. They were established at the time the test was standardized by administering the test to representative groups of students for whom the test was constructed. Thus, they indicate the typical performance of students in these standardization groups and nothing more. They should not be viewed as standards or goals to be achieved by other students.

Test norms enable us to answer questions such as the following:

1. How does a student's test performance compare with that of other students?
2. How does a student's performance on one test (or subtest) compare with performance on another test (or subtest)?
3. How does a student's performance on one form of a test compare with performance on another form of the test administered at an earlier date?

These comparisons of test scores make it possible to predict a student's probable success in various areas, to diagnose strengths and weaknesses, to measure educational growth, and to use the test results for other instructional and guidance purposes. Such functions of test scores would be severely curtailed without the use of the derived scores provided by test norms.

A summary of the most common types of test norms is presented in Table 19.1. To interpret and use test results effectively, we need a good grasp of the characteristics, advantages, and limitations of each of these types of norms.

GRADE NORMS

Grade norms have been widely used with standardized achievement tests, especially at the elementary school level. The grade equivalent that corresponds to a particular raw score identifies the grade level at which the typical student obtains that raw score. Grade equivalents are based on the performance of students in the norm group in each of two or more grades. For example, suppose the mathematics test that Michael Adams took had been administered to fourth- and fifth-grade students in the norm group in October and in May. We would expect that the group who took the test in May of the fifth grade would generally get higher scores than the group who took the test in October of the fourth grade.

As we see in Table 19.2, this expected pattern is obtained. In October of grade 4, 50% of the students have raw scores below the median score of 28, but this value goes up to 35 in May of grade 4, to 37 in October of grade 5, and to 41 in May of grade 5. Thus, Michael would need to have a higher raw score (41) to obtain a grade equivalent of 5.8 (which corresponds to the typical performance of the grade 5 student in May) than he would to obtain a grade equivalent of 4.1 (the typical performance of the grade 4 student in October). Because Michael's raw score was actually 35, he would receive a grade-equivalent score of 4.8: the grade at which the typical student receives a raw score of 35. As is suggested by this example, grade equivalents are expressed by two numbers: The first indicates the year and the second the month. Grade equivalents for the fifth grade, for example, range from 5.0 to 5.9, or, if the decimal point is omitted, as is the practice for some tests, from 50 to 59. This division of the calendar year into tenths, starting with September = .0 and ending with June = .9, is based on the traditional school year and assumes little or no growth in achievement test performance during the summer vacation months.

Table 19.2 provides all that is needed to convert Michael's raw score to a grade equivalent because he happened to get a raw score equal to the median of one of the grade norm groups. To obtain grade equivalents for Bob Brown, who got a raw score of 31, and Teresa Chavez, who got a raw score of 45, however, we would need some more information. We could see that Bob should have a grade equivalent somewhere between 4.1 and 4.8, but to determine a specific score we would need to interpolate (i.e., decide how far to go above 4.1 toward 4.8) to account for the fact that Bob did better than the typical fourth-grade student did in October but not as well as the typical fourth-grade student in May. Similarly, we could see that Teresa's raw score of 45 should be converted to a grade-equivalent score above 5.8 but would have to extrapolate (i.e., project the rate of increase with grade level beyond the point where data were collected) to give Teresa a specific grade equivalent.

Fortunately, we do not need to know the details of interpolation and extrapolation to convert Bob's and Teresa's raw scores to grade equivalents. Test publishers perform those

Table 19.2
Illustration of the construction of grade-equivalent scores

Grade	Time of Administration (Month)	Median* Raw Score	Grade Equivalent
4	October (.1)	28	4.1
4	May (.8)	35	4.8
5	October (.1)	37	5.1
5	May (.8)	41	5.8

*50% of the students in the norm group score below, and 50% score above the median raw score (see Appendix A).

operations and produce tables showing the grade equivalent corresponding to each possible raw score. To convert to grade equivalents with a table of grade norms, all one needs to do is find the students' raw scores in the table and read off the corresponding grade equivalents. Using this procedure, for example, we might find that Bob's grade equivalent is 4.4 and that Teresa's grade equivalent is 6.5. Grade norms are popular largely because test performance is expressed in units that are easy to understand and interpret. To illustrate, assume that we obtained the following grade equivalents for Jennifer, who is in the middle of the fifth grade.

Mathematics   5.5
Language   6.5
Reading   9.0

In examining these scores, teachers, parents, and students alike would recognize that Jennifer is exactly average in mathematics, 1 year advanced in language, and 3½ years advanced in reading. Grade equivalents provide a common unit with which we all are familiar. The only difficulty is that this familiarity leads those who are unaware of the numerous limitations of grade norms to misleading or inaccurate interpretations. Concern about misinterpretations of grade equivalents has led to sharp criticisms of the scores. Indeed, an earlier version of the *Standards* (American Psychological Association, 1974) suggested that the use of grade-equivalent scores should be discouraged. On the other hand, some measurement experts (Hoover, 1984) have argued that grade equivalents are useful and no more subject to misinterpretation than other types of scores. In any event, nothing indicates their popularity is declining. It is important to understand their limitations so that misinterpretations can be avoided.

Six possible misinterpretations of grade equivalents are worthy of consideration. Each of these misinterpretations is based on an unjustified assumption about the meaning of the scores. These inappropriate assumptions are (1) assuming that norms are standards of what should be, (2) assuming that grade equivalents indicate the appropriate grade placement for a student, (3) assuming that all students should be expected to grow one grade-equivalent unit per year, (4) assuming that the units are equal throughout the score range, (5) assuming that grade equivalents for different tests are comparable, and (6) assuming that the scores that are based on extrapolations to grades well above or below the test level are meaningful. Let's briefly consider each of these faulty assumptions and the resulting misinterpretation of grade equivalents.

1. Don't confuse norms with standards of what should be. For any particular grade equivalent, 50% of the students in the standardization group are above this norm, and 50% are below. Consequently, we should not interpret a particular grade norm as something all our students should attain. If half our students are above norm and half are below, we may conclude that our students compare favorably with the students in the norm group. Whether this is good or bad depends on a number of factors, such as our students' ability, the extent to which the learning outcomes measured by the test reflect our curriculum emphasis, and the quality of the educational facilities at our disposal. If we are teaching students with above-average ability under conditions comparable to those of schools in the norm group, merely matching the norm would be cause for concern. On the other hand, if our students have a history of low achievement in previous grades, reaching the norm might call for considerable pride. In any case, it is well to remember that the norm is merely an average score made by the students in the standardization group. As such, it represents the typical performance of average students in average schools and should not be considered a standard of excellence to be achieved by others.

2. Don't interpret a grade equivalent as an estimate of the grade where a student should be placed. One potential misinterpretation of grade norms, although not because of weaknesses in the scoring system itself, is to assume that students who earn certain grade-equivalent scores are ready to do work at that level. For example, we might conclude that a fourth-grade student should be doing sixth-grade work in language skills if she earns a grade equivalent of 6.0 on a language skills test. This assumption overlooks the fact that she can obtain a grade-equivalent score well above her grade level by doing the less difficult test items more rapidly and accurately than the average fourth-grade student. The grade-equivalent score of 6.0 may represent nothing more than a thorough mastery of language skills taught in the first four grades. Thus, grade equivalents should never be interpreted literally; at best, they are only rough guides to the level of test performance. Students at different grade levels who earn the same grade-equivalent score are apt to be ready for quite different types of instruction.

3. Don't expect that all students should gain 1.0 grade equivalent each year. It seems natural to think that if Jane and Sara had grade equivalents of 4.7 and 2.5, respectively, at the end of grade 3, they should be expected to each gain 1.0 and have scores of 5.7 and 3.5 at the end of grade 4. This expectation is inappropriate not only because norms should not be confused with standards but also because a gain of 1.0 per year is typical only of students scoring close to the average for their grade. On average, students who score well above their grade placement gain more than 1.0 grade equivalent per year, whereas students who score well below the norm gain less than 1.0 per year. Thus, if students in a remedial reading program show an average gain of 1.0 in a year's time, that actually would be better than is typical of students with low initial scores.

4. Don't assume that the units are equal at different parts of the scale. A year of growth in mathematics achievement from grade 2.0 to 3.0, for example, might represent a much greater improvement than an increase from grade 4.0 to 5.0 or grade 8.0 to 9.0. Thus, being advanced or behind in terms of grade units has a different meaning on different parts of the grade scale. Students who earn grade equivalents several grades above their grade placement might be demonstrating either vastly superior achievement or performance just slightly above average.

5. Don't assume that scores on different tests are comparable. A grade-equivalent score of 8.0 on one test publisher's fifth-grade reading comprehension test may not represent the same degree of superior performance as an 8.0 on another publisher's fifth-grade reading comprehension test. We know that in both cases an 8.0 is well above the average for a fifth grader. However, an 8.0 might be one of the highest possible scores for one publisher's test, whereas the scores provided by the other publisher might go considerably higher.

The lack of comparability also applies to a single publisher's tests in different subjects. Patterns of growth vary from subject to subject, and so our grade-equivalent units stretch and contract at different points on the scale for different subjects. Although it would be tempting to conclude that a fourth grader who received a grade equivalent of 7.2 in reading and a grade equivalent of 6.3 in mathematics was better at reading than mathematics, such a conclusion is likely to be inappropriate. In comparison with other fourth-grade students, the two scores may actually represent equally superior performance because the range of grade-equivalent scores for fourth-grade students is generally greater in reading than in mathematics.

   6. Don't interpret extreme scores as dependable estimates of students' performance level. Grade-equivalent scores that are several years above or below the student's actual grade placement and the grade levels where the test is normally used are based on extrapolation. This results in artificial units that do not correspond to the achievement of students in any particular group. Estimating these grade equivalents is frequently necessary because the younger students do not have the needed skills to take the test and because growth in the basic skills tends to level off in the eighth and ninth grades. In interpreting grade equivalents at the extremes, therefore, it is well to keep in mind that they do not represent the actual performance of students at these levels.

   In summary, grade norms are based on the average performance of students at various grade levels. They are widely used at the elementary school level largely because of the ease with which they can be interpreted. As we have seen, however, grade equivalents have a number of limitations that can lead to misinterpretations. In general, grade norms are most useful for reporting growth in the basic skills during the elementary school period. They are least useful for comparing a student's performances on different tests. For whatever purpose grade norms are used, however, the inequality of grade units must be considered during interpretation of the results.

PERCENTILE RANK

   One of the most widely used and easily understood methods of describing test performance is percentile rank. A percentile rank (or percentile score) indicates a student's relative position in a group in terms of the percentage of students scoring lower. Thus, if we consult a table of norms and find that a student's raw score of 29 equals a percentile rank of 70, we know that 70% of the students in the reference group obtained a raw score lower than 29. Stating it another way, this student's performance surpasses that of 70% of the group. Percentile rank is sometimes interpreted as the percentage of individuals receiving scores equal or lower than a given score. The specific interpretation depends on the methods of computation used, but for all practical purposes, the meaning is the same.

   One method of presenting percentile norms is shown in Table 19.3. These norms are for the three mathematics subtests of the *Stanford Achievement Test, Eighth Edition.* Percentile norms for other subtests and for the Mathematics Total score are presented in similar tables. The raw scores for each subtest are listed in the first column, and the corresponding percentile rank is listed in the second column under the subtest heading. Corresponding stanine scores, grade-equivalent scores, and scaled scores are also listed in

Table 19.3
Partial norms for the *Stanford Achievement Tests*, Advanced Level 1, Form J, for students tested in the spring of grade 7

Concepts of Number					Mathematics Computation					Mathematics Applications					Mathematics Applications*				
Raw Score	%-ile Rank	Sta-nine	Grade Equiv.	Scaled Score	Raw Score	%-ile Rank	Sta-nine	Grade Equiv.	Scaled Score	Raw Score	%-ile Rank	Sta-nine	Grade Equiv.	Scaled Score	Raw Score	%-ile Rank	Sta-nine	Grade Equiv.	Scaled Score
34	99	9	PHS	818	44	99	9	PHS	818	40	99	9	PHS	814	40	99	9	PHS	808
33	99	9	PHS	794	43	99	9	PHS	795	39	99	9	PHS	791	39	99	9	PHS	785
·	·	·	·	·	·	·	·	·	·	·	·	·	·	·	·	·	·	·	·
20	53	5	8.1	676	30	62	6	8.7	687	26	55	5	8.3	679	26	48	5	7.7	671
19	50	5	7.8	672	29	59	5	8.5	683	25	52	5	8.0	675	25	44	5	7.4	667
18	45	5	7.5	667	28	56	5	8.3	679	24	48	5	7.7	671	24	41	5	7.1	663
17	41	5	7.2	663	27	53	5	8.1	675	23	44	5	7.4	667	23	37	4	6.7	659
16	36	4	6.8	658	26	50	5	7.9	672	22	41	5	7.1	663	22	34	4	6.5	655
15	31	4	6.5	653	25	47	5	7.6	668	21	37	4	6.7	659	21	30	4	6.2	651
·	·	·	·	·	·	·	·	·	·	·	·	·	·	·	·	·	·	·	·
					5	1	1	3.5	579										
					4	1	1	3.2	570	4	1	1	3.1	572	4	1	1	2.8	563
					3	1	1	2.8	559	3	1	1	2.7	561	3	1	1	2.6	552
2	1	1	2.7	558	2	1	1	2.5	543	2	1	1	2.4	545	2	1	1	2.3	536
1	1	1	2.2	532	1	1	1	2.0	518	1	1	1	1.9	520	1	1	1	1.7	511

*For students tested using calculators.

the third, fourth, and fifth columns under each subtest. Grade-equivalent scores have already been discussed, and stanine and scaled scores are described later.

A student with raw scores of 20 on the Concepts of Number subtest and 25 on the Mathematics Computation subtest would have percentile ranks of 53 and 47, respectively, on those two subtests. It is not surprising that the higher raw score converts to a lower percentile rank in this example because there are fewer items on the Concepts of Number subtest than on the Mathematics Computation subtest. Note that these two percentile ranks of 53 and 47 for a test administered in the spring of grade 7 convert to grade-equivalent scores slightly above (8.1) and slightly below (7.6) grade level.

Several points are worth noting about the example in Table 19.3. (a) The conversion of raw scores to percentile scores is specific to each subtest (a raw score of 20 corresponds to a percentile rank of 53 on Concepts of Number but only 33 on Mathematics Computation). (b) The conversion is specific to the particular level and form of the test (see table title, Advanced Level 1, Form J). (c) The conversion is specific to a particular grade and time of year (spring of grade 7). Different tables would be needed if another form of the test had been administered or if the test had been administered at another time of year or grade. (d) The percentile ranks are for a particular norm group. In this case, these are the national norms for students tested in the spring of 1988. Different percentile ranks would be obtained for specialized norms (large-city norms or private schools) or for different norming years. (e) As can be seen in Table 19.3, conversions on the Mathematics Applications subtest depend on whether the students used a calculator when taking this section of the test. A Mathematics Applications raw score of 25, for example, yields a percentile rank of 52 for a student who took the test without a calculator but a percentile rank of only 44 for a student who was tested using a calculator.

A desirable feature of percentile norms is that we can interpret a student's performance in terms of various groups. Most commonly, performance is reported in terms of relative standing in the student's own grade or age group. In some instances, however, we are more interested in how a student compares with those who have completed second-year French, are majoring in home economics, or are enrolled in the college preparatory program. Such comparisons are possible with percentile norms. The interpretations of a particular score are limited only to the types of decisions we want to make and the availability of the appropriate sets of norms.

The wide applicability of percentile norms is not without its drawbacks. When interpreting a percentile rank, we must always refer to the norm group on which it is based. A student does not have a percentile rank of 80, but a percentile rank of 80 *in some particular group*. A raw score on a scholastic aptitude test, for example, may be equivalent to a percentile rank of 80 in a general group of high school seniors, 63 in a group of college-bound seniors, and 25 in a group of college freshmen in a highly selective college. Relative standing varies with the ability of the reference group used for comparison.

A related inconvenience with percentile norms is that numerous sets of norms are usually required. We need a set of norms for each group with which we wish to compare a student. This is not especially troublesome at the elementary school level, where a student's own grade and age mates provide a suitable basis for comparison. At the high school level, however, where the curriculum becomes diversified and students pursue different courses, it becomes rather difficult. Here we need sets of norms for students who have completed varying numbers of courses in each subject area.

The main limitation of percentile norms is that percentile units are not equal on all parts of the scale. A percentile difference of 10 near the middle of the scale (e.g., 45–55) represents a much smaller difference in test performance than the same percentile difference at the ends (e.g., 85–95) because a large number of students receive scores near the middle, whereas relatively few students have extremely high or low scores. Thus, a student whose raw score is near average can surpass another 10% of the group by increasing the raw score just a few points. But a student with a relatively high score will need to increase the raw score by a great many points in order to surpass another 10% simply because there are so few students at that level.

The inequality of units requires special caution when using percentile ranks. First, a difference of several percentile points should be given greater weight at the extremes of the distribution than near the middle. In fact, small differences near the middle of the distribution generally can be disregarded. Second, percentile ranks should not be averaged arithmetically. The appropriate average when using percentile norms is the 50th percentile. This is the midpoint of the distribution and is called the median, or counting average.

In summary, percentile norms are widely applicable, easily determined, and readily understood. A percentile rank describes a student's performance in terms of the percentage of students in some clearly defined group that earn a lower score. This might be a grade or age group or any other group that provides a meaningful comparison (e.g., college freshmen). More than one set of norms is usually required, and percentile ranks must be interpreted in terms of the norm group on which they are based. The most severe limitation of percentile ranks is that the units are unequal. This can be offset somewhat by careful interpretation, however, because the inequality of units follows a predictable pattern.

STANDARD SCORES

Another method of indicating a student's relative position in a group is by showing how far the raw score is above or below average. This is the approach used with standard scores. Basically, standard scores express test performance in terms of standard deviation units from the mean. The mean (M) is the arithmetical average, which is determined by adding all the scores and dividing by the number of scores. The standard deviation (SD) is a measure of the spread of scores in a group. Because the method of computing the standard deviation is not especially helpful in understanding it, the procedure is not presented here (see Appendix A for computation). The meaning of standard deviation and the standard scores based on it can best be explained in terms of the normal probability curve (also called the normal distribution curve or simply the normal curve).

The Normal Curve and the Standard Deviation Unit

The normal curve is a symmetrical bell-shaped curve that has many useful mathematical properties. One of the most useful from the viewpoint of test interpretation is that when it is divided into standard deviation units, each portion under the curve contains a fixed percentage of cases. This is shown in the idealized normal curve presented in Figure 19.1.

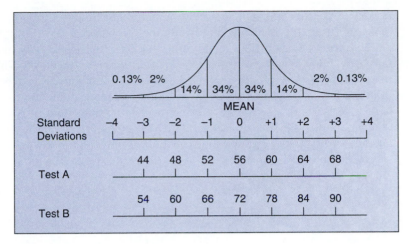

Figure 19.1

Normal curve, indicating the approximate percentage of cases falling within each standard deviation interval

(For the moment, disregard the raw scores beneath the figure.) Note that 34% of the cases fall between the mean and +1 SD, 14% between +1 SD and +2 SD, and 2% between +2 SD and +3 SD. (All percentages have been rounded.) The same proportions, of course, apply to the standard deviation intervals below the mean. Only 0.13% of the cases fall below −3 SD or above +3 SD. Thus, for all practical purposes, a normal distribution of scores falls between −3 and +3 standard deviations from the mean.

To demonstrate the value of standard deviation units for expressing relative position in a group, raw scores from two different tests have been placed beneath the row of deviations along the baseline of the curve in Figure 19.1. The tests have the following means and standard deviations:

	Test A	Test B
M	56	72
SD	4	6

In Figure 19.1, the mean raw scores of both tests have been placed at the zero point on the baseline of the curve. Thus, they have been arbitrarily equated to zero. Notice that +1 SD is equivalent to 60 (56 + 4) on Test A and 78 (72 + 6) on Test B and that −1 SD is equivalent to 52 (56 − 4) on Test A and 66 (72 − 6) on Test B. If we convert all the raw scores on the two tests to the standard deviation units in this manner, we can directly compare performance on the tests. For example, raw scores of 62 on Test A and 81 on Test B are equal because both are 1.5 standard deviation units above the mean. When converted to standard deviation units, the raw scores are, of course, no longer needed. A +2.5 SD on Test A is superior to a +2.0 SD on Test B regardless of the size of the raw scores from which they were derived. The only restriction for such comparisons is that the conversion to standard deviation units be based on a common group.

The utility of the standard deviation is that it permits us to convert raw scores to a common scale that has equal units and that can be readily interpreted in terms of the normal curve. At this point, it should be helpful to review a few of the characteristics that make the normal curve so useful in test interpretation.

Referring to Figure 19.1 again, note that 68% (approximately two thirds) of the cases fall between −1 and +1 standard deviations from the mean. This provides a handy benchmark for interpreting standard scores and the standard error of measurement, as both are based on standard deviation units. The fixed percentages in each interval make it possible to convert standard deviation units to percentile ranks. For example, −2 SD equals a percentile rank of 2 because 2% of the cases fall below that point. Starting from the left of the figure, each point on the baseline of the curve can be equated to the following percentile ranks.

$$-2 \text{ SD} = 2\%$$
$$-1 \text{ SD} = 16\% \ (2 + 14)$$
$$0 \text{ SD} = \text{Mean} = 50\% \ (16 + 34)$$
$$+1 \text{ SD} = 84\% \ (50 + 34)$$
$$+2 \text{ SD} = 98\% \ (84 + 14)$$

This relationship between standard deviation units and percentile ranks enables us to interpret standard scores in simple and familiar terms. When used for this purpose, we must, of course, be able to assume a normal distribution. This is not a serious restriction in using standard score norms, however, because the distribution of scores on which they are based usually closely approximates the normal curve. In many instances, the standard scores are normalized; that is, the distribution of scores is made normal by the process of computing percentiles and converting directly to their standard score equivalents. Although it is generally safe to assume a normal distribution when using standard scores from tables of norms in test manuals, it is usually unwise to make such an assumption for standard scores computed directly from a relatively small number of cases, such as a classroom group.

Types of Standard Scores

There are numerous types of standard scores used in testing. Because they all are based on the same principle and are interpreted in somewhat the same manner, only the most common types are discussed here.

Z-Score.   The simplest of the standard scores, and the one on which others are based, is the z-score. This score expresses test performance simply and directly as the number of standard deviation units a raw score is above or below the mean. The formula for computing a z-score is

$$\text{z-score} = \frac{X - M}{SD}$$

where

$X =$ any raw score

$M =$ arithmetic mean of raw scores

$SD =$ standard deviation of raw scores

You can quickly become familiar with this formula by applying it to various raw scores in Test A or Test B of Figure 19.1 and then visually checking your answer along the baseline of the curve. For example, z-scores for the raw scores of 58 and 50 on Test A (M = 56, SD = 4) would be computed as follows:

$$z = \frac{58 - 56}{4} = .5 \text{ and } z = \frac{50 - 56}{4} = -1.5$$

A z-score is always negative when the raw score is smaller than the mean. Forgetting the negative sign can cause serious errors in test interpretation. For this reason, z-scores are seldom used directly in test norms but are usually transformed into a standard score system that uses only positive numbers.

T-Score.   The term **T-score** was originally given to a type of normalized score based on a group of unselected 12-year-old children. However, it has come to refer to any set of normally distributed standard scores that has a mean of 50 and a standard deviation of 10. T-scores (linear conversion) can be obtained by multiplying the z-score by 10 and adding the product to 50. Thus,

$$T\text{-score} = 50 + 10 \text{ (z)}$$

This formula will provide T-scores only when the original distribution of raw scores is normal, because with this type of conversion, the distribution of standard scores retains the same shape as the original raw score distribution. Some people call any set of scores derived from this formula T-scores; others call them linear T-scores or z-scores to distinguish them from normalized T-scores. Applying this formula to the two z-scores computed earlier (z = .5, z = −1.5), we would obtain the following results:

$$T = 50 + 10 \text{ (.5)} = 55 \text{ and } T = 50 + 10 \text{ (−1.5)} = 35$$

One reason that T-scores are preferred to z-scores for reporting test results is that only positive integers are produced. It seems preferable, for example, to report a person's test performance as a T-score of 33 than to report the same performance as a z-score of −1.7. The two scores are equivalent, however. Because T-scores always have a mean of 50 and a standard deviation of 10, any T-score is directly interpretable. A T-score of 55, for example, always indicates one half a standard deviation above the mean and so on. Once the concept of T-scores is grasped, interpretation is relatively simple.

Normalized Standard Scores.   Normalized T-scores are calculated by (a) converting the distribution of raw scores into percentile ranks, (b) looking up the z-score each percentile rank would have in a normal distribution and assigning these z-scores to the corresponding raw scores, and (c) converting the z-scores to T-scores, using the formula presented earlier. The procedure of going from raw score to percentile to the corresponding z-score in a normal distribution is called an **area conversion** and yields normalized z-scores, which are then transformed directly into normalized T-scores. This results in a normally distributed set of standard scores regardless of the shape of the original distribution of raw scores. Normalizing is used by test publishers to remove minor irregularities in the raw score distributions.

Many other normalized standard scores are computed in the same way that normalized T-scores are determined, but different values are used for the mean and standard deviation. For example, standard scores with a mean of 100 and a standard deviation of 15 are used with some aptitude tests. Consequently, on these tests a score of 115 means one standard deviation above the mean, the same as a T-score of 60. Standard scores can be assigned any arbitrarily selected mean and standard deviation, and the interpretation will be the same because the basic frame of reference is the standard deviation unit.

Stanines.   Stanines (pronounced *stay-nines*) are a simple type of normalized standard score that illustrates the process of normalization. Stanines are single-digit scores ranging from 1 to 9. This system of scores is so named because the distribution of raw scores is divided into nine parts (standard nines). Stanine 5 is precisely in the center of the distribution and includes all cases within one-fourth of a standard deviation on either side of the mean Table 19.4). In a normal distribution, percentile ranks of 40 and 60 correspond to one-fourth of a standard deviation below and above the mean. Any score with a percentile rank of at least 40 but less than 60 is converted to a stanine score of 5. Thus, raw scores corresponding to percentile ranks between 40 and 59 all convert to stanine scores of 5. The remaining stanines are evenly distributed above and below stanine 5. Each stanine, with the exception of stanines 1 and 9, which cover the tails of the distribution, includes a band of raw scores the width of one half of a standard deviation unit. Thus, for all practical purposes, stanines present test norms on a 9-point scale of equal units. These standard scores have a mean of 5 and a standard deviation of 2. The conversion from percentile ranks to stanines is straightforward for a normal distribution (see Figure 19.2).

The following points summarize the major strengths of stanine scores.

1. The stanine system uses a 9-point scale, in which 9 is high, 1 is low, and 5 is average. Thus, the system is easily explained to students and parents, and they can readily visualize where test performance (e.g., 7) falls on a scale of 1 to 9.

Table 19.4

Normal curve, indicating the approximate percentage of cases falling within each standard deviation interval (correspondence of percentile ranks and stanine scores in a normal distribution)

Range of Percentile Ranks	Stanine
96 or higher	9
89–95	8
77–88	7
60–76	6
40–59	5
23–39	4
11–22	3
4–10	2
Below 4	1

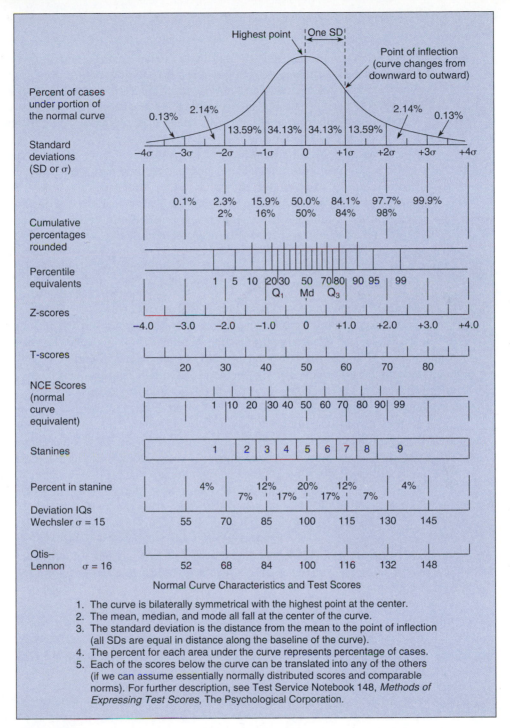

Figure 19.2

Corresponding standard scores and percentiles in a normal distribution. (Test Service Notebook No. 148, September 1980, of The Psychological Corporation. Reproduced by permission.)

2. Stanines are normalized standard scores that make it possible to compare a student's performance on different tests (if based on a common group). Typically, a difference of two stanines represents a significant difference in performance between tests (assuming test reliability is satisfactory). Thus, a student with a stanine of 7 in arithmetic and 5 in spelling is probably demonstrating superior performance in mathematics.

3. The stanine system makes it easy to combine diverse types of data (e.g., test scores, ratings, and ranked data) because stanines are computed like percentile ranks but are expressed in standard score form. Thus, the conversion to stanines is simple, and the standard score feature makes it possible to add stanine scores from various measures to obtain a composite score. A simple summing of stanines will give equal weight to each measure in the composite.

4. Because the stanine system uses a single-digit score, it is easily recorded and takes up less space than other scores. (It was originally developed to fit into a single column on an IBM card.)

The main limitation of stanine scores is that growth cannot be shown from one year to the next. If a student's progress matches that of the norm group, then the same position in the group will be retained and the same stanine will be assigned. Percentile ranks and other standard scores used to indicate relative position in a particular group share this shortcoming. To determine growth, we need to examine the increase in the raw scores or in developmental scale scores (e.g., grade equivalents).

Stanines are sometimes criticized on the grounds that they are rather crude units because they divide a distribution of scores into only nine parts. On the plus side, however, these crude units prevent the overinterpretation of test scores. Although greater refinement might be desirable for some special purposes (e.g., identifying gifted students), stanines provide satisfactory discrimination for most educational purposes. With a more refined scoring system, there is always the danger that minor, chance differences in scores will be interpreted as significant differences.

Normal-Curve Equivalent.   The normal-curve equivalent (NCE) is another normalized standard score that was introduced in order to avoid some of the pitfalls of grade-equivalent scores. Because school districts need NCE scores to fulfill the requirements of some federally supported compensatory education programs, publishers of the major standardized achievement tests have added this score to their list of score reporting options.

Like T-scores, NCE scores have a mean of 50; however, the standard deviation of NCE scores is 21.06 rather than the 10. This seemingly strange choice for a standard deviation was selected so that NCE scores would range from 1 to 99. As can be seen from the following list of NCE scores and their corresponding percentile ranks in Table 19.5, NCE scores of 1, 50, and 99 are equivalent to percentile ranks of the same numerical values. At other points on the scale, however, NCE scores have different numerical values than the corresponding percentile ranks. Compared to percentile ranks, they are more spread out at the extremes (e.g., an NCE difference of 90 to 99 corresponds to a percentile rank difference of only 97 to 99) and less spread out near the middle (e.g., an NCE difference of 50 to 75 corresponds to a percentile rank difference of 50 to 88).

Standard Age Scores. Another widely used standard score for ability tests is the standard age score (SAS). Here the mean is set at 100 and the standard deviation at 16. Thus, a student with an SAS of 84 has scored one standard deviation below the mean (T-score = 40), and a student with an SAS of 116 has scored one standard deviation above the mean (T-score = 60). Scores on ability tests could just as easily be expressed as T-scores or NCEs. However, in the past these tests reported scores as deviation IQ scores with a mean of 100 and a standard deviation of 16 (15 on some tests). The SAS (or similar scales, such as the Cognitive Skills Quotient or School Ability Index) has replaced deviation IQ scores in an attempt to avoid some of the misinterpretations associated with the terms *intelligence* and *IQ*.

Comparison of Score Systems

The equivalence of scores in various standard score systems and their relation to percentiles and the normal curve are presented in Figure 19.2. This figure illustrates the interrelated nature of the various scales for reporting relative position in a normally distributed group. A raw score one standard deviation below the mean, for example, can be expressed as a z-score of −1.0, a percentile rank of 16, a T-score of 40, an NCE score of 29, a deviation IQ of 85, an SAS of 84, or a stanine of 3. Thus, the various scoring systems are merely different ways of saying the same thing, and we can easily convert from one scale to another if we assume a normal distribution and comparable norm groups.

The relationships among the scoring systems shown in Figure 19.2 are especially helpful in understanding a particular standard score scale. Until we fully understand T-scores, for example, it is helpful to convert them, mentally, into percentile ranks. A T-score of 60 becomes meaningful when we note that it is equivalent to a percentile rank of 84. This conversion to percentile ranks, which are more easily understood, is also useful for interpreting standard scores to parents and students.

In summary, standard scores indicate a student's relative position in a group in terms of standard deviation units above or below the mean. In a normal distribution, the various standard score scales and the percentile scale are interrelated, making it possible to convert from one to another. Standard scores have the special advantage of providing

Table 19.5
Correspondence between percentile ranks and normal-curve equivalents

NCE Score	Corresponding Percentile Rank	Percentile Rank	Corresponding NCE Score
99	99	99	99
90	97	90	77
75	88	75	64
50	50	50	50
25	12	25	36
10	3	10	23
1	1	1	1

roughly equal units. Thus, unlike percentiles, 10 standard score points represent approximately the same difference in test performance anywhere along the scale. In addition, standard scores can be averaged mathematically. One drawback of standard scores is that they are not readily understood by students and parents. A more serious limitation is that interpretation is difficult unless the scores are normally distributed. This is not a problem in using standard score norms, however, because norm tables are generally based on normalized standard scores.

One of the best ways to become familiar with the various scoring systems and the relationships among them is to review the corresponding scores below a selected point in Figure 19.2.

PROFILES

One advantage of converting raw scores to derived scores is that a student's performance on different tests can be compared directly. This is usually done by means of a test profile, like the one presented in the top half of Figure 19.3. Such a graphic representation of test data makes it easy to identify a student's relative strengths and weaknesses. Most standardized tests have provisions for plotting test profiles.

The profile shown in the top half of Figure 19.3 indicates a desirable trend in profile construction. Instead of plotting test scores as specific points on the scale, test performance is recorded in section D by means of bands that extend one standard error of measurement above and below the student's obtained scores. Recall from our discussion of reliability that there are approximately two chances out of three that a student's true score will fall within one standard error of the obtained score. Thus, these confidence bands indicate the ranges of scores within which we can be reasonably certain of finding the student's true standings. Plotting them on the profile enables us to take into account the inaccuracy of the test scores when comparing performance on different tests. Interpreting differences between tests is simple with these score bands. If the bands for two tests overlap, we can assume that performance on the two tests does not differ significantly, and if the bands do not overlap, we can assume that there is probably a real difference in performance. Thus, performance on Verbal Reasoning, Numerical Reasoning, Perceptual Speed and Accuracy, and Language Usage subtests does not differ significantly for the example in Figure 19.3. The performance on the Abstract Reasoning subtest is clearly higher than that on the Mechanical Reasoning or Spatial Relations subtests.

The score bands used with *The Differential Aptitude Tests* can be plotted by hand or by computer. The computer-produced profile shown in Figure 19.3 is based on the same-sex percentiles. These are recorded in section C of the form, under the column heading "PR." Also shown, under the column head "S," are the corresponding stanine scores. The opposite-sex percentiles and stanines as well as those for the combined group of males and females are listed down the right side of the report to show how the scores compare with the female norms and to total group norms. The difference in male and female percentiles for some tests (e.g., Mechanical Reasoning and Language Usage) highlights the importance of reporting scores in terms of both male and female norms.

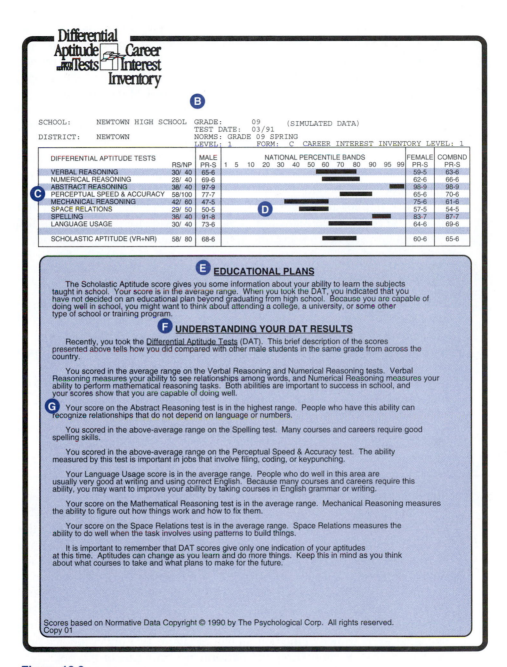

Figure 19.3

DAT™ Student Profile and Narrative Summary. (Reproduced from *The Differential Aptitude Tests*, 5th ed., by permission. Copyright 1990, The Psychological Corporation. All rights reserved.)

Not all test publishers make provisions for plotting score bands, but more will probably do so in the future. In the meantime, it is possible to plot these bands for any test for which we have a standard error of measurement. All we need to do is determine the error band in raw score points and refer to the norm table with these figures. For example, if a student has earned a raw score of 74 and the standard error of measurement is 3, then the error band in raw score points will range from 71 to 77. By locating these two numbers in the norm table, we can obtain the corresponding range in percentiles, standard scores, or whatever derived score is being used and plot the results directly on the profile. The use of such bands minimizes the tendency of test profiles to present a misleading picture. Without the bands, we are apt to attribute significance to differences in test performance that can be accounted for by chance alone.

When profiles are used to compare test performance, it is essential that the norms for all tests be comparable. Many test publishers provide for this by standardizing a battery of achievement tests and a scholastic aptitude test on the same population.

Profile Narrative Reports

Narrative reports that describe how well the student is achieving are also available from publishers of many tests. As illustrated in Figure 19.3, profile reports are frequently accompanied by a narrative report. The graphic profile provides a quick view of the student's strengths and weaknesses, and the narrative report aids in interpreting the scores and identifying areas in which instructional emphasis is needed.

Narrative reports are especially useful in communicating test results to parents. They are, of course, also helpful to those teachers who have had little or no training in the interpretation and use of scores from published tests.

SKILL ANALYSIS

Some test publishers provide profiles that include reports for skill objectives as well as for full subtests. An example of such a report is shown in Figure 19.4. The "Performance on Objectives" scores shown on the bottom of the figure are based on the *TerraNova*. It presents a comprehensive, detailed description of each individual's test results. The norm-referenced scores and profile (using percentile bands) are shown in the top half of the report for the full subtests. Section B in the figure can be tailored to report up to six norm-referenced scores. Section C displays percentile bands. The student's national percentile rank is indicated by the diamond for each subtest, and the bands extend one standard error of measurement on each side of the diamond. The criterion-referenced skill analysis is shown in the bottom half of Figure 19.4 under the heading "Performance on Objectives." Section D reports performance in terms of the objectives measured by the *TerraNova*, and section E displays an "Objectives Performance Index" (OPI) for each objective. Users are told that "an OPI of 75 or higher indicates Mastery, an OPI between 50 and 74 indicates Partial Mastery, and an OPI of 49 or less indicates Non-Mastery" (CTB/McGraw-Hill, 1997, p. 149).

Report forms like this yield a wealth of information for the instructional use of test results. The norm-referenced scores indicate how the student's test performance compares

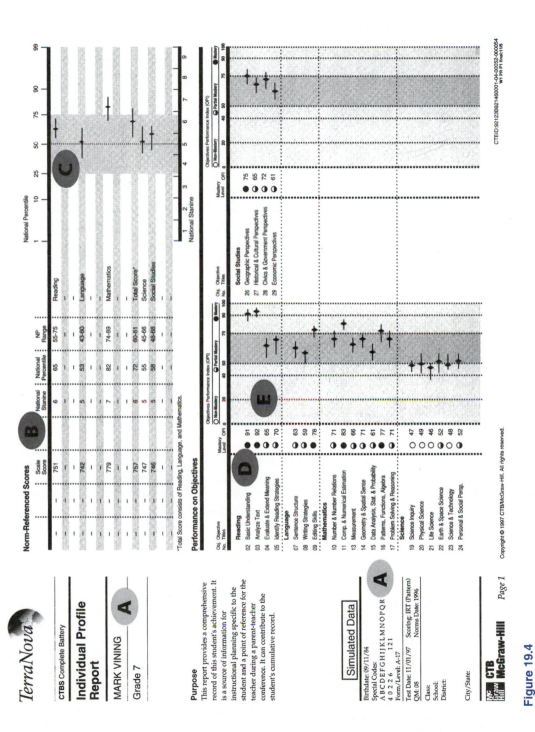

Figure 19.4

Illustrative score report for the *TerraNova*. (Reproduced by permission. Copyright 1997, CTB/McGraw-Hill. All rights reserved.)

with that of others, the subtest profile identifies strengths and weaknesses in each general content area, and the objectives performance scores and profile, by detailed objectives, identify strengths and weaknesses in specific skills in each general content area. As noted earlier in this chapter, however, caution is necessary when interpreting performance on content clusters based on a small number of test items. In these instances, the results are best interpreted as clues for further study.

In addition to detailed reports for individuals, many publishers also offer profile and skill analysis by class, school, and school system. By using computer scoring and reporting services, test results can be obtained in almost any form desired.

JUDGING THE ADEQUACY OF NORMS

As noted earlier, test norms can be expressed in terms of several different types of derived scores. Regardless of the type of derived score used, the main purpose is to make possible an interpretation of students' test performance in terms of a clearly defined reference group. This should not be just any reference group, however, but one that provides a meaningful basis for comparison.

The adequacy of test norms is a basic consideration during test selection and a factor to be reckoned with during the interpretation of test scores. The following criteria indicate the qualities most desired in norms.

1. Test norms should be relevant. Test norms are based on various types of groups. Some represent a national sample of all students at certain grade or age levels, whereas others are limited to samples from a given region or state. For special purposes, the norms also might be confined to a limited group, such as high school students in independent schools, girls who have completed secretarial training in a commercial high school, or college freshmen in engineering. The variety of groups available for comparison makes it necessary to study the norm sample before using any table of norms. We should ask whether these norms are appropriate for the students being tested and for the decisions to be made with the results. If we merely want to compare our students with a general reference group in order to diagnose strengths and weaknesses in different areas, national norms may be satisfactory. Here our main concern is with the extent to which our students are similar to those in the norm population on such characteristics as scholastic aptitude, educational experience, and cultural background. The more closely our students approximate those in the norm group, the greater will be our certainty that the national norms are a meaningful basis for comparison.

But when we are trying to decide such things as which students should be placed in an accelerated group, who should be encouraged to select the college preparatory curriculum, or whether a particular student should pursue a career in engineering, national norms are much less useful. For such decisions, we need norms for each of the specific groups involved. A student can have an above-average aptitude and achievement when compared with students in general and still fall short of the ability needed to succeed in highly select groups. When decisions involve predictions of future success in a particular area, comparing a student with potential competitors is more meaningful than comparisons with grade or age mates.

2. Test norms should be representative. Once we are satisfied that a set of test norms is based on a group with which comparisons are desired, it is appropriate to ask whether the norms are truly representative of that group. Ideally, the norms should be based on a random sample of the population they represent. This is extremely difficult and expensive, however, so we must usually settle for something less. At minimum, we should demand that all significant subgroups of the population be adequately represented. For national norms, it is desirable to have a proper proportion of students from such subgroups as boys and girls, geographic regions, rural and urban areas, socioeconomic levels, racial groups, and schools of varying size. The most adequate representation in these areas is obtained when the norm sample closely approximates the population distribution reported by the United States Census Bureau.

3. Test norms should be up to date. One factor that is commonly neglected in judging the adequacy of norms is whether they are currently applicable. The age of norms became a major issue in the late 1980s, when John Cannell (1988; also Linn, Graue, & Sanders, 1990) reported that all states and most school districts where norm-referenced tests were used were reporting scores above the national average in the elementary grades. This result came to be known as the "Lake Wobegone effect"—a reference to Garrison Keillor's radio program about a fictitious place where all the children are above average. The Lake Wobegone effect led to the charge that the public was being misled and caused a minor scandal in the popular press. One of the major reasons for this effect—though not the only one—was the use of old norms. When achievement is going up, a given raw score will yield a higher percentile rank when compared to old norms than when compared to new norms. With the rapid changes that are taking place in education, we can expect test norms to become out of date much sooner than they did in the past.

It is generally unsafe to use the copyright date on the test manual as an indication of when the norms were obtained, as this date may be changed whenever the manual is altered, no matter how slightly. To find the year in which the norm groups were tested, consult the description of the procedures used in establishing norms. When a test has been revised, make certain that the norms are based on the new edition.

4. Test norms should be comparable. It is often necessary or desirable to directly compare scores from different tests, such as when we make profile comparisons of test results to diagnose a student's strengths and weaknesses or when we compare aptitude and achievement test scores to detect underachievers. Such comparisons can be justified only if the norms for the different tests are comparable. We can be assured of comparability when all tests have been normed on the same population. This is routinely done with the tests in an achievement battery, and test publishers also usually administer a scholastic aptitude test to the same norm group. Whenever the scores from different tests are to be compared directly, the test manuals should be checked to determine whether the norms are based on the same group and, if not, whether they have been made comparable by other means.

5. Test norms should be adequately described. It is difficult to determine whether these norms provide a meaningful basis of comparison unless we know something about the norm group and the norming procedures used. The type of information we might expect to find in a test manual includes (a) method of sampling; (b) number and distribution of cases in the norm sample; (c) characteristics of the norm group with regard to such factors as age, sex, race, scholastic aptitude, educational level, socioeconomic status, types of schools represented, and geographic location; (d) extent to which standard conditions of administration and motivation were maintained during the testing; and (e) date of the testing (i.e., whether in the fall or the spring). Other things being equal, we should always favor the test for which we have detailed descriptions of these and other relevant factors. Such information is needed if we are to judge the appropriateness of test norms for our particular purposes.

USING LOCAL NORMS

In some cases, it may be desirable to compare students with local norms. If our students deviate markedly from those in the published norms on such characteristics as scholastic aptitude, educational experience, or cultural background, for example, comparison with a local group may be more meaningful. Local norms can also be useful for making within-class comparisons in special groups (e.g., remedial class in reading) and for determining how well particular children (e.g., handicapped children being mainstreamed) are succeeding in the regular classroom group. When we wish to make profile comparisons of scores obtained from tests standardized on different populations, local norms can also be used to obtain comparable scores by administering all tests to a common local group. Local norms can, of course, also be computed for classroom tests and are especially useful for departmental examinations used in several sections of a course.

Local norms are typically prepared using either percentile ranks or stanines. Most test publishers will provide local norms if requested, but they also can be prepared locally.

CAUTIONS IN INTERPRETING TEST SCORES

Interpreting test scores with the aid of norms requires an understanding of the type of derived score used and a willingness to study the characteristics of the norm group. The standards listed in Table 19.6 provide good advice that can increase the likelihood that scores will be interpreted correctly. In addition, keep in mind the following general cautions that apply to the interpretation of any test score.

1. **A test score should be interpreted in terms of the specific test from which it was derived.** No two scholastic aptitude tests or achievement tests measure exactly the same thing. Achievement tests are especially prone to wide variation, and the differences are seldom reflected in the test title. For example, one mathematics test may be limited to simple computational skills, whereas another may contain a number of reasoning problems. Similarly, one science test may be confined largely to items measuring knowledge of terminology, whereas another with the same title stresses the application of scientific principles. With such variation, it is misleading to interpret a student's test score

Table 19.6
Standards for interpreting and reporting scores

Test Developers	*Test Users*
Test developers should report test results accurately and provide information to help test users interpret test results correctly.	*Test users should report and interpret test results accurately and clearly.*
C-1. Provide information to support recommended interpretations of the results, including the nature of the content, norms or comparison groups, and other technical evidence. Advise test users of the benefits and limitations of test results and their interpretation. Warn against assigning greater precision than is warranted.	C-1. Interpret the meaning of the test results, taking into account the nature of the content, norms or comparison groups, other technical evidence, and benefits and limitations of test results.
C-2. Provide guidance regarding the interpretations of results for tests administered with modifications. Inform test users of potential problems in interpreting test results when tests or test administration procedures are modified.	C-2. Interpret test results from modified test or test administration procedures in view of the impact those modifications may have had on test results.
C-3. Specify appropriate uses of test results and warn test users of potential misuses.	C-3. Avoid using tests for purposes other than those recommended by the test developer unless there is evidence to support the intended use or interpretation.
C-4. When test developers set standards, provide the rationale, procedures, and evidence for setting performance standards or passing scores. Avoid using stigmatizing labels.	C-4. Review the procedures for setting performance standards or passing scores. Avoid using stigmatizing labels.
C-5. Encourage test users to base decisions about test takers on multiple sources of appropriate information, not on a single test score.	C-5. Avoid using a single test score as the sole determinant of decisions about test takers. Interpret test scores in conjunction with other information about individuals.
C-6. Provide information to enable test users to accurately interpret and report test results for groups of test takers, including information about who were and who were not included in the different groups being compared, and information about factors that might influence the interpretation of results.	C-6. State the intended interpretation and use of test results for groups of test takers. Avoid grouping test results for purposes not specifically recommended by the test developer unless evidence is obtained to support the intended use. Report procedures that were followed in determining who were and who were not included in the groups being compared and describe factors that might influence the interpretation of results.
C-7. Provide test results in a timely fashion and in a manner that is understood by the test taker.	C-7. Communicate test results in a timely fashion and in a manner that is understood by the test taker.

Table 19.6 (Continued)
Standards for interpreting and reporting scores

Test Developers	Test Users
Test developers should report test results accurately and provide information to help test users interpret test results correctly.	Test users should report and interpret test results accurately and clearly.
C-8. Provide guidance to test users about how to monitor the extent to which the test is fulfilling its intended purposes.	C-8. Develop and implement procedures for monitoring test use, including consistency with the intended purposes of the test.

Source: Code of Fair Testing Practices in Education, 2004, Washington, DC: Joint Committee on Testing Practices. (Mailing address: Joint Committee on Testing Practices, American Psychological Association, 750 First Street NE, Washington, DC 20002-4242.)

as representing general achievement in any particular area. We need to look beyond test titles and evaluate the student's performance in terms of what the test actually does measure.

2. A test score should be interpreted in light of all of the student's relevant characteristics. Test performance is influenced by the student's aptitudes, educational experiences, cultural background, emotional adjustment, health, and the like. Consequently, when a student performs poorly on a test, first consider factors such as language background, prior educational experiences, improper motivation, or similar factors that might have interfered with the student's response to the test.

3. A test score should be interpreted according to the type of decision to be made. The meaningfulness of a test score is determined to a considerable extent by the use to be made of it. For example, a Scholastic Aptitude stanine score of 4 on the DAT™ would have quite different meaning if we were wanting to predict achievement in the senior year of high school than if we were counseling a student about submitting an application to a highly selective college. We will find test scores much more useful when we stop considering them as high or low in general and begin evaluating their significance in relation to the decision to be made.

4. A test score should be interpreted as a band of scores rather than as a specific value. Every test score is subject to error that must be allowed for during test interpretation. One of the best means of doing this is to consider a student's test performance as a band of scores one standard error of measurement above and below the obtained score. For example, if a student earns a score of 56 and the standard error is 3, the test performance should be interpreted as a band ranging from score 53 to score 59. Such bands were illustrated in the profiles presented earlier. Even when they are not plotted, however, we should make allowances for these error bands surrounding each score. This will prevent us from making interpretations that are more precise than the test results warrant. Treating small chance differences between test scores as though they were significant can lead to erroneous decisions.

5. A test score should be verified by supplementary evidence. When interpreting test scores, it is impossible to determine fully the extent to which the basic assumptions of testing have been met (i.e., maximum motivation, equal educational opportunity, and so on) or to which the conditions of testing have been precisely controlled (i.e., administration, scoring, and so on). Consequently, in addition to the predictable error of measurement, which can be taken into account with standard error bands, a test score may contain an indeterminate amount of error caused by unmet assumptions or uncontrolled conditions. Our only protection against such errors is not to rely completely on a single test score. As Cronbach (1970) pointed out,

> The most helpful single principle in all testing is that test scores are data on which to base further study. They must be coordinated with background facts, and they must be verified by constant comparison with other available data. (p. 381)

The misinterpretation and misuse of test scores would be substantially reduced if this simple principle were more widely recognized. But this caution should not be restricted to test scores; it is merely a specific application of the more general rule that no important educational decision should ever be based on one limited sample of performance.

SUMMARY

Test interpretation is complicated because the raw scores obtained for a test lack a true zero point (point where there is no achievement at all) and equal units (such as feet, pounds, and minutes). In an attempt to compensate for these missing properties and to make test scores more readily interpretable, various methods of expressing test scores have been devised. In general, we can give meaning to a raw score either by converting it into a description of the specific tasks that the student can perform (criterion-referenced interpretation) or by converting it into some type of derived score that indicates the student's relative position in a clearly defined reference group (norm-referenced interpretation). In some cases, both types of interpretation can be made.

Criterion-referenced test interpretation permits us to describe an individual's test performance without referring to the performance of others. This is typically done in terms of some universally understood measure of proficiency (e.g., speed or precision) or the percentage of items correct in some clearly defined domain of learning tasks. The percentage-correct score is widely used in criterion-referenced test interpretation, but it is primarily useful in mastery testing where a clearly defined and delimited domain of learning tasks can be most readily obtained. Although criterion-referenced interpretation is frequently possible with standardized tests, such interpretations must be made with caution because these tests were typically designed to discriminate among individuals rather than describe the specific tasks they can perform. Test publishers are attempting to produce tests that are more amenable to criterion-referenced interpretation.

Expectancy tables also provide a type of criterion-referenced interpretation. Instead of describing an individual's performance on the test tasks, it indicates expected performance in some situation beyond the test (e.g., success in college). Expectancy tables provide a simple and direct means of interpreting test results without the aid of test norms.

Standards-based score reports convert scores into a few broad categories of performance. For example, scores below a specified level may be called below basic, those from that level to another specified level basic, and those above that level proficient or advanced.

Standardized tests typically have been designed for norm-referenced interpretation, which involves converting the raw scores to derived scores by means of tables of norms. These derived scores indicate a student's relative position in a particular reference group. They have the advantage of providing more uniform meaning from one test to another and from one situation to another than raw scores.

Test norms merely represent the typical performance of students in the reference groups on which the test was standardized and consequently should not be viewed as desired goals or standards. The most common types of norms are grade norms, percentile norms, and standard score norms. Each type has its own characteristics, advantages, and limitations that must be taken into account during test interpretation.

Grade norms describe test performance in terms of the particular grade group in which a student's raw score is just average. These norms are widely used at the elementary school level largely because of the ease with which they can be interpreted. Depicting test performance in terms of grade equivalents can often lead to unsound decisions, however, because of the inequality of the units and the invalid assumptions on which they are based. Grade-equivalent scores must be interpreted with caution.

Percentile norms and standard score norms describe test performance in terms of the student's relative standing in some meaningful group (e.g., grade or age group). A percentile rank indicates the percentage of students falling below a particular raw score. Percentile units are unequal, but the scores are readily understood by persons without special training. A standard score indicates the number of standard deviation units a raw score falls above or below the group mean. It has the advantage of providing equal units that can be treated mathematically, but persons untrained in statistics find it difficult to interpret such scores. Some of the more common types of standard scores are z-scores, stanines, T-scores, NCE scores, and standard age scores.

With a normal distribution of scores, we can readily convert between standard scores and percentiles, using the special advantages of each. Standard scores can be used to draw on the benefits of equal units, and we can convert to percentile equivalents when interpreting test performance to students, parents, and those who lack statistical training.

A student's performance on several tests that have comparable norms may be presented in the form of a profile, making it possible to readily identify areas of strength and weakness. Profile interpretation is apt to be more accurate when standard error bands are plotted on the profile. Some test profiles also include narrative reports and/or detailed analysis of the results by content or skill clusters. This criterion-referenced analysis is especially useful for the instructional use of test results.

The adequacy of test norms can be judged by determining the extent to which they are (a) relevant, (b) representative, (c) up to date, (d) comparable, and (e) adequately described. In some instances, it is more appropriate to use local norms than published norms. When local norms are desired, percentile and stanine norms can be easily computed.

In addition to a knowledge of derived scores and norms, the proper interpretation of test scores requires an awareness of (a) what the test measures, (b) the student's characteristics and background, (c) the type of decision to be made, (d) the amount of error in the score, and (e) the extent to which the score agrees with other available data. No important educational decision should ever be based on test scores alone.

LEARNING EXERCISES

1. Describe the cautions needed in making criterion-referenced interpretations of standardized achievement tests.
2. Describe the meaning of raw scores and derived scores.
3. A fifth-grade student received an average grade-equivalent score of 6.8 on a standardized achievement battery administered in the fall of the year. What arguments might be presented for and against moving the student ahead to the sixth grade?
4. What advantages do stanines have over T-scores? What disadvantages?
5. Explain each of the following statements.
   a. Standard scores provide approximately equal units.
   b. Percentile scores provide systematically unequal units.
   c. Grade-equivalent scores provide unequal units that vary unpredictably.
6. Assuming that all the following test scores were obtained from the same normally distributed group, which score would indicate the highest performance? The lowest performance?
   a. z-score = .65
   b. T-score = 65
   c. NCE score = 65
   d. Percentile score = 65
7. Consult the section on norms in *Standards for Educational and Psychological Testing* (American Educational Research Association, American Psychological Association, & National Council on Measurement in Education, 1999) and review the types of information that test manuals should contain. Compare a recent test manual with the *Standards*.
8. What is the difference between a norm and a standard? Why should test norms not be used as standards of good performance?
9. What is the value of using national norms? Under what conditions is it desirable to use local norms?
10. What are the relative advantages and disadvantages of using local norms for disadvantaged students? For what purposes are more general norms (e.g., national) useful with these students?

REFERENCES

American Educational Research Association, American Psychological Association, & National Council on Measurement in Education. (1999). *Standards for educational and psychological testing.* Washington, DC: American Educational Research Association.

American Psychological Association. (1974). *Standards for educational and psychological tests.* Washington, DC: Author.

Cannell, J. J. (1988). Nationally normed elementary achievement testing in America's schools: How all 50 states are above the national average. *Educational Measurement: Issues and Practice, 7*(2), 5–9.

Cronbach, L. J. (1970). *Essentials of psychological testing* (3rd ed.). New York: Harper & Row.

CTB/McGraw-Hill. (1997). *Teacher's Guide to TerraNova.* Monterey, CA: CTB/McGraw-Hill.

Hoover, H. D. (1984). The most appropriate scores for measuring educational development in elementary schools: GE's. *Educational Measurement: Issues and Practice, 3*(4), 8–14.

Linn, R. L., Graue, M. E., & Sanders, N. M. (1990). Comparing state and district test results to national norms: The validity of claims that everyone is above average. *Educational Measurement: Issues and Practice, 9*(3), 5–14. Discusses the reasons behind the Lake Wobegone effect.

FURTHER READING

American Psychological Association. (1985). *Standards for educational and psychological testing.* Washington, DC: Author. See Part 1 for what to look for in test manuals and Parts 2 and 3 for material on the effective interpretation and use of tests in various areas.

Anastasi, A., & Urbina, S. (1996). *Psychological testing* (7th ed.). New York: Macmillan. Chapters, "Norms and the Interpretation of Test Scores," describes the various types of norms, computer interpretation of test scores, and criterion-referenced testing.

Gronlund, N. E. (2005). *Assessment of student achievement* (8th ed.). Boston: Allyn and Bacon. Chapters 10, "Interpreting Standardized Achievement Test Results," describes simplified methods for use with classroom tests.

Lyman, H. B. (1997). *Test scores and what they mean* (6th ed.). Englewood Cliffs, NJ: Prentice Hall. A well-written and interesting description of the various types of test scores and how to interpret them, with emphasis on norm-referenced interpretation.

Petersen, N. S., Kolen, M. J., & Hoover, H. D. (1989). Scaling, norming, and equating. In R. L. Linn (Ed.), *Educational measurement* (3rd ed.). New York: Macmillan. A comprehensive and technically advanced treatment of scales, norms, and equating scores.

APPENDIX A

ELEMENTARY STATISTICS

Statistics is concerned with the organization, analysis, and interpretation of test scores and other numerical data. At minimum, teachers should know those statistical techniques that enable them to (a) analyze and describe the results of measurement obtained in their own classrooms, (b) understand the statistics used in test manuals and research reports, and (c) interpret the various types of derived scores used in testing.

Many teachers shy away from statistics because they think it requires advanced mathematics and tedious calculations. However, the elementary statistical concepts and skills we shall deal with require neither. The calculations that can be quite tedious if conducted by hand can be done quite readily with a simple, inexpensive, handheld calculator. Calculators costing $20 or so not only can do all the intermediate calculations but often have built-in procedures for all of the statistics we shall discuss. Computation of the statistics we consider as well as much more complicated ones obviously can also be readily performed on a personal computer with easy-to-use statistical software or spreadsheet software. Hence, we have reduced the emphasis on calculation that was present in previous editions. We also have kept the mathematics to a minimum and will emphasize interpretation.

The statistics that we shall be concerned with here are known as descriptive statistics. As the term suggests, the emphasis is on describing a set of scores. The description may take the form of tables, graphs, or a single number (e.g., an average). Some of these modes of description are seen routinely in newspapers, magazines, and the evening television news. The purpose of these statistics is to summarize sets of numbers so that interesting features may be seen and understood more easily. For example, given a list of the high and low temperatures for each of the 365 days of a year, it would be possible to read them all and get a sense of how temperate the climate was and of seasonal changes. However, a graph of the average high and low temperatures for each of the 12 months of the year could convey the information much more efficiently and effectively.

We shall begin with a brief discussion of organizing data and displaying results in tables and graphs. We shall then turn to a discussion of three types of statistical measures:

1. Measures of central tendency (averages)
2. Measures of variability (spread of scores)
3. Measures of relationship (correlation and regression)

The first two measures provide a convenient means of analyzing and describing a single set of test scores, and the third category of measures can be used to indicate the agreement between two sets of test scores obtained for the same students. All three are widely used in educational measurement and should be mastered by anyone working with test data.

ORGANIZING AND DISPLAYING SCORES

When test scores are obtained for a group of students they are usually in haphazard order as shown in Table A.1. After careful inspection of the scores on the midterm exam for the 24 students we see that scores in the 70s and 80s are fairly common, that only three students had scores in the 90s, and that one student had a score less than 50. Similar statements might be made after inspecting the scores on the final exam. We might even note that there is a tendency for the scores on the final to be slightly higher than those on the midterm and that there is a tendency for students with high scores on the midterm to receive relatively high scores on the final, though the relationship is far from perfect. For example, Student E, who had the highest score on the midterm, had the fourth-highest score on the final, whereas Student W, who had the fifth-highest score on the midterm, had the highest score on the final.

From our detailed inspection of the scores in Table A.1, we could actually get a rough idea of all three of the statistical concepts of concern here. These are the central tendency, or the score obtained by the average student; the variability of the scores (e.g., the midterm scores range from a high of 97 to a low of 45, but most of the students have scores between 60 and 90); and the relationship between performance on the midterm and performance on the final. None of these characteristics of the scores is very easy to see from the haphazard arrangement of the scores, however, nor are they very precise. If we were working with 200 scores for all seventh-grade students at a junior high school or 3,000 scores

Table A.1

Set of scores for a class of 24 students

Student	Midterm	Final	Student	Midterm	Final
A	78	85	M	65	80
B	67	71	N	92	93
C	88	78	O	53	69
D	74	71	P	65	75
E	97	91	Q	83	76
F	84	88	R	79	74
G	57	76	S	45	63
H	65	68	T	95	80
I	81	94	U	62	58
J	58	67	V	74	80
K	70	72	W	85	96
L	81	87	X	76	81

for all third-grade students in a school district, the difficulty of seeing interesting characteristics and communicating them in a precise way would be much greater than it was for our class of 24 students. But even for our 24 students, we need to organize and display the scores to see these characteristics more easily, and we need to do some simple calculations to quantify the information in a more precise fashion.

Simple Ranking

For some uses, it may be sufficient to arrange a set of scores in order of size and to assign a rank to each score. This will indicate the relative position of each score in the group. Ordinarily, the largest score is given a rank of 1, the second largest a rank of 2, and so on until all scores are ranked. The midterm scores from Table A.1 have been rearranged in order of size and assigned ranks to illustrate the procedure. The results are presented in Table A.2. Note that when two or more students have the same score (the two 81s, the two 74s, and the three 65s), the average of the ranks for those students is given to each. Thus, the two students who received scores of 81 on the midterm would have been ranked 8 and 9. They are both given the average of these two ranks (8.5) because there is no basis for giving one of the students a rank of 8 and the other one a rank of 9. Using Table A.2, it is obviously much easier than it was with Table A.1 to find the highest and lowest midterm scores and the number of students with scores above 90 or below 70 and to see that scores in the 70s are obtained by students who rank close to the middle of the class. It is also easy to see that half the students score above 75 and half of them score below 75. Creating a rank order list for the final exam scores would make it easy to see similar characteristics of those scores. For example, it would make it easier to see that while nine students had scores below 70 on the midterm, only five had scores below 70 on the final.

With only 24 scores, there is no great need to go beyond a rank order display of scores. With more scores, however, it is often helpful to construct grouped frequency

Table A.2
Ranking test scores

Midterm	Rank		Midterm	Rank	
97	1		74	13.5	Tied ranks
95	2		74	13.5	13 and 14
92	3		70	15	
88	4		67	16	
85	5		65	18	Tied ranks
84	6		65	18	17, 18, and 19
83	7		65	18	
81	8.5	Tied ranks	62	20	
81	8.5	8 and 9	58	21	
79	10		57	22	
78	11		53	23	
76	12		45	24	

Table A.3
Frequency distributions of midterm and final scores

Midterm			Final	
Class Interval	Tally	Frequency	Class Interval	Frequency
95–99	//	2	95–99	1
90–94	/	1	90–94	3
85–89	//	2	85–89	3
80–84	////	4	80–84	4
75–79	///	3	75–79	4
70–74	///	3	70–74	4
65–69	////	4	65–69	3
60–64	/	1	60–64	1
55–59	//	2	55–59	1
50–54	/	1	50–54	0
45–49	/	1	45–49	0
N		$N = 24$	N	$N = 24$

distributions and graphs of the score distributions. Grouped frequency distributions of the midterm and final scores are shown in Table A.3. Note that the scores have been grouped into class intervals, the number of scores falling in each interval has been tallied, and the tallies have been counted to obtain the frequency, or number of scores in each interval. Thus, there were two students with midterm scores in the interval 95–99, one student with a score in the interval 90–94, and so on. The total number (N) is the sum of the numbers in the frequency column. In the finished table, the tally column is usually omitted as it has been for the final exam scores.

To construct a grouped frequency distribution, it is conventional to choose a class interval that is an odd number and that will result in approximately 10 to 12 intervals. This makes the midpoint of each interval an integer. For our example, the class interval is 5 (e.g., 95, 96, 97, 98, and 99 in the highest interval), and the midpoint of each interval is an integer (e.g., 97 is the midpoint of the highest interval). The lower bound of each interval starts with a multiple of the width of the interval (e.g., the lowest interval starts with 45, the next with 50, and so on). All class intervals should be the same size.

To decide on the width of the interval that will result in a reasonable number of intervals, the range can be divided by 12 and the nearest odd number used as the width of the class interval. For example, the highest midterm score is 97, and the lowest is 45, for a range of 52 (97 − 45 = 52). Since 52/12 = 4.33, the class interval was set at 5, the nearest odd number. Note that applying the same process for the final scores would have suggested using a class interval of 3; however, using the same interval makes it easier to compare the two sets of scores.

The grouped frequency distributions provide a good summary of the results. Features of the two distributions that already have been mentioned can be easily seen, but there is some loss of information. For example, from the grouped frequency distribution, we see that two students had scores in the interval 95–99 on the midterm, but we can no longer tell that one of these students had a 95 and the other one had a score of 97.

Graphic Presentations of Frequency Distributions

A frequency distribution presents test data in a clear, effective manner, and it is satisfactory for most classroom purposes. If we want to study the distribution of scores more carefully or to report the results to others, however, a graphic representation may be more useful. The two most commonly used graphs are the histogram (or bar graph) and the frequency polygon (or line graph). Both graphs are presented in Figure A.1, based on the midterm scores in Table A.3. The scores are shown along the baseline, or horizontal axis, and are grouped into the same class intervals used in Table A.3. The vertical axis, to the left of the graphs, indicates the number of students earning each score and thus corresponds to the frequency column in Table A.3. The histogram presents the data in the form of rectangular columns. The base of each column is the width of the class interval, and the height of the column indicates the frequency, or the number of students falling within that interval. It is as if each student earning a score within a given class interval were standing on the shoulders of the student beneath to form a human column.

The frequency polygon is constructed by plotting a point at the midpoint of each class interval at a height corresponding to the number of students, or frequency, within that interval and then joining these points with straight lines. As can be seen in Figure A.1, the frequency polygon and histogram are simply different ways of presenting the same data. In actual practice we would use only one of the graphs, the choice being somewhat arbitrary.

Histograms or frequency polygons allow us to see the shape of the distribution of scores as well as some of the features we have seen before. With a small number of students, such as the 24 in our example, the shape of the distribution is often jagged, going

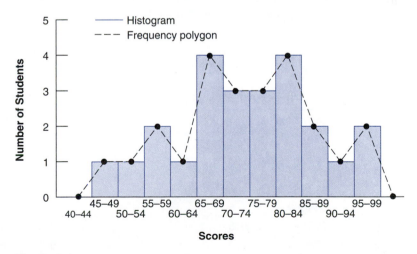

Figure A.1
Histogram and frequency polygon plotted from midterm exam scores in Table A.3

up and down and up again as you go from left to right. With a large number of scores, however, distributions of scores generally look smoother than the one shown in Figure A.1. Distributions of scores for many students on standardized tests often appear bell shaped, not unlike the shape of a normal distribution, and in many cases normal distribution is assumed or used as an approximation. See Chapter 19 for a description of the normal distribution and illustrations of some of its uses.

Stem-and-Leaf Display

An approach to displaying data that has become increasingly popular in recent years is the stem-and-leaf display. Like grouped frequency distributions, frequency polygons, and histograms, stem-and-leaf displays show the shape of a distribution of scores. In addition, they preserve all the information about the individual scores that is lost when scores are grouped into class intervals.

Tables A.4 and A.5. show two versions of stem-and-leaf displays for the midterm and final exam scores in Table A.1. The "stem" in Table A.4 is simply the tens digit for each score and the "leaf" is the units digit. On the midterm there were three scores in the 90s (92, 95, and 97). These three scores all have a stem of 9, and the individual scores are represented by the string of numbers 257 for the three leaves of 2, 5, 7. Similarly, six students with scores in the 80s (81, 81, 83, 84, 85, and 88) are represented by the common stem of 8 and the string of numbers 113458 for the six leaves. The numbers in the columns labeled "count" simply record the number of scores with a given stem. As can be seen, the stem-and-leaf displays retain the detail that two students received a score of 81 while giving a general summary of the type provided by a grouped frequency distribution or frequency polygon.

The stem-and-leaf displays in Table A.5 show exactly the same information as is shown in Table A.4. The stem now corresponds to 5-point intervals, however. Thus, 9* represents a stem for the numbers 95 to 99, 9: represents the stem for the numbers 90 to 94, and so on. By using two stems for each tens digit, the shape of the distribution can be seen more easily.

Table A.4
Stem-and-leaf displays of midterm and final exam scores (Data from Table A.1)

	Midterm Exam				Final Exam		
Stem	*Leaf*	*Count*			*Stem*	*Leaf*	*Count*
9	257	3			9	1346	4
8	113458	6			8	0001578	7
7	044689	6			7	11245668	8
6	25557	5			6	3789	4
5	378	3			5	8	1
4	5	1					
		$N = 24$					$N = 24$

Table A.5
Stem-and-leaf displays of midterm and final exam scores (Data from Table A.1)

Midterm Exam				Final Exam		
Stem	*Leaf*	*Count*		*Stem*	*Leaf*	*Count*
9*	57	2		9*	6	1
9:	2	1		9:	134	3
8*	58	2		8*	578	3
8:	1134	4		8:	0001	4
7*	689	3		7*	5668	4
7:	044	3		7:	1124	4
6*	5557	4		6*	789	3
6:	2	1		6:	3	1
5*	78	2		5*	8	1
5:	3	1				
4*	5	1				
		$N = 24$				$N = 24$

Scatter Plots

The graphs and displays we have presented have highlighted all but one of the features that was discussed concerning the data in Table A.1. Because the tables, graphs, and displays have focused on one type of score at a time, they have not done anything to make it easier to see the relationship between scores on the midterm and the final. To see the relationship better than can be seen from a simple listing of the scores, we need to construct a plot that displays pairs of numbers. Such a plot is called a scatter plot (or scattergram). The scatter plot for the scores in Table A.1 is shown in Figure A.2. Each dot in Figure A.2 represents a pair of scores for an individual student. Thus, there are 24 dots corresponding to the students. A student's score on the midterm is shown on the horizontal, or X, axis, and the student's score on the final is shown on the vertical, or Y, axis. For example, Student A had a score of 78 on the midterm and a score of 85 on the final. That student's score is represented by the dot that is shown by the arrow and the letter A. It is directly above the point on the horizontal line corresponding to a score of 78 and directly to the right of the point on the vertical axis corresponding to a score of 85. Points representing the remaining 23 students are plotted in a similar fashion.

By looking at the plot, we see that a swarm of dots tends to run from the lower-left-hand corner to the upper-right-hand corner of the figure. This shows that there is a positive relationship between the scores on the midterm and the scores on the final. That is, students with relatively low scores on one test tend to have relatively low scores on the other test, whereas students with relatively high scores on one test tend to have relatively high scores on the other test. For example, there are nine dots to the right of 80 on the horizontal axis. These represent the nine students with midterm scores higher than 80. We see that all nine of these points are above 75 on the vertical scale, indicating that no

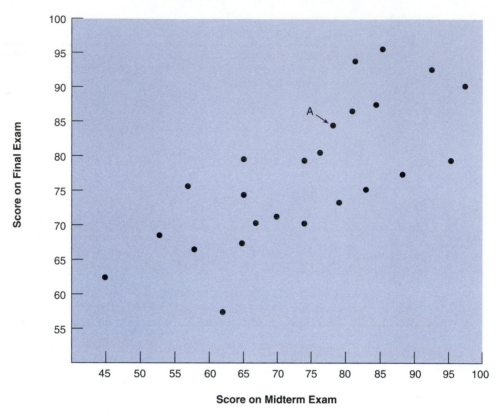

Figure A.2

Scatter plot of midterm and final exam scores (scores from Table A.1)

student who had a score of 80 or higher on the midterm had a score of 75 or less on the final. On the other hand, we can see by looking at the lower-left-hand corner of the scatter plot that six of the eight students who had midterm scores of 65 or less had scores of 75 or less on the final.

Although there clearly is a relationship between scores on the two tests, it is also clear that the relationship is far from perfect. That is, a student who has the highest or one of the highest scores on one test is not always ranked as highly on the other test. Indeed, the four students with scores of 90 or higher on the final had scores ranging all the way from 81 to 97 on the midterm, while one of the three students who had scores of 90 or higher on the midterm received a score of only 80 on the final.

Scatter plots and the graphs considered here can be produced easily with a personal computer. The version of the scatter plot shown in Figure A.3, for example, was produced using Microsoft EXCEL. The scores on the midterm and final examinations were entered into the spreadsheet as shown in Table A.8. (The spreadsheet entries and statistics in Table A.8 are discussed after the basic statistics shown there have been discussed.) The scatter plot was then produced by pointing and clicking with a mouse and specifying that the column of midterm scores would be used as the X axis and the column of final scores would be used as the Y axis for the scatter plot.

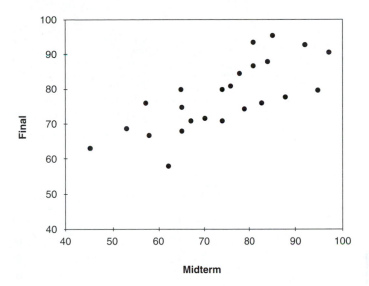

Figure A.3
Scatter plot of midterm and final exam scores produced by Microsoft EXCEL.

MEASURES OF CENTRAL TENDENCY

A measure of central tendency is simply an average or typical value in a set of scores. We all are familiar with the arithmetic average obtained by adding all the scores in a set and dividing this sum by the number of scores. In statistics, this type of average is called the mean and is represented by the letter M (or $\bar{X}$). Two other commonly used measures of central tendency are the median (represented by Mdn or P_{50}) and the mode. The median is the midpoint of a set of scores, that is, the point on either side of which half the scores occur. The mode (fashion) is the score that occurs most frequently. Because the mean, median, and mode are different types of averages, the word *average* should be avoided when describing data. Preciseness requires that the specific type of average be indicated.

The method of determining each measure of central tendency is described next and is illustrated in Table A.6.

The Mean (M or $\bar{X}$)

The **mean**, or arithmetic average, is the most widely used measure of central tendency. Because it is calculated by adding a series of scores and then dividing this sum by the number of scores, the computation can be represented by the following formula.

$$\bar{X} = \frac{\text{Sum of all scores}}{\text{Number of scores}}$$

$$\bar{X} = \frac{\Sigma X}{N}$$

where

Σ = the sum of
X = any score
N = number of scores

Applying this formula to the scores in Table A.6 produces a mean of 73.92 for the midterm and 78.04 for the final. The mean takes into account the value of each score, and so one extremely high or low score could have an appreciable effect on it.

Table A.6
Measures of central tendency

	Midterm Score (X)	Final Score (Y)	
	97	96	
	95	94	
	92	93	
	88	91	
	85	88	
50% of	84	87	50% of
scores	83	85	scores
	81	81	
	81	80	
	79	80	
	78	80	
	76	78	
Median = 75	→ ←		Median = 77
	74	76	
	74	76	
	70	75	
	67	74	
	65	72	
50% of	65	71	50% of
scores	65	71	scores
	62	69	
	58	68	
	57	67	
	53	63	
	45	58	
	Sum of X = 1,774	Sum of X = 1,873	
	Mean = (1,774/24)	Mean = (1,873/24)	
	= 73.92	= 78.04	

Note: Scores are rank ordered separately for the midterm and the final.

The Median (*Mdn* or P_{50})

The median is a counting average. It is determined by arranging the scores in order of size and counting up to (or down to) the midpoint of the set scores. If the number of scores is even (as in Table A. 6), the median will be halfway between the two middle most scores. When the number of scores is odd, the median is the middle score.

The median is a **point** that divides a set of scores into equal halves, and thus the same number of scores falls above the median as below the median, regardless of the size of the individual scores. Because it is a counting average, an extremely high or low score will not affect its value.

The Mode

The **mode** is simply the most frequent or popular score in the set and is determined by inspection. In Table A.6, the mode is 65 for the midterm because the largest number of persons made that score. The mode is the least reliable type of statistical average and is frequently used merely as a preliminary estimate of central tendency. A set of scores sometimes has two modes and is called **bimodal**.

MEASURES OF VARIABILITY

A set of scores can be more adequately described if we know how much they spread out above and below the measure of central tendency. For example, we might have two groups of students with a mean test score of 70, but in one group the span of scores is from 60 to 80 and in the other the span is from 50 to 100. These represent quite different spreads of performance. We can identify such differences by numbers that indicate how much scores spread out in a group. These are called measures of variability, or dispersion. The three most commonly used measures of variability are the **range**, the **quartile deviation**, and the **standard deviation**.

The Range

The simplest and crudest measure of variability is the range, calculated by subtracting the lowest score from the highest score. In the preceding example, the range of scores in the first group is 20 points and in the second 40 points. The range provides a quick estimate of variability but is undependable because it is based on the position of the two extreme scores. The addition or subtraction of a single score can change the range significantly. In the preceding example, the ranges of the two groups would become equal if we added two students to the first group: one with a score of 50 and another with a score of 100. It is obvious that a more stable measure of variability would be desirable. For our example with the midterm and final exam scores, however, the smaller range for the final (96 − 58 = 38) than for the midterm (range = 97 − 45 = 52) accurately reflects the smaller variability in scores on the final exam that we have previously noted and that will be quantified by the other measures of variability.

The Quartile Deviation (Q)

The quartile deviation is based on the range of the middle 50% of the scores, instead of the range of the entire set. The middle 50% of a set of scores is called the interquartile range, and the quartile deviation is simply half of this range. The quartile deviation is also called the semi-interquartile range.

The middle 50% of the scores is bounded by the 75th percentile and the 25th percentile. These points are called quartiles and are indicated by Q_3 and Q_1, respectively. Quartiles are merely points that divide a set of scores into quarters. The middle quartile, or Q_2, is the median.

To compute the quartile deviation, we simply determine the values of Q_3 and Q_1 and apply the following formula.

$$Q = \frac{Q_3 - Q_1}{2}$$

We use the same counting procedure to locate Q_3 and Q_1 that we used to find the median. With the scores arranged in order of size, we start from the lowest score and count off 25% of the scores to locate Q_1 and 75% of the scores to locate Q_3. Because we have 24 students in our example, Q_1 is equal to the score that is higher than that achieved by 6 students (25%) and lower than that achieved by 18 students (75%). For the midterm, $Q_1 = 65$, and for the final, $Q_1 = 71.5$. Note that Q_1 is 71.5 on the final because it falls halfway between 71, the sixth lowest score, and 72, the seventh lowest score. The values of Q_3 are 83.5 for the midterm (halfway between 83 and 84) and 86 for the final (halfway between 85 and 87).

Given the 75th and 25th percentiles (Q_1 and Q_3), the quartile deviation (Q) is easily computed. As would be expected from what we have already seen, Q is larger for the midterm scores [Q = (83.5 − 65)/2 = 9.25] than it is for the final scores [Q = (86 − 71.5)/2 = 7.25]. These quartile deviation values simply quantify the fact that the midterm scores are more variable than the final scores.

Although quartiles are points on the scale (like averages and percentiles), the quartile deviation represents a distance on the scale. It indicates the distance we need to go above and below the median to include approximately the middle 50% of the scores.

The Standard Deviation (SD, S, or σ)

The most useful measure of variability, or spread of scores, is the standard deviation. The computation of the standard deviation does not make its meaning readily apparent, but essentially it is an average of the degree to which a set of scores deviates from the mean. Because it takes into account the amount that each score deviates from the mean, it is a more stable measure of variability than either the range or quartile deviation.

Because the procedure for calculating a standard deviation involves squaring each score, summing the scores and the squares of the scores, as well as taking a square root, the help of a handheld calculator is highly desirable for any reasonably sized problem. Better yet, a calculator with built-in statistical procedures or a microcomputer with a simple statistical package is recommended for anyone who wants to compute statistics such as standard deviations and correlations on a routine basis. To perform the calculations by hand or with a handheld calculator that does not offer statistical procedures, however, the following steps are involved.

1. Find the sum of the scores (ΣX) as was done to compute the mean.
2. Square each score (X^2).
3. Find the sum of the squared scores (ΣX^2).
4. Square the sum of the scores obtained in Step 1; that is, multiply (ΣX) times (ΣX).
5. Divide the square obtained in Step 4 by N, the number of students, ($\Sigma X)(\Sigma X)/N$.
6. Subtract the result in Step 5 from the sum of the squared scores obtained in Step 3, $[\Sigma X^2 - (\Sigma X)(\Sigma X)/N]$.
7. Divide the result in Step 6 by ($N-1$), one less than the number of students, $[\Sigma X^2 - (\Sigma X)(\Sigma X)/N]/(N-1)$.
8. Find the square root of the result of Step 7. This number is the standard deviation (SD) of the scores.

Thus, the formula for the standard deviation (SD) is

$$SD = \sqrt{\frac{[\Sigma X^2 - (\Sigma X)(\Sigma X)/N]}{N-1}}$$

The square of each midterm score and the square of each final score is listed in Table A.7. Also shown are the sums of the scores and of the squared scores. The last column of the table lists the product of the midterm score times the final score for each student. Those numbers are not used for calculating standard deviations but will be used later to calculate the correlation. Using the numbers for the midterm exam in the eight steps just listed, the standard deviation is obtained as follows:

1. From Table A.7, $\Sigma X = 1,774$.
2. See Table A.7 for a listing of X^2 for each student.
3. From Table A.7, $\Sigma X^2 = 135,342$.
4. $(\Sigma X)(\Sigma X) = (1,774)(1,774) = 3,147,076$.
5. $(\Sigma X)(\Sigma X)/N = 3,147,076/24 = 131,125.1667$.
6. $[\Sigma X^2 - (\Sigma X)(\Sigma X)/N] = 135,342 - 131,125.1667 = 4,213.8333$.
7. $[\Sigma X^2 - (\Sigma X)(\Sigma X)/N]/(n-1) = 4,213.8333/23 = 183.2101$.
8. $SD = \sqrt{\dfrac{[\Sigma X^2 - (\Sigma X)(\Sigma X)/N]}{N-1}} = \sqrt{183.2101} = 13.54$

Applying the same steps to the scores on the final exam, we find that the SD for the final is 10.04. What do these standard deviations of 13.54 on the midterm and 10.04 tell us? First, it should be no surprise that the midterm scores have a larger standard deviation than the final scores. We have already noted that the midterm scores are more spread out. The midterm scores have a larger range and a larger quartile deviation than the final scores. The larger standard deviation is one more way of quantifying the fact that the midterm scores have greater variability than the final scores do.

The standard deviation, like other measures of variability, represents a distance. If we move the distance equal to one SD above and below the mean, we will find that somewhere between 60% and 75% of the scores fall in that region for most distributions of scores. In a normal distribution, 68% of the scores are included between the mean minus one SD and the mean plus one SD. For example, the midterm had a mean of 73.92 and a standard deviation of 13.54. Thus, the mean minus one SD is 73.92 − 13.54 = 60.35,

Table A.7
Intermediate calculations for standard deviation (*SD*) and product-moment correlation coefficient (*r*)

Student	Midterm Score		Final Score		
	X	X²	Y	Y²	XY
E	97	9,409	91	8,281	8,827
T	95	9,025	80	6,400	7,600
N	92	8,464	93	8,649	8,556
C	88	7,744	78	6,084	6,864
W	85	7,225	96	9,216	8,160
F	84	7,056	88	7,744	7,392
Q	83	6,889	76	5,776	6,308
I	81	6,561	94	8,836	7,614
L	81	6,561	87	7,569	7,047
R	79	6,241	74	5,476	5,846
A	78	6,084	85	7,225	6,630
X	76	5,776	81	6,561	6,156
D	74	5,476	71	5,041	5,254
V	74	5,476	80	6,400	5,920
K	70	4,900	72	5,184	5,040
B	67	4,489	71	5,041	4,757
H	65	4,225	68	4,624	4,420
M	65	4,225	80	6,400	5,200
P	65	4,225	75	5,625	4,875
U	62	3,844	58	3,364	3,596
J	58	3,364	67	4,489	3,886
G	57	3,249	76	5,776	4,332
O	53	2,809	69	4,761	3,657
S	45	2,025	63	3,969	2,835
	1,774	135,342	1,873	148,491	140,772
Column sum	*SD* = 13.54		*SD* = 10.04		*r* = .74

and the mean plus one *SD* is 73.92 + 13.54 = 87.46. Looking at Table A.7, we see that 16 of the 24 students (67%) have midterm scores between these two limits. Although the distribution of midterm scores is not the same shape as a normal distribution, the percentage of cases that fall between the mean plus and minus one *SD* is very close to the 68% that would be found for a true normal distribution. This result is not unusual, and it is reasonable to expect that roughly two thirds of the cases will have scores between the mean minus one *SD* and the mean plus one *SD*.

Finding the mean and standard deviation is quite easy with a personal computer or a calculator with statistical functions. This is illustrated using a Microsoft EXCEL spreadsheet. The student identification letters and their associated midterm and final scores were entered into an EXCEL spreadsheet, which is shown in Table A.8.

In EXCEL the student column is denoted column A and the midterm and final columns are denoted columns B and C, respectively. The rows are numbered and cells are referred to by column letters and row numbers. Thus, the "Student" label is entered in cell A1, the student designation "A" is entered in cell A2, and the student designation "X" is entered in cell A25. The midterm scores for the 24 students are in cells B2 through B25, and the final scores are in cells C1 through C25.

The sum of the midterm scores displayed in cell B26 as 1774 was obtained by typing "=SUM(B2:B25)" in the B26 cell. (Note: Only the material between the quotation marks is entered.) Other statistics are obtained by similarly simple statements. For example, the standard deviation for the final scores (shown as 10.041 in cell C32) was obtained by entering "=STDEV(C2:C25)."

Which Measure of Dispersion to Use

The quartile deviation is used with the median and is satisfactory for analyzing a small number of scores. Because these statistics are obtained by counting and thus are not affected by the value of each score, they are especially useful when one or more scores deviate markedly from the others in the set.

The standard deviation is used with the mean. It is the most reliable measure of variability, and is especially useful in testing. In addition to describing the spread of scores in a group, it serves as a basis for computing standard scores, the standard error of measurement, and other statistics used in analyzing and interpreting test scores.

COEFFICIENT OF CORRELATION

The next statistical measure that we shall consider is the correlation coefficient. The meaning of the correlation coefficient and its use in describing the validity and reliability of test scores can be found in Chapters 4 and 5. Basically, a coefficient of correlation expresses the degree of relationship between two sets of scores by numbers ranging from -1.00 to $+1.00$. A perfect positive correlation is indicated by a coefficient of $+1.00$ and a perfect negative correlation by a coefficient of -1.00. A correlation of .00 indicates no relationship between the two sets of scores. Obviously, the larger the coefficient (positive or negative), the higher the degree of relationship expressed.

Recall that from the scatter plot shown in Figure A.2 we concluded that there was a positive relationship between scores on the midterm and scores on the final exam. The relationship was far from perfect, however. Thus, we should expect from an inspection of the scatter plot that the correlation coefficient should be greater than .00 but less than $+1.00$. As we shall see, the correlation between the midterm and final scores is .74. This value reflects a relatively strong but less-than-perfect relationship between these two sets of scores.

Table A.8
Example of EXCEL spreadsheet with midterm and final test scores with basic statistics

Student	Midterm	Final		
A	78	85		
B	67	71		
C	88	78		
D	74	71		
E	97	91		
F	84	88		
G	57	76		
H	65	68		
I	81	94		
J	58	67		
K	70	72		
L	81	87		
M	65	80		
N	92	93		
O	53	69		
P	65	75		
Q	83	76		
R	79	74		
S	45	63		
T	95	80		
U	62	58		
V	74	80		
W	85	96		
X	76	81		
Sum	1,774	1,873	Correlation =	0.744
Average	73.917	78.042	Regression	
Maximum	97	96	Slope =	0.552
Minimum	45	58	Intercept =	37.239
Range	52	38		
Variance	183.210	100.824		
SD	13.536	10.041		

Just as there are several measures of central tendency and several measures of variability, there are several different measures of relationship expressed as correlation coefficients. We shall consider only one of these, the product-moment correlation coefficient. This is by far the most commonly used and most useful correlation coefficient. It is the one that is most likely to be reported in test manuals and research studies. Indeed, if it is not specified otherwise when a correlation coefficient is reported, it is ordinarily assumed to be a product-moment correlation. The product-moment correlation coefficient is indicated by the symbol r.

As was true of a standard deviation, computation of a product-moment correlation coefficient is best done by a calculator or computer. Fortunately, much of the work for our example of 24 students with scores on a midterm and a final exam has already been done in Table A.7 because many of the intermediate values needed to compute the standard deviations of the two sets of scores are also used to compute the correlation coefficient. The following steps are involved in computing the correlation coefficient, r_n:

1. Begin by writing the pairs of scores to be studied in two columns, as was done in the columns labeled X and Y in Table A.7. Make certain that the pair of scores for each student is in the same row.
2. Square each of the entries in the X column and enter the result in the X^2 column, as was done to compute a standard deviation.
3. Square each of the entries in the Y column and enter the result in the Y^2 column.
4. In each row, multiply the entry in the X column by the entry in the Y column and enter the result in the XY column (see the right-hand column of Table A.7).
5. Sum the entries in each column and note the number (N) of pairs of scores. From Table A.7, then,

$$\Sigma X = 1{,}774$$
$$\Sigma X^2 = 135{,}342$$
$$N = 24$$
$$\Sigma Y = 1{,}873$$
$$\Sigma Y^2 = 148{,}491.$$
$$\Sigma XY = 140{,}772.$$

6. Substitute the obtained values in the formula:

$$r = \frac{[\Sigma XY - (\Sigma X)(\Sigma Y)/N]}{\sqrt{[\Sigma X^2 - (\Sigma X)(\Sigma X)/N][\Sigma Y^2 - (\Sigma Y)(\Sigma Y)/M}}$$

This formula looks complex, but it requires only simple arithmetic. For the scores in Table A.7, the most tedious part of the calculations has already been done. All that remains is to substitute numerical values for the appropriate symbols in the previous formula for r and do the arithmetic operations. The substitutions and intermediate steps are illustrated by the following:

The numerator for r is

$$\begin{aligned}[\Sigma XY - \Sigma(X)(\Sigma Y)/N] &= 140{,}772 - (1{,}774)(1{,}873)/24 \\ &= 140{,}772 - 3{,}322{,}702/24 \\ &= 140{,}772 - 138{,}445.9167 \\ &= 2{,}326.0833\end{aligned}$$

The part of the denominator involving X already has been used as part of the calculation of the standard deviation. It is

$$[\Sigma X^2 - \Sigma X)(\Sigma X)/N] = 135{,}342 - (1{,}774)(1{,}774)/24$$
$$= 135{,}342 - 3{,}147{,}076/24$$
$$= 135{,}342 - 131{,}125.1667$$
$$= 4{,}213.833$$

The part of the denominator involving Y is

$$[\Sigma Y^2 - (\Sigma Y)(\Sigma Y)/N] = 148{,}491 - (1{,}873)(1{,}873)/24$$
$$= 148{,}491 - 3{,}508{,}129/24$$
$$= 148{,}491 - 146{,}172.0417$$
$$= 2{,}318.9583$$

Putting these three parts together in the formula for r, we have

$$r = \frac{2{,}326.0833}{\sqrt{(4{,}213.8333)(2{,}318.9583)}}$$
$$r = .74$$

Although it is not readily apparent from the preceding formula, the computations involve most of the steps needed to find the mean and the standard deviation of each set of scores (X and Y). Thus, the formula also can be written as

$$r = \left(\frac{\frac{\Sigma XY}{n} - \overline{XY}}{(SD_X)(SD_Y)}\right)\left(\frac{N}{N-1}\right)$$

where

$\overline{X}$ = mean of scores in X column
$\overline{Y}$ = mean of scores in Y column
SD_x = standard deviation of scores in X column
SD_y = standard deviation of scores in Y column

Thus, for the same data,

$$r = \left(\frac{5{,}865.5 - (73.92)(78.04)}{(13.54)(10.04)}\right)\left(\frac{24}{23}\right)$$
$$r = .74$$

If the means and standard deviations are already available for the two sets of scores, then this latter formula will be easier to apply. If they are not available, the first formula can be used, and the means and standard deviations of the two sets of scores can also be computed during the process, if needed.

As was already stated, it is obviously much easier to compute a correlation with the help of a calculator with statistical functions or with a computer. The command to compute the correlation as well as the regression equation is equally simple. The correlation that is shown as .744 in cell E26 of the EXCEL spreadsheet displayed in Table A.8 was obtained by entering "=CORREL(B2:B25,C2:C25)" in cell E26, which tells the spreadsheet to correlate the midterm scores in cells B2 through B25 with the corresponding final scores in cells C2 through C25.

LINEAR REGRESSION COEFFICIENTS

Correlation coefficients provide an indication of the strength of relationship between two sets of scores. In many situations, however, we are interested in using one set of scores to predict the scores that would be obtained on another measure. For example, we might want to predict the grades that students will obtain from their test scores. Or we might want to predict scores on an achievement test from scores obtained on an aptitude test. In the example used in this appendix, we can show how linear regression is used to make such predictions.

The linear regression equation for predicting Y (the final) from X (the midterm) is

$$\hat{Y} = a + bX$$

where a and b are the regression coefficients. The caret (^) over the Y indicates that it is the predicted Y score rather than the one that is actually achieved. The coefficient b is known as the slope, and the coefficient a is known as the intercept. They can be computed using the following formulas:

$$b = \frac{r\,(SD_Y)}{SD_X}$$

and

$$a = \bar{Y} - b\,(\bar{X})$$

where

r is the correlation coefficient
SD_X and SD_Y are the standard deviations of X and Y
$\bar{X}$ and $\bar{Y}$ are the means of X and Y, respectively

For the midterm and final scores, the coefficients are

$$b = \frac{(.7441)(10.0411)}{13.5355} = .5520$$

and

$$a = 78.0417 - (.5520)(73.9167) = 37.24$$

Hence, the predicted scores on the final from scores on the midterm are given by the following equation.

$$\hat{Y} = 37.24 + .552(X)$$

Using this formula for Students A, B, and C, who had midterm scores of 78, 67, and 88, respectively, yields the following predicted scores on the final:

Student A: $\hat{Y} = 37.24 + .552(78) = 80.3$
Student B: $\hat{Y} = 37.24 + .552(67) = 74.2$
Student C: $\hat{Y} = 37.24 + .552(88) = 85.8$

The actual final exam scores for Students A, B, and C are 85, 71, and 78, respectively. Thus, Student A did somewhat better on the final than predicted, whereas Students B and C did somewhat worse than predicted. The difference between the actual Y scores and the predicted ones is known as the error of prediction. The errors of prediction get smaller in comparison to the standard deviation of *Y* as the correlation increases. Thus, the higher the correlation, the more accurate the prediction will be.

Of course, if we already know the scores on *Y*, there is no need to predict them, other than to see who did better or worse than would have been predicted from previous performance. A more common use of the regression equation for making predictions occurs when the equation that is obtained for one group of students (e.g., the freshman class of 1995) is used to predict the performance of another group (e.g., the applicants for freshman class of 1996). For example, we could use the regression of freshman grades on test scores obtained for the 1995 freshman class to predict the grade that 1996 applicants would obtain if they are admitted.

The regression coefficients are also shown in the EXCEL spreadsheet displayed in Table A.8. The slope, which appears in cell E28, was obtained by entering "=SLOPE(C2:C25, B2:B25)" in that cell, and the intercept was obtained by entering "=INTERCEPT(C2:C25, B2:B25)" in cell E29.

A FINAL CAUTION

Correlation indicates the degree of relationship between two sets of scores but not causation. If *X* and *Y* are related, there are several possible explanations: *X* may cause *Y*, *Y* may cause *X*, or *X* and *Y* may be the result of a common cause. For example, the increase in incidence of juvenile delinquency during the past decade has been paralleled by a corresponding increase in teachers' salaries. Thus, the correlation between these two sets of figures would probably be quite high. Obviously, further study is needed to determine the cause of any particular relationship.

REFERENCES

Coladarci, A., & Coladarci, T. (1979). *Elementary descriptive statistics: For those who think they can't.* Belmont, CA: Wadsworth. A witty and precise introduction to the basic concepts and procedures in elementary statistics.

Downie, N. M., & Health, R. W. (1984). *Basic statistical methods* (5th ed.). New York: Harper & Row. An introductory textbook designed for nonmathematics majors.

Glass, G. V., & Hopkins, K. D. (1996). *Statistical methods in education and psychology* (3rd ed.). Needham Heights, MA: Allyn & Bacon. Provides a comprehensive and rigorous discussion of the descriptive statistics discussed in this appendix as well as broad coverage of inferential statistics.

Hopkins, K. D., Glass, G. V., & Hopkins, B. R. (1987). *Basic statistics for the behavioral sciences* (2nd ed.). Upper Saddle River, NJ: Prentice Hall. Provides an introduction to statistics with a good discussion of interpretations of correlation coefficients and factors that influence them.

Jaeger, R. (1990). *Statistics: A spectacular sport* (2nd ed.). Newbury Park, CA: Sage Publications. Explains what statistics are, what they mean, and how they are used and interpreted. Emphasizes understanding rather than computation.

Townsend, E. A., & Burke, P. J. (1975). *Using statistics in classroom instruction.* New York: Macmillan. Offers step-by-step directions and practice in using simple descriptive statistics with test scores.

PROFESSIONAL JOURNALS FOR LOCATING MEASUREMENT AND ASSESSMENT ARTICLES

Articles on educational and psychological measurement and assessment appear in many different types of professional journals. List A includes those journals that focus most directly on measurement and assessment articles. List B contains journals that sometimes have relevant articles. List C contains selected on-line newsletters, publications, and reports dealing with testing and assessment issues.

List A
Applied Measurement in Education

Applied Psychological Measurement

Educational Assessment

Educational Measurement: Issues and Practice

Educational and Psychological Measurement

Journal of Educational Measurement

Journal of Personality Assessment

Measurement and Evaluation in Counseling and Development

List B
American Educational Research Journal

Educational Leadership

Educational Researcher

Journal of Applied Psychology

Journal of Counseling Psychology

Journal of Educational Psychology

Journal of School Psychology

Journal of Special Education

Psychology in the Schools

Phi Delta Kappan

Review of Educational Research

List C

Educational Policy Analysis Archives—http://olam.ed.asu.edu/epaa

ERIC Clearinghouse on Assessment and Evaluation—http://ericae.net

The Evaluation Exchange—http://www.gse.harvard.edu/hfrp/eval.html

CRESST—http://www.ces.ucla.edu/

CONTENT STANDARDS

For an overview of content standards in various subjects, see

Kendall, J. S., & Marzano, R. J. (1997). *A compendium of standards and benchmarks for K–12 education* (2nd ed.). Available at the McREL Web site: http://www.mcrel.org/standards-benchmarks.

References to selected content standards described in greater detail by Kendall and Marzano (1997) are listed below followed by a listing of the Web sites of subject area professional associations supporting content standards.

REFERENCES

Consortium of National Arts Education Associations. (1994). *National standards for arts education: What every young American should know and be able to do in the arts.* Reston, VA: Music Educators National Conference.

Economics America: National Council on Economic Education. (1997). *Voluntary national content standards. In virtual economics version 2.0 [CD-ROM].* New York: Author.

Geography Education Standards Project. (1994). *Geography for life: National geography standards.* Washington, DC: National Geographic Research and Exploration.

Joint Commitee on National Health Education Standards. (1995). *National health education standards: Achieving health literacy.* Reston, VA: Association for the Advancement of Health Education.

National Association for Sport and Physical Education. (1995). *Moving into the future, national standards for physical education: A guide to content and assessment.* St. Louis: Mosby.

National Business Education Association. (1995). *National standards for business education: What America's students should know and be able to do in business.* Reston, VA: Author.

National Center for History in the Schools. (1996). *National standards for history* (Basic ed.). Los Angeles: Author.

National Council for the Social Studies. (1994). *Expectations of excellence: Curriculum standards for social studies.* Washington, DC: Author.

National Council of Teachers of English and the International Reading Association. (1995, October). *Standards for the English language arts* (draft). Urbana, IL: National Council of Teachers of English.

National Council of Teachers of Mathematics. (1989). *Curriculum and evaluation standards for school mathematics.* Reston, VA: Author.

National Research Council. (1996). *National science education standards.* Washington, DC: National Academy Press.

National Standards in Foreign Language Education. (1995, April). *Standards for foreign language learning: Preparing for the 21st century* (draft). Yonkers, NY: Author.

National Standards in Foreign Language Education Project. (1996). *Standards for foreign language learning: Preparing for the 21st century*. Lawrence, KS: Author.

New Standards. (1997a). *Performance standards: English language arts, mathematics, science, applied learning: Vol. 1. Elementary school*. Washington, DC: National Center on Education and the Economy.

New Standards. (1997b). *Performance standards: English language arts, mathematics, science, applied learning: Vol. 2. Middle school*. Washington, DC: National Center on Education and the Economy.

New Standards. (1997c). *Performance standards: English language arts, mathematics, science, applied learning: Vol. 3. High school*. Washington, DC: National Center on Education and the Economy.

Project 2061, American Association for the Advancement of Science. (1993). *Benchmarks for science literacy*. New York: Oxford University Press.

Secretary's Commission on Achieving Necessary Skills. (1991). *What work requires of schools: A SCANS report for America 2000*. Washington, DC: U.S. Department of Labor.

Speech Communication Association. (1996). *Speaking, listening, and media literacy standards for K through 12 education*. Annandale, VA: Author.

Web Sites for Professional Subject-Area Associations with Materials Related to Content Standards

CONTENT AREA	WEBSITE ADDRESS
The Arts	http://www.menc.org
Civics and Government	http://www.civiced.org
Economics	http://www.nationalcouncil.org
Foreign Language	http://www.actfl.org
Health Education	http://www.aahperd.org/index.cfm
History	http://www.sscnet.ucla.edu/nchs
Language Arts	http://www.reading.org
Mathematics	http://www.nctm.org
Physical Education	http://www.aahperd.org/index.cfm
Science	http://www.nap.edu/readingroom/books/nses
Social Studies	http://www.ncss.org
Technology Education	http://www.iteaconnect.org
Vocational Education	http://vocserve.berkeley.edu

STANDARDS FOR TEACHER COMPETENCE IN EDUCATIONAL ASSESSMENT OF STUDENTS

The professional education associations began working in 1987 to develop standards for teacher competence in student assessment out of concern that the potential educational benefits of student assessments be fully realized. The Committee* appointed to this project completed its work in 1990 following reviews of earlier drafts by members of the measurement, teaching, and teacher preparation and certification communities. Parallel committees of affected associations are encouraged to develop similar statements of qualifications for school administrators, counselors, testing directors, supervisors, and other educators. These statements are intended to guide the preservice and in-service preparation of educators, the accreditation of preparation programs, and the future certification of all educators.

A standard is defined here as a principle generally accepted by the professional associations responsible for this document. Assessment is defined as the process of obtaining information that is used to make educational decisions about students, to give feedback to the student about his or her progress, strengths, and weaknesses, to judge instructional effectiveness and curricular adequacy, and to inform policy. The various assessment techniques include, but are not limited to, formal and informal observation, qualitative analysis of pupil performance and products, paper-and-pencil tests, oral questioning, and analysis of student records. The assessment competencies included here are the knowledge and skills critical to a teacher's role as educator. It is understood that there are many competencies beyond assessment competencies which teachers must possess.

*The Committee that developed this statement was appointed by the collaborating professional associations: James R. Sanders (Western Michigan University) chaired the Committee and represented NCME along with John R. Hills (Florida State University) and Anthony J. Nitko (University of Pittsburgh). Jack C. Merwin (University of Minnesota) represented the American Association of Colleges for Teacher Education, Carolyn Trice represented the American Federation of Teachers, and Marcella Dianda and Jeffrey Schneider represented the National Education Association.

Developed by the American Federation of Teachers, National Council on Measurement in Education, National Education Association.

By establishing standards for teacher competence in student assessment, the associations subscribe to the view that student assessment is an essential part of teaching and that good teaching cannot exist without good student assessment. Training to develop the competencies covered in the standards should be an integral part of preservice preparation. Further, such assessment training should be widely available to practicing teachers through staff development programs at the district and building levels.

The standards are intended for use as:

- a guide for teacher educators as they design and approve programs for teacher preparation,
- a self-assessment guide for teachers in identifying their needs for professional development in student assessment,
- a guide for workshop instructors as they design professional development experiences for inservice teachers,
- an impetus for educational measurement specialists and teacher trainers to conceptualize student assessment, and
- teacher training in student assessment more broadly than has been the case in the past.

The standards should be incorporated into future teacher training and certification programs. Teachers who have not had the preparation these standards imply should have the opportunity and support to develop these competencies before the standards enter into the evaluation of these teachers.

The Approach Used to Develop the Standards

The members of the associations that supported this work are professional educators involved in teaching, teacher education, and student assessment. Members of these associations are concerned about the inadequacy with which teachers are prepared for assessing the educational progress of their students, and thus sought to address this concern effectively. A committee named by the associations first met in September 1987 and affirmed its commitment to defining standards for teacher preparation in student assessment. The Committee then undertook a review of the research literature to identify needs in student assessment, current levels of teacher training in student assessment, areas of teacher activities requiring competence in using assessments, and current levels of teacher competence in student assessment.

The members of the Committee used their collective experience and expertise to formulate and then revise statements of important assessment competencies. Drafts of these competencies went through several revisions by the Committee before the standards were released for public review. Comments by reviewers from each of the associations were then used to prepare a final statement.

The Scope of a Teacher's Professional Role and Responsibilities for Student Assessment

There are seven standards in this document. In recognizing the critical need to revitalize classroom assessment, some standards focus on classroom-based competencies. Because of teachers' growing roles in education and policy decisions beyond the classroom, other standards address assessment competencies underlying teacher participation in decisions related to assessment at the school, district, state, and national levels.

The scope of a teacher's professional role and responsibilities for student assessment may be described in terms of the following activities. These activities imply that teachers need competence in student assessment and sufficient time and resources to complete them in a professional manner.

Activities Occurring Prior to Instruction

    a. Understanding students' cultural backgrounds, interests, skills, and abilities as they apply across a range of learning domains and/or subject areas;

    b. understanding students' motivations and their interests in specific class content;

    c. clarifying and articulating the performance outcomes expected of pupils; and

    d. planning instruction for individuals or groups of students.

Activities Occurring During Instruction

    a. Monitoring pupil progress toward instructional goals;

    b. identifying gains and difficulties pupils are experiencing in learning and performing;

    c. adjusting instruction;

    d. giving contingent, specific, and credible praise and feedback;

    e. motivating students to learn; and

    f. judging the extent of pupil attainment of instructional outcomes.

Activities Occurring After the Appropriate Instructional Segment (e.g., lesson, class, semester, grade)

    a. Describing the extent to which each pupil has attained both short- and long-term instructional goals;

    b. communicating strengths and weaknesses based on assessment results to students, and parents or guardians;

    c. recording and reporting assessment results for school-level analysis, evaluation, and decision making;

    d. analyzing assessment information gathered before and during instruction to understand each student's progress to date and to inform future instructional planning;

    e. evaluating the effectiveness of instruction; and

    f. evaluating the effectiveness of the curriculum and materials in use.

Activities Associated with a Teacher's Involvement in School Building and School District Decision Making

    a. Serving on a school or district committee examining the school's and district's strengths and weaknesses in the development of its students;

    b. working on the development or selection of assessment methods for school building or school district use;

    c. evaluating school district curriculum; and

    d. other related activities.

Activities Associated with a Teacher's Involvement in a Wider Community of Educators

    a. Serving on a state committee asked to develop learning goals and associated assessment methods;

    b. participating in reviews of the appropriateness of district, state, or national student goals and associated assessment methods; and

    c. interpreting the results of state and national student assessment programs.

Each standard that follows is an expectation for assessment knowledge or skill that a teacher should possess in order to perform well in the five areas just described. As a set, the standards call on teachers to demonstrate skill at selecting, developing, applying, using, communicating, and evaluating student assessment information and student assessment practices. A brief rationale and illustrative behaviors follow each standard.

The standards represent a conceptual framework or scaffolding from which specific skills can be derived. Work to make these standards operational will be needed even after they have been published. It is also expected that experience in the application of these standards should lead to their improvement and further development.

Standards for Teacher Competence in Educational Assessment of Students

1. Teachers should be skilled in choosing assessment methods appropriate for instructional decisions. Skills in choosing appropriate, useful, administratively convenient, technically adequate, and fair assessment methods are prerequisite to good use of information to support instructional decisions. Teachers need to be well acquainted with the kinds of information provided by a broad range of assessment alternatives and their strengths and weaknesses. In particular, they should be familiar with criteria for evaluating and selecting assessment methods in light of instructional plans.

Teachers who meet this standard will have the conceptual and application skills that follow. They will be able to use the concepts of assessment error and validity when developing or selecting their approaches to classroom assessment of students. They will understand how valid assessment data can support instructional activities such as providing appropriate feedback to students, diagnosing group and individual learning needs, planning for individualized educational programs, motivating students, and evaluating instructional procedures. They will understand how invalid information can affect instructional decisions about students. They will also be able to use and evaluate assessment options available to them, considering, among other things, the cultural, social, economic, and language backgrounds of students. They will be aware that different assessment approaches can be incompatible with certain instructional goals and may impact quite differently on their teaching.

Teachers will know, for each assessment approach they use, its appropriateness for making decisions about their pupils. Moreover, teachers will know where to find information about and/or reviews of various assessment methods. Assessment options are diverse and include text- and curriculum-embedded questions and tests, standardized criterion-referenced and norm-referenced tests, oral questioning, spontaneous and structured performance assessments, portfolios, exhibitions, demonstrations, rating scales, writing samples, paper-and-pencil tests, seatwork and homework, peer- and self-assessments, student records, observations, questionnaires, interviews, projects, products, and others' opinions.

2. Teachers should be skilled in developing assessment methods appropriate for instructional decisions. While teachers often use published or other external assessment tools, the bulk of the assessment information they use for decision making comes from approaches they create and implement. Indeed, the assessment demands of the classroom go well beyond readily available instruments.

Teachers who meet this standard will have the conceptual and application skills that follow. Teachers will be skilled in planning the collection of information that facilitates the decisions they will make. They will know and follow appropriate principles for developing and using assessment methods in their teaching, avoiding common pitfalls in student assessment. Such techniques may include several of the options listed at the end of the first standard. The teacher will select the techniques which are appropriate to the intent of the teacher's instruction.

Teachers meeting this standard will also be skilled in using student data to analyze the quality of each assessment technique they use. Since most teachers do not have access to assessment specialists, they must be prepared to do these analyses themselves.

3. The teacher should be skilled in administering, scoring, and interpreting the results of both externally produced and teacher-produced assessment methods. It is not enough that teachers are able to select and develop good assessment methods; they must also be able to apply them properly. Teachers should be skilled in administering, scoring, and interpreting results from diverse assessment methods.

Teachers who meet this standard will have the conceptual and application skills that follow. They will be skilled in interpreting informal and formal teacher-produced assessment results, including pupils' performances in class and on homework assignments. Teachers will be able to use guides for scoring essay questions and projects, stencils for scoring response-choice questions, and scales for rating performance assessments. They will be able to use these in ways that produce consistent results.

Teachers will be able to administer standardized achievement tests and be able to interpret the commonly reported scores: percentile ranks, percentile band scores, standard scores, and grade equivalents. They will have a conceptual understanding of the summary indexes commonly reported with assessment results: measures of central tendency, dispersion, relationships, reliability, and errors of measurement.

Teachers will be able to apply these concepts of score and summary indices in ways that enhance their use of the assessments that they develop. They will be able to analyze assessment results to identify pupils' strengths and errors. If they get inconsistent results, they will seek other explanations for the discrepancy or other data to attempt to resolve the uncertainty before arriving at a decision. They will be able to use assessment methods in ways that encourage students' educational development and that do not inappropriately increase students' anxiety levels.

4. Teachers should be skilled in using assessment results when making decisions about individual students, planning teaching, developing curriculum, and school improvement. Assessment results are used to make educational decisions at several levels: in the classroom about students, in the community about a school and a school district, and in society, generally, about the purposes and outcomes of the educational enterprise. Teachers play a vital role when participating in decision making at each of these levels and must be able to use assessment results effectively.

Teachers who meet this standard will have the conceptual and application skills that follow. They will be able to use accumulated assessment information to organize a sound instructional plan for facilitating students' educational development. When using assessment results to plan and/or evaluate instruction and curriculum, teachers will interpret the results correctly and avoid common misinterpretations, such as basing decisions on scores that lack curriculum validity. They will be informed about the results of local, regional, state, and national assessments and about their appropriate use for pupil, classroom, school, district, state, and national educational improvement.

5. Teachers should be skilled in developing valid pupil grading procedures which use pupil assessments. Grading students is an important part of professional practice for teachers. Grading is defined as indicating both a student's level of performance and a teacher's valuing of that performance. The principles for using assessments to obtain valid grades are known and teachers should employ them.

Teachers who meet this standard will have the conceptual and application skills that follow. They will be able to devise, implement, and explain a procedure for developing grades composed of marks from various assignments, projects, in-class activities, quizzes, tests, and/or other assessments that they may use. Teachers will understand and be able to articulate why the grades they assign are rational, justified, and fair, acknowledging that such grades reflect their preferences and judgments. Teachers will be able to recognize and to avoid faulty grading procedures such as using grades as punishment. They will be able to evaluate and to modify their grading procedures in order to improve the validity of the interpretations made from them about students' attainments.

6. Teachers should be skilled in communicating assessment results to students, parents, other lay audiences, and other educators. Teachers must routinely report assessment results to students and to parents or guardians. In addition, they are frequently asked to report or to discuss assessment results with other educators and with diverse lay audiences. If the results are not communicated effectively, they may be misused or not used. To communicate effectively with others on matters of student assessment, teachers must be able to use assessment terminology appropriately and must be able to articulate the meaning, limitations, and implications of assessment results. Furthermore, teachers will sometimes be in a position that will require them to defend their own assessment procedures and their interpretations of them. At other times, teachers may need to help the public to interpret assessment results appropriately.

Teachers who meet this standard will have the conceptual and application skills that follow. Teachers will understand and be able to give appropriate explanations of how the interpretation of student assessments must be moderated by the student's socioeconomic, cultural, language, and other background factors. Teachers will be able to explain that assessment results do not imply that such background factors limit a student's ultimate educational development. They will be able to communicate to students and to their parents or guardians how they may assess the student's educational progress. Teachers will understand and be able to explain the importance of taking measurement errors into account when using assessments to make decisions about individual students. Teachers will be able to explain the limitations of different informal and formal assessment methods. They will be able to explain printed reports of the results of pupil assessments at the classroom, school district, state, and national levels.

7. Teachers should be skilled in recognizing unethical, illegal, and otherwise inappropriate assessment methods and uses of assessment information. Fairness, the rights of all concerned, and professional ethical behavior must undergird all student assessment activities, from the initial planning for and gathering of information to the interpretation, use, and communication of the results. Teachers must be well versed in their own ethical and legal responsibilities in assessment. In addition, they should also attempt to have the inappropriate assessment practices of others discontinued whenever they are encountered. Teachers should also participate with the wider educational community in defining the limits of appropriate professional behavior in assessment.

Teachers who meet this standard will have the conceptual and application skills that follow. They will know those laws and case decisions which affect their classroom, school district, and state assessment practices. Teachers will be aware that various assessment procedures can be misused or overused, resulting in harmful consequences such as embarrassing students, violating a student's right to confidentiality, and inappropriately using students' standardized achievement test scores to measure teaching effectiveness.

Invitation to Users

The associations invite comments from users to improve this document. Comments may be sent to:

Teacher Standards in Student Assessment
American Federation of Teachers
555 New Jersey Avenue, NW
Washington, DC 20001

Teacher Standards in Student Assessment
National Council on Measurement in Education
1230 Seventeenth Street, NW
Washington, DC 20036

Teacher Standards in Student Assessment
Instruction and Professional Development
National Education Association
1201 Sixteenth Street, NW
Washington, DC 20036

This is not copyrighted material. Reproduction and dissemination are encouraged.

TEST PUBLISHERS

The following is a list of the test publishers and distributors whose tests are mentioned in this book (the tests are listed in Appendix F, with the publisher's number that appears here in boldface). All will provide catalogs of their current tests.

The names and addresses of other test publishers and distributors can be obtained from the latest volume of the *Mental Measurements Yearbook*.

1. American Guidance Service, Inc.
   4201 Woodland Rd.
   Circle Pines, MN 55014
2. C.P.S., Inc.
   P.O. Box 83
   Larchmont, NY 10538
3. CTB/McGraw-Hill
   20 Ryan Ranch Rd.
   Monterey, CA 93940-5703
4. Consulting Psychologists Press, Inc.
   3803 E. Bayshore Rd.
   Palo Alto, CA 94303
5. Educational Testing Service
   Princeton, NJ 08540
6. Harcourt Brace Educational
   Measurement
   555 Academic Court
   San Antonio, TX 78204-2498
7. Institute for Personality and Ability
   Testing
   P.O. Box 188
   Champaign, IL 61820

8. Psychological Assessment
   Resources (PAR)
   P.O. Box 998
   Odessa, FL 33556
9. PRO-ED
   8700 Shoal Creek Blvd.
   Austin, TX 78757
10. Riverside Publishing Co.
    425 Spring Lake Drive
    Itasca, IL 60143-2079
11. Scholastic Testing Service
    480 Meyer Road
    Bensenville, IL 60106
12. Science Research Associates
    155 N. Wacker Drive
    Chicago, IL 60606

SELECTED PUBLISHED TESTS

TEST NAME (PUBLISHER'S NO.)[1]	GRADE LEVEL COVERED[2]
Achievement Batteries	
California Achievement Tests (3)	K–12
Iowa Tests of Basic Skills (11)	K–9
Iowa Tests of Educational Development (11)	9–12
Metropolitan Achievement Tests (6)	K–12
Stanford Achievement Tests (6)	1–12
TerraNova [Comprehensive Tests of Basic Skills] (3)	K–12
The 3-Rs Test (11)	K–12
Diagnostic Tests	
California Diagnostic Mathematics Tests (3)	1–12
California Diagnostic Reading Tests (3)	1–12
Metropolitan Achievement Tests	
Language Diagnostic Tests (6)	1–9.9
Mathematics Diagnostic Tests (6)	1–9.9
Reading Diagnostic Tests (6)	K.5–9.9
Stanford Diagnostic Mathematics Test (6)	1.5–12
Stanford Diagnostic Reading Test (6)	1.5–12
Individual Achievement Tests	
Basic Achievement Skills Individual Screener (6)	1–A
Peabody Individual Achievement Test—R (1)	K–A
KeyMath Diagnostic Arithmetic Test—R (1)	P–6
Woodcock Reading Mastery Test—R (1)	K–A

[1]The publisher's number in parentheses refers to the list in Appendix E.
[2]Gives total span only, not the number of separate levels available (P = preschool, K = kindergarten, A = adult).

Criterion-Referenced Tests

DMI Mathematics System (3)	K–8.9
National Proficiency Survey Series (11)	8–12
PRI Reading Systems (3)	K–9

Reading Tests

Gates–McGinitie Reading Tests (11)	K–12
Iowa Silent Reading Tests (6)	6–14
Nelson Reading Skills Test (11)	3–9
Nelson–Denny Reading Test (11)	9–16, A

(See also Achievement Batteries and Diagnostic Tests)

Learning Ability Tests

Cognitive Abilities Test (11)	K–12
Culture-Fair Intelligence Test (6)	4–16, A
Henmon–Nelson Tests of Mental Ability (11)	K–12
Otis–Lennon School Ability Test (6)	K–12
School and College Ability Tests, SCAT (3)	3.5–12.9
Tests of Cognitive Skills (3)	2–12

Multiaptitude Batteries

Armed Services Vocational Aptitude Test (Dept. of Defense)	10–12, A
Differential Aptitude Tests (6)	8–13, A
General Aptitude Test Battery (U.S. Employment Service)	A

Readiness Tests

Boehm Test of Basic Concepts (6)	K–2
Cooperative Preschool Inventory (3)	P–K
Metropolitan Readiness Test (6)	K–1
Stanford Early School Achievement Test (6)	K–1
Tests of Basic Experience (3)	P–1

Attitude Scales

Estes Attitude Scales (8)	3–12
School Interest Inventory (11)	7–12
Survey of School Attitudes (6)	1–8

Interest Inventories

Holland Self-Directed Search	10–A
Kuder General Interest Survey (13)	6–12
Kuder Occupational Interest Survey (13)	10–A
Strong–Campbell Interest Inventory (6)	11–A

TAXONOMY OF EDUCATIONAL OBJECTIVES

Table G.1
Major categories in the cognitive domain of the taxonomy of educational objectives (Bloom, 1956)

Descriptions of the Major Categories in the Cognitive Domain

1. **Knowledge**. Knowledge is defined as the remembering of previously learned material. This may involve the recall of a wide range of material, from specific facts to complete theories, but all that is required is the bringing to mind of the appropriate information. Knowledge represents the lowest level of learning outcomes in the cognitive domain.

2. **Comprehension**. Comprehension is defined as the ability to grasp the meaning of material. This may be shown by translating material from one form to another (words or numbers), by interpreting material (explaining or summarizing), and by estimating future trends (predicting consequences or effects). These learning outcomes go one step beyond the simple remembering of material and represent the lowest level of understanding.

3. **Application**. Application refers to the ability to use learned material in new and concrete situations. This may include the application of such things as rules, methods, concepts, principles, laws, and theories. Learning outcomes in this area require a higher level of understanding than those under comprehension.

4. **Analysis**. Analysis refers to the ability to break down material into its component parts so that its organizational structure may be understood. This may include the identification of the parts, analysis of the relationships between parts, and recognition of the organizational principles involved. Learning outcomes here represent a higher intellectual level than comprehension and application because they require an understanding of both the content and the structural form of the material.

5. **Synthesis**. Synthesis refers to the ability to put parts together to form a new whole. This may involve the production of a unique communication (theme or speech), a plan of operations (research proposal), or a set of abstract relations (scheme for classifying information). Learning outcomes in this area stress creative behaviors, with major emphasis on the formulation of *new* patterns or structures.

6. **Evaluation**. Evaluation is concerned with the ability to judge the value of material (statement, novel, poem, research report) for a given purpose. The judgments are to be based on definite criteria. These may be internal criteria (organization) or external criteria (relevance to the purpose) and the student may determine the criteria or be given them. Learning outcomes in this area are highest in the cognitive hierarchy because they contain elements of all of the other categories plus value judgments based on clearly defined criteria.

Table G.2

Examples of general instructional objectives and clarifying verbs for the cognitive domain of the taxonomy

Illustrative General Instructional Objectives	Illustrative Verbs for Stating Specific Learning Outcomes
Knows common terms Knows specific facts Knows methods and procedures Knows basic concepts Knows principles	Defines, describes, identifies, labels, lists, matches, names, outlines, reproduces, selects, states
Understands facts and principles Interprets verbal material Interprets charts and graphs Translates verbal material to mathematical formulas Estimates consequences implied in data Justifies methods and procedures	Converts, defends, distinguishes, estimates, explains, extends, generalizes, gives examples, infers, paraphrases, predicts, rewrites, summarizes
Applies principles to new situations Applies theories to practical situations Solves mathematical problems Constructs charts and graphs Demonstrates correct usage of a procedure	Changes, computes, demonstrates, discovers, manipulates, modifies, operates, predicts, prepares, produces, relates, shows, solves, uses
Recognizes unstated assumptions Recognizes logical fallacies in reasoning Distinguishes between facts and inferences Evaluates the relevancy of data Analyzes the organizational structure of a work (art, music, writing)	Breaks down, diagrams, differentiates, discriminates, distinguishes, identifies, illustrates, infers, outlines, points out, relates, selects, separates, subdivides
Writes a well-organized theme Gives a well-organized speech Writes a creative short story (or poem) Proposes a plan for an experiment Integrates learning from different areas into a plan for solving a problem Formulates a new scheme for classifying objects (or events or ideas)	Categorizes, combines, compiles, composes, creates, devises, designs, explains, generates, modifies, organizes, plans, rearranges, reconstructs, relates, reorganizes, revises, rewrites, summarizes, tells, writes
Judges the consistency of written material Judges the adequacy with which conclusions are supported by data Judges the value of a work (art, music, writing) by use of internal criteria Judges the value of a work (art, music, writing) by use of external standards	Appraises, compares, concludes, contrasts, criticizes, describes, discriminates, explains, interprets, justifies, relates, summarizes, supports

Table G.3
Major categories in the affective domain of the taxonomy of educational objectives (Krathwohl et al., 1964)

Descriptions of the Major Categories in the Affective Domain

---

1. **Receiving**. Receiving refers to the student's willingness to attend to particular phenomena or stimuli (classroom activities, textbook, music, etc.). From a teaching standpoint, it is concerned with getting, holding, and directing the student's attention. Learning outcomes in this area range from the simple awareness that a thing exists to selective attention on the part of the learner. Receiving represents the lowest level of learning outcomes in the affective domain.

2. **Responding**. Responding refers to active participation on the part of the student. At this level he not only attends to a particular phenomenon but also reacts to it in some way. Learning outcomes in this area may emphasize acquiescence in responding (reads assigned material), willingness to respond (voluntarily reads beyond assignment), or satisfaction in responding (reads for pleasure or enjoyment). The higher levels of this category include those instructional objectives that are commonly classified under *interest;* that is, those that stress the seeking out and enjoyment of particular activities.

3. **Valuing**. Valuing is concerned with the worth or value a student attaches to a particular object, phenomenon, or behavior. This ranges in degree from the more simple acceptance of a value (desires to improve group skills) to the more complex level of commitment (assumes responsibility for the effective functioning of the group). Valuing is based on the internalization of a set of specified values, but clues to these values are expressed in the student's overt behavior. Learning outcomes in this area are concerned with behavior that is consistent and stable enough to make the value clearly identifiable. Instructional objectives that are commonly classified under *attitudes* and *appreciation* would fall into this category.

4. **Organization**. Organization is concerned with bringing together different values, resolving conflicts between them, and beginning the building of an internally consistent value system. Thus, the emphasis is on comparing, relating, and synthesizing values. Learning outcomes may be concerned with the conceptualization of a value (recognizes the responsibility of each individual for improving human relations) or with the organization of a value system (develops a vocational plan that satisfies his need for both economic security and social service). Instructional objectives relating to the development of a philosophy of life would fall into this category.

5. **Characterization by a Value or Value Complex**. At this level of the affective domain, the individual has a value system that has controlled his behavior for a sufficiently long time for him to have developed a characteristic *lifestyle*. Thus, the behavior is pervasive, consistent, and predictable. Learning outcomes at this level cover a broad range of activities, but the major emphasis is on the fact that the behavior is typical or characteristic of the student. Instructional objectives that are concerned with the student's general patterns of adjustment (personal, social, emotional) would be appropriate here.

Table G.4

Examples of general instructional objectives and clarifying verbs for the affective domain of the taxonomy

Illustrative General Instructional Objectives	Illustrative Verbs for Stating Specific Learning Outcomes
Listens attentively Shows awareness of the importance of learning Shows sensitivity to social problems Accepts differences of race and culture Attends closely to the classroom activities	Asks, chooses, describes, follows, gives, holds, identifies, locates, names, points to, selects, sits erect, replies, uses
Completes assigned homework Obeys school rules Participates in class discussion Completes laboratory work Volunteers for special tasks Shows interest in subject Enjoys helping others	Answers, assists, complies, conforms, discusses, greets, helps, labels, performs, practices, presents, reads, recites, reports, selects, tells, writes
Demonstrates belief in the democratic process Appreciates good literature (art or music) Appreciates the role of science (or other subjects) in everyday life Shows concern for the welfare of others Demonstrates problem-solving attitude Demonstrates commitment to social improvement	Completes, describes, differentiates, explains, follows, forms, initiates, invites, joins, justifies, proposes, reads, reports, selects, shares, studies, works
Recognizes the need for balance between freedom and responsibility in a democracy Recognizes the role of systematic planning in solving problems Accepts responsibility for own behavior and limitations Understands and accepts own strengths Formulates a life plan in harmony with his abilities, interests, and beliefs	Adheres, alters, arranges, combines, compares, completes, defends, explains, generalizes, identifies, integrates, modifies, orders, organizes, prepares, relates, synthesizes
Displays safety consciousness Demonstrates self-reliance in working independently Practices cooperation in group activities Uses objective approach in problem solving Demonstrates industry and self-discipline Maintains good health habits	Acts, discriminates, displays, influences, listens, modifies, performs, practices, proposes, qualifies, questions, revises, serves, solves, uses, verifies

Table G.5
A classification of educational objectives in the psychomotor domain (Simpson, 1972)

Description of the Major Categories in the Psychomotor Domain

1. **Perception**. The first level is concerned with the use of the sense organs to obtain cues that guide motor activity. This category ranges from sensory stimulation (awareness of a stimulus), through cue selection (selecting task-relevant cues), to translation (relating cue perception to action in a performance).

2. **Set**. Set refers to readiness to take a particular type of action. This category includes mental set (mental readiness to act), physical set (physical readiness to act), and emotional set (willingness to act). Perception of cues serves as an important prerequisite for this level.

3. **Guided Response**. Guided response is concerned with the early stages in learning a complex skill. It includes imitation (repeating an act demonstrated by the instructor) and trial and error (using a multiple-response approach to identify an appropriate response). Adequacy of performance is judged by an instructor or by a suitable set of criteria.

4. **Mechanism**. Mechanism is concerned with performance acts where the learned response has become habitual and the movements can be performed with some confidence and proficiency. Learning outcomes at this level are concerned with performance skills of various types, but the movement patterns are less complex than at the next higher level.

5. **Complex Overt Response**. Complex overt response is concerned with the skillful performance of motor acts that involve complex movement patterns. Proficiency is indicated by a quick, smooth, accurate performance, requiring a minimum of energy. This category includes resolution of uncertainty (performs without hesitation) and automatic performance (movements are made with ease and good muscle control). Learning outcomes at this level include highly coordinated motor activities.

6. **Adaptation**. Adaptation is concerned with skills that are so well developed that the individual can modify movement patterns to fit special requirements or to meet a problem situation.

7. **Origination**. Origination refers to the creating of new movement patterns to fit a particular situation or specific problem. Learning outcomes at this level emphasize creativity based upon highly developed skills.

Table G.6

Examples of general instructional objectives and clarifying verbs for the psychomotor domain

Illustrative General Instructional Objectives	*Illustrative Verbs for Stating Specific Learning Outcomes*
Recognizes malfunction by sound of machine Relates taste of food to need for seasoning Relates music to a particular dance step	Chooses, describes, detects, differentiates, distinguishes, identifies, isolates, relates, selects, separates
Knows sequence of steps in varnishing wood Demonstrates proper bodily stance for batting a ball Shows desire to type efficiently	Begins, displays, explains, moves, proceeds, reacts, responds, shows, starts, volunteers
Performs a golf swing as demonstrated Applies first aid bandage as demonstrated Determines best sequence for preparing a meal	Assembles, builds, calibrates, constructs, dismantles, displays, dissects, fastens, fixes, grinds, heats, manipulates, measures, mends, mixes, organizes, sketches
Writes smoothly and legibly Sets up laboratory equipment Operates a slide projector Demonstrates a simple dance step	(Same list as for Guided Response)
Operates a power saw skillfully Demonstrates correct form in swimming Demonstrates skill in driving an automobile Performs skillfully on the violin Repairs electronic equipment quickly and accurately	(Same list as for Guided Response)
Adjusts tennis play to counteract opponent's style Modifies swimming strokes to fit the roughness of the water	Adapts, alters, changes, rearranges, reorganizes, revises, varies
Creates a dance step Creates a musical composition Designs a new dress style	Arranges, combines, composes, constructs, creates, designs, originates

REFERENCES*

Bloom, B. S., et al. (Eds.). (1956). *Taxonomy of educational objectives: Handbook I, Cognitive domain.* New York: D. McKay. Describes the cognitive categories in detail and presents illustrative objectives and test items for each.

Harrow, A. J. (1972). *A taxonomy of the psychomotor domain.* New York: D. McKay. Provides a model for classifying learning outcomes in the psychomotor domain and presents illustrative objectives.

Krathwohl, D. R., et al. (Eds.). (1964). *Taxonomy of educational objectives: Handbook II, Affective Domain.* New York: D. McKay. Describes the affective categories in detail and presents illustrative objectives and test items for each.

Simpson, E. J. (1972). The classification of educational objectives in the psychomotor domain. In *The psychomotor domain* (vol. 3.). Washington: Gryphon House. Describes the psychomotor domain in detail and presents illustrative objectives.

*Tables G.1 through G.6 are reprinted from N.E. Gronlund, *Stating Objectives for Classroom Instruction,* 3rd ed. (New York: Macmillan, 1985).

RELATING ASSESSMENT PROCEDURES TO INSTRUCTIONAL OBJECTIVES

Instructional objectives encompass a variety of learning outcomes, and assessment includes a variety of procedures. The key to effective assessment of student learning is to relate the assessment procedures as directly as possible to the intended learning outcomes. This is easiest to accomplish if the general instructional objectives and the specific learning outcomes have been clearly stated in terms of student performance. It is then simply a matter of constructing or selecting assessment instruments that provide the most direct evidence concerning the attainment of the stated outcomes.

The sequence of steps shown in Figure H.1 summarizes the general procedure for relating assessment techniques to instructional objectives.

RELATING TEST ITEMS TO INSTRUCTIONAL OBJECTIVES

Preparing test items that are directly relevant to the instructional objectives to be measured requires matching the performance measured by the test items to the types of performance specified by the intended outcomes. Stating the outcomes as specifically as possible is useful in this regard, but good judgment is still needed. If the intended learning outcomes call for *supplying* the answers (e.g., *name, define*), the test items should also require that the answers be supplied rather than selected. If the intended learning outcomes call for *identifying* a procedure, the test items should be concerned only with identifying, rather than with more complex outcomes. If the intended learning outcomes call for *performing* a procedure, the test items should require actual performance rather than a verbal description of how to do it. Issues such as these highlight the care needed in determining whether there is a good match between the stated outcomes and the expected responses to the test items.

Constructing relevant test items was considered in earlier chapters. Here we are simply pointing out the importance of matching test items and assessment tasks as closely as possible to the learning outcomes they are intended to measure. The following examples, from various content areas, show reasonably good matches between intended outcomes and test items. In each example, the specific learning outcome describes the performance the student is to demonstrate, and the test item presents a task that demands that type of performance.

General Instructional Objectives
Intended outcomes that direct our teaching.
↓

Specific Learning Outcomes
Types of student performance we are willing to accept
as evidence of the attainment of objectives.
↓

Assessment Techniques
Procedures for obtaining samples of student
performance like those described in the specific
learning outcomes.

Figure H.1
Relation of assessment techniques to objectives

EXAMPLES   *Specific Learning Outcome:*   Defines common terms. (Elementary Mathematics)

Directions: In one or two sentences, define each of the following words:

1. Interest
2. Premium
3. Dividend
4. Collateral
5. Profit

Specific Learning Outcome: Identifies procedure for converting from one measure to another.
(Elementary Mathematics)

1. The area of a rug is given in square yards. How should you determine the number of square
   feet?
   A Multiply by 3
   Ⓑ Multiply by 9
   C Divide by 3
   D Divide by 9

Specific Learning Outcome: Differentiates between relative values expressed in fractions.
(Elementary Mathematics)

1. Which of the following fractions is smaller than one half?
   A 2/4
   B 4/6
   Ⓒ 3/8
   D 9/16

Specific Learning Outcome: Distinguishes fact from opinion. (Elementary Social Studies)

Directions: Read each of the following statements carefully. If you think the statement is a *fact*,
circle the F. If you think the statement is an *opinion*, circle the O.

Ⓕ   O   1. George Washington was the first president of the United States.
F   Ⓞ   2. Abraham Lincoln was our greatest president.

Ⓕ O   3. Franklin Roosevelt was the only president elected to that office three times.
Ⓕ O   4. Alaska is the biggest state in the United States.
F   Ⓞ   5. Hawaii is the most beautiful state in the United States.

Specific Learning Outcome: Identifies common uses of weather instruments. (Elementary Science)

1. Which one of the following instruments is used to determine the speed of the wind?
   A Wind vane
   B Anemometer
   Ⓒ Altimeter
   D Radar

Specific Learning Outcome: Identifies cause-and-effect relationships. (Elementary Science)
Directions: In each of the following statements, both parts of the statement are true. Decide whether the second part explains *why* the first part is true. If it does, circle Yes. If it does not, circle No.

Examples:

Ⓨes   No   1. People can see   *because*   they have eyes.
Yes   Ⓝo   2. People can walk   *because*   they have arms.

In the first example, the second part of the statement explains *why* "people can see," and so Yes was circled. In the second example, the second part of the statement does *not* explain *why* "people can walk," and so No was circled. Read each of the following statements and answer in the same way.

Yes   Ⓝo   1. Some desert snakes   *because*   the weather is hot in
                are hatched   the desert.
                from eggs
Ⓨes   No   2. Spiders are   *because*   they eat harmful
                very useful   insects.
Ⓨes   No   3. Some plants do not   *because*   they get their food from
                need sunlight   other plants.
Yes   Ⓝo   4. Water in the ocean   *because*   it contains salt.
                evaporates
Ⓨes   No   5. Fish can get   *because*   they have gills.
                oxygen from
                the water

Specific Learning Outcome: Identifies reasons for an action or event. (Biology)

1. Which one of the following best explains why green algae give off bubbles of oxygen on a bright sunny day?
   A Transpiration
   B Plasmolysis
   Ⓒ Photosynthesis
   D Osmosis

Specific Learning Outcome: Identifies the relevance of arguments. (Social Studies)

Directions: The items in this part of the test are to be based on the following resolution:

Resolved: The legal voting age in the United States should be lowered to eighteen. Some of the following statements are arguments *for* the resolution, some are arguments *against* it, and some are *neither* for nor against the resolution. Read each of the following statements and circle

F if it is an argument *for* the resolution.

A if it is an argument *against* the resolution.

N if it is *neither* for nor against the resolution.

Ⓕ	A	N	1. Most persons are physically, emotionally, and intellectually mature by the age of eighteen.
F	A	Ⓝ	2. Many persons are still in school at the age of eighteen.
F	A	Ⓝ	3. In most states it is legal to drive an automobile by the age of eighteen.
F	Ⓐ	N	4. The ability to vote intelligently increases with age.
F	A	Ⓝ	5. The number of eighteen-year-old citizens in the United States is increasing each year.

These examples are sufficient to show how test items should be related to specific learning outcomes. Although not all subject-matter areas and all types of learning outcomes are represented, the basic principle is the same. State the desired learning outcomes in measurable terms and select or develop test items that demand that specific type of performance.

RELATING PERFORMANCE ASSESSMENT TASKS TO INSTRUCTIONAL OBJECTIVES

There are many areas in which testing procedures are not useful. In assessing some performance skills (e.g., singing, dancing, or speaking), it is necessary to observe the students as they perform and to judge the effectiveness of the performance. In other instances, it is possible to assess students' skill by judging the quality of the product resulting from the performance (e.g., a theme, a painting, a typed letter, or a baked cake). In assessing students' social adjustment, it may be necessary to observe the students in formal and informal situations in order to judge their tendencies toward aggression or withdrawal, relations with peers, and the like. In fact, whenever we assess how students typically behave in a situation, some type of observational procedure is usually called for.

As with testing procedures, the selection or development of a performance-based assessment task or an observational technique should evolve from the objectives and specific learning outcomes. In the case of rating scales or checklists, the specific learning outcomes become the dimensions to be observed. In the following examples, note how the specific learning outcomes require only a slight modification to become items in a rating scale.

EXAMPLES **SPEECH**

Specific Learning Outcome: Maintains good eye contact with audience.

Rating Scale Item: How effective is the speaker in maintaining eye contact with the audience?

1	2	3	4	5
Ineffective	Below average	Average	Above average	Very effective

THEME WRITING

Specific Learning Outcome: Organizes ideas in a coherent manner.

Rating Scale Item: Organization of ideas.

1	2	3	4	5
Poor organization		Fair organization		Clear, coherent organization

GROUP WORK

Specific Learning Outcome: Contributes worthwhile ideas to group discussion.

Rating Scale Item: How often does the student contribute worthwhile ideas to group discussion?

1	2	3	4	5
Never	Seldom	Occasionally	Fairly often	Frequently

More complete rating scales and checklists are presented in Chapter 13. It is our purpose here merely to illustrate how assessment tasks and other observational procedures can be related to the learning outcomes we wish to assess. The specific learning outcomes specify the characteristics to be observed, and the rating scale provides a convenient method of recording our judgments. Such judgments are, of course, still subjective, but we have made them as objective as possible by defining the samples of student responses we wished to observe and then observing those responses.

RELATING ASSESSMENT PROCEDURES USING AN EXPANDED TABLE OF SPECIFICATIONS

When using multiple techniques to assess classroom learning, it is usually desirable to expand the table of specifications used in test construction to include both test and nontest procedures. This provides an overall plan that clarifies how each assessment technique relates to the instructional objectives. Including all objectives and assessment procedures in a single table makes clear the relative emphasis given to each objective and each method of assessment and prevents an overemphasis on testing procedures. A simplified version of such a table is presented in Table H.1.

Table H.1

Table of specifications for evaluation of a weather unit in junior high school science

Content	Knows — Symbols and Terms	Specific Facts	Understands — Influence of Each Factor on Weather Formation	Interprets — Weather Maps	Skill in — Using Measuring Devices	Constructing Weather Maps	Total Number of Items
Air pressure	2	3	3	3	Observe pupils	Evaluate maps	11
Wind	4	2	8	2	using measuring	constructed	16
Temperature	2	2	2	2	devices (rating scale)	by pupils (checklist)	8
Humidity and precipitation	2	1	2	5			10
Clouds	2	2	1				5
Total number of items	12	10	16	12			50
Percentage of evaluation	12%	10%	16%	12%	25%	25%	100%